World Religions

Western Traditions

Fourth Edition

World
Religions
Western Traditions

Edited by

Willard G. Oxtoby

Amir Hussain

Roy C. Amore

OXFORD
UNIVERSITY PRESS

OXFORD
UNIVERSITY PRESS

Oxford University Press is a department of the University of Oxford.
It furthers the University's objective of excellence in research, scholarship,
and education by publishing worldwide. Oxford is a registered trade mark of
Oxford University Press in the UK and in certain other countries.

Published in Canada by
Oxford University Press
8 Sampson Mews, Suite 204,
Don Mills, Ontario M3C 0H5 Canada

www.oupcanada.com

First Edition published in 1996
Second Edition published in 2002
Third Edition published in 2011

Library and Archives Canada Cataloguing in Publication

World religions : Western traditions / edited by Willard
G. Oxtoby, Amir Hussain, Roy C. Amore. — Fourth edition.

Includes index.
ISBN 978-0-19-900287-0 (pbk.)

1. Religions—Textbooks. I. Amore, Roy C., 1942–, editor of
compilation   II. Oxtoby, Willard G. (Willard Gurdon), 1933–, editor
of compilation   III. Hussain, Amir, editor of compilation

BL80.2.W672 2014   200   C2013-907204-7

Cover image: Frank Fell/Robert Harding World Imagery/Getty Images

Printed and bound in the United States of America

1 2 3 4 — 17 16 15 14

Brief Contents

Contents

3 | Jewish Traditions 74

4 | Christian Traditions 148

8 | Current Issues   402

Contributors

Roy C. Amore is professor and an associate dean in the Faculty of Arts, Humanities and Social Sciences at the University of Windsor in Ontario. His extensive research in the areas of comparative religion and Asia has enabled him to author *Two Masters, One Message*, a book comparing the lives and teachings of Christ and Buddha, and co-author *Lustful Maidens and Ascetic Kings: Buddhist and Hindu Stories of Life*.

Ken Derry received his PhD from the University of Toronto's Centre for the Study Religion with a thesis on religion, violence, and First Nations literature. Since 1996 he has been teaching courses on religion, culture, literature, and film, and he is currently a Lecturer in the Department of Historical Studies at the University of Toronto.

Michael Desrochers is adjunct professor of history at California State University, Dominguez Hills, and received his PhD from UCLA in the history of Mesopotamia. He is currently at work on two book-length projects: an overview of the religions of antiquity and an examination of historical irony.

Wendy L. Fletcher is professor of the History of Christianity and the past Dean (2000–5) and past Principal and Dean (2005–12) of the Vancouver School of Theology. She has published extensively in the areas of women and Christianity, spirituality, and religion and ethnicity.

Amir Hussain is professor in the Department of Theological Studies at Loyola Marymount University in Los Angeles, where he teaches courses on Islam and world religions. A Canadian of Pakistani origin, he is the author of *Oil and Water: Two Faiths, One God*, an introduction to Islam for North Americans. He is also the editor of the *Journal of the American Academy of Religion* (JAAR).

Michele Murray is a professor in the Department of Religion at Bishop's University, where she holds the William and Nancy Turner Chair in Christianity. She obtained her M.A. from Hebrew University of Jerusalem in Jewish history of the Second Temple period, and her PhD in Religion from the University of Toronto.

The late Willard G. Oxtoby, the original editor of this work, was professor emeritus at the University of Toronto, where he launched the graduate program in the study of religion. His books include *Experiencing India: European Descriptions and Impressions* and *The Meaning of Other Faiths*.

Important Features of This Edition

World Religions: Western Traditions, fourth edition, is a readable and reliable introduction to Western religions. Expert contributors thoroughly investigate Jewish, Christian, Muslim, ancient, Indigenous, and new traditions. Highlights of the fourth edition include:

 NEW Jewish Traditions chapter by Michele Murray, Bishop's University

 NEW Christian Traditions chapter by Wendy L. Fletcher, Vancouver School of Theology

 NEW "Recent Developments" sections addressing contemporary issues and practices

 NEW learning tools in the form of chapter outlines, chapter summaries, discussion questions, and Sacred/Foundational Texts tables

 NEW content on the roles and experiences of women

Dynamic pedagogical program

Traditions at a Glance boxes give readers a summary of the basics at the start of each chapter.

Traditions at a Glance

Numbers

Reliable statistical information on Indigenous religions is virtually impossible to come by. According to the United Nations, there are approximately 370 million Indigenous people in the world. On average perhaps 15 to 20 per cent practise their ancestral traditions, but the figures are much higher in some communities and much lower in others.

Distribution

Indigenous religious traditions can be found almost everywhere: there are more than 5,000 distinct Indigenous cultures in some 90 countries around the world. By far the largest Indigenous populations are in Asia and Africa; fewer than 10 per cent live in Central and South America, approximately 2 per cent in North America and Oceania, and just a small fraction in Europe.

Recent Historical Periods

Extant written records of most Indigenous traditions begin only after contact with non-Indigenous people occurred, so the only developments we can trace with any certainty are those that have taken place since then. It's important to keep in mind, however, that Indigenous religions had been changing and adapting for millennia before that time.

600–700	First contact between Muslims and Indigenous Africans
1450–1850	First contact between Europeans and Indigenous people of Africa, North America, and Oceania; development of Atlantic slave trade and other colonial practices that devastated Indigenous populations
1930–1960	Several governments begin to reduce restrictions on Indigenous people and religion

1960–present	Revival of many Indigenous traditions around the world; development of global pan-Indigenous movements

Founders and Leaders

Few pre-contact Indigenous traditions identify a human founder, although most attribute key features of their religious life to superhuman ancestors. Virtually all traditions also contain religious authority figures such as elders, as well as ritual specialists such as diviners and healers who invoke spiritual powers to aid their communities. In response to colonialism, several new movements were founded by specific people, such as Wovoka (Paiute) or Nongqawuse (Xhosa).

Deities

Indigenous traditions vary widely in their conceptions of gods. Some recognize a single supreme deity as the source of all life and power. Others do not recognize such a being, but attribute creation to a series of gods, spirits, or ancestors. Almost all Indigenous traditions, however, believe that personal deities (or spirits or ancestors) have an active, ongoing impact on the world.

Authoritative Texts

Most pre-contact Indigenous religions passed along their sacred stories orally. These stories often include accounts of the creation of the present world and/or the origins of the community. Many also recount the ongoing activity of personal spiritual forces in the world. New tales continue to be told (and written), particularly about trickster figures, and some post-contact movements (such as the Handsome Lake religion of the Iroquois) have their own sacred texts.

Noteworthy Teachings

Indigenous traditions are typically bound to specific places where important spiritual forces have

◄ Chief Arvol Looking Horse (see p. 343) at the Cheyenne River Sioux Reservation in South Dakota (© National Geographic Image Collection/Alamy).

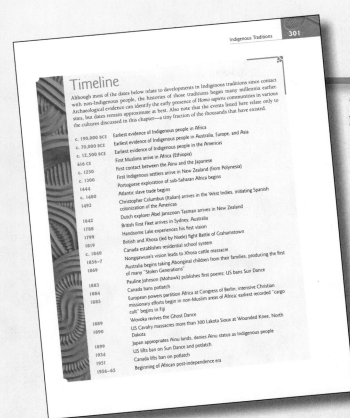

Indigenous Traditions   301

Timeline

Although most of the dates below relate to developments in Indigenous traditions since contact with non-Indigenous people, the histories of those traditions began many millennia earlier. Archaeological evidence can identify the early presence of *Homo sapiens* communities in various sites, but dates remain approximate at best. Also note that the events listed here relate only to the cultures discussed in this chapter—a tiny fraction of the thousands that have existed.

c. 190,000 BCE	Earliest evidence of Indigenous people in Africa
c. 70,000 BCE	Earliest evidence of Indigenous people in Australia, Europe, and Asia
c. 12,500 BCE	Earliest evidence of Indigenous people in the Americas
616 CE	First Muslims arrive in Africa (Ethiopia)
c. 1250	First contact between the Ainu and the Japanese
c. 1300	First Indigenous settlers arrive in New Zealand (from Polynesia)
1444	Portuguese exploration of sub-Saharan Africa begins
c. 1480	Atlantic slave trade begins
1492	Christopher Columbus (Italian) arrives in the West Indies, initiating Spanish colonization of the Americas
1642	Dutch explorer Abel Janszoon Tasman arrives in New Zealand
1788	British First Fleet arrives in Sydney, Australia
1799	Handsome Lake experiences his first vision
1819	British and Xhosa (led by Nxele) fight Battle of Grahamstown
c. 1840	Canada establishes residential school system
1856–7	Nongqawuse's vision leads to Xhosa cattle massacre
1869	Australia begins taking Aboriginal children from their families, producing the first of many "Stolen Generations"
1883	Pauline Johnson (Mohawk) publishes first poems; US bans Sun Dance
1884	Canada bans potlatch
1885	European powers partition Africa at Congress of Berlin; intensive Christian missionary efforts begin in non-Muslim areas of Africa; earliest recorded "cargo cult" begins in Fiji
1889	Wovoka revives the Ghost Dance
1890	US Cavalry massacres more than 300 Lakota Sioux at Wounded Knee, North Dakota
1899	Japan appropriates Ainu lands, denies Ainu status as Indigenous people
1934	US lifts ban on Sun Dance and potlatch
1951	Canada lifts ban on potlatch
1956–65	Beginning of African post-independence era

Timelines help to place religious developments in historical context.

Informative **maps** provide useful reference points.

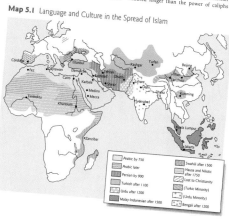

268   World Religions: Western Traditions

confirms the scriptures that preceded it, notably the Torah and the Gospels. Historically, Muslims from the beginning responded to and interacted with the communities of other faiths, particularly Christians and Jews. As a religio-political power, therefore, Islam had to regulate its relations with non-Muslim citizens.

As People of the Book, Jews and Christians living in Muslim lands were promised full freedom to practise their faith in return for paying a poll tax that also guaranteed them physical and economic protection and exemption from military service. Legally such communities came to be known as **dhimmis** ("protected people"). In the course of time,

this designation was extended to other communities with sacred scriptures, including Zoroastrians in Iran and Hindus in India.

In its first century Islam spread through conquest and military occupation. Much of the Byzantine and Roman world and all of the Sasanian Persian domains yielded to the Arab armies and came under Umayyad rule. In subsequent centuries, politico-military regimes continued to contribute to Islam's dominance, especially in regions under Arab, Iranian, or Turkish rule.

Over time, however, the influence of mystics, teachers, and traders has reached farther and endured longer than the power of caliphs and

Map 5.1 Language and Culture in the Spread of Islam

A rich and vibrant **art program** highlights practitioners' lived experience.

2

Religions of
Antiquity

Michael Desrochers

Sacred/Foundational Texts tables give students
a convenient summary of the most important
texts in each tradition, how and when they were
composed, and the uses made of them.

Sacred Texts

Religion	Text	Composition/Compilation	Compilation/Revision	Use
Christianity	Old Testament (Genesis, Exodus, Leviticus, Numbers, Deuteronomy, Joshua, Judges, Ruth, 1 Samuel, 2 Samuel, 1 Kings, 2 Kings, 1 Chronicles, 2 Chronicles, Ezra, Nehemiah, Esther, Job, Psalms, Proverbs, Ecclesiastes, Song of Solomon, Isaiah, Jeremiah, Lamentations, Ezekiel, Daniel, Hosea, Joel, Amos, Obadiah, Jonah, Micah, Nahum, Habakkuk, Zephaniah, Haggai, Zechariah, Malachi)	Composed by various individuals and schools, from approximately 625 BCE to the 1st century BCE.	Individual books and sections revised from the 6th to 1st century BCE. At the Council of Yavne (70–90 CE) these writings were brought together and the canon reached final form. However, later writings suggest that debates were ongoing as to which texts belonged in the canon.	Doctrinal, ritual, inspirational, educational
	New Testament: Undisputed Pauline Epistles (1 Thessalonians, Galatians, Philippians, 1 Corinthians, 2 Corinthians, Romans, Philemon)	Composed between approximately 51 and 63 CE, over the course of Paul's career in Ephesus, Corinth, Philippi, Macedonia, and Rome.		Doctrinal, ritual, inspirational, educational
	New Testament: Disputed Pauline Epistles (2 Thessalonians, Colossians, Ephesians)	Composed in Macedonia and Asia Minor between approximately 60 and 85 CE. Scholars doubt that they were actually written by Paul.		Doctrinal, ritual, inspirational, educational
	New Testament: Pastoral Epistles (1 Timothy, 2 Timothy, Titus)	Composed in Asia Minor and perhaps Crete between approximately 90 and 140 CE. These letters are named after the people to whom they were addressed and traditionally attributed to Paul, but their actual authors are unknown.		Doctrinal, ritual, inspirational, educational

Continued

Sites

Sites boxes draw attention to locations of special significance to each tradition.

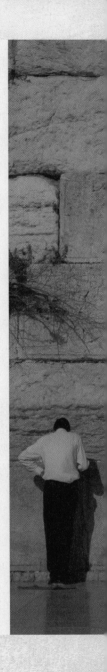

Document

Document boxes provide a generous selection of excerpts from scripture and other important writings.

Focus

Focus boxes offer additional information on selected subjects.

End-of-chapter discussion questions enhance students' critical understanding of key concepts; glossaries explain key terms; and further readings and recommended websites provide excellent starting points for further research.

Discussion Questions

1. What kinds of social and economic factors may contribute to the rise of new religious movements?

2. Why is the line between a "cult" and a "religion" so difficult to define?

3. Why do Eastern religions appeal so strongly to many people in the West?

4. Do all "religions" have to involve belief in deities?

5. Can a set of beliefs and practices centred on extraterrestrial aliens be considered a "religion"?

6. What do you think are some of the factors that might attract some people to new religious movements?

7. How do new religious movements gain acceptance?

8. How do new religious movements tend to change over time?

Glossary

Bab The individual expected to appear as the "Gateway" to the new prophet in the Baha'i Faith.

Baha'i The religious tradition of those who call themselves Baha'i, meaning "adherents of Baha ('u 'llah)"

bhakti Devotional faith, the favoured spiritual path in ISKCON.

Church of Jesus Christ of Latter-day Saints The formal name of the largest Mormon organization, abbreviated as "LDS."

cult Term for a new religion, typically demanding loyalty to a charismatic leader.

dianetics L. Ron Hubbard's term for the system he developed to clear mental blocks.

Eckankar A new religion based on the teachings of Paul Twitchell.

E-meter A device used in Scientology to detect mental blocks.

engrams The term for mental blocks in Scientology.

Falun Dafa A "law wheel" said to be acquired through Dafa practice.

Free Zoners Individuals or groups teaching Hubbard's thought independently of Scientology International.

Hare Krishnas Informal name for the members of ISKCON, based on their chant.

ISKCON International Society for Krishna Consciousness.

Kabbalah Traditional Jewish mysticism.

Komeito A Japanese political party loosely associated with Soka Gakkai.

Mormons Another name for members of the Church of Jesus Christ of Latter-day Saints.

millenarian Term used to refer to the belief that the current social order will soon come to an end.

Nation of Islam (NOI) An African-American movement that originated in Detroit in 1930. Its practice of Islam has become more aligned with the Sunni tradition in recent years.

New Age A vague term embracing a diversity of religious or spiritual movements providing alternatives to mainstream Western religions.

qi (or **chi**) Spiritual energy.

qigong Exercises to cultivate qi.

Raëlian Movement A new religion originating in France in the 1970s, based on the belief that an alien revealed previously unknown information about the creation of life on earth to a man named Raël.

Scientology A new religion devoted to clearing mental blockages; founded by L. Ron Hubbard.

sect A sociological term for a group that breaks away from the main religion.

Soka Gakkai A lay movement that originated in the 1930s among Japanese adherents of Pure Land Buddhism; now an independent new religion teaching the power of chanting homage to the Lotus Sutra.

spherot The ten attributes of God in Kabbalah.

thetan Term for the soul or mind in Scientology.

Vaishnava A Hindu who worships Vishnu and related deities.

Wicca A name for witchcraft or the Craft.

Further Reading

Baha'u'llah. 1952. *Gleanings from the Writings of Baha'u'llah*, rev. edn. Wilmette, IL: Baha'i Publishing Trust. A good selection of Baha'i writings.

Barrett, David V. 2003. *The New Believers: A Survey of Sects, Cults and Alternative Religions*. London: Octopus Publishing Group. A good place to start on the topic of cults versus new religions.

Das, Joseph. 2005. *Kabbalah: A Very Short Introduction*. Oxford: Oxford University Press. A useful introduction.

Drew, A. J. 2003. *The Wiccan Bible: Exploring the Mysteries of the Craft from Birth to Summerland*. Franklin, NJ: Career Press. An overview of Wicca.

Esslemont, John E. 1979. *Baha'u'llah and the New Era: An Introduction to the Baha'i Faith*. 4th edn. Wilmette, IL: Baha'i Publishing Trust. The standard survey researched by Baha'is.

Gallagher, Eugene V., William M. Ashcraft, and W. Michael Ashcraft, eds. 2006. *An Introduction to New and Alternative Religions in America*. 5 vols. Westport: Greenwood Press. Scholarly introductions to religious movements from colonial era to the present.

Headley, Marc. 2009. *Blown for Good: Behind the Iron Curtain of Scientology*. Burbank: BFG Books. The autobiography of a former Scientologist turned critic.

Hubbard, L. Ron. 1956. *Scientology: The Fundamentals of Thought*. 2007. Los Angeles: Bridge Publications. The basic introduction, by Scientology's founder.

Lewis, James R., and J. Gordon Melton, eds. 1992. *Perspectives on the New Age*. Albany: State University of New York Press. One of the best assessments of the New Age phenomenon.

Li Hongzhi. 2000. *Falun Gong*. 3rd edn. New York: University Publishing Co. Master Li's introduction to Falun Dafa.

Miller, William McElwee. 1974. *The Baha'i Faith: Its History and Teachings*. Pasadena: William Carey Library. An outsider's view of Baha'i.

Muster, Nori J. 2001. *Betrayal of the Spirit: My Life behind the Headlines of the Hare Krishna Movement*. Champaign: University of Illinois Press. A former member's critical view of ISKCON.

Ostling, Richard, and Joan K. Ostling. 2007. *Mormon America—Revised and Updated Edition: The Power and the Promise*. New York: HarperOne. An overview of the issues.

Porter, Noah. 2003. *Falun Gong in the United States: An Ethnographic Study*. N.p.: Dissertation.Com. Argues against the "cult" label based on interviews and publications.

Seager, Richard H. 2006. *Encountering the Dharma: Daisaku Ikeda, Soka Gakkai, and the Globalization of Buddhist Humanism*. Berkeley: University of California Press. A scholarly overview.

Shinn, Larry D. 1987. *The Dark Lord: Cult Images and the Hare Krishnas in America*. Philadelphia: Westminster Press. An objective account, based on extensive interviews.

Starhawk. 1982. *Dreaming the Dark*. Boston: Beacon Press. One of many works by an important Wicca leader.

White, Vibert L., Jr. 2001. *Inside the Nation of Islam: A Historical and Personal Testimony by a Black Muslim*. Gainesville: University Press of Florida. Particularly interesting because the author was involved both in the NOI and in the organization of the 1995 March.

Wright, Lawrence. 2013. *Going Clear: Scientology, Hollywood, and the Prison of Belief*. New York: Alfred A. Knopf. A balanced but critical overview of Scientology, its leaders and celebrity followers.

Recommended Websites

www.bahai.org
Site of the Baha'i religion.

www.falundafa.org
Site of Falun Dafa.

www.finalcall.com
News site of the Nation of Islam.

www.internationfreezone.net
Portal for the Free Zoner alternative to Scientology.

www.iskcon.com
Site of the International Society for Krishna Consciousness.

www.kabbalah.com
Site of the Kabbalah Centre International.

www.lds.org
Site of the Church of Jesus Christ of Latter-day Saints, the Mormons.

www.komei.or.jp
Site of the New Komeito party, loosely affiliated with Soka Gakkai.

www.rael.org
Site of the International Raëlian Movement.

www.scientology.org
Site of the international Scientology organization.

www.sgi.org
Site of Soka Gakkai International.

www.wicca.org
Site of the Church and School of Wicca.

Extensive ancillary package

Instructors benefit from a suite of ancillaries designed to support their teaching goals:

- **Instructor's Manual** containing chapter overviews, lecture outlines, and tutorial discussion questions.
- **Test Generator** producing multiple-choice, true/false, short-answer, and essay questions.
- **PowerPoint Slides** covering all key concepts, easily adapted to suit your course.
- **NEW Image Bank** containing all images and captions, maps, and boxed features.

Students have access to a wealth of additional information in the **Student Study Guide**, which offers chapter summaries, multiple-choice and short-answer questions with answers, research questions, reflection questions, fieldwork guidelines, and a bonus chapter on Zoroastrianism.

www.oupcanada.com/Western4e

Preface

I first met the late Will Oxtoby in 1987, as a student in the undergraduate course on world religions at the University of Toronto that he taught with Joe O'Connell and Julia Ching. Eventually, I became one of many teaching assistants for that course. I also took numerous other courses with Will, and he supervised my MA as well as my PhD dissertation. Whereas I came from a working-class background (both my parents were factory workers), Will had a consummate academic pedigree. The son and grandson of scholars, he held degrees from Stanford and Princeton and taught at McGill, Harvard, and Yale before arriving at the University of Toronto. He was also an outstanding researcher. But I think that Will's true excellence was as a teacher. It is no coincidence that the publication for which he will be best remembered is a textbook.

Will wrote and edited several chapters of the original *World Religions: Eastern Traditions* and *World Religions: Western Traditions*. The work was first used in draft form for students in his world religions class in 1994–5. After some fine tuning, it was published in 1996 and then revised for the second edition in 2002. The project was Will's gift to those who did not have the privilege of studying with him.

Will believed that only those who loved classroom teaching should write textbooks. Therefore every author he recruited had to be an excellent teacher. He also made sure that his fellow authors were not just academic authorities but sympathetic observers, if not members, of the traditions they were writing about.

This fourth edition of the Western Traditions volume, like the new Eastern volume edited by Roy C. Amore, takes advantage of the enhanced colour format; text, site, and focus boxes; and discussion questions of the single-volume *A Concise Introduction to World Religions* (2007, 2012). The two new volumes also share their opening and concluding chapters, on the nature of religion and current trends respectively.

With the death of Alan Segal in 2011, a new author for the chapter on Jewish Traditions was required. Michele Murray, who knew both Will and Alan, was able to provide us with a wonderful new chapter. Another new author, Wendy Fletcher, was brought in to rewrite the chapter on Christian Traditions. In recruiting Michele and Wendy, I kept Will's criteria firmly in mind. Together, Roy Amore and I have tried to stay true to his vision.

In his original foreword, Will wrote that people often used to ask him why he would waste his life on something as unimportant as religion, but that no one ever asked that question after the Islamic revolution in Iran. I have had the same experience: since the terrorist attacks of 9/11, not a single student has raised the issue of relevance. On the contrary, the study of world religions is more important today than ever before.

Acknowledgements

At Oxford University Press I would like to thank Katherine Skene and Stephen Kotowych for their encouragement, Meagan Carlsson for her developmental guidance, and Sally Livingston for her hands-on editorial work. I also need to thank Roy Amore for all his help in making this volume a reality and a tribute to Will's legacy. Of course, my thanks to Ken Derry, Michael Desrochers, Wendy Fletcher, and Michele Murray for their fine contributions.

Finally, I am grateful to all the reviewers whose comments helped to shape this volume, both those whose names are listed below and those who wished to remain anonymous:

Clarence Bolt, Camosun College
Zeba Crook, Carleton University
David Galston, Brock University
Ernest P. Janzen, University of Winnipeg
Robert P. Kennedy, St Francis Xavier University
David Perley, University of Toronto Scarborough
Michelle Rebidoux, Memorial University of Newfoundland

With the death of Joe O'Connell in 2012, all three of the instructors who first taught me have now passed on. I'm privileged to continue their work, and I dedicate this edition to them.

Amir Hussain
February 2013
Loyola Marymount University
Los Angeles

1

About Religion

Roy C. Amore and Amir Hussain

In this chapter you will learn about:

- some basic characteristics of human religion from ancient times
- a number of patterns that can be observed in more than one religious tradition
- various theories of why humans are religious
- some reasons for studying religion

Basic Human Religion: Looking Both Ways from Stonehenge

Standing on the west side of **Stonehenge**, we watch the sun rise through the circle of massive standing stones. Within the outer circle is a grouping of paired stones capped by lintels and arranged in a horseshoe pattern, opening towards the rising sun. At the centre of the horseshoe lies a flat stone that was once thought to have served as an altar for sacrifices. Today, however, it is believed that the centre stone originally stood upright, marking the spot where an observer would stand to watch the movements of the sun and stars.

The Stonehenge we know today is what remains of a structure erected between 3,500 and 4,000 years ago. But the site had already been used as a burial ground for centuries before that time: researchers believe that the remains of as many as 240 people, probably from a single ruling family or clan, were interred there between roughly 3000 and 2500 BCE.[1] The structure itself is generally believed to have been used for ceremonial purposes, and its orientation—towards the point where the sun rises at the summer solstice—has led many to think it might have been designed to serve as a kind of astronomical observatory. Another recent theory, based on excavations of a nearby Neolithic village, Durrington Walls, with a similar circular arrangement of timber posts, suggests that the two sites represented the living and the dead respectively, with Stonehenge serving as the permanent dwelling place of the ancestors. If so, there are parallels in other ancient cultures.[2]

Ignoring the crowd of tourists, we position ourselves behind the central stone to note the position of the rising sun in relation to the "heel stone" on the horizon more than 60 metres (200 feet) away. Today, on the morning of the summer solstice, the sun rises in the northeast, just to the left of the heel stone. It's easy to imagine that this day—the longest of the year and the only one on which the sun rises to the north side of the heel stone—would have been the occasion for some kind of ceremony in ancient times; that the entire community would have gathered at dawn to watch as someone with special authority—perhaps a priest, perhaps the local chief or ruler—confirmed the position of the rising sun. It's also easy to imagine the sense of order in the universe that would have come from knowing exactly when and where the sun would change course.

Tomorrow the sun will rise behind the heel stone, and it will continue its (apparent) journey towards the south for the next six months. Then in late December, at the winter solstice, the sun will appear to reverse course and begin travelling northwards again. Many centuries after people first gathered at Stonehenge, the Romans would celebrate this day as marking the annual "rebirth" of the sun—the high point of the festival they called Saturnalia. And in the fourth century CE, the Christians in Rome would choose the same time of year to celebrate the birth of their risen lord. Christmas would combine the unrestrained revelry of the Roman midwinter festival, marked by feasting, gift-giving, and general merriment, with the celebration of the coming to earth of a deity incarnate.

Looking Back from Stonehenge

There are a few concepts, shared by virtually all human cultures, which seem fundamental to what we call religion: powerful gods, sacred places, a life of some kind after death, the presence in the physical world of spirits that interact with humans in various ways. These concepts are so old and so widespread that no one can say where or when they first emerged.

Birds over Stonehenge (Tore Johannesen/Getty Images).

Three Worlds

Historically, it seems that humans around the globe have imagined the world to consist of three levels—sky, earth, and underworld. The uppermost level, the sky, has typically been considered the home of the greatest deities. Exactly how this concept developed is impossible to know, but we can guess that the awesome power of storms was one contributing factor. The apparent movement of the sun, the stars, and the planets across the sky was very likely another. Observing the varying patterns could well have led early humans to believe that the heavenly bodies were living entities animated by their own individual spirits—in effect, gods and goddesses.

The very highest level, in the heavens above the clouds and stars, was thought to be the home of the highest deity, typically referred to by a name such as Sky Father, Creator, or King of Heaven. This deity—invariably male—was the forerunner of the god of the monotheistic religions. Under the earth lived the spirits of serpents (surviving as the cobras, or **nagas**, in the religions of India) or reptilian monsters (surviving in dragon lore); perhaps because they were associated with dark and hidden places, they were usually imagined as evil. Finally, between the sky and the underworld lay the earth: the intermediate level where humans lived.

Sacred Places

Around the world, there are certain types of places where humans tend to feel they are in the presence of some unusual energy or power. Such places are regarded as set apart from the everyday world and are treated with special respect. Among those sacred places ("sacred" means "set aside") are mountains and hilltops—the places closest to the sky-dwelling deities. In the ancient Middle East, for instance, worship was often conducted at ritual centres known simply as "**high places**." People gathered at these sites to win the favour of the deities by offering them food, drink, praise, and prayer. One widely known example is the altar area on the cliff above the ancient city of Petra in Jordan (familiar to many people from the Indiana Jones films).

Great rivers and waterfalls are often regarded as sacred as well. And in Japan virtually every feature of the natural landscape—from great mountains and waterfalls to trees and stones—was traditionally believed to be animated by its own god or spirit (*kami*).

Animal Spirits

Another common and long-standing human tendency has been to attribute spirits to animals, either individually or as members of a family with a kind of collective guardian spirit. For this reason, traditional hunting societies have typically sought to ensure that the animals they kill for food are treated with the proper respect, lest other members of those species be frightened away or refuse to let themselves be caught.

In addition, body parts from the most impressive animals—bulls, bears, lions, eagles—have often been used as "power objects," to help make contact with the spirits of these animals. People in many cultures have attributed magical properties to objects such as bear claws or eagle feathers, wearing them as amulets or hanging them in the doorways of their homes as protection against evil spirits.

Death and Burial

From ancient times, humans have taken great care with the burial of their dead. The body might be positioned with the head facing east, the "first direction," where the sun rises, or placed in the fetal position, suggesting a hope for rebirth into a different realm. These burial positions in themselves would not be enough to prove a belief in an afterlife; however, most such graves have also contained, along with the remains of the dead, "grave goods" of various kinds. Some of these provisions for the afterlife likely belonged to the person in life; some appear to be specially made replicas; and some are rare, presumably costly items such as precious stones. Apparently the living were willing to sacrifice important resources to help the dead in the afterlife.

The belief that deceased ancestors can play a role in guiding the living members of their families appears to be especially widespread. Traditions such as the Japanese **Obon**, the Mexican **Day of the Dead**, and the Christian **All Saints Day** and **Hallowe'en** all reflect the belief that the souls of the dead return to earth once a year to share a ritual meal with the living.

Why Are Humans Religious?

The reasons behind human religiosity are complex and varied. All we can say with any certainty is that religion seems to grow out of human experiences: from the fear of death to the hope for a good afterlife, from the uncertainty surrounding natural events to the sense of control over nature provided by a priest capable of predicting the change of seasons and the movement of the planets. Religion emerges through the experience of good or bad powers that are sensed in dreams, in sacred spaces, and in certain humans and animals.

Religion has many emotional dimensions, including fear, awe, love, and hate. But it also has intellectual dimensions, including curiosity about what causes things to happen, a sense of order in the universe that suggests the presence of a creator, and the drive to make sense out of human experience.

The nature of religious belief and practice has changed through the centuries, so we must be careful not to take the religion of any particular time and place as the norm. What we can safely say is that religion is such an ancient aspect of human experience that it has become part of human nature. For this reason some scholars have given our species, *Homo sapiens*, a second name: *Homo religiosus*.

🦋 Looking Forward from Stonehenge

Looking forward from ancient Stonehenge, we can see a number of patterns emerge in different parts of the world, some of them almost simultaneously.

Since most of the chapters in this book focus on individual religions, it may be useful to begin with a broader perspective. What follows is a brief overview of some of the major developments in the history of what the late Canadian scholar Wilfred Cantwell Smith (1916–2000) called "religion in the singular," meaning the history of human religiosity in the most general sense.

Shamanism

One very early pattern involves a ritual specialist—in essence, a kind of priest—that we know today as a **shaman**. The word "shaman" comes from a specific central Asian culture, but it has become the generic term for a person who acts as an intermediary between humans and the spirit world. Other terms include "medicine man," "soul doctor," and "witchdoctor."

Hunting Rituals

Many ancient cave drawings depict hunting scenes in which a human figure seems to be performing a dance of some kind. Based on what we know of later hunting societies, we can guess that the figure is a shaman performing a ritual either to ensure a successful hunt or to appease the spirits of the animals killed.

It's not hard to imagine why such societies would have sought ways to influence the outcome of the hunt. Indeed, it seems that the more dangerous the endeavour, the more likely humans were to surround it with rituals. As the anthropologist Bronislaw Malinowski pointed out in his book *Magic, Science and Religion*, the Trobriand Islanders he studied did not perform any special ceremonies before fishing in the lagoon, but they never failed to perform rituals before setting out to fish in the open ocean. This suggests that religious behaviour is, at least in part, a way of coping with dangerous situations.

In addition, though, as we have seen, early humans believed that the spirits of the animals they hunted had to be appeased. Thus a special ritual might be performed to mark the first goose kill of

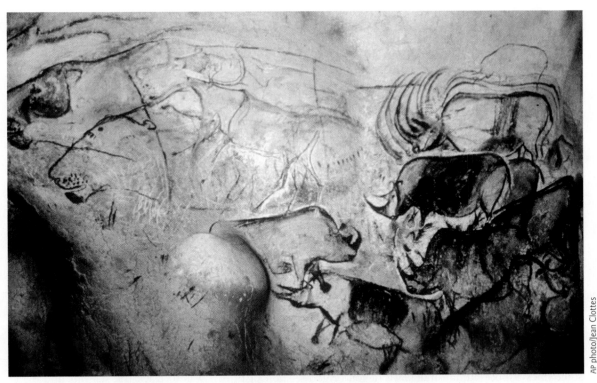

Animal images from the Chauvet cave in southern France, dated c. 30,000 BCE.

AP photo/Jean Clottes

the season, in the hope that other geese would not be frightened away from the hunting grounds.

Such rituals reflect humans' concern over the future food supply, but they also reveal something about the nature of human belief in spirits. From very ancient times, it seems, humans have believed that the spirit—whether of an animal killed for food or of a human being—survives death and can communicate with others of its kind.

Coping with Unfriendly Spirits

The spirits associated with natural phenomena—whether animals or storms, mountains or rivers—have typically been thought to behave towards humans in the same ways that humans behave towards one another. Strategies for dealing with unfriendly spirits, therefore, are usually based on what works with humans.

Many cultures have believed wild, uninhabited areas to be guarded by resident spirits. In some cases,

these spirits have taken the form of monsters or mythical beasts; in others, of "little people" such as trolls (common in the folklore of Scandinavia, for example).

Unfriendly spirits were of particular concern to those who ventured into the forest as hunters or gatherers, but they were not confined to the wilderness. Pain and disease of all kinds—from toothache to appendicitis to mental illness—were also attributed to possession by malevolent spirits or demons. In Sri Lanka, those suffering from certain illnesses were advised to have a shaman sacrifice a chicken as an offering to the "graveyard demon," effectively bribing him to go away; in such cases a second chicken, still alive, would be given to the shaman who performed the ritual. Another approach was to frighten the demon away, either by threatening to invoke another, stronger spiritual power, such as the spirit guide of the shaman, to drive him off, or by making threatening gestures or loud noises. The firecrackers still used in some East Asian rituals are examples of the latter approach.

The Shaman

The most important resources of all, however, have been the shamans themselves. Shamans are still active in a number of cultures today. The way they operate varies, but certain patterns seem to be almost universal, which in itself suggests that the way of the shaman is very ancient. Sometimes the child of a shaman will follow in the parent's footsteps, but more often a shaman will be "called" to the role by his or her psychic abilities, as manifested in some extraordinary vision or revelation, or perhaps a near-death experience.

Candidates for the role of shaman face a long and rigorous apprenticeship that often includes a vision quest, in the course of which they are likely to confront terrifying apparitions. Typically the quester will acquire a guiding spirit, sometimes the spirit of a particular animal (perhaps a bear or an eagle, whose claws or feathers the shaman may wear to draw strength from its special powers) and sometimes a more human-like spirit (a god or goddess). That spirit then continues to serve as a guide and protector throughout the shaman's life.

To communicate with the spirit world, the shaman enters a trance state (often induced by rhythmic chanting or drumming). According to Mircea Eliade in his classic *Shamanism: Archaic Techniques of Ecstasy*, contact is then made in one of two ways. In the first, the shaman's soul leaves his body (which may appear lifeless) and travels to the realm where the spirits live; this way is described as "ecstatic" (from a Greek root meaning to "stand outside"). In the second, the shaman calls the spirit into her own body and is possessed by it; in such cases the shaman may take on the voice and personality of the spirit, or mimic its way of moving.

In either case, after regaining normal consciousness the shaman announces what he has learned about the problem at hand and what should be done about it. Typically, the problem is traced to the anger of a particular spirit; the shaman then explains the reason for that anger and what must be done to appease the spirit: in most cases the appropriate response is to perform a ritual sacrifice of some kind.

Connecting to the Cosmos

A second pattern is the one that inspired the building of structures like Stonehenge. People of the Neolithic ("new rock") era went to extraordinary lengths to create sacred areas by assembling huge stones in complex patterns. In some cases the motivation may have been political: perhaps a leader wanted to demonstrate his power over the people under his command. In others, however, the main reason undoubtedly had something to do with religion—for instance, the need for a public space where the rituals essential to the society—weddings, puberty rites, funerals—could be performed.

Discerning the Cosmic Cycles

Ritual centres such as Stonehenge may also have served purposes that we might think of as scientific or technical, but that their builders would have associated with religion. One very important function of priests was to track the seasons and determine the best time for seasonal activities such as planting. In addition to tracking the north–south movements of the sun, the people of the Neolithic era paid careful attention to the phases of the moon and the rising positions of certain constellations. The horizon was divided into segments named after the planet or constellation associated with that section. What we now call astrology developed as a way of understanding the cycle of the seasons and how humans fitted into it, collectively and individually. In ancient times no important decision would have been made without consulting an expert in the movements of the sun, moon, planets, and constellations. Even in modern times, many people, including political leaders, will consult an astrologer before making a major decision.

Hilltop Tombs

We suggested earlier that two powerful reasons behind human religion are the fear of death and the idea of an afterlife. Ancient cultures around the world appear to have favoured high places as burial sites. Where there were no hills, artificial ones were sometimes built, at least for the most important members of the society. The pyramids of Egypt and the stupas of Asia are both examples of this practice. In the pyramids, shafts extending from the burial chambers towards important stars connected the deceased with the cosmos. Similarly in Buddhist stupas, a wooden pole—later, a vertical stone structure—extended above the burial mound to connect the earth with the heavens. Scholars refer to this kind of symbolic link between earth and sky as an *axis mundi* ("world axis").

Animals and Gods

Another common feature of Neolithic religion was a tendency to associate certain animals with specific deities. One very early example comes from the ancient (c. 7000–5000 BCE) city of Catalhoyuk ("forked mound"), near Konya in modern Turkey, where a small sculpture was found of a woman flanked by two large felines. James Mellaart, the archaeologist who first excavated the site in the 1960s, believed she represented a mother goddess seated on a throne. Although this interpretation has been disputed, we know that the ancient Egyptians had a cat goddess named Bast who was revered as a symbol of both motherliness and hunting prowess. And the fierce Hindu goddess Durga is usually depicted riding either a lion or a tiger. (One Christmas card from modern India shows the Virgin Mary riding a tiger in the same fashion.)

The Bull God

A similar pattern of association links the most powerful male deities with the strength and virility of the bull. In Greek mythology, the great god Zeus took the form of a white bull when he abducted the Phoenician princess Europa. A creature known as the minotaur—half man, half bull—was said to have been kept in a labyrinth beneath the ancient palace of Knossos, on the island of Crete, where frescos show people leaping over the horns of a bull. Greek temples often displayed bull horns near their altars. And in India a bull named Nandi is the sacred mount of the great god Shiva.

The association of the bull with the creator god can be seen even in Judaism, which strictly forbade the use of any image to represent its invisible deity. When Moses returns from the mountain and finds that his brother Aaron, the first high priest, has allowed the people to worship an image of a golden calf or bullock, he denounces this practice as idolatry. Centuries later, one of Solomon's sons is severely chastised for installing bull images in the temples he has built.

Temple Religion

A third pattern features larger temples, more elaborate sacrificial rituals, and the development of a priestly class endowed with unusual power, prestige, and wealth. This pattern, beginning at least 3,000 years ago, played an enormous role in shaping many traditions, including Judaism, Chinese religion, and Hinduism.

Indo-European Priests

"Indo-European" is a modern term referring to a language family and cultural system that eventually stretched from India all the way through Europe; it does not designate any particular ethnic group. The Indo-European (IE) cultural system has been one of the most important in human history. It may have originated in the region around the Black Sea, but that is only one of many theories that scholars have proposed. From the vocabulary of "proto-IE," as reconstructed by linguists, it is clear that the IE people hunted, practised metallurgy, rode horses, drove chariots, and waged war, among other things. Farming, however, appears not to have been part of their culture: the fact that the IE vocabulary related to agriculture differs from one place to another suggests that in farming the Indo-Europeans simply adopted existing local practices.

Everywhere the IE warriors conquered, they set up a social system with four basic divisions, the top three of which consisted of priests, warriors, and

Document

The Sacrifice

When they divided the Man [*Purusha*, the primal Person sacrificed by the gods to create the world], into how many parts did they disperse him? What became of his mouth, what of his arms, what were his two thighs and his two feet called? His mouth was the brahmin, his arms were made into the nobles, his two thighs were the populace, and from his feet the servants were born (Doniger O'Flaherty 1975: 26).

Three times a year all your males shall appear before the Lord your God at the place which he will choose: at the feast of unleavened bread, at the feast of weeks, and at the feast of booths. They shall not appear before the Lord empty-handed: All shall give as they are able, according to the blessing of the Lord your God that he has given you (from Moses' instructions to the people of Israel; Deuteronomy 16: 16–17).

middle-class commoners. In India these groups are known respectively as the brahmins, kshatriyas, and vaishyas. In ancient times each of these groups had a special clothing colour; thus today in India *varna* ("colour") is still the standard term for "class." The priests performed rituals, kept the calendar, taught the young, and advised the kings; within the warrior class, the top clans were the rulers, while the middle-class "commoners" earned their living as merchants or farmers. Finally, all people of local origin, no matter how wealthy or accomplished, were relegated to the servant (shudra) class.

The four-level social system was given mythic status in the *Rig Veda*, according to which the world came into being through the sacrifice of a "cosmic person" (*Purusha*). Out of his mouth came the brahmin priests, whose job was to chant the sacred hymns and syllables. The warriors came from his arms, the middle class from his thighs, and the servants from his feet. Even today, this ancient hymn continues to buttress the social class structure of India.

Over a period of about a thousand years, beginning around 2500 BCE, the Indo-Europeans took control of the territories that are now Afghanistan, northwest India, Pakistan, Turkey, Greece, Rome, central Europe, and, for a while, even Egypt. Their religious culture was similar to most of its counterparts four to five thousand years ago, with many deities, including a "sky father" (a name that survives in Greek Zeus Pater, Latin Jupiter, and Sanskrit Dyaus Pitar) and a storm god (Indra in India, Thor in Scandinavia); they sang hymns to female deities, such as the goddess of dawn; and they had a hereditary priesthood to offer sacrifices to the gods.

Although the IE people did not necessarily invent the system of hereditary priesthood, they certainly contributed to its spread. In addition to Hindu brahmins, examples include the ancient Roman priests and Celtic Druids. These priests enjoyed great power and prestige, and sometimes were resented by non-priests. (One ancient Indian text includes a parody in which dogs, acting like priests, dance around a fire chanting "*Om* let us eat, *om* let us drink."[3])

Priests and Temples Elsewhere

We actually know when the first Jewish temple was built. After David had been chosen as king of both the northern kingdom of Israel and the southern kingdom of Judah, he captured the Jebusite city now known as Jerusalem. He transformed the city into a proper capital, complete with a grand palace for himself and an organized priesthood. His son Solomon took the next step, building the first temple in the mid-tenth century BCE. The priests attached to the temple soon made it the only site where sacrificial rituals could be performed.

The Jewish priesthood was hereditary. All those who served in the temple as assistants to the priests were required to be Levites (from the tribe of Levi), and priests themselves had to be not only Levites but direct descendants of Aaron, the brother of Moses who was the original high priest.

Priests became a powerful social class in many other parts of the world as well, including Africa, Asia, and the Americas. In some cultures they were a hereditary class, and in others they were recruited. Typically, the role of priest was reserved for males, females being considered impure because of the menstrual cycle; the Vestal Virgins of ancient Rome, who tended the sacred fires and performed rituals, were among the very few exceptions to the general rule.

Prophetic Religion

By 700 BCE or even earlier, several new religious traditions had begun to form under the leadership of a great prophet or sage. The word "prophet" derives from Greek and has two related meanings, one referring to a person who speaks on behalf of a deity and one referring to a person who foresees or predicts the future. The terms are often conflated because prophets delivering messages from the deity often warned of disasters to come if God's will was not obeyed. The site of the temple at Delphi, Greece, where a virgin priestess under

Document

Ritual Sacrifice in the Hebrew Bible

Long before the establishment of the temple in Jerusalem, where priests would perform ritual sacrifices, God commanded the Hebrew patriarch Abram (later renamed Abraham) to sacrifice several animals to mark the covenant that was about to be made between them.

Then [God] said to [Abram], "I am the Lord who brought you from Ur of the Chaldeans, to give you this land to possess." But he said, "O Lord God, how am I to know that I shall possess it?" He said to him, "Bring me a heifer three years old, a female goat three years old, a ram three years old, a turtledove, and a young pigeon." He brought him all these and cut them in two, laying each half over against the other; but he did not cut the birds in two. And when birds of prey came down on the carcasses, Abram drove them away.

As the sun was going down, a deep sleep fell upon Abram, and a deep and terrifying darkness descended upon him. Then the Lord said to Abram, "Know this for certain, that your offspring shall be aliens in a land that is not theirs, and shall be slaves there, and they shall be oppressed for four hundred years; but I will bring judgment on the nation that they serve, and afterward they shall come out with great possessions. As for yourself, you shall go to your ancestors in peace; you shall be buried in a good old age. . . ."

When the sun had gone down and it was dark, a smoking fire pot and a flaming torch passed between these pieces [the halved carcasses]. On that day the Lord made a covenant with Abram, saying, "To your descendants I give this land, from the river of Egypt to the great river, the river Euphrates, the land of the Kenites, the Kenizzites, the Kadmonites, the Hittites, the Perizzites, the Rephaim, the Amorites, the Canaanites, the Girgashites, and the Jebusites" (Genesis 15: 7–21).

the inspiration of Apollo delivered prophecies, had been considered sacred for centuries, maybe millennia, before the glory days of classical Greece. It must have seemed a natural spot for making contact with the divine and receiving sacred knowledge: high up a mountainside, close to the gods, with a natural cave that resembled the entrance to a womb (*delphys* in Greek, representing the mysterious female energy) and a standing stone or *omphalos* (navel of the earth), representing the male energy and the connection between heaven and earth.

This sacred site dates back at least 3,000 years, to a time before the rise of classical Greece, when the oracle was believed to be inspired not by Apollo but by the earth goddess Gaia. Eventually males took control of the sacred site, but even in classical times the virgin priestesses would prepare themselves to receive Apollo's message by bathing in an artesian spring and breathing intoxicating fumes from a fissure in the earth—both water and fumes issuing from Gaia, the earth.

Those wishing to consult the oracle had to climb the mountain, make known their request, pay a fee, and sacrifice a black goat before their question would be put to the oracle. The priestess would take her place over the fissure and, in an ecstatic trance, deliver Apollo's message, which was typically unintelligible and had to be translated into ordinary language by a male priest. Interpreting the real-world significance of a prophecy was not so simple, however. In one famous case, a Greek leader who asked what would happen if he went to war with another state was told that a great country would fall; accordingly, he went to war—but the country that fell was his own. Similarly in the Oedipus myth, the oracle's prophecy that the infant would grow up to kill his father and marry his mother was fulfilled in spite of the measures taken to avoid that fate.

Abrahamic Prophetic Traditions

In 586 BCE the people of Israel were forcibly removed from their homeland and exiled to Babylon. The centuries that followed the "Babylonian captivity" were the defining period for the concept of prophecy as it developed in the three monotheistic traditions that trace their origins to the prophet Abraham. Often, the Jewish prophets' messages were directed towards the people of Israel as a whole, warning of the disasters that loomed if they did not follow God's demands. Christianity saw Jesus and certain events surrounding his life as the fulfillment of Hebrew prophecies. And Islam in turn recognized the Hebrew prophets, beginning with Abraham and including Jesus, as the forerunners of the Prophet Muhammad, the last and greatest of all, the messenger (*rasul*) who received God's final revelations. Muslims understand Muhammad to have been the "seal of the prophets": no other prophet will follow him, since he has delivered the message of God in its entirety. As with earlier prophetic traditions, the Day of Judgment (or Day of Doom) and the concepts of heaven and hell are central to Islam.

Zarathustra, Prophet of the Wise Lord

Zarathustra (or Zoroaster) was a prophet figure who lived more than 2,500 years ago, probably in the region of eastern Iran or Afghanistan. Although we know little about his life, he left behind a collection of poems devoted to a "wise lord" called Ahura Mazda. The religion that developed around his teachings, which came to be known as Zoroastrianism, played an important part in the development of monotheism. The concepts of heaven and hell also owe a lot to the Zoroastrians, who believed that evil-doers were condemned to hell at their death, but that eventually a great day of judgment would come when the souls of all the dead would be made to pass through a fiery wall. Those who had been virtuous in life would pass through the fire without pain, while the rest would be cleansed of their remaining sin and permitted to enter paradise (a term believed to derive from a Persian word meaning garden). The threat of hell and the promise of heaven were powerful tools for any prophet seeking to persuade people to behave as they believed the deity demanded.

Sites

Tell Megiddo, Israel

Tell Megiddo is an archeological mound in Israel, southeast of the modern city of Haifa. The ancient city of Megiddo was strategically located near a pass used by the trade route connecting Egypt and Assyria. The site of a battle with Egypt in the sixteenth century BCE, Har ("Mount") Megiddo is mentioned numerous times in the Hebrew Bible, and is referred to by the Greek version of its name, Armageddon, in the Book of Revelation 16: 16—a passage that some Christians interpret to mean that a final battle will be fought there at the end of time.

© Richard T. Nowitz/Corbis

The remains of Har Megiddo, the site known to Christians as Armageddon. The circular rock structure is thought to have been an altar.

The Energy God

Yet another important pattern emerged around 2,500 years ago. In it the divine is understood not as a human-like entity but as the energy of the cosmos. The Energy God does not issue commandments, answer prayers, or in any way interact with humans as a human. It does not create in the usual fashion of gods; it does not direct the course of history, or dictate the fate of individuals. In fact, some have suggested that this god may have more in common with the principles of modern physics than with

Document

Divine Energy

The Dao that can be told of
Is not the Absolute Dao;
The Names that can be given
Are not Absolute Names.
The Nameless is the origin of Heaven and Earth;
The Named is the Mother of All Things
(from Laozi in the *Daodejing*; Lin Yutang 1948: 41).

This finest essence, the whole universe has it as its Self: That is the Real: That is the Self: That *you* are, Svetaketu! (from the *Chandogya Upanishad* 6.9; Zaehner 1966: 110).

the traditional gods of most religions. This divinity simply exists—or rather, "underlies" everything that exists. Among the traditions that developed around the Energy God concept were Chinese Daoism, the Upanishadic wisdom of India, and the pre-Socratic philosophy of the early Greek world.

Finding the Dao Within

The sage who became known as Laozi ("Master Lao") lived in northern China around 600 BCE. According to legend, he worked for the government as an archivist. At night students would visit his home to hear his words of wisdom about life, especially how to live in harmony with one's inner nature. But Lao had what we might call a mid-life crisis. Dissatisfied with his job and the social and political life of his time, he is said to have left home and set out to the west, riding on a water buffalo (an event that became a favourite subject for artists). Apparently he had not even said goodbye to his students, but one of them happened to be working as a guard at the border. Shocked to learn that his master was leaving China, he begged Lao to record his teachings before leaving.

So Lao paused at the border long enough to write down the fundamentals of his thought in a series of beautiful, if cryptic, verses that were eventually collected in a small volume called **Daodejing** (or *Tao De Ching*), meaning the book (*jing*) about the

Dao and its power (*de*). It became and remains one of the world's most influential books.

What did Laozi write that has spoken to so many through the millennia? He begins with what became one of the most famous opening lines in history: "The Dao that can be described is not the eternal Dao. The name that can be named is not the eternal name." In general usage the word "Dao" means "the way," but here it refers to the mysterious energy that underlies all things. Laozi is warning readers that words cannot adequately describe the Dao. Ogden Nash, a twentieth-century poet noted for combining insight and humour, captured the same idea this way: "Whatever the mind comes at, God is not that."

In traditional cultures, people talk about the characteristics of various deities—their loving nature, or anger, or jealousy, or desire for a particular kind of behaviour. But the absolute, the eternal Dao, has no such attributes. Thus Laozi uses poetic imagery to give us some insights into its nature. Unlike Athena, Zeus, Yahweh, or Indra, the Dao does not have a "personality," and there is no reason for humans to fear, love, or appease it.

Rather, Laozi says, the Dao is like water: it will take on the shape of whatever container we pour it into. Falling from the sky, it may seem content to lie in the hollow made by the hoof of an ox in the muddy road. Raining on the rocky mountaintop, it tumbles all the way down. Water seems malleable, passive and without a will of its own. Yet a mountain will be worn down by the water over time. The water in the hoofprint will evaporate and return to the sky, to fall again when the time is right.

"That Is You": Sitting near the Sages of Old India

A worldview similar to that of Daoism took shape in northern India around the same time. It is reflected in the **Upanishads** (a Sanskrit term meaning literally "sitting-up-near" the master), a series of philosophical texts composed beginning around 600 BCE.

What the Daoist sages called the Dao the Upanishadic masters called *sat* (usually translated as "being," "truth," or "the real"). One Upanishad tells the story of a young man named Svetaketu who has just completed his studies with the brahmin priests. Back at home, his father, who is a king and therefore a member of the warrior class, asks Svetaketu what his priestly teachers taught him about the original source of all things. When Svetaketu admits that he was not taught about that subject, his father undertakes to instruct him in the secret wisdom.

The first lesson has to do with the need for sleep and food; then the real teaching begins. The father has Svetaketu bring a bowl of water and taste it. Then he has him put a lump of sea salt into the water. The next morning Svetaketu sees that the lump of salt is no longer visible; he tastes the water and finds it salty. We can imagine his impatience at being instructed in something he already knows. But his father has a bigger point in mind. He tells Svetaketu that just as the salt is invisible yet present in the water, so also there is a hidden essence present throughout the world. That hidden essence, the force that energizes everything, is the highest reality, the father says, and that reality is you (*tat tvam asi*; "that you are"). The Upanishadic master is initiating his son into a new religious worldview that understands "god" as an energy hidden within and sustaining everything. And that great energy, that ultimate reality, "*tat tvam asi*"—that is you.

The First Principle: Greek Philosophy before Socrates

Around 2,500 years ago the Greek-speaking philosophers of Ionia (now southwestern Turkey) began to ask the same questions as Svetaketu's father: What is the first principle, the first cause, the source from which all else comes? Starting from the science of the day, which held there to be four primal elements—earth, air, fire, and water—they wanted to determine which of the four came first. Although their methods were those of philosophy rather than scientific experimentation, their attempt to understand the causal principle underlying all things—without bringing in a god as the final cause—marked a major advance towards the development of the scientific worldview.

Later Theistic Mysticism

European religious thought eventually reflected mysticism as well. German Christian mystics such as Jacob Böhme (1575–1624) would use terms such as *Ungrund* ("ungrounded") or *Urgrund* ("original ground") to refer to the divine as primal cause. Christian, Jewish, and Muslim mystics all believed in a god beyond the reaches of human understanding.

Purity and Monasticism

At almost the same time that the "Energy God" worldview was establishing itself in China, India, and Greek culture, another spiritual movement of great importance was developing in India. The earliest historical records come from the region of what is now northern India around 2,500 years ago, but the tradition itself claims to have much older roots. Its followers typically sought spiritual enlightenment through asceticism—intense bodily discipline. Their ethic was one of non-violence towards all creatures, and their goal was perfect purity of mind.

Ganges Spirituality

English has no specific term for the new type of religion that came into bloom in the region of the Ganges river around 500 BCE. By that time the Indo-European cultural system, including the religion of the brahmin priests, was firmly established in what is now northern India. We can never know for certain what earlier traditions that religion displaced, since the written sources we rely on were the products of the brahmins themselves. However, linguistic and archaeological data lend support to the theory that two of the world's great living religions—Jainism and Buddhism—were rooted in the pre-brahminic traditions of the Ganges region.

Along the banks of the river were many camps where spiritual masters of various persuasions operated what were in effect open-air seminaries. Though some of the teachers were brahmins, others were committed to the idea that it was wrong to harm any living creature. Their followers rejected the killing of animals for food, and some even objected to farming, because hoeing and plowing would harm organisms living in the soil. While the brahmin masters continued to perform their animal sacrifices, the masters committed to the principle of non-harm (ahimsa) denounced that tradition. Some of the latter—among them the Jaina master Mahavira—went so far as to require their disciples to cover their mouths and noses and strain their drinking water, in order to avoid causing harm to microscopic insects.

Leaving the world of day-to-day life to follow the path of spiritual enlightenment through rigorous ascetic discipline, the students who gathered around these masters took vows of poverty and celibacy, and considered themselves to have "departed the world." The Buddhist and Jaina monastic traditions trace their roots to these ascetics, and it is possible that Indian monasticism played a role in the development of Western monasticism as well.

One more difference between the Indo-European and "Gangetic" cultural systems is worth mentioning here. In the IE system, priests were recruited only from the brahmin social class. In the Ganges tradition, by contrast, the notion of a hereditary priesthood is rejected entirely: anyone, however humble, can choose to lead the life of a holy person. As the Buddha would teach his followers, the status of the "true brahmin" is not a birthright, but must be earned through meritorious conduct.

Mystery Religion

"Mystery religion" refers to a type of Greek and Roman tradition in which the core teachings and rituals were kept secret from outsiders and were revealed only to those who were prepared to undergo initiation in the hope of securing blessings during this life and a heavenly paradise in the afterlife. Such religions became so popular during the Roman period that they presented a threat to the power and influence of the official Roman priesthood (not to be confused with the Roman Catholic priesthood).

The Eleusinian mystery tradition may be the oldest. Named for an ancient Greek town called Eleusis, it grew out of the myth of the young Persephone or Kore ("girl") who is abducted by the god of the dead (Hades) and taken down into the underworld. With the disappearance of this young girl—a potent symbol of growth and fertility—everything on earth begins to die. This imperils not only humans but the gods themselves, who depend on humans to feed them through sacrifices. The girl's mother, Demeter, is therefore allowed to descend into the underworld and bring her back. Scholars understand the Persephone myth to be based on the seasonal cycles of stagnation during the winter and renewal in the spring. Members of her cult believed that by identifying themselves with the dying and rising goddess through the celebration of seasonal rituals, they too would triumph over death.

Initiates into the mysteries associated with the god Dionysus were also following a very ancient tradition. Through rituals that included the drinking of wine, ecstatic dancing, and, perhaps, the eating of mind-altering plants, participants were able to enter into ecstatic states of consciousness in which they believed that their god would ensure

Document

Avatar Gods

For the protection of the good,
For the destruction of evildoers,
For the setting up of righteousness,
I come into being, age after age.
(Krishna to Arjuna in the *Bhagavad Gita*; Zaehner 1966: 267).

Have this mind among yourselves, which you have in Christ Jesus, who, though he was in the form of God, did not count equality with God a thing to be grasped, but emptied himself, taking the form of a servant, being born in the likeness of men. And being found in human form he humbled himself. . . . (St Paul to the Christians of Philippi: Philippians 2: 6–7).

a pleasant afterlife. Another popular mystery cult, dedicated to the goddess Isis, had Egyptian origins.

Many scholars have suggested that mystery cults such as these may have influenced the development of Christianity. The early Christians were initiated into the new cult by undergoing baptism. They then joined an inner circle of people whose faith centred on the death and resurrection of Jesus and who hoped that by following Christ they would secure blessings during this life and a place in heaven after death. Although Christianity developed out of Judaism, its theological structure does seem to have been influenced, however indirectly, by mystery religion.

Avatar: God on Earth

The Avatar

Long before anyone thought of an "avatar" as either a blue-skinned movie humanoid or the on-screen image representing a player in a computer game, *avatar(a)* was a Sanskrit theological term for the "coming down" to earth of a god. By the first century of the Common Era, the idea of a god born in human form was taking root in many parts of the world. In the earlier stages of religion there were many stories of gods and goddesses who came down to earth, but there are two major differences in the avatar stories.

First, whereas the ancient gods came down to earth as gods, the avatar is a god in a truly human form—as a later Christian creed put it, "fully God and fully man." For example, in the ancient Indian story of Princess Dhamayanti, her father holds a party to which he invites all the marriageable princes from various kingdoms. Four gods also attend the party, however, all disguised as the handsome prince Nala, whom the princess already plans to choose. At first she is disturbed to see five look-alikes, but finally finds that she can distinguish the four divine imposters because they do not sweat and are floating slightly above the ground. She marries the human prince, and they live happily ever after.

Unlike the gods at Dhamayanti's party, the avatar gods walk on the ground, sweat, get hungry, sleep, and are in every way human. They are incarnated in a human womb, are born, grow up, teach, save the world from evil, and eventually die. As a Christian layman once explained, "You have to understand that we Christians worship a god in diapers." His choice of words was unusual, but his theology was solid, and it leads us to the second major innovation that came with the concept of the avatar god.

This second innovation is the idea that the avatar god is a saviour figure in at least two ways. Not only does he save the world from some evil power, such as Satan or a demonic king: he also saves from hell those who put their faith in him and secures them a place in heaven. In avatar religions, the ritual of sacrifice is replaced by the ritual of placing faith in the saviour god.

The biography of the saviour gods follows a well-known pattern. Typically, the avatar god has a special, non-sexual conception. His mother is chosen to bear him because she is exceptionally pure, and an angel or prophet announces to her that the child she is carrying has a special destiny. The saviour's birth, usually in a rustic setting, is surrounded by miracles, which often include a fortuitous star or constellation pattern in the night sky. Wise persons foresee the child's greatness. An evil king tries to kill the baby, but kills another baby, or other babies,

instead. The child has special powers, and as an adult is able to work miracles. He typically marries and has a child before embarking on his religious mission. His death represents a triumph over evil and the cosmos responds with earthquakes and other natural signs. Upon dying, he returns to the heavens to preside over a paradise in which his followers hope to join him after they die.

The avatar concept took root in Asia and the Middle East at least two thousand years ago. Among Hindus its impact was reflected in the worship of Krishna; among Buddhists in the veneration of Amitabha Buddha (the figure who would become Amida in Japan); and among Jews in the rise of Christianity.

© Art Directors & TRIP/Alamy

The name Krishna means "dark one," and he is usually pictured as dark blue or black. Here the youthful Krishna and his older brother Balarama are pictured stealing ghee (Indian-style butter) from storage pots, thus earning his nickname "The Butter Thief." He is both an avatar of God and a naughty human boy.

Krishna, Avatar of Vishnu

In some Hindu stories Vishnu is the ultimate deity, the god who lies at the origin of everything there is, including the creator god Brahman. Vishnu lies on his cosmic serpent, sometimes identified with the Milky Way, and out of his navel grows a lotus plant. From the lotus Brahman is born as the first of all creations; then the universe and all its material and spiritual energies follow. This is not exactly a mythic version of the big bang theory, but it comes close. Life evolves, over an unimaginable number of years, out of the divine energy at the centre of the universe. After the universe has run its allotted course, the process reverses from evolution to involution. Over an equally long period of time, eventually all things return into Vishnu, as if crossing the event horizon into a black hole. There all energy lies dormant as Vishnu sleeps, before the whole process begins again.

Another story about Vishnu sees him as the protector of the world. When earth gets into trouble, he comes down to save us. The first five *avatars* of Vishnu take the form of animals that protect the world from natural disasters in its formative millennia. The next four avatars are humans, the most important of whom is Krishna. His exploits are narrated in several different Hindu sources. The most famous is the *Bhagavad Gita*—the "Song of the Lord." A small section of the epic *Mahabharata*, the *Gita* tells of a great war between two houses of the royal family. Krishna is a relative of both houses and is recruited by both armies, but chooses to fight for neither. Instead, he agrees to drive the chariot of Arjuna, one of the five princes who lead one army.

At the beginning of the *Gita*, just before the battle, Arjuna asks Krishna to drive the chariot into the neutral zone between the two great armies, so that he can get a better look at the enemy. But when he sees his adversaries more closely, he loses his will to fight, telling Krishna that he recognizes among them his cousins, his old teachers, and others he remembers from childhood.

Krishna counsels him to take up his bow and fight, for that is his duty as a warrior. Arjuna has misgivings, however, and they begin a long conversation about morality or duty (*dharma*) and the eternal soul that cannot die even though the body may be killed in battle. Krishna teaches with such great authority that soon Arjuna asks how he knows so much. Krishna replies that he is a god of gods, that he is the energy behind all the categories of spirits and gods. When Arjuna asks for proof, Krishna grants him the eye of a god, with which he sees the splendours and mysteries of the universe as a god would.

In the end, Arjuna accepts the divinity of his chariot-driving cousin, acts on his advice, fights alongside his brothers, and wins the war. More important, however, is what Arjuna learns from Krishna about the many ways to lead a good religious life. These include the *yoga* (way) of good works (*karma yoga*), the way of deep spiritual wisdom (*jnana yoga*), and the way of faithful devotion to Krishna (*bhakti yoga*). Of these, the path of faithful devotion is the most highly recommended because it is the easiest and the most certain. The real saving power comes not from the wisdom or discipline of the individual, but from the saving power of the god. Krishna promises that those who practise devotion to him will go to his heaven when they die.

Another source offers stories about other parts of Krishna's life. We learn from it that Krishna was born under the rule of an evil king who was secretly part of a demonic plot to take over the world. One day King Kamsa is driving the wedding chariot of a female relative when an old man—a prophet figure—yells out to the king and tells him he is assisting in the marriage of a woman whose eighth child will grow up to kill him. The king is about to call off the wedding, but the bride pleads with him to reconsider, even promising that when she has children, Kamsa can do with them as he wishes. Kamsa agrees, the marriage takes place, and he proceeds to kill her children as they are born. On the night of the fateful eighth birth, the father is told in a dream to take the baby to safety with relatives across the river. This he does, replacing his child with a baby girl born the same evening.

When the king's guards hear the baby crying, they awaken the king, who smashes the infant's head on the ground. As the baby's soul rises towards heaven, it tells Kamsa that the baby who will grow up to kill him is still alive. That child is Krishna, and when he grows up he fulfills his destiny, saving the world from the evil represented by Kamsa and his demons.

Amitabha, the Buddha of Saving Grace

The avatar concept gave Buddhism the story of Amitabha Buddha, in which a prince intent on achieving buddhahood makes 48 vows, a number of which focus on helping others towards the same goal. Among them is a promise to establish a paradise free of all suffering, disease, and ill will, in which those who put their trust in Amitabha Buddha will be reborn after their death. His followers hope that if they sincerely profess their faith in his saving power, they will be rewarded with rebirth in that "Pure Land."

Jesus the Christ: God Come Down

The Christian doctrine of the trinity affirms that the one God exists in three persons: those of the father, the son, and the holy spirit. In formulating this doctrine, the Christians departed radically from the theology proclaimed by Abraham and Moses. There is no room in Jewish thought for an avatar god, but that was the direction in which Christian thought developed. The prologue to the Gospel of John identifies Jesus with the divine Logos—the word of God that was present before creation. The New Testament says that Jesus "emptied himself of divinity" and came down for the salvation of the world. He is conceived in the womb of a virgin by the spirit of God. An angel announces the pregnancy and its significance to his mother. The birth is associated with a special star. Shepherds overhear the angels rejoicing and come to revere the infant, according to Luke's gospel. In Matthew's gospel, magi (wise men) from the East follow a special star and bring gifts to the child.

For Christians, Jesus became the ultimate god who died on the cross on behalf of his followers and rose on the third day. By participating in the sacred rituals—the sacraments of baptism and the eucharist (in which consecrated bread and wine are consumed in commemoration of the Last Supper)—and placing their trust in Jesus as Lord, Christians hoped to secure a place in heaven after their death.

So Christianity starts with the Hebrew scriptures and the monotheism of Moses and incorporates into them the avatar pattern, along with elements of the mystery traditions, to form a new religion. Many Jews resisted these changes, but some accepted them in the belief that God had in fact offered the world a new dispensation.

Scriptural Religion

The beginning of scriptural religion is hard to date. The earliest scriptures we have are the Zoroastrian Avesta of Persia, the Hindu Vedas, and the Torah of Judaism, all of which took shape approximately 3,000 years ago. Religions based primarily on scripture came much later, however, when different groups began to insist that their particular scriptures were the literal words of God, and to make adherence to those scriptures the focus of their religious life.

Scripturalism manifested itself in Rabbinic Judaism in the centuries that followed the destruction of the Jerusalem temple in 70 CE. It emerged in full force with the rise of Islam, destined to become one of the two most influential religions of all time, in the seventh century. It also played a large role in Protestant Christianity, starting in the sixteenth century, in which the authority of scripture replaced that of tradition and the papacy.

Living by Torah

During the Jews' exile in Babylon the priests were not able to perform the traditional temple rituals, and so the Jews turned to the rabbis—scholars of the Torah with special expertise in Jewish law and

Document

The Word of God

We have sent it down as an Arabic Qur'an, in order that you may learn wisdom (from the Qur'an, 12: 2).

In the beginning was the Word, and the Word was with God, and the Word was God. The same was in the beginning with God. All things were made by him, and without him was not any thing made that was made (John 1: 1–3, KJV).

And the Word was made flesh and dwelt among us (John 1: 14, KJV).

ritual. In this way scripture began to play a more important role in Jewish life, a role that became even more important after the destruction of the second temple in 70 CE. Since that time, Jewish religious life has centred on interpretation of the scripture.

The Word of God

The gospels were not written until two or three generations after the death of Jesus, and the Christian canon did not take final shape until well into the third century CE. But once the books of the canon were fixed, the Church came to emphasize scripture as a divinely inspired source of faith and practice. The Bible became as central to Christianity as the Torah was to Judaism. Christians commonly refer to the scripture as the word of God, and some believe that the Bible was literally dictated by God to its human authors.

God's Final Prophet

The scriptural approach to religion reached its greatest height in Islam. The *surahs* that make up the Qur'an are believed to be the sacred words of God as revealed to the Prophet Muhammad by an angel, recorded by scribes, and compiled as a collection after his death. In its essence, therefore, the Qur'an is considered to be an oral text, meant to be recited—always in the original Arabic—rather than read. Nevertheless, the written Qur'an is treated with great respect. No other book is to be placed on top of the Qur'an, and before opening the book, the reader is expected to be in the same state of ritual purity required to perform the daily prayers.

The Lotus Sutra

The teachings of the Buddha were transmitted orally for centuries before they were first written down, some 2,000 years ago. Although Buddhists revered these texts, their practice did not centre on them. Later, the Mahayana and Vajrayana schools added many more texts to their respective canons, but Buddhists in general did not attribute any special properties to the scriptures themselves. That changed in the 1200s, when a Japanese monk named Nichiren instructed his followers to place their faith in the power of his favourite scripture, the *Lotus Sutra*, and chant their homage to it, just as followers of the Pure Land school chanted homage to Amitabha/Amida Buddha.

Creation through the Word of God

A number of scriptural traditions have maintained that their scriptures were in existence before the world was created. The medieval book of Jewish mysticism known as the *Zohar*, for example, teaches that the Torah played a role in the creation. The prologue to the Gospel of John in the New Testament talks about creation through the Word (*logos*

School children in Ibadan, Nigeria, learning to read the Arabic of the Qur'an.

© Paul Almasy/Corbis

in Greek). And Islam understands the Qur'an to have existed in the mind of God before the world itself was brought into existence.

This idea has very old roots. In ancient Israel, Egypt, India, and elsewhere, it was assumed that the deities would not have performed the physical work of creation themselves, like ordinary humans: rather, like kings, they would have commanded that the work be done: "Let there be light." Thus the divine word took on a special role in later theologies. In traditional Hindu thought, the goddess of speech, Vac, played this role. How could the scriptures—the actual words of the Torah, Bible, or Qur'an—be present in the mind of God at the time of creation, thousands of years before the historical events they describe? The answer for believers is that God knows the future. Outsiders might argue that this calls into question the concept of free will: If the deity knows everything in advance, how can humans be free to choose? What use is it to try to persuade people to do the right thing if the deity

has already determined what each of them will do? Such questions have led to lively theological debates in many religious traditions.

Some branches of scriptural religions place such total authority in their scripture that outsiders have branded them **fundamentalists**. As we will see in Chapter 8, the term "fundamentalism" was first used in the early twentieth century to refer to a variety of American Protestantism characterized by a fervent belief in the absolute, literal truth of the Bible. Similar movements exist within most religious traditions.

What Is Religion?

Many scholars trace the derivation of the word "religion" to the Latin verb *religare*, "to bind." Yet others argue that the root is *relegere*, "to go over again." From the beginning, then, there is no universal definition of religion. We can describe religion as being concerned with the divine, but even that raises questions. Is there one god that is worshipped, or many gods? What about atheism, or no gods? Most of us would probably not think of atheism as a religion, but what about Theravada Buddhism, which is clearly a religion but has nothing to do with an Abrahamic-style god? The same problem arises with religious texts. Is there one text or a set of texts that is particularly authoritative for a particular tradition? Is that set a closed "canon," or can new materials be added to it? What are the distinctions between established religions and newer ones (sometimes referred to pejoratively as "cults")? We may accept, for example, the validity of a man (Moses) receiving revelations from God on Mount Sinai 3,200 years ago, or another man (Muhammad) receiving similar revelations in Mecca 1,400 years ago, but reject the idea of a third man (Joseph Smith) receiving revelations in upstate New York 200 years ago. There is some truth in the saying "today's cult, tomorrow's religion." Although this text focuses mainly on established traditions, it will discuss several newer religious movements in Chapter 7.

Another way of looking at religion is in terms of its functions. For example, a simple functional definition might be that religion is a way of creating community. For some people, "church" has less to do with piety or Sunday worship than with a community that offers a sense of belonging and activities to participate in. Karl Marx defined religion in terms of economics; Sigmund Freud, in terms of interior psychological states. Other scholars have approached the question from the perspective of sociology or anthropology, looking at religion as a social phenomenon or a cultural product. The academic study of religion is usually a secular, non-confessional enterprise, undertaken without a particular faith commitment. One of the key scholars in this area is Jonathan Z. Smith at the University of Chicago. His work on the history of religions has had a profound impact on scholarly understanding of key terms such as "myth" and "ritual," and the way comparisons are made both within a single religious tradition and across different traditions.

Why Study Religion?

The first and most obvious reason to study religion is that it exists. Not all humans would lay claim to religious beliefs, but humans in general have been religious from time immemorial.

A closely related reason is that religion has played such an important role in human affairs. People organize their communities around religious identities, go to war over religious beliefs, make great art in the service of religion, seek to change social norms, or to prevent change, out of religious conviction. In short, religion so pervades the human world that it demands our attention regardless of whether it plays a direct role in our own lives.

It is also common to study religion for more personal reasons. You may want to know more about the tradition you, or someone close to you, grew up in. You may want to study other religions in order to understand other people's beliefs, or to look at your own beliefs from a different perspective. You may also want to arm yourself with knowledge in order to bring others around to your way of thinking, or to defend your beliefs against the arguments of those who might try to convert you to theirs.

Insider versus Outsider

Most people learn about their own religion from their parents, their teachers at religious schools, or other members of the same religious community. Naturally, we tend to accept the teachings of our own religion as true and assume that the teachings of other religions are false, or at least less true. As "insiders" we may find it disturbing when "outsiders" challenge our beliefs or suggest that the history of "our religion" may not be exactly as we have been taught. In his 1962 book *The Meaning and End of Religion*, Wilfred Cantwell Smith famously wrote: "Normally persons talk about other people's religions as they are, and about their own as it ought to be."

One of the advantages of a book such as this is that it helps us appreciate our own traditions from both insider and outsider points of view. When approaching an unfamiliar religious tradition, outsiders need to be sensitive to the ways in which it serves the needs of its followers. For their part, insiders need to understand how their own tradition looks from the outside.

The insider–outsider matter is more complex than we might imagine, for there are many kinds of insiders. Is your Muslim friend a Sunni or a Shi'i? If a Shi'i, does she belong to the Twelver branch or one of the Sevener branches? Which variety of Buddhism does your classmate practise—Theravada, Mahayana, or Vajrayana? If Mahayana, which school? Is your Christian neighbour Protestant, Catholic, or Orthodox? A Protestant may well be an "outsider" to other Protestant groups, let alone to Catholic Christianity. A Zen Buddhist could have trouble seeing any connection between his practice and an elaborate Vajrayana ritual. Because each religion has many subdivisions, in these volumes we will speak of traditions in the plural. We hope our readers will keep in mind the diversity behind the monolithic labels.

Some Practical Matters

The East–West division of our two volumes is quite conventional, but it's problematic for several reasons. For one thing, the so-called "Western" religions arose in what we now term the Middle East: they are Western only in the sense that they were widely adopted in the West. A related problem is that there is no clear dividing line between East and West. As the late Will Oxtoby pointed out in an earlier edition of this text,

> Well into the twentieth century, the East was everything to the east of Europe. The Orient began where the Orient Express ran: Istanbul. For some purposes, it even included North Africa and began at Morocco. A century ago, Islam was thought to be an Eastern religion, and Westerners who studied it were called orientalists.

For those of us living in the twenty-first century, the biggest problem with the East–West division is that all the religions discussed in these volumes may be found anywhere in the world. In any event, our Eastern volume focuses on traditions that developed in the East and are still centred there, while its Western counterpart focuses mainly on traditions that developed in the Middle East and now predominate in the Middle East, Europe, Africa, and the Americas.

For dates we use BCE ("Before the Common Era") rather than BC ("Before Christ"), and CE ("Common Era") rather than AD ("Anno Domini," Latin for "in the year of our lord"). For dates that are obviously in the Common Era, the "CE" will be implied.

Finally, it is difficult to decide whether a book like this should use diacritical marks on foreign words. Scholars of religion writing for other scholars typically use diacritics for precision in transliterating foreign terms into English. Since this is an introductory text, we have chosen not to use diacritics because students often find them more confusing than helpful. Anyone who wishes to do more research on a religious tradition will soon encounter them, however.

Whether or not you are religious yourself, we invite you to delve into the study of several religious traditions that have played central roles both in the lives of individual humans and in the civilizations they have built around the world.

Discussion Questions

1. What are some concepts that are fundamental to what we call religion?

2. What are some of the major developments or patterns in the history of human religiosity?

3. What is an avatar? Give an example from both an Eastern and a Western tradition to illustrate your answer.

Glossary

All Saints Day A Christian festival honouring all the departed saints; held in the West on 1 November.

Daodejing The Daoist "Classic of the Way and Power," compiled roughly 2,500 years ago and traditionally attributed to Laozi.

Day of the Dead A Mexican festival honouring the dead.

fundamentalists/fundamentalism Persons who ascribe total authority to their scriptures or doctrines, rejecting any conflicting secular or religious alternatives.

Hallowe'en Now a popular secular holiday, held on 31 October; originally celebrated as the "Eve" of All Saints Day.

high places Sacred areas located on hill- or mountain tops; such places existed throughout the ancient Near East.

naga A mythical cobra living in the underworld, often associated with water and fertility in Indian religions.

Obon A Japanese festival honouring ancestors.

shaman A type of priest, widespread among hunter-gatherer societies, who communicates with the spirit world on behalf of the people.

Stonehenge One of several ancient rock structures thought to have been constructed for ritual purposes.

Upanishads Hindu religious texts thought to have been composed around 600 BCE.

References

Ballter, Michael. 2005. *The Goddess and the Bull: Catalhoyuk: An Archaeological Journey to the Dawn of Civilization*. New York: Free Press.

Doniger O'Flaherty, Wendy. 1975. *Hindu Myths: A Source Book*. Translated from the Sanskrit. Harmondsworth: Penguin Classics.

Eliade, Mircea. [1951] 1964. *Shamanism: Archaic Techniques of Ecstasy*. Translated by Willard R. Trask. Princeton: Princeton University Press.

Lin, Yutang. 1948. *The Wisdom of Laotse*. New York: The Modern Library.

Malinowski, Bronislaw. 1948. *Magic, Science and Religion*. Boston: Beacon Press.

Zaehner, R.C., ed. 1966. *Hindu Scriptures*. London: Everyman's Library.

Notes

1. Marc Kaufman, "Researchers Say Stonehenge Was a Family Burial Ground," *Washington Post*, 30 May 2008: A1.

2. Mike Parker Pearson, *Stonehenge: Exploring the Greatest Stone Age Mystery* (London: Simon and Shuster, 2012).

3. *Chandogya Upanishad* I, xii, in Zaehner 1966: 84.

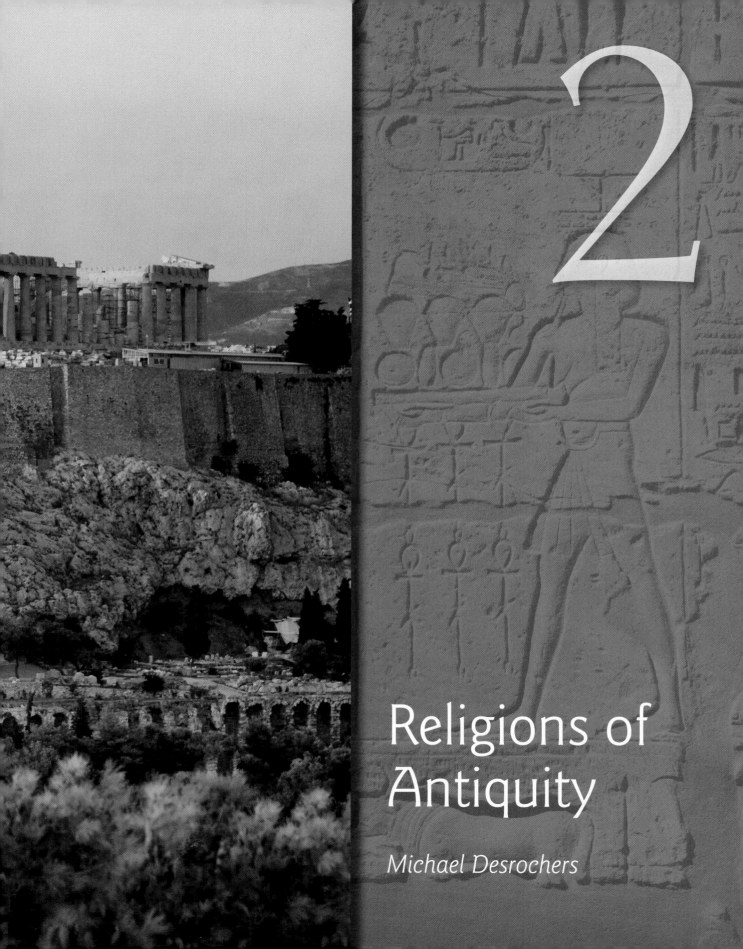

2

Religions of Antiquity

Michael Desrochers

Traditions at a Glance

In the Western context, "antiquity" refers to the general region of the Near East and the Mediterranean as it existed from the late fourth millennium BCE to the mid-first millennium CE. In that time many religious traditions emerged and evolved, sometimes independently and sometimes intersecting with one another.

Founders and Principal Leaders

None of the traditions examined in this chapter had founders or leaders.

Names of the Deity

Each tradition recognized hundreds, if not thousands, of deities, many of which also had multiple aspects, expressed in various epithets.

Authoritative Texts

None of the ancient traditions had a central text even remotely comparable to the scriptures of the Abrahamic religions. However, certain texts did become essential components of a canonic tradition: The *Epic of Gilgamesh* for Mesopotamia, Homer's *Iliad* for Greece, and Virgil's *Aeneid* for Rome.

Noteworthy Doctrines

All the ancient traditions were polytheistic, worshipping multiple gods, and all of them sought to promote moral/ethical behaviour. In practice, however, they all placed equal or greater emphasis on ritual of various types.

In this chapter you will learn about:

- the fundamental attributes of the religions of ancient Mesopotamia, Egypt, Greece, and Rome
- the nature and purposes of myth and ritual in antiquity
- shared and conflicting interpretations of the divine
- the variety of ways in which ancient peoples expressed their religiosity
- the reasons for both the longevity of the ancient traditions and their ultimate collapse.

"If we would be wise," states a character in the *Saturnalia* of the fifth-century-CE author Macrobius, "we must always revere antiquity" (Ando 2008: 178). Yet the same "antiquity" was castigated as "the mother of all evils" in a Christian sermon of the period (cited in Brown 1995: 24). In Deuteronomy 12:1–3 the Lord commands the Israelites not simply to destroy any Canaanite place of worship, altar, pillar, or idol but also to obliterate the memory of that tradition by erasing the very names of the Canaanites' gods. Surah 9, verse 113, of the Qur'an admonishes "believers" to extend neither forgiveness nor compassion to *mushrikun* ("polytheists" or "idolaters"), even if they are their own relatives; and verse 63 of the same *surah* declares that opponents of Allah will be condemned to the eternal fires of hell. The Wisdom of Solomon (one of the non-canonical books of the Bible known as the Apocrypha) identifies some of the evils of antiquity:

> All is in chaos—bloody murder, theft and fraud, corruption, treachery, riot, injury, honest men driven to distraction, ingratitude, moral corruption, sexual perversion, breakdown of marriage, adultery, debauchery. For the worship of idols, whose names it is wrong even to mention, is the beginning, cause, and end of every evil. Men either indulge themselves to the point of madness, or produce inspired utterance which is all lies, or live dishonest lives, or break their oath without scruple. They perjure

The Acropolis, Athens (Scott E Barbour/Getty Images).

themselves and expect no harm because the idols they trust in are lifeless (xiv: 25–30; Johnson 2009: 2–3).

What the two passages above condemned would be ridiculed in the early fifth century CE by the Christian philosopher Augustine of Hippo:

[L]et us inquire which gods, of all that host of gods . . . , they believed to be specially responsible for the extension and preservation of the Roman Empire. . . . [T]hey do not dare to assign any part to . . . Cloacina [goddess of sewers], or to Volupia [voluptuousness] or to Lubentina [lust], . . . or to Cunina [goddess of cradles]. How could Cunina have even given a thought to [weapons], when her authority was not permitted to range beyond cradles? (1972: 143–4; H. Bettenson, trans.).

Why should we examine the long-dead religious traditions (variously labelled as gentile, pagan, polytheist, or idolatrous, but all subsumed under the rubric "antiquity" in this chapter) within which Judaism, Christianity, and Islam developed, against which they identified themselves, which they cursed as wicked, and which they overcame? An elegant answer comes from a character in Robertson Davies' novel *Fifth Business*:

A serious study of any important body of human knowledge, or theory, or belief, if undertaken with a critical but not a cruel mind, would in the end yield . . . some valuable permanent insight into the nature of life and the true end of man.

A more modest answer might be that learning about those ancient traditions can help us appreciate and respect both commonalities and differences in the ways of being religious among various peoples. Another position, representative of antiquity's moralizing tendencies, comes from the Greek historian **Herodotus** (484–425 BCE), who held that every religious tradition should be respected.

Herodotus characterized the Persian ruler Cambyses as demented for mocking Egyptian priests by plunging his knife into the thigh of Egypt's sacred Apis-bull and asking, "Do you call that a god, you idiots?" On his return from Egypt to Persia, Cambyses died of a self-inflicted wound to his own thigh—a fate that ancient Greeks and Egyptians, among others, would have interpreted as divine justice. Sensitivity, based on knowledge, matters.

Terminology

We need to call on our sensitivity when we consider the term "religion" itself. Is the understanding of "religion" among contemporary adherents of the three monotheistic faiths comparable to that of the ancient Greeks, Egyptians, and Mesopotamians, none of whom had a single-word equivalent to the term "religion"? The word itself derives from the Latin *religio*, but even the Romans disagreed on what *religio* meant. Some associated it with the verb *religare* ("to bind"), as in the unbreakable bond between humans and gods; others, with *relegere* ("to go over again"), as in the meticulous repetition of a sacred ritual. In fact, the two notions were complementary. The community sought the continuing support of its gods by faithfully adhering to ancestral customs; each community had its own religious traditions, hence its own *religio*, as long as it participated in what the Roman philosopher Cicero (106–43 BCE) called "the pious **cult** of the gods"—"cult" being defined as ritual worship and "piety" as "giving the gods their due."

The ancient Greeks distinguished between the public expression of piety (*to hosion*) and privately felt reverence (*eusebia*), and spoke of "honouring the gods by participating in traditional practices" (*hiera kai hosia*) in roughly the same way that the Romans would speak of practising *religio*. A comparable Mesopotamian phrase translates as "fear of god," an attitude of reverence for gods manifested in cultic observances. An early Mesopotamian word for "prayer" consisted of a cuneiform sign for "grain" inside the sign for "calf." Prayer and sacrifice were inseparable. Anyone who prayed and sacrificed to the gods was "pious" and "wise." For the Egyptians, characterized by Herodotus as the most pious of the ancient peoples, the **Book of the Dead** (properly *The Book of Going Forth by Day*) set out what was expected: true religious practitioners would "propitiate the gods with the breath of their mouths, give proper offerings to the gods and render supplication offerings to the dead." But Egyptian religion also included ethics—doing justice to other humans. Thus in addition to requiring the proper respect for the gods and the dead, the *Book of the Dead* emphasized truth in human relationships: the truly religious "judge poor and rich," "live on truth and feast on truth, [their] hearts do not lie, [they] detest falsehood" (von Dassow 1994: 116; R. Faulkner, trans.).

In the second century CE, the Roman grammarian Festus defined religious people as those who participated in the state's traditional rituals and avoided superstition (*superstitio*)—"irrational" behaviour that might include anything from intentional disregard of standard state practices to improper pursuit of secret knowledge, overly emotional engagement with a particular god, or placation of gods based on fear of their malevolence rather than trust in their beneficence. *Superstitio* was a Latin translation of the Greek *deisidaimonia*: literally, "fear of the gods," especially the numerous minor deities (*daimones*) who played more active roles in the daily life of humans than the major gods did.

According to an expanded definition in Book 3 of Cicero's *On the Nature of the Gods*:

> The entirety of the *religio* of the Roman people is divided into rites and auspices, to which is added a third thing, namely whatever warnings the interpreters of the Sibylline books or haruspices issue for the sake of foreknowledge on the basis of portents and dreams. I hold that none of these *religiones* should ever be neglected (Ando 2008: 3).

The passage makes three important points. First, Roman religion consisted of three practices: cult/ ritual, divination, and prophecy. Second, it did not concern itself with belief (a position it shared with the other religions of antiquity). Third, each of those practices was itself a separate religion, hence the plural *religiones*. Plurality, "polyreligiousness," outweighed singularity.

When Christians co-opted the term *religio* in the fourth century CE, they redefined it to refer solely to their own "true" faith in a single god and in so doing reclassified the old traditions as false—not religion but superstition. In 384 CE, Symmachus, prefect of Rome, attempted to defend the original pluralistic meaning of *religio*, arguing that "everyone has his customs, everyone his own rites; the Divine Mind has designated different guardians and different cults to different cities." He further suggested that "if a long period gives authority to religious customs, we ought to keep faith with so many centuries and to follow our ancestors, as they happily followed theirs" (Schaff and Wace 1885: 415). Four decades later, the Theodosian Code (a compilation of all the laws enacted since the time of the first Christian emperor, Constantine) outlawed those traditional modes of piety as superstitions and legally defined religion from the single perspective of the Christian church.

✤ Religiosity

This chapter examines the religious views and practices of four ancient civilizations (Mesopotamian, Egyptian, Greek, and Roman) to the exclusion of others. Eschewing a chronological approach ("antiquity" covers more than 4,000 years), it focuses on three distinct groups within each of those civilizations—common people, officials (both government and religious), and intellectuals (court or temple scribes, poets, philosophers)— and explores how they were involved with the divine. The chapter identifies four types of such involvement: understanding the world (*cosmos* in Greek), negotiating the world, communing with the divine, and transcending the world. Each of the three groups—individual householders, officials, and intellectuals—understood, negotiated,

Timeline

	Mesopotamia	Egypt	Greece	Rome
3000 BCE	Sumerian Era			
2700 BCE		**Old Kingdom** Pyramid Age Pyramid Text		
2300 BCE	Sargon			
2000 BCE		**Middle Kingdom** *Merikare*		
1800 BCE	Hammurabi *Epic of Gilgamesh*	Coffin Texts		
		New Kingdom *Book of the Dead*		
1300 BCE		Akhenaten		
	Enuma Elish			
1100 BCE				
	Omen collections			
700 BCE			Homer Hesiod	
				Roman Republic
500 BCE	Persian Conquest	Persian Conquest	Xenophanes	
400 BCE			Plato	
	Alexander's Conquest	Alexander's Conquest	Alexander	
300 BCE				
200 BCE			*Hymn to Zeus*	Cybele imported
100 BCE				
BCE/CE	Last cuneiform text	Roman conquest		Cicero Augustus Caesar Virgil Ovid
100 CE				Epictetus
300 CE				Constantine
400 CE				Theodosius Sack of Rome Augustine

Map 2.1 Classical World of Greece and Rome

communed, and sought transcendence in different ways. The vehicle for understanding the cosmos was myth, while the fundamental, though not exclusive, means of negotiating it was ritual/cult. To commune with the gods was to feel profound awe and wonder in their presence. Finally, to transcend the world was to overcome the material conditions of human existence, including death. Evidence for institutional and intellectual responses to the divine is available in the wealth of written material they have bequeathed us, while archaeology fills in the gaps for the common people.

Prehistory

Before examining antiquity, we should take a brief glance at prehistory. In the absence of documentary evidence we must rely on material remains; thus our interpretations of prehistory will always be conjectural.

The origins of anatomically modern humans have recently been pushed back as far as 200,000 years ago. Some scholars contend that human symbolic behaviour, such as the association of red ochre with burials—hence the very origins of religion—can be traced to an equally distant time, making religion inherent to our species. The spectacular cave paintings created over a span of 25 millennia—from roughly 35,000 to 10,000 BCE—seem to include many symbolic elements associated with religion, even if there is no consensus on how they should be interpreted. Four more recent sites in southwestern Asia and northeast Africa offer somewhat clearer evidence of the types of symbolic

Map 2.2 Ancient Near East

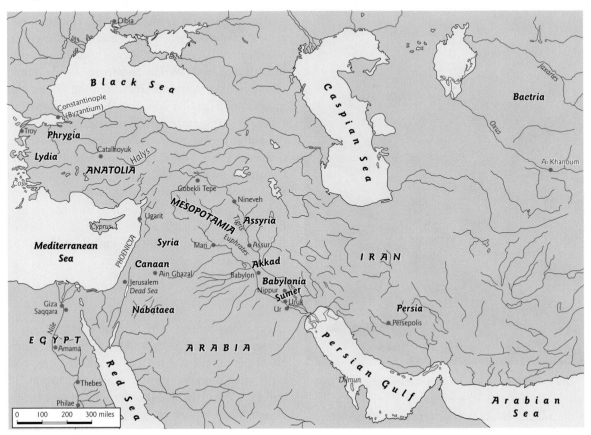

behaviour associated with religion in the period from approximately 9500 to 3500 BCE.

Gobekli Tepe

Dating from 9500 to 8000 BCE, Gobekli Tepe in southeastern Turkey consisted of a series of rings or circles, edged by benches that connected massive T-shaped pillars whose sides resembled human arms. It is the oldest known example of monumental architecture, and if its excavator is correct in claiming that Gobekli was a temple complex, it is also the oldest known religious structure. Since similar features have been found at several contemporary sites nearby, Gobekli represents what may be termed the oldest known religious tradition (second oldest if one counts the cave paintings).

Gobekli's builders were pre-agricultural foragers. Given the meagre evidence that anyone lived there, the complex must have served as a central meeting place for social functions, including feasts and ceremonies. One interesting hypothesis suggests that it was the necessity of feeding large numbers of workers and pilgrims that served as the catalyst for the development of agriculture; the earliest evidence for the domestication of wheat, dated to 9000 BCE, was found at a site barely 30 kilometres (20 miles) from Gobekli. If this hypothesis is valid, it reverses the long-held position that organized religion began in response to the needs of settled agricultural life. Religion, in this new view, may have been the inspiration for agriculture and, ultimately, the beginnings of "civilization."

Uncovered by the German archaeologist Klaus Schmidt, Gobekli Tepe in Turkey is believed to be the world's oldest temple, predating the pyramids and Stonehenge. Its discovery has called into question many long-held ideas about prehistoric peoples.

Catalhoyuk

Catalhoyuk, 480 km (300 miles) west of Gobekli, was an early agricultural town, inhabited from 7400 to 6000 BCE. Its growth seems to have coincided with the desertion of other nearby settlements, and its unusual layout may reflect a new approach to social integration, prompted by the need to absorb disparate groups of people. Catalhoyuk's structures are clearly residential, divided into two distinct zones: a drab domestic space and a "sacred" area with platforms superimposed over burials and walls painted with scenes of humans baiting wild animals and often adorned with bulls' heads.

Burials, platforms, thresholds, and plaster-covered animal skulls were all painted with red ochre.

Catalhoyuk was as much a ritual centre as it was a place of production, and as much a cemetery as a settlement. Many of the homes contain evidence of both numerous burials and frequent rebuilding. In effect, they were archives, holding bones and material objects that appear to have functioned as symbolic texts, preserving transgenerational memory and bringing ancestors temporarily back to life with each rebuilding. Catalhoyuk exemplifies many features of religious significance: the role of religion as an integrator of both families and communities; boundaries between the mundane and the sacred; rituals and memorialization; as well as the use of figurines and a repertoire of symbols used in the region for several millennia.

'Ain Ghazal

Excavations at the 'Ain Ghazal site in Jordan, inhabited from 7250 to 5000 BCE, revealed burials of 32 plaster statues, some half life-size, and busts with prominent eyes, in addition to human remains. What the statues represented (ancestors, ghosts, worshippers, or gods) is unclear, as is the reason for their burial, although the fact that the most prominent figure is a female holding her breasts, a pose found in Near Eastern iconography for the next five millennia, suggests an association with fertility. It's possible that the statues played a role in public observances of some kind, perhaps seasonal ceremonies associated with the agricultural year.

Nabta Playa

Nabta Playa, in the western desert of southern Egypt, was a meeting place for Saharan cattle herders, who erected a series of significant monuments there between the late seventh and mid-fourth millennia BCE. One part of the complex, labelled the Valley of Sacrifices, held several burials, including the remains of entire cattle. One burial even contained a life-sized stone sculpture of a cow.

Sites

Babylon, Mesopotamia

Literally the "gateway of/to the gods," Babylon was for many centuries the political and religious centre of Mesopotamia. Its sixth king, Hammurabi (c. 1750 BCE) claimed that, with the construction of his temple complex dedicated to the god Marduk, Babylon had supplanted the one-time Sumerian religious centre, Nippur, as the "navel of the universe."

Next to the Valley of Sacrifices were several megalithic complexes, including standing stones with **anthropomorphic** (human-shaped) shoulders (as at Gobekli), oriented to the brightest stars of the northern sky. There was also a "calendar circle" used to predict the summer solstice, when life-giving rains would arrive. Abandoned around 3400 BCE, Nabta was foundational for much of what would become central to Egyptian civilization, including religion, for the next several millennia. Egypt's most widely adored deity was the goddess **Hathor**: depicted as a cow, she was considered the patron of rulers. Of course, the best-known Egyptian burials are the royal pyramids. Every pyramid had a series of internal passageways that opened to the outside and were oriented to the very same stars as the stones at Nabta, the stars that were understood to be the home of the gods and the ultimate destination of deceased pharaohs.

🐚 Deities

Nothing so characterized antiquity as the omnipresence of the divine. Antiquity was, in the words of the early-sixth-century-BCE Greek philosopher Thales, a "world full of gods." The best-known are the major Greek deities and their Roman counterparts: **Zeus**–Jupiter, **Hera**–Juno, Aphrodite–Venus, Ares–Mars, Athena–Minerva, Poseidon–Neptune, Artemis–Diana, Hermes–Mercury, Hephaestus–Vulcan, **Demeter**–Ceres, plus Apollo and Dionysus. These were the 12 great gods who, according to the ancient Greeks, inhabited Mount Olympus. But 12 is a paltry number compared to the hundreds and even thousands of gods invoked by other ancient civilizations. The Babylonian epic of creation **_Enuma Elish_** described the city of Babylon as the meeting place of 300 gods from "on high" and 300 more from "below"; Egyptian texts and

Sites

Olympia, Greece

The site of the ancient Olympic games, on the southwestern peninsula known as the Peloponnese. Its sanctuary contained numerous structures, including temples to Zeus and Hera, as well as a monumental statue of Zeus that was among the "seven wonders" of the ancient world. According to legend, the Olympic Games were instituted in 776 BCE and the festival continued to be held every four years until 393 CE, when the Roman emperor Theodosius I outlawed it as a pagan tradition.

monuments named at least 1,500 deities; the Mesopotamians had some 2,500; one early **Sumerian** text referred to 3,600 gods (3,600 being a symbolic number signifying totality); and in Rome, as Augustine mockingly noted in the passage quoted earlier, there was a specific "little god" for almost every aspect of life.

Not all deities were equally god-like, of course. Divinity was a continuum along which great gods, secondary gods, minor gods, demigods such as heroes, personified abstractions, and special groups such as nymphs, the dead, and divinized emperors all occupied different locations. Even among the great gods—the 12 Olympians, for instance, or the "seven great gods" of Mesopotamia—one was supreme: Olympian Zeus, Mesopotamian Enlil (until he was supplanted by **Marduk**), Egyptian **Amun-Ra**, or Roman Jupiter.

Early Gods

The earliest gods corresponded to natural phenomena: sun, moon, planets, sky, grain, fresh water, storm. Mesopotamia's Enlil was "Lord Wind." The Sumerian goddess Inanna, depicted in the fourth millennium BCE as a reed gatepost, guarded the storehouses on which a community's survival depended. The oldest Sumerian cuneiform sign for "god" was an eight-sided star. As the Tigris–Euphrates floodplain became urbanized in the late fourth millennium BCE, the deified elements of nature acquired social and political functions. Each city had its own patron deity, typically accompanied by a spouse and counsellors. Over time the gods of several cities or districts were connected to one another through complex family relationships, eventually leading to the development of a pantheon ("totality of gods").

The early patron gods were the equivalent of petty rulers, but as the more successful cities came to dominate entire regions, their gods were elevated accordingly. For instance, the status of Marduk, the previously unimportant patron god of Babylon, received an important boost under Hammurabi (r. 1792–1750 BCE) and thereafter continued to rise until, in the Babylonian creation epic (composed towards the end of the second millennium BCE), he became the supreme ruler of the Mesopotamian pantheon. Egypt's New Kingdom rulers similarly elevated Amun, the patron of their home city of Thebes, linking him, as Amun-Ra, with the sun-deity Ra, the dominant god of the Old Kingdom.

Power

The defining characteristic of pre-eminent gods was their supreme power; the **Akkadian** word for god was *ilum*, whose root had to do with power. It was from *ilum* that the Hebrew *el(ohim)* and Arabic *Allah* were derived. The greatest power was associated with the fiercest forces of nature—in particular, storms. Enlil, Zeus, and even the early Yahweh were storm gods. The most powerful humans being rulers, the supreme gods were rulers as well. Secondary gods played supporting roles, acting as judges dispensing justice to humans or as advisors to the sovereign god, seeking to contain his "stormy" power. Minor gods served as a kind of

Sites

Thebes (modern Luxor), Egypt

The political and religious capital of the New Kingdom. The great temples of Luxor and nearby Karnak were dedicated to Amun-Ra. The Valley of the Kings, where New Kingdom rulers were buried, is located on the west bank of the Nile, on the opposite shore from Thebes.

staff, carrying out unpleasant tasks for the more powerful deities. In Greece these *daimones* were understood to be agents of calamity and punishment. Like subordinate administrators serving the ruler, numerous deities—each with a different local base and area of responsibility, under the direction of one pre-eminent leader and assisted by numerous divine servants—collectively ensured societal order. Multiplicity secured unity, of the cosmos and of the state.

Divine Light

Intrinsic to Mesopotamian deities was "divine splendour" (*melammu*; literally, "luminous power"), an awesome and fearsome supernatural brilliance emanating from the gods, portrayed as a halo surrounding their heads. At Marduk's birth, the "auras of the gods" clothed his body and encircled his head. The narrator of the Roman poet **Ovid**'s *Fasti*, while praying to the goddess **Vesta**, "felt the influence of celestial divinity, and the glad earth gleamed with a purple light" (Feeney 1998: 99). A comparable Egyptian term was *akhu*, "radiant power." Amun was praised: "How great is your power! Your appearance is noble. You have surrounded me with your radiance" (Assmann 2001: 117). In Egypt it was the custom to place under the head of the deceased a disk-shaped object inscribed with an incantation in the belief that this would enflame head and body and thereby stimulate the process of divinization. Gilded veneers made Mesopotamian statues of deities appear to scintillate, and the Assyrians depicted gods with flames emerging from their heads and torsos. The Greek word for god, *theos*, is likely to have originally meant "bright"; thus the gods were "the shining ones." When, in the *Homeric Hymn to Demeter*, the mother goddess reveals herself to the royal family of **Eleusis**,

> beauty spread around her and a lovely fragrance was wafted from her sweet-smelling robes, and from the divine body of the goddess a light shone afar, while golden tresses spread down over her shoulders so that the

strong house was filled with brightness as with lightning (Bowden 2010: 21–2).

So awesome is this vision that queen Metaneira collapses to the ground.

Omniscience

A third major characteristic of gods was their superior knowledge. The deeply religious Greek historian Xenophon (430–354 BCE) noted in his *Cyropedia* that "The gods, who always exist, know all things, both the things that have taken place, the things that are, and whatever shall come to pass" (Flower 2008: 106). According to a Mesopotamian work from the second millennium BCE known as the *Babylonian Theodicy*, "The divine mind, like the centre of heaven, is remote. Knowledge of it is difficult; humans do not know it" (Lambert 1960: 87).

Appropriation of Gods

Third-millennium-BCE Sumerians began to organize their thousands of gods in lists, typically with two columns: names in the left column and descriptions in the right. Later, bilingual lists correlated Sumerian with Semitic gods in the same way that the Romans correlated their gods with those of the Greeks: the Sumerian goddess Inanna, for instance, was linked with the Semitic **Ishtar**, the Sumerian sun-god Utu with the Semitic Shamash, and the Sumerian Enki with the Semitic Ea.

Eventually, Mesopotamians produced multilingual lists, recording multiple names for the same god. As political boundaries expanded and contact among different peoples increased, correlations among the gods of different cultures became increasingly frequent. Berossus, a Babylonian priest in the third century BCE, wrote that the Persian ruler Artaxerxes II erected a statue of Aphrodite Anaitis (Greek for Persian Anahita) in Babylon and encouraged her worship throughout his empire. Herodotus had already equated certain Egyptian gods with their closest counterparts in the Greek pantheon. Especially after Alexander's conquests in the fourth century BCE, the Greeks identified foreign gods with their own: Amun and Marduk with Zeus, Ishtar with Aphrodite, the Egyptian deities **Isis** and Thoth with Demeter and Hermes. Some scholars see this trend as marking a fusion of religious traditions termed syncretism; others interpret it simply as a reflection of the need for peoples from different traditions to communicate with one another.

Whatever the motivation, the Roman historian Tacitus (56–117 CE) captured the phenomenon in his discussion of the Greco-Egyptian god Serapis, who appears to have been deliberately created in the third century BCE in an effort to reconcile Egyptians to their Greek rulers, the Ptolemys:

> As for the identity of [Serapis], he is equated by many with Aesculapius [the Latin form of the Greek **Asclepius**] because he heals the sick, by some with **Osiris**, who is the oldest deity known to the Near East, by [others] with Jupiter[,] owing to his all-embracing powers (1964: 266; K. Wellesley, trans.).

Gods and Goddesses

There were household gods, such as the Roman Penates and Lares; there were gods of the countryside, such as Pan in Greece; cities had their own patron gods, such as Athena in Athens or Marduk in Babylon; and different political regimes promoted specific state gods, as Egypt's New Kingdom rulers promoted Amun-Ra. All these were male

Inanna–Ishtar, goddess of love and war, was one of many Mesopotamian goddesses. This terracotta relief was crafted in approximately 2000 BCE.

Eileen Tweedy/The Art Archive at Art Resource, NY

deities, but there were as many goddesses as gods. The two most important female deities in Egypt were Isis and Hathor.

Worshipped in Egypt as early as the Old Kingdom, Isis became so popular that in time her

Sites

Athens, Greece

The city-state that was the cultural heart of the ancient Greek world. The Parthenon, the temple dedicated to the city's patron deity, the goddess Athena, was erected in the fifth century BCE and overlooks the city from the rocky outcrop called the Acropolis. The city was also home to the Temple of Hephaestus and the Temple of Olympian Zeus (at one time the largest temple in mainland Greece).

worship spread throughout the Greek and Roman worlds. One reason for her popularity was her role as a nurturing mother, captured in the many statues that show her nursing her son, Horus.

That maternal role led to her assimilation to Hathor, who represented beauty, love, and motherhood. In her guise as the lion-headed goddess Sekhmet, Hathor also represented violent destruction, although she was normally depicted as either a cow or a woman wearing a crown with a sun disk between cow horns. One scholar has suggested that the most significant feature of Mesopotamian religion was its many powerful goddesses. Some were nurturers, such as Ninsun, literally the "mistress of wild cows," who was the mother of **Gilgamesh**, and Ninhursaga, described as the wet-nurse of kings whom she nourished on her lap, or the even more prominent Inanna–Ishtar, who like Hathor

Focus

The *Epic of Gilgamesh*

There was an actual third-millennium-BCE Sumerian king named Gilgamesh. Proclaimed a god shortly after his death, he became the subject of a series of tales. During the Old Babylonian period the stories were reorganized into a single composition that would be recast throughout later Mesopotamian history and would spread across the ancient Near East. Unfortunately, no complete version of *Gilgamesh* has survived, but the two main versions—the Old Babylonian and the first-millennium-BCE Standard—are sufficiently complete to allow modern readers to follow the plot.

The story opens with the citizens of the city of Uruk appealing to the gods for relief from their oppressive king. The gods respond by creating a wild, "uncivilized" man named Enkidu to serve as a counterweight to Gilgamesh. The two become friends, however, and decide to gain lasting fame by killing the demon known as the Guardian of the Cedar Forest. The plan succeeds, but the fact that they kill the creature as it begs for its life turns what might have been an honourable victory into an act of murder.

News of their adventure attracts the interest of Ishtar, the goddess of love and fertility. When Gilgamesh rejects her amorous advances, she shows her other side, as the goddess of destruction. She threatens to open the gates to the underworld and unleash the restive spirits on the world unless her father sends the Bull of Heaven to punish not just Gilgamesh but his people. Accordingly, the bull is sent, only to be slain by Gilgamesh and Enkidu. Then Enkidu makes a fatal mistake: instead of offering the animal as a sacrifice, he tears off the thighbone and hurls it at the gods. For this sacrilege Enkidu must die.

Enkidu's death transforms Gilgamesh, for now he has to face his own mortality—a reality that this son of a goddess has not previously considered. He sets out to discover the secret of immortality. Although several characters along the way warn him that he will not find the object of his quest, he is undaunted. Finally he reaches the island where the immortal Utnapishtim lives with his wife—the only survivors of the annihilating flood sent by the god Enlil in his rage against humans. Utnapishtim tells Gilgamesh the story of the flood, revealing that he did not achieve his immortality but was given it as a divine gift. In parting, Utnapishtim gives Gilgamesh a plant named "Old Man Grown Young"—an early version of the fountain of youth. But Gilgamesh loses even that consolation prize when a snake steals it from him. Returning home chastened, wiser, and resigned to his mortality, he dedicates the rest of his life to being the best ruler, husband, and father he can.

was simultaneously a goddess of love and war and who like both Isis and Hathor granted and guaranteed kingship. The most popular Greek goddesses were "kourotrophic," "child-nourishing." To the common people, Hera (who was also symbolized by a cow) was not the nagging scold depicted in epic poetry but, like Demeter and Artemis, a solicitous guardian of women. The male deity most favoured by Greek women was **Asclepius** because of his assistance in the most critical issues in a woman's life—fertility, pregnancy, and childbirth. An Egyptian "child-nourishing" goddess named Taweret, especially popular in the homes of commoners, was depicted as a hippopotamus, a species whose females were known for their ferocity in protecting their young. It is not surprising that Strabo, a Greek geographer and historian of the first century CE, remarked: "All agree that women are the chief founders of religion; it is women who encourage men to more attentive worship of the gods" (Connelly 2007: 166–7).

🐾 Understanding the World

The people most interested in understanding the cosmos were antiquity's intellectuals. The earliest of them were tellers of oral tales, but the works that have been preserved were produced by a literate elite that, though typically anonymous in Mesopotamia and Egypt, included many familiar Greek and Roman names. The intellectuals' mode of explanation was myth. In addition to explaining, myth entertained, moralized, legitimated, inspired, and even mocked. It offered insights into human nature, social and political relations, and cosmic operations. It even attempted to translate into human terms the seemingly untranslatable. Myth touched on the everyday even as it addressed the ultimate human questions: how the world originated (cosmogony); how it was structured (cosmology); how the gods came into being (theogony); the nature of the gods (theology); how humans came into existence (anthropogony); the conditions of human life (anthropology); the relationship between fate and free will; how the gods could be seen as just when

they allowed evil to exist in the world (theodicy); the end of life and what would come next (eschatology). Myth offered no single explanation for any of those concerns: it was open-ended, comfortable with several possibilities. At a certain point, however, the poets' mythic accounts of the world would be challenged by the accounts proposed by a rival set of intellectuals—the philosophers.

Cosmogony: How the World Originated

In their myths the ancients used analogy to address several of the "big" questions, especially those concerning origins and identity. There was no creation *ex nihilo* (out of nothing). Creation represented the transformation of shapeless pre-existence ("before two things had developed") into substantial existence, of potentiality into actuality. Creation gave shape to the amorphous, which Egyptians and Mesopotamians alike envisioned as primeval waters. To explain how that transformation came about, both civilizations used two analogical models.

Nature

The first analogical model for creation was nature, as in the daily circuit of the sun or the annual changes of season. Since life in Egypt depended on the annual flooding of the Nile to irrigate the land, one Egyptian creation story envisioned an earthen mound with a lotus plant emerging from the receding primeval waters. By the New Kingdom, sun and lotus were merged iconographically. The sanctuary of every Egyptian temple replicated that primeval mound.

Human Behaviour

The second analogical model for creation was human behaviour. Some things came into being through sexual intercourse, some through the spoken word, and some through labour. One Egyptian creation myth personified the undifferentiated

Sites

Memphis, Egypt

Located just south of contemporary Cairo, Memphis was the capital of Egypt during the Old Kingdom, when the three great pyramids were constructed at the city's nearby **necropolis** of Giza/Gizeh. Designated a World Heritage Site in 1979, today its ruins are an open-air museum. The major religious structure in Memphis itself was the Great Temple of Ptah, dedicated to the patron god of the city.

waters as the primeval god named Atum, whose name meant both "nonexistent" and "completed." But in fact he was far from complete: aware of his lone(li)ness, he impregnated himself and gave birth to twin gods, a male named Shu ("air") and a female named Tefnut ("moisture"), also known, respectively, as Ankh ("life") and Ma'at ("order"). Androgynous Atum passed on to his sexually dimorphic offspring his "life force" (*ka*), which they in turn implanted in their children Geb ("earth") and Nut ("sky"). In this way singularity became duality became plurality, which in time became complexity and diversity, including deadly competition. Indeed, it was the rivalry among the fourth-generation descendants of Geb and Nut—**Osiris** and Seth, with their sister-consorts Isis and Nephthys—that formed the basis of Egypt's most pervasive myth. (Osiris, murdered by Seth, was temporarily resurrected by Isis, who managed to conceive their son Horus before Osiris returned forever to

Document

From the Mesopotamian Creation Epic, *Enuma Elish*

Enuma Elish *(the first two words of the piece, translated as "When on high") was probably composed towards the end of the second millennium* BCE *as literary propaganda in support of Babylonian claims to supremacy in Mesopotamia. Crediting Marduk, the patron of Babylon, with the defeat of the primordial creatures whose remains he used to fashion the universe (essentially by naming everything), it elevated him to the position of supreme god and thereby legitimized Babylon's rise to dominance. The opening lines (I: 1–10), which allude to pre-existent potentiality, include references to several of the concepts that were also fundamental to Egyptian creation myths: procreation, naming, fashioning, and land emerging from primeval waters (the female* **Tiamat** *represented salt water; the male Apsu, fresh underground water).*

When on high heaven had yet no name,
Nor below had earth received its name,
Primordial Apsu, their begetter,
And fashioner Tiamat, who bore them all,
Mingled their waters together;
No pastures had yet formed, no reedbeds had emerged;
No single god had yet appeared,
No name spoken, no destiny decreed;
Then the gods within them came to life.
Their names pronounced, Lahmu and Lahamu emerged.

the underworld; when Horus was grown, he took up the struggle with Seth.) Eventually Atum was further differentiated into Ra, the sun-god whose daily passage represented eternal recurrence; Heka, transformational power; Sia, imagination; and Hu, the word that turned image into creature. The creator, "the one who made himself into millions," initiated differentiation and multiplication.

Ptah, the city-god of Memphis, was another Egyptian creator-deity who brought everything into existence through thought and speech. In the beginning was the thought; then came the word. Creation stories themselves multiplied to the point that every late-Egyptian temple had a different story in which its own god played the role of creator. Isis was "mistress of the word in the beginning." Another goddess created the entire world by proclaiming just seven magic words. Words—the union of name and object—were the basis of identity.

Cosmology: How the World is Structured

In Greek accounts such as **Hesiod**'s *Theogony*, as in their Mesopotamian and Egyptian counterparts, the first order of creation was the divine. Cosmogony started with theogony. Next came cosmology, the organization of the universe. Egyptians, Greeks, and Mesopotamians all envisioned a tripartite cosmos: heaven, earth, and a **netherworld** of some kind. According to a Mesopotamian text known as *Atrahasis*, the process of organization began with a lottery in which Anu won heaven, Enlil the earth, and Ea the underground waters.

Cosmic order was the goal, but conflict was the norm. So threatening was Tiamat (who gave birth to a brood of sea monsters) that Marduk killed her and fashioned the universe out of her carcass. In Greece, Zeus led his generation of gods in overthrowing the older Titans, headed by his father Cronus, who in his time had unseated his own progenitor, Uranus. Similarly in Egypt, the rivalry that led Seth to murder his brother Osiris continued with Horus, the

son of the murdered Osiris. Ma'at (order) waged an unending struggle against Isfet (chaos). And the sun-god Ra, whose light represented life, descended into the netherworld every night to do battle with the serpent-monster Apophis, who symbolized evil in that he threatened the source of life itself.

In a world where order was so tenuous, it was essential to establish institutions, protocols, and responsibilities for the gods. One Sumerian myth listed 94 components of the cosmic state, including kingship, governorship, power, knowledge, triumph, rebellion, godhood, priesthood, temple servant, sanctuary, truth, slander, righteousness, dishonesty, and justice (that is, political and religious institutions and ethical standards). Within this cosmic state, every god was assigned a specific responsibility. The goddess Ninti, whose name literally meant "Lady (*nin*) rib (*ti*)," had the single duty of nursing the sore rib of Enki, the Sumerian god of wisdom. One god was assigned to serve as the divine inspector of canals, another as the divine architect, yet another as the guardian of boundaries. Such appointments were made permanent when they were inscribed on the Tablet of Destinies, which played a role in several myths. In one, the goddess Inanna stole Enki's tablet by getting him drunk. In another, the cosmic state ceased operating when the tablet was hidden. According to *Enuma Elish*, once Marduk had defeated the forces of chaos, he secured the tablet, thereby legitimizing both his claim to kingship of the gods and his decrees for reorganizing the cosmos.

In cloudless Egypt, the most visible manifestation of order was the sun's daily course across the sky. As Ra's earthly representative, the king was responsible for ensuring order. Thus each day his regimen re-enacted the sun's routine. Egypt's temples were not only the homes of particular gods but models of the cosmos itself. The walls that enclosed them separated order from chaos; processional passageways replicated the course of the sun; dim inner sanctums corresponded to the primeval darkness from which life and order emerged. In maintaining their kingdom's temples, Egyptian rulers secured *ma'at*, the continuing order of the cosmos.

© Glen Allison/Alamy

The Great Temple at Abu Simbel in Nubia (southern Egypt) was commissioned by Ramesses II. Four colossal statues of the pharaoh guard the entrance, while Ra-Horakhty is shown above the entrance. The entrance was positioned so that on two occasions each year the sun could penetrate some 60 metres (200 feet) into the innermost sanctuary and illuminate its four statues: the deified Ramesses, Ra-Horakhty, Amun-Ra, and Ptah.

Socrates (*Gorgias*) observed, "Wise men say that heaven and earth and gods and men are bound together by communion and friendship, orderliness, temperance, and justice, and it is for this reason that they call this whole a cosmos" (F. Rochberg, in Snell 2005: 339). The speaker may have been Greek, but his ideas capture the "wisdom" of Mesopotamian and Egyptian myth.

Anthropogony: How Humans Came to Exist

In Mesopotamia, the more important gods might have enjoyed their existence, but the lesser gods faced eternal drudgery on their behalf. Eventually the latter rebelled, forcing the major gods to find substitutes. Thus humans were created, formed of clay lubricated with the blood of a rebel leader. Humans (*awilum*) were partly divine (*ilum*), but they were flawed from the start because their progenitor had challenged the cosmic order. Just as their life-source had been put to death for his "original sin," humans would one day die and become spirit (*etemmu*). At the same time, because humans had inherited the mind (*temu*) of their dead ancestor, they knew that they were created to serve the gods, to toil daily on their behalf. Name and ancestry defined human nature; divine will determined human function.

The creation of humans was not a major theme in ancient Egypt. Among the few references to the subject are two **Coffin Texts** (spells inscribed on coffins during the Middle Kingdom to assist the deceased in the afterlife). Coffin Text 1130, a speech by the sun-god Ra, includes what is essentially a play on words: "I created gods from my sweat while humans [*rmt*] are the tears [*rmwt*] of my eye" (Assmann 2001: 177). Coffin Text 714 explains that the creator wept because the other gods were angry at him. Tears streaming, he became temporarily blind, unable to see what his tears had produced. Humans were thus the imperfect products of blind anger and self-pity—quintessential "human" qualities.

Classical myth also regarded humanity as flawed from the beginning. One tradition, recounted in Ovid's *Metamorphoses*, traced human ancestry to the Titans, the representatives of brute force, barbarism, and chaos, who were defeated by the Olympians, the proponents of law, order, and civilization.

Thus humans were variously described as sprouting from soil irrigated by the Titans' blood, materializing out of their incinerated remains, or being formed from their flesh and blood and brought to life by the lightning bolt of Zeus. Ovid reproved humans for being—like the Titans—"contemptuous of the gods."

Another set of traditions associated human beginnings with an "original offence" of some kind. When Prometheus ("Forethought"), who fashioned humans from water and earth, stole fire for them, he gave them the ability to offer sacrifices to the gods, but that ability was tainted inasmuch as it was the result of a transgression. Similarly, Pandora ("Allgift") was entrusted with a "box" (actually a jar) by Hermes, who instructed her never to open it; but she disobeyed, opened the jar, and let loose all the evils that would afflict humans for ever after. So dismal was Hesiod's view of humanity that, in his

Focus

The *Iliad*

The *Iliad*, composed by Homer in the eighth century BCE, describes the events of several days towards the end of the ten-year war between the Greeks and the Trojans. The war pits not only humans but also gods against one another. Hera, Poseidon, and Athena, for instance, favour the Greeks, while Apollo, Ares, and Aphrodite side with the Trojans. The gods—who do not have to face death—are depicted as considerably less noble than the human characters. Lying, browbeating, carping, threatening, promiscuous, and generally petty, the gods are hardly suitable models for humans to emulate. Their dominant characteristic is their vastly superior power, most evident in Zeus, who shows no concern for human death and anguish.

The human who most resembles the gods is Achilles, the most powerful Greek warrior, whose father was human but whose mother was a minor goddess. The *Iliad* is his story above all, its first line announcing the theme of "Achilles' wrath." When aroused, Achilles projects the power of a god, and in the concluding chapters he is truly uncontrollable, willing to go to his own prophesied death once he has unleashed his deadly fury on as many Trojans and gods as possible. Even after he kills Hector, the greatest and most noble of the Trojan heroes and the specific target of his "mankillings," Achilles' wrath is undiminished. He straddles Hector's corpse, abusing it and refusing to release it for burial. His anger is still seething when Priam, Hector's aging father, crawls in terror towards him to plead for the release of his son's body. Reminded of his own father, Achilles sets aside his wrath and grants Priam his wish. This act of compassion tames Achilles' "god-like" anger and restores his humanity.

Works and Days, he lamented the contrast between the humans of his time, the so-called "Iron Race," condemned to toil and misery, and those of the first "Golden Race," who neither toiled nor aged but feasted and lived like gods. Decline was inherent in the human condition.

Anthropology: The Conditions of Human Life

Greek literature, in particular, confronted the fundamental flaws that humans could not overcome. In myth, epic, tragedy, and history, Greeks examined the truth of Zeus' remark to Athena, near the beginning of **Homer**'s *Odyssey*, that greed and folly doubled the suffering that was the lot of humans. Humans always wanted more than they had and consistently overrated their own intelligence. Their arrogant pride ("hubris") led them to ignore divine warnings, think they can deceive the gods, and refuse to accept the limits imposed on them. Greek authors delineated those limits and demonstrated the tragic consequences of ignoring them. An example is the tale of Daedalus and Icarus, made famous by Ovid in his *Metamorphoses*. To escape from Crete, Daedalus constructed feather-and-wax wings for himself and his son. As they departed, he warned Icarus to "fly a middle course. If you're too low, sea spray may damp your wings; and if you fly too high, the heat is scorching" (Mandelbaum 1993: 255). But hubristic Icarus ignored his father; he soared higher and higher until the sun's fiery rays melted the wax and he plunged to his death in the sea.

Mesopotamian myths reflected a similar view of human nature. In *Atrahasis*, for instance, the first humans did not recognize any limit on procreation, and their numbers multiplied so rapidly that they disturbed the divine rest of Enlil. He then sent a great flood to drown them all, but relented—allowing the hero Atrahasis and his family to survive—when Ea offers two solutions to the population problem: miscarriage and death. (There is an echo of this story in the *Epic of Gilgamesh* when

the hero encounters Utnapishtim, another flood survivor who owes his life to the intercession of Ea.) The same pattern can be seen in Greece, where the Olympian gods were said to have sent a "liquidating" flood in retaliation for a deceitful sacrifice. In that case the survivors, Deucalion and Pyrrha, revived humanity (*laos*) by tossing stones (*laas*) over their shoulders.

According to Egyptian myth, humans and gods originally lived together until some humans rebelled against their subservient status. Enraged at this betrayal, Ra decided to wipe out the entire species but was advised by other gods to vent his wrath only against the rebels. Accordingly, Ra dispatched the goddess Hathor to punish the offenders, but she flew into an uncontrollable rage and began killing humans indiscriminately. To prevent the complete annihilation of humans, Ra tricked Hathor by mixing ochre into beer until it resembled blood. Bloodthirsty Hathor consumed the beer and became inebriated, losing her focus and ferocity. The surviving humans were thus spared, but before long they again attracted the wrath of Ra. This time, instead of punishing them, Ra decided on separation, leaving the earth and moving all the gods to the heavens.

Like the later biblical story of the "paradise lost," this myth explained humanity's separation from the divine as the consequence of the deity's displeasure with human behaviour, although in this case, instead of expelling the humans, the gods removed themselves. At the same time, it confronted the conflict between justice and power. Similarly in *Gilgamesh*, Enlil thundered when he learned that humans had survived his flood. But the other gods, upset because human sacrifices had ceased during the flood, chastised him: "How could you so lack judgment as to inundate [all humans]? Punish [only] transgressors; punish [only] wrongdoers." Cosmic justice was indispensable to limit otherwise unlimited cosmic power. But the criticism directed at Enlil also applied to Gilgamesh, who had abused his powers as the earthly ruler of Uruk. Both divine and human justice were considered essential to prevent abuses of human power.

Legitimation

If the *Gilgamesh* myth sought, on one level, to temper power, power also used myth for its own purposes. Nothing so effectively legitimized a ruler as association with a god. Royally sponsored mythmakers asserted that kingship "came down from heaven," and thus that rulers functioned either as divine agents or as gods themselves. Egyptian rulers had claimed a direct relationship with the gods since the inception of historical kingship; according to Egyptian myth, Atum, usually depicted wearing the double crown of kingship, was the creator of the ordered political system as well as the ordered cosmos. As early as the fifth dynasty (c. 2400 BCE) they were referring to themselves as "sons of Ra," and even before that time one king had given himself the title "the perfect god." A New Kingdom royal myth attributed the conception of Amenhotep III directly to the god Amun. Attracted to the queen, the god entered her bedchamber. She awakened and exclaimed "Your sweet fragrance stiffens all my limbs." After impregnating her, Amun announced: "Amenhotep-ruler-of-Thebes is the name of the child I have placed in your womb. . . . He shall exercise potent kingship in this entire land. . . . He shall rule the Two Lands [Egypt] like Ra forever" (Wilkinson: 2010, 250). The boy was fashioned in Amun's image by the potter-god Khnum, and after his birth (attended by deities) he was raised among the gods until he was ready to be presented to the Egyptians as their new king. Centuries later, Alexander the Great—who was identified as the son of Zeus–Amun when he entered Egypt—circulated a similar story, claiming that a god had visited his mother at his conception.

Eventually that Alexandrian model in turn made its way to Rome. No ruler was more astute in the use of myth to justify his political regime than Octavian, better known as Augustus Caesar. Augustus transformed foundation myth into legitimation myth. Rome's principal foundation myth centred on the legend of Romulus, whose choice of the Palatine hill as the site of the future city had been validated by the appearance of 12 vultures. Accordingly, Octavian made it known that 12 vultures had also appeared to him, clearly implying that he would re-establish Rome (as he in fact did at the conclusion of the civil wars in 28 BCE).

Augustus used religious props throughout his reign, including a second foundation myth that was the subject of the greatest literary work of the Augustan Age. Virgil's *Aeneid* traced Rome's origins to Aeneas, a refugee from Troy who was the son of a human father and a divine mother identified as Aphrodite/Venus (Augustus's clan, the Julians, had long claimed Aeneas and Venus as ancestors).

As *pontifex maximus* ("high priest"), Augustus was expected to live next to the house of the Vestal Virgins, the guardians of Rome's hearth, but he didn't want to give up his own home. Therefore he rededicated his house as public property and

Sites

Rome, Italy

The religious as well as the political capital of the Roman world, ancient Rome contained hundreds of temples. Among them was the magnificent Pantheon, commissioned by the emperor Hadrian in the second century CE to replace a temple built under the Augustan-era consul Marcus Agrippa. Although the earlier temple had burned down, its façade survived and was incorporated into the new building, which was eventually converted into a Christian church.

Focus

The Magna Mater (Cybele)

Worship of the Magna Mater ("Great Mother") had a long and distinguished history. The origins of her cult are most commonly traced to seventh-century-BCE Phrygia (a land in western Turkey), but its roots went back at least to the early first millennium BCE and quite possibly to the mid-second. From Phrygia the cult spread to Greece in the sixth century BCE and from there to Rome. By the second century CE her sanctuaries covered the breadth of the Roman Empire and beyond, from the Vatican hill to Lugdunum in Gaul (Lyons, France) to Ai Khanoum in northern Afghanistan.

In Phrygia she was known simply as Matar, Mother, but one of her epithets, associating her with mountains, was *kubileya*, which the Greeks rendered as Kybele/Cybele. She was the only Phrygian deity to be depicted iconographically. In many of those images she was accompanied by a lion—a symbol of her power.

turned part of it into a shrine to Vesta. In this way he not only brought Rome's hearth, the symbol of the empire's divine favour, into his own home but also reinforced his connection with the foundation myth, in which the fire of Vesta was first transferred from Troy to Italy by Aeneas and then brought into Rome by Romulus. Augustus also rebuilt the neighbouring temple of the goddess called Magna Mater or Cybele, whose cult had originated near Troy and had been introduced into Rome from Greece in 204 BCE. In all, Augustus boasted of restoring 82 temples and (re)building another 14 during his reign.

Finally, the very name "Augustus" was part of the emperor's plan to legitimize his rule. Until he took the name for himself, "August" had been an epithet attached to places touched by a god and subsequently consecrated by priests known as augurs. By renaming himself Augustus, Octavian emphasized his heaven-sent good fortune. Sacrifices were offered to both his *genius* (the personification of his innate qualities) and his *numen* (divine power). He would be elevated to divine status on his death in 14 CE, when a senator—his vision sharpened by an extremely large bribe from Augustus's widow, the empress Livia—declared under oath that he had witnessed Augustus physically ascending to heaven.

Households

The common people did not generate myth, but they were familiar with it, typically learning the stories through re-enactments at public festivals or, in Athens, at the theatre. Myth could also enter their houses in tangible form. A common item found in Egypt was a carved hand. This was the hand of god—more specifically, the hand into which the primeval god Atum "spat" (a euphemism for "masturbated") to conceive Shu and Tefnut. The hand symbolized the feminine role in creation. By the New Kingdom, influential women were given the title "hand of god," and ivory hands featuring a depiction of the goddess Hathor were used in dances honouring her: a dancer would hold the ivory hand above her head so that it was reflected in a mirror (another symbol associated with Hathor) held in her other hand. A number of Hathor-handled mirrors have been uncovered in Middle Kingdom homes. Any woman looking into such a mirror would equate the disk of the mirror on top of the handle with the disk of the sun that traditionally formed part of Hathor's headdress—and thereby also gaze momentarily on the face of the goddess herself.

Mothers and children were envisioned as reflections of Isis and Horus, and numerous spells sought

Getty Villa Museum

A Roman statue of Cybele/Magna Mater from the first century CE, in the collection of the Getty Villa. Here she sits on a throne accompanied by a lion. Her headdress in the shape of a city wall symbolizes her relationship with the urbanized Roman Empire, which, as her horn of plenty suggests, benefits from her role as provider. The model for the statue was likely Livia, the wife of Augustus.

Isis's protection for human children. Some of those spells were recited over an amulet, which often contained a seal inscribed with a hand, to be worn by the child. Figurines depicting Isis as a "madonna" cradling the infant Horus in one arm spread from her Egyptian homeland throughout the ancient world, where she came to epitomize motherhood. One memorable scene in Egyptian myth had Isis, upon finding the child Horus near death, accusing Ra of imperious disregard of suffering and death. Stung by her attack, Ra restored Horus to health.

Isis's life-saving intercession figured prominently on a type of small stela, no more than a metre in height, called a *cippus*. Found in both homes and tombs, *cippi* were typically engraved with images of the child Horus combatting dangerous animals that threatened both cosmic order and family tranquility. Any mother who gave her child water that had been poured over a *cippus* could preserve him just as Isis had preserved Horus. Finally, Egyptian homes were filled with the scent of incense—aromatic substances that were burned not only to please the senses but (as the Egyptian term for "incense" indicated) "to make divine."

Questioning Myth

Certain intellectuals, especially early Greek philosophers, first questioned and then challenged the way traditional myths presented the gods. A major shift in thinking about the gods has been attributed to the sixth-century-BCE Greek poet, philosopher, and social critic named **Xenophanes**. Only fragments of his work have survived, but in them he rejected the anthropomorphic view of the divine, according to which "mortals suppose that gods are born, wear their own clothes and have voice and body." He was particularly contemptuous of those—notably Homer and Hesiod—who "attributed to the gods all sorts of things which are matters of reproach and censure among men: theft, adultery, and mutual deceit." In place of those all-too-human gods Xenophanes proposed a supreme universal god:

One god is greatest among gods and men, not at all like mortals in body or in thought.

Whole he sees, whole he thinks, and whole he hears.

Always he abides in the same place, not moving at all, nor is it seemly for him to travel to different places at different times.

But completely without effort he shakes all things [keeps everything moving] by the thought of his mind (Lesher 1992: 23, 25, 31, 33).

The debates set off by these ideas have yet to end. Anaxagoras, following Xenophanes, wrote that "All living things, both great and small, are controlled by Mind" (E. Hussey, in Freeman 1996: 227). Protagoras disagreed: "Concerning the gods I am unable to discover whether they exist or not, or what they are in form; for there are many hindrances to knowledge, the obscurity of the subject and the brevity of life" (W. Guthrie, in Freeman 1996: 227). Other Greeks, such as the Athenian playwright Critias, were downright cynical: "I believe that a man of shrewd and subtle mind invented for men the fear of gods so that there might be something to frighten the wicked even if they acted, spoke, or thought in secret" (R. Muir, in Freeman 1996: 227). Certainly the most influential Greek philosopher to reflect on the nature of the divine was **Plato** (c. 425–347 BCE), who could not envision divinity as evil.

His position put him in conflict with the poets, whom he decried in *The Republic* and whom his *Laws* would banish from the state; in particular he challenged the greatest of all Greek poets, Homer, who at the end of the *Iliad* had Achilles address Priam as follows:

> The gods have woven thus for happy mortals,
> That they live in sorrow, but they themselves
>   have no cares.
> For on Zeus's threshold stand two urns,
> For the gifts he sends: one of evils, the
>   other of blessings (Foley 2009: 310; M.
>   Edwards, trans.).

Since for Plato the divine was good, it could not introduce evil into the world. The Stoics took up this positive appreciation of the god(s), whom they termed the Divine Mind, and thus came to view Zeus first as the embodiment of the divine and later as a synonym for it.

Myth could also be used to challenge myth. Ovid's *Metamorphoses* was a direct challenge to Augustus's legitimation myth and Rome's developing imperial cult. Ovid's gods, far from concerning themselves with justice, used their power to prey on the weak. Male gods, Jupiter in particular, regularly resorted to sexual violence. The only truly compassionate deity was the female Isis, self-described as *dea auxiliaris*, who, when called on for help and hope, brought comfort. It was no coincidence that Augustus exiled Ovid shortly afterwards.

Thirteen centuries before Ovid, an Egyptian pharaoh challenged the traditional Egyptian worldview by offering an alternative myth. He announced the change visually at the beginning of his reign, when he was still known officially as Amenhotep IV, by ordering the construction of a monumental complex at the centre of which was a temple named Gempaaten ("the Aten is found"), its courtyard lined with towering statues of the king and his wife, Nefertiti, wearing distinctive crowns that identified them as Shu (light), the eldest son of Atum, and Tefnut, the sister of Shu. The building program was followed by a name change: Amenhotep ("Amun is content") became **Akhenaten** ("Effective for Aten" or "Illuminated Manifestation of Aten") and Nefertiti assumed the epithet Neferneferuaten ("Beautiful are the beauties of the Aten"). More building ensued, and a new capital named Akhetaten ("Horizon of Aten"; modern Amarna) transformed what had been virgin desert into a grand open-air temple to Aten. Represented as the disk of the sun with rays ending in human hands holding signs of life and bounty, Aten—light itself—was henceforth to be worshipped in the open rather than in some dark inner sanctuary.

Akhenaten's religious revolution has been the subject of countless modern interpretations. The standard view derives from the so-called Restoration Stele of his successor, the boy king Tutankhamun, especially the following passage:

> The temples of the gods and goddesses, from Aabu [Aswan] down to the marshes of the Delta, had fallen into decay, their shrines had become desolate ruins overgrown with weeds, and their chapels as though they had never existed. Their halls were used as footpaths. The land was disorderly and the

gods turned their back on it. . . . If anyone abased himself before a god to petition him, he did not respond; if a prayer was made to a goddess, she did not reply (Watterson 1999: 121).

According to Tutankhamun (or his advisors) Akhenaten was a "heretic" who not only overturned Egypt's religious traditions (closing temples, ending festivals, forbidding worship of deities other than Aten) but threatened the security of Egypt itself by alienating all the other gods. He was charged with having the names of other gods expunged from monuments (the earliest attested act of iconoclasm), forbidding personal names that included elements of other divine names, and, most astoundingly, ordering the eradication of any plural form of "god." The reaction against Akhenaten was dramatic, beginning with a name change for his son (from Tutankhaten to Tutankhamun) that signalled a return to Egypt's traditional religion, and concluding with a campaign to obliterate any vestige or memory of Akhenaten.

Was Tutankhamun's Restoration Stela fact, propaganda, or a combination of the two? Akhenaten did make a determined effort to get rid of two gods, ordering that the names of Amun and Mut (Amun's consort) be removed from temple inscriptions and that individuals whose names included "Amun" and "Mut" rename themselves. But this component of his reforms was limited to the gods most closely associated with kingship and Thebes. Moreover,

Akhenaten's own inscriptions used the plural "gods," and almost all the houses excavated in Amarna have shrines dedicated to gods other than Aten. If there was a component of monotheism to Akhenaten's reforms, it was restricted to the official state religion.

At first Akhenaten identified Aten with Atum, the primeval god who initiated the creation of the world, and he presented himself and his wife Nefertiti as the first-born children of Atum. Later, Akhenaten switched Aten's identification from Atum to Ra. Both Ra and Atum represented creation. The Great Hymn to Aten (see p. 52) emphasized Aten's role as creator. Moreover, the way Akhenaten had himself portrayed, with a body that seems to blend male and female features, symbolized his role as sustainer of Egypt's fertility. What lay behind his elevation of Aten remains uncertain, however. One possibility is that he disdained the anthropomorphic representation of Amun-Ra, and by focusing attention on the source of light (and renewal) itself, sought to purify the representation of the supreme deity.

Akhenaten's counter-myth challenge to two of the most deeply entrenched Egyptian myths failed to take hold, and his opponents created a counter-counter-myth, encapsulated in the Restoration Stela, to discredit him. Although they did not succeed in removing every reference to him, they did a good job: by the time his tomb was discovered in the late nineteenth century, he was virtually unknown to history.

Sites

Akhetaten (modern Amarna), Egypt

Literally "the horizon of Aten," Akhetaten was the short-lived city created by Akhenaten as his capital in the fourteenth century BCE. Archaeologists continue to study the structure and purpose of the city. The "Amarna Letters"—some 400 cuneiform tablets discovered at the site—shed light on Egypt's relations with its neighbours.

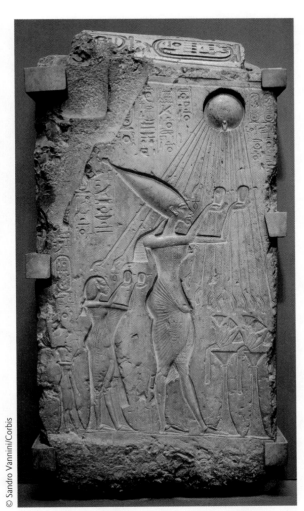

© Sandro Vannini/Corbis

Akhenaten (r. 1353–1336 BCE) with his wife Nefertiti and one of their six daughters worshipping the sun-disk, Aten.

🜲 Negotiating the World

Ritual

The people of the ancient world knew that theirs was a world full of gods; they were also aware that it was a dangerous, unstable place, and that to navigate it safely required the help of the gods. "Pious" humans therefore fed, clothed, and sheltered their deities; bestowed gifts on them; glorified

and obeyed them, in exchange for crops, progeny, economic security, health, and safety—practical benefits in a world where subsistence was hard and people were lucky if they lived to the age of 30. The means through which humans performed their part in this exchange was ritual: "the things done" in Sumerian, "what is customary" or "public duties" in Greek, *cultus* in Latin. Temples provided places for gods to spend their time on earth. In Mesopotamia and Egypt, gods dwelt in their temples as living statues, entering them through "Opening of the Mouth" rituals. The word for "god" in Egyptian derived from a term for "image." Priests began each day by greeting and worshipping the divine statue in its inner sanctum, then anointing and dressing it; in Egypt the clothing rite alone required 45 separate steps.

In the most important of all the daily rituals, the statue was offered the first of two (in Mesopotamia) or three (in Egypt) daily meals, which mysteriously nourished the gods even though they were not consumed. So close was the association between ritual and mystery that the Egyptians referred to ritual itself as *shetau*, "mystery." Most rituals were performed in secret, away from public scrutiny, and required the meticulous performance of a sequence of steps that simultaneously imitated the cosmic order and helped to secure it by pleasing the gods.

Sacrifice

The foremost ritual act was sacrifice (from the Latin meaning "to make sacred"; the Mesopotamian equivalent meant "gift"; the Greek, "to make smoke"). Sacrifice transformed profane objects into holy ones. Sacrificial offerings ranged from simple foods (fruits, vegetables, honeyed barley cakes) and libations (wine, milk, or oil) to animals, ritually slaughtered by priests and then cooked and eaten by devotees. As in Mesopotamia, animal sacrifice was the central ritual in Greece and Rome, the highlight of public festivals. The altars on which sacrifices were performed were more important than temples to Greeks and Romans. Since the smoke from the

Document

The Great Hymn to Aten

Found in the tomb of the priest-administrator Ay, the Great Hymn to Aten has often been compared to the Hebrew Bible's Psalm 104. After an introductory dedication to Nefertiti and the king under three of his official names (In-his-name-Shu-who-is-Aten, Sole-one-of-Ra, and Akhenaten), the poem begins:

O living Aten, creator of life!
When you have dawned in eastern lightland,
You fill every land with your beauty.
You are beauteous, great, radiant,
High over every land;
Your rays embrace the lands,
To the limits of all that you made.

. . .

Earth brightens when you dawn in lightland,
When you shine as Aten of daytime;
As you dispel the dark,
As you cast your rays,
The Two Lands [Egypt] are in festivity.
Awake they stand on their feet;
You have roused them;
Bodies cleansed, clothed,
Their arms adore your appearance.
The entire land sets out to work,
All beasts browse on their herbs;
Trees, herbs are sprouting,
Birds fly from their nests,
Their wings greeting your *ka*.

. . .

Who makes seed grow in women,
Who creates people from sperm;
Who feeds the son in his mother's womb,
Who soothes him to still his tears.

Nurse in the womb,
Giver of breath,
To nourish all that he made.
When he comes from the womb to breathe,
On the day of his birth,
You open wide his mouth,
You supply his needs.

. . .

How many are your deeds,
Though hidden from sight,
O Sole God beside whom there is none!
You made the earth as you wished, you alone,
All peoples, herds, and flocks;

. . .

You set every man in his place,
You supply their needs;
Everyone has his food,
His lifetime is counted.
Their tongues differ in speech,
Their characters likewise;
Their skins are distinct,
For you distinguished the people.

. . .

Your rays nurse all fields;
When you shine they live, they grow for you;
You made the seasons to foster all that you made,
Winter to cool them, heat that they taste you,
You made the far sky to shine therein,
To behold all that you made;
You alone, shining in your form of living Aten,
Risen, radiant, distant, near.
You made millions of forms from yourself alone.

. . .

You are in my heart . . . (Lichtheim 1976: 96–9).

sacrifices had to rise to heaven to reach the gods, the altars were open to the elements. Offerings destined for the gods of the underworld were poured on the ground. Greek and Roman temples were treasuries housing the gifts offered to the gods by their devotees, either in thanks for favours granted or in fulfillment of vows ("votive" gifts). Altars and temples were parts of a sanctuary, an area

Document

Cleanthes' Hymn to Zeus

The Hymn to Zeus, though written 1,000 years after the Great Hymn to Aten, is strikingly similar in theme. Its author, the Stoic philosopher Cleanthes (331–230 BCE), lauds the universal dominion of a single omniscient god (Zeus, in this case) and his role in dispensing universal justice.

Noblest of immortals, many-named, always all-powerful
Zeus, first cause and ruler of nature, governing everything with your law,
greetings! For it is right for all mortals to address you:
for we have our origin in you, bearing a likeness to god,
we, alone of all that live and move as mortal creatures on earth.
Therefore I shall praise you constantly; indeed I will always sing of your rule.
This whole universe, spinning around the earth, truly
obeys you wherever you lead, and is readily ruled by you;
such a servant do you have between your unconquerable hands,
the two-edged, fiery, ever-living thunderbolt.
For by its stroke all works of nature are guided.
With it you direct the universal reason, which permeates
everything, mingling with the great and the small lights.
Because of this you are so great, the highest king for ever.
Not a single thing takes place on earth without you, god,
nor in the divine celestial sphere nor in the sea,
except what bad people do in their folly.
But you know how to make the uneven even
and to put into order the disorderly; even the unloved is dear to you.
For you have thus joined everything into one, the good with the bad,
that there comes to be one ever-existing rational order for everything.
This all mortals that are bad flee and avoid,
the wretched, who though always desiring to acquire good things,
neither see nor hear god's universal law,
obeying which they could have a good life with understanding.
But they on the contrary rush without regard to the good, each after different things,
some with a belligerent eagerness for glory,
others without discipline intent on profits,
others yet on indulgence and the pleasurable actions of the body.
They desire the good, but they are born now to this, then to that,
while striving eagerly that the complete opposite of these things happen.
But all-bountiful Zeus, cloud-wrapped ruler of the thunderbolt,
deliver human beings from their destructive ignorance;
disperse it from their souls; grant that they obtain
the insight on which you rely when governing everything with justice;
so that we, having been honoured, may honour you in return,
constantly praising your works, as befits
one who is mortal. For there is no greater privilege for mortals
or for gods than always to praise the universal law of justice (Thom 2005: 40–1).

separated from its surroundings by a sacred boundary. Everything within the boundary belonged to the god.

Festivals

A typical festival would begin with a procession in which the god's statue was displayed to the public, followed by hymns to the deity, the sacrifice ritual, games or competitions while the sacrificial animals cooked, and a communal banquet. The first three stages were solemn while the last two were celebratory. Humans revelled in one another's company, confirmed communal bonds, re-established connections with the gods, and acknowledged the pre-eminence of the divine. The Greek philosopher Democritus pronounced that a life without festivals was a long road without inns. In Athens the religious calendar set aside 170 festival days every year. The Roman calendar distinguished between Fasti, days of the month for conducting public business, and Nefasti, "sacred" days set aside for religious festivals. Attendance lists noted that workmen in Egyptian royal necropolises took time off to attend family festivals, in addition to celebrating the two major public festivals and at least 65 lesser ones.

Alfredo Dagli Orti/The Art Archive at Art Resource, NY

Dionysus, the god of wine, with two maenads (female revellers); detail of an Attic red-figure krater (a large vessel used to mix wine and water), 460 BCE. One of many festivals held in Athens in honour of Dionysus was Anthesteria. The celebration lasted three days and included parades, feasts, and drinking competitions.

Priests

Except during public festivals, ritual was the exclusive prerogative of priests. In Mesopotamia and Egypt, priests were originally private citizens appointed for limited periods of service, but in time priesthood became a full-time profession. Priests were scrupulous in the performance of their duties, which included ensuring the absolute integrity of sanctuaries. Egyptian priests, "pure ones," were circumcised, dressed in white, and observed food taboos; to remove physical pollution and restore spiritual purity, they washed themselves several times each day, often in basins located at temple entrances. Mesopotamians, too, ritually removed surface and internal impurities in "bathing houses" before entering temple grounds. Such ritual cleansing was referred to as "making holy"; it was often reinforced with pleasant-smelling incense.

Anyone entering a sacred place had to be pure, both morally and physically. The Greek physician Hippocrates wrote, "We ourselves mark out the precincts of the temples so that no one should enter without purifying himself; as we go in, we sprinkle ourselves with holy water" (Chadwick and Mann 1950: 240). When a local benefactor in North Africa dedicated a shrine to Asclepius during the early Roman Empire, he set the following conditions: "Whoever wishes to ascend into the shrine, let him abstain from women, pork, bean, barber, and public bath for three days; do not enter the enclosure wearing shoes" (Rives 2007: 102). A first-century-BCE inscription posted outside a temple in Ephesus prohibited entry to anyone who had murdered, robbed, remained silent about a crime, committed adultery, or used a contraceptive or abortion-inducing drug or charm. The entrance to the Egyptian temple at Edfu warned: "Whoever enters by this door must beware of entering impurely, for god loves purity more than millions of rituals." Inside the temple were further injunctions: "Do not utter falsehood in his house, do not covet things, do not slander, do not accept bribes, do not be partial as between a poor man and a great, . . . do not reveal what you have seen in the

mysteries of the temple" (H. te Velde, in Sasson, ed., 1995: 1733).

Attached to late Egyptian temples were two "Houses," one of Life and one of Books, in which priests passed on their knowledge to neophyte priests and preserved the sacred writings, written in hieroglyphs (Greek for "holy writing," from the Egyptian "words of the god"). Each temple library contained 42 indispensable books—42 being the number of Egyptian provinces, hence symbolic of perfection or totality. Among them were books explaining how to inscribe texts on temple walls. The priests who began this process of codifying their cultic knowledge were transforming the "words of god" into holy scripture.

Female Priests

Since there were as many goddesses in the ancient world as there were gods, it is no surprise that women had significant roles and responsibilities in ancient religion. Women were particularly devoted to goddesses associated with marriage, pregnancy, and birth. Greek and Roman women served female deities, maidens attending virgin goddesses and matrons attending mother-goddesses such as Demeter, and they celebrated their own festivals. Sumerian women held high priestly office. The highest-ranking priestess was literally the "lady goddess." Sargon, a third-millennium-BCE ruler, installed his daughter Enheduana as high priestess of the moon-god of Ur. So integral were women to their religion that Mesopotamians dismissed as uncivilized any people whose god knew no priestess.

During both the Old and Middle Kingdoms of Egypt, statues identified women as "priestess of Hathor." The best-known Roman priestesses were the six Vestals, who were chosen as young girls to serve for 30 years. They performed three functions that were considered essential to the city's survival: preparing the objects to be used in public sacrifices, guarding Rome's symbolic storehouse, and, above all, preserving the sacred fire. Greek priestesses kept the keys to temples, groomed cult statues, led prayers, and even took part in sacrifices—activities paralleling the duties for which the ordinary Greek woman would be responsible in her own home.

Divination

An Assyrian incantation text described the gods as "drawing the cosmic designs." The ability to "divine" the gods' wishes and plans was crucial, especially for rulers. Gods communicated their designs, but rarely in a form that was immediately obvious. Humans almost always had to work to uncover and interpret them. The exceptions to that rule were cases of inspiration or revelation—a phenomenon typically associated with the holy scriptures of Judaism, Christianity, and Islam. Among the ancient texts that claimed divine inspiration was the *Iliad*, whose opening line—"Sing, goddess, of Achilles' wrath"—suggested that Homer was merely the mouthpiece for a divine muse. Mesopotamians also claimed to receive revelations in dreams. The conclusion of the Babylonian *Poem of Erra* stated that during the night a god had revealed the story to the author, who recorded it word for word.

Prophecy

The significance of prophecy lay above all in its impact on the state. Our knowledge of Mesopotamian prophecy derives mainly from some 80 prophecies found in two official archives, one from the Old Babylonian period and the other from the Assyrian Empire. The latter refers to a number of prophets, mostly women, whose names associated them with Ishtar. Prophecies that touched on the affairs of king or state were reported to rulers and had to be confirmed via various forms of divination, especially extispicy—examination of the inner organs (*exta*), primarily livers, of sacrificed animals. For the Romans the most important prophecies were the Sibylline Oracles, a collection of texts associated with the Sibyl (from the Greek for "prophetess") of Cumae, a Greek colony near Naples. By the late third century BCE the Sibylline Oracles had been relocated to Rome, where they were guarded by priests. All other prophecies, whatever their source, had to be "tested" against the Sibylline Oracles in order to establish their legitimacy.

The word "oracle" (from the Latin verb "to speak") may refer not only to gods' answers to questions but also to the places where they were delivered or to the individuals through whom the gods spoke. Egyptian festival processions, in which gods' statues made public appearances, provided opportunities to ask them "yes–no" questions. The answers were relayed via movement: "yes" if the statue advanced, "no" if it retreated. Rulers' questions concerned matters of state, especially military campaigns, while commoners asked about issues of everyday life: whether a sick child would recover,

Sites

Delphi, Greece

Home to the most important oracle in the Greek world, located on Mount Parnassus and dedicated to Apollo. Inside the Temple of Apollo, which was one component of the grand Sanctuary of Apollo, was the *adyton*, the seat of the Pythia. Delphi also housed numerous treasuries, filled with spoils of victory that had been offered to Apollo; they were sacked on several occasions. A number of festivals were held at Delphi, the most famous being the Pythian games, second in importance only to the Olympic games. Both the games and the oracle were outlawed by Theodosius I.

Sites

Dodona, Greece

The site of the oldest Greek oracle, originally associated with a mother goddess but later dedicated to Zeus. Though located in an isolated region of northwestern Greece, Dodona was mentioned in both the *Iliad* and the *Odyssey*, and in time it became second in importance only to Delphi. The earliest oracles were obtained by interpreting the rustling of the leaves of a sacred oak tree or the cooing of doves.

whether to plant a particular crop, whether the person accused of a theft was in fact guilty.

The best-known oracle of antiquity was at Delphi in Greece, where the god Apollo spoke through a priestess called the Pythia. On "oracle days," enquirers would pay a substantial fee to line up with a sacrificial goat, on which a priest sprinkled water; if the animal shook off the water, Apollo would hear the enquiry. On entering the temple, the enquirer presented a question to a priest who passed it on to the Pythia. Apollo then spoke through her. Responses were often ambiguous, and questioners were expected to put considerable effort into interpreting them.

Most of our knowledge regarding the questions posed to the Pythia comes from Herodotus and **Plutarch**, both of whom were interested mainly in matters of state. Evidence of other types of questions is available, however, on lead tablets from the oracle of Zeus at Dodona. The majority of the queries recorded on those tablets reflected the everyday concerns of ordinary people—the same kinds of concerns expressed in Egypt or Mesopotamia: should I wed? will he love me in return? is it really my child? will I get my rations? Plutarch (45–120 CE), a priest of Delphi, complained of the trivial, mundane questions posed to the Pythia in his day.

Messages and Omens

In Mesopotamia and Rome, virtually anything could contain a message from the gods: stars, storms, smoke, oily water, sacrificed animals, chance meetings, even human hair. Divination was a matter of reading signs. The Akkadian term for sign was *ittu*, related to Hebrew *'oth* and Arabic *aya*. All entries in the numerous Mesopotamian collections of omens were identified as *ittu*, messages from the gods, just as all verses of the Qur'an are referred to as *aya*, messages from Allah.

Omens were divine messages understood as warnings. Mesopotamians recorded two types of omen: diagnostic and predictive. Diagnostic omens were based on physical or behavioural characteristics: a mole on the right thigh, for instance, might indicate prosperity, while a generous person could expect to be treated generously. Predictive omens, by contrast, hinted at one's fate or *shimtu* ("that which has been decreed"). Sometimes these omens were discovered through observation of natural phenomena: movements of the stars, unusual births, thunder on a cloudless day, a sudden appearance of birds. Assyrian rulers required that every unusual sighting throughout the empire be reported to the court.

Predictive omens could also be solicited by various means. Pouring oil on water was one common, inexpensive method. Eventually, lengthy treatises were written explaining how different effects should be interpreted. For example: "If I pour oil on water and the oil sinks, surfaces, and covers the water: [then] for the campaign, disaster; for the sick person, the hand of god is heavy [he will die]." Examination of a sacrificial sheep's liver was the most common method of divination in Mesopotamia (and eventually in the Roman world), but the most influential and enduring was astrology, translating the "heavenly writing" of the gods.

The divine "inscriptions" that recorded human destiny were analogous to royal decrees. In the same way that citizens could appeal to rulers to reconsider their decisions, humans could appeal to gods to reconsider theirs. One could pray to Ishtar, for instance, to use her power to transform an unfortunate *shimtu* into a favourable one. More commonly, people resorted to **apotropaic** incantations or rituals, so-called because they were specifically designed to ward off or drive away (exorcise) evil, or to remove its effects. An Egyptian text called the *Instruction for [King] Merikare* even suggested that the creator gave humans magic (*heka*) specifically as a weapon to ward off whatever evil might come their way.

Ethics

The gods represented only one-half of the cosmos; human society, too, needed negotiation. One important function of Egyptian tombs was to serve as monuments to the virtue of the deceased. During the Old Kingdom, tombs of high-ranking Egyptians often bore "autobiographical" inscriptions attesting to their virtue. In later periods, however, the dead had to prove themselves to a divine tribunal that included Osiris and Anubis, the jackal-headed god who acted as the divine undertaker. The third member of this tribunal was Ma'at, the goddess of truth, justice, and order, who used the scales of justice to weigh the heart of the deceased against her own "feather of truth." Presented with a list of 80 possible "sins" (offences against social norms), the deceased was expected to respond with avowals of innocence. Each lie or transgression caused the heart's side of the scale to sink. If it sank too far, the deceased would disappear forever into the maw of a monster, but if the heart stayed level with Ma'at's feather, the person would gain eternal life among the gods.

Autobiographical tomb inscriptions emphasized the values central to human social interaction: responsibility, compassion, and justice. An early Mesopotamian ruler named Urukagina introduced a series of reforms, at the end of which he declared that the fundamental responsibility of a ruler was to protect widows and orphans from "the strong man." Hammurabi of Babylon's so-called "law code" proclaimed that he "brought justice to the land." And a famous Egyptian story from the Middle Kingdom praised the wisdom of an "eloquent peasant" who urged the powerful to "Speak and perform justice, for it is mighty. It is great; it endures; its worth is proven; it leads one to be revered" (Lichtheim 1973: 181).

Several Egyptian texts, known as "instructions," were designed to inculcate the fundamental values of the society: self-control, acceptance of limits,

Document

An Egyptian Tomb Inscription

The following text is from an Old Kingdom tomb.

I spoke truly, I did right;
. . .
I judged between two so as to content both;
I rescued the weak from one stronger
As much as I had power.
I gave bread to the hungry, clothes to the naked;

I brought the boatless to land;
I buried him who had no son;
I made a boat for him who lacked one.
I respected my father, I pleased my mother,
I raised their children.
So says he whose nickname is Sheshi (Lichtheim 1973: 17).

trust in other humans and, especially, the gods. Social superiors should be obeyed and social inferiors treated with generosity. Above all, Egyptian society valued balance.

In Greece the message was much the same, summed up in Apollo's Delphic admonition: "Nothing in excess." The *Histories* of Herodotus offered numerous instances of the dire consequences of excess, and Greek tragedians made careers of demonstrating those consequences on the stage. Cosmic justice would ensure that every transgression was eventually punished. Retribution was inescapable. If the perpetrator of an offence was not punished, a descendant would be.

A major figure in Herodotus was Croesus, king of Lydia, a powerful state in western Turkey. When the rising Persian Empire under Cyrus the Great began to encroach on his domain in the mid-sixth century BCE, Croesus asked Apollo's oracle at Delphi about the consequences of waging war against Cyrus. Informed that "a great empire would be destroyed" if he went into battle, the ambitious Croesus closed his inner ear to the oracle's ambiguity. Taking the oracle's answer as a guarantee of victory, Croesus fought Cyrus, only to be defeated. Afterwards, when he complained that Apollo had misguided him, the Pythia responded that Croesus should have asked which empire would be defeated.

Croesus' failure to ask the question was his responsibility, not Apollo's. Humans were responsible for their own actions and for whatever consequences followed.

Once a sin had been committed, could its stain be removed? In Mesopotamia three different rituals were used for purification. Approximately 200 sins required cleansing, among them ignoring food taboos, slandering, bearing false witness, oppressing the weak, dishonouring parents, stealing, committing adultery, murdering, swearing false oaths, scorning the gods, and failing to name the god while making offerings. In one way or another, all these sins involved disrespect, either towards the gods or towards other humans. The list of sins is strikingly similar to the list in the Egyptian *Book of the Dead*. How humans treated one another was no less important than how they treated the gods. Social order depended on the former, cosmic order on the latter.

If improper actions incurred punishment, then proper actions could reap rewards. As a Mesopotamian text known as the "Moral Canon" explained:

> If he is just, and nevertheless things go
>   wrong, later on things will get better.
> If he speaks according to justice, he will
>   have good recompense.

Document

Counsels of Wisdom

The following extract (lines 135–45) comes from a Mesopotamian text summarizing proper religious behaviour and its rewards. It dates from the mid-second millennium BCE.

Praise your god every day.
Prayer and sacrifice complement incense.
Generously offer gifts to your god,
For this is piety towards the gods.

Prayer, supplication, and prostration
Will be repaid a hundredfold;
You will find favour with your god.
Reverence secures grace,
Sacrifice prolongs life,
And prayer atones for guilt.
Whoever honours the gods is never despised
    (M. Desrochers, trans., based on Lambert
    1960: 105).

If he loves what is good, only goodness will
    follow him all the time.
If he is merciful, he will die in abundance.
If he is concerned about helping others, the
    gods will follow him all the time (Sasson,
    ed., 1995: 1690–1; G. Buccellati, trans.).

The religious behaviours listed in the *Counsels of
Wisdom* identified various ways of negotiating with
the gods. Rooted in the belief that humans and
gods interacted within a system of reciprocity, the
practice of negotiation was based on an underlying
logic or rationale that is captured in the "if X, then
Y" phrasing of omens:

1. Omens and prophecy: if this is the "word"
    (will) of the gods, then the following will
    occur.
2. Apotropaic and exorcistic rituals: if those are
    the threats, then this is how to remove them.
3. Supplication: if I give you something, then
    you'll give me something in return.
4. Votive offerings: if you do something for me,
    then I'll give you something.
5. Prayer could be simultaneously praise and
    supplication (if I praise you, then you should
    meet my request) or praise and thanksgiv-
    ing (since you answered my previous prayer,
    then I praise you even more).
6. Sacrifice: if the gods are content, then they'll
    care for us.
7. Intercession: if you are my (deceased) rela-
    tive, then you'll do the following for me.
8. Insurance (the requirement to verify oracles
    and prophecies by means of divination): if
    it is really as they say, then extispicy will
    prove it.
9. Tradition: if it worked in the past, then it will
    work now.

Wisdom

Sometimes the if–then logic failed. Hence theodicy:
if matters did not turn out as they were supposed
to—if the gods no longer upheld their part of the

if–then bargain—then they were unfair. Even
the most pious must sometimes have wondered
whether their devotion would ever be rewarded.
Disappointment gave rise to a literary genre called
"wisdom literature." In one of these texts, the
Babylonian Theodicy, a speaker who had faithfully
fulfilled all his religious obligations, exactly as
prescribed in the *Counsels of Wisdom*, expressed his
frustration:

Those who neglect the god go the way of
    prosperity,
While those who pray to the goddess are
    impoverished and dispossessed.
In my youth I sought the will of my god;
With prostration and prayer I followed my
    goddess,
But I was bearing a profitless corvée [forced
    labour] as a yoke.
My god decreed instead of wealth destitu-
    tion (Lambert 1960: 75–7).

In another Mesopotamian text (*Ludlul bel nemeqi*;
"I will praise the lord of wisdom"), a Job-like "righteous sufferer" had performed all the prescribed rituals to no avail. He lamented the impossibility of
understanding the ways of the gods:

I wish I knew that these things were pleas-
    ing to one's god!
What is proper to oneself is an offence to
    one's god;
What in one's heart seems despicable is
    proper to one's god.
Who knows the will of the gods in heaven?
Who understands the plans of the under-
    world gods?
Where have mortals learned the way of a
    god? (Lambert 1960: 41)

The "wisdom" conveyed by these texts is resignation to the inscrutable will and superior power of
the gods.

Similar themes ran through Greek literature. No
character was more tragic than Sophocles' Oedipus,

a good man and a good ruler but, being human, of limited knowledge and power. At the close of *Oedipus The King*, the chorus asked, "What god, what dark power [*daimon*] leapt beyond all bounds, / beyond belief, to crush your wretched life?" (Fagles, trans. 1984). A character in Euripides' play *Heracles* accused Zeus of being heartless or unjust. Yet in his *Phoenician Women* (another take on the Oedipus story) the same playwright had Oedipus conclude that humans had no choice but to endure whatever the gods decreed. Humans had to learn to live within their limitations.

Criticism of Sacrifice

The fourth-century-BCE Greek comedian Menander lampooned sacrifice, suggesting humans deliberately offered the inedible portions of an animal to the gods while saving the finest meat for themselves. A more serious criticism came from the **Neoplatonist** philosopher Porphyry (234–305 CE):

> The lover of the body is always a lover of wealth; the lover of wealth is necessarily unjust; the unjust person is both irreverent toward God and parents and immoral toward everyone else. Consequently, even if he sacrifices hecatombs and adorns shrines with countless votive offerings, he is impious and ungodly (Wicker 1987: 59).

Porphyry was rephrasing Plato's *Laws*:

> For the wicked man is unclean of soul, whereas the good man is clean. From him that is defiled no good man or god can ever rightly receive gifts. Therefore, all the great labour that impious men spend upon the gods is in vain, but that of the pious is most profitable to them all (D. Ullici in Knust and Varhelyi 2011: 64).

The Instruction of Merikare said it more simply: "The loaf [of bread] of the upright is preferred to the ox of the evildoer" (Lichtheim 1973: 106).

None of these critics argued for an end to sacrifice, but they set the stage for later attacks, beginning with an imperial law of 341 CE that ordered an end to the "madness of sacrifices." Archaeologists have found no evidence of animal sacrifice in Italy after 400 CE. That timing corresponds with the banning of sacrifices, temple visits, and the worship of images ("idolatry") by Theodosius I.

✿ Communing with the Divine

The preceding section may suggest that the religions of antiquity were concerned exclusively with pragmatic issues, based on a system of reciprocity

David Lees/Corbis

Three Sumerian statuettes, c. 2900–2370 BCE, show male worshippers with their hands clasped over their chests in prayer. Their large eyes—a feature of many Mesopotamian sculptures—were meant to represent the awe that worshippers felt in the presence of the gods.

between humans and deities. For many people that was the case. But for Greek and Roman philosophers, especially those influenced by Plato, the idea of bargaining was downright offensive to the gods. Most philosophers approved of traditional religious practice to the extent that it served the interests of social and political order. However, they also sought "real" spirituality.

For millennia people had "believed" that the statues of the gods were literally the gods. Hidden from the general public in the innermost sanctum of the temple, identified as "the holy of holies" in Egypt, the statues rarely made public appearances, and when they did it was always a time of celebration. People could look at their gods, share a meal with them, and also share those pleasures with family and neighbours. Plutarch captured the popular sentiment:

> No visit delights us more than a visit to a temple; no occasion than a holy day; no act of spectacle than what we see and what we do ourselves in matters that involve the gods, whether we celebrate a ritual or take part in a choral dance or attend a sacrifice or ceremony of initiation. . . . When [humans] believe that their thoughts come closest to God as they do him honour and reverence, it brings pleasure and sweetness of a superior kind (Johnson 2009: 107).

Public festivals aside, the most common way for humans to make contact with the divine was through prayer. We have already seen examples of "sweetness of a superior kind" in Cleanthes' *Hymn to Zeus* and *The Great Hymn to Aten*, both of which evoked the blessings bestowed upon humans and their deeply felt reverence for divine majesty.

One of the great intellectuals of the Roman world was the Stoic philosopher **Epictetus** (50–120 CE). Born a slave, he praised divine providence:

> Why, if we had any sense, ought we be
> doing something else, publicly or
> privately, than hymning and praising the
> deity and rehearsing his benefits?

> Ought we not, as we dig and plough and eat,
> to sing the hymn of praise to God?
> Great is God that he hath furnished us these
> instruments wherewith we shall till
> the earth. Great is God that he hath given us
> hands, and power to swallow,
> and a belly, and power to grow uncon-
> sciously, and to breathe while asleep.
> That is what we ought to sing on every occa-
> sion, and above all to sing the
> greatest and divinest hymn, that God hath
> given us the faculty to comprehend
> these things and to follow the path of rea-
> son. What then? Since most of you
> have become blind, ought there not to be
> someone to fulfill this office for you
> and in behalf of all sing of praise to God?
> Why, what else can I, a lame old man,
> do but sing hymns to God? If, indeed, I were
> a nightingale, I should be singing
> as a nightingale; if a swan, as a swan. But as
> it is, I am a rational being; therefore,
> I must be singing hymns of praise to God.
> This is my task; I do it and will not
> desert this post so long as it may be given to
> me to fill it; I enjoin you to join me
> in the same song (Oldfather 1925: 111).

The common people could not use such soaring words, but they could demonstrate their deep devotion to divinity in the names they gave their children. An Egyptian might name a child Meryra ("Beloved of Ra"), Paraherwenemef ("Ra is his right hand"), or Horemheb ("Horus is in festival"). Mesopotamian names served as miniature prayers: Ana-ilia-atkal ("I trusted in my god"), Kabti-ilani-Marduk ("Marduk, most honoured of the gods"), Aramma-il-abi ("I love the god of my father"), or Ishtar-remet ("Ishtar is merciful").

Overcoming the World

Antiquity sought to transcend the material world in two basic respects: overcoming death and overcoming matter itself. Some traditions, especially the

Mesopotamian, viewed death as an ending, while others, particularly the Egyptian, saw death as a transition, a passage into another world. Overcoming the fear of death was important to certain groups in the Greco-Roman world. Inspired by Plato's dualism of material body and immaterial spirit, Stoics and Neoplatonists attempted to liberate pure spirit from its imprisonment in matter.

Death as an Ending

One of the main topics in the *Epic of Gilgamesh* is death. The central event in the story is the death of Enkidu, which threw Gilgamesh into emotional turmoil: he had to experience the full range of disbelief, rage, and grief before he could accept it. He ordered craftsmen to fashion a statue of Enkidu; had valuable items from his own treasury interred with his friend so that Enkidu could impress the netherworld gods; and held a funeral that included a sacrifice of animals for a banquet at which Gilgamesh ordered further offerings to the gods.

Ancient funeral rites institutionalized the sequence of emotional responses to death that Gilgamesh illustrated. Greek rites, for instance, included several phases. In the "laying out" phase, women washed, anointed, and dressed the body, wrapped it in cloth, and placed in its mouth or hand a coin to pay Charon for ferrying it across the river Styx to the land of the dead; then they positioned the body on a bier where family members paid their final respects. The following night, accompanied by mourners, a family procession "carried out" the deceased to the burial site, where it was cremated and then interred with offerings of food, wine, and other items deemed useful in the afterlife. The family then returned home for a funeral banquet that typically included animal sacrifices.

Families showed their respect for the dead by maintaining their gravesites and making offerings on the anniversaries of their deaths. These family "cults of the dead" were complemented by community observances such the Athenian festivals of Genesia and Anthesteria and the Roman festivals known as the Parentalia and Lemuria (the latter was dedicated specifically to those who had not received proper burial).

Mesopotamians, like other peoples of the ancient world, believed that the spirits of the dead lived on, but depictions of the afterlife were so consistently gloomy that no one looked forward to it. Most Greeks and Romans shared that view. In Book 11 of the *Odyssey*, the spirit of the dead Achilles told Odysseus that he would rather toil as a hired hand on someone else's dirt than rule the underworld. Surviving funerary inscriptions suggest that most Greeks did not envision any meaningful existence after death.

Document

A Tavern-keeper's Advice to Gilgamesh

In this Old Babylonian version of the tale, Siduri advises Gilgamesh to "seize the day" ("carpe diem" in Latin).

You'll never find the life you seek.
When the gods created humankind,
they assigned them death,
retaining immortality for themselves.
Gilgamesh, fill your belly,

enjoy yourself day and night!
Savour every day,
dance merrily day and night!
Wear clean clothes, anoint your head, bathe in
    water!
Dote on the child who holds your hand;
tender your wife loving embraces.

Death as a Passage

In Mesopotamian thinking, this world mattered more than the next, so life should be lived to its fullest. The Egyptians also enjoyed this world, so much so that they never wanted it to end. During the Old Kingdom that possibility extended only to the rulers and their immediate court circles. Tomb scenes emphasized the presentation of offerings, both life's necessities (bread and beer) and elite status symbols (furniture and jewellery). If the actual grave offerings ever ran out, the offerings depicted on the tomb walls would come to life. The **Pyramid Texts** of the Old Kingdom, Egypt's oldest religious literature, included prayers, spells, and hymns to assist the deceased ruler on his afterlife journey to the cosmic realm of the gods.

Major changes occurred during the Middle Kingdom. No longer was afterlife divinity restricted to rulers: any member of the elite could achieve that status. With this "democratization of the afterlife," the main focus of mortuary religion shifted from Ra to Osiris, ruler of the underworld. The deceased were expected to undertake a treacherous journey, from their Land of Life to the Field of Offering. To complete the journey the deceased had two aids: the 1,200 spells known as Coffin Texts and maps of the underworld sketched on their coffins. Lastly, the deceased had to prove their worthiness to enter the realm of Osiris by vindicating themselves before a divine tribunal. These beliefs continued to be held for the remainder of ancient Egyptian history.

Mastering Death

Not everyone feared death. The Greek philosopher Epicurus wrote, "The most terrifying of evils, death, is nothing to us, since when we exist, death does not. But when death is present, then we do not exist." A favourite epitaph in Roman times consisted of a simple sequence of verbs: "I was not; I was; I am not; I care not." The Stoic philosopher Seneca left this epigram: "Death is either an end or a transition," hence not to be feared (all three cited in Segal 2004: 222–3). Seneca was known as a moralist. Moralists sought to transform the inner life through moral endeavour. For them "salvation" entailed the triumph of the human spirit over ignorance and moral malaise.

Other thinkers, including Neoplatonists, viewed moral reform as insufficient. To them the human world was illusion, the body a tomb. Salvation required purifying the body and gaining sufficient knowledge to escape, or transcend, the corrupt world of illusion and to enter the soul's true home, the divine presence. This could only be accomplished by a select few individuals who participated in a program of enlightenment. Neoplatonists took their cues from Plato, whose *Phaedrus* described souls after they had separated themselves from their bodies:

> They could see beauty shining, when with the divine chorus they beheld the blessed sight and vision—we following after Zeus

Sites

Eleusis, Greece

Located just to the west of Athens, Eleusis was home to the mystery cult of Demeter and her daughter Persephone. The tradition centred on the myth of Persephone's abduction to the underworld by Hades and her rescue by Demeter. Initiates took part in rituals designed to ensure a favourable stay in the netherworld.

and others after other gods—and we went through the initiations which it is right to call the most blessed, which we celebrated in complete wholeness . . . seeing, as initiates (*mystai*), entire and whole and calm and happy visions of pure light (Bowden 2010: 205).

Plato's words captured the experience of participants in the "mystery religions" associated with deities such as Demeter, Dionysus, and Isis. Unlike most Greek ritual traditions, these cults were non-exclusive, equally accepting of males and females, slaves and free citizens.

Three notable features of mystery cults were secrecy, specialized knowledge, and direct experience of the divine. Initiates were required to swear oaths of secrecy (the same was true of priests in Egypt and Mesopotamia). At some point (as in Egypt) the initiates would be given directions, on gold-leaf tablets, for navigating the "Sacred Way" of the underworld. They encountered the divine twice: immediately in the brilliant light described by Plato and ultimately at the end of their journey through the underworld.

✤ The End of Antiquity

The Latin word *traditio* was dichotomous in that it could mean either "handing down" or "betrayal." Respect for tradition was based on the notion that if something had worked in the past, then it should continue to work. If it no longer worked, however, then it was time for a change. In 42 BCE, a 30-year-old mother of four named Taimhotep died. Her husband commissioned a funerary **stela** that showed her worshipping all the traditional Egyptian gods. Part of the inscription read:

> Oh my brother, my husband,
> Friend, High Priest,
> Weary not of drink and food,
> Of drinking deep and loving!
> Celebrate the holiday,
> Follow your heart day and night,

> Let no care enter your heart,
> Value the years spent on earth!
> The west, it is a land of sleep;
> Darkness weighs on the dwelling-place
> [i.e., darkness covers the land of the dead]
> (Lichtheim 1980: 62–3).

That *carpe diem* advice—the same advice that Siduri gave Gilgamesh—repudiated the 2,000-year-old Egyptian religious tradition that looked forward

The stela of Taimhotep, Late Ptolemaic Period, 43–42 BCE.

to a pleasurable afterlife. The real speaker was not Taimhotep but rather the commissioner of the stela, her high-priest spouse, the archetypal upholder of tradition. Perhaps he had a premonition of the darkness that would descend on Egypt within the decade, when it would be forcibly incorporated into the Roman Empire. Four centuries later, darkness would enshroud antiquity itself.

Christianity did not displace the ancient traditions of Rome overnight: the process of transition was long and complex. A study of Roman sarcophagi from the period between 270 and 400 CE provides one measure of the time required: it identified 778 pagan and 71 Christian sarcophagi for the years between 270 and 300 CE; 313 pagan and 463 Christian for 300–330; and 12 pagan and 325 Christian for 330–400 (cited in Cameron 2011: 183). The major shift occurred during the reign of Constantine (r. 312–337). Although he did not prohibit traditional religious practices, he supported (in his words) the "shining houses of God's truth" against "the powers of darkness" (Kahlos 2009: 60).

Historians looking for the event that marked the definitive end of antiquity have many choices: the emperor Theodosius's ban on traditional sacrifices in 391 CE; his decree, the following year, forbidding anyone "to go to the sanctuaries, walk through the temples, or raise his eyes to statues created by human labour"; the death of the last traditional Roman priest in 402; the sack of Rome in 410; the closing of the Academy in Athens by Justinian in 529. Just as beginnings—the first time a god was given a name, the first time a structure was erected to serve as a temple, the first time a sacrifice was offered to a god—are impossible to pinpoint, so are endings. In the 470s a prefect of Rome restored an image of Minerva; two decades later a bishop of Rome suppressed the ancient festival of Lupercalia. Meanwhile, despite repeated prohibitions, Christians continued to offer sacrifices to an image of Constantine, the first Christian emperor.

As the increasingly Christian Roman state took steps first to reduce and then to eliminate the influence of "paganism," an intriguing exchange of letters took place between Maximus of Madauros and

A column in the Temple of Hathor at Dendera, Egypt, defaced by Christians.

Bob Young Photo/AGPix

Augustine of Hippo. Maximus, insisting that there was more than one path to God, advocated religious pluralism and what he called "harmonious discord," with pagans and Christians worshipping their common Father in thousands of ways. But Augustine's monolithic religion—one exclusive path, one exclusive truth, one exclusive God—won out. Laws proscribing traditional practices helped, as did denunciatory sermons. Still, perhaps the most effective tactic in the campaign against antiquity was the withholding of imperial monies from "pagan" temples and shrines. By 400, anyone wanting to commune with the divine in the presence of others had nowhere to go but a Christian church.

If we seek a symbolic moment, however, we might select the following. In 389 CE Serena, the adopted niece of Theodosius I and a committed Christian, entered the Augustan temple of Magna

Mater (the Great Mother, Cybele), removed a necklace from the cult image of the goddess, and placed it around her own neck. Observing this transfer of religious symbols and power from antiquity to the "modern" day was Coelia Concordia, Rome's last Vestal Virgin. The priestess responsible for keeping Rome's eternal flame alive, who had taken refuge in the Mother's sanctuary, protested. But her protests met deaf ears, and she was never heard from again. The age of the "mother of all evils" was over; the reign of the Father had begun.

Recent Developments

The study of ancient religion(s) today reflects the influence of several relatively recent developments. First, archaeological evidence has both complemented textual evidence and in some cases suggested challenges to interpretations derived exclusively from texts (especially texts produced by the literary elite). Relatedly, archaeological evidence has also permitted the emergence of much more detailed pictures of everyday religious life. Much greater attention has been paid to the roles of women in religion in the ancient world. Another important development has been a greater emphasis on the features that the religions of antiquity share in common with Judaism and Christianity (there are many fewer commonalities with Islam). This emphasis has had two results: a greater effort to contextualize practices and concepts, and a greater appreciation that differences between religious traditions are more often differences of degree than of kind. Finally, a number of religious practices, such as divination, are now being interpreted in the light of cognitive psychology.

Summary

This chapter has demonstrated that the religious traditions of antiquity sought to address every aspect of what most lay people today would consider "religion": a "belief" in the supernatural, an effort to understand the interaction between the divine and the human planes of existence, consideration of what makes a person worthy of divine support, the idea of a conflict between good and evil, contemplation of the ultimate end of material existence. The four traditions examined in this chapter all reached similar conclusions. The questioning of those conclusions that began in several of the traditions around 600 BCE, however, would set the stage for a challenge to the most fundamental components of the religions of antiquity: the number of gods and the most proper form of worship. Eventually, a different set of answers, which formed the basis of the three monotheistic Western traditions, would supplant the ancients' answers.

Sacred Texts
Foundational Texts

Religious Tradition	Text	Composition/ Compilation	Compilation/ Revision	Use
Egypt	Pyramid Texts	24th century BCE		mortuary ritual myth
Egypt	Coffin Texts	22nd–17th centuries BCE		mortuary ritual myth

Continued

Sacred Texts (Continued)

Foundational Texts

Religious Tradition	Text	Composition/ Compilation	Compilation/ Revision	Use
Egypt	*Book of the Dead* (*Book of Going Forth by Day*)	16th century BCE		mortuary ritual myth
Mesopotamia	*Enuma Elish*	12th century BCE (Babylonian version)	7th century BCE (Assyrian version)	ritual myth
Mesopotamia	*Gilgamesh*	18th century BCE (Old Babylonian Version)	13th–10th centuries BCE (Standard Version)	myth
Mesopotamia	*Atrahasis*	18th century BCE		myth
Mesopotamia	*Erra* (also known as *Erra and Ishum*)	8th century BCE		myth magic
Greece	*Iliad* and *Odyssey* of Homer	8th–7th centuries BCE		myth
Greece	*Theogony* of Hesiod	8th–7th centuries BCE		myth
Rome	Ovid's *Metamorphoses*	1st century CE		myth
Rome	Ovid's *Fasti*	1st century CE		ritual

Discussion Questions

1. How did gods differ from humans in antiquity?

2. What radically new understanding of the divine did the Greek philosophers introduce?

3. Which of the following aspects of ancient religion would prove most offensive to Jews, Christians, and Muslims? (a) The worship of statues of gods as if they were the actual gods themselves (idolatry); (b) The practice of offering sacrifices to the gods; (c) The recognition of numerous gods (polytheism); or (d) The ancients' general openness to diverse explanations of how the universe operated.

4. Many late-antique defenders of "pagan" religion argued that since God was ultimately unknowable to humans, all reasonable ways to reach some understanding of the divine were legitimate. "The paths to God are many," according to that view. Is it defendable?

5. Which are more important: the differences between the religions of antiquity and the three major monotheisms, or the similarities? Why?

6. In what ways were the religions of antiquity more inclusive than the major monotheistic faiths?

7. Were the religions of antiquity any less "moral" than the religions of today?

Glossary

Akhenaten Controversial ruler of Egypt in the fourteenth century BCE whose exclusive devotion to the sun-disk Aten has led some scholars to claim that he was the world's first monotheist. The centre of Aten worship was Akhenaten's new capital city, Akhetaten (modern Amarna).

Akkadian The name given to the Semitic languages (Babylonian and Assyrian) of Mesopotamia.

Amun/Amun-Ra The principal Egyptian state god during the Middle and New Kingdoms.

anthropomorphism The attribution of a human form or character to non-human phenomena.

apotropaic A type of ritual practice whose goal is to ward off evil.

Asclepius A god of healing, worshipped throughout the classical Mediterranean world. His most important cult centres were at Epidaurus in Greece and Pergamum in Asia Minor.

Atrahasis A long narrative poem from Mesopotamia, composed during the Old Babylonian period and named for its hero, Atrahasis (meaning "exceptionally wise"). It includes mythological accounts of the creation of humans, their almost complete annihilation in a flood, and the re-creation of humanity through the life cycle of birth, marriage, and death.

Book of the Dead A New Kingdom collection of spells (based on the earlier **Coffin Texts**) designed to ensure the resurrection of the dead and their security in the afterlife. "Book of the Dead" is a modern designation; the actual title translates as *The Book of Going Forth by Day*.

Coffin Texts Essentially spells, based on the earlier **Pyramid Texts**, inscribed on the coffins of non-royal elite Egyptians during the Middle Kingdom, intended to protect the dead traversing the netherworld and to secure them an afterlife comparable to that of the (divinized) dead rulers.

cult A synonym for "ritual worship."

Demeter A Greek "mother goddess" associated with the harvest whose principal centre of worship was Eleusis.

Eleusis The town near Athens that was the site of the Eleusinian mysteries. The tradition centred on the myth of Persephone's abduction to the underworld by Hades and her rescue by her mother Demeter. Initiates took part in rituals designed to ensure a favourable stay in the netherworld. Unlike most Greek ritual traditions, the Eleusinian cult was non-exclusive, equally accepting of males and females, slaves and free citizens.

Enuma Elish The Mesopotamian creation epic, written in the late second millennium BCE, in which the Babylonian god Marduk triumphed over the forces of chaos, "created" and ordered the universe, and became ruler of the Mesopotamian pantheon. The title (literally, "when on high") comes from the first two words of the composition.

Epictetus (55–135 CE) Influential Stoic philosopher.

Gilgamesh Historical ruler of the city of Uruk, c. 2700 BCE, who became the subject of a series of Sumerian stories that were reformulated during the Old Babylonian period to create the unified narrative commonly known as the *Epic of Gilgamesh*. The tale was revised several centuries later in a "Standard Version."

Hathor Egyptian cow goddess associated with both creation (love, sex, and fertility) and violent destructive power.

Hera The wife of Zeus in Greek mythology and a patron of marriage and motherhood.

Herodotus The fifth-century-BCE Greek known as the "Father of History"; his *Histories* described the religious practices of numerous peoples.

Hesiod The eighth-century-BCE author of *Works and Days* and *Theogony*; one of the two primary sources for the "standard" portraits of the Greek gods (the other was **Homer**).

Homer The eighth-century-BCE author of the *Iliad* and the *Odyssey*; the other primary source for the "standard" portraits of the Greek gods (see also **Hesiod**).

Ishtar A Mesopotamian goddess of both love and war, early identified with her Sumerian counterpart Inanna.

Isis The best known Egyptian goddess, first mentioned in Old Kingdom texts that associated her with rulers in both life and death. In later myth she was the devoted sister and wife of Osiris and the loving mother of Horus. During the Ptolemaic and Roman eras, Isis took on the functions of numerous other deities and became a universal goddess, worshipped throughout the Mediterranean world.

Marduk The patron god of Babylon, first promoted by Hammurabi and later elevated to the supreme position in the Mesopotamian pantheon.

necropolis Literally, "city of the dead"; a synonym for "cemetery."

Neoplatonism A school of philosophy that was most influential between the third and sixth centuries CE. Many of its concepts regarding divinity and cosmology intersected with Jewish, Christian, and Islamic thought.

Netherworld The region that the spirits of the dead were believed to enter, also known as the afterworld or afterlife. While "netherworld" suggests that it lies beneath the earth, the land of the dead could also be located in the heavens.

Osiris The Egyptian god, depicted as a mummy wearing a crown, elevated to the position of ruler of the realm of the dead during the Middle Kingdom. New Kingdom texts portray him as the pre-eminent judge of the dead, a belief that gained in significance in the later periods of Egyptian history and presumably influenced the understanding of divine judgment in Judaism and Christianity.

Ovid (43 BCE–17 CE) The Roman author of *Metamorphoses* and *Fasti*, among other works.

Plato (c. 425–347 BCE) The Greek philosopher whose most important contribution to religious thought was his separation of the world into the conflicting realms of the material and the spiritual.

Plutarch (46–120 CE) A senior priest of Apollo at Delphi and a prolific author. Among his works was the *Moralia*, which included "On the Decline of the Oracles" and "On the Worship of Isis and Osiris"—the most complete version of the principal Egyptian myth.

Pyramid Texts Spells or incantations (literally, "utterances") carved on the walls of the royal burial suites of late Old Kingdom rulers; recited by priests to guarantee the resurrection and well-being of dead rulers.

stela An inscribed stone sculpture; plural "stelas" or "stelae."

Sumer The urban civilization of southernmost Mesopotamia (Sumer) in the late fourth millennium BCE; Sumerian religion was the substratum of Mesopotamian religion.

Tiamat The female monster who represented primeval chaos/disorder and was subdued by Marduk in *Enuma Elish*. (The name "Tiamat" is related to *tehom*, the Hebrew word usually translated as "the void" or "nothing" in the first verses of *Genesis*.)

Vesta The Roman goddess of household and hearth, served by priestesses known as the Vestal Virgins, who maintained the sacred fire that secured the safety of Rome itself. Vesta's Greek equivalent was named Hestia ("hearth").

Xenophanes (c. 570–c. 475 BCE) Early Greek philosopher who challenged the anthropomorphic depictions of the gods in Greek myth.

Zeus The most powerful of the Greek gods, who ruled from Mount Olympus. His principal shrine was at Olympia, the site of the ancient Olympic games.

Further Reading

General

Armstrong, Karen. 2006. *The Great Transformation: The Beginnings of Our Religious Traditions.* New York: Alfred A. Knopf. A synthesis focused on the Axial Age, the era (from roughly 900 to 200 BCE) when various religious and philosophical traditions that survive to the present began to challenge longstanding practices and behaviours.

Bellah, Robert N. 2011. *Religion in Human Evolution: From the Paleolithic to the Axial Age.* Cambridge, MA: Harvard University Press. A sociological interpretation of ancient religion.

Hinnels, John R., ed. 2007. *A Handbook of Ancient Religions.* Cambridge: Cambridge University Press. Several chapters devoted to the ancient Near East and the Classical worlds.

Johnston, Sarah Iles, ed. 2004. *Religions of the Ancient World: A Guide.* Cambridge: Harvard University Press. A single-volume compendium that includes sections on 11 major aspects of religion, the histories of 11 religious traditions, and comparative examinations of 20 important topics.

Ancient Near East: General

Snell, Daniel C. 2011. *Religions of the Ancient Near East.* Cambridge: Cambridge University Press. An excellent introduction for beginners.

Ancient Near East: Mesopotamia

Bottéro, Jean. 2001. *Religion in Ancient Mesopotamia.* Chicago: University of Chicago Press. A sophisticated, topical overview.

Dalley, Stephanie. 2000. *Myths from Mesopotamia: Creation, the Flood, Gilgamesh, and Others.* Revised edn. New York: Oxford University Press. Translations of key Mesopotamian texts.

Jacobsen, Thorkild. 1976. *The Treasures of Darkness: A History of Mesopotamian Religion.* New Haven: Yale University Press. A chronological treatment based on Jacobsen's translations and interpretations of numerous early texts.

Schneider, Tammi J. 2011. *An Introduction to Ancient Mesopotamian Religion.* Grand Rapids, MI: William B. Eerdmans. An acceptable starting point for students.

Ancient Near East: Egypt

David, Rosalie. 2002. *Religion and Magic in Ancient Egypt.* London: Penguin Books. A straightforward presentation of 3,000 years of Egyptian religion.

Wilkinson, Richard H. 2003. *The Complete Gods and Goddesses of Egypt.* London: Thames and Hudson. An illustrated guide to Egyptian deities.

Classical World: General

Kraemer, Ross Shepard, ed. 2004. *Women's Religions in the Greco-Roman World: A Sourcebook.* Oxford: Oxford University Press. A wide-ranging collection of Jewish, Christian, and "pagan" documents.

Ogden, Daniel, ed. 2009. *Magic, Witchcraft, and Ghosts in the Greek and Roman Worlds: A Sourcebook.* 2nd edn. Oxford: Oxford University Press. A fascinating collection of texts.

Classical World: Greece

Buxton, Richard. 2004. *The Complete World of Greek Mythology.* London: Thames & Hudson. An illustrated guide to Greek deities.

Dillon, Matthew. 2002. *Girls and Women in Classical Greek Religion.* London: Routledge. A thorough overview.

Mikalson, Jon D. 2005. *Ancient Greek Religion.* Oxford: Blackwell. A basic, topical introduction.

Ogden, Daniel, ed. 2007. *A Companion to Greek Religion.* Oxford: Blackwell. A collection of articles on eight major aspects of Greek religion.

Classical World: Rome

Beard, Mary et al. 1998. *Religions of Rome.* 2 vols. Cambridge: Cambridge University Press. A thoughtful assessment in Vol. 1, supplemented by hundreds of texts in Vol. 2.

Rives, James B. 2007. *Religion in the Roman Empire.* Oxford: Blackwell. A topical introduction, suitable for upper-division students.

Recommended Websites

Mesopotamia

www.etana.org

ETANA (Electronic Tools and Ancient Near Eastern Archives) offers a range of materials, including texts in translation.

Egypt

www.uee.ucla.edu

The Encyclopedia of Egyptology offers short articles on dozens of topics.

Greece and Rome

www.perseus.tufts.edu

The Perseus Digital Library provides texts in Greek, Latin, and English.

General

www.fordham.edu.halsall/ancient/asbook.HTML

The Internet Ancient History Sourcebook provides easy access to Egyptian, Mesopotamian, Persian, Greek, and Roman texts.

References

Ando, Clifford. 2008. *The Matter of the Gods: Religion and the Roman Empire*. Berkeley: University of California Press.

Assmann, Jan. 2001. *The Search for God in Ancient Egypt*. Ithaca: Cornell University Press.

Augustine, Saint. 1972. *City of God*. Henry Bettenson, trans. London: Penguin.

Bowden, Hugh. 2010. *Mystery Cults of the Ancient World*. Princeton: Princeton University Press.

Brown, Peter. 1995. *Authority and the Sacred Aspects of the Christianisation of the Roman World*. Cambridge: Cambridge University Press.

Cameron, Alan. 2011. *The Last Pagans of Rome*. Oxford: Oxford University Press.

Chadwick, J. and W.N. Mann. 1950. *Hippocratic Writings*. London. Penguin.

Cicero. 1997. *The Nature of the Gods*. P.G. Walsh, trans. Oxford: Oxford University Press.

Connelly, Joan Breton. 2007. *Portrait of a Priestess: Women and Ritual in Ancient Greece*. Princeton, NJ: Princeton University Press.

Epictetus. 1925. *Discourses, Books 1 & 2*. W.H. Oldfather, trans. Cambridge: Harvard University Press.

Fagles, Robert, and Bernard Knox. 1984. *The Three Theban Plays: Antigone, Oedipus the King, and Oedipus at Colonus*. New York: Penguin.

Feeney, Denis. 1998. *Literature and Religion at Rome: Cultures, Contexts, and Beliefs*. Cambridge: Cambridge University Press.

Flower, Michael Attyah. 2008. *The Seer in Ancient Greece*. Berkeley: University of California Press.

Foley, John Miles, ed. 2009. *A Companion to Ancient Epic*. Oxford: Wiley-Blackwell.

Freeman, Charles. 1996. *Egypt, Greece, and Rome: Civilizations of the Ancient Mediterranean*. Oxford: Oxford University Press.

Johnson, Luke Timothy. 2009. *Among the Gentiles: Greco-Roman Religion and Christianity*. New Haven: Yale University Press.

Kahlos, Maijastina. 2009. *Forbearance and Compulsion: The Rhetoric of Religious Tolerance and Intolerance in Late Antiquity*. London: Duckworth.

Kemp, Barry. 2012. *The City of Akhenaten and Nefertiti: Amarna and Its People*. London: Thames and Hudson.

Knust, Jennifer, and Zsuzsanna Varhelyi, eds. 2011. *Ancient Mediterranean Sacrifice*. Oxford: Oxford University Press.

Lambert, W.G. 1960. *Babylonian Wisdom Literature*. Oxford: Oxford University Press.

Lesher, J.H. 1992. *Xenophanes of Colophon*. Toronto: University of Toronto Press.

Lichtheim, Miriam. 1973–80. *Ancient Egyptian Literature*. 3 vols. Berkeley: University of California Press.

Mandelbaum, Allen. 1993. *The Metamorphoses of Ovid*. San Diego: Harcourt, Inc.

Pinch, Geraldine. 2002. *Egyptian Mythology: A Guide to the Gods, Goddesses, and Traditions of Ancient Egypt*. Oxford: Oxford University Press.

Rives, James B. 2007. *Religion in the Roman Empire*. Oxford: Blackwell.

Sasson, Jack M., ed. 1995. *Civilizations of the Ancient Near East*. Vol. III. New York: Charles Scribner's Sons.

Schaff, Philip, and Henry Wace, eds. 1885. *Nicene and Post-Nicene Fathers*. Series II, Volume X. Edinburgh: T & T Clark. Accessed 12 Feb. 2010 at <www.ccelorg/ccel/schaff/npnf210.html>.

Scheid, John. 2003. *An Introduction to Roman Religion*. Bloomington: Indiana University Press.

Segal, Alan F. 2004. *Life after Death: A History of the Afterlife in Western Religions*. New York: Doubleday.

Snell, Daniel C., ed. 1995. *A Companion to the Ancient Near East*. Oxford: Blackwell.

Tacitus. 1964. *The Histories*. Kenneth Wellesley, trans. New York: Penguin.

Thom, Johan. 2005. *Cleanthes' Hymn to Zeus*. Tubingen, Germany: Mohr Siebeck.

von Dassow, Eva, ed. 1994. *The Egyptian Book of the Dead: The Book of Going Forth by Day*. San Francisco: Chronicle Books.

Watterson, Barbara. 1999. *Amarna: Ancient Egypt's Age of Revolution*. Stroud, UK: Tempus.

Wicker, Kathleen O'Brien. 1987. *Porphyry the Philosopher: To Marcella*. Atlanta: Scholars Press.

Wilkinson, Toby. 2010. *The Rise and Fall of Ancient Egypt*. New York: Random House.

3

Jewish
Traditions

Michele Murray

Traditions at a Glance

Numbers
Approximately 14 million.

Distribution
The majority of Jews live in either the United States (5–6 million) or Israel (6 million). There are about 1.5 million Jews in Europe, 400,000 in Latin America, and 375,000 in Canada.

Founders and Leaders
Abraham, his son Isaac, and Isaac's son Jacob are considered the patriarchs of the Jews, and the prophet Moses, who is said to have received the Torah from God and revealed it to the Israelites at Mount Sinai, is known as the Lawgiver. There is no credible evidence outside the Bible, however, that any of them actually existed.

Deity
Yahweh.

Authoritative Texts
Hebrew Bible (Tanakh); Mishnah; Talmud.

Noteworthy Teachings
Deuteronomy 6: 4–9: "Hear O Israel, the LORD our God, the LORD is One. You shall love the LORD your God with all your heart and with all your soul and with all your strength. These words which I command you this day are to be kept in your heart. You shall repeat them to your children, speaking of them indoors and outdoors, morning and night. You shall bind them as a sign upon your hand and wear them as signs upon your forehead; you shall write them on the doorposts of your houses and on your gates."

Leviticus 19: 18: "You shall not take vengeance or bear a grudge against any of your people, but you shall love your neighbour as yourself: I am the LORD."

In this chapter you will learn about:

- Jewish history from biblical times to the present day
- the diverse expressions of Jewish identity through that history
- how Jews responded to struggle and adversity in their past, how their responses shaped Judaism, and how Judaism affected their responses
- Jewish rituals and practices, and their connections to events in Jewish history
- how it is possible to identify oneself as a Jew, and even take part in religious services, without necessarily believing in God
- how Jewish women are now challenging some ancient traditions within Judaism.

Jewish Identity as Ethnicity and Religion

Introducing Three Jews

Having removed the ornately wrapped Torah scroll from the Holy Ark, the rabbi carefully slid the velvet curtains closed. As she turned to face her congregation, she placed the scroll gently on the table before her and began to recite in Hebrew the first blessing.

*

Normally it was not so blustery in Jerusalem, but the weather had been stormy all day. The young man was thankful for the warmth of his long black coat and vest as he hurried along the narrow pathway to

Jerusalem: view from the Old City over the Western Wall and the Dome of the Rock (© FredFroese/Getty Images).

his Talmud study class. The wind tossed his curly sidelocks wildly behind him as he dipped his head low against the wind, one hand grasping his wide-brimmed black hat.

*

Rashel walked into her favourite greasy spoon in downtown Montreal and sat down at her usual table. Every Saturday morning she came here for breakfast, with the local paper in hand to read as she ate. She didn't even need to put in her order, because it was the same every time: a ham and cheese omelette with a side order of bacon.

Each of the three people described above is Jewish. And Judaism has room for all three. Some Jews, such as the first two, feel their Jewishness to be inseparable from Jewish religious practices

and customs. Others—in fact, the majority of Jews living in North America and Israel—are more like Rashel in that they rarely if ever attend **synagogue** (the place of congregational worship) and make no attempt to follow the rules set down by **Halakhah** (Jewish law). They consider themselves to be ethnically Jewish because they were born to Jewish parents, and they may or may not identify with aspects of secular Jewish culture (music, literature, food, and so on), but the religious dimension is not important to them. Thus Jewishness can be grounded in religious, ethnic, or cultural elements, or any combination of them.

For some Jews the mere idea of a female **rabbi** ("teacher") is preposterous and contrary to Halakhah. They believe that women have important roles in the Jewish community, but that the role of rabbi is reserved for men alone. For others, a female rabbi is completely acceptable and natural; in fact, some Jews might be attracted to a particular synagogue precisely because it has a female rabbi. Similarly, some Jews might perceive the dress and lifestyle of the young man described above—a member of a rigorously observant sub-group of Orthodox Jews known as **Haredim**—to be antiquated and unnecessary, while others would consider the devotion of such men, whose lives revolve around the study of ancient Jewish texts, to be one of the reasons for the survival of Judaism, and therefore worthy of deep respect. Jews holding the latter perspective would likely maintain that eating pork and consuming meat and dairy together—as Rashel does—are serious transgressions of Jewish law. Yet if you asked Rashel if she identified herself as Jewish, she would respond fervently in the affirmative. And there are many Jews (particularly in Canada, the United States, and Israel) who would say the same.

The spectrum of Jewish identity is broad, and what one Jew considers an essential part of that identity may not hold any significance for another. Who ought to be called Jewish and what constitutes acceptable Jewish behaviour are subjects of ongoing debate among Jews themselves.

© Ingo Wagner/dpa/Corbis

Alina Treiger—the first female Rabbi to be installed in Germany since the Holocaust—introduces herself to her parish at the synagogue in Oldenburg on 1 February 2011.

Timeline

c. 1850 BCE	Abraham (Abram) arrives in Canaan
c. 1260	Moses leads the Exodus from Egypt and Yahweh reveals the Torah to the Israelites
c. 1000	David takes Jerusalem and makes it his capital
921	Northern kingdom separates following Solomon's death
722	Assyrians conquer northern kingdom and disperse its people
586	Babylonians conquer Jerusalem and deport its leaders
539	Persians conquer Babylonia, permitting exiles to return in 538 BCE
c. 515	Rededication of the Second Temple
c. 333	Alexander the Great's conquests in the eastern Mediterranean begin the process of Hellenization
c. 200	The Torah is translated from Hebrew into Greek; the translation is called the Septuagint
167–164	Maccabean Revolt
70 CE	Romans lay siege to Jerusalem and destroy the Second Temple
132–135	Bar Kochba Revolt
c. 220	The Mishnah of Rabbi Judah ha-Nasi
c. 400	The Palestinian (or Jerusalem) Talmud
c. 500	The Babylonian Talmud
1135	Birth of Moses Maimonides, author of *The Guide of the Perplexed* (d. 1204)
1492	Jews expelled from Spain
1569	Kabbalah scholar Isaac Luria establishes a centre of Jewish mysticism in the northern Palestinian city of Safed
1666	Sabbatai Zvi is promoted as the messiah
1698	Birth of Israel ben Eliezer, the Baal Shem Tov, in Poland (d. 1760)
1729	Birth of Moses Mendelssohn, pioneer of Reform Judaism in Germany (d. 1786)
1881	Severe pogroms in Russia spur Jewish emigration
1889	Conservative Judaism separates from Reform Judaism in the United States
1897	Theodor Herzl organizes the first Zionist Congress
1935	Nuremberg Laws revoke many rights of Jews in Germany
1938	November 9–10 *Kristallnacht*, the "Night of Broken Glass": Jewish businesses and synagogues attacked across Germany in prelude to the Holocaust
1939–45	Second World War (including the Holocaust)
1947	Discovery of the Dead Sea Scrolls
1948	Establishment of the state of Israel

❧ Earliest Jewish History: The Biblical Story

The place to commence a discussion of Jewish history is with the **Hebrew Bible**, which is also known to Jews as the **Tanakh** and to Christians as the Old Testament (Jews do not use the latter term, which reflects the Christian idea that the Hebrew Bible was superseded by the New Testament). Although often described as a book, the Hebrew Bible is in fact an anthology of 24 books, many of which were initially separate. The writings they contain represent a variety of literary forms, including poems, songs, legal prose, and vivid narratives full of drama and supernatural events. Most scholars believe that they were composed by a variety of authors from different segments of society over some 800 years, from approximately the tenth to the second century BCE, although a few scholars, usually called the Minimalists, argue that few if any of the Hebrew Bible's contents were written before the sixth century BCE. Eventually the separate books were assembled in a single canonical collection. There were many additional Jewish writings that could have been selected, but the Jewish community had come to recognize only a certain set of documents as theologically meaningful and authoritative.

The Hebrew Bible is divided into three sections: Torah, Nevi'im, and Ketuvim. ("TaNaKh" is

Document

The Tanakh

The books comprising the three sections of the Tanakh are as follows:

I. Torah (הָרוֹת, "Law"):
1. (תִּישׁאָרְבְ / Bərē'shît) Genesis
2. (תומש / Shemot) Exodus
3. (ארקיו / Vayikra) Leviticus
4. (רבדמב / Bəmidbar) Numbers
5. (סירְבְד / Dəbhārîm) Deuteronomy

II. Nevi'im (סיאיבְנ, "Prophets"):
6. (עֲשׁוֹהִי / Yěhôshúa') Joshua
7. (סיטפוש / Shophtim) Judges
8. (לֵאומְשׁ / Shěmû'ēl) Samuel (I & II)
9. (סיכלמ / M'lakhim) Kings (I & II)
10. (הָיְעַשְׁי / Yěsha'ǎyāhû) Isaiah
11. (הָיְמְרִי / Yirměyāhû) Jeremiah
12. (לאֵיקְזֶחְי / Yěkhezqiēl) Ezekiel
13. (רשע ירת / The Twelve Prophets
    a. (עֲשׁוֹה / Hôshēa') Hosea
    b. (לֵאוֹי / Yô'ēl) Joel
    c. (סומָע / 'Āmôs) Amos

d. (עַבְדַיְה / 'Ōbhadhyāh) Obadiah
e. (הָנוֹי / Yônāh) Jonah
f. (הָכִימ / Mîkhāh) Micah
g. (נַחתוס / Naḥûm) Nahum
h. (קוקבַח / Ḥăbhaqqûq) Habakkuk
i. (הָיַנְפֶצ / Ṣěphanyāh) Zephaniah
j. (יַגַּח / Ḥaggai) Haggai
k. (הָיַרְכֶז / Zěkharyāh) Zechariah
l. (יכִאָלמ / Mal'ǎkhî) Malachi

III. Ketuvim (סִיבוּתְכ, "Writings"):
14. (סילהת / Tehillim) Psalms
15. (ילשמ / Mishlei) Proverbs
16. (בוֹיִּא / Iyyôbh) Job
17. (רִישׁ סִירִישׁׁה / Shîr Hashîrîm) Song of Songs
18. (תור / Rûth) Ruth
19. (הכיא / Eikhah) Lamentations
20. (תלֶהֹק / Qōheleth) Ecclesiastes
21. (רֵתְסֵא / Estēr) Esther
22. (לאֵיַנָּד / Dānī'ēl) Daniel
23. (ארזע הימחנו / Ezra v'Nechemia) Ezra-Nehemiah
24. (ירבד סימיה / Divrei Hayamim) Chronicles (I & II)

an acronym based on the first letters of the three section names, separated by the vowel "a"; the "h" indicates that the final "k" is pronounced with a guttural sound.) The name of the first section, "Torah," is a Hebrew word that has two meanings. In its broad sense it designates the law or instruction of God, and as such is another way of referring to the Hebrew Bible as a whole; in its narrow sense it refers specifically to the first five books: Genesis, Exodus, Leviticus, Numbers, and Deuteronomy. These books cover the history of the **Israelites** from the creation of the world until the entry into the Promised Land, and they instruct the people on how to live moral and ritually acceptable lives. Also known collectively as the **Pentateuch** (Greek for "five books"), these books are considered the most sacred part of the entire Hebrew Bible. "Nevi'im" is the Hebrew word for "prophets": men such as Moses, who were believed to speak for God to the Israelites. The third section, "Ketuvim"—"writings"—contains a variety of material, including songs, prayers, and wisdom literature (i.e., the books of Job, Proverbs, and Ecclesiastes, each of which offers practical advice for dealing judiciously with common human concerns) as well as historical texts.

The Biblical Narrative as Sacred History

The biblical people of Israel, the Israelites, were the precursors of modern Jews, and the majority of Jewish festivals, rituals, and customs are derived from biblical stories. Yet the accuracy of those stories is a matter of debate among scholars, since in most cases there is no extra-biblical evidence to confirm that the events they describe ever occurred, or even that the people involved in them actually existed. But it was not the goal of the human authors of the biblical stories to record an objective account of historical events. Rather, their writings were intended to convey a theological message and teach the Israelites how to live their lives devoutly both in action and in attitude. Although some of the accounts

found in the Tanakh do contain accurate historical information, modern readers ought not to assume that every story is historically factual.

The biblical narrative is more properly understood to be "sacred" history: it was because the stories served the theological agenda of the writers that they were valued and incorporated in the Tanakh. What the Hebrew Bible does is provide insight into the characters and events that came to be considered theologically meaningful for the Jewish community. Whether or not the biblical stories are accurate, they are essential for understanding the development of Judaism.

The material eventually included in the Hebrew Bible may have originated as oral stories or songs that were transmitted by word of mouth from one generation to the next until eventually they were written down. Among the central characters in Israelite history whose existence cannot be confirmed are Abraham, his son Isaac, Isaac's son Jacob, and Moses. The earliest biblical figure for whom we may have archaeological evidence is the lowly shepherd-turned-king of Israel, David. Yet even this evidence—an inscription on the Tel Dan stela (an upright monumental stone), discovered in 1993 in northern Israel—is disputed by a few scholars.

The Creation of Humanity

In fact, there are two different accounts of the creation of humans in the Hebrew Bible, and each of them has its own repercussions for gender relations. The first one is found in the Book of Genesis 1: 26–7:

> Then God said, "Let us make humankind in our image, according to our likeness; and let them have dominion over the fish of the sea, and over the birds of the air, and over the cattle, and over all the wild animals of the earth, and over every creeping thing that creeps upon the earth." So God created humankind in his image, in the image of God he created them; male and female he created them.

In this account, man and woman are created at exactly the same time in "the image of God": thus they are equals. In the second creation story, however, man is created first out of the earth, and woman is created later out of one of his ribs as a "helper" for him (Genesis 2: 7, 18, 21–4):

> Then the Lord God formed man from the dust of the ground, and breathed into his nostrils the breath of life; and the man became a living being. . . . Then the Lord God said, 'It is not good that the man should be alone; I will make him a helper as his partner." . . . So the Lord God caused a deep sleep to fall upon the man, and he slept; then he took one of his ribs and closed up its place with flesh. And the rib that the Lord God had taken from the man he made into a woman and brought her to the man. Then the man said, "This at last is bone of my bones and flesh of my flesh; this one shall be called Woman, for out of Man this one was taken." Therefore a man leaves his father and his mother and clings to his wife, and they become one flesh.

This second creation account is by far the better known of the two; indeed, many people take it for granted that this account, in which Eve is a secondary creation, made from one of Adam's ribs, is the only creation story. Rabbis through the centuries have tried to explain the significance of the rib. One **midrash** (rabbinic commentary or interpretation) dated to the fourth or fifth century CE proposes that "the rib is a hidden part of the body, and therefore it was chosen to teach women modesty" (*Bereshit Rabbah* 18). This is an example of circular reasoning: the rabbinic account of why God chose to create the woman out of a rib (so that she will be modest) is used to justify the rabbinic view of the way women ought to behave (modestly). In rabbinic literature, women are excluded from numerous leadership roles on the grounds that it would be immodest for a woman to perform a public role of any kind. In fact, this creation story has been used throughout history to justify the dominance of men over women. The "appropriate" hierarchy of male and female is explicitly presented in this version of humanity's creation. Some interpretations suggest that because the female was created from a bone rather than from the earth, women were "lesser" creations whose central obligation was to serve men, not God. This understanding shapes everything from the marital tasks of a wife to the imagery used to express the relationship between God and Israel, in which God takes the role of husband and Israel takes the role of wife.

So where was the first woman, made together with Adam in Chapter 1 of Genesis, when Eve was created in Chapter 2? The rabbis devised a creative answer with the midrash of Lilith, the original female being (see document box). In early rabbinic references, Lilith appears as a long-haired, winged demon of the succubae class—that is, a female demon who has sexual relations with sleeping men: "Rabbi Hanina said, 'One [male] may not sleep alone in a house, for Lilith takes hold of whoever sleeps alone in a house" (BT Shabbat 151b). Later, succubae were said to be particularly envious of human wives, and to hate the children born of ordinary human relations. Thus Lilith became known as an enemy of women, and all problems related to pregnancy and childbirth, including infertility and miscarriage, were blamed on her. In the late Middle Ages, amulets warding off the jealousy of Lilith were used to protect pregnant mothers and their babies.

The earliest reference to the people of Israel outside the Bible is found on the victory stela of the Egyptian pharaoh Merneptah, which dates from approximately 1208 BCE. Discovered in 1896, it is a black granite stone inscribed with a hymn recording the pharaoh's triumphs. One verse reads: "Israel is wasted, its seed is not . . ." (Hallo 2003: 41). "Israel," here, almost certainly refers to an ethnic group or people: instead of the hieroglyphic sign for "country," the inscription uses the sign for "people." By the end of the thirteenth century BCE, then, it seems that a people calling itself "Israel" existed in Canaan (a term designating roughly the region of

Document

The Story of Lilith

The Alphabet of Ben Sira, *written between the eighth and tenth centuries* CE, *is the earliest written version of the rabbinic explanation for the two different creation stories in Genesis. According to this text, Adam's first wife, Lilith, expected to share power equally with Adam since both were made of the same substance. Thus Lilith refused to lie below Adam during sex: she wanted to be on top. Adam refused and Lilith left him, necessitating the creation of a second wife, Eve:*

When the first man, Adam, saw that he was alone, God made for him a woman like himself, from the earth. God called her name Lilith, and brought her to Adam. They immediately began to quarrel. Adam said: "You lie beneath me." And Lilith said: "You lie beneath me! We are both equal, for both of us are from the earth." And they would not listen to one another.

As soon as Lilith saw this, she uttered the Divine name and flew up into the air and fled. Adam began to pray before his Creator, saying: "Master of the universe, the woman that you gave me has fled." God sent three angels and said to them: "Go bring back Lilith. If she wants to come, she shall come, and if she does not want to come, do not bring her against her will."

The three angels went and found her in the sea at the place where the Egyptians were destined to drown. There they grabbed her and said to her: "If you will go with us, well and good, but if not, we will drown you in the sea."

Lilith said to them: "My friends, I know God only created me to weaken infants. . . . From the day a child is born until the eighth day, I have dominion over the child, and from the eighth day onward I have no dominion over him if he is a boy, but if a girl, I rule over her twelve days."

They said: "We won't let you go until you accept upon yourself that each day one hundred of your children will die." And she accepted it. That is why one hundred demons die every day. They would not leave her alone until she swore to them: "In any place that I see you or your names in an amulet, I will have no dominion over that child." They left her. And she is Lilith, who weakens the children of men. . . .

Alphabet of Ben Sira 23a–b; trans. N. Bronznick in D. Stern and M.J. Mirsky 1990: 183–4.

---

modern-day Israel, the Palestinian territories, Lebanon, and part of Syria).

The Origins of "Israel," "Hebrew," "Jew," and "Semitic"

The origins of the term "Israel" are not certain, although one interpretation ("the one who struggled with God") links it with a story in which Abraham's grandson Jacob wrestled with a divine being and was then renamed "Israel." Two other terms used on occasion in the Hebrew Bible are

"Hebrew(s)" and "Jew(s)." Abraham, for example, is called a Hebrew, and the prophet Jonah identifies himself as a Hebrew. This term might come from the Akkadian word *hab/piru* (Canaanite *apiru*), which referred to fugitives, mercenaries, and people living on the periphery of regular society. It may be that this was a term used to refer to early Israelites, signifying that they were somehow removed from a conventional society. Modern-day usage of the term "Hebrew" is reserved for languages: the ancient Hebrew of the Bible and other religious Jewish literature, and the modern Hebrew that is one of the two official languages of the modern state of Israel (the other is Arabic). The word "Jew" is derived from "Judah," the name of the territory that in ancient times was considered to be the Jewish homeland. The word "Semitic" is derived from "Shem": the name of the man from whom both Jews and Arabs were said to have descended. (According to the biblical story, Shem was one of three sons of the legendary Noah, builder of the Ark that survived the great flood sent by God to destroy the creation.)

When Was the Torah Written Down?

There has been a good deal of scholarly debate over when the material in the Torah was written down. Traditional Jews (for example, those belonging to the Orthodox branch of Judaism) hold that the Torah was divinely revealed to Moses, the legendary leader of the Israelites, at Mount Sinai and written down by him as a single document. Most contemporary biblical scholars strongly disagree with this view. They argue that the Torah is a composite text, comprising various documents composed at different times by human beings. The theory that still dominates modern discussions of the Torah question is the **Documentary Hypothesis**, which was proposed in 1883 by the German scholar Julius Wellhausen. Based on observations from earlier investigators as well as his own insights, it argues that the Five Books of Moses consist of material from four different authors (or schools of authors) that can be identified through their differences in style and vocabulary as well as theological viewpoint. The basic assumption that the Bible is a human rather than a divine creation has drawn vigorous criticism of the Documentary Hypothesis from traditional Jews, Christians, and Muslims alike. Scholars holding a more liberal perspective have also been critical of the theory, in particular regarding the dates and other details pertaining to the composition of the documents. Nevertheless, the Documentary Hypothesis has had a powerful influence: it is now widely accepted that multiple voices are represented in the texts of the Torah.

The second book of the Torah, Exodus, tells how Moses led the Israelites out of slavery in Egypt and eventually, after 40 years of wandering in the desert, to the Promised Land of Canaan. Some scholars suggest that part of the book may have been written as early as the thirteenth century BCE—the time that most scholars would associate with any event resembling the **Exodus**. According to the biblical story, Moses, with divine help in the form of ten horrible plagues, convinced the Egyptian pharaoh to liberate the enslaved Israelites and let them leave Egypt.

Other scholars suggest that the writing process may have begun during a time of crisis, when there was reason to fear that the oral traditions might be lost if they were not recorded. Two periods of tumult that have been suggested as possible candidates are the eighth century BCE, after the northern kingdom of Israel fell to the Assyrians, and the sixth century BCE, after Jerusalem fell to the Babylonians and the leaders of the Israelites were sent into exile in Babylonia.

It is probably safe to assume that the earliest material to have been committed to the page (or, more correctly, the papyrus or parchment) was the Torah (the five books of Moses). The first five books likely took their final form in the post-exilic period, sometime between the sixth and fourth centuries BCE. The Nevi'im were probably finalized around 200 BCE, and the Ketuvim by the second century CE. The latest book in the Hebrew Bible is the Book of Daniel, whose final chapters (7–12) were written after 167 BCE (even though the narrative is written as if the events it describes took place during the time of the Exile in Babylonia).

Relationship as Covenant: The Israelites and their God

The Bible identifies the Israelites as God's chosen people. On the one hand, they were chosen by Yahweh, as it says in the fifth book of the Torah: "For you are a people holy to the LORD your God; the LORD your God has chosen you out of all the

Focus

Passover

Passover (*Pesach* in Hebrew) commemorates the supposed liberation of the Israelites from slavery in Egypt. It falls in the spring and is one of the major Jewish festivals. The focal point of this festival is the ritual meal called a **Seder** ("order"), during which a text called the **Haggadah** is read aloud. Relating the story of the Exodus from Egypt, it celebrates the fact that death passed over the Israelites when God struck down the Egyptian firstborn in the tenth plague. During the Seder meal Jews eat unleavened bread to remind them of the speed with which the Israelites left Egypt; in fact, it is forbidden to eat any yeast or cereal products, which could ferment throughout the holiday. This means that no bread or bread products are eaten during Passover; only matsoh—unleavened bread (without yeast)—is allowed. This is why Passover is also known as the Feast of Unleavened Bread.

A Seder is a joyous occasion, a gathering of family and friends that should include not only the recitation of the Haggadah, but a spirited discussion with many questions and debates about the meaning of the holiday. The evening can stretch into the early hours of the morning, and in Orthodox households the meal may not even be served until well past midnight.

The centrepiece of the Seder table is a plate with five or six symbolic foods on it. The *karpas* (vegetable) is typically a piece of parsley or celery, and represents spring or hope. It is dipped in salt water, which symbolizes the tears of the Israelites, before it is eaten. *Maror* (bitter herb) is usually represented by horseradish, and is meant to remind one of the bitterness of slavery. The *kharoset*, a mixture often made of apples, nuts, wine, and spices, relates to the mortar from which the Israelite slaves made bricks for the pharaoh's buildings. The *zeroa* (shankbone) echoes the lamb's blood with which Israelites marked the lintels of their doorways, signalling their presence to God so that he would "pass over" without taking their firstborn. The *baytzah* (hard-boiled egg) is understood to symbolize

peoples on earth to be his people, his treasured possession" (Deuteronomy 7: 6). On the other hand, the Israelites themselves chose Yahweh: "Then Joshua said to the people, 'You are witnesses against yourselves that you have chosen the LORD, to serve him.' And they said, 'We are witnesses'" (Joshua 24: 22). It is unlikely that the Israelites understood their selection by Yahweh to mark them out as superior to other peoples; rather, it obliged them to assume the responsibilities of serving God. Nor was the notion of being a "chosen people" unique to the Israelites; there is evidence that other peoples in the ancient world also understood themselves to have been chosen by their deities.

One of the central themes in the Bible's account of the relationship between the Israelites and their God is that of the **covenant**. The Hebrew word for "covenant" is **brit**, which can also be translated as "treaty," "alliance," or "pact." It refers to an agreement between two parties, in which promises are made under oath either to carry out or to abstain from certain specified actions; marriage is a modern example of this type of agreement. The first biblical covenant, described in Genesis 9: 8–17, is made when God promises Noah that he will never again send a flood to destroy the world.

The fact that the Israelites are described as participating in covenants is not unusual for the place and time in which they lived. A multitude of international treaties are preserved in texts from the ancient Near East. Covenants were important for the governing and stabilization of ancient social either fertility or mourning for the loss of the two historic Temples in Jerusalem (because hard-boiled eggs are relatively easy to digest, they were often eaten during periods of mourning). Finally, *hazeret* (bitter vegetable) is an optional second symbol of the harsh life of a slave; a piece of romaine lettuce is commonly used. Jews are to retell the story of the Exodus as if everyone gathered around the table had been liberated from slavery in Egypt themselves.

At the table, it is the custom to reserve some wine in a special cup for the prophet Elijah, whose return to earth will herald the coming of the Messianic Age, a time of peace and prosperity for all. At one point in the evening the door to the house is even held open for him to come in and partake of the Passover meal.

The Torah indicates that *Pesach* is to last seven days and that the first and last days of the holiday are to be special. For Reform and Reconstructionist Jews, and for those living in Israel, that means holding services on the first and seventh days. Conservative and Orthodox Jews living outside Israel typically observe the holiday for eight days.

Passover is the first of three major festivals known collectively as the *Shalosh Regalim* ("Three

A Seder plate makes a colourful centrepiece for the Passover table. Starting from the top and moving in a clockwise direction are the six symbolic foods: a hard-boiled egg (*baytzah*); a shankbone (*zeroa*); a "mortar" mixture made of apples, nuts, wine, and spices (*kharoset*); a piece of lettuce (*hazeret*); parsley (*karpas*); and horseradish (*maror*).

Pilgrimages"), for which the Torah commanded the ancient Israelites to make a pilgrimage to Jerusalem; the other two are Shavuot and Sukkot.

and political life. Typically such agreements were made between two parties of unequal power: thus a powerful ruler would promise protection to a less powerful one on condition that the latter fulfilled certain obligations. One way of ritualistically sealing such a treaty was to have a number of animals cut in half and their carcasses lined up in rows. The two parties would then walk in between the bodies, symbolically indicating their understanding of the contract: if either party did not fulfil its obligations, it would suffer the same fate as the animals.

What was unusual about the Israelites' covenants was that they were made with a deity and involved promises to live in accordance with a moral code in exchange for that deity's protection and presence in their lives. Other Near Eastern

peoples offered sacrifices to their national or tribal deities in hopes of receiving rainfall, fertility, and prosperity, as well as protection, but they did not promise to behave in an ethical manner as part of the pact.

The Book of Genesis traces Israelite ancestry back to a single patriarch, a descendant of Noah through his son Shem. This man, Abraham, has left his birthplace in the region between the Tigris and Euphrates Rivers (later known by the Greek name Mesopotamia, "between the rivers," in present-day Iraq and Syria), and been travelling with his extended family, including his wife Sarah, towards the land of Canaan. At a midway point called Haran, where much of his family decides to settle, Abraham is called by God to continue on

Focus

Circumcision

Judaism, like other religious traditions, uses rituals to commemorate important transitional moments in a person's life. Circumcision is one of the best-known of these rituals, and the first one performed on a Jewish male, usually eight days after birth unless it would put the infant's life in danger. Just as Abraham underwent circumcision as a sign of the covenant between him and God, so too does every male born into a Jewish family. Known as a *Brit milah* ("covenant of circumcision") in Hebrew, in **Yiddish** (the vernacular language of Central and Eastern European Jews) it is called a "**Bris**." It involves the removal of the foreskin from the penis by a **mohel**, a ritual circumciser who is hired for the occasion. Usually the ceremony is conducted at home in the presence of family members and friends who gather to celebrate the birth, although it can also take place in a synagogue. The only people who are required to be present are the father, the mohel, and the *sandek*, the person who holds

the baby while the circumcision is performed. Traditionally, the baby is then named and a celebratory meal is served so that the presence of a new life in the world is connected with the joy of sharing food with family and friends. Blessings for the child and his parents are recited as part of the ritual.

Nowadays, more and more Jewish families are finding formal ways of expressing their joy on the birth of daughters as well as sons. The more liberal branches of Judaism now hold a naming ceremony for girls called a **Simchat Bat** ("joy of a daughter"). Basically, it celebrates the bringing of a daughter both into the family and into the covenant with God. Since there is no explicit ritual formula to follow, families tend to create their own traditions: some invite relatives and friends to their home or to a hall simply to share a meal, while others make the event more of a traditional ceremony in which various prayers and blessings are recited.

to Canaan. Once in Canaan, God enters into a covenant with Abraham that shares many of the elements outlined above. God, who is obviously the more powerful of the two parties, promises Abraham that he will give the land of Canaan to Abraham's still unborn offspring for their own, on condition that Abraham shows perfect obedience to God. When Abraham asks for a guarantee that God will keep his promise, the ceremonial splitting of animal carcasses is performed, and God, whose presence is symbolized by a smoking fire pot and flaming torch, "passe[s] between these pieces" (Genesis 15: 17–18).

Many years later, at the advanced age of 99, Abraham agrees to God's request that he undergo circumcision (removal of the foreskin of the penis) as a sign of their covenant (Genesis 17). Then, in

fulfillment of another promise that God makes to Abraham, Sarah miraculously produces a son, Isaac, even though she has always been "barren" and is now well past childbearing age. A few chapters later, in Genesis 22, God asks Abraham to sacrifice the young Isaac as a burnt offering, and Abraham prepares to fulfill his part of the bargain. But just as he is about to plunge his knife into his son's body, an angel intervenes, instructing him to free Isaac and sacrifice a ram instead. Abraham, who has now shown that he was willing to obey God even if it meant sacrificing his beloved son, becomes the model par excellence of obedience for the Israelite people.

Abraham's son Isaac and Isaac's son Jacob in turn make further covenants with God, but it is only centuries later, after the Exodus from Egypt,

Document

The Decalogue (Ten Commandments)

The terms of the covenant into which Yahweh and the Israelites enter are presented in the Decalogue or Ten Commandments. The Decalogue appears twice in the Torah: in the second book, Exodus (20: 2–17) and in the fifth, Deuteronomy (5: 6–21). The first five commandments concern responsibilities to God; the second, to fellow human beings.

I am the LORD your God who brought you out of Egypt, out of the land of slavery.

You shall have no other god to set against me.

You shall not make a carved image for yourself nor the likeness of anything in the heavens above, or on the earth below, or in the waters under the earth. You shall not bow down to them or worship them; for I, the LORD your God, am a jealous god. I punish the children for the sins of the fathers to the third and fourth generations of those who hate me. But I keep faith with thousands, with those who love me and keep my commandments.

You shall not make wrong use of the name of the LORD your God: The LORD will not leave unpunished the man who misuses his name.

Remember to keep the sabbath day holy. You have six days to labour and do all your work. But the seventh day is a sabbath of the LORD your God; that day you shall not do any work, you, your son or your daughter, your slave or your slave-girl, your cattle or the alien within your gates; for in six days the LORD made heaven and earth, the sea, and all that is in them, and on the seventh day he rested. Therefore the LORD blessed the sabbath day and declared it holy.

Honour your father and mother, that you may live long in the land which the LORD your God is giving you.

You shall not commit murder.

You shall not commit adultery.

You shall not steal.

You shall not give false evidence against your neighbour.

You shall not covet your neighbour's house; you shall not covet your neighbour's wife, his slave, his slave-girl, his ox, his ass, or anything that belongs to him (Exodus 20: 2–17.)

that the legendary leader and prophet Moses makes a covenant with God on behalf of the Israelites. The Decalogue—the Latin translation of the Hebrew *aseret hadevarim* ("ten words"; also known as the Ten Commandments), which Moses transmits to the Israelites at Mount Sinai, stipulates not only the people's duties to God, but also their duties to one another. This aspect of the Torah confirms that ethical behaviour was an obligatory component of the Israelites' covenant with God.

The second book of the Torah, Exodus, is called *Shemot* ("Names") in Hebrew, from its first sentence, "These are the names of. . . ." It describes how God, through Moses, led the Israelites out of Egypt to Mount Sinai and then, amid thunder and lightning, spoke out of a cloud to reveal his commandments, beginning with the Decalogue. Shortly after, Moses went up the mountain and stayed there for 40 days and 40 nights.

Lost without their leader, the Israelites persuaded Aaron, Moses' brother, to make them a god to take Moses' place. Having collected the people's gold earrings, Aaron melted them down and used the gold to create an idol in the form of a golden

Focus

Shavuot

Shavuot celebrates God's revelation of the Torah to Moses, although its origins can be traced to the barley harvest in the ancient Land of Israel. Also known as the Festival of Weeks (because seven weeks pass between the second day of Passover and the day before Shavuot), the holiday is the second of the *Shalosh Regalim* ("Three Pilgrimages").

By the middle of the second century CE, it had become the tradition to mark Shavuot by reading the Decalogue (a crucial part of the Law) and the Book of Ruth (set during the barley harvest). Another tradition, still observed today among religious Jews, is to stay up the entire night of Shavuot reading from a special volume that contains passages from every book of the Bible and every section of the rabbinic commentary on it (the Mishnah); this ritual, introduced by sixteenth-century mystics, represents devotion to the Torah. A third tradition is to eat sweet dairy foods such as cheesecake and blintzes filled with cheese on Shavuot, possibly because they

recall the description of the Torah as "honey and milk . . . under your tongue" (Song of Songs 4: 11).

Usually falling in late May or early June, Shavuot is celebrated for just one day in Israel, but for two days by most Jews living outside Israel. The reason for the two-day celebration is that in antiquity the Jewish calendar was set on a month-by-month basis, and the beginning of a new month was not established until two witnesses had observed the new moon. This information was then communicated by lighting signal fires. Since this means of communication was slow, Jews living outside Israel were sometimes not sure exactly when the *Shalosh Regalim* began, so to be on the safe side they added an extra day to the celebrations. Even though the Jewish calendar is now fixed and there is no longer any risk of missing the correct festival day, the tradition has been maintained by the majority of Jews outside Israel (the exceptions are members of the Reform branch).

---

calf. They were worshipping the calf when Moses descended from the mountain with the stone tablets on which God had engraved his commandments—the second of which forbade the making of idols. Enraged, Moses hurled the Tablets of the Law to the ground, shattering them; he destroyed the golden idol, and, with help of the faithful Israelites who had not taken part in the idol worship, put to death 3,000 who had. According to the Bible, Moses and the Israelites spent the next 40 years wandering in the desert; then, within sight of the Promised Land of Canaan, Moses died.

Leadership of the people of Israel was transferred to Joshua, who guided them across the Jordan River to take possession of Canaan.

According to the book of Joshua, the Israelites annihilated the people of Canaan. Yet there is no

archaeological evidence to support this account, and many biblical scholars argue that it was constructed to convey the theologically important idea of the Israelites' taking full possession of the land that had been promised to their ancestors. Archaeological findings in fact reveal that the earliest Israelite communities were not built on the ruins of Canaanite settlements, but rather on formerly uninhabited land in the central highlands. As a result, most scholars now understand the Israelite acquisition of Canaan to have been accomplished through settlement rather than military conquest.

The Personal Name of God

The God with whom all these biblical figures made their covenants has a personal name, which is

Focus

Sukkot

Sukkot commemorates the Israelites' wanderings in the wilderness. It is an eight-day holiday during which—weather permitting—Jews eat and sleep in the open air in a temporary structure called a *sukkah* ("booth" or "tabernacle" in Hebrew; *sukkot* is the plural form). The *sukkah* should have a roof made of organic material "grown from the ground," such as palm leaves, bamboo sticks, or pine tree branches, and it must be possible to see the sky through the gaps in the roof. This symbolizes the willingness of the people using the *sukkah* to put themselves directly under divine protection. Usually falling in September or October, Sukkot is said to have taken its name from the temporary shelters in which farmers would stay in autumn to keep watch over their ripening crops. It is the third and last of the *Shalosh Regalim*.

represented in Hebrew by four letters (*yod, hay, vav, hay*): YHWH. This **Tetragrammaton** ("four-letter word") is conventionally written as "Yahweh." In fact, it is not known how those four letters ought to be pronounced, since there are no vowels between the consonants (in its origins, the Hebrew alphabet is entirely consonantal). In Exodus 3: 14, YHWH tells Moses, "I am who I am," which suggests a possible linkage with the Hebrew verb *hayah*, "to be." This might mean that YHWH denotes something like "he [who] causes to be," but there is no strong consensus on this interpretation. In any case, many religious Jews consider the Tetragrammaton too sacred to ever be pronounced. Indeed, one of the commandments of the Decalogue warns that God's name is not to be taken in vain. Modern Jews who encounter YHWH in the text while reading aloud say the word "Adonai" ("Lord") or "haShem" ("the Name") instead. English translations of the four Hebrew letters normally use capital letters (the LORD or GOD).

In the sixteenth century, a mistaken belief that the vowels of "Adonai" were those belonging to the Tetragrammaton, YHWH, produced the name "Jehovah." Protestants were in a power struggle against the Catholic Church of Rome at that time, and to buttress their arguments they turned to the ancient biblical texts in the original Hebrew and Aramaic. But they were not well-versed in these languages, and did not realize that the vowels they were combining with the Tetragrammaton were in fact those of another word altogether. To this day, certain Christians (in particular, Jehovah's Witnesses) continue to use the name Jehovah, but it was never used by Jews.

Of Kings and Messiahs

It is possible that the biblical David—an obscure shepherd who, according to one tradition, killed the giant Goliath with his slingshot and became king—is based on a historical figure. David, whose reign is said to have begun around 1000 BCE, is identified as the Israelites' greatest king, the ruler against whom every future leader of Judah is compared. As part of the inauguration ritual, the new king was anointed with oil by the prophet Samuel. The Hebrew term *mashiach*, from which the English **messiah** is derived—as is the Greek form "Christos," hence "Christ"—is directly related to this ritual, as it means "anointed [one]." Thus David was a messiah. He was also a warrior king who, with his soldiers, was said to have conquered an impressive number of the Israelites' neighbouring enemies, establishing an empire of sorts that his son and successor as king, Solomon, inherited.

Focus

Samaritans

The Samaritans are an ancient people who still inhabit what is today the modern state of Israel. For the most part they live now, as they did then, in Samaria, in the centre of the country. They identify themselves as Jews, but there have always been Jews who consider them "half-Jews" at best. This is primarily because of the uncertainty of their origins: some believe that the Samaritans were the product of intermarriage between the people who were not deported by the Assyrians and those brought to the region from other locations. In any event, the Samaritans broke off from mainstream Jewish tradition in about the fifth century BCE and have distinct beliefs and practices. For example, the Jerusalem Temple was never their holy place: they had their own temple on Mount Gerizim in Samaria, although it was destroyed in the second century BCE and was never rebuilt. Their Bible consists of the Torah or Pentateuch alone. And their Torah differs from the standard Hebrew text in several ways; for example, in the Samaritan tradition, the Tabernacle (also sometimes called the Tent of Meeting) in which the Israelites are said to have worshipped God in the wilderness during the Exodus, is set up on Mount Gerizim rather than in Shiloh (Joshua 18: 1).

Samaritans exist in Israel in dwindling numbers today (there are approximately 600 of them). And to this day, during Passover, they continue to hold sacrifices at the foot of Mount Gerizim, which makes them the longest-sacrificing group in the Middle East—and possibly the world. When Israeli authorities feel that the area is safe enough, tourists can go there to observe the sacrifice ritual.

© www.BibleLandPictures.com/Alamy

Samaritan priests prepare a fire pit for their Passover sacrifices, held at the foot of Mount Gerizim in Samaria.

Solomon built the first Temple in Jerusalem as a focal point for national identity and Israelite worship, the latter primarily in the form of sacrifices. The creation of a centralized place to venerate their God was intended, at least in part, to put an end to the worship of Yahweh in the "high places" where the Canaanites too worshipped their gods. Apparently it did not entirely succeed, however, since biblical writers continued to condemn "high places" worship even after the establishment of the Temple. Following the death of Solomon, in the second half of the tenth century BCE, the kingdom split into two: Israel in the north and Judah in the south. From this point on, the historicity of events described in the Hebrew Bible is on firmer ground.

The Exile in Babylonia

Some two centuries later (c. 722 BCE), the northern kingdom fell to the superpower of the region, the Assyrians. The victors deported some of the Israelites to other parts of their empire, and imported people from elsewhere into Israel, destroying its national cohesion. The Israelites remaining in the south fell to a later superpower, the Babylonians, in 586 BCE, at which time the Temple in Jerusalem was destroyed. Like the Assyrians, the Babylonians did not utterly destroy the population; instead, they deported its political and religious leaders to Babylonia (modern-day Iraq) to prevent them from stirring up trouble in their homeland. Thus began the Babylonian captivity or "**Exile**."

The Exile is of paramount importance in Israelite–Jewish history. Marking the beginning of the **Diaspora**—the dispersion of Jews outside Israel—it reverberates throughout the Hebrew Bible in passages evoking the trauma of alienation from their homeland, which Jews have dealt with throughout their history (see Document box). One important theological development associated with the Exile was the first unambiguous statement of monotheism. Scholars theorize that, far from their homeland, the exiles recast their national deity as universal. The earliest writer to describe Yahweh as the only god in the universe is the unnamed prophet who is believed to have composed chapters 40 to 55 of the Book of Isaiah: in Isaiah 45: 21, for example, he has Yahweh declare that "There is no

Document

From Psalm 137: 1–6

The Psalms are poetic prayers whose central purpose is to praise God. Although tradition attributes them to the tenth-century-BCE King David, modern scholars believe that the linguistic evidence points to a multitude of authors and editors working in the post-exilic period (sixth century BCE) and later. Indeed, the exile is a frequent theme in the collection. Psalm 137, for example, expresses the longing of an exile in Babylon for his city, Jerusalem. It is often recited on the Ninth of Av, the day of mourning for the destruction of the two temples.

By the rivers of Babylon,
   there we sat,
   sat and wept,

as we thought of Zion.
There on the poplars
   we hung up our lyres,
   for our captors asked us there for songs,
   our tormentors, for amusement,
   "Sing us one of the songs of Zion."
How can we sing a song of the Lord
   on alien soil?
If I forget you, O Jerusalem,
   let my right hand wither;
   let my tongue stick to my palate
   if I cease to think of you,
   if I do not keep Jerusalem in memory
   even at my happiest hour.

other god besides me, a righteous God and a Saviour; there is no one besides me."

The Exile lasted for nearly fifty years, but it came to an end in 539 BCE, when Babylonia itself was conquered by yet another superpower—the Persian Empire. The victor, Cyrus of Persia (modern-day Iran), allowed all the Babylonians' captives to return to their homelands, among them the people from Judah. Not all of them did return, however. A sizeable number had put down roots in Babylonia and felt no need to go back to their ancestral home. In time, Babylonia would become one of the most vibrant intellectual centres of Judaism, and it would remain so until the tenth century. In fact, it was the Babylonian Jewish community that would produce one of the central texts in the history of Judaism: the **Babylonian Talmud**, completed in the sixth century CE.

The Second Temple Period (515 BCE–70 CE)

Those who did return to their ancestral homeland found that their territory had been reduced to the area immediately around Jerusalem. Nevertheless, they were able to rebuild the Temple and (with the help of the Persians) furnish it with many of the gold and silver items that had been taken by the Babylonians. Rededicated in 515 BCE, the "Second Temple" would endure until 70 CE, when it was destroyed in the course of a Roman siege that left much of Jerusalem in ruins.

The Impact of Alexander the Great

Alexander the Great (356–323 BCE) brought major cultural shifts to the ancient Near East. The son of the king of Macedon, on the northern Greek peninsula, as a youth Alexander had been tutored by the Greek philosopher Aristotle, and he had no doubt that Greek culture surpassed all others. When his father died, the 20-year-old Alexander set out to become the master of the then known world.

As he and his troops travelled across Asia Minor (modern-day Turkey) and down into the eastern Mediterranean basin, Alexander introduced Greek culture to the lands he conquered. He established more than 30 cities (20 named after himself), in each of which he established facilities central to Greek civilization, such as theatres and gymnasia. Before long, *koine* or "common" Greek became the new lingua franca of the region. One consequence of Alexander's diffusion of Greek culture was that

Focus

The Septuagint

The arrangement of the books in the Christian "Old Testament" is based on the Greek version of the Hebrew text, which was translated around the beginning of the third century BCE to serve the Greek-speaking Jewish community in Alexandria, Egypt. (By that time in their history, even Jews living in the Land of Israel reserved Hebrew for religious purposes and used Aramaic as their day-to-day language.)

The Greek text is known as the **Septuagint** (Latin for "seventy") or LXX (70) because legend had it that the Torah (the first section) was translated by 70 (or 72) Jewish sages. According to the legend, the sages worked independently, and yet all of them came forward with precisely the same text. This was taken as evidence that their work was divinely sanctioned.

people from one part of the empire, such as Asia Minor, could travel to a very different part, such as north Africa, and be sure to find people with whom they shared a common language; they would also see many recognizable Greek structures and architectural forms, and so feel a measure of familiarity even in an otherwise foreign city. In this way Alexander laid the foundations for the *cosmopolis* ("world city") and made possible a new sense of interconnectedness among peoples and areas that were formerly disparate and distinct.

Hellenization and the Jews

Scholars refer to the spread of Greek culture outside the borders of Greece as Hellenization, from the Greek word for Greece (*Hellas*). Jewish responses to Hellenization varied widely. The fact that some Jews enthusiastically embraced Greek ideas and customs, while others forcefully rejected them as contrary to the Jewish way of life, created serious tensions in the Jewish community. Certain Jews became so enamoured of Greek culture that they abandoned their ancestral traditions and rituals and began living like Greeks. There were Jewish men who so desired to blend in with non-Jewish (uncircumcised) males at the gymnasium that they underwent a special surgery to hide the evidence of circumcision so that when they exercised nude, they would not stand out as different. On the other hand, there were many Jews, particularly in non-urban areas, who staunchly rejected all Greek ideas and customs.

The Maccabean Revolt

Meanwhile, Judea's rulers worked to break down Jewish resistance to Hellenization. For over a century, Judea was controlled by the Ptolemies, the Greek dynasty—descended from one of Alexander's generals—that had ruled Egypt since 305 BCE. In 198 BCE, however, a rival Greek dynasty named the Seleucids, who already ruled Syria, took control of Judea. The territory around Jerusalem became known in Greek as *Ioudaia*, and a person from there was a *Ioudaios*.

Antiochus IV Epiphanes (r. 175–163 BCE) was a Seleucid who strongly advocated assimilation to Greek culture among the inhabitants of the territories he ruled. To that end, he prohibited both the reading and the teaching of the Mosaic Law, commanded that Torah scrolls be burned, and made observation of the **Sabbath** (the seventh day) a crime punishable by death. He also ordered that women who had had their sons circumcised be put to death; the First Book of Maccabees (one of several texts excluded from the Hebrew and Protestant canons but included in Catholic and Eastern Orthodox Bibles) contains gruesome stories of mothers executed with their sons' bodies tied around their necks (e.g., I Macc. 1: 60–1).

All this was extremely painful for Jews to endure, but the most egregious actions of all were directed against the Temple, where Antiochus erected altars to other gods and placed a statue of Zeus in the sanctuary courtyard. On Yahweh's altar he sacrificed pigs—animals considered inappropriate for Israelites to eat, let alone to offer in veneration of their deity. It was this act that the Book of Daniel described as an "abomination" (9: 27). Antiochus also intervened in the selection of the Temple's high priest, replacing the legitimate priest, Onias III, with his more Hellenized brother Jason; then, when offered an even larger bribe by an even more Hellenized candidate named Menelaus, Antiochus promptly replaced Jason in turn. When Jews revolted against this interference, Antiochus further restricted Jewish practices. His ultimate goal might well have been to promote political unity rather than to eradicate the Judeans' religion, but since religion in antiquity was intertwined with all aspects of life, the Judeans interpreted his actions as a comprehensive attack on their way of life.

Jews who refused to transgress the laws of their faith (for example, by eating pork or leaving their sons uncircumcised) were often tortured and put to death. The graphic descriptions of the persecution in 1 and 2 Maccabees suggest that some of these people understood it to be a sign that the end of the world was imminent. This **apocalyptic** perspective is also reflected in chapters 7–12 of the Book of Daniel, which describe the toppling of Antiochus from his throne; as we noted earlier, these chapters are thought to have been written in that period.

The Hasmonean Family

In 167 BCE, a family of priests known as the Hasmoneans mounted a successful uprising against Antiochus Epiphanes and Hellenized Jews. From a village on the outskirts of Jerusalem, they were led by Judah, who with his brothers coordinated a band of fighters who knew the hills and gullies of the land well. Together they engaged in a guerilla-style warfare that proved unexpectedly effective against the Syrian army. Judah's impressive power as a fighter and leader earned him the nickname "Maccabee" ("the Hammer"), from which the revolt as a whole derives its name. The Maccabeans recaptured the Temple, purged it of foreign idols and impure animals, and rededicated it to its rightful deity in 164 BCE. It is this rededication of the Temple that is recalled by the annual Hanukkah holiday (see Focus box).

Establishing themselves as client kings of the Seleucids, the Hasmoneans ruled from 164 to 63 BCE in precarious semi-independence during a time of profound sectarian discord and civil war. In time many of them willingly adopted Hellenistic culture. In 63 BCE, however, the Roman general Pompey secured Jerusalem and made the state a vassal of Rome, bringing Jewish self-rule to an end.

A Variety of Judaisms

An astonishing variety of Jewish groups emerged during the latter part of the Hasmonean period. Then as now, there were competing views about who was a Jew, what it meant to be a Jew, and how Jews should relate to non-Jews. Because of this diversity, it is more accurate to refer to "Judaisms" than "Judaism" in the Second Temple period. A brief look at some of the groups active near the end of that period will demonstrate this diversity.

Sadducees and Pharisees

The Sadducees came primarily from the upper echelons of society, and most were wealthy. They made up most of the membership of the Sanhedrin, the local Jewish council. Sadducees had close

Focus

Hanukkah

Hanukkah, the festival of lights, commemorates the return of the Temple to the Jews by Judah the Maccabee and his brothers. According to the Talmud (B. Shabbat 22b), when the Temple was purified, only one vial of oil with the seal of the High Priest could be found to light the seven-branched oil lamp called the **menorah**. This amount of oil should have run out after one day, but—miraculously—it lasted for eight days. For this reason Hanukkah is celebrated by lighting a candle on a special menorah called a Hanukkiah for eight consecutive days and eating foods cooked in oil, such as potato latkes (pancakes)

and *sufganiot* (doughnuts with jam or caramel in the centre). Gambling games with spinning tops called dreidels are frequently played at Hanukkah. Dreidels made outside Israel have a single Hebrew letter on each of their four sides: *nun*, *gimel*, *hay*, and *shin*. These letters stand for the Hebrew words meaning "A great miracle happened there," in reference to the miraculous event of the oil. On dreidels made in Israel, the letter *shin* is replaced by *pay*, indicating that the events took place in Israel itself: "A great miracle happened *here*."

Document

Josephus on Jewish Sects

Born to a priestly family in Jerusalem, Josephus (37 CE–c. 100) was a Jewish historian who described to Roman readers the complicated religious situation in the Judea of his day.

Now at this time there were three schools of thought among the Jews, which held different opinions concerning human affairs; the first being that of the Pharisees, the second that of the Sadducees, and the third that of the Essenes. As for the Pharisees, they say that certain events are the work of fate, but not all; as to other events, it depends upon ourselves whether they shall take place or not. The sect of Essenes, however, declares that Fate is mistress of all things, and that nothing befalls men unless it be in accordance with her decree. But the Sadducees do away with Fate, holding that there is no such thing and that human actions are not achieved in accordance with her decree, but that all things lie within our power, so that we ourselves are responsible for our well-being, while we suffer misfortune through our own thoughtlessness (Josephus, *Jewish Antiquities* 13: 171–3, trans. Thackeray et al., 1927–65: 311–13).

connections with the priests in charge of the Temple cult, and most of them were priests themselves. Sadducees were responsible for the smooth running of the Temple, in particular the sacrificial system. They emphasized the need for Jews to be properly involved in this cultic worship in accordance with the Torah. For the Sadducees, the Torah—that is, the Pentateuch, or Five Books of Moses—was the only authoritative text, and they demanded a narrow, literal interpretation of the law. They did not believe in a future resurrection of the dead, nor did they believe in a future day of judgment when humans would be held accountable for their deeds on earth: in their view, this life was the only one.

The Pharisees, for their part, sought to apply Halakhah to everyday life. The New Testament, particularly the Gospel of Matthew, interprets this focus as narrow and legalistic, even hypocritical (the *Oxford English Dictionary* lists "hypocrite" as one of the meanings of "Pharisee"). What has often been overlooked, however, is the competitive context in which the Gospels were written: from the perspective of the Gospel writers, the Pharisees were their rivals. And one of the most effective ways to undermine the power of rivals is to portray them in a negative light. Thus readers familiar with the New Testament ought not to accept at face value its portrayal of Pharisees as nit-picking legalists.

The Pharisees sought to understand how a Jew should live in order to please God. In a modern setting, they would be the people holding Bible study classes and poring over the scriptures in an effort to understand what God intended human beings to do. They had a social conscience and were concerned with what it meant to live their daily lives in accordance with the Torah. In contrast to the Sadducees, the Pharisees tended to interpret the scriptural text broadly. They practised alms-giving, prayer, and fasting, and they believed in the resurrection and future day of judgment. For them the entire Tanakh was sacred and worthy of study.

Among their concerns were the Torah's instructions regarding matters such as food purity, Sabbath observance, and family issues. The Pharisees took it on themselves to clarify points that were vague or confusing. For example, in the Decalogue Jews are instructed to keep the Sabbath day holy (Exodus 20: 8–11; Deuteronomy 5: 12–15). But what did that mean in practical terms? If it meant refraining from work on the Sabbath, how did one define "work"? The Pharisees provided interpretations and formulated answers to such questions; they also established rules and instructions to help Jews observe the law. In due course, these teachings attained the status of divinely revealed law, and came to be known as the Oral Law or Oral Torah. In developing their interpretations and regulations, the Pharisees were not trying to split hairs: their goal was to understand what God had commanded so that they could obey and help other Jews do likewise.

In 70 CE the Romans destroyed the Second Temple, and it was never rebuilt. The Pharisees were one of the only groups to survive; by the second century CE, those who would have been called Pharisees in an earlier time were referred to as **rabbis** (from *rav*, "teacher" in Hebrew). Their oral tradition likewise survived, and developed further under the rabbis, who inherited the pharisaic interpretations and added their own. According to rabbinic tradition, God gave Moses the Oral Torah at the same time as the written version. Finally, the Oral Torah was written down and codified around the year 220 CE, by Judah haNasi ("Judah the Prince") and in this written form is called the **Mishnah**.

Essenes

The Essenes are generally held to have been the authors of the Dead Sea Scrolls: a collection of texts produced between the second and first centuries BCE that were discovered accidentally by a Bedouin shepherd searching the Judean hills for a lost sheep in 1947. These important manuscripts shed light on how the Essenes—a monastic community of meticulously observant priests—were organized, initiated newcomers, and viewed the world. In addition, the Dead Sea Scroll library contains the earliest manuscripts of every book of the Hebrew Bible (some in fragmented form only) except, for unknown reasons, the Book of Esther.

Cultic purity—a bodily state in which one is sufficiently pure to be acceptable in the sacred spaces of God—was of the utmost importance for the Essenes; like the Pharisees, they sought to apply the Bible to daily life, but in a much more rigorous manner. They established their community at Qumran in the Judean desert after expressing their disapproval of the way the Hasmoneans were running the Temple cult. They held an **apocalyptic** worldview, believing that the world was under the control

Focus

Purim

Purim is a joyful and exuberant minor holiday that falls around March. The Book of Esther tells how the Jews of Persia were saved from the evil plot of a Persian official named Haman, who sought to exterminate them (the word "purim" means "lots," a reference to the lottery by which Haman determined the date of his attack on the Jews). At the centre of the story are Esther, a wise and beautiful Jewish woman, and her uncle, Mordecai, who together prevent the destruction of the Jews. Since the holiday celebrates deliverance from a physical threat, it calls for great happiness and merriment, with a focus on material rather than spiritual things. When the Book of Esther is read in the synagogue, members of the congregation use noise-makers or bang pots and pans to drown out every mention of Haman's name. There is also a festive meal, at which guests are expected to drink enough wine that they cannot distinguish between "Blessed be Mordecai" and "Cursed be Haman." As in the North American celebration of Halloween, there are costume parties and gifts of food, especially *hamantashen*: cookies (traditionally filled with poppy seeds) that are supposed to resemble the ears of Haman.

of evil forces and that God would soon intervene to defeat the powers of darkness. The Essenes thought of themselves as the new children of Israel, biding their time until the day when, with God's help, they would take back the Promised Land from what they saw as the corrupt leadership of Hellenized Jews.

Therapeutae

The Therapeutae were a monastic group living near Lake Mareotis in Egypt. In sharp contrast to the monastic Essenes of Qumran, the Therapeutae included women as well as men in their community, and although the sexes lived and ate separately, they would meet to worship, sing hymns, and dance together. Members of the community renounced private property and family life, lived their lives in devotion to God, prayed at sunrise and sunset, and spent the rest of their time in study or worship.

Zealots

The Zealots did not exist as an organized group until well into the first century CE. In contrast to the Sadducees, who found ways of mollifying the Roman authorities, the Zealots vehemently refused to cooperate with Rome; in fact, they encouraged fellow Jews to engage in violent rebellion. The result was the First Jewish Revolt (66–73 CE), in the course of which most of Jerusalem, including the Temple, would be destroyed and much of the Jewish population either killed or forced into slavery.

Other Temples

Although the Temple in Jerusalem was supposed to be the central focus of Jewish worship, in fact it was not the only Jewish temple in existence. In addition to the Samaritan temple on Mount Gerizim, there were two temples in Egypt. One was built on Elephantine (an island in the Nile) in the fifth century BCE to serve a Jewish military colony in service to the pharaoh; it appears to have been destroyed within a century. The other was constructed in the second century BCE at Leontopolis (north of modern Cairo) by the high priest (Onias III) who had been removed from his office by Antiochus IV Epiphanes, and lasted until 73 CE. The existence of these other places of worship is often overlooked by scholars.

Other Visions of the Future

Further expressions of diversity can be seen in the varied expectations for the future held by Jews in this period. Some hoped for a **messiah** to lead them out from under the oppressive hand of the Romans. As we have seen, the term "messiah" comes from the Hebrew *mashiach*, "anointed one." Until the end of Judean monarchic rule in 586 BCE, the term referred exclusively to the current Hebrew king; some time later, the Persian king Cyrus, who allowed the return of the people exiled in Babylonia, was also honoured as a *mashiach* (Isaiah 45). By Hellenistic times, however, the idea of an "anointed" king had moved out of the world of current possibility and into the realm of anticipation: now the *mashiach* was the ideal future king whom God would raise up and empower to lead Israel to victory over its enemies. The Essenes, in fact, awaited two messiahs: one a king, and one a priest.

Not all expectations centred on a messiah, however. Some Jews hoped for the establishment of a new covenant between God and his people, while others looked forward to a new era of justice and equality. There were also those who looked forward to a time when Jerusalem would become central to the world, and all peoples would worship God at Mount Zion. The range of thought regarding the future is similarly broad among modern Jews.

Points of Consensus

Diversity of expectations notwithstanding, a degree of consensus did exist concerning certain fundamental factors. The majority of Jews, regardless of sect, believed in:

1. The oneness of God. By the Second Temple period, Judaism was a monotheistic tradition centred on the idea of a single, all-powerful creator God.

2. The authority and sacred nature of the Torah.
3. The special status of Israel as the chosen "people of God." Who exactly was included in the "people of God" was a point of contention (as it continues to be in the modern state of Israel). But there was a general belief not only in a "people of God" but also in a "land of God." The latter point is illustrated by the tradition, still practised today, of giving all the agricultural land in Israel a "sabbath" every seven years, when it is to lie fallow.
4. The status of the Temple in Jerusalem as the place where God and his people met.

Finally, it is important to note that the majority of Jews in late antiquity did not belong to any of the sects discussed above. Most people went about their daily lives observing the aspects of the Torah law that their parents, and their parents' parents before them, had deemed important.

Enter the Romans (63 BCE)

Conflicts among the Hasmonean leaders eventually led to a bloody civil war. In 63 BCE the Roman general Pompey was called to Judea settle the rivalry among the various contenders for the Hasmonean throne. Instead, he took control of the land. Thus began approximately four centuries of repressive Roman rule over Judea.

Herod the Great

In 37 BCE the Romans put an end to the Hasmonean dynasty by appointing Herod the Great as king of Israel. Herod's governance style was marked by extravagant self-indulgence, brutality, and deception; yet he was one of the most vibrant and successful leaders in all of Jewish history, cleverly balancing Roman and Jewish interests. Nevertheless, because he was not of Judean descent—his ancestors were Idumeans, converts to Judaism who inhabited the territory just south of Judea—many Jews did not accept Herod's rule as legitimate.

Herod was indeed devoted to Rome and Hellenistic culture, but he made many advances on behalf of Judean culture and religion. He also greatly improved the quality of life for the peasantry by extending irrigation and reducing lawlessness and banditry. The kingdom of Judea prospered under his leadership. At the same time, he was

Focus

Monotheism

Monotheism—the belief in and worship of a single god, creator of the universe—is a central feature of Judaism, and is considered one of the fundamental teachings of the Torah. Yet there is evidence in the Hebrew Bible that polytheism (the belief in and worship of multiple gods) was not only practised by the Israelites during the pre-exilic period, but was acceptable to much of the population. Israelites worshipped fertility gods such as Ba'al and Asherah along with Yahweh, who was initially perceived as a national deity. Through their battles with other peoples and their gods, as well as their internal struggles with allegiances to multiple deities, the Israelites eventually became persuaded that Yahweh was the sole god of the universe. The belief in one god is a central tenet today not only for Jews, but also for Christians and Muslims.

pathologically suspicious, prepared to kill any member of the former Hasmonean dynasty who might possibly threaten his power, including his wife Mariamme and three of his sons. After their murders he was frequently tormented with guilt. Perhaps it is no wonder that Augustus, who was Emperor of Rome from 27 BCE to 14 CE, and a friend of Herod's, is said to have declared that he "would rather be Herod's pig than Herod's son."

Herod enriched his kingdom by establishing new cities, such as Caesarea Maritima on the Mediterranean coast, and new fortresses including the Antonia in Jerusalem, Herodion just south of Jerusalem, and Masada. He built many impressive public structures, including temples, aqueducts, and theatres. But his most famous project was the renovation of the Temple in Jerusalem. He replaced what had been a rather modest building, more than four centuries old, with a stunningly beautiful structure on a much-enlarged site. Even those who

did not particularly like Herod were moved by this project honouring the national religion.

The Rabbinic Period (70–700 CE)

The traditions of the Pharisees outlived those of all the other groups, except for the Samaritans. The interpretations of the **rabbinic movement**, which incorporated the Pharisaic traditions, have defined Jewish beliefs and practices for the past 2000 years. The teachers and religious leaders who helped to steer Jewish communities after the devastating loss of the Temple, in 70 CE, replaced sacrificial worship—never practised again—with liturgical prayer and a new emphasis on ethical behaviour, such as the giving of alms.

Synagogues (the term comes from the Greek for "gathering together") already existed while the Temple still stood; the earliest archaeological evidence comes from Egypt, in the late third century

© Vladimir Khirman/Alamy

Solomon's Temple was destroyed by the Babylonians in 586 BCE, but it was rebuilt and rededicated following the return from the Exile. Five centuries later, that Second Temple was renovated and expanded on the orders of Herod the Great. A model of Jerusalem in his day (the late first century BCE), including the refurbished Second Temple (above; scale 1:50) was constructed under the direction of Michael Avi-Yonah, former professor of Archaeology at the Hebrew University, and opened to the general public in 1966. Now located at the Israel Museum in Jerusalem, it is a popular attraction and educational site.

Sites

The Western Wall, Israel

The only remnant of Herod's temple still standing is one of the outer retaining walls, today known as the "Western Wall" (*kotel* in Hebrew). Religious Jews around the world consider it a sacred place because of its association with the Temple, and it is treated with great respect. When leaving the wall, for example, people walk backwards, to avoid turning their backs on it. Large rectangular stones with borders around their perimeters, located at the wall's base, date to the time of Herod the Great. Subsequent layers were added by the various Islamic regimes that controlled the area between the seventh century and 1967. After the State of Israel gained control of East Jerusalem in the Six-Day War of that year, the wall area was designated an open-air synagogue; as a consequence no photos of the Wall may be taken on the Sabbath.

The area in front of the wall is sex-segregated, with men praying on the left and women on the right. Traditionally, people write personal prayers and leave these notes in the cracks of the wall. Since antiquity Jews have gathered before the Western wall to mourn the loss of the Temple that once stood behind it. On the ninth day of Av (**Tisha b'Av** in Hebrew)—the day on which, according to legend, both the First and Second Temples were destroyed—thousands of Jews gather in the plaza in front of the wall to express their sorrow. Leather shoes are not worn on this day, since the comfort of leather is a luxury that is considered inappropriate at a time of mourning. On Tisha b'Av, therefore, one often sees the incongruous sight of Haredi men wearing plastic flip-flops or white tennis shoes under their long black coats.

© Michele Murray

A woman deep in prayer on the women's side of the Western Wall. Also visible are some of the many prayer requests that the faithful have stuffed into the cracks.

BCE. But they gained in importance once the Temple was gone. Communal gathering places in which Jews met to read the Torah, to pray, and to study, by the first century CE synagogues were scattered across the Roman Empire, wherever there was a community of Jews.

The fact that texts and interpretations, rather than a particular place, became the central focus of Judaism helped those scattered communities maintain a sense of unity regarding religious culture, language, and customs. Because of the centrality of Torah study to Judaism, literacy rates tended to be higher among Jewish males than among their non-Jewish counterparts. If most Jewish boys learned to read, however, it seems that girls and women were—with one possible exception—excluded from Torah study on the grounds that women's primary domain was the home.

A possible exception was Beruriah, the daughter of one great scholar and the wife of another. According to the Babylonian Talmud, she learned 300 laws from 300 scholars in one day (BT Pesah 62b). According to another story (BT Berakhot 10a), when her husband prayed that some local trouble-makers would die, Beruriah rebuked him: "Why would you pray for that? Because the psalm (104: 35) says 'Let sins cease'? Does it say 'sinners'? No—it says 'sins.' Besides, look at the end of the verse: 'And they are wicked no more.' Once sins have ceased, the people won't be wicked any more. So you should be praying that they will repent and be wicked no more." He prayed for them, and they repented.

Another example exhibits Beruriah's superior awareness of the rabbinic law, as well as her supreme confidence in demonstrating this awareness to well-established rabbinic scholars. Rabbi Yosi the Galilean was going along the road when he met Beruriah. He said to her, 'By which road shall we go to Lod?' She said to him, 'Galilean fool! Did not the sages say, 'Do not talk too much with a woman' [Mishnah Avot 1:5, BT Nedarim 20a]? You should have said, 'By which to Lod?' (BT 'Eruvin 53b).

Was Beruriah a historical figure? If so, does this mean that women in rabbinic circles were indeed permitted to study Torah? Or did the rabbis invent her in order to demonstrate the danger of educating women? According to one medieval tradition, Beruriah committed suicide after being seduced by one of her husband's students; undoubtedly that story was meant as a warning against permitting women to study Torah.

The limiting of Torah study to males was not unusual for the era in which the rabbis were writing (between roughly the second and sixth centuries CE). What may be somewhat surprising is that the Talmud contains rulings concerning a husband's sexual obligations to his wife. The rabbis outlined a set of laws (based on Exodus 21: 10) in which three necessities are highlighted as rights that a wife can expect from her husband: food, clothing, and marital rights. The last of the three, "marital rights," is understood to refer to sexual relations. The Talmud, in its commentary on this verse, specifies how often a man must provide sex for his wife based on his profession, since what he does for a living will affect how long he is away from her and how physically tired he is: "Men of independent means: every day; workmen: twice a week; ass drivers: once a week; camel drivers: once a month, and sailors: at least once every six months" (BT, Ketubbot 5: 6). If a husband does not fulfill his duty, he must divorce his wife so that she can remarry and have her sexual needs met by someone else. On the one hand, given the period in which the Talmudic commentary was composed, this acknowledgement of women's sexual needs seems rather progressive. On the other hand, these laws may have been based on the understanding that women's sexuality was so passive that they were not capable of asking for sex, or, alternatively, that women were not capable of controlling their sexuality, thus must be satisfied. The same laws, by prohibiting men from taking vows of abstinence, increased the likelihood of procreation. This is hardly surprising: after all, the rabbis of the Talmudic period considered Genesis 1: 28 to be the first **mitzvah** (commandment) in the Bible. And what is that commandment? "Be fruitful and multiply, and fill the earth. . . ."

By the end of the first century CE, the majority of Jews were living outside Judea. The total Jewish population was probably between 5 and 6 million, and Jewish communities could be found in every major city of the Roman Empire. The Jewish quarter of Alexandria, which was one of the three largest cities in the Empire (after Rome and Antioch, in what is now southern Turkey), had approximately 200,000 inhabitants by the first century CE.

Another Clash with Rome

The last major Jewish revolt against Roman rule took place between 132 and 135 CE. It is associated with a messianic figure named Shimon Bar Kosiba, whom his supporters called Bar Cochba ("son of the Star," a messianic title from Numbers 24: 17) but who was known to his critics as Bar Koziba ("son of the Lie" or "Liar"). The revolt was likely prompted by the emperor Hadrian's plan to establish a Roman city on the remains of Jerusalem, and a temple to Jupiter Capitolinus on what had been the site of the Temple. The revolt—a last gasp of revolutionary fervour on the part of the Jews—failed miserably, and Hadrian's plans were carried out. Those Jews who had been living within the precincts of Jerusalem were now driven out, and if they tried to return to the city they faced death. It was at this time that, in an attempt to rid Judea—a Roman province since 6 CE—of any reminders of its Jewish inhabitants, the Romans renamed it "Syria-Palestina." Until the establishment of the state of Israel in 1948 Judaism would be predominantly a religion of the Diaspora.

Rabbi Hillel

Rabbi Hillel was a popular teacher who was active between 30 BCE and 10 CE, hence an older contemporary of Jesus of Nazareth. He was a humble woodworker who became the leader of a religious school (**yeshiva**) and was renowned for his piety. According to a famous story, an impertinent non-Jew once came to Hillel and said that he would convert to Judaism if the Rabbi could recite all of the Torah while standing on one foot. Hillel reportedly

told him: "What is hateful to you, do not do to your neighbour: that is the entire Torah. The rest is commentary; go and learn it!" Whereas Hillel was said to have been lenient in his interpretation of the Torah, his compatriot and rival, Rabbi Shammai, took a stricter, more literal view. More than 300 arguments between the House of Hillel and the House of Shammai are recorded in the Talmud, and in most cases it was Hillel's interpretation that the rabbinic scholars followed.

The Androcentric Perspectives of the Rabbis

The foundational literature of rabbinic Judaism reflects the interests and concerns of the male rabbis. Women generally were excluded from the rabbinic hierarchies of achievement and exempt from the rituals and activities considered to be the most meritorious, such as the study of Torah and the performance of mitzvot ("commandments," the plural of "mitzvah"). Women were typically expected to fulfill only those commandments that were negative ("you shall not . . .") and not time-bound (that is, rituals that did not have to be performed at a certain time). While rabbinic Halakhah gave women more freedom and protection than biblical law did, and the rabbis made it possible for some women to inherit, control, and dispose of property, the status of most women—in particular wives and unmarried minor daughters—was clearly subordinate to that of men in all areas of life: judicial, religious, sexual, and economic.

On the other hand, non-rabbinic evidence such as inscriptions demonstrates that some women did serve as heads of synagogues (*archisynagogos*) in the ancient world, particularly in the Greco-Roman Diaspora, and that others were patrons and benefactors of both civic and religious institutions. While it is true that these women would have belonged to the elite, and so been afforded opportunities that most women were not, they remind us of how important it is to differentiate between the idealized life of the Jewish woman that the rabbis prescribed in their writing and the realities of the

Focus

Mishnah and Gemarah: The Talmud

The written version of the Oral Torah, the Mishnah, is divided into six "orders," each of which deals with a particular sphere of life and the laws that govern it, although some also address other subjects. The names of the orders reveal their central topics: Seeds (laws of agriculture); Appointed Seasons (laws governing festivals, fast days, and the Sabbath); Women (laws governing marriage, divorce, betrothal, and adultery; this section also includes Vows); Damages (civil and criminal law, and the most commonly read section of the Mishnah, the "Sayings of the Fathers," a collection of ethical maxims); Holy Things (temple-related matters such as sacrifices, ritual slaughter, and the priesthood rituals); and Purities (issues of ritual purity and impurity).

The writing of the Mishnah in the early third century CE did not mark the end of rabbinic commentary, however. Over the next few centuries, rabbis in both Babylonia and the Land of Israel continued to study and interpret traditional teachings, including the Mishnah. Their commentaries are referred to as **Gemarah** (from an Aramaic root that means "teaching"), and they were transmitted orally from teacher to student (just as the Oral Law had been). The Gemarah contains both Halakhah (legal material) and **Aggadah** (narrative material). Aggadah includes historical material, biblical commentaries, philosophy, theology, and wisdom literature.

Eventually, this commentary also was written down. The Gemarah produced in Palestine was written down in the early fifth century, and in its written form is called the Palestinian (or Jerusalem) Talmud. About a century later, the Gemarah produced by Babylonian rabbis was written down; logically enough, it is referred to as the Babylonian Talmud. It was the latter that gained predominance in the Jewish world, so that any general reference to "the Talmud" is understood to refer to the Babylonian Talmud. The two Talmuds are compendia of law, interpretation, and argument that offer what may be described as a "slice of life" from the rabbinic academies of the time, since the discussions they present (in stream-of-consciousness fashion) often go round and round before reaching a conclusion.

lives that actual Jewish women lived in antiquity. It was—alas—the idealized image, not the flesh and blood reality, that would determine the norms, roles, and expectations for Jewish women in subsequent centuries.

Two Main Rabbinic Centres: Palestine and Babylonia

After the Bar Kochba revolt, Judaism developed under the guidance of the rabbis, the successors of the priestly leaders of the previous period. There were two main centres of development: in the Galilee region of northern Palestine, and in Babylonia, which was now ruled by the Parthians. Relations between Palestinian Jews and the Romans eventually calmed, and an arrangement was forged between the two former enemies in which the Jews were granted the same treatment as other minorities of the empire, with the extra privilege of exemption from pagan cultic observances. Roman leaders recognized the Jewish Patriarch, a descendant of Rabbi Hillel, as the central political leader of the Jewish community. But the situation for Jews deteriorated as the third century progressed, primarily because of a general decline in economic and political circumstances across the Roman Empire that left Palestine relatively impoverished.

In general, conditions were better for Babylonian Jews at that time. When the Persian Sassanids replaced the Parthians in 226 CE, Jews experienced some persecution as a result of the Sassanids' efforts to promote their own religion (Zoroastrianism), but by the middle of the century their zeal for conversion had waned. Thereafter, the Persian rulers allowed the Jews extensive autonomy under their communal leader in exile, the exilarch. Intellectual activity flourished as a result of the efforts of two third-century rabbis named Samuel and Rav. Samuel was a wealthy Babylonian scholar on good terms with the Persian emperor, and eventually he established an academy in Nehardea that was later moved to Pumbeditha. Rav (whose full name was Abba Arika) was a Palestinian rabbi who arrived in Babylonia in 219 and introduced Babylonian Jews to the Mishnah. He founded an academy at Sura. These schools rivalled and eventually surpassed in prestige the rabbinic schools of Palestine, thriving as centres of Jewish scholarship until the eleventh century.

The Rise of Christianity

When the Roman emperor Constantine I gave Christians the liberty to practise their faith in the year 313, he began a process that led to Christianity's becoming, in 380, the official religion of the Roman Empire. Henceforth all inhabitants of the Byzantine Empire were expected to follow the Christian faith. Obviously, this did not bode well for Jews.

Christian attitudes towards Jews had been shaped in large part by the earliest history of Christianity, including the incontrovertible fact that Christianity had begun as a Jewish sect. Jesus was Jewish, as were his earliest disciples, but his message had had only modest success among Jews. By the end of the second century, most of the people who were joining the movement were Gentiles (non-Jews). In time, as leaders of Christian communities sought to differentiate their movement from Judaism, tensions developed, especially with certain Gentiles who identified themselves as Christians but chose to adopt Jewish practices such

as circumcision, observance of Jewish dietary laws, or synagogue attendance. Since these "Judaizers" were undermining Christian efforts at differentiation, Christian leaders such as Paul sought to dissuade them. In his letter to the Galatians (c. 50 CE), for example, he urged Gentile Christians not to tie themselves to "a yoke of slavery" (5: 1) by observing the law; and the author of the late first-century Epistle of Barnabas chastised the Judaizers in his own community for "heaping up your sins and saying that the covenant is both theirs and ours" (4: 6).

Others argued that Christianity had superseded Judaism: Justin Martyr, author of the second-century *Dialogue with Trypho*, declared that Christians had replaced Jews as "the true and spiritual Israelite nation, and the race of Judah and of Jacob and Isaac and Abraham" (11: 5); elsewhere he asserted that circumcision was commanded of the Jews to set them apart for suffering: "that you alone should suffer the things you are rightly suffering now, and that your lands should be desolate and your cities burned with fire, and that foreigners should eat up the fruits before your face, and none of you go up unto Jerusalem" (16: 2). In response to Christians in Antioch, Syria, who were still attending synagogue services in the fourth century, the bishop of that city, John Chrysostom, preached some of the most vehement anti-Jewish sermons in Christian history, condemning the synagogue as "a whorehouse and a theatre . . . a den of thieves and a haunt of wild animals" (*Against the Judaizers* 1.3). Although this rhetoric was originally directed at Christian Judaizers, it would eventually be repurposed for use against Jews.

Other early Christian literature, such as the Gospel of Matthew, explicitly blamed the Jews for the death of Jesus (e.g., 24: 26); this charge would be recycled in later centuries, whenever tensions between Jews and Christians were high. The same gospel contains a diatribe against Jewish leaders that has unfortunately been influential in the formation of anti-Jewish attitudes: "Woe to you scribes and Pharisees, hypocrites! for you are like whitewashed tombs, which outwardly appear beautiful, but within they are full of dead men's bones and all uncleanness. . . . You serpents, you brood of vipers,

Focus

The Jewish Calendar

The Gregorian calendar used in the Western world is a solar calendar, based on the solar year of 365¼ days. The Jewish calendar is a lunar calendar, based on 12 months of 29½ days. Since this adds up to 354 days for a lunar year—about 11 days less than a solar year—any given date in the lunar calendar will move backwards each year by 11 days. In order to ensure that holidays and festivals consistently fall around the same time of the year, the Jewish calendar adds a thirteenth "leap month" (called Adar Sheni, "second Adar") on a fixed schedule of 7 years out of every 19. In ancient times the rabbis used to set the calendar based on the direct observations of witnesses who had seen the new moon, but around the fourth or fifth century CE a calibrated written calendar rendered this system unnecessary. Today trained experts make the astronomical calculations, and festival dates and leap months are established far in advance.

According to the Gregorian solar calendar, a new day begins at midnight—the first moment of the morning. By contrast, the Jewish day begins at nightfall, which is defined as the time when at least three stars can be seen in one glimpse of the sky. A Jewish day goes from one evening to the next; thus the Sabbath begins at nightfall on Friday evening and ends at nightfall on Saturday. This is in accordance with the description of the first day of creation in Genesis 1: 5—"And there was evening and there was morning, the first day"—in which evening is mentioned first.

By convention, the Jewish calendar counts the years from the creation of the universe, based on the life spans and time periods mentioned in the biblical text. This number is not taken too literally, though, since even people who consider the creation story in Genesis to be an accurate account of events acknowledge that the biblical references to time periods may not be reliable. All Jews, however, accept the system as a matter of convenience. The Gregorian calendar year "2015–16" is the year "5776 Since the Creation" in the Jewish calendar (Wylen 1989: 67).

how are you to escape being sentenced to hell?" (Matthew 23: 27, 32).

By the early fifth century the Roman Empire was decidedly Christian, and the continuing vitality of Judaism was seen by some as contrary to Christian interests. Now laws were introduced to restrict Jewish religious and commercial activities. Jews were forbidden to hold public office, build new synagogues, or marry Christians. They were also prohibited from owning Christian slaves. Biblical law offered certain protections to Jewish slaves (including the possibility of manumission), and, although it was forbidden for a master to force the conversion of a slave, the fact that many slaves voluntarily converted to Judaism may have been one of the reasons behind the prohibition. At a time when slavery was an integral part of the agricultural system in the Roman Empire, this injunction meant that Jews had no hope of competing economically with Christian farmers (Efron et al. 2009: 134). It also represented a first step in the alienation of Jews from the land, a development that by the Middle Ages would transform them into an almost entirely urban people.

Certain Christian leaders favoured banning Judaism entirely and presenting Jews with the same options that the Romans had given Christians themselves in the third century CE: conversion or death. In fact, the Visigothic king Sisebut, ruler of Spain from 612 to 621, implemented this approach as official policy when he forced Jews to choose between conversion to Christianity, exile, and death. A much longer-lasting approach, first formulated in the fifth century by Augustine of Hippo in his *City of God* and later accepted by Pope Gregory I (r. 590–604) as Church policy, was less radical but nonetheless devastating for Jews. Augustine wished Jews to serve as an example of the consequences of not accepting Jesus as messiah. To that end, he proposed that Jews should not be eradicated: rather, they should be allowed to live in suffering. To justify his position, Augustine quoted a verse from Psalms 59: 11, in which David, the ancient king of the Israelites, says of his enemies: "Do not destroy them, lest my people forget."

🐌 Jewish Life under Islam: Seventh–Twelfth Century

In the early seventh century a new force appeared that would shape the course of Jewish history: Islam. Within a few short decades, Islam had seized Palestine and Egypt from the Christian Byzantine Empire, and Persia from the Persian Empire, and by the end of that century most of the world's Jews resided in a unified Islamic empire encompassing territory from the Iberian Peninsula in the west to India in the east. As a consequence Jews in Palestine, Egypt, and Spain were liberated from the injustice and oppression they had tolerated under antagonistic Christian rulers. Muslims considered Judaism and Christianity their partners in monotheism and respected them for possessing, as did Islam, a divinely revealed book. Thus Jews and Christians living under Islam were defined as *dhimmis* ("protected peoples") and guaranteed protection of their lives and property, as well as the right to practise their religion, as long as they paid special taxes and adhered to certain rules stipulated in a document called the Pact of Umar.

For Jews, life under Muslim rule was considerably better than it had been under Christian Rome. Without the complicated history shared by Christianity and Judaism (discussed above), Jewish–Muslim relations were less fraught with tension. In addition, Muslims understood that with Jews they shared not only belief in a single god, but

opposition to the use of images in the worship of Yahweh/Allah. Hence they tended to be less suspicious of Jews than of Christians, whose doctrine of the Trinity, and pervasive use of crucifixes, overtly contradicted Islamic principles.

The period of European decline often called the "Dark Ages," from the seventh to the thirteenth century, was a time of great advances for Islam. And since the majority of the world's Jews lived in the Islamic empire, they were beneficiaries of its prosperity. Jewish involvement in urban trade and commerce increased; by the end of the eighth century more Jews in the Muslim world were active in commerce than in agriculture. Arabic, formerly the language of a small tribal population, was now the language of a vast culture, and replaced Aramaic as the Jewish lingua franca.

The Gaonic Period

In 750 CE, the Abbasid dynasty overthrew the Umayyads, and as a result the capital of the Muslim Caliphate moved from Damascus to Baghdad. The academies of Pumbeditha and Sura likewise moved to Baghdad in the ninth and tenth centuries respectively, and attracted Jewish students from all over the Muslim world. They also attracted letters from rabbis, who asked the leaders of the academies, known as **Gaonim**, questions about problematic cases involving such diverse issues as divorce, inheritance, and commercial enterprises. Their answers to these questions, called **responsa**, reflected their interpretations of Talmudic laws, and provided the foundation for later legal and philosophical developments.

The main opposition to the Gaonim came from the **Karaites** ("scripturalists"; from the Hebrew *qara'*, "to read"). Founded in Iraq in the eighth century by Anan ben David, the Karaite movement maintained that only the Tanakh was authoritative and rejected the principle that the rabbinic interpretations of the Oral Torah/Talmud had the status of divinely revealed truth. Ben David sought to make the Bible the exclusive source of legal authority, encouraging individual Jews to read and interpret the (written) Torah for themselves, and to favour the plain meaning of the words in their context over creative rabbinic explanations such as the midrash of Lilith. The Karaites gained significant popular support, and from the tenth to twelfth centuries even threatened to surpass the rabbis in status. Jews supportive of Talmudic scholarship were referred to as "Rabbanites" in order to distinguish them from the Karaites. Because of the Karaites' emphasis on individual interpretation, their movement was characterized by division and disunity. Nevertheless, their impact on the rabbinic world was important: they were the first Jews to make an intensive study of Hebrew grammar and the manuscript traditions of the Bible, and they influenced the codification of the Hebrew text of the Bible in the tenth century. It was largely because the Muslim authorities recognized the Rabbanites as the official representatives of Judaism that they were eventually able to prevail over the Karaites. But small communities of Karaites still exist today in Israel, Turkey, and elsewhere in the Diaspora.

Maimonides

By the beginning of the eleventh century, the Islamic Empire had fractured into a number of regional powers, and as a consequence Iraq no longer dominated the Muslim world. At the same time the influence of the Gaonim was waning, and instability in Baghdad prompted many Jews to leave Babylonia for more promising lands.

Focus

Ashkenazim, Sephardim, and Mizrahim

Over time, three distinct cultural traditions took shape among the world's Jews. The oldest by far originated in Babylonia with the exiles who did not return to Judea in the sixth century BCE—the first members of the Diaspora. These Jews, and all the others whose ancestors remained in the general region of the Middle East, eventually came to be known as Mizrahim (from the Hebrew meaning "East"). Since many Mizrahi Jews come from Arab countries, the language most closely associated with them is Arabic, but other languages are also spoken among them, such as Persian and Kurdish. Other Jews made their way west to Europe. Those who settled on the Iberian Peninsula (modern Spain and Portugal) came to be known as Sephardim (from the Hebrew for "Spain"), while those who turned north towards France and Germany became the Ashkenazim (from the Hebrew for "Germany"). From the eighth century until the fifteenth, the Sephardic communities fared significantly better under the Muslim rulers of Al-Andalus than did the Ashkenazic communities of Christian-dominated Europe.

These two groups are distinctive from one another in language, food, and certain religious rituals. **Ladino** (a blend of medieval Spanish and Hebrew that is written in Hebrew characters) is traditionally associated with Sephardic Jews, while Yiddish (a German-based language with influences from Hebrew and other languages, written in Hebrew characters) is the lingua franca of the Ashkenazic community. In terms of culinary differences, at Passover Sephardic Jews eat rice, corn, and beans—all foods that lack leaven as an ingredient, and so comply with the Passover prohibition on foods made with yeast (such as bread)—but Ashkenazic Jews avoid such foods because when they are cooked they rise and expand just as leavened foods do. In addition to lighting two candles on Sabbath eve, Sephardic Jews light candles in honour of family members who have died. Mizrahi Jews tend to follow Sephardic religious practices.

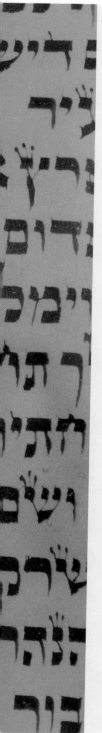

Document

From Maimonides, *Guide of the Perplexed: On Image* (tzelem) *and Likeness* (demut)

People have thought that in the Hebrew language *image* denotes the shape and configuration of a thing. This supposition led them to the pure doctrine of the corporeality of God, on account of His saying: "Let us make man in our image, after our likeness" (Gen. 1: 26). For they thought that God has a man's form, I mean his shape and configuration. The pure doctrine of the corporeality of God was a necessary consequence to be accepted by them. They accordingly believed in it and deemed that if they abandoned this belief, they would give the lie to the biblical text; that they would even make the Deity to be nothing at all unless they thought that God was a body provided with a face and a hand, like them in shape and configuration. However, His [body] is, in their view, bigger and more resplendent than they themselves, and the matter of which He is composed is not flesh and blood. As they see it, this is as far as one can go in establishing the separateness of God from other things. Now with respect to that which ought to be said in order to refute the doctrine of the corporeality of God and to establish His real unity—which can have no true reality unless one disproves His corporeality—you shall know the demonstration of all of this from this treatise. However, here, in this chapter, only an indication is given with a view to elucidating the meaning of *image* and *likeness*.

As for the term *likeness* (demut), it is a noun derived from the verb *damah* (to be like), and it too signifies likeness in respect of a notion. For the Scriptural dictum, "I am like a pelican in the wilderness" (Ps. 102: 7), does not signify that its author resembled the pelican with regard to its wings and feathers, but that his sadness was like that of the bird. In the same way in the verse, "Nor was any tree in the garden of God like it in beauty" (Ezek. 31: 18), the likeness is with respect to the notion of beauty. Similarly the verses, "Their venom is in the likeness of the venom of a serpent" (Ps. 58: 5), and "His likeness is that of a lion that is eager to tear in pieces" (Ps. 17: 12), refer both of them to a likeness in respect of a notion and not with respect to a shape and a configuration. In the same way it is said, "the likeness of a throne . . . the likeness of the throne" (Ezek. 1: 26), the likeness referred to being in respect of elevation and sublimity, not in respect of a throne's square shape, its solidity, and the length of its legs, as wretched people think. A similar explanation should also be applied to the expression, "the likeness of the living creatures" (Ezek. 1: 13). Now man possesses as his proprium something in him that is very strange as it is not found in anything else that exists under the sphere of the moon, namely, intellectual apprehension. In the exercise of this, no sense, no part of the body, none of the extremities are used; and therefore this apprehension was likened to the apprehension of the Deity, which does not require an instrument, although in reality it is not like the latter apprehension, but only appears so to the first stirrings of opinion. It was because of this something, I mean because of the divine intellect conjoined with man, that it is said of the latter that he is "in the image of God and in His likeness" (Gen. 1: 26–7), not that God, may He be exalted, is a body and possesses a shape (*Guide of the Perplexed*, Part one, Chapter one; I. Twersky [1972]: 246–7).

Some Babylonian Jews headed to Spain, a country in which, under the Umayyads (who had established themselves there after their defeat by the Abbasids in the eighth century), Jewish culture was blossoming. But that period too came to an end when a puritanical Muslim sect from Morocco called the Almohads invaded during the twelfth century and banned both Judaism and Christianity. Many Jews fled Spain as a result.

Among the Jewish families that escaped the Almohad persecution was that of a judge named Maimon. His son, Moses ben Maimon, better known as **Moses Maimonides** (1135–1204), would become one of the most famous Jewish philosophers and legal scholars of the Islamic age, identified in religious texts as "Rambam" (R-M-B-M, the acronym of "Rabbi Moses ben Maimon").

Moses ben Maimon was only a child when his family left Spain, going first to Morocco and then to Palestine. As an adult he ultimately established himself in Egypt—one of the central hubs of Jewish life and at that time under the control of the renowned Salah al-Din (Saladin), the first Sultan of Egypt. Jews were generally treated well at Saladin's court, and Maimonides became the personal physician to a high official.

Maimonides was a prolific writer, producing the famous 14-volume code of Jewish law called **Mishneh Torah** (in Hebrew) as well as various treatises on medicine and logic. His most important philosophical work, however, was *The Guide of the Perplexed*, originally written in Arabic. Presented as if addressing a single student's uncertainties about the truth of Judaism, the *Guide* was directed to Jews at large who were "perplexed" by the challenges of living in a cosmopolitan and philosophically sophisticated environment that tested their faith. Using Greek philosophy, particularly that of Aristotle, Maimonides sought to diminish the tension between faith and knowledge and emphasized that science (i.e., learning) ought not to undermine faith. He believed that all the biblical commandments were rational, although some were easier to understand than others, and he argued against the literal interpretation of Scripture. As he explains

in the boxed excerpt from the *Guide*, biblical language that describes God anthropomorphically— that is, language that attributes human qualities to God—is intended only to make God understandable to humans and should not be interpreted literally.

Medieval Jewish thought was deeply influenced by Islam. Muslim writers and thinkers had translated into Arabic scientific and philosophical works of the Greeks (such as Plato, Aristotle, and Plotinus), and these works emphasized the primacy of rational thought and human reason over revelation as the best source of knowledge about the world. Muslims considered the Greek philosophical tradition to be part of their culture, and did not see it as alien or threatening to the revelatory foundation of Islam. Jewish intellectuals such as Maimonides were also inspired by Muslim thinkers to undertake the challenge of connecting philosophy to religion. In turn, Jewish thinkers in the Islamic world then influenced Jewish thought in Christian Europe.

Jews in the Christian World: Seventh to Fifteenth Century

Christian Europe between the seventh and twelfth centuries was largely a feudal agricultural society in which peasants farmed land owned by the wealthy in exchange for their protection. Jews, however, belonged mainly to the urban merchant class and relied on protection from the government. Jewish intellectual life flourished in France and Germany, but elsewhere in Europe Jews faced undercurrents of hostility that at times would surge into waves of persecution, expulsion, or both.

Perhaps the best-known expulsion was the one ordered by the Christian monarchs of Spain, Ferdinand and Isabella, in 1492. Having finally taken the last Muslim stronghold, in Granada, they completed their "reconquest" of the land by commanding that the Jewish population either convert to Christianity or leave the country that had been their home

Map 3.1 Expulsion and Migration of Jews from Europe, c. 1000–1500 CE

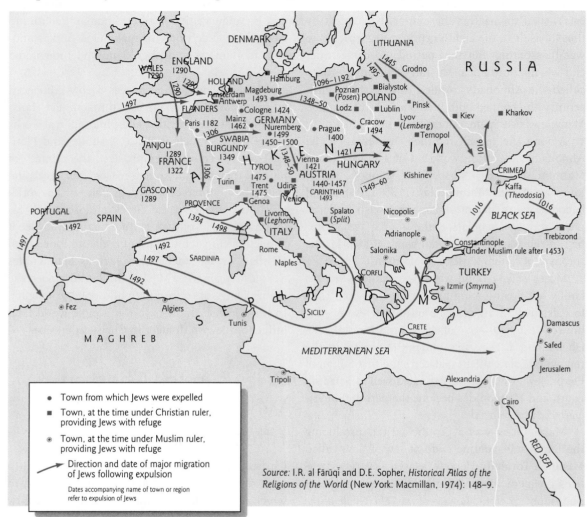

Source: I.R. al Fārūqī and D.E. Sopher, *Historical Atlas of the Religions of the World* (New York: Macmillan, 1974): 148–9.

• Town from which Jews were expelled

■ Town, at the time under Christian ruler, providing Jews with refuge

⊚ Town, at the time under Muslim ruler, providing Jews with refuge

→ Direction and date of major migration of Jews following expulsion

Dates accompanying name of town or region refer to expulsion of Jews

for centuries. When Christopher Columbus left Spain on the voyage that would take him to the "new world," in August 1492, he was forced to set sail from a small port in the south because all the country's major ports were so congested by departing Jews. Of the tens of thousands who left, most sought refuge in the Ottoman Turkish Empire. There they were welcomed by Sultan Bayazid II, who recognized the potential value to his empire of what were, in many cases, highly skilled refugees. To this day, some Turkish Jews still speak the Sephardic language, Ladino.

The Spanish Inquisition

In order to avoid expulsion, other Spanish Jews did convert to Christianity, but some of these "Conversos" (and their descendants) would continue to practise Jewish rites in secret. They were not the first. As early as the 1481, Ferdinand and Isabella had petitioned the Pope for permission to establish an Inquisition to root out and punish such heresy. Known for the ruthlessness of both its interrogation methods and the punishments it imposed, the Spanish Inquisition established tribunals in many cities with the goal of finding and executing those Conversos (also referred to as Marranos, "swine") who had not abandoned all Jewish traditions. More than 13,000 Conversos were put on trial during the first 12 years of the Spanish Inquisition.

The Kabbalah

Perhaps in response to the pain caused by the expulsion, many Jews took a renewed interest in mysticism, particularly the tradition known as **Kabbalah** (from the Hebrew meaning "to receive"). Although Kabbalah itself appears to date from the twelfth century, some of its teachings are said to have been passed from teacher to student from as far back as Moses, and perhaps earlier. Certainly the biblical Book of Ezekiel abounds in prophecies and mystical visions of the divine, and there was a long tradition of **Hekhalot** ("Palaces") literature recounting visionary ascents into the heavenly palaces of the divine. In the Jewish mystical tradition, the devout individual can experience direct revelation of God, usually through meditation or ecstatic prayer. This tradition developed in new ways in the Middle Ages, influenced in part by the Islamic mystical tradition of Sufism.

The most authoritative Kabbalah text (actually a collection of texts) is a commentary on the Five Books of Moses called the Zohar ("splendour" or "radiance" in Hebrew). Though written as if its author was the second-century rabbinic sage Shimon bar Yochai, it is generally thought to have been written (in Aramaic) by Moses de Leon, a thirteenth-century Spanish–Jewish mystic who was immersed in the great Jewish thinkers of the Islamic world, including Maimonides.

Kabbalists refer to God as the *Ayn Sof* ("Without End" or "Infinite" in Hebrew), for God is considered to be beyond thought, beyond form, beyond gender—in effect, the unknowable creator. What *can* be known about God are aspects of his divine being that connect the created world with the unknowable divine source of all creation; in other words, the powers of the *Ayn Sof* flow through them, revealing him to the world. Kabbalists call these aspects—of which there are ten—Sefirot, which literally means "numbers" but is usually translated as "emanations" or "channels" of God's creative energy and power. The sefirot are *Keter*/Crown, *Hokhmah*/Wisdom, *Binah*/Understanding, *Hesed*/Lovingkindness, *Gevurah*/Might, *Tiferet*/Beauty, *Hod*/Splendour, *Netzakh*/Victory, *Yesod*/Foundation, and *Malkhut*/Sovereignty. Each is an aspect of the *Ayn Sof* that radiates from the divine sphere into the created, material realm, and each one is interlinked with the others. Kabbalists are to spend their lives seeking not only to understand the Sefirot and their interrelations, but also (through the Kabbalists' own actions, thoughts, and words) to modify these interrelations.

But why should humans intervene in such divine matters? And how can they possibly do so? The Zohar answers these questions by explaining that at the beginning of creation (in the Garden of Eden), the powers of the Sefirot were perfectly in balance. But this balance was disturbed when humans began to disobey God (when Adam and Eve ate of the forbidden fruit). According to the Zohar, the Torah was given to Israel to provide a way of restoring the Sefirot to their original harmony. Each time a Jew fulfills a commandment of the Torah, a small positive shift occurs that helps to bring the Sefirot into balanced alignment. Likewise, every time a commandment is not fulfilled, the Sefirot are pushed into further disarray. When perfect balance is achieved, the divine powers will flow unhindered, just as they did at the beginning of creation. Some of the earthly manifestations of harmony among the Sefirot include the return of the Jewish people to the Land of Israel and the ascension of all humankind (including non-Jews) to Mount Zion in Jerusalem in order to worship God—the *Ayn Sof*—through sacrificial offerings at the Temple. Henceforth, all will live in love, unity, and obedience to God.

Isaac Luria

An enormously influential later scholar of the Kabbalah was **Isaac Luria** (1534–72), who was born in

Jerusalem and, after some time in Egypt, moved to the northern Palestinian city of Safed in 1569. He did not live there for long—he died just three years later, at the age of 38—yet he and his disciples transformed the city into the centre of Jewish mysticism that it remains to this day. Unfortunately, Luria did not write his teachings down—what we know about them has come down through his students' writings—but they were extremely complicated and creative.

One of the better-known components of Lurianic mysticism is the concept of *tikkun* ("mending" or "restoration" in Hebrew). The basis of this idea is Luria's understanding of how the universe was created. First there was the *tzimtzum* ("contraction"): in order to make room for the world, the Ayn Sof had to create an empty space. Since he was everywhere, it was necessary for God to contract parts of himself—a step that Luria interpreted as a type of divine exile. Next, divine light surged from God into the empty space, taking the form of the ten Sefirot as well as the first man: Adam Kadmon ("primal man"). Out of the eyes, nose, and mouth of Adam Kadmon the light streamed, and this created vessels that held the light. But the vessels were unable to contain such divine power, and so they exploded into luminous fragments that became trapped in the created world. In this way, thought Luria, evil entered creation.

Like the Zohar, Luria held that Jews had the capacity to reverse this dismal situation, for the divine sparks longed to be liberated from their material abode and returned to their original state; through prayer, study, and the performance of mitzvot, Jews could assist in the process of "restoring the world," or *tikkun olam*. For the generation of Jews struggling with the aftermath of their community's expulsion from Spain, the idea that individual religious acts made a difference was empowering. At the same time, the concept of the

Document

Welcoming the "Sabbath Queen"

Isaac Luria developed a number of mystical rituals that are still practised today even by Jews who have no interest in mysticism. One example is the ritual of Kabbalat Shabbat, welcoming the "Sabbath Queen." On Friday night, the eve of the Sabbath, Luria and his disciples would go to the periphery of the city of Safed and turn their faces towards the setting sun. There they would welcome the "Sabbath Queen" by reciting several psalms and then singing a poem called "L'cha Dodi" ("Come my Beloved"). Composed in 1529 by the Kabbalist scholar Solomon Alkabez, it invites Jews to gather and greet the Sabbath, which is personified as a bride. Today congregations of all types continue to sing this song at Friday night services just before the official beginning of the Sabbath. In many synagogues, members of the congregation stand for the final stanza and turn to face the door in order to "greet" the Sabbath bride.

Below is a translation from the Hebrew of the first and last stanzas:

Come, my beloved, with chorus of praise,
Welcome Bride Sabbath, the Queen of the days.
'Keep and Remember'!—in One divine word
He that is One, made his will heard;
One is the name of him, One is the Lord!
His are the fame and the glory and praise!

Come in thy joyousness, Crown of thy lord;
Come, bringing peace to the folk of the Word;
Come where the faithful in gladsome accord,
Hail thee as Sabbath-Bride, Queen of the days
Come where the faithful are hymning thy praise;
Come as a bride cometh, Queen of the days!
(Hertz 1960: 357, 259).

Ayn Sof's fragmentation during the creation process, and the introduction of evil into the world as a result, offered a way of understanding the suffering that Jews were experiencing in their lives.

Sabbatai Zvi

Messianic expectations swelled in the year 1666, when a student of Lurianic Kabbalah named **Sabbatai Zvi** was declared the messiah in Izmir, Turkey. A number of mystically oriented Jews aligned themselves with him, and together they marched on the sultan in Istanbul, where they camped outside the city walls. The sultan initially paid no attention, but when the group did not leave, he had Zvi put in prison. Ultimately, Zvi was offered the choice of conversion to Islam or death. He chose to convert, and changed his name to Aziz Mehmed Effendi. Although the majority of his followers became disillusioned and abandoned him, some of them interpreted Zvi's conversion as a divinely sanctioned act. Therefore they too converted to Islam, but continued to follow Jewish mystical practices in secret. Descendants of this sect still live in modern Turkey, where they are known as the Dönmeh ("returners" in Turkish).

Eastern Europe

For centuries, Ashkenazic Jews had tended to live in their own communities, separated to some extent from the Christian mainstream of European life. By the early sixteenth century, however, many places were beginning to enforce segregation. Among them was the Republic of Venice, whose name for its Jewish quarter, the "ghetto," became the common term for such districts, some of which were enclosed by high walls. Meanwhile, persecution had been pushing many Jews farther east. The feudal leaders in Poland welcomed them, and several areas of Eastern Europe became home to a vibrant Ashkenazic Jewish culture in which the vernacular was Yiddish. Jews lived in largely Jewish urban areas where they could practise their faith without obstruction.

In 1648, however, a revolt against the Polish Roman Catholic nobility by Ukrainian Greek Orthodox Cossack peasants brought this peaceful period to an end. Jews, who had developed ties with the nobility through commercial activities, were also targeted by the rebels. This prompted many Ashkenazim to leave Poland and move west, back into the regions from which their ancestors had fled.

Hasidism

In the mid-eighteenth century, in the southeastern Polish province of Podolia, a highly influential movement emerged to counter the rabbinic leaders of the day who exaggerated the necessity of scholarship as a means of knowing God, and as a result dismissed uneducated Jews. Members of this group called themselves Hasidim (from the Hebrew word for "piety"). The charismatic founder of **Hasidism**, Israel ben Eliezer (1698–1760), came to be known as the **Baal Shem Tov** ("Master of the good name" in Hebrew) or "Besht" (an acronym). An itinerant healer and teacher, the Besht encouraged his fellow Jews to worship God with joy and delight, from the heart rather than the head. Little is known about his personal life, as he left no written record apart from a few letters. What is known comes from the stories of his disciples, who claimed that he had supernatural powers, including the ability to heal illness and even to revive the dead. A collection of those stories, entitled *In Praise of the Baal Shem Tov*, first published in 1815, is an early example of one of the most valuable legacies of Hasidic culture: storytelling. Today the movement continues to flourish in certain Jewish communities. Hasidic men in particular are easily identified by their long black coats, black hats, and substantial beards and **sidelocks**.

In keeping with the Besht's emphasis on deep religious feeling rather than scholarship, Hasidic leaders are not rabbinic scholars but charismatic individuals known as tzaddikim ("righteous men") whose authority is based on what are believed to be their supernatural powers; Hasidic teaching goes

Document

A Rabbi for a Day

Jacob ben Wolf Kranz, the famous "Preacher of Dubno," was born in Lithuania around 1740 and died in 1804. He was known both for his scholarly ability and for his down-to-earth, often humorous, stories that subvert conventional assumptions. In the following tale, for example, one might assume that the distinguished rabbi would be more clever than his driver . . .

The famous Preacher of Dubno was once journeying from one town to another delivering his learned sermons. Wherever he went he was received with enthusiasm and accorded the greatest honours. His driver, who accompanied him on this tour, was very much impressed by all this welcome.

One day, as they were on the road, the driver said, "Rabbi, I have a great favour to ask of you. Wherever we go people heap honours on you. Although I am only an ignorant driver I'd like to know how it feels to receive so much attention. Would you mind if we were to exchange clothes for one day? Then they'll think I am the great preacher and you the driver, so they'll honour me instead!"

Now the Preacher of Dubno was a man of the people and a merry soul, but he saw the pitfalls awaiting his driver in such an arrangement.

"Suppose I agreed—what then? You know the rabbi's clothes don't make a rabbi! What would you do for learning? If they were to ask you to explain some difficult passage in the Law, you'd only make a fool of yourself, wouldn't you?"

"Don't you worry, Rabbi—I am willing to take that chance."

"In that case," said the preacher, "here are my clothes."

And the two men undressed and exchanged clothes as well as their callings.

As they entered the town all the Jewish inhabitants turned out to greet the great preacher. They conducted him into the synagogue while the assumed driver followed discreetly at a distance.

Each man came up to the "rabbi" to shake hands and to say the customary: *Sholom Aleichem*, learned Rabbi!"

The "rabbi" was thrilled with his reception. He sat down in the seat of honour surrounded by all the scholars and dignitaries of the town. In the meantime the preacher from his corner kept his merry eyes on the driver to see what would happen.

"Learned Rabbi," suddenly asked a local scholar, "would you be good enough to explain to us this passage in the Law we don't understand?"

The preacher in his corner chuckled, for the passage was indeed a difficult one. "Now he's sunk!" he said to himself.

With knitted brows the "rabbi" peered into the sacred book placed before him, although he could not understand one word. Then, impatiently pushing it away from him, he addressed himself sarcastically to the learned men of the town, "A fine lot of scholars you are! Is this the most difficult question you could ask me? Why, this passage is so simple even my driver could explain it to you!"

Then he called the Preacher of Dubno: "Driver, come here for a moment and explain the Law to these 'scholars'!" (Ausubel 1961: 21–2).

so far as to assert that "Whatever God does, it is also within the capacity of the tzaddik to do" (Efron et al. 2009: 264). Hasidim believe that through a personal relationship with a **tzaddik** it is possible for an ordinary person to attain a state of *devekut* ("attachment" or "cleaving" to God). Thus the relationship between a tzaddik and his disciples tends to be very close, and Hasidim address their tzaddik by the Yiddish title **Rebbe** instead of the more formal "Rabbi." By the early nineteenth century it was believed that a tzaddik could transmit his charisma to his sons, and in this way Hasidic leadership became dynastic.

With the passage of time, many subgroups of Hasidism developed. Of those that have survived, the largest and best-known today is Chabad. Named for three concepts that it considers central—*chokhmah* (wisdom), *binah* (reason), and *da'at* (knowledge)—it was founded in the late eighteenth century by Rebbe Shneur Zalman (1745–1813) and today is widely known as Chabad–Lubavitch, after the Russian town that was its base for many years. Chabad's adherents, often referred to as Lubavitchers, follow many of the traditions and prayers established by Isaac Luria. For example, like Luria they attribute human suffering to the fragmentation of the Godhead, and their *siddur* (prayer book) follows the same arrangement as Luria's. In 1940

A poster in Jerusalem shows the "Lubavitcher Rebbe," the late Menachem Mendel Schneerson (1902–94), and proclaims that "The King, the Messiah Lives!".

the community fled wartime Europe and set up a synagogue in New York; its official headquarters are in the Crown Heights section of Brooklyn. Menachem Mendel Schneerson (1902–94), who assumed the leadership in 1951, turned the movement into a dominant force in Judaism by significantly expanding its international activities and founding a worldwide organization whose goal is to reach out to Jews and, in so doing, hasten the coming of the Messianic Age. In fact, some of Rebbe Schneerson's followers believed he was the Jewish messiah (although he denied it) and called him the "Moshiach" (the Lubavitcher pronunciation of "Mashiach"). All Lubavitcher homes displayed his portrait, and followers regularly sought his blessing. Even now, 20 years after his death, some devotees still consider him the messiah, though others firmly reject the idea. The reverence with which he was treated by his followers led many Jewish critics, from both the right and the left, to decry what appeared to be the personality cult that had developed around him. Despite the criticism, and the fact that no successor has yet emerged to replace Schneerson, Chabad continues to grow: it now claims more than 200,000 adherents, and up to a million Jews attend Chabad services at least once a year.

Hasidim vs Mitnagdim

The eighteenth century was a dark time for Eastern European Jews. Poor, downtrodden, and politically disenfranchised, they needed hope to revive them, and Hasidism provided it. The Baal Shem Tov taught that everyone, no matter how impoverished or uneducated, could commune with God, for God was everywhere. The Hasidic emphasis on community and equality also struck a chord. Hasidic worship was marked by swaying prayer, ecstatic dancing, and joyous singing to melodies that would eventually shape the musical styles of synagogues across denominational lines, as well as secular Jewish music (especially klezmer).

Initially, learned scholars resisted Hasidism. A group called Mitnagdim ("Opponents" in Hebrew) objected in particular to the introduction of

Kabbalah—traditionally the preserve of Talmudic masters and mystical adepts—into the daily life of the masses; they saw the tzaddik as a threat to the authority of the rabbis; and they were disturbed that the Hasidim paid little attention either to Torah study or to dignified deportment during prayer. To curtail the spread of the movement, the Mitnagdim urged Jewish communities to shun Hasidim. But their efforts were in vain. By the early nineteenth century almost two-thirds of Eastern European Jewry had joined the movement, and today Hasidim make up an important component of Orthodox Judaism (see below).

The Modern Period

Haskalah: The Jewish Enlightenment

In the eighteenth century, a number of European philosophers articulated a program for the radical freedom of individual thought. At a time when Europe was dominated by monarchic governments in league with Christian authorities, Enlightenment thinkers argued that individuals should be able to judge for themselves what was right and wrong. The French Revolution (1789–99) ended feudalism and overturned the Catholic alliance with the French monarchy in favour of freedom, equality, and brotherhood. As the Enlightenment swept Western Europe, Jews benefited from its emphasis on reason, tolerance, and material progress. Restrictions were lifted: the walls of the ghettos fell, and Jews were free to live where they wished. Some countries gave Jews citizenship, which opened up opportunities for them to vote, attend universities, and choose their own occupations in life.

It was in response to these developments that one of the most important movements in the history of European Jewry was launched: the **Haskalah** (Jewish Enlightenment). As doors began opening for Jews, leaders of the Haskalah advocated a restructuring of Jewish education to devote less time to the Talmud and more to other subjects, such as modern languages and practical skills, which would help Jews integrate (without assimilating) into European society. The German philosopher Moses Mendelssohn (1729–86) recognized that, after so many years of living behind ghetto walls, Jews had become inward-looking and segregated from the rest of society. He urged his fellow German Jews "to be a Jew at home and a German on the street," and encouraged them to speak German rather than Yiddish—a language he considered to be a degraded form of German. To facilitate the latter, Mendelssohn published his own German translation of the Bible (in Hebrew characters), along with a Hebrew commentary. The "new Jew" envisioned by proponents of Haskalah would be both a committed adherent of Judaism and a full participant in modern culture.

Modern Branches of Judaism

The adaptation of traditional Jewish thought and practice to the modern world laid the foundation for the emergence of the diverse movements that we know today as the Reform, Orthodox, Conservative, Reconstructionist, and Humanistic branches of Judaism. Each of these movements originated in an effort to reconcile centuries-old traditions with the new ways of thinking and living promoted by the European Enlightenment.

Reform

Reform Judaism began with the goal of making Jewish practice meaningful for Jews living in eighteenth-century Germany. Its pioneers explicitly supported Enlightenment ideals and drew attention to their compatibility with Judaism. The man known as the father of Reform was Israel Jacobson (1768–1828), who in 1815 opened his Berlin home for worship services with sermons by other leaders of the movement. Three years later the New Israelite Temple Association opened the Hamburg Temple for Sabbath services that used the everyday German of the community rather than Hebrew, eliminated the traditional references to the hoped-for restoration of the Temple in Jerusalem, and featured choral music with organ accompaniment. (The latter was quite a daring innovation: although music, vocal and instrumental, had been a part of Jewish worship as long as the Temple stood, instrumental music had been banned after its destruction, as a sign of mourning.) It took two generations for Reform Judaism to find its niche among German congregations, however. Reform synagogues did not have a meaningful presence in Germany until the 1830s, and a German-language prayer book was not introduced until 1848.

The spiritual leader of the Reform movement was Abraham Geiger (1810–74). He studied Near Eastern languages and philosophy and devoted his life to the history of Judaism, using his scholarship to argue that Jewish culture had been adapting to its surroundings throughout history, and hence that reform was natural to Judaism. Geiger used critical textual analysis to argue that the contents of the Hebrew Bible reflected the concerns and perspectives of post-biblical Jewish movements. He also demonstrated the connections among the three major monotheistic faiths of Judaism, Christianity, and Islam.

Today Reform Jews do not generally observe the dietary laws (see p. 118) although over the last decade growing numbers have been becoming more observant. The Reform branch understands Judaism to be a flexible, living religion that remains relevant to its adherents because it evolves as the realities of human life change. Interfaith dialogue is encouraged in order to achieve understanding and peaceful interaction among those of different

AP Photo/Michal Fattal/CP

In April 2013, while attending the monthly women's prayer service at the Western Wall, this woman was arrested for wearing a tallit (prayer shawl), which the Haredi community insists is reserved for men. Four other women were also detained.

Focus

Dietary Laws

Some Jews jokingly suggest that Judaism is a way of eating. That may not be far from the truth. Food—and how it is prepared and eaten—is an essential part of Jewish observance. Jewish dietary laws (*kashrut*) stipulate the foods that are acceptable and those that must be avoided, as well as how to cook the acceptable foods, and the types of food that can be eaten together in the same meal. Food is considered **kosher** if it is "fit" or "proper" in accordance with Jewish law. The term is not limited to food: a **tallit** (prayer shawl) with its fringes cut off would no longer be kosher.

There are two places in the Torah where the types of food Jews can eat are discussed: Leviticus 11 and Deuteronomy 14: 2–21. These verses instruct that, among land animals, only those that have split hooves and chew their own cud are acceptable (this means that cows and goats can be eaten, but pigs and rabbits cannot). Among sea creatures, only those with both scales and fins are permitted; thus mussels and crustaceans such as shrimp are prohibited. When it comes to birds, the Torah simply lists the species that are acceptable (chicken, turkey, goose, and duck) and those that are not (birds of prey such as the vulture, owl, and hawk). The products of non-acceptable animals are likewise considered unkosher (except for honey, which is understood to derive from flowers rather than bees, which fall into the forbidden category of "winged swarming things").

Even meat that is permitted must be prepared and cooked correctly if it is to be considered kosher. For example, an animal that has died a natural death is not to be eaten; only animals that are slaughtered in accordance with the law are acceptable. This means that an animal must be put to death humanely, by slitting the throat with a sharp knife. The blood from the carcass must be drained completely either by soaking and salting the meat, or by grilling it until no trace of blood remains.

Once the meat is prepared in accordance with the law, there are rules about how to eat it. For example, meat is not to be consumed at the same time as dairy. Thus cheeseburgers are never on the menu for observant Jews. This stipulation is drawn from an instruction that appears twice in the Torah: "you shall not boil a kid in its mother's milk" (Exodus 23: 19 and Deuteronomy 14: 21). It was the rabbis who interpreted this rule as forbidding the combination of meat and dairy, and from it they derived a number of additional laws: thus one must wait between one and six hours, depending on the cultural tradition, after eating meat before having (for example) ice cream for dessert. Some Jews consider it so important to keep meat and dairy separate that they have two sets of dishes and cutlery (one for meat, one for dairy), as well as two sinks and two dishwashers.

Manufacturers of kosher food or drink products use various symbols to inform consumers of the product's status. One of the most common is a capital U (for "Union of Orthodox Jewish Congregations") inside a circle, which indicates that a body of rabbis has inspected the plant at which the product was prepared and deemed it to be kosher.

religions. Reform also allows women to serve as rabbis; in 1972, when Sally Priesand became the first female rabbi in North America, it was a Reform seminary—Hebrew Union College in Cincinnati, Ohio—that ordained her.

Orthodox Judaism

It was the spread of Reform Judaism that stimulated the establishment of the Orthodox branch, a traditionalist reaction that was largely spearheaded by Samson Raphael Hirsch (1808–88). Hirsch sought to prove that traditional Judaism was compatible with modernity, and coined the Hebrew phrase *Torah im derekh erets* ("Torah with the way of the land") to refer to the application of Torah in all aspects of everyday life. The term "Orthodox" was not used to distinguish traditional Jews from those associated with Reform Judaism until the next century.

Orthodox Jews believe that the Hebrew Bible is the revealed word of God, and understand the Mishnah and two versions of the Talmud to be written forms of Oral Law that originated with Moses; they follow rabbinic Halakhah and observe the laws of Torah. The most conservative members of the Orthodox branch are called Haredim, "trembling ones" (from Isaiah 66: 5: "Hear the word of the Lord, you who tremble at his word"). While all Orthodox Jews are rigorously observant, the more liberal among them do participate to some degree in non-Jewish society. By contrast, Haredi Jews tend to live and work in segregated communities, and every part of their lives, without exception, is governed by Halakhah. The Hasidim are a subgroup of the Haredim.

Conservative

The third branch of Judaism to emerge in the mid-nineteenth century was founded by Zacharias Frankel (1801–75) under the name "Positive-Historical Judaism." An attempt to find middle ground between rigid Orthodoxy and the radical liberalism of Reform Judaism, it eventually developed into what is known today as Conservative Judaism. Frankel argued that the core teachings of Judaism (for example, the oneness of God) were divinely revealed, but at the same time he acknowledged that Judaism had developed within history, and therefore that its traditions were open to moderate reinterpretation and modification. Conservative Jews interpret the text more literally than do their Reform counterparts, but more liberally than the Orthodox. In contrast to Reform Jews, Conservative Jews typically do follow the dietary laws. Since they are not Orthodox, however, they also allow for some restructuring in order to keep current and relevant in modern times. Conservative synagogues vary in their attitudes towards women's roles: the more liberal Conservative congregations allow female rabbis and full female participation in synagogue services, whereas the more traditional ones do not.

Reconstructionism

Whereas the Reform, Orthodox, and Conservative movements all originated in Germany, the Reconstructionist movement was created in North America. Its founder, Mordechai Kaplan (1881–1983), began his career as an Orthodox rabbi,

Focus

Kosher Cola

Rabbi Tobias Geffen (1870–1970) was an Orthodox rabbi who lived near the Coca-Cola headquarters in Atlanta, Georgia. In response to the many inquiries he received from rabbis across the United States asking whether Coke was kosher for Passover, Rabbi Geffen asked the company for a list of the ingredients and was given the secret formula, on the condition that he not disclose it. After persuading the company to replace a non-kosher glycerin with a vegetable-based substitute, and to use a sweetener that was not derived from grain, Geffen in 1935 declared that Coca-Cola was kosher for year-round consumption by observant Jews.

but soon grew uncomfortable with the Orthodox movement. He then obtained a teaching position at the Jewish Theological Seminary (a Conservative institution), which he kept until 1963 while at the same time working as a rabbi at the Society for the Advancement of Judaism, a Reconstructionist synagogue that he established in 1922. His book *Judaism as a Civilization* (1934), in which he argues that Judaism was not supernaturally revealed, but is an ever-changing religious civilization involving language, literature, art, social organization, and symbols as well as certain beliefs and practices, provided the fundamental framework for the Reconstructionist movement. Kaplan called for the synagogue to be a social and cultural centre (rather than a religious one), and he introduced the idea of the Jewish Community Centre—an institution that has become a regular part of the North American Jewish environment. He also argued that the scriptures were not divinely revealed, but created by the Jewish people themselves; and that the traditions existed for the people, not the other way around, and so could be modified. As an example, in 1922 Kaplan marked his daughter Judith's coming of age by conducting the world's first bat mitzvah for her; this ceremonial equivalent to the **bar mitzvah** ceremony for boys is now practised regularly not only by Reconstructionists, but in Reform and Conservative synagogues as well. Thus Kaplan's influence is felt well beyond the movement he established.

Since the Reconstructionist movement developed primarily out of the Conservative movement (Kaplan had in fact intended to change Conservative Judaism from within rather than launch an entirely new movement), it preserved a number of traditional features, such as the dietary laws and the custom of wearing the **kippah** (skullcap) for men, as well as a significant amount of Hebrew in the liturgy. As a consequence, its practice tends to look very much like Conservative practice. But its rejection of the idea of the Jews as the chosen people, its gender-neutral prayer book, and the fact that some of its adherents may well describe themselves as atheists clearly distinguish Reconstructionism from Conservative Judaism. What matters to Reconstructionists more than individual faith is active participation in a community and the effort to honour Jewish history by retaining meaningful symbols and customs.

Humanistic Judaism

The American rabbi Sherwin Wine (1929–2007) took Kaplan's ideas several steps further, removing God from the picture altogether. He initially served as a rabbi in the Reform synagogue, but as his belief in the existence of God waned, he looked for a more congenial community. Finding none, in 1963 he himself established a secular congregation called the Birmingham Temple that continues to function today with some 400 members in Farmington Hills, Michigan. In 1969 this congregation united with several like-minded others to form the Society for Humanistic Judaism (SHJ), which now includes congregations from across North America. According to its website, the goal of the SHJ is "to foster a positive Jewish identity, intellectual integrity, and ethical behaviour."

Over the years Wine developed a new liturgy, in both Hebrew and English, which makes no reference to God. He also found new focal points for the various Jewish holidays (for example, the Humanist Passover Seder ritual includes readings from a new haggadah that links aspects of the Exodus story to contemporary social concerns). Humanistic Jews welcome everyone to participate in their services, regardless of gender, sexual orientation, or religious background. From the perspective of Humanists, Jewish identity is largely a personal decision. Not surprisingly, Humanist rabbis and *Madrichs* or *Madrichas* (trained "guides") will officiate at marriages between Jews and non-Jews.

The Modern Synagogue

The synagogue is at the heart of the Jewish religious community: it is a place for prayer and study of sacred texts, a venue for communal worship, and a place to learn. It also functions as a centre for social interaction and charitable activity (for example, certain synagogues run soup kitchens and offer

Focus

The High Holidays

The High Holidays, also called the High Holy Days and the Days of Awe, encompass the ten days from the beginning of Rosh Hashanah through the end of Yom Kippur. **Rosh Hashanah** is considered the Jewish New Year, and usually falls in September or October. On this day God is said to open the "Book of Life," in which he will inscribe the individual's fate for the year on Yom Kippur. This is the time of the year when Jews are supposed to examine their consciences, for Rosh Hashanah is followed by "ten days of penitence" that culminate on the Day of Atonement, **Yom Kippur**. According to the Babylonian Talmud, God says: "On Rosh Hashanah I open the book of life and at the end of Yom Kippur I shall close it again, and your fate will be sealed for the coming year!" Historically, this was the only time when the Divine Name of God was pronounced—by the high priest before the ark in the Jerusalem Temple's most sacred place, the Holy of Holies—in order to make atonement for the people. Apples dipped in honey are customarily eaten at Rosh Hashanah as an expression of the hope for a "sweet" new year. The traditional greeting during this time is *L'shanah tova tikatevu* ("May you be inscribed for a good new year").

Nowadays Yom Kippur is spent at the synagogue in prayer and supplication, asking for God's forgiveness. Fasting—no eating or drinking from sundown on the evening of Yom Kippur until the following nightfall (a period of 25 hours)—is compulsory for adults, with three exceptions: pregnant women, the elderly, and the ill are exempt. It is understood that God forgives sins against himself; however, if a family member or neighbour has been wronged, that person must be asked for forgiveness. The word for "sin" is *chet*, which means "missing the mark," as in archery. Thus one can think of a sin as a "missed opportunity" for a kind word or a righteous act. The liturgy during the High Holy Days makes frequent references to the many ways in which human beings hurt each other through unkindness and lack of generosity, both in speech and in action. The time between Rosh Hashanah and Yom Kippur is meant for contemplative reflection on one's own words and behaviour. Yet these days of penitence should not be sad, because Jews are supposed to have confidence in the power of repentance and the mercy of God.

Most members of the Jewish community, including those who are not very observant, mark Yom Kippur to some degree and many go to synagogue, even if they do not go again for the rest of the year. At intervals throughout the synagogue service, the shofar (usually a ram's horn) is sounded. This tradition has been ascribed many symbolic meanings, including a "wake up" call to reflect on one's sinfulness and need for repentance, a summons to war against evil inclinations, and a reminder of the ram that God told Abraham to sacrifice instead of his son Isaac. Whatever the interpretation, for Jews the plaintive sound of the shofar is one of the most stirring aspects of Yom Kippur.

beds for the homeless). In Hebrew it is called a Beit K'nesset (literally, "house of assembly); "synagogue" is the Greek equivalent. Orthodox and Hasidic Jews typically use the Yiddish term "Shul" (from the German for "school") and emphasizes the synagogue's role as an intellectual hub. Whereas Conservative Jews tend to use the term "synagogue," Reform Jews call their local place of assembly a "temple" because they consider it to have definitively replaced the Temple in Jerusalem.

Typically, a board of directors made up of laypeople is responsible for supervising the synagogue

Document

The Shema

Among the prayers recited daily in Judaism, the oldest and most highly revered is the **Shema***. Composed of three paragraphs from the Torah (Deuteronomy 6: 4–9 and 11: 13–21, and Numbers 15: 37–41), it is known by its first word: "Shema" ("Hear"). The Shema commands that these Torah passages be recited "morning and night;" and from days of old, Jews have fulfilled this commandment by reciting the Shema twice a day, once in the morning and once at night:*

Hear, O Israel: The Lord is our God, the Lord alone. You shall love the Lord your God with all your heart, and with all your soul, and with all your might. Keep these words that I am commanding you today in your heart. Recite them to your children and talk about them when you are at home and when you are away, when you lie down and when you rise. Bind them as a sign on your hand, fix them as an emblem on your forehead, and write them on the doorposts of your house and on your gates.

If you will only heed his every commandment that I am commanding you today—loving the Lord your God, and serving him with all your heart and with all your soul— then he will give the rain for your land in its season, the early rain and the later rain, and you will gather in your grain, your wine, and your oil; and he will give grass in your fields for your livestock, and you will eat your fill. Take care, or you will be seduced into turning away, serving other gods and worshipping them, for then the anger of the Lord will be kindled against you and he will shut up the heavens, so that there will be no rain and the land will yield no fruit; then you will perish quickly from the good land that the Lord is giving you.

You shall put these words of mine in your heart and soul, and you shall bind them as a sign on your hand, and fix them as an emblem on your forehead. Teach them to your children, talking about them when you are at home and when you are away, when you lie down and when you rise. Write them on the doorposts of your house and on your gates, so that your days and the days of your children may be multiplied in the land that the Lord swore to your ancestors to give them, as long as the heavens are above the earth.

The Lord said to Moses: Speak to the Israelites, and tell them to make fringes on the corners of their garments throughout their generations and to put a blue cord on the fringe at each corner. You have the fringe so that, when you see it, you will remember all the commandments of the Lord and do them, and not follow the lust of your own heart and your own eyes. So you shall remember and do all my commandments, and you shall be holy to your God. I am the Lord your God, who brought you out of the land of Egypt, to be your God: I am the Lord your God.

and all its activities, as well as hiring a rabbi for the community. Although most synagogues have a rabbi, some do not: instead, they invite different members of the community to lead the service. Synagogues tend to derive the majority of their financial income from annual membership dues, voluntary donations, fees for memorial plaques to be hung on the walls of the sanctuary in honour of deceased relatives, and the sale of tickets for seats at services during the High Holidays (see box, p. 121), when the building can become very crowded.

Synagogues do not have to be a particular shape or size; nor is there any architectural style requirement. Usually the building is designed so that members of the congregation face Jerusalem when they pray, although Reform synagogues tend to be oriented to suit the land they sit on. There are several ritual objects that will be found in any synagogue, no matter which branch of Judaism it belongs to. In modern synagogues the Holy Ark (or Ark of the Covenant) in which the Torah scrolls are kept symbolizes the place that stored the tablets given to Moses at Mount Sinai. It can be a cabinet, or even a hollow indentation in the wall, and different people are given the honour of opening and closing it. Usually it is situated at the front of the room, and has doors as well as an inner curtain that are opened or closed during certain prayers. When the Ark is opened, all members of the congregation stand. In liberal (i.e., Reform and most Conservative) synagogues, where the rabbi leads the service, the *bimah*, or pulpit, is set before the ark, facing the congregation. By contrast, where the **cantor** (*hazzan* in Hebrew) leads the worship and faces in the same direction as the congregation, the *bimah* is in the centre. In front of the Ark is the *ner tamid* ("Eternal Lamp"), which represents the fulfillment of the commandment (in Exodus 27: 20–1) to future generations of Israelites to keep a light perpetually burning outside the curtain covering the Holy Ark in the tent of meeting—the place where the Israelites met with God.

Once the Torah scrolls are opened, a pointer is used to aid in the reading; often in the shape of a hand, it is called a *yad* ("hand" in Hebrew). Human hands never touch the parchment, since sweat contains acids that could damage it. The scrolls are stored in a fabric cover (often velvet) that may be ornately decorated with silver or gold.

Prayer Services

Jewish prayers take two forms: pre-set (determined in advance, typically from the ancient period) and spontaneous (created on the spot by the individual Jew). Prayer services revolve around the former type. Three times a day practising Jews daven (Yiddish for "pray") in communal worship services: in the evening (Ma'ariv), in the morning (Shacharit), and in the afternoon (Minchah). These services correspond to the three daily sacrifices that were performed at the Temple in Jerusalem. A book called a *siddur*, which means "order" (and is related to the word for the Passover meal, seder), contains a collection of prayers in the order in which they are recited through the week. Prayers are also recited during mundane activities, such as when getting up in the morning and before washing one's hands, as well as before and after eating.

Every Sabbath morning service includes readings from the Torah and the Prophets (the latter readings are called *haftarah*, "conclusion," because they conclude the worship service). The Torah has 54 sections (*parashot*), each of which is read and studied for a week, so that the entire Torah is covered in an annual cycle. Every *parasha* is further divided into seven sections (*aliyah*), all of which are read during the Sabbath morning service. (Although the Torah is also read on Monday and Thursday mornings as well as Saturday afternoon, only one *aliyah* of the seven is recited at those services.) On the days when the Torah is read, there is a formal ritual in which the scrolls are paraded around the room and then placed on the *bimah*. On the Sabbath, each of the seven readings is preceded and followed by a special blessing; to be asked to recite one of them is an honour.

A regular weekday morning service in an Orthodox synagogue lasts about an hour; the afternoon and evening weekday services (which are usually performed back-to-back) are about half that long. A Shabbat or holiday morning service will usually start early and run for three or four hours; evening services on Shabbat (Friday night) and festivals are about 45 minutes. Conservative services are very similar, though there may be minor variations in the content of the prayers; for example, instead of praying for the restoration of the Temple with its "offerings and prayers," Conservative Jews pray only for the restoration of its prayers. Reform services are usually shorter, but follow the same basic structure.

Tradition teaches that it is better to pray in a group than alone. Thus in Orthodox practice at least ten adult males are needed to make up a quorum for public prayer; this group of ten is called a **minyan** ("number" in Hebrew). Certain Conservative synagogues allow women to be part of the minyan, and Reform Judaism does not require a minyan at all.

In most Conservative and Orthodox synagogues, male members of the congregation wear the skullcap known as a kippah in Hebrew and a **yarmulke** in Yiddish. The **tallit** is a fringed prayer shawl, typically worn by men during the morning prayers (the only time it is worn in the evening is on Yom Kippur). The tallit fulfills the commandment to the Israelites to "make fringes on the corners of their garments throughout their generations and to put a blue cord on the fringe at each corner" so that

they will "remember all the commandments of the Lord and do them" (Numbers 15: 37–41). Likewise, for weekday morning prayer men put on **tefillin** (or **phylacteries**): small black leather boxes containing words of scripture (Exodus 13: 1–10, 11–16; Deuteronomy 6: 4–9, 11: 13–21), which are tied to the forehead and upper arm by leather thongs. Worn in literal fulfillment of the instruction in the Shema to "Bind them [these words] as a sign on your hand, fix them as an emblem on your forehead," the tefillin must be wrapped onto the forehead and arm in a particular way, in order to concentrate the mind, and the box on the arm is then held toward the heart during prayer. Traditionally, only men have worn the tallit and tefillin, but in modern times some Conservative women have begun wearing

© Michele Murray

As this storefront display in Jerusalem shows, the kippah (skullcap; literally: "dome" in Hebrew) can be a colourful and creative vehicle for personal expression, including expressions of support for favourite sports teams.

them as well. In Reform congregations, more and more women as well as men are now wearing the tallit and kippah, although the tefillin ritual is not generally practised by either sex. This could change, however: ritual observance has been increasing in the Reform movement in recent years.

In Reform and Conservative synagogues, all members of the congregation sit together, but Orthodox men are not permitted to pray in the presence of women, lest they be distracted from their prayers. For this reason Orthodox women have their own section at the back or side of the room, or in an upper-floor balcony, that is separated from the men's section by a wall or a curtain. Language is another area of difference. In Orthodox and many Conservative synagogues, every part of the service is in Hebrew, but Reform services in North America are conducted mainly in English— although the use of Hebrew has been increasing in the last decade or so.

Finally, it is interesting to note that Conservative and Reform services are more tightly organized than their Orthodox counterparts. This might seem odd, but in Conservative and Reform synagogues, people tend to arrive at the beginning of the service, and those who arrive late simply join in with the rest of the group. The Orthodox service is more relaxed and fluid, and may even look like a free-for-all to the first-time observer. People arrive on their own schedule and catch up to the group at their own pace, so there tends to be a loud din of both prayer and talk, and a lot of movement as people enter and leave the sanctuary. Still, those who get used to this sometimes say that they find it more natural to pray this way than to try for unison.

Anti-Semitism

In the aftermath of the Enlightenment, the nineteenth century at first seemed to offer Jews a better life: as they moved out of the ghettos throughout Western Europe, they began to participate more fully in the culture and society around them. But a new debate arose over what came to be known as "the Jewish Question." In an 1843 essay on the subject, a German Protestant theologian named Bruno Bauer claimed that Jews as a group were scheming against the rest of the world, and that they were to blame for the hostility they encountered in modern society because they refused to relinquish their ancestral culture. Underpinning these accusations was the long-standing Christian practice of disparaging the Jews as "Christ killers." In fact, European society was undergoing major changes in the second half of the nineteenth century, and with those changes came severe tensions. Workers were beginning to demand more rights as well as better living and working conditions, while middle-class shopkeepers and skilled workers were watching the growth of department stores and factories with mounting concern. Competition among England, France, and Germany was increasing, and nationalism and racism added to the tensions leading up to the outbreak of the First World War.

At a time of anxiety and division, commonalities were needed to bring different sectors of society together, and politicians used opposition to Jews to unify disparate groups in society. In Central and Western Europe, political parties from across the spectrum exploited people's anxieties to gain votes and popular support. No matter how illogical and contradictory the charges, Jews were to blame, whether for Marxism, liberalism, communism, or rampant capitalism. And even if they were not pinpointed as the catalysts behind the unsettling shifts in European society, Jews were said to be completely undeserving of the benefits of emancipation.

Political parties were established specifically to promote anti-Semitism; Jews were openly derided and caricatured in cartoons, posters, and pamphlets all over Europe. Germany produced more of this propaganda than any other country, and the organizations that distributed it were located not on the periphery of society, but at its very centre. In this way anti-Semitic attitudes were made acceptable, even respectable.

The central difference between the anti-Judaism of the ancient world (including that of early Christians) and the anti-Semitism of the modern world was the racial dimension associated with the latter.

In the modern world, Jews were publicly attacked for being racially "other": whereas ancient writers had focused on the distinctive religious practices and customs of the Jews, nineteenth-century propaganda portrayed them as racially alien. Even when they converted to Christianity, they remained racially tainted.

The German writer credited with coining the term "anti-Semitism," Wilhelm Marr (1819–1904), noted that Jewish financial investors emerged from the economic depression of 1873 in better shape than non-Jewish investors, and suggested in his book *The Victory of the Jews over the Germans* (1879) that the problem was not that Jews lacked connection with European society, but rather that they were so well integrated into it that they were taking over. These views were promoted in various ways, including at the First International Anti-Semites' Congress held in Dresden in 1882.

The Dreyfus Affair

In France, hostility towards the changes brought about by the Revolution of 1789 and nostalgia for the strong monarchy, nobility, and church of the past were reflected in anti-Semitic attitudes. French Jews, who had been granted legal equality in 1791, came to be seen as symbols of all that was wrong with post-revolutionary France, and anti-Semitism served as a rallying point for the discontented. In 1894 a Jewish army officer named Alfred Dreyfus (1859–1935) was falsely accused of spying for Germany, based on forged documents and a military cover-up. The "Dreyfus Affair," as it came to be known, was motivated by overt anti-Semitism. Dreyfus asserted his innocence but was found guilty and sentenced to life imprisonment. Four years later, his cause was taken up by the novelist Émile Zola in an open letter ("J'accuse!") to the President of the French Republic in which he charged the French army with a cover-up. The army tried Dreyfus again, and again he was found guilty, but this time under "extenuating circumstances" (Efron et al. 2009: 378). In 1899, after the details of the army cover-up were made public, he was

granted a pardon, and eventually he was restored to his former military rank and awarded the Legion of Honour.

The Russian Context

Anti-Semitism in Russia spilled over into violence. In Tsarist Russia, church and state alike labelled Jews both as outsiders to Russian society and as enemies of Christianity. Jews, most of whom lived in poverty in small towns and cities, became targets of violent popular persecutions called **pogroms**, especially in the political chaos that followed the assassination of Tsar Alexander II in 1881. In southern Russia, Jews were beaten, tortured, and killed; their houses were burned and their businesses ransacked. The government did not organize these pogroms, but neither did it intervene to stop them. Russia's most lasting contribution to modern anti-Semitism, however, was *The Protocols of the Elders of Zion*, a fiction created by members of the Russian secret police, sometime between 1896 and 1898, which purported to be the minutes of a meeting at which members of a Jewish conspiracy had discussed a secret plan for global domination. It enjoyed widespread distribution in Western Europe, especially in the years after the First World War, and was published in the United States by the automobile entrepreneur Henry Ford. Although it was exposed as fraudulent not long after its composition, the document resonated with anti-Semites around the world and is still in circulation today.

Zionism

The pogroms and poverty faced by Jews in Eastern Europe, and the growth of political and racial anti-Semitism in Western Europe, triggered the development of the movement called **Zionism**, which sought to return Jews to the ancient land of Israel to establish a nation there. The idea was not a new one: the words of the Passover Seder, "Next year in Jerusalem," indicate an enduring desire for return to the ancient Land of Israel, whether in the present or in some future messianic age. Zion is the biblical name of a hilltop in Jerusalem that is described as God's dwelling place and is known today as the Temple Mount; the formation known as Mount Zion is a hill just outside the walls of the Old City of Jerusalem. In ancient times the name "Zion" had a variety of associations, and could be used to refer to the land around Jerusalem, the people, or their religious and political traditions.

Jewish Nationalism

Zionism as a political movement was formally established by the Austro-Hungarian journalist and playwright Theodor Herzl (1860–1904) in 1897, following the publication of his book *Der Judenstaat* ("The Jewish State"). Herzl had become persuaded that a Zionist movement was necessary during the Dreyfus affair and the resulting rise in anti-Jewish sentiment, when he was serving as the Paris correspondent of a daily paper in Vienna. In August of that year he spearheaded the first Zionist Congress, held in Basel, Switzerland, which attracted 200 people. Out of that meeting came a platform calling for a Jewish national home in what was at the time Ottoman-controlled Palestine. In 1903 the British government offered parts of Uganda for Jewish settlement, but after some investigation, that offer was rejected. Other places, including Australia and Canada, were also considered. But Herzl insisted that Palestine was the only suitable location, and that the future state would have to be recognized by international law. It was to be half a century before that state—Israel—was established, by which time the need for it could no longer be disputed.

🐾 The Holocaust (1933–1945)

Of all the adversities that the Jewish people have experienced in their long history, the most shattering took place between 1933 and 1945 under Adolf Hitler's National Socialist German Workers' Party, the NSDAP, soon better known as the "Nazi" Party (from the first two syllables of the German

word for "National," *Nazional*). By the end of the Second World War at least 6 million Jews were dead, and the vibrant Ashkenazic and Sephardic cultures established on European soil over the previous millennia had been all but eradicated. Now widely known as the **Holocaust** (from the Greek meaning "whole" and "burnt"), the Nazi program of genocide is referred to in Hebrew as the **Shoah** ("catastrophe").

The Rise of Hitler

In the aftershock of Germany's defeat in 1918 and the grim economic conditions that followed as a result of the humiliating reparations demanded by the allies, the Nazi party attracted enthusiastic popular support. Radical anti-Semitism was central to Hitler's political platform from the start; he placed the blame for Germany's defeat in the war squarely on the Jews, and he was determined to teach them a lesson.

During one of his stays in prison (for a failed attempt to seize power in Munich), Hitler began to write the story of his life and thought. The first volume of that book, called *Mein Kampf* ("My Struggle"), was published in 1925. Hitler recounts how as a young man in Vienna before 1914 he learned about the Jewish conspiracy to use the Social Democratic Party to infiltrate German politics in order to destroy the "Aryan" world. The term "Aryan" was in fact a linguistic term referring to the Indo-European family of languages, but it had already been given a racial meaning by other late-nineteenth-century writers and been used to argue the supremacy of Aryans over people of Semitic stock ("Semitic" too originally referred to languages, such as Hebrew, Arabic, and Aramaic). Hitler associated "Aryan" with purity and "Semitic" with impurity. His goal, outlined in *Mein Kampf*, was first to reveal the threat that the Jews posed to Aryans, and then to destroy that threat. He cast his project as a service to God: "In standing guard against the Jew I am defending the handiwork of the Lord" (cited in Gilbert 1985: 28).

As soon as Hitler became chancellor of Germany, on 30 January 1933, he began enacting legislation designed to overturn the emancipation of Germany's Jews, eliminate them from public life, and divest them of their citizenship. On 11 March Jewish-owned department stores were ransacked in Braunschweig, and two days later all Jewish lawyers were expelled from court in Breslau. On 1 April the government orchestrated a day-long boycott of Jewish-owned stores and businesses, during which Hitler's soldiers, the Stormtroopers, stood with signs advising "Germans" not to enter shops owned by Jews, and wrote *Jude* ("Jew") across their windows, often with a Star of David (the six-pointed star Jewish symbol). New discriminatory laws were introduced almost daily thereafter: on 4 April, for example, the German Boxing Association excluded all Jewish boxers; on 5 April the systematic dismissal of Jewish faculty and teaching assistants at the universities began; on 7 April, the government announced the "retirement" of all civil servants who were "not of Aryan descent" (Gilbert 1985: 36); and on 10 May books written by Jews were publicly burned at universities across the country (Efron et al. 2009: 377–8).

Some Jews began making plans to leave the country, but as yet there was no widespread panic: of the roughly 525,000 Jews in Germany in 1933 only 37,000 left in that year (ibid.: 378). Those who remained hoped that the wave of persecution would subside. Given *Mein Kampf*'s references to Jews as "cockroaches," "maggots," and *Untermenschen* ("subhumans"), they hoped in vain.

A new phase in Hitler's offensive against the Jews was introduced with the passage of the Nuremberg Laws on 15 September 1935. These edicts revoked Jews' German citizenship, deprived them of legal and economic rights, and prohibited intermarriage between people of allegedly "pure" Nordic blood and Jews. On 20 October 1935, the *New York Times* reported that a Jewish doctor named Hans Serelman, who had transfused his own blood to save the life of a non-Jew, had been charged with "race defilement" and sent to a concentration camp for seven months (Gilbert 1985: 50).

Jewish businesses were taken over by "Aryans"—what the Nazis called the "master race"—in two stages. From 1933 to 1938 Jews could "voluntarily" transfer their businesses; then after November 1938, they were compelled to hand them over. Again, many Jews left Germany; but again, many others stayed. Although the Nazis programs also targeted gays and lesbians, Roma (Gypsy) people, communists, and the disabled, all of Germany's hardships were described as the fault of the Jews alone.

The first burning of a synagogue (the central one in Munich) took place on 9 June 1938; afterwards, more than 2,000 Jews were incarcerated throughout Germany. In October of the same year, approximately 17,000 Polish Jews were expelled from German territory; Poland then refused them entry, leaving them in a no-man's land. Barely a week later, on 6 November, 17-year-old Hershel Grynszpan, whose parents had been among the deported Polish Jews, entered the German Embassy in Paris and assassinated the third secretary. In revenge for the murder, Hitler ordered that free rein be given to "spontaneous" anti-Jewish demonstrations, and on the night of 9 November a series of riots took place across Germany that came to be known as *Kristallnacht*, the "Night of Broken Glass." More than 1,000 synagogues were plundered and some 300 burned; Jewish homes and businesses were destroyed by storm troopers and ordinary German citizens. Ninety-one Jews were killed, and approximately 26,000 were rounded up and placed in concentration camps (Efron et al. 2009: 384).

The S.S. St Louis

Thousands of Jews left Germany over the months that followed. In May 1939, the German passenger ship *St Louis* left Hamburg for Cuba with 936 Jews aboard seeking asylum from Nazi persecution. Although all had paid $150 for a tourist visa, on their arrival the Cuban government refused them entry either as tourists (laws related to tourist visas had recently been changed) or as refugees unless they paid an additional fee of $500 each—money that most of the refugees did not have. Captain Gustav Schröder, the non-Jewish commander of the ship, decided to sail to Florida in hopes that the United States would accept his passengers, but ultimately the US too refused, having enacted quotas on immigrants from eastern and southern Europe in 1924.

When the *St Louis* was turned away from the US, a group of academics and clergy in Canada tried to persuade Prime Minister Mackenzie King to offer the passengers sanctuary, as the ship was a mere two days from Halifax. But Canadian immigration officials and cabinet ministers opposed to Jewish immigration persuaded King not to intervene. Among the officials was Frederick Charles Blair, director of the Immigration Branch, who argued that Canada "had already done too much for the Jews" and that "the line must be drawn somewhere" (Abella and Troper 1991: 8, 64).

Thus the ship returned to Europe, docking at Antwerp, Belgium, in June 1939. Various European countries (the United Kingdom, France, Belgium, and Holland) agreed to provide refuge to the passengers, and they seemed to be safe. But in 1940 Germany invaded Belgium and France, putting the lives of all the Jews in those countries in jeopardy. It is estimated that of the 936 refugees who returned to Europe 227 were killed by the Nazis in concentration camps (G. Thomas and M.M. Witts 1974: 135–217).

The Second World War

The Second World War began on Friday 1 September 1939, when, in the early morning hours, German forces invaded Poland. Immediately Poland's Jews were subjected to random public humiliation. By the end of September they were being herded into ghettos that were essentially prisons, surrounded by fences or walls that were locked from

During the two-minute siren that sounds throughout Israel on Holocaust Memorial Day, people cease whatever they are doing—including driving—to stand at attention and honour those who died during the Holocaust.

the outside by German guards. Typhus, tuberculosis, and dysentery ran rampant because of overcrowding and, along with starvation, killed many inhabitants.

In Germany the enactment of anti-Semitic laws continued. Jews increasingly were moved into "Jews' Houses," which were separate apartment buildings; Germans writing Ph.D. dissertations were permitted to quote Jews only when unavoidable, and Jewish authors had to be listed in a separate bibliography. As of 23 November 1939 all Polish Jews over the age of ten were required to wear a yellow badge in the shape of the star of David to identify them, and on 1 September 1941 German Jews were ordered to follow suit.

The Death Camps

To facilitate what they called the "final solution to the Jewish problem," the Nazis built a network of large-scale death camps in Poland. There were hundreds of Nazi concentration and labour camps across Europe, but only six extermination camps, all of them in Poland. The gassing of Jews began at the Chelmno camp in December 1941. One after another, groups of Jewish and Roma prisoners were placed in a sealed van and driven away to be gassed by the exhaust fumes that were channelled back into the compartment where they were held. In this way many were killed, but not fast enough for the Nazis. The first camp to use gas chambers was Belzec, in southeastern Poland, in March 1942. But the largest extermination camp was Auschwitz-Birkenau, where more than 1 million Jews as well as tens of thousands of Roma, Poles, and Soviet prisoners of war were killed using Zyklon B, a cyanide-based insecticide. Up to 7,000 Jews were gassed each day at Auschwitz-Birkenau alone. Scholars estimate that 60 per cent of Holocaust victims were murdered in the six death camps. When it became clear that the allied forces were advancing on Poland in the winter of 1944, prisoners were removed from

Focus

Holocaust Memorial Day

Holocaust Memorial Day, or Yom HaShoah, was inaugurated in 1953. It falls on the 27th of the Hebrew month of Nisan (usually in March or April, according to the Gregorian calendar). Most Jewish communities across the world hold a solemn ceremony on this day, but there is no institutionalized ritual that is accepted by all Jews. In Israel, Yom HaShoah begins at sundown with a state ceremony at Yad Vashem, Israel's official memorial to the Jewish victims of the Holocaust, in Jerusalem. The national flag is lowered to half-mast, the President and Prime Minister both deliver speeches, Holocaust survivors light six torches symbolizing the approximately 6 million Jews who died in the Holocaust, and the Chief Rabbis recite prayers. At 10 the next morning, sirens are sounded throughout Israel for two minutes, during which people cease whatever they are doing and stand at attention. Cars stop and drivers emerge from them, even on the highways, and the whole country comes to a halt as Israelis pay silent tribute to the dead. Ceremonies and services are held at schools, military bases, and other community institutions. Places of public entertainment are closed by law, television broadcasters air Holocaust-related documentaries and talk shows, and subdued songs are played on the radio. In the Diaspora, commemorations range from synagogue services to communal vigils and educational programs featuring talks by Holocaust survivors or their descendants and recitation of appropriate psalms, as well as Holocaust-themed songs, readings, and films.

Sites

The Great Synagogue of Aleppo, Syria

It is hard to imagine today, but the city of Aleppo was once one of Judaism's most important intellectual and spiritual centres. Jews had lived there since biblical times, and the city was home to several synagogues. Although they had flourished in the past, however, life became difficult for Syrian Jews in the twentieth century. After the founding of the state of Israel in 1948, Jews in Syria were not only banned from government employment and political office, but virtually forbidden to leave the country (out of fear that they would immigrate to Israel, and because the president thought that the presence of Jews in Syria would prevent Israel from attacking it). Of all the minorities in Syria they were the only ones to have their religion identified on their passports and identity cards. When the travel restriction was finally lifted in 1992 (at the urging of the United States) an estimated 4,000 Jews immediately left for Turkey, Europe, and North America. By 2011 there were no more than 150 Jews remaining in Syria, most of them elderly and living in and around the city of Damascus.

Before the outbreak of civil war in 2011, the Great Synagogue of Aleppo stood as a testament to an earlier time (its fate as of 2013 is unknown). Peering through the bars on the windows, a visitor could see dusty, broken lamps, and a plaque engraved with the Decalogue. It was in this synagogue that the Aleppo Codex, the earliest manuscript containing the entirety of the Tanakh, was stored for approximately six centuries (c. 1400–1947). When the synagogue was burned by anti-Zionist groups in 1947, the codex was rescued, but it remained hidden until 1958, when it was smuggled out of Aleppo and presented to the president of Israel. Several pages of the codex, however, are missing.

© Michele Murray

the Polish concentration camps and sent back to Germany both by train and on foot; such "death marches" killed approximately 250,000 prisoners. British and American forces liberated the rest of the camps between April and May 1945 (Efron et al. 2009: 385–405).

The State of Israel

When the horrors perpetrated against the Jews of Europe came to light, the United Nations voted to create a Jewish state in Palestine. The decision to provide a physical refuge for the thousands displaced by the Nazis gave hope to Jews around the world. It created a new refugee problem, however,

for the indigenous Palestinian Arab people living in the territory, many of whom would be forced out of their homes. The original UN plan partitioned the land between the Jews and the Arabs, with Jerusalem to be administered by a United Nations Trusteeship Council for the first decade, after which the city's fate would be negotiated. Neither the Palestinian Arab community nor the Arab League accepted the partition plan, and Jewish leaders themselves had reservations, although they accepted it because the need for a Jewish homeland was so great.

The Jewish state of Israel came into being on 14 May 1948 and was attacked the following day by Egypt, Jordan, Syria, and Iraq. This was the start of decades of battles between Israel and the

Sites

Jerusalem

Jerusalem, nestled upon the mountains of Judaea between the Mediterranean Sea and the northern side of the Dead Sea, is one of the most beguiling of the world's great cities. Within its boundaries are monuments sacred to all three Abrahamic faiths (Judaism, Christianity, and Islam). It was this city that, according to the Bible, King David captured and made his capital at the beginning of the tenth century BCE, and in which his son Solomon built the First Temple. Destroyed in 586 BCE by the Babylonians, the Temple was rebuilt under the Persian ruler Cyrus the Great, and rededicated in 515 BCE. But in 70 CE the Second Temple too was destroyed, and now the Western Wall is all that remains of this holy site. The city became a centre of worship for Christians with the construction of the Church of the Holy Sepulchre (begun in 326). Then in 637 Jerusalem fell to the new power of Islam, and in 691 the Muslim shrine known as the Dome of the Rock was completed on the Temple Mount.

Jerusalem has three sections, each possessing its own distinctive character: the ancient Old City

with its four quarters (Jewish, Muslim, Christian and Armenian); East Jerusalem, whose population is predominantly Arab; and the Israeli New City, which is also known as West Jerusalem.

Frequent socio-political turbulence makes the atmosphere of day-to-day life vibrant and intense. Jerusalem is Israel's largest city in both population and area. It is also the country's capital, although it is not internationally recognized as such. The status of Jerusalem remains one of the most contentious issues in the Israeli–Palestinian conflict. During the 1948 Arab–Israeli War, West Jerusalem was among the areas captured and later annexed by Israel, while East Jerusalem, including the Old City, was captured by Jordan. Israel took East Jerusalem during the 1967 Six-Day War and subsequently appropriated it. Although Israelis call Jerusalem Israel's "undivided capital," the international community has rejected the annexation of East Jerusalem as illegal and considers it Palestinian territory held by Israel under military occupation.

Idan Raichel is an Israeli singer-songwriter and musician whose group, the Idan Raichel Project, sings in Amharic, Arabic, Spanish, and Swahili as well as Hebrew.

Palestinians, as well as neighbouring Arab countries. While peace treaties have been signed with Egypt and Jordan, and some of the territory that Israelis gained in later conflicts has been given back, the region continues to be extremely volatile. Most residents of the territory, whether Israeli or Palestinian, now support a two-state solution. Negotiating the boundaries and the security challenges of each state, however, continues to be inordinately difficult.

The electoral system in Israel is based on proportional representation, which means that even the most popular parties never win a clear majority of the seats. Thus to form a government, the party with the most votes must gain the support of one or more smaller parties, usually in return for promises of special treatment. This makes for a rather unpredictable and insecure political system, and tends to give religious parties influence well beyond their size.

In 1950 the Israeli government adopted the Law of Return, which granted "Every Jew . . . the right to immigrate to the country." The Israel Central Bureau of Statistics put the country's 2013 population at approximately 8 million, of whom perhaps 75 per cent are Jews and just over 20 per cent Arabs. In the early years most Jewish Israelis were of European Ashkenazi decent, but demographics have changed and now the majority are of Middle Eastern origin (termed "Mizrachi" since the 1990s). Just over a million Israeli Jews are immigrants from the former Soviet Union; they are now well established in the country both socially and politically, with their own political parties and Russian-language media. Another 130,000 Israeli Jews are Beta Israel ("House of Israel"): Ethiopian Jews, many of whom were evacuated to Israel by the Israeli government between the late 1970s and 1991. Although the process of integration has not been easy, especially for older people, the community now has a strong presence in Israeli society—a presence that is reflected in the fact that popular entertainers such as the Idan Raichel Project now include songs in the Ethiopian language, Amharic, in their repertoire.

❧ Life-Cycle Events

How Jews Deal with Death

Jews consider death to be a natural part of the life cycle. As the Book of Ecclesiastes 3: 1–2 says, "To everything there is a season, and a time to every purpose under heaven—a time to be born, and a

time to die. . . ." Death is to be faced head-on, with unflinching realism. If possible, members of the immediate family should maintain a constant presence in the room of a dying person. The reasoning behind this custom is that we do not enter the world alone, and therefore ought not to depart it alone.

Jewish customs associated with the bereavement process, which are followed rigorously by the Orthodox and to a lesser degree by less observant Jews, are highly structured and serve a twofold purpose. First, they allow mourners the opportunity to express their grief at being separated from their loved ones; second, they facilitate the mourners' return to regular life. Friends and relatives outside the deceased person's immediate family—spouse, brothers and sisters, parents, and children—are expected to comfort the bereaved and provide for their needs.

Pre-Burial Customs

The mourning is divided into two stages: before and after burial. The ritual of *kiriah* ("tearing") is done

Map 3.2 Jewish Populations around the World

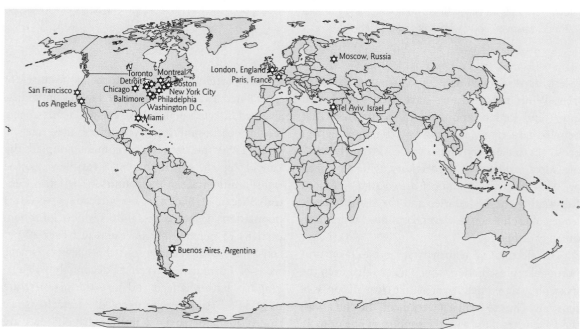

during the first stage; numerous biblical stories describe Israelites tearing their garments to express their anguish and grief—for example, in 2 Samuel 1: 11, when David hears about Saul's death. Eventually this custom attained the force of law, and nowadays Orthodox mourners rend their shirts, while liberal Jews make a tear in a black ribbon supplied by the funeral home. The ripping is done while standing, on the left side when the deceased is one's parent, and the right side for all others.

Preparation of the Body

Jewish law and tradition require that the body be buried as soon as possible after death, preferably within 24 hours. After death, the eyes and mouth of the deceased are closed and a sheet is placed over the body and pulled up over the face. Members of the local burial society then wash and dry the body while reciting prayers and psalms, and then wrap it in a simple white shroud. Out of respect, the body is always kept face up. Care is also taken to ensure that the feet face towards the door, and that any standing water in the house is poured out. The latter customs probably reflect traditional superstitions: in the first case, the belief that if the eyes of the corpse were to look back into the home, the spirit might decide to remain there; in the second, the belief that spirits could not cross water, which meant that the spirit of the deceased could be trapped in the house if there were any water blocking the exit path. Candles, symbolic of the resplendent soul, are lit and placed at the head of the body, and the body is never left alone. Until the time of the funeral, an attendant is hired to stand by and read psalms continuously; Psalm 91, which refers to God taking humans "under the shelter of his wings," is considered particularly appropriate at this time of sorrow and loss.

Burial

No consolation visits are made before the funeral, and there is no public viewing of the body. The deceased is simply buried in the ground, in accordance with Genesis 3: 19: "you are dust, and to dust you shall return." The corpse is not embalmed, as that would be considered a desecration of the body, and if a coffin is used, it is expected to be simple, in plain wood. But coffins are rarely used in Israel: the body is simply lowered into the ground on a stretcher or a bed of reeds. Instead of purchasing flowers for the funeral or for the mourners, comforters will often make a charitable donation in honour of the deceased: Jews living in the Diaspora, for example, will often contribute to the planting of a tree in Israel.

The funeral can take place entirely at the graveside, but part of the service may be conducted at a funeral home. The eulogy, or *hesped*, is an important part of the mourning process, and may be delivered either by family and friends or by the officiating rabbi. A memorial prayer is recited as the congregation stands, and at the graveside the liturgy *Tsidduk Hadin*, "justification of the Divine judgment," is delivered. After the body is lowered into the grave, the first shovels of earth are placed on it by the bereaved, and then the comforters. After the burial, the children of the deceased (in Orthodox families, only the sons) recite the Kaddish: a prayer that is part of every synagogue service, but that since the Middle Ages has also been used as a mourner's prayer; intriguingly, it does not mention death or loss, but praises the name of God.

What if the deceased committed suicide? Since Jewish law forbids the taking of one's own life, it was traditional, especially among Orthodox Jews, not to give those who had committed suicide a full funeral service, and to bury them in an area of the cemetery that was at least 1.83 metres (6 feet) from other graves. More recently, however, as understanding of suicide and mental illness has increased, even traditional Jews have begun providing full funeral services and regular burial for those who have taken their own lives.

Post-Burial Rituals

After the funeral, the mourners and comforters gather for what is called the "meal of consolation."

Document

The Kaddish Prayer

Reader: Hallowed and enhanced may He be throughout the world of His own creation. May He cause His sovereignty soon to be accepted, during our life and the life of all Israel. And let us say: Amen.

Congregation and Reader: May He be praised throughout all time.

Reader: Glorified and celebrated, lauded and worshipped, acclaimed and honoured, extolled and exalted may the Holy One be, praised beyond all song and psalm, beyond all tributes that mortals can utter. And let us say: Amen.

May the prayers and praise of the whole House of Israel be accepted by our Father in Heaven. And let us say: Amen.

Let there be abundant peace from Heaven, with life's goodness for us and for all the people Israel. And let us say: Amen.

He who brings peace to His universe will bring peace to us and to all the people Israel. And let us say: Amen.

In the Talmud, the rabbis stipulate that friends must provide the first meal for the bereaved after the burial of a loved one. Typically the food offered is simple and easy to digest, in order to encourage mourners—who often have no desire to eat, and may even wish to die themselves—to partake of the food and gently to begin to engage with life again.

The post-burial period has three stages. During the seven days of "sitting shiva" (from the Hebrew for "seven"), the mourning family members receive visitors who wish to pay their respects. These visits are considered an important part of the healing process. Typically, visitors stay for no more than 30 or 40 minutes, and their primary duty is to listen: Jewish tradition encourages them to remain silent until the bereaved person has spoken. It is recognized that silence can often be healing and calming for those suffering profound emotional distress. Especially at this time, family and friends try to help the bereaved family by cooking and dropping off food, or taking care of other mundane responsibilities so that the mourners are free to focus on their grief. Mourners do not go to work, and are not expected to keep up appearances: the mirrors in the home are covered to reinforce the idea they need not care about how they look. The women do not put on makeup, and the men do not shave during this time. It is customary (particularly among Orthodox Jews) for members of the immediate family to sit on low stools or even on the floor.

The second stage of mourning consists of the 30 days (including the seven days of shiva) that follow the burial. The bereaved are not expected to abruptly return to regular life after only seven days. For the month of *sheloshim*, the mourners return to work but do not participate in social activities.

With the end of the month, the standard mourning period is considered complete: only the children of the deceased are expected to observe the third stage. A brief memorial service is held, during which a few words are spoken about the deceased and Kaddish is recited; then mourners may return to a full schedule of work and social life. Children of the deceased, however, recite the Kaddish every day for a year. In the Orthodox context, sons are expected to attend synagogue every day to recite the Kaddish, and social restrictions remain in force for both sons and daughters for the entire year.

Mourning rituals do not continue beyond the first anniversary; indeed, after a year, the mourners are expected to return to living a full life. Widows may remarry after 90 days—the minimum time required to determine the paternity of a child born soon after the death of the husband. Widowers are to wait until three festivals pass, or about seven months. The shorter time period for women who lose their husbands probably reflects the recognition in ancient times that women without husbands were particularly vulnerable to poverty.

Yharzeit—"anniversary" in both Yiddish and German—is the annual commemoration of a loved one's death. Lighting a 24-hour yharzeit candle on the eve of the anniversary is a common practice, even among otherwise non-practising Jews, though for safety reasons many people today use electric candles. Typically this ritual is performed at home rather than in a communal setting. However, the name of the deceased is read aloud during a service, and a memorial plaque bearing his or her name is illuminated on the anniversary of the death. Other ways to mark the date include fasting, reciting Kaddish, visiting the grave, and making a donation to a charity in the name of the loved one. To mark their visits to a grave site, Jews place small stones on top of the tombstone.

Marriage

Marriage in Judaism is regarded as a natural and highly desirable state for human beings. Indeed, as we have seen, the rabbis considered Yahweh's very first mitzvah or commandment to humans to be "Be fruitful and multiply, and fill the earth . . ." (Genesis 1: 28): thus everyone is encouraged to marry and raise children. Sexual relations within the sanctified bounds of marriage are encouraged both for the purpose of reproduction and for the pleasure they bring to the couple; as we noted earlier, sexual fulfillment is generally considered something that a husband owes to his wife.

The Ketubah

Jewish marriages are occasions for happy celebration in a framework of religious seriousness and sanctity. A wedding can take place almost anywhere: in a home, a synagogue, a hotel, or outdoors. A rabbi

is present in a legal capacity, to make sure that the marriage contract, called the ketubah, is properly prepared and the appropriate procedures are followed. The early rabbis introduced this contract in particular to protect the economic rights of wives. To provide for a woman in the case of a divorce, or if her husband died before her, the contract would stipulate a "bride price" to be paid to her from the husband's estate. The ketubah also established the dowry (such as bedding and linens) that the bride's family would provide to help the young couple set up a home. Today the dowry and bride-price customs are no longer observed, since wedding gifts and savings are used to help establish new households, and the ketubah does not have much official

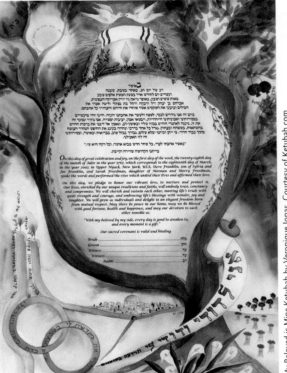

My Beloved is Mine Ketubah by Veronique Jonas. Courtesy of Ketubah.com

A beautiful ketubah is a work of art that is often framed and hung prominently in the home as a reminder of the spouses' vows and responsibilities to each other. Today even non-Jewish couples are commissioning ketubahs.

power in North America, since the legal obligations of spouses are set by the laws of the land. However, traditional Jews continue to sign a ketubah written in Aramaic (the lingua franca in the era when the ketubah was first created), while liberal Jews sign a more modern version of the contract.

Under the Chuppah

For the marriage ceremony, the couple stands under a chuppah, a wedding canopy supported by four poles that may be either free-standing or held by friends. Its origins are not certain, but the chuppah is most often understood to symbolize the home that the couple will create. The canopy itself can be plain or ornately decorated, and is sometimes made of a tallit. In Orthodox and Conservative weddings, the bride and her family circle the groom under the chuppah either three or seven times; this custom derives from the instruction in Jeremiah 31: 22 that "A woman shall court a man," which the rabbis interpreted to mean that she should "go around" him.

Traditionally the ring is placed on the index finger of the bride's right hand, because the index is the most prominent finger and can be seen by the official witnesses to the wedding; and the ring is moved to the more familiar position (third finger of the left hand) after the ceremony. The rabbi, cantor, or friends then recite the *sheva berachot*, "seven blessings," which include a blessing over a cup of wine and expressions of hope for the future happiness of the couple; then the bride and groom drink from the cup.

The conclusion of the wedding comes with one of the best-known rituals associated with Jewish weddings: the breaking of the glass. At Orthodox and some Conservative weddings the glass is broken under the foot of the groom, while at Reform, Reconstructionist, and Humanistic weddings both of the newlyweds typically step on a glass (or sometimes a light bulb) wrapped in a napkin. The sound of the shattering glass is greeted with joyful shouts of "Mazel tov!" ("Congratulations!") throughout the wedding place. The glass-breaking ritual has multiple interpretations: some understand it to be

a reminder of the destruction of the Jewish Temple—and the realization that even in happy times one must be aware that life also brings sadness and pain; others suggest that in the breaking of the glass the couple is reminded that life and love are fragile and must be protected. At Orthodox and some Conservative weddings, the newlyweds spend a few minutes alone after the ceremony, sharing some bread and wine before joining their family and friends at the reception.

Divorce

Divorce is mentioned several times in the Bible (particularly in Deuteronomy 24: 1–4) and Judaism accepts it as a legal institution. The Bible gives the power of divorce to the husband, and today it remains the case that a divorce must be initiated by the husband of his own free will. The husband presents the divorce decree, called a **get**, to the wife. Obtaining a divorce was traditionally rather easy under Jewish law; on the other hand, no woman can be divorced against her will, as mutual consent is required. In practice, divorce is strongly discouraged, and this contributes, at least in part, to the fact that in North America divorce rates are lower among Jews than in the general population.

The text of the get often stipulates a financial settlement and provisions for the return of property that rightfully belongs to the wife. Among non-religious and many liberal Jews, civil divorce is deemed sufficient and a get is not pursued. Orthodox and certain Conservative Jews must obtain a get if either party wishes to remarry; but it is not provided until the civil divorce is completed.

The Agunah: A Woman Chained

The fact that granting a get remains within the power of the husband places certain observant women in a very unfortunate situation. These women are referred to as Agunot (from *agunah*, literally "chained" or "anchored"). Historically, a wife could find herself "chained" to her marriage if her husband had left on a journey and not returned, had died in battle and not been found, or had become mentally incapacitated. Nowadays, many *agunah* cases arise because the husband refuses to grant his wife a get even when ordered to do so by a rabbinic court. There may be several motivations for refusal; for example, the husband might want to obtain a better divorce settlement, or deal his wife a vindictive parting blow.

Focus

The Mezuzah

Many Jewish homes have a mezuzah ("doorpost") affixed beside the front entrance as a reminder of God's presence and God's commandments. This is done to fulfill in a literal way the commandment to write God's laws "on the doorposts of your house and upon your gates" (Deuteronomy 6: 9). Inside the decorative container is a piece of rolled parchment (animal skin) inscribed with hand-written verses from the "Shema" prayer (see box, p. 122).

Photowitch/Dreamstime.com/GetStock

Inside the decorative container of the mezuzah is a piece of rolled parchment with hand-written verses from the Shema prayer. Religiously observant Jews touch the mezuzah and then kiss their fingers as they pass through the doorway.

An *agunah* (a religious woman who is "chained" to her marriage) cannot remarry, and if she were to have a child with another man, that child would be considered a "mamzer"—a child of forbidden relations. Mamzer status is attached to anyone born of incest, of adultery between a married Jewish woman and a Jewish man who is not her husband, or of a parent who is a mamzer. But it is not synonymous with illegitimacy, since it does not apply to a child born to an unmarried woman. Jewish men are not permitted to marry before being divorced either, but because polygamy was practised in the past (even quite recently in certain Sephardic and Mizrahi communities), a child born to a man who has not granted a divorce to his wife will not be considered a mamzer. Although mamzerim (plural) are not disadvantaged in any other way, they do face restrictions with respect to marriage: for example, a mamzer is not permitted to marry someone with a priestly lineage.

Various *agunah* groups have been formed to support women in these painful situations. So far no solution has found widespread acceptance, although the "Prenuptial Agreement for the Prevention of Get-Refusal" is one remedy that modern Orthodox Jewish communities use, and it is accepted by moderate rabbinic authorities as well.

Recent Developments

In the course of its history, Judaism became the foundation for two other major monotheistic religions. Christianity and Islam, like Judaism, are referred to as "Abrahamic traditions" because they too trace their spiritual lineage back to the biblical Abraham. Judaism is by far the smallest of the three, with only 1 to 2 per cent the number of adherents that Christianity and Islam have. In total, there are approximately 14 million Jews in the world, the vast majority of whom live in either the United States or Israel. Each of the latter has a Jewish population of around 6 million. There are about 1.5 million Jews in Europe (including more than

Focus

Conversion to Judaism

Although Judaism, for most of its history, has not actively sought to convert non-Jews, a person who wishes to become a Jew may do so. The conversion process depends on which branch of Judaism one is joining. The Orthodox process is the most rigorous, and can take between one and three years of study with a rabbi, while the more liberal branches typically require roughly one year of study. Ultimately, though, the time required for an individual convert is determined by the supervising rabbi. Rabbinic law establishes three requirements for conversion: circumcision (for men), immersion in a mikveh (the ritual bath), and acceptance of the yoke of the commandments. When the student is ready, the first step for a male is the circumcision ritual. If he is already circumcised, he must nonetheless undergo a ritual in which a symbolic drop of blood is drawn. It may be because of this operation that conversion to Judaism has generally been more common among women than men. A court of rabbis (typically three) is called to meet at the mikveh; if any of the rabbis are not of the same sex as the convert, they gather in a room adjoining the bath. Then, as the convert stands in the water of the mikveh, the rabbis pose questions (if necessary from the adjoining room) to confirm his or her knowledge of Judaism. After the questioning, the convert fully immerses him- or herself in the water and emerges as a Jew to receive the Hebrew name that he or she has selected.

100,000 in Germany), 400,000 in Latin America, and 375,000 in Canada, which has the fourth-largest Jewish population after Israel, the United States, and France. Toronto, Montreal, and Vancouver are home to the largest Canadian Jewish communities (in descending order).

The Jewish Bloodline

One issue of concern in Jewish communities today is patrilineal versus matrilineal descent. According to Halakhah, it is the mother's status as a Jew that determines the status of her children: to be a Jew by birth, one must be born to a Jewish mother. Orthodox and Conservative branches consider Halakhic rules binding, and thus accept a child as Jewish only if the mother is Jewish either by birth or by conversion in an Orthodox or Conservative synagogue. Reform and Reconstructionist Judaism do not consider the Halakhic rules binding. They accept a child as Jewish if either parent is Jewish, as long as the child is raised as a Jew and adopts a Jewish identity. Because different branches of Judaism follow different conversion processes, conversions performed by more liberal denominations are not accepted by rigorously observant groups.

Conversion has been a matter of contention in Jewish communities around the world, but perhaps particularly in Israel, where the Chief Rabbinate, an institution dominated by Orthodox Judaism, has jurisdiction over many personal status issues including marriage and conversion. The Chief Rabbinate does not accept non-Orthodox converts, nor may rabbis perform a marriage involving converts from non-Orthodox branches of Judaism. For this reason many Israelis choose to marry outside Israel, often in nearby Cyprus. Secular Israelis—the majority of the country's Jewish population—as well as Jews from non-Orthodox branches have expressed strong objections to the Chief Rabbinate's strict control over weddings, divorce proceedings, conversions, and rulings as to who qualifies as Jewish for the purpose of immigration. In May 2012, the attorney general of Israel consented to recognize Miri Gold, a Reform rabbi, as the first rabbi of a non-Orthodox congregation in the history of Israel. This means that Rabbi Gold can receive payment for her work, in the same way that thousands of Orthodox rabbis do, and that the state will recognize her as a rabbi. It is believed that this decision will help to pave the way for dozens of Reform and Conservative rabbis in Israel to receive a salary from the government for their work, and that it is a step towards levelling the playing field between the Orthodox and non-Orthodox branches of Judaism in Israel.

Attitudes Towards Gays and Lesbians

Another subject of contention in modern Judaism has been attitudes towards gays and lesbians. Traditionally, male homosexual intercourse has been considered unacceptable (based on Leviticus 18: 22; 20: 13), and this is still the Orthodox position. The Reform and Reconstructionist branches, however, advocate full equality and accept both same-sex marriage and ordination of gays and lesbians as rabbis. The Conservative branch's Committee on Jewish Law and Standards took the same view as the Orthodox branch until recently, but since 2006 has recognized multiple positions in support of its pluralistic philosophy. One position upholds the Orthodox view but another is significantly more relaxed regarding homosexual sex and relationships, although it continues to regard certain sexual acts as prohibited.

The Hebrew Bible makes no reference to lesbianism, and rabbinic tradition considers it a minor offence: an example of immoral behaviour, but nowhere near as serious a transgression as male homosexuality. This is a reflection of the androcentric perspective of rabbinic law. Since, from the rabbinic perspective, the definition of a sexual act is penetration by the male member, sexual activity between women cannot violate the law.

Gender Equality: A Distance Yet to Go

Finally, extraordinary strides have been taken in the last several decades towards full gender egalitarianism. The Conservative, Reform, and Reconstructionist branches now ordain women to the rabbinate and allow full female participation in synagogue worship. Orthodox women, by contrast, cannot become rabbis, they do not count as members of a minyan, and they cannot be called to read from the Torah in synagogue services. Yet increasing numbers are studying Torah with other women—an activity formerly limited to males. As Jewish feminists point out, gender equality means that gendered traditions, images, regulations, rites, and rituals deeply embedded in Judaism must be recreated in the spirit of gender equality. This process of transformation is underway in all branches of Judaism, and is far from finished.

❧ Summary

In this chapter you have learned about the development of Judaism from its sacred beginnings as recorded in the Bible through its varied expressions during the Second Temple period to the innovations introduced in late antiquity by the rabbis. The importance of both oral and written texts was discussed, as well as the diverse types of literature produced through the centuries by Jewish communities. You have also learned about the history of the Jewish people, and their often creative responses to difficult times. Finally, you have seen how the challenges of the Enlightenment and modernity were reflected in the development of the multiple, frequently incompatible, approaches to Jewish law, practice, and identity that are manifest in the various branches of Judaism that exist today.

Sacred Texts of Judaism

Religion	Text	Composition/ Compilation	Compilation/ Revision	Use
Judaism	Hebrew Bible (Tanakh): 24 books organized in three sections: Teaching or Law (Torah), the Prophets (Nevi'im), and sacred Writings (Ketuvim).	Written in the first millennium BCE.	Canon fixed sometime between 200 BCE and 100 CE.	Doctrinal, inspirational, educational, liturgical.
	Mishnah	Teachings of rabbis in the land of Israel between 100 BCE and 220 CE.	Compiled by Rabbi Judah the Prince c. 220 CE.	One of the foundations of Jewish law; the object of ongoing study.
	Babylonian Talmud	Teachings of rabbis in the land of Israel and in Babylonia between 100 BCE and 500 BCE.	Compiled in Babylonia in 6th century CE.	Another foundation of the law; also the object of ongoing study.
	Zohar	Mystical teachings of various rabbis.	Composed/edited in the 13th century.	Study, inspiration, contemplation.

Discussion Questions

1. Explain how Jewish identity can be based on religious, ethnic, or cultural elements—or any combination of them.

2. The Jewish Exile in Babylonia is of paramount importance in Israelite–Jewish history, reverberating in Hebrew literature and providing a framework for dealing with the displacement and feeling of alienation from their homelands that Jews have dealt with throughout their history. How so?

3. How did the Enlightenment affect Jews living in Europe?

4. What is anti-Semitism, and how does it differ from anti-Judaism? What were some of the circumstances in Europe in the nineteenth and early twentieth centuries that gave rise to anti-Semitism?

5. Describe the life-cycle rituals that provide a "framework of meaning" for Jews as they pass through different stages of their lives.

6. What are some of the religious traditions that Jewish women today are challenging?

7. How do different Jewish rituals and practices reflect the importance that Judaism attributes to its historic past?

Glossary

Aggadah Anecdotal or narrative material in the Talmud; see also **Halakhah**.

agunah (Hebrew, "chained" or "anchored") A Jewish woman who is "chained" to her marriage because her husband refuses to give her a divorce ("get"); plural "agunot."

apocalyptic Refers to the belief that the world is under the control of evil forces, but that God will intervene and defeat the powers of darkness at the end of time; from "apocalypse," a Greek term meaning "unveiling" (the Latin equivalent is "revelation"). Apocalyptic literature flourished in the Hellenistic era.

Ashkenazim Jews of Central and Eastern European ancestry, as distinguished from **Sephardim** and **Mizrahim**.

Baal Shem Tov (Hebrew, "Master of the good name") Rabbi Israel ben Eliezer (1698–1760), the founder of **Hasidism**; also known as "the Besht" (an acronym).

bar mitzvah "Son of the commandment;" the title given to a 13-year-old boy when he is initiated into adult ritual responsibilities; some branches of Judaism also celebrate a **bat mitzvah** for girls.

bris The Yiddish form of the Hebrew **brit**.

brit "Treaty" or (most commonly) "covenant" in Hebrew; the special relationship between God and the Jewish people. **Brit milah** is the covenant of circumcision.

cantor The liturgical specialist who leads the musical chants in synagogue services; *hazzan* in Hebrew.

covenant See **brit**.

Diaspora A collective term for Jews living outside the land of ancient Israel; from the Greek meaning "dispersal." The Diaspora began with the Babylonian Exile, from which not all Jews returned to Judea.

Documentary Hypothesis The theory that the Pentateuch was not written by one person (Moses) but was compiled over a long period of time from multiple sources; proposed by the German scholar Julius Wellhausen in 1883.

Exile The deportation of Jewish leaders from Jerusalem to Mesopotamia by the conquering Babylonians in 586 BCE; disrupting local Israelite political, ritual, and agricultural institutions, it marked the transition from Israelite religion to Judaism.

Exodus The migration of Hebrews from Egypt under the leadership of Moses, understood in later Hebrew thought as marking the birth of the Israelite nation.

Gaonim The senior rabbinical authorities in Mesopotamia under Persian and Muslim rule; singular "Gaon."

Gemarah The body of Aramaic commentary attached to the Hebrew text of the Mishnah, which together make up the Talmud (both the Jerusalem Talmud and the Babylonian Talmud).

Haggadah The liturgy for the ritual Passover dinner.

Halakhah Material in the Talmud of a legal nature; see also **Aggadah**.

Haredim A rigorously observant subgroup of Orthodox Judaism.

Hasidism Movement founded in Eastern Europe by the eighteenth-century mystic known as the **Baal Shem Tov**. Today the movement encompasses many subgroups, each of which has its own charismatic leader. The Hasidim (Hebrew, "pious ones") make up a significant part of Orthodox Judaism.

Haskalah The Jewish Enlightenment.

Hebrew Bible The sacred canon of Jewish texts, known to Jews as the **Tanakh** and to Christians as the Old Testament.

Hekhalot A genre of esoteric and revelatory writing produced sometime between late antiquity and the early Middle Ages; the term *hekhalot* ("palaces") refers to visions of ascent into heavenly palaces.

Holocaust The mass murder of approximately 6 million European Jews by the Nazi regime of Adolf Hitler during the Second World War; from the Greek words meaning "whole" and "burnt." The Hebrew term is **Shoah** ("catastrophe").

Israelites The biblical people of Israel.

Kabbalah The medieval Jewish mystical tradition; its central text is a commentary on scripture called the *Zohar*, which is thought to have been written by Moses of León (d. 1305) but is attributed to Rabbi Shimon bar Yohai, a famous second-century rabbinic mystic and wonder-worker.

Karaites "Scripturalists"; an eighth century anti-rabbinic movement that rejected the Talmud, taking only the Bible as authoritative.

kippah "Dome" or "cap;" the Hebrew word for skullcap that Jewish men wear; see also **yarmulke**.

kosher Term for food that is ritually acceptable, indicating that all rabbinic regulations regarding animal slaughter and the like have been observed in its preparation.

Ladino A language composed mainly of old Spanish and Hebrew, spoken by some Sephardic Jews.

Luria, Isaac (1534–72) Influential scholar of the Kabbalah who was born in Jerusalem and eventually taught in the northern Palestinian city of Safed.

Maimonides, Moses Latinized name of Moses ben Maimon (1135–1204), one of the most famous Jewish philosophers and legal scholars of the Islamic age, identified in religious texts as "Rambam" (from R-M-B-M, the acronym of "Rabbi Moses ben Maimon").

menorah The seven-branched oil lamp that has been a Jewish symbol since ancient times, well before the widespread adoption of the six-pointed star; the nine-branched menorah used at Hanukkah is sometimes called a hannukiah.

messiah From the Hebrew *Mashiach*, "anointed [one]." The Greek translation is "Christos," from which the English term "Christ" is derived.

midrash Rabbinic commentary on scripture.

minyan The quorum of ten required for a prayer service in the synagogue. In more rigorously observant synagogues, only adult males qualify; in more liberal synagogues adult women may also participate in the minyan.

Mishnah The Oral Law—inherited from Pharisaism and ascribed to Moses—written down and codified by topic; edited by Rabbi Judah haNasi around 220 CE, it has an authority paralleling that of the written Torah.

Mishneh Torah A topically arranged code of Jewish law written in the twelfth century by **Maimonides**.

mitzvah A commandment (plural "mitzvot"); in the Roman era, the rabbinic movement identified exactly 613 specific commandments contained within the Torah.

Mizrahim Jews of Middle Eastern ancestry, as distinguished from **Ashkenazim** and **Sephardim**.

mohel A ritual circumciser.

Passover A major spring festival that began as a celebration of agricultural rebirth, but came to commemorate the supposed liberation of the Israelites from slavery in Egypt under Moses' leadership.

Pentateuch The Greek name for the first five books of the Hebrew Bible, ascribed by tradition to Moses but regarded by modern scholars as the product of several centuries of later literary activity.

phylacteries The usual English term for tefillin.

Purim Literally "lots"; the holiday commemorating the escape of the Jews of Persia from an evil plot of a Persian official named Haman, as described in the Book of Esther. Haman used a lottery system to determine the date for the destruction of the Jews, hence the name of this holiday.

rabbi Literally "teacher," but by the second century CE the official title of an expert on the interpretation of Torah; once priestly sacrifices had ended with the destruction of the Temple in 70 CE, the rabbi became the scholarly and spiritual leader of a Jewish congregation.

rabbinic movement Legal teachers and leaders who inherited the teachings of the Pharisees and became the dominant voices in Judaism after the destruction of the Temple in 70 CE.

responsa From the Latin for "answers"; accumulated rulings on issues of legal interpretation issued by rabbinical authorities in response to questions from rabbis.

Rosh Hashanah The new year festival, generally falling in September; the day when God is said to open the Book of Life in which he will inscribe the individual's fate for the year on Yom Kippur.

Sabbath The seventh day of the week, observed since ancient times as a day of rest from ordinary activity.

Seder "Order"; the term used for the ritual Passover dinner celebrated in the home; the six divisions of the **Mishnah** are also called orders or seders.

Sephardim Jews of Spanish–Portuguese ancestry, as distinguished from **Ashkenazim** and **Mizrahim**.

Septuagint The Greek translation of the Hebrew scriptures, made in Alexandria during the Hellenistic period, beginning in the third century BCE.

Shavuot A one-day festival (two days in the Diaspora, except for Reform and Reconstructionist Jews) in late May or early June that celebrates the revelation of the Torah by God to Moses on Mount Sinai; also known as the Festival of Weeks for the seven weeks that separate the second day of Passover and the day before Shavuot.

Shema, the The oldest and most sacred fixed daily prayer in Judaism, found in Deuteronomy 6: 4–9; and 11: 13–21, and Numbers 15: 37–41. "Shema" ("Hear") is its first word.

Shoah "Catastrophe"; the Hebrew term for the **Holocaust**.

sidelocks Long curls of hair in front of the ears worn by some Orthodox men and boys in literal fulfillment of the command in Leviticus 19: 27 against shaving the "corners" of one's head.

Simchat Bat ("Joy of a daughter"); the naming ceremony for girls that more liberal branches of Judaism have adopted as an equivalent to the Brit ceremony conducted for boys.

Sukkot The Feast of "Tabernacles" or "Booths"; probably named for the temporary shelters that were constructed by farmers in autumn to protect their ripening crops and later given a historical interpretation commemorating the wanderings of the Israelites in the wilderness after the Exodus.

synagogue From the Greek for "gathering together"; the local place of assembly for congregational worship, which became central to the tradition after the destruction of the Jerusalem Temple.

tallit A shawl with fringes at the corners, worn for prayer; usually white with blue stripes.

Tanakh The entire Hebrew Bible, consisting of Torah (Law), Nevi'im (Prophets), and Ketuvim (sacred Writings); the name is an acronym of the initial letters of those three terms.

tefillin Small black leather boxes, also termed **phylacteries**, containing parchment scrolls on which the words of four paragraphs from the Torah (Exodus 13: 1–10, 11–16; Deuteronomy 6: 4–9, 13–21) are written, tied to the forehead and upper arm by leather thongs.

Tetragrammaton "Four-letter" word, the personal name of the Jewish deity, consisting of the four Hebrew letters *yod, hay, vav, hay* (YHWH); conventionally written as "Yahweh."

tikkun olam "Restoration of the world": the Kabbalistic concept, introduced by Isaac Luria, that the world can be restored through prayer, study, meditation, and the observance of commandments.

Tisha b'Av "Ninth day of Av," a day of mourning for the destruction of both the First and Second Temples.

tzaddik "Righteous person," a title conveying the Hasidic ideal for a teacher or spiritual leader; plural "tzaddikim."

yarmulke The Yiddish word for the **kippah** or skullcap worn by Orthodox Jewish males.

yharzeit "Anniversary" in Yiddish and German; specifically, the anniversary of a person's death.

yeshiva A traditional school for the study of the scriptures and Jewish law.

Yiddish The language spoken by many Central and Eastern European Jews in recent centuries; although it is written in Hebrew characters and contains some words derived from Hebrew, it is essentially German in its structure and vocabulary.

Yom Kippur The "Day of Atonement," dedicated to solemn reflection and examination of one's conduct; falls ten days after Rosh Hashanah, usually in September.

Zion In biblical times, the hill in Jerusalem where the Temple stood as God's dwelling place; by extension, the land of the Israelites as the place of God's favour; in modern times, the goal of Jewish migration and nation-state settlement (Zionism).

Zionism The modern movement, initiated by the Austro-Hungarian journalist and playwright Theodor Herzl in 1897, for a Jewish nation-state in the ancient land of Israel.

Zvi, Sabbatai A student of Lurianic Kabbalah who was declared the messiah in the year 1666; given the choice between death and conversion to Islam, he chose to convert.

Further Reading

Abella, Irving, and Harold Troper. 1991. *None Is Too Many: Canada and the Jews of Europe 1933–1948*. Toronto: Lester Publishing. An eye-opening must-read for Canadians.

Ausubel, Nathan, ed. 1961. *A Treasury of Jewish Folklore: The Stories, Legends, Humor, Wisdom and Folk Songs of the Jewish People*. New York: Crown Publishers. To get a sense of the Jewish penchant for story-telling, read this book.

Baskin, Judith, ed. 1999. *Jewish Women in Historical Perspective*. Detroit: Wayne State University Press. A collection of insightful research.

Berlin, Adele, and Marc Zvi Brettler, eds. 2004. *The Jewish Study Bible*. Oxford: Oxford University Press. The best translation of the Hebrew scriptures currently available.

Biale, Rachel. 1984. *Women and Jewish Law: The Essential Texts, Their History and Their Relevance for Today*. New York: Schocken Books. An excellent source of insight into issues of concern to observant Jewish women.

Brooten, Bernadette J. 1982. *Women Leaders in the Ancient Synagogue: Inscriptional Evidence and Background Issues*. Chico, CA: Scholars Press. Ground-breaking research findings argue against the long-standing assumption that women could not have held leadership roles in the Judaism of late antiquity.

De Lange, Nicholas. 2003. *Judaism*. 2nd edn. Oxford: Oxford University Press. An accessible overview of Jewish history.

Diamant, Anita. 1997. *The Red Tent*. New York: Wyatt Books for St Martin's Press. A historical novel that centres on a minor female character in the Book of *Genesis*; a fascinating glimpse into what life might have been like for girls and women in the time of the ancient Israelites.

Diamant, Anita, and Howard Cooper. 1991. *Living a Jewish Life: Jewish Traditions, Customs and Values for Today's Families*. New York: HarperCollins. An easy-to-read guide written from a liberal perspective.

Goldstein, Elyse. 1998. *ReVisions: Seeing Torah Through a Feminist Lens*. Toronto: Key Porter Books. An insightful, accessible analysis of biblical writings by a female Reform rabbi.

———, ed. 2009. *New Jewish Feminism: Probing the Past, Forging the Future*. Woodstock, VT: Jewish Lights. An excellent anthology of feminist writings from a variety of denominational perspectives.

Greenberg, Irving. 1988. *The Jewish Way: Living the Holidays*. New York: Simon & Schuster. A comprehensive exploration of Judaism through its holy days.

Magness, Jodi, 2012. *The Archaeology of the Holy Land: From the Destruction of Solomon's Temple to the Muslim Conquest*. Cambridge: Cambridge University Press. A lucid, engaging overview of the archaeology of ancient Palestine by a specialist.

Plaskow, Judith, 1991. *Standing Again at Sinai: Judaism from a Feminist Perspective*. New York: Harper One. A classic of Jewish feminism.

Scholem, Gershom G., 1974. *Kabbalah*. Jerusalem: Keter. A survey of the medieval mystical tradition by one of its most respected modern interpreters.

Spiegelman, Art, 1986, 1992. *Maus I and II*. New York: Pantheon Books. A powerful graphic novel that tells the story of Spiegelman's father, a survivor of the Holocaust.

Steinsaltz, A. 1989. *The Talmud, the Steinsaltz Edition: A Reference Guide*. The "go-to" source for understanding the Talmud.

Wiesel, Elie, 1960. *Night*. New York: Bantam. A short, compelling memoir by a writer who, as a teenager, survived the concentration camps at Auschwitz, Buna, and Buchenwald.

Recommended Websites

www.centuryone.com/hstjrslm.html
A chronological history of Jerusalem

www.ushmm.com
United States Holocaust Memorial Museum

www.idanraichelproject.com/en/
Idan Raichel's group performs in multiple languages, including Arabic, Amharic, and Swahili as well as Hebrew, and has been described as providing a "window the young, tolerant, multi-ethnic Israel taking shape away from the headlines" (*Boston Globe*)

www.jbooks.com
The Online Jewish Book Community

www.jewishfilm.com
Publishes an annual list of films concerning Jewish themes and issues

www.tikkun.orgTikkun Magazine
An excellent source of articles on politics, religion, and creating a meaningful life from a progressive Jewish perspective.

http://jwa.org
A comprehensive archive of Jewish women's issues

www.myjewishlearning.com/
Useful information on Jewish life

www.jewishvirtuallibrary.org
A vast collection of information and resources, with more than 13,000 entries and 6,000 photos.

References

Abella, Irving, and Harold Troper. 1991. *None Is Too Many: Canada and the Jews of Europe 1933–1948*. Toronto: Lester Publishing.

Ausubel, Nathan, ed. 1961. *A Treasury of Jewish Folklore: The Stories, Legends, Humor, Wisdom and Folk Songs of the Jewish People*. New York: Crown Publishers.

Efron, John, Steven Weitzman, Matthias Lehmann, Joshua Holo. 2009. *The Jews: A History*. Upper Saddle River, NJ: Pearson Education.

Gilbert, Martin. 1985. *The Holocaust: A History of the Jews of Europe during the Second World War*. New York: Holt, Rinehart and Winston.

Goldstein, Elyse. 1998. *ReVisions: Seeing Torah Through a Feminist Lens*. Toronto: Key Porter Books.

Hallo, William W., ed. 2003. *The Context of Scripture*. Vol. 2. *Monumental Inscriptions from the Biblical World*. Leiden: Brill.

Hertz, Joseph H. 1960. *The Authorised Daily Prayer Book*. New York: Bloch Publishing Company.

Josephus. *Jewish Antiquities*. Trans. H. St. J. Thackeray, Ralph Marcus, Allen Wikgren, Louis Feldman. 6 vols. Loeb Classical Library. Cambridge, MA: Harvard University Press, 1930–65.

Manning, Christel, and Phil Zuckerman. 2005. *Sex & Religion*. Belmont, CA: Thomson Wadsworth.

Murray, Michele. 2004. *Playing a Jewish Game: Gentile Christian Judaizing in the First and Second Centuries CE*. Waterloo, ON: Wilfrid Laurier University Press.

Robinson, George. 2000. *Essential Judaism: A Complete Guide to Beliefs, Customs, and Rituals*. New York: Pocket Books.

Segal, Alan F. 2012. "Jewish Traditions." Pp. 80–139 in Willard G. Oxtoby and Alan F. Segal, eds. *A Concise Introduction to World Religions*, 2nd edn. Toronto: Oxford University Press.

Thomas, Gordon, and Max Morgan-Witts. 1974. *Voyage of the Damned*. London: Hodder & Stoughton.

Twersky, Isadore. 1972. *A Maimonides Reader*. New York: Behrman House.

Wylen, Stephen M. 1989. *Settings of Silver: An Introduction to Judaism*. New York: Paulist Press.

4

Christian
Traditions

Wendy L. Fletcher

Traditions at a Glance

Numbers

2.2 billion around the world.

Distribution

Christians constitute the majority of the population in Europe and the Americas, Oceania, sub-Saharan Africa, Russia, and the Philippines, and nearly a quarter of the population of Asia.

Founders and Leaders

Founded by the followers of Jesus of Nazareth, called the Christ, on the basis of his teachings and resurrection. Among the early founders, the Apostles Peter and Paul were especially important.

Deity

One God, called "God" or "Lord."

Authoritative Texts

The Christian Bible consists of the Old Testament (the Hebrew Bible) and the New Testament. The Roman Catholic and Orthodox churches include as part of the Old Testament a number of books from the Septuagint (the Greek translation of the Hebrew Bible) that Protestants set apart as Apocrypha. In addition, Roman Catholics hold the teaching office (magisterium) of the Church to be authoritative.

Noteworthy Teachings

According to the doctrine of the Trinity, the One God exists in three persons, as Father, Son, and Holy Spirit. Jesus, the second person of the Trinity, is truly God as well as truly man, and his resurrection is the sign that those who believe in him will have eternal life. The authority of the Church has been passed down from the Apostles.

In this chapter you will learn about:

- The development of Christianity from the beginnings of the Jesus movement through the Greco-Roman period to the modern era
- The Christian literature, including the Gospels, Paul, and theological writings from different periods of Christian history
- Issues relating to Church structure: governance, authority, the relationship between Church and state
- The debate over "right belief," which occupied the first several councils of the Church, concluding with the Council of Chalcedon in 451
- How Christians use outward expressions, such as liturgy, art, and architecture, to express their faith and theological beliefs
- The changing role of women in the Church
- How Christianity has adapted to the challenges of the modern era.

Christianity as we know it today is the product of what could be characterized as a 2,000-year-long conversation in diversity. From its beginnings as a small movement within Palestinian Judaism, Christianity has grown to become the world's largest religion. But it is far from homogeneous. Comprising more than 25,000 distinct denominational groups whose ethnic and cultural diversity reflects its wide geographic distribution, today's Christianity is a study in complexity and adaptation. This is not new. From the beginning, Christianity has evolved through negotiation of difference in belief, practice, and ecclesiastical form.

Those who identify themselves as Christians profess the faith commitment that Jesus of Nazareth was the Son of God, both human and divine, the lord and saviour of the world; that he died on a cross for the sins of all; and that he was resurrected two days later, demonstrating the power of God over death. From these propositions an "atonement theology" was developed, according to which

Christ in Majesty: detail of a thirteenth-century mosaic in Hagia Sophia, Istanbul (© Cultura Creative (RF)/Alamy).

Jesus' suffering and death atoned for the sins of the world and in so doing reconciled humanity with God, thus assuring the possibility of what Christians call salvation: going home to God after death. What that faith commitment means and how it is expressed vary widely, depending on period in history, socio-political context, geographical location, theological perspective, and cultural-ethnic identity. Nevertheless, there are two rituals that virtually all Christians practise. These rituals, known as **sacraments** (outward and visible signs of God's grace and action among them), are **baptism**, the rite of initiation into the community, and the **Eucharist** (also known as Holy Communion or the Mass), which commemorates the last meal that Jesus shared with his disciples before his death.

❧ Origins

Given the importance of the figure of Jesus to Christianity, some consideration of his life and work is a necessary starting point. There is very little that we can say definitively about the historical Jesus. However, it is generally agreed that he was born in Palestine around the year 3 BCE, was raised as a Jew in an Aramaic-speaking family, and began his public ministry around the age of 30. From the **Gospels** written some years after his death, we conclude that he was an itinerant teacher in the prophetic tradition of his day. He both chose and gathered followers who accompanied him as he moved from place to place, teaching and preaching, as well as healing, casting out demons, and on occasion raising the dead—activities that were relatively common for the itinerant religious leaders of the age. At the age of about 33, he was arrested by the Romans and sentenced to death by crucifixion. The nature of his crime is unclear. Pontius Pilate, the Roman official who presided over his trial, found him guilty of nothing. However, those who had handed him over to Pilate insisted he be put to death for the blasphemy of claiming to be the son of God. What distinguished Jesus from other prophetic leaders of his type was his followers' claim that two days after his execution he rose from the dead and showed

himself to them, commissioning them to carry on the work he had begun.

The main sources of information on the life, teachings, and intentions of Jesus are found in the writings that make up the New Testament, especially the four Gospels (Matthew, Mark, Luke, and John) and the Pauline Epistles (letters from the Apostle Paul to the Christian communities around the Mediterranean). The first Gospel, Mark, was likely written at least thirty years after Jesus' death, and overlapping themes, words, and phrases indicate that it was the basis for Matthew and Luke. As a consequence, these three books are known as the "synoptic" Gospels (from the Greek *syn*, "together," and *optic*, "seen"). Although they were named after three followers of Jesus, their actual authors are not known, and it was only in the second century that they came to be associated with eye-witnesses to the events they recount. They were written not to provide historians with an accurate biography of Jesus, but to sustain and inform a later generation of Christian believers. Nevertheless, scholars agree that some of the material they contain does go back to Jesus of Nazareth: sayings, **parables** (simple stories illustrating a moral or spiritual lesson), and accounts of his miracles, as well as stories of his death and resurrection. The fact that the sayings and parables recur, often verbatim but in differing contexts, in Matthew and Luke has led scholars to hypothesize an early common source named Q (for *Quelle*, German for "source"), and has played a key role in modern efforts to discern the historical figure behind the Gospels.

Compared with these narratives, the Gospel of John is a major theological essay. Its purpose is to set out not just the narrative itself but its cosmic significance. Far from simply recounting the teachings and actions of Jesus, the writer of the Gospel of John proclaims Jesus' identity as messiah and saviour. The opening passage makes the author's theological interest plain: "In the beginning," he writes (recalling the opening words of Genesis in the Hebrew Bible) "was the **logos**, and the logos was with God, and the logos was God; all things were made through him" (John 1: 1). This logos is the

Timeline

c. 3 BCE	Birth of Jesus
c. 30 CE	Death of Jesus
c. 65	Death of Paul
312	Constantine's vision of the cross
325	First Council of Nicaea
c. 384	Augustine's conversion experience
529	Benedict establishes monastery
842	Iconoclast controversy ends
862	Cyril and Methodius in Moravia
c. 1033	Birth of Anselm (d. 1109)
1054	Break between Rome and Constantinople
1095	Urban II calls for the first crusade
c. 1225	Birth of Thomas Aquinas (*Summa Theologiae*) (d. 1274)
1517	Luther posts his 95 theses
1534	Henry VIII proclaims himself head of the Church of England
1536	Calvin's *Institutes*
1563	Council of Trent concludes
1738	John Wesley's conversion experience
1781	Immanuel Kant's *Critique of Pure Reason*
1830	*Book of Mormon*
1859	Charles Darwin's *On the Origin of Species*
1870	First Vatican Council concludes
1910	Publication of *The Fundamentals*
1944	Florence Li Tim-Oi becomes the first woman ordained as a priest in the Anglican Church
1948	First assembly of the World Council of Churches
1965	Second Vatican Council concludes
1980	Roman Catholic Archbishop Oscar Romero is killed in El Salvador
1982	"Baptism, Eucharist, and Ministry" (BEM) document published
1984	Archbishop Desmond Tutu is awarded the Nobel Peace Prize for his role in opposing apartheid in South Africa
1988	United Church of Canada declares that homosexuality in itself is not an impediment to ordination
1992	Porvoo Common Statement is signed, facilitating cooperation between a number of Lutheran and Anglican churches
2013	Benedict XVI becomes the first pope in 600 years to resign.

"word" with a capital W, used by John to declare Jesus to be the **incarnation** of that divine Word: "The logos became flesh and dwelt among us, full of grace and truth; we have beheld his glory, glory as of the only Son from the Father" (John 1: 14). As John's Gospel unfolds, Jesus and his followers are continually challenged by Jewish opponents, and Jesus prophesies that his followers will be expelled from synagogues. These details are important because they draw attention to Christianity's origins as a movement within Judaism. For John, the true inheritors of Abraham's faith are those who believe that the Word became flesh in Jesus, that the risen Jesus lives among them, and that it is their mission to declare those beliefs to a largely hostile world.

The Gospels are not journalistic biographies. Their authors selected certain actions, teachings, and events from the life of Jesus to address the early Christian community's need for a context in which to understand the events it professed to have experienced. They took particular care to situate Jesus amid conflict and tell stories that foreshadowed his death and resurrection. The Gospels are especially important for understanding Christianity as it was developing in the second half of the first century.

The second set of writings central to the New Testament corpus is known as the **Pauline Epistles**: a series of letters written by the Apostle Paul to various early Christian communities around the Mediterranean world discussing issues of theology, community practice, and discipline. The man they were named for, who would come to be known as Saint Paul, had a profound influence on the shape that early Christian life took. It is worth noting that Paul (d. c. 35) himself never met the historical Jesus; in fact, he had persecuted Christians on behalf of the Pharisees. But one day on the road to Damascus he was unexpectedly overcome with an experience of the risen Christ, which led him to believe that Jesus was the Messiah that many Jews had been waiting for, the Son of God who had been raised from the dead in order to extend the promises that God first made to Israel to all who believed that Christ had reconciled the world to God.

Not all the Epistles called Pauline are actually believed to have been written by Paul. The undisputed letters—Romans, I and II Corinthians, Galatians, Philippians, 1 Thessalonians, Philemon—emphasize Paul's understanding of Jesus as the Jewish Messiah and divine Son of God whose death and resurrection were ordained by God. By contrast, the disputed Epistles—Ephesians, Colossians, 2 Thessalonians, and the Pastorals (1 and 2 Timothy and Titus)—focus on life in the Church and the Church's place in the larger world, and were most likely written by followers of Paul who wanted to inscribe their interpretation of his message in their own communities. Contemporary with the Gospels, these documents are valuable testimony to the institutionalization of beliefs, practices, and emerging leadership structures. In them Paul's more radical teachings are domesticated. Whereas Paul believed that the end of the world was imminent, the later letters suggest a longer perspective in which that prospect had receded to a relatively distant future.

The Epistles give clear instructions to the early followers of Jesus as to the shape that a Christian life should take. Paul did not write a systematic treatise on his thought: rather, he wrote letters to churches he had founded in order to instruct, admonish, and exhort them to right belief and practice. Since these letters address conflicts related to Paul's teachings, we know that there was a variety of opinions about the meaning of Jesus' life, death, and resurrection. Paul alerts us to some of the earliest features of the new belief system, sometimes quoting hymns to Christ or liturgical sayings that in due course, together with the Old Testament, the Gospels, and other New Testament materials, would become the basis for Christian theology. Paul is a valuable witness to the extension of the Jesus movement through the Roman Empire. Although his beliefs became normative, it is probable that this early period was marked by diversity, conflict over how to understand Jesus' message and intentions, and differences in both ethics and religious practices.

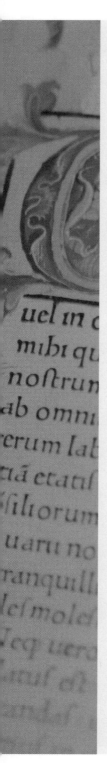

Document

Excerpts from the Epistles of Paul

The uncontested letters of Paul show his mind in action, encouraging and exhorting his readers. By contrast, the contested letters seem more formulaic. The contested passage from 2 Timothy below, for example, casts Paul as a hero looking back at his life and celebrating his faithfulness; it expresses the esteem in which he was held by a later generation of believers. And although the passage from Ephesians presents a version of Paul's thinking about the importance of faith, as opposed to good works, it lacks the long and often complex arguments characteristic of the uncontested letters.

Uncontested

Romans 8: 38 For I am convinced that neither death, nor life, nor angels, nor rulers, nor things present, nor things to come, nor powers, nor height, nor depth, nor anything else in all creation, will be able to separate us from the love of God in Christ Jesus our Lord.

1 Corinthians 12: 27–32 Now you are the body of Christ and individually members of it. And God has appointed in the church first apostles, second prophets, third teachers; then deeds of power, then gifts of healing, forms of assistance, forms of leadership, various kinds of tongues. Are all apostles? Are all prophets? Are all teachers? Do all work miracles? Do all possess gifts of healing? Do all speak in tongues? Do all interpret? But strive for the greater gifts.

1 Corinthians 13: 1–3 If I speak in the tongues of mortals and of angels, but do not have love, I am a noisy gong or a clanging cymbal. And if I have prophetic powers, and understand all mysteries and all knowledge, and if I have all faith, so as to remove mountains, but do not have love, I am nothing. If I give away all my possessions, and if I hand over my body so that I may boast, but do not have love, I gain nothing.

Philippians 2: 6–11 Let the same mind be in you that was in Christ Jesus, who, though he was in the form of God, did not regard equality with God as something to be exploited, but emptied himself, taking the form of a slave, being born in human likeness. And being found in human form, he humbled himself and became obedient to the point of death—even death on a cross. Therefore God also highly exalted him and gave him the name that is above every name, so that at the name of Jesus every knee should bend, in heaven and on earth and under the earth, and every tongue should confess that Jesus Christ is Lord, to the glory of God the Father.

Contested

2 Timothy 4: 6–8 As for me, I am already being poured out as a libation, and the time of my departure has come. I have fought the good fight, I have finished the race, I have kept the faith. From now on there is reserved for me the crown of righteousness, which the Lord, the righteous judge, will give to me on that day, and not only to me but also to all who have longed for his appearing.

Ephesians 2: 8–10 For by grace you have been saved through faith, and this is not your own doing; it is the gift of God—not the result of works, so that no one may boast. For we are what he has made us, created in Christ Jesus for good works, which God prepared beforehand to be our way of life.

Sites

Jerusalem

Jerusalem, a holy city for all three Abrahamic traditions, is sacred to Christians as the place where Jesus died. Tradition holds that he carried the cross along the Via Dolorosa to the hill where he was to be crucified.

An Easter procession along the Via Dolorosa.

Documents Beyond Scripture

Many of the documents that we now rely on to help us interpret the life of the early Christians were not discovered until the late nineteenth century, in the course of the archaeological exploration of the Mediterranean world. These documents shed new light on early Christianity.

The Didache

The document known as the *Didache* ("Teaching"; from the first line in the manuscript: "Teaching of the Lord to the Gentiles by the Twelve Apostles") was probably written in Syria in the first century and is the first known example of a Church Order (a set of instructions for organization and worship in the early Church). Its contents include a **liturgy** (a prescribed form) for the sacrament of the Eucharist in the context of a fellowship meal and prayers that are clearly adapted from earlier Jewish models.

Apostolic Traditions

This work, often attributed to a third-century bishop of Rome named Hippolytus, gives us our earliest example of the full text of a Eucharistic prayer. It indicates that there was still no fixed liturgical form at the time when it was written (215 CE): whoever presided over the ritual could ad lib. It also offers a broad window onto the development of the Christian ministry.

The Apostolic Constitutions

The *Apostolic Constitutions* are eight treatises relating to Church Orders, including teaching on discipline, worship, and doctrine. Although the author is not known, it is generally thought that the text was written by a bishop from Syria, probably in Antioch, in the late fourth century.

Internal Conflicts in the Early Church

It took approximately 400 years for Christianity to evolve from a movement within Judaism to an organized religion in its own right. The process of institutional development involved fundamental questions of identity, authority, belief, and organizational structure, and it absorbed much of the time and attention of early Christians and their leaders.

Jews or Gentiles?

One of the first points of controversy for the emerging religion was the matter of inclusion. Was the Jesus movement only for Jews, or could it accommodate Gentiles? Jesus of Nazareth probably conceived of himself as an emissary sent to Israel alone (Matthew 10: 6; Mark 7: 19–29). But his reinterpretation of the Torah resulted in a radical reformulation of the idea that God's covenant applied only to members of the Jewish community. Paul dramatically expanded Jesus' teachings by interpreting them, along with his crucifixion and resurrection,

Focus

Christian Sacraments

From the beginning, members of the Christian community gathered regularly for worship, prayer, and teaching from community leaders. As well, very early on the Christians developed the rituals that they called "sacraments." A sacrament is defined as an outward and visible sign of an inward and spiritual grace—something you can see in the physical world that demonstrates the love and action of God. All Christians accept baptism and the Eucharist as necessary for the practice of their faith, but the Roman Catholic and Anglican churches

recognize five more: ordination (the setting apart of some individuals for particular work or positions of authority in the community); unction (the anointing of people who are sick or dying); confirmation (the public confession of faith in adulthood by people who were baptized as infants or children); marriage; and penance (the confession of sins and receiving of forgiveness). Most sacraments must be administered by an ordained minister of the Church, and each church has its own laws regulating them.

as part of a universalizing plan whereby membership in the community of the faithful would depend not on adherence to laws at all, but on faith in Jesus (Romans 3: 21–31). By the time the Gospels were written, this universalism had become emblematic for certain followers: Matthew's Jesus commands his disciples to baptize Gentiles and teach them what he taught (Matthew 28: 19); in Acts they are commissioned to be his witnesses "to the ends of the earth" (Acts 1: 6–9). A movement that began with a message directed solely to Israel expanded to embrace all the peoples of the earth as potential followers, with the consequence that ultimately a faith centred on a Jewish prophet was transformed into a worldwide religion distinct from Judaism.

A second point of controversy was whether, if Gentiles were to be included, they should be required to conform to traditional Jewish norms. In this context, the two most critical issues were circumcision and the Jewish laws regarding food and ritual purity. We see these controversies played out most notably in Paul's epistle to the Galatians (c. 50 CE), in which he provocatively calls down a curse on those who require Gentiles to be circumcised (Galatians 1: 9). The Book of Acts (c. 85), attributed to Luke and written by a later follower of Paul, reveals a consensus that neither circumcision nor observance of Jewish dietary laws is required of Gentiles. In Galatians (2: 11–14) Paul accuses Peter of flip-flopping on the question of the food laws, while in Acts Peter champions dispensing with them (10: 9–14; 11: 1–11; 15: 22–9)! The author of Acts reflects a continuing debate over these matters in his own day, and although Paul's interpretation prevailed, the debates continued. Perhaps it is not surprising that a movement that dispensed with the chief markers of Jewish religious and ethnic identity—circumcision and dietary observance—developed into a religion that is not only separate from Judaism but, tragically, has often been actively hostile to Jews.

A member of the Westboro Baptist Church, a Kansas-based independent Baptist group that is notorious for its protests against homosexuals and Jews, pickets a Jewish high school for girls in Los Angeles.

Relations between Church and Society

The religious climate of the age into which Jesus was born was, to a significant degree, otherworldly and escapist. Greco-Roman religion was an amalgam of beliefs and cults from many lands and stages of cultural development. Outside of particular cults, religious practice was largely unorganized, and people were free to worship the gods they chose. However, at the head of the pagan pantheon stood the state gods of Rome, most notably the Emperor himself. This was not an innovation: civilizations of the eastern Mediterranean had venerated their rulers as gods for millennia. Designed specifically to foster the right relationship between the gods and the people, the imperial cult made loyalty to the empire a primary social and religious norm.

As monotheists, Jews and Christians could not acknowledge any god but theirs. Thus they refused to offer sacrifices to the Emperor, and it was this refusal, more than anything else, that led to overt acts of persecution against Christians, particularly in the third century. By refusing to perform this civic duty, the early Christians destabilized the civic order.

Sporadic local incidents aside, the first empire-wide persecutions of Christians began in 250. By that time civil wars, barbarian invasions, famines, and plagues were widely interpreted as signs that the gods were angry at the empire. As a consequence, the Emperor Decius ordered that all inhabitants of the empire make sacrifices to the gods and obtain official certification that they had done so. Christians interpreted this edict as a systematic attempt to enforce universal worship of pagan gods and thereby to extirpate Christianity. Some Christians converted to paganism, others went into hiding, and still others were martyred. Seven years later, in 257, the Emperor Valerian moved to cut the head off the emerging institution by ordering first the deportation and then the execution of many Christian clergy. The result was a serious loss of leadership for the young Church.

On Valerian's death, his son Gallienus ordered the return of deported clergy and the restoration of vandalized churches and cemeteries. Forty years of peace followed, during which time the Church, though technically illegal, was tolerated by both emperors and provincial governors. This made possible a consolidation of the Church's organization, and regular meetings of regional leaders moved the Church towards greater unity.

One last great persecution would challenge the Christians when the Emperor Diocletian took power. In 298 he ordered all members of the imperial court to offer sacrifices to the emperor on pain of flogging. Throughout the empire, soldiers and civil servants were required to offer sacrifices or forfeit their jobs, churches were dismantled, copies of scripture were confiscated and burned, gatherings of Christians for worship were banned, and clergy were arrested.

Constantine

The external fortunes of Christianity underwent a significant change in direction in 312, after the Emperor of the Western segment of the Roman Empire, Constantine (c. 272–337), won a major battle at a bridge over the Tiber. According to legend, he had seen the image of a cross symbol (the Chi Rho) over his head before the battle and taken this as a sign that God would give him the victory. With the realization of that victory, Constantine confirmed his loyalty to the Christian God.

Although he was not baptized until shortly before his death, Constantine's policies became increasingly favourable to the Christians. Beginning in 313 he exempted North African clergy from taxation and used imperial money to enlarge churches, laying the foundation for the accumulation of vast ecclesiastical fortunes. As well, bishops were given the same power as magistrates, and a significant number of Christians were called to upper-level posts in his administration.

Between 320 and 330 Constantine thrust the Church to the forefront of public life, guaranteed religious toleration, and forbade both the erection and the worship of statues of himself, thus undermining the essential political function of the pagan religious system. Later Constantine declared that the Church had the right to emancipate slaves belonging to Christians, and empowered its bishops to exercise juridical authority with reference to litigation among its adherents.

For these actions Constantine has been regarded as the first great Christian Emperor. His impact on the form and direction of Christianity cannot be overestimated. With Constantine Christianity began its journey from persecuted sect to power-holder in Western culture. No longer did affiliation with Christianity come with a negative stigma, socially and politically; now it promised status and opportunity. Membership expanded accordingly,

Portrait medallion of Constantine the Great, c. 320. The Chi Rho symbol (☧) on his headdress is one of the earliest symbols of the cross used by Christians. It represents Christ by overlaying the Greek letters for ch (X) and r (P).

with troubling implications for the climate within a community that until then had been characterized by its capacity for self-sacrifice. In retrospect, many have raised questions about what it meant for Christianity to become a power-holding partner of the state rather than a humble servant of the world.

❧ Authority in the Early Church

With the rapid expansion of the Christian movement, questions of authority became a primary focus. That these questions had been less pressing in the early years was a reflection of the very private nature of Christian practice at that stage. In its infancy Christian worship was conducted in the privacy of the household, as distinct from the public arena of the city. This was the norm in the Greco-Roman period. Even though there were public spaces dedicated to religious expression—temples for pagans and synagogues for Jews—devotional activity was still largely centred in the home. It was only when Christianity grew large enough to take up space in the public realm that formal structures and conventions began to develop.

Authority Structures and Leadership Roles

From the beginning, Christians understood their faith to demand active engagement with the world. To be a follower of Jesus was to live out the meaning of God's commandment to love one's neighbour as oneself. This concrete expression of an internal faith was called ministry. Baptism signalled the Christian's entry into the ministry of Christ himself. In other words, membership in the community of Christians implied living a life of self-giving love, consonant with Christ's own. During the lifetimes of the **Apostles** (those who had seen the risen Christ and received his commission to continue his work), ministry was largely a matter of **charism**: a spiritual gift that surfaced in the context of the local community. By the end of the first century, however, the need for a more structured system of ministry and a recognized chain of authority was evident. To cast the Apostolic and post-Apostolic periods respectively as the age of charism and the age of ministry as office would be to make too stark a distinction; nevertheless, those terms do shed some light on the differences between them.

The early Christians believed that the end times, when Jesus would return in the "second coming," were imminent, and organized their communal lives accordingly. As it became clear that Jesus was not returning in the expected timeframe, a broader vision became necessary, especially as the numbers of Christians and the size of the geographical area involved continued to grow. Together, the external threat of persecution and the internal threat of theological division made it essential for the early Christians to standardize the structures of their institutional life, as well as their doctrine.

The foundational office in Christianity was the **episcopacy** (literally, "oversight"). Perhaps drawing on the historic notion of the 12 tribes of Israel, the writers of the New Testament named 12 disciples (the list of names varies slightly between the Gospels and the Book of Acts) who, having seen the risen Christ and accepted his commission, became travelling evangelists who carried the good news of his resurrection to new regions. As they moved from one place to the next, they appointed local people to oversee the nascent community of believers. These local leaders, or *episcopoi*, were what the early Church came to call bishops. Although there is no record of literal manumission (formal passing of authority through the laying on of hands in the act of ordination to a particular office), this concept became the seed of the Church's structure of authority. The role of bishop as it has been passed on in Christian tradition is to preach the Word, preside at sacraments, and administer discipline, providing oversight for the continuity and unity of the Church.

As the numbers of Christians and Christian communities grew, individual *episcopoi* found that they needed to delegate some of their authority—specifically, the authority to administer sacraments—to others. Those others, appointed for their particular spiritual gifts, were known as **presbyters** (literally, "elders"). Over time, the role of presbyter evolved to become the role of the priest as we understand it today. As late as 416, Innocent I was explaining that in the towns the bread and wine for the Eucharist would be consecrated (blessed) by the bishop and sent to parish priests for distribution, but that in rural areas priests would have to do the consecrating themselves. In the authority structure of the Church, the priest continues to be subordinate to the bishop.

A third office that (judging from the letters of Paul) dates from the earliest days of the Church—even earlier than the office of the bishop—is that of the deacon (from *diakonia*, service). The deacon's work supported that of the bishops and often took the form of service to the poor and the destitute.

Centralized Authority

With regional expansion, it also became necessary to decide how authorities in different parts of the Christian world should relate to one another. Five major episcopal areas or **sees** developed—Rome, Constantinople, Alexandria, Antioch, and Jerusalem—whose authority reflected both their place in the development of the early Church and the administrative structure of the Roman Empire. From the time of the Emperor Justinian I (r. 527–565), the Eastern regions of the Empire generally accepted this pentarchy of authority; however, Rome insisted on its own primacy from very early on.

Conflict was particularly intense between Rome and Constantinople, each of which aspired to be the primary centre of power. The nature of the conflict was both theological and institutional, and eventually led to a permanent schism between Eastern and Western Christianity. Between the fourth and seventh centuries, as the power of the Roman Empire declined, the power of the Church and its hierarchy grew, while in the East, which became the new political centre of the Empire, the world held steady. This meant that the Eastern and Western branches of the Church developed in different directions and ultimately became institutionally separate.

In the East, a system of oversight developed in which the secular emperor was invested with both *imperium* (secular power) and *sacerdotium* (priestly or religious authority). This led to the concept of a single society in which the sacred and the secular lived in harmony, preserved by the Holy Spirit from all doctrinal error and presided over by an emperor who was the earthly counterpart of the divine monarch, God. In the ancient Eastern Church, the term **pope** (*papae*) was reserved for the bishop of Alexandria, but today it applies to all Orthodox priests.

Over time, the bishop of Rome, whom we identify today as the pope or the head of the Western (Roman Catholic) Church, gradually assumed primary authority over all churches in the West. As in the East, however, the word *papae* ("pope") originally referred to any bishop. When the Bishop of

Rome rebuked another bishop for using the title, in 988, it was generally assumed by his peers that he had the right to object, but it was not until 1073 that Pope Gregory VII formally prohibited use of the title by any bishop other than himself and his successors as bishop of Rome. From that point until the Protestant Reformation, Rome's claim to primary authority in Western Christianity was accepted on the grounds that the bishop of Rome was the direct successor of Peter, the "prince of Apostles," who was said to have arrived in Rome as early as the year 42. Although there is little or no evidence to support that tradition, we do know that when Paul wrote his Epistle to the Romans,

Sites

St Peter's Basilica, Rome

St Peter's Basilica is a late-Renaissance church in Vatican City that is one of the most sacred places in the Roman Catholic tradition. The tradition according to which it sits on the burial site of St Peter—the disciple said to have been martyred, along with Paul, during the persecution of 64—makes it a site of pilgrimage for Catholics from around the world.

The famous square outside St Peter's Basilica was designed by the great Baroque sculptor and architect Gian Lorenzo Bernini between 1656 and 1667.

around the year 58, there was already a large Christian community in the city.

The model of Church–state relations that developed in this period and flowered in the Middle Ages was strikingly different from its Eastern counterpart. In the West a fundamental dualism between sacred and secular led to a situation where consistent antagonism between religious leaders and secular princes set the stage for much of both political and ecclesiastical life.

Women in Ministry

As the centre of Christianity shifted from the private household to the public square, the place of women in the Church also shifted, particularly with respect to leadership roles. In the context of the household women held significant authority, in some cases even buying and selling land, orchards, and vineyards. However, the separation between the private and public spheres meant that as ministry and Church authority became more deeply embedded in the public world, the roles that women could fill in and for the Church were increasingly restricted.

In the gospels we see Jesus welcoming women as his followers. The letters of Paul indicate that during the apostolic age women as well as men performed diaconal (service) roles for the community. Individual women were also acknowledged as prophets and identified by Paul as co-preachers with men in the work of evangelization (Acts 2: 17–18). Paul also wrote about the equality of all before God, including male and female.

By the end of the apostolic age, however, it seems that women were expected to be largely silent in worship. The extra-Pauline letters known as the Pastoral Epistles admonish women to be silent in church. And as the three orders of ministry (bishop, priest, deacon) developed, women were excluded from all three leadership roles. Two lesser offices were open to women, however: those of **widow** and **deaconess**.

The earliest known order for women in Christianity, the order of widows originated as a response to the needs of poor widows in the community.

Because the Church supported them, only a limited number of women were allowed to assume the role of widow within the Church structure. To qualify for this designation a woman had to be at least 60 years of age, have no other means of support, have had only one husband, and be known for her domesticity, compassion, and continence (abstinence from sexual activity). In return for support, the widows lived lives of contemplation and intercession, praying for the Church.

Although both took their names from *diakonia*, deaconesses were not female equivalents of deacons, and it was only over time that their role developed into an ecclesiastical office. Different regions had different practices, but it is known that by the third century women were ordained through the laying on of hands in the sanctuary (the area around the altar) during the Eucharist (as were their male counterparts; male subdeacons were ordained outside the sanctuary). Beyond this, we know only that deaconesses assisted with the preparation of female candidates for baptism, visited sick women and children, and prayed for the Church and for those who suffered; and that the office of deaconess had died out almost entirely by the sixth century. Essentially, it was a ministry sanctioned by the Church for women and children. There were no deaconesses in the Greek-speaking world until the fifth century, and even then the category existed only as an honorific title. The idea of women in ordained ministry would not surface again until the nineteenth century.

Ecclesiastical Virgins

In the third and fourth centuries several upper-class Christian women established their own spiritual communities for women. Particularly famous were Macrina, Melania the Younger, and Marcella. These women—some widowed, some never married—used their wealth to support a community of female relatives and friends, as well as orphaned girls and poor women with no means of support, to live with them. The "*mater familias*" was the head of the household and set the rules for the common life to be lived there; in addition to establishing the schedule for common prayer, she determined what kinds charitable work the women performed, as well as the cottage industries they engaged in to support the community. These women voluntarily withdrew from society, and their consecration to the religious life was informal, but their asceticism was often rigorous. Their households existed under the protection of the Church and served as prototypes for the female monastic communities that would emerge in the Middle Ages.

The Development of Orthodoxy

By the end of the second century the Church was developing an institutional form, but it did not yet have a clearly defined system of doctrine and belief. The Christ-centred self-image of the early Church meant that clarifying its **Christology**, its understanding of who Jesus was, would be pivotal to all other theological and doctrinal activity. Passions ran high for centuries as Church leaders and theologians disputed what would eventually become the Church's normative theological positions. Early theological controversies were addressed through the establishment of a scriptural canon, the compilation of **Rules of Faith** based on bishops' teachings, and the use of councils to settle disputes. As we will see, the heresies that engaged the Church's attention ranged across many issues, but all of them in some way touched on the fundamental question of what would be understood as authoritative for the emerging Church.

The Scriptural Canon

To guarantee the integrity of its tradition and preserve its legitimacy as the successor to the Church of the Apostles, the early Church decided to recognize as "scripture" only writings that were associated in some way with an Apostle and were "orthodox in doctrine" (although **orthodoxy** itself was still in the process of being defined). Efforts to verify the origins of the various books under consideration reflected the idea that the tradition of the Church was trustworthy in general, but could be wrong in detail.

Eventually, 27 books were recognized as constituting the official canon of New Testament scriptures. By the early third century, the theologian and biblical scholar Origen was already using the same 27 books that would be confirmed as scripture by **Athanasius**, Bishop of Alexandria, a century and half later, in 367, and Pope Damasus of Rome in 382. It seems that, from the fourth century in the West and the fifth century in the East, there was a general consensus as to which writings would be considered authoritative for the Christian tradition. As well, in both the Eastern and Western traditions the sacred texts of the Jewish people in the form of the Greek translation known as the Septuagint were also considered authoritative.

Rules of Faith

Early in the life of the community, Christian leaders collected the main teachings of the bishops and compiled them as Rules of Faith. This practice was grounded in the idea that the "monarchial bishop" was the guarantor of an oral tradition that could be relied upon. The earliest example of such a rule is found in the writings of Irenaeus, second-century Bishop of Lugdunum in Gaul.

Councils of the Church

Very early in the Church's history, bishops began to meet in councils known as synods to discuss common problems and work out common solutions. The first synod we know of took place in Asia between 160 and 175. In time, as we noted above, five churches acquired special status: Rome, Alexandria, Constantinople, Antioch, and Jerusalem. This distribution of authority would hold over many centuries, even as the Western and Eastern branches gradually evolved into separate entities with their own distinct authority structures: Rome as the centre of the Western Church and the other four comprising key regions of what became the Eastern Church. It was in councils that representatives of the five distinct churches met to settle their theological disputes, particularly in the earliest centuries of the Church's existence.

Four councils held between 325 and 451 are called "ecumenical," from a Greek word meaning "worldwide," because they were accepted by both the Eastern and Western branches of Christianity as part of their respective official histories.

Council of Nicaea, 325

The first significant agreements as to the nature of Christ were reached at the **Council of Nicaea**, convened by the Emperor Constantine in 325. Athanasius and **Arius** represented the two sides of a debate on the question of whether Jesus was of the same substance (*homoousious*) as God the Father or of similar substance (*homoiousious*). The debate was resolved in favour of the Athanasians and a statement of belief was formulated that came to be called the **Nicene Creed**.

Councils of Antioch, 341, and Constantinople, 381

Although it had seemed that the question of Jesus' divine nature was settled at Nicaea, debates continued to rage, particularly in the Eastern churches. The Council of Antioch was summoned in an attempt to reverse the decision made at Nicaea and produce a creedal statement more reflective of the Arian position, but the result was further division in the Eastern churches. Four decades later, the Council of Constantinople also failed to resolve the matter.

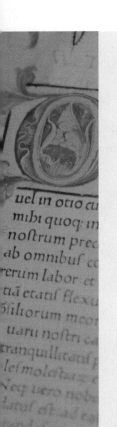

Document

The Nicene Creed

The Nicene Creed affirms the humanity and the divinity of Jesus in one person, as the second person of the Trinity. In so doing, it expresses the understanding of his nature that is shared by all Christian traditions, Western and Eastern. However, the text was modified more than once after the Council of Nicaea, and the version that follows includes three words—"and the Son"—that have never been accepted by the Eastern churches. At issue is the nature of the relationship of the Holy Spirit to the Father and the Son (see also p. 169).

We believe in one God, the Father almighty, maker of heaven and earth, and of all things visible and invisible; and in one Lord Jesus Christ, the only-begotten Son of God, begotten of the Father before all worlds, God of God, light of light, very God of very God, begotten not made, being of one substance with the Father, by whom all things were made, who for us men and for our salvation came down from heaven, and was incarnate by the Holy Spirit of the Virgin Mary, and was made man, and was crucified for us under Pontius Pilate. He suffered and was buried, and the third day he rose again according to the scriptures, and ascended into heaven, and sits on the right hand of the Father, and he shall come again with glory to judge both the living and the dead; whose kingdom shall have no end. And we believe in the Holy Spirit, the Lord and giver of life, who proceeds from the Father *and the Son*, who with the Father and Son together is worshipped and glorified, who spoke by the prophets. And we believe in one holy catholic and apostolic church. We acknowledge one baptism for the remission of sins. And we look for the resurrection of the dead, and the life of the world to come.

[handwritten annotation:] shows of same substance Father, Son, Holy Spirit

[handwritten annotation:] "universal" not capitalized

Focus

Christianity in Egypt, Ethiopia, and Armenia

The indigenous Christians of Egypt, the Copts, believe that their faith was taken to Egypt by the gospel writer Mark, and that their ancestors were pioneers in the development of monasticism (see p. 172). After the Islamic conquest in the seventh century, Egyptians who remained Christian were a minority, but a significant one. The Copts have retained a sense of cultural pride as "original" Egyptians. By the fourth century, Coptic Christian influence had extended to Ethiopia. A few centuries later, Ethiopia gave asylum to Muslim emigrants, but remained Christian, recognizing the authority of the Coptic **patriarch** in Cairo and maintaining a window on the world through its own priests and monks in Jerusalem. The Ethiopian Church has remained essentially Coptic, though it has been formally independent of Cairo since the mid-twentieth century. In Armenia, as in Egypt, legend traces the introduction of Christianity to the missionary activity of the Apostles, in this case Thaddeus and Bartholomew.

Armenian Christians maintain that their king Tiridates III, who was baptized by Gregory the Illuminator around 301, was the first ruler anywhere to establish Christianity as a state religion.

© Philippe Lissac/Godong/Corbis

One of 11 rock-hewn churches on UNESCO's World Heritage list, Bieta Ghiorghis (Saint George's House) in Lalibela, Ethiopia, was carved from volcanic rock in the thirteenth century. It is an important pilgrimage site for members of the Ethiopian Orthodox Tewahedo Church.

Council of Ephesus, 431 *CE*

The Council of Ephesus was convened by Theodosius I in response to a theological movement called **Nestorianism**, which was eventually declared a **heresy** (a belief or practice contrary to the accepted doctrinal teachings of the Church.) Nestorius and his followers argued that the incarnate Christ had two natures, one fully divine (Christ) and one fully human (Jesus), and that the human Mary—the mother of the human Jesus—could not be the mother of God (the divine Christ). The Council of Ephesus decided against Nestorius, and Mary was affirmed as *Theotokos* ("God bearer").

Council of Chalcedon, 451 *CE*

Disputes over the nature of Jesus were finally resolved at the **Council of Chalcedon** in response to the argument, advanced by a churchman from Constantinople named Eutyches, that Christ had two natures (human and divine) prior to the incarnation but only one divine nature after it. His view was a variation on a position known as **monophysitism**, according to which Christ had only one nature (in this case divine). The Council of Chalcedon affirmed the decisions of both Nicaea and Ephesus and adopted as orthodoxy for both the Western and Eastern Christian churches the position known as **dyophysitism**: that the two natures of Jesus, human and divine, are united in the second person of the Trinity. Although monophysitism persisted in breakaway branches such as the Coptic Church, the dyophysite belief affirmed at Chalcedon became normative thereafter.

Other Early Heresies

Nestorianism was not the only movement that came to be defined as heretical as the Church gradually worked out what constituted Christian orthodoxy. Other heresies involved not only Christology but views of salvation and matters of institutional authority.

Gnosticism

Gnosticism was a worldview that influenced many ancient religions, including Christianity. Its root is *gnosis*, meaning knowledge. Based on a radical dualism, which gave priority to reason and spirit over the physical, Gnosticism took Neoplatonic metaphysics as its point of departure for interpreting the relationship between God the Father and Jesus the Son. Gnostics separated the idea of God the creator from God the supreme being, positing that the creator was a lower being or "demi-urge." This idea contradicted the developing Christian orthodoxy of the Trinity, which conceived of God as three co-equal persons of one divine substance: Father, Son, and Holy Spirit.

Among the texts generally considered Gnostic gospels today is the "Gospel of Mary": an incomplete document, discovered in 1896, it recounts the conversation a female disciple had with Jesus in a vision, and the opposition she encountered from some male disciples when she told them about it. Other Gnostic gospels include similar accounts.

Montanism

Montanism was an apocalyptic sect in second-century Asia Minor that spread rapidly through the Roman Empire and in some areas persisted until the sixth century. Its founders, a Christian priest named Montanus and two prophetesses, Maximilla and Priscilla, believed that the second coming of Christ was imminent long past the time when the mainstream Church had abandoned that expectation. Its emphasis on the idea that the end of days was near made it less problematic for women to hold significant leadership roles.

Docetism

This Christological heresy, which developed in the late second and third centuries, held that God could not have been humiliated on a cross, and therefore that the apparent suffering of Jesus could not have been real. The Council of Nicaea categorically rejected this position.

Pelagianism

The early Church taught that the sin of the first humans, Adam and Eve—disobedience of God's command not to eat of the tree of knowledge of good and evil—was passed down to all their descendants, and that because of this **original sin**, no human being was capable of living a moral life without God's grace. The British theologian Pelagius (354–c. 420) rejected that teaching, arguing that humans were not so tainted as to be unable to choose the good of their own free will. His opponents, most notably Augustine of Hippo, believed that Pelagius attributed too much autonomous agency to humans and too little dependence on God's grace, and in 418 he was declared a heretic. Pelagianism was a salvation heresy.

Apollinarianism

In the late fourth century, Apollinaris of Laodicea maintained that Jesus' humanity was not exactly the same as our own, since in addition to a human body and soul, Jesus had a divine mind. This position can be classified as one of the monophysite heresies, denying the two full natures of Jesus.

Map 4.1 The Spread of Christianity

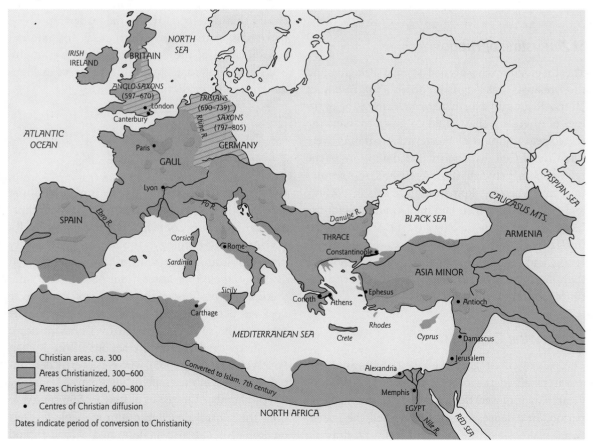

- Christian areas, ca. 300
- Areas Christianized, 300–600
- Areas Christianized, 600–800
- • Centres of Christian diffusion

Dates indicate period of conversion to Christianity

Apollinarianism was declared heretical in 381 by the first Council of Constantinople.

Donatism

Donatism was an institutional heresy of the fourth and fifth centuries, related to authority structures within the Church. The Donatists were a schismatic group from North Africa that had separated from Rome because they refused to recognize as valid consecrations performed by *traditores* (bishops who had recanted their faith during the Diocletian persecutions). The Donatists argued that the Church must be a church of saints, not sinners, and that sacraments administered by *traditores* could not be valid. By contrast, the Roman Church held that sinners could be restored to full communion through penance and reconciliation, and that sacraments administered by restored penitents were valid.

St Augustine of Hippo

The theologian who argued against Pelagius and the Donatists was Augustine (354–430), Bishop of Hippo Regius in North Africa. Among the writings of Augustine that would do much to shape the theological tradition of Western Christianity were *The City of God*, which articulated a vision for the relationship between the sacred and the secular in a time when the Roman Empire was in decline, and *De Trinitate*, which laid the foundations for the basic categories of theology in the West. Augustine's thought in the areas of original sin, grace, suffering, and just war shaped the emerging scholastic tradition, which would reach its full flower in the thirteenth century with Thomas Aquinas.

Gregory the Great

The papacy of Gregory the Great (540–604) was a watershed in the development of the Western Church as it moved from antiquity to the medieval period. In a sense, Gregory embodied the transitional character of the late sixth century, drawing on the traditions of late antiquity while heralding the Rome-centred clerical culture of the medieval West. This is not to suggest that he had some preconceived notion of the Roman Church as the leader of Western Christendom; that idea was developed slowly and hesitantly over the course of several hundred years. However, Gregory's letters do reveal efforts to strengthen Christian authority over secular rulers in the West, to establish bishops as leaders of Christian communities at every level, to eradicate the habits of crass superstition and idolatry that had been retained from ancient religious practices, and to bolster the authority of the see of Rome by promoting the cults of St Peter and St Paul.

Gregory's measures were adopted in piecemeal fashion. They did not constitute a master strategy to achieve Roman supremacy, but his strong stance against temporal authority, his assertion of Roman authority against Byzantium (the tradition of Christianity that developed under the leadership of the patriarchs of the four Eastern sees), his internal consolidation of the bureaucracy, and his careful oversight of internal Church life did serve as foundations for the medieval papacy.

❧ Relations between East and West

Doctrinal disputes related to the person of Christ led to power struggles over primary authority. Although the Council of Chalcedon upheld a non-Arian Christology, the Arian controversy persisted, leading to a schism between Rome and Constantinople that lasted from 486 to 518. After the breach was closed, the bishops of Rome were deprived of the liberty they had enjoyed during the schism. The pressure exerted by Constantinople was sharply reflected in the actions of the Roman Pope Vigilius (r. 537–555), who was overtly deferential to the Byzantine emperor Justinian.

The Lombard invasion of Italy in 586 served to limit the control that Byzantium was able to exert on Rome, but it also inaugurated a long period during which the Roman Church had to cope with a complicated and often violent landscape of secular princes. Rome was no longer under the thumb of Byzantium, but it had to negotiate power with secular rulers from the north and west. This meant that by the early seventh century, the Byzantine Church was more stable than its Western counterpart and had been able to develop its infrastructure, theology, art, institutions, and social mission to a degree that the West had not.

Constantinople and Rome

After the Council of Chalcedon, Greek and Latin Christianity grew further and further apart. The underlying reasons probably had more to do with politics and cultural differences, but once again a theological formulation provided a rallying point. At issue was a single word, *filioque* (Latin, "and the son"). Did the Holy Spirit "proceed" from God the Father alone, as the original version of the Nicene Creed had it, and as the Greek Church continued to hold, or from the Father "and the Son," as the Latin church came to maintain from the time of Charlemagne in the ninth century? Photius, the patriarch of Constantinople, in 867 denounced both the intrusion of Latin missionaries into Bulgaria, which he took to be Greek territory, and the insertion of *filioque* into the creed. For the next two decades, one party in Constantinople repudiated the term and condemned the pope, while another supported the term and condemned Photius. Behind the theological niceties lay the basic issue of authority, for Rome had added *filioque* to the creed without the consent of a universal Church council. In so doing, Rome had staked its claim to be the centre of authority against the Greek view of it as just one among five equally important patriarchates, and the Roman notion of papal authority against the Greek understanding of authority as vested in councils of bishops. The final break between Rome and Constantinople is conventionally dated to 1054, though it was in the making before then and attempts were made after that date to heal it.

The *filioque* was not the only issue that separated the Orthodox and Roman traditions. In addition, the Orthodox tradition venerated icons (see p. 177), permitted married clergy, used languages other than Latin in Bible readings and liturgy, and—most important—refused to recognize the Roman pontiff as supreme.

Eastern-rite Catholic Churches

Rome's efforts to recruit new adherents among Eastern Orthodox Christians led to the formation of new churches that, even though they were aligned with Rome rather than Constantinople, retained important elements of the Eastern tradition, from the use of local languages (rather than Latin) to immersion baptism. Significantly, they also continued to have married priests, although their higher ecclesiastical officers were generally drawn from the celibate clergy. Since most of the Eastern Catholic churches had Orthodox roots, most of them continue to have Orthodox counterparts today. The exception is the Maronite Church of Lebanon. Named after its fifth-century founder Maron, it has always been part of the Roman Catholic rather than the Orthodox world.

🐾 Practice

Worship Spaces

Because Christianity began as a small movement, private dwellings were the logical places to gather for worship organized around a shared meal. Such gatherings usually took place in the larger homes of the group's wealthiest members, although poorer urban Christians are known to have met on the upper levels of the multi-family dwelling spaces known as *insulae*. This kind of domestic worship continued well into the Constantinian era. However, from that point on the worship spaces used by Christians became more diverse.

From the mid-second century, some houses used for Christian worship were re-modelled to accommodate as many as 75 people in a single large room. This type of building is known as a house church (*domus ecclesiae*). As well, rooms known

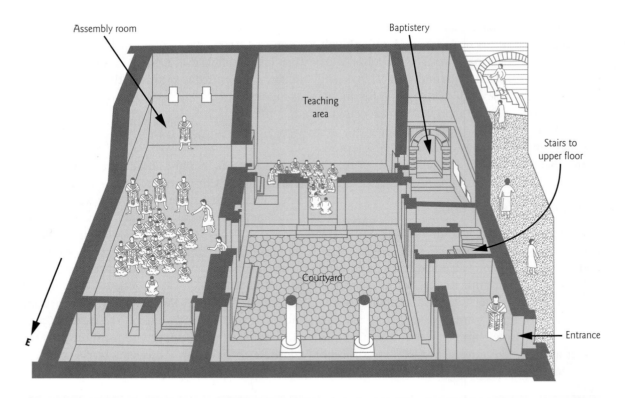

Figure 4.1 Diagram of the house church at Dura-Europos, Syria.
Source: Adapted from http://www.deeperstudy.com/link/dura_church.html.

as baptisteries were added, providing space for full-immersion baptism rituals. The Dura-Europos house church in Syria, built in the third century, is the earliest known example.

Constantine's pro-Christian initiatives led to the construction of much larger and grander worship spaces known as basilicas. (The term was adopted from an earlier type of building used to conduct the business of government.) Constantine had several of these buildings—in the shape of long rectangles with side aisles—constructed as spaces for Christian worship, usually adorned with wall paintings and gilded mosaics.

The earliest records suggest that two rituals with their roots in Judaism were critical to the identity of the first communities: baptism, the rite of initiation into the Christian community, and the Eucharist,

the shared symbolic meal, which became part of the weekly worship life of the community.

Baptism

In the Jewish world of the first century there were several rituals involving the use of water. Some were designed to wash away impurities and restore the worshipper to fitness for contact with God. In Jewish communities outside Palestine, converts to Judaism would prepare for reception in the Jewish faith through instruction, male circumcision, and a water bath. Although the early Christians abandoned the Jewish practice of circumcision, they did retain the ideas of instruction and immersion in water as a symbolic purification in preparation for initiation into the faith. Their baptism ritual also reflected the

A fourth-century mosaic in the basilica of Santa Pudenziana in Rome shows Jesus teaching the Apostles in the heavenly Jerusalem.

influence of two Greco-Roman customs: the newly baptized were anointed with oil, like athletes (Jewish prophets and leaders were also anointed) and given milk and honey, like newborn infants.

In the Synoptic Gospels, the story of Jesus' baptism by his cousin, a holy man known as John the Baptist, is generally understood to signal the beginning of his public ministry. Early Christians developed their baptism ritual in keeping with the story of Jesus' own baptism. It is in the act of baptism that the Christian life begins and the path of discipleship is undertaken.

The meaning of baptism for early Christians is usually understood to have been threefold:

- soteriological (involving salvation): baptism washes away sin
- Christological: baptism plunges us into a new identity in Christ

- ecclesiological: baptism initiates us into a new community, the **Body of Christ**.

Eucharist

We know that the early Christians usually gathered around a shared meal at which scripture was read, prayers were offered, and, finally, the consecrated bread and wine of the Eucharist were distributed. This structure was modelled on that of Jewish gatherings for prayer and worship.

The idea of the Eucharist drew on the Synoptic Gospels' accounts of the night before Jesus was arrested. At supper with his friends, he took bread, gave thanks to God, blessed the bread, broke it, and shared it with them. He then took a cup of wine, gave thanks, blessed it, and shared it with his followers. As Jesus shared the wine and bread he said, "Do this in memory of me." This ritual act of remembering Jesus' life and death became central to Christian life and worship.

Written some time after Paul's letters, the Synoptics reflect the assumption that the last supper was a Passover meal, although it does not follow the pattern of a Seder. Over time, the form of the Eucharist became fairly predictable, and that form was then established as liturgical practice.

Early Christian Art

The earliest art of the Christian community reflects the influence of classical Greco-Roman models. Most of what has survived is funerary art: sarcophagi (coffins) decorated with scenes from Jesus' life, biblical stories of various kinds, and images of the deceased; statues representing Jesus as the good shepherd carrying a lamb across his shoulders; wall and funerary plaque inscriptions with names and symbols such as the Chi Ro; peacocks representing eternal life; doves representing peace and happiness for the soul; the ICHTHYS symbol, representing Christ; portraits of the deceased with their arms raised in prayer; representations of early Christian martyrs; scenes depicting both the last supper and the symbolic heavenly banquet at which Jesus' followers would gather after the second coming. These symbols suggest the frame of meaning that early Christians placed around their practice.

The Rise of Monasticism

As the centuries passed, many churches became substantial landowners and assumed the responsibility of caring for poor members of the community. A career in the episcopate became something to which men might aspire for reasons not entirely religious. Bishops became influential patrons, often interceding with the state on behalf of individuals. From the third century forward, questions began to arise from some quarters within the Christian community: Should the Church occupy a position of influence in places of social power? Could the Church fill that role without losing some of its moral agency and independence?

Figure 4.2 ICHTHYS (Greek, "fish") is an acronym formed from the initial letters of a Greek phrase meaning "Jesus Christ, God's Son, Saviour."

Questions such as these contributed to the rise of the monastic movement. The idea of living under an ascetic discipline was not unique to Christianity. In the Jewish tradition, some Jews during the Maccabean revolt refused to fight even to save their lives; the Essenes were an ascetic sect with a rigorous, highly organized communal lifestyle; and the Therapeutae practised a severe discipline, abjuring money and living in seclusion near Alexandria. Pagan religious traditions had their own versions of ascetic discipline: particularly among philosophers, there were many who embraced solitude, a strictly celibate life, and often a vegetarian diet.

External societal factors also contributed to the rise of the monastic life in Christianity. Because Christians were no longer persecuted, the chances of dying a martyr's death—a prospect that many cherished—were greatly diminished. The crushing weight of imperial taxes drove small landholders to abandon their farms and flee, often to the desert. And as the Empire fragmented, social, political, and economic chaos combined with serious epidemics to create a climate of instability that gave rise to new ways of both surviving and living in community. Among those ways were two streams of monastic life known as **anchoritic** and **cenobitic**.

Anchoritic Monasticism

An anchorite is someone who withdraws from society. The term was commonly used to refer to hermits, people who devoted their lives to silence, prayer, and sometimes mortification of the flesh. The first significant Christian example of this way of life was Anthony of Egypt (251–356). The son of wealthy Christian farmers, he is said to have given up all his possessions at the age of 18 and retired to the desert, where he attracted disciples who joined him in the ascetic life.

Thousands of others, including some women, followed suit. The writings of Evagrius Ponticus (346–399) give us a window onto the life and wisdom of the "desert fathers and mothers." From his work we see that the desert path was understood to be the way of detachment or letting go. Through a life of silence, refusal of illusions and other forms of attachment (both material and spiritual), recitation of psalms from the Hebrew Bible, continual prayer, a simple lifestyle, hospitality, and self-supporting work, those who followed the desert path sought to move more deeply into communion with the heart of God.

Cenobitic Monasticism

"Cenobitic" means "communal." The monastic who chose the cenobitic path lived in community with others committed to the religious life. The founder of cenobitic monasticism is understood to be St Pachomius (290–346), who was raised by pagan parents and experienced a conversion to Christianity in his mid-twenties. He began his Christian life as a hermit on the Nile River in Upper Egypt but felt himself drawn toward community life. Accordingly, he built a monastery, or community house, and many came to join him. By the time of his death the movement or "order" he founded counted nine monasteries and two nunneries. Large settlements that supported themselves on the income produced by a variety of trades and occupations, they became models for the religious communities which would follow.

In communal monasticism the Bible was the foundation of all learning. Every member of the community was under the direction of a senior

Document

The Desert Fathers and Mothers

Although the desert fathers and mothers lived mainly as recluses, they would share their wisdom with pilgrims who sought them out, often in the form of anecdotal stories designed to help the person find his or her own way forward.

Someone asked Abba [Father] Anthony, "What must one do in order to please God?" The old man replied, "Pay attention to what I tell you: whoever you may be, always have God before your eyes; whatever you do, do it according to the testimony of the holy Scriptures; in whatever place you live, do not easily leave it. Keep these three precepts and you will be saved" (Anthony the Great in Ward 1975: 2).

One of the old men said, "When Saint Basil came to the monastery one day, he said to the abbot, after the customary exhortation, "Have you a brother here who is obedient?" The other replied, "They are all your servants, master, and strive for their salvation." But he repeated, "Have you a brother who is really obedient?" Then the abbot led a brother to him and Saint Basil used him to serve during the meal. When the meal was ended, the brother brought him some water for rinsing his hands and Saint Basil said to him, "When I enter the sanctuary, come, that I may ordain you deacon." When this was done, he ordained him priest and took him with him to the bishop's palace because of his obedience (Basil the Great in Ward 1975: 39–40).

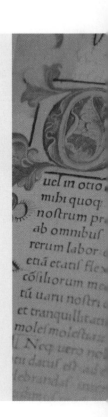

member, and all wore a standardized form of clothing that eventually became known as a "habit." The tradition developed further in the East under the influence of St Basil Bishop of Caesarea (330–379) and in the West under the Italian St Benedict (480–550). Basil wrote a rule (code of discipline) of life that still forms the basis of Eastern monasticism, the fundamental aim of which is to live a common life of devotion to God. Basil's monasteries tended to be small (no more than 40 people) and all property and dress was held in common. No excesses of asceticism were allowed, and local bishops maintained control over orders in their area. Finally, each Basilian community was expected to be of service to the larger community around it.

More than a century later, Benedict developed the prototype for monastic communities in the West. Little is known of him except that he lived first as a hermit, but after twelve monks had gathered around him, he developed a rule to govern their communal life: **Benedict's Rule** was grounded in the principle that the central activity of the community was the divine office: the devotional services held at specified hours throughout the day and the night. As in the East, all possessions were held in common, and moderation and balance were key aspects of the religious life.

⚜ Eastern Orthodoxy

The Cappadoccian Fathers

As important as Augustine was to the Western tradition, so the **Cappadoccian Fathers** were to the development of Eastern Christian theology. The Cappadoccians came from a region of what is now Turkey that was known for its desert monasticism. Basil, the founder of Eastern monasticism, his younger brother Gregory of Nyssa (332–395), and their friend Gregory of Nanzianzus (329–389), who became the patriarch of Constantinople, all made significant contributions to the theology of Eastern Orthodoxy.

As a theologian, Basil supported the opposition to the Arians and their monophysite Christology. He was also known for his preaching, work with the poor, and care for the sick.

The most significant of the three in terms of theology was Gregory of Nyssa. Influenced by the earlier work of Origen, he wrote on the Trinity, universal salvation (the resurrection of all people at the end time), and theological anthropology, defending the capacity of human beings to move closer to God.

Gregory of Nanzianzus was a prolific writer who contributed much to the development of dyophysite Christology and furthered thinking about the doctrine of the Trinity through his original argument for the relationship between the Holy Spirit and God the Father.

The Greek Orthodox Tradition

Most of the Greek-speaking Byzantine (or Eastern Roman) Empire remained orthodox in the terms of Chalcedon's doctrinal formulation: Jesus was the Son of God both human and divine, of the same substance as his Father. The eastern Mediterranean was a comparatively stable and prosperous region in the seventh and eighth centuries, and therefore far more conducive to intellectual life than its Western counterpart, which was still struggling after the barbarian invasions. Byzantium lasted more than 1,000 years after Constantine. Even the slow but steady spread of the Turks, who took control of Constantinople in 1453, did not mean the end of the Greek Church. Formally tolerated under Islam, though now forbidden to proselytize, Orthodox Christians became a self-governing religious community under the Ottoman Turks, with the patriarch as their civil ruler.

Theology

Representative of the eastern Mediterranean's cultural sophistication was the Greek theologian John of Damascus (c. 675–c. 749), who for a time followed in his father's footsteps as the representative of the Christians to the Muslim caliph. His most important work, *Pege gnoseos* ("The Fountain of Wisdom"), is a comprehensive treatise on theological topics. Medieval Byzantine theology included a rich vein of devotional practice and mysticism. Simeon (949–1022), who headed a monastery in Constantinople, wrote of the profundities of the spiritual life. A pervasive theme in his work is God's closeness to the faithful:

> I know that the Immovable comes down;
> I know that the Invisible appears to me;
> I know that he who is far outside the whole creation
> Takes me into himself and hides me in his arms. . . .
> I know that I shall not die, for I am within the Life,
> I have the whole of Life springing up as a fountain within me.
> He is in my heart, he is in heaven
> (McManners 1990: 147–8).

By the fourteenth century a group calling themselves the Hesychasts (from a Greek word meaning "inner stillness") had developed a devotional practice centred on repetition of a mantra-like formula known as the Jesus Prayer: "Lord Jesus Christ, son of God, have mercy on me, a sinner." When their practical spiritual discipline was challenged by Barlaam the Calabrian, a philosopher who held that one could know God directly only in the next life, another great Byzantine theologian came to their defence. Gregory Palamas distinguished between God's essence and his energies, agreeing with Barlaam that God transcends this realm, but arguing that God's energies come through to humans like the radiance of the transfigured Christ described in Mark 9 and Matthew 17. Palamas held divine transcendence and divine contact with humans in balance:

> He is being and not being; he is everywhere and nowhere; he has many names and cannot be named; he is both in perpetual movement and immovable; he is absolutely everything and nothing of that which is (Meyendorff 1964: 209).

Christianizing the Slavs

Eastern Orthodoxy is the form of Christianity that was carried from Byzantium to various peoples in Eastern Europe. Orthodox missionaries to the Slavic peoples made significant headway in the ninth century. Language played an important part in their success, for they used local vernaculars rather than Greek, and this encouraged the development of independent local churches with a strong sense of national identity based on language. This missionary effort was pioneered by two brothers, Cyril (826–869) and Methodius (c. 815–885). In 862 they travelled to Moravia (the region of today's Czech Republic), where they preached in the vernacular and translated the Bible and liturgy into Slavonic. When, after Cyril's time, a new alphabet (based on the Greek) was created for Slavic languages such as Bulgarian, Serbian, Ukrainian, and Russian, it was named Cyrillic in his honour. Romania, which was originally colonized by Rome as the province of Dacia, was Christian from the fourth century and adopted the Latin alphabet, but its church was eventually brought into the Eastern Orthodox orbit during a period of Bulgarian rule. Other parts of Eastern Europe were converted by Roman Catholic missionaries, who instituted a Latin liturgy and more centralized Church control. Thus the languages of mainly Catholic peoples such as the Croats, Slovenes, Czechs, Slovaks, Poles, Lithuanians, and Hungarians use the Latin alphabet.

The early centre of Russian Orthodoxy was Kiev, in Ukraine, whose non-Christian ruler Vladimir apparently converted in order to marry the sister of the Byzantine emperor and thereby form an advantageous alliance. Whatever his motives, he became a vigorous promoter of Christianity, though it seems the methods he used among his subjects may have been more coercive than persuasive. It was only after Kiev fell to Mongol invaders in 1237 that Moscow replaced it as the centre of Russian religion and politics. Russian ecclesiastical and diplomatic interests coincided in the nineteenth century when, as part of its effort to establish a presence in the Holy Land, Moscow established churches and convents while strengthening diplomatic ties with the Turkish Empire. Likewise, Russian political expansion in Siberia was aided by missionaries to the indigenous peoples of the region. From 1917 to 1989 the communist state was hostile to religion of any kind. But Christianity survived, often transmitted from grandmother to grandchild. After 1989, the Russian Orthodox Church slowly reasserted its traditional role as the church favoured by the state, while Catholics and Protestants were allowed more freedom. Since the late 1990s, however, the state has been less than welcoming to foreign missionaries. A 2006 law brought the bank accounts of foreign-backed organizations under scrutiny, in effect cutting off most outside support for missionary work in Russia. In protest against the Catholic Church's "expansionism," the Russian Orthodox Patriarch Alexy II refused to meet with Pope Benedict XVI during his 2007 trip to Russia. Protestants find their religious life even more restricted in the former Soviet republics of Belarus and Uzbekistan.

Secular Yugoslavia disintegrated in the 1990s into religio-ethnic strife among Catholic Croats, Muslim Bosnians and Albanians, and Orthodox Serbs. Today the leadership of the Serbian Orthodox Church continues to espouse Serbian nationalist policies, while the civil government wants good relations with its neighbours and closer integration with the European Union. To appease the influential Orthodox clergy, the Serbian government has introduced religious instruction in the school system, by Orthodox priests or others they approve. In 2006 a law was passed to return the properties of all religious communities previously nationalized under the Nazi or Communist regimes. The Jewish community alone has requested the denationalization of more than 500 properties confiscated during the Nazi period. So far, however, only the Orthodox Church has regained possession of its properties.

Worship in the Greek Church

In the first centuries of Christianity, religious services must have included chanting. The evidence is only fragmentary, but similarities in medieval Roman Catholic, Greek Orthodox, Muslim, and Jewish melodies and harmonies point to a common background, and the signs used for musical notation in the Byzantine era are virtually identical to those recording Jewish cantorial traditions in medieval Hebrew manuscripts.

Many Christians celebrate the eve of **Easter** with a vigil service in which a flame symbolizing Jesus' resurrection is passed from candle to candle among the congregation. The ceremony is particularly spectacular in the Greek Orthodox service at the Church of the Holy Sepulchre in Jerusalem. Hundreds of worshippers, each carrying a candle, pack the church's rotunda. A priest is ritually searched to ensure that he is carrying no matches. He then enters the chamber at the centre of the rotunda, which marks the traditional site of Jesus' tomb. After a time he extends his arm from the chamber with a miraculously burning taper. The people closest to him light their candles from his and then share the fire with others, so that within moments the vast rotunda is a sea of flame. Outside the church, the fire is carried by runners to Orthodox congregations elsewhere. This ritual graphically symbolizes the spreading of the Easter light and the going forth of the gospel message.

Byzantine Art

The influence of the Byzantine imperial tradition can be seen in pictorial representations of Jesus. After Constantine made Christianity mainstream, Jesus began to appear in art not as the young shepherd of the early centuries, but as an older, bearded man, a king or a judge, attired in robes reflecting the dignity of his office. It was also around this time that he began to be depicted with a halo or nimbus representing the glory and radiance of the sun. (Halo imagery goes back a long way: third- to seventh-century Sasanian kings were portrayed with halos; similar imagery was used throughout Asia in representations of the Buddha.) By the sixth century, Byzantine mosaics were depicting Christ enthroned in heaven as the ruler of creation. Usually located in a place of honour, such as directly above an altar, these formal Byzantine representations position Christ in the centre, flanked by attendant figures in a kind of heraldic symmetry. The cosmic-ruler Christ generally has a far more mature and distinguished appearance than the young preacher from Nazareth who was crucified.

Icons in the Orthodox Church

The Orthodox churches developed a distinctive form of portraiture for depicting Jesus, Mary, and other religious figures. These portraits are known as icons, from the Greek word for "image." An icon might be an entirely two-dimensional painting, often on a piece of wood, or it might be overlaid in low relief, in wood or precious metal and ornamented with jewels. While the robes clothing the figure were executed in relief, the hands and face were typically two-dimensional, so that the parts of the image representing flesh appeared to exist on a different plane from the material world around them. Nevertheless, in the seventh and eighth centuries these images became the subject of a heated dispute known as the iconoclastic controversy.

Pitting a faction called the iconoclasts ("icon breakers") against one called the iconodules ("icon worshippers"), the controversy served in part as a vehicle for other antagonisms (political, regional, etc.). But points of principle were also at stake, and Byzantine intellectuals engaged in serious theological discussions concerning the role of images in worship. In the end the Second Council of Nicaea in 787 decided that icons were permissible and could be venerated, as long as the faithful did not actually worship them.

Some historians continue to wonder whether the dispute might also have had something to do with the success of Islam, which rejects any kind of iconography, since the iconoclastic movement seems to have been particularly strong in the regions bordering Syria. In any event, their opponents prevailed in the end, and Eastern Christendom retained its distinctive tradition. In Orthodox sanctuaries today, a massive screen in front of the altar shields it from the main portion of the sanctuary. The

A shop selling religious icons in Monastiraki, Athens.

screen is called an iconostasis ("place for icons") and is designed to hold a row of large icons. Smaller icons are hung in private homes; some, as small as a pocket diary, are equipped with folding covers so that they can be carried on the person, especially when travelling.

Medieval Christianity

Decline and Expansion

The first widespread decline in Christian influence began about the year 600 and continued until the mid-tenth century. It was not rapid, nor was it without spurts of revival, but by 950 Christianity was far less prominent in the West than it had been in 500.

Both internal and external factors contributed to the decline. Internally the Western Church was weakened by poor leadership and various forms of corruption. External factors included the decline of the Roman Empire and the ensuing socio-political and economic turmoil, and Islam's rise to power in various parts of the Euro-Mediterranean theatre.

The rapid spread of Islam following the death of the prophet Mohammad in 632 changed the religious map. After only three centuries it was as geographically widespread as Christianity and was the official faith of states much more powerful than many that professed to be Christian. Byzantine Christianity in particular struggled in the face of Islam.

And then the tide turned. Near the end of the tenth century, the invasions that had racked Western Europe for 500 years simply ceased. There were no further incursions of non-Christians into Western Christendom, even though Muslim populations were well established on the Iberian peninsula. Later invasions by the Ottoman Turks and the Mongols did not penetrate substantially beyond the eastern and southern borders of Europe. The resulting stability was conducive to economic growth, development of commerce and wealth, the beginnings of modern states and an increase in the number and population of cities.

Between 950 and 1050 CE, Christianity made the greatest geographic advances in its history. Scandinavia—Denmark, Norway, and parts of Sweden, Iceland, and Greenland—which had formerly been a passionate enemy of Christianity, was converted. Czechs, Poles, and Hungarians were Christianized, as were all the inhabitants of Kiev, and Sicily and northern Spain were "recovered" from Islam. This is not to say that by 1050 all inhabitants of Western and Central Europe thought of themselves as Christians; Christians co-existed with Muslims, Jews, and occasional enclaves of paganism. By 1350, however, most of Europe had converted to Christianity except for the Lithuanians, the Finns, and the remaining Jewish and Muslim communities in Spain.

In Western Europe, nascent nations were emerging from feudalism. In 911 Germanic tribal princes elected a king; in 987 feudal princes chose a king of France; and in 1066 William the Conqueror began establishing a strong state in England. Across territories previously conquered by Islam, political power shifted from Muslim to Christian rulers exercising political control over discrete territories.

The Crusades

After the Arab Muslims captured Jerusalem in 637, the Christians who lived there were tolerated, and Christian pilgrims from outside the Islamic word were still allowed to visit. In 1071, however, the city was captured by the Seljuq Turks, who as recent converts to Islam were less accommodating than the Arabs had been. The Byzantine emperors felt threatened and appealed to the West for help. In 1095 Pope Urban II responded by proclaiming what would become the first in a series of "crusades" to liberate the holy places of Palestine. Participation was framed as a sacred pilgrimage and encouraged by promises that those who died in the attempt to free the Holy Land would be honoured as martyrs—a prospect that was still highly valued. At the same time, the prospect of worldly adventure and profit encouraged both peasants and nobles to "take the cross."

In all, the Crusades spanned nearly four centuries, but the most significant period ended in 1204, when crusaders headed for Egypt attacked the Christian city of Constantinople instead, plundering it and placing a ruler from Flanders on the throne. Although the Byzantines recaptured the city in 1261, relations between Western and Eastern Christians did not recover.

Punishing Heresy

The use of violence by the Church in the Middle Ages was not limited to action against "infidels" (non-Christians). Beginning in the thirteenth century, the Church also undertook to discover and punish those—theologians and ordinary believers—whose views differed from Church teaching. This chapter in Christian history is known as the time of the Inquisitions. Like the Crusades, the Inquisitions unfolded in various regions over hundreds of years. Until the twelfth century the punishment for heresy was excommunication: exclusion from participation in the Christian community. By the early thirteenth century, however, the attitude of the Church had changed, largely because the secular powers were now closely aligned with it in maintaining the social order. This gave the Church access to state power, including military power, to enforce its decisions.

The first Inquisition was established in 1232, after the Emperor Frederick II issued an edict entrusting the hunt for heretics to state officials. Pope Gregory IX, fearing Frederick's ambitions, claimed this responsibility for the Church and appointed papal inquisitors to travel the countryside admonishing those guilty of heresy to confess voluntarily, in which case they would be required to do penance. After about a month of grace during which the accused were given the opportunity to confess, actual trials began. The Inquisitor was assisted by a jury and evidence was heard from at least two witnesses. (The famous Spanish Inquisition had a different character, as it was established by the state specifically to investigate Jewish and Muslim converts to Christianity. Its grand inquisitor, Tomás de Torquemada, ordered more than 2,000 executions and was a major force behind the expulsion of the Jews and Muslims from Spain in 1492.) Penalties for those found guilty of heresy ranged from confiscation of goods to imprisonment to, in the worst case, execution; those sentenced to death were handed over to secular authorities and burned at the stake.

The Inquisition in Toulouse, France, established a trial procedure that lasted for centuries. Those accused of heresy, even by anonymous informers, were presumed guilty unless they could prove their innocence. Those who confessed were assigned penances and penalties, but those who maintained their innocence were returned to prison to "discover" their heresy. In 1252 Pope Innocent IV ruled that torture could be used and that heretics handed over to the secular authorities should be executed within five days.

The same pope who made Torquemada the Grand Inquisitor, Innocent VIII, issued a papal bull calling for the eradication of witchcraft. To that end, a German Dominican named Heinrich Kraemer, with the assistance of Johann Sprenger, published a handbook for Christian witch-hunting entitled the *Malleus Maleficarum* ("Hammer of Witches") in 1486. Peasant superstition contributed to the tendency to identify certain individuals as practitioners of malevolent magic, agents of the devil who had intimate sexual relations with him. Often, personal grudges led to accusations of witchcraft. In sixteenth- and seventeenth-century England, the most frequent charge was that the alleged witch, usually a neighbour, often an old woman, had caused some misfortune to befall the accuser. Widows and women with knowledge of herbal cures were particularly likely to attract accusations of witchcraft. (It's possible that the symptoms of "demonic possession" suffered by some accusers may have been physiological; records of the witchcraft trials of 1692 in Salem, Massachusetts, have suggested to some modern researchers that the accusers were accidentally poisoned by ergot—a grain fungus that produces a hallucinogen similar to LSD. People who ingest ergot-infected grain often die, but those who survive report strange experiences and wild visions.)

Development of Papal Authority

Innocent III

One of the most significant popes of the Middle Ages was Innocent III (c. 1160–1216). After several weak predecessors, he asserted the authority of the papacy over secular power, and under his leadership, the activities of the Church became more organized. There was a rapid development of the bureaucracy and systems of ecclesiastical government. The papacy became a consultative focal point for the Church, maintaining communication with churchmen across Europe, Byzantium, and Russia.

Boniface VIII

By the later Middle Ages, however, the pope and Church councils were competing for power and authority within the Church. This also implied a contest with the secular authority as councils allowed opportunities for secular challenges to papal authority.

Some of the strongest claims for papal authority in the temporal as well as the spiritual realm were made by Pope Boniface VIII (1235–1303). He immediately asserted his authority by imprisoning his ineffectual predecessor, who had resigned, and involving himself in foreign affairs of a secular nature. In the papal bull *Unam Sanctam*, issued in 1302, Boniface proclaimed it "absolutely necessary for salvation that every human creature be subject to the Roman pontiff." This pronouncement, along with Boniface's involvement in secular matters, led to conflict with secular rulers, most notably King Philip IV of France.

During this period the monarchs of Europe were competing for power, and the kings of both England and France decreed that Church revenues in their countries should be used to support their respective governments (and help pay for

their wars against one another). Boniface issued the bull *Clericos Laicos* (1296), in an effort to prevent these kings from appropriating Church monies, but both Philip IV of France and Edward I of England asserted their higher authority to exact tax from the Church. In response to *Clericos Laicos*, Philip prohibited the export of gold, silver, precious stones, or food from France to the Papal States, which cut off major revenue sources for the papacy. Eventually a more moderate bull, *Etsi de Statu* (1297) decreed that kings could tax the Church in an emergency. Despite the compromise, this struggle demonstrates the extent to which the struggle for pre-eminence between Church and state occupied the medieval imagination.

The Avignon Papacy

When Boniface's successor died after only eight months in office, the conclave to choose his successor was deadlocked for nearly a year before finally electing Clement V in 1305. Clement, who was French, refused to move to Rome and had the papal court moved to Avignon in southern France. The Avignon period, sometimes known as the Babylonian captivity, continued for 67 years, during which papal administration was increasingly influenced by the French Crown.

Finally in 1377 Pope Gregory XI chose to return the papacy to Rome. On his death, however, the cardinals (senior clergy) established a second line of popes while Urban remained in Rome. Although the Church considered them illegitimate, the new Avignon pope and his successor were able to stay in power until 1398, when the latter lost the support of the French king. The "Western schism" would not be officially brought to an end until in 1417, at the Council of Constance.

The Conciliar Movement

The Avignon years gave rise to a critique of papal authority in the Church itself. For example, a theologian named Marsilius of Padua (1290–1343) held that the pope could teach salvation and right behaviour but had no right to command obedience. Speaking against the misuse of papal power, he argued that the Apostles elected Peter as their spokesperson, not as the all-powerful authority that the bishop of Rome had become. Marsilius took the view that power flowed from God to the people and from the people to the king in the realm of worldly affairs and to the pope with reference to spiritual matters.

With Marsilius we see the kernel of medieval conciliar theory, according to which the councils of the Church represented the people and the popes depended on the councils for their power. In the old model, God invested both spiritual and worldly authority in the pope, who in turn invested worldly power in the secular ruler; then the two of them, each in his own sphere, ruled the people. In the new model, the direction was reversed so that power travelled from God to the people through the councils to the pope.

It was the Council of Constance that, with the decree *Sacrosancta* (1415), declared the council itself the supreme authority within the Church. It then used its new power to demonstrate conciliar authority over the papacy, deposing the competing popes and electing a single successor. Concluding that the only guarantees of reform in the Church were constant vigilance and frequent communication, the Constance council also decreed that a new council should be called within five to seven years and every ten years thereafter.

The conciliar theory did not mean lay enfranchisement. However, it did provide for a more broadly based sharing of power. The relationship between the councils of the Church and the Pope after the investiture of authority was not clear; the theory was never fully developed as a working model of power sharing and accountability; and the movement was crushed by a revived papal monarchy by the mid-fifteenth century. Nevertheless, the Council of Constance would influence both the development of representative governments in emerging nation-states and the thinking of religious reformers, both inside and outside the Catholic Church, over the centuries that followed.

The more radical Council of Basel in 1431 introduced a model of the people's right to enforce standards of conduct on both political and religious rulers. The paradox of this model was that leaders within the conciliar movement were committed to strong papal authority, as is reflected by the fact that a council was used to depose a pope only as a last resort. Interestingly, canon law, as a mirror of Roman law, had always anticipated the possibility of clerical abuses and had preserved the principle that the people were the ultimate source of a ruler's absolute power.

Reason and Revelation

The most critical intellectual issue of the Middle Ages was framed as an epistemological question: How do we know what we know? That question was answered by two competing (or complementary) perspectives: scholasticism and mysticism.

Scholasticism

Scholasticism was a school of thought that developed in an effort to reconcile the philosophy of ancient Greece and then Rome with Christian theology. In effect, it was a method of philosophical and theological speculation that came to characterize medieval learning. Institutionally, scholasticism is defined as the teaching of the clergy in the "schools"—that is, the emerging universities. Theology was a central part of the curriculum in the great schools of Paris, Bologna, and Oxford. The clerical foundations of scholarship, 1,000 years ago, are reflected in the academic hoods and gowns, similar to monks' robes, that are still common today.

Intellectual definitions, on the other hand, characterize scholasticism in terms of its assumptions and goals. Faith and reason, for scholastics, were mutually confirming; philosophy was called the "handmaid" of theology. The idea that theology was "faith seeking understanding" can be seen in the early fifth century in Augustine, and in early sixth-century Italy in the government administrator Boethius, who urged his readers to, "As far as you are able, join faith to reason." He was perhaps the last important layman in Christian philosophy for 1,000 years, for in 529 the emperor Justinian closed the Platonic academy in Athens and in the same year Benedict founded his abbey at Monte Cassino. The centre of gravity shifted to the clergy as custodians of faith and learning.

John Scotus Erigena, who was born in Ireland around 810 and taught in Paris, expanded on Augustine's understanding of the relationship between reason and scriptural revelation. For Erigena, scripture was the source of authority, but it was the duty of reason to examine and expound it. Early scholastic teaching was based on the reading of scripture in an effort to arrive at a rational grasp of its meaning. In time, however, scholastic teaching developed a dialectical structure in which a proposition of doctrine was stated and then objections to it were raised and systematically addressed.

Some two centuries later, **Anselm** (c. 1033–1109) moved away from the principle of scriptural authority, asserting that faith itself has a kind of rationality. One of the formulations for which he is famous is the statement "I believe so that I may understand." The most tantalizing of the medieval proofs for the existence of God is Anselm's "**ontological argument**." Unlike later proofs that infer God's existence from inspection of the universe, Anselm's reasoning finds it implied in the very idea of God.

Thomas Aquinas

As scholastic thinking developed, so did the philosophical resources at its disposal. The tradition on which the early scholastics relied came through Augustine and Boethius: based on the thought of Plato, it was dominated by abstract ideas. In the twelfth century, however, Latin Christianity discovered the thought of Plato's contemporary Aristotle, who developed a model of rational argument that gave more scope for examination of the material world. The greatest of the Aristotelian scholastics was the Dominican Thomas Aquinas (1225–74).

In his *Summa Theologiae* ("Summation of Theology") and other writings, Aquinas sharpened the distinction between reason and faith. He believed some Christian faith assertions, such as the doctrine of the Trinity and the incarnation of God in Christ, to lie beyond reason in the realm of faith (though that did not mean they were contrary to reason). Other Christian affirmations, however, such as the existence of God, he did think to be provable by reason. Aquinas identified five "ways" of proving God's existence, most of which involved describing some feature of the material world and arguing that such a world could not exist without a God. For example, for his second proof he argued that the pattern of cause and effect necessarily implies the existence of a First Cause that itself is uncaused, and that that First Cause must be God.

Because the new rational approach was based on logic first, rather than faith, its exponents sometimes became suspect in the eyes of Church authorities. Shortly after Aquinas died, the archbishop of Paris formally condemned a list of propositions reminiscent of his. Nevertheless, it was used to explore the key theological questions of the age: How can reason be present in the soul? What is the right relationship between reason and revelation? What is the basis of knowledge?

Mysticism

The fourteenth-century reaction to Thomas's views included further discussion of the limits of reason in matters of faith. But there was another development afoot that rendered those limits to some extent irrelevant. The late Middle Ages saw a remarkable flowering of mysticism.

To describe something as "mystical" is not simply to say that it involves mystery. **Mysticism** is a specific tradition that emphasizes the certainty of profound personal experience. Typically, mystics are certain of God not because of some logical proof but because they have experienced a moment of intense, vivid awareness. At such a moment we may experience ecstasy (from Greek, "standing outside oneself"), or displacement from our ordinary mode of awareness. One characteristic of that experience is a sense of union with the divine through a temporary dissolving or bridging of the gulf that normally separates the human person from God. The mystic then re-engages ordinary time with new perspectives. Accounts of mystic experience are inevitably written from memory, after the moment of ecstasy has passed.

A number of medieval Christian mystics nevertheless described in vivid detail what they had experienced. Medieval mysticism was part of a long tradition of cultivation of the interior life. In Christianity, that life is usually termed "spirituality." It complements the ethical life where virtue is practised in one's relationship with others. In spirituality, the heart or conscience opens itself to the divine through prayer and contemplation.

For many Christians, spirituality is the essence of religious experience. They credit it to the action of the Holy Spirit on the individual self or soul. Christian spirituality had roots in the Jewish tradition of contemplating the mystery of God's presence with his people. It was cultivated by the desert fathers and mothers whose ascetic practice was the foundation of medieval monasticism, and was central to the monastic life.

In medieval Europe, one of the most notable systematizers of mystical thought was the German Dominican Johannes ("Meister") Eckhart (c. 1260–1327). Eckhart believed that human beings are created in the image of God, but our divine nature is obscured because our life is finite and creaturely. However, the mind of the spiritual person permits an actualization of the divine nature that the human soul contains. The individual mystic becomes aware of the divinity of his or her being. Eckhart's mysticism is unitive, seeking to dissolve distinctions between self and God.

In the fourteenth century, the Flemish mystic Jan van Ruysbroeck took up the problem of differentiation and related it to the persons of the Trinity. God as Father, he said, is the One. But the other parts of the Trinity are related to the movement of creation in the cosmos and a movement of awareness in the self.

Whereas Eckhart and Ruysbroeck sought to identify the self with the image of God, others saw God in all the nearness of humanity. The French Cistercian Bernard of Clairvaux likened the awareness of God to the awareness of one's beloved. Unity of the spirit with God, he said, is a concurrence of wills, not a union of essences. Like the ecstasy of love, this union is fleeting, but no less intensely experienced:

> To lose yourself so that you are as though you were not, to be unaware of yourself and emptied of yourself, to be, as it were, brought to nothing—this pertains to heavenly exchanges, not to human affection (O'Brien 1964: 122).

Bonaventure (1221–74), an Italian Franciscan who taught at Paris, wrote a text entitled *Journey of the Mind to God* in which meditation on the humanity of Christ becomes the point of experiential contact with the divine.

Female Mystics

A striking feature of late medieval mysticism was the scope it afforded women. Although they were forbidden to participate fully in clerical activities, and were limited to supporting roles even in female religious orders, there was no limit to the experiential depth and profundity they could attain in their devotion.

Hildegard of Bingen (1098–1179) was a Benedictine abbess who had a creative life in writing and music but was also involved in politics and diplomacy. Feudal nobles as well as clergy sought the advice of the "Sybil of the Rhine," as she was called. When she became abbess in 1141, she had a vision of tongues of flame from the heavens settling on her, and over the next ten years she wrote a book of visions entitled *Scivias* ("Know the ways [of God]").

Catherine of Siena (1347–80 or 1333–80) in Italy was a member of a Dominican lay order. She was actively involved in the religious politics of the day, but her *Dialogue* records her mystical visions.

The English mystic Julian of Norwich (c. 1342–c. 1413) was 30 when she experienced a series of visions during a severe illness. After two decades of reflection, she wrote an analysis of her visions in

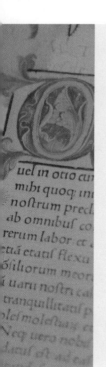

Document

Julian of Norwich

The written texts recording the revelations received by Julian of Norwich have attracted new attention in recent years, as the wisdom they carry speaks to the anxiety so prevalent in the world today. Her revelations gave her assurance that all that is created is known, loved, and held by God. The following text from the Showings uses the image of the hazelnut to express this understanding.

And at the same time I saw this corporeal sight, our Lord showed me a spiritual sight of his familiar love. I saw that he is to us everything which is good and comforting in our help. He is our clothing, for he is that love which wraps and enfolds us, embraces us and guides us, surrounds us for his love, which is so tender that he may never desert us. And so in this sight I saw truly that he is everything which is good, as I understand. And in this he showed me something small, no bigger than a hazelnut, lying in the palm of his hand, and I perceived that it was as round as a ball. I looked at it and thought: What can this be? And I was given this general answer: It is everything which is made. . . . In this little thing I saw three properties. The first is that God made it, the second that he loves it, the third is that God preserves it. It is that God is the Creator and the lover and the protector (Colledge and Walsh, ed. and trans., 1978: 130–1).

her *Showings* (also known as *Sixteen Revelations of Divine Love*. To Julian, evil was a distortion, introduced by the human will, that served to reveal the divine love of God all the more clearly.

Medieval Religious Communities

Monastic Orders

Monastic communities developed a highly structured religious discipline in the medieval period. Monks (male) and **nuns** (female) were required to take solemn vows of poverty, chastity, and obedience, to stay within the physical precincts of the community, and to follow its code of discipline.

Monks played an important part in both the Greek and Latin traditions. Technically, since monasticism had begun as an alternative to established religion, monks were laymen rather than priests, but a demanding schedule of prayer and worship was central to their practice. A distinction was drawn between "religious" (or "regular") clergy, who followed a monastic rule, and "secular" clergy, who worked in the world and in the Greek Church (unlike the Roman) were permitted to marry. (Members of the ecclesiastical hierarchy were always celibate, however.) An important centre of Byzantine spirituality is Mount Athos, a peninsula in northern Greece that projects into the Aegean Sea. It is dotted by 20 monasteries founded at different times over the last thousand years. The entire peninsula is a preserve of male monks, and women are not permitted there even today.

Cluniac Fathers

Founded in 910 by William the Pious, Duke of Aquitaine, the monastery at Cluny, north of Lyon in France, became the centre of a movement to reform Benedictine monasticism by bringing its institutions under the control of religious rather than secular authorities. Cluny became a centre of revitalization that inspired other efforts at renewal; over the next two and a half centuries, the Cluniac order established a network of more than 300 satellite houses across Europe. Within a century of its founding, however, Cluny itself was growing rich and abandoning the rigorous simplicity that Benedict had called for.

Cistercians

Robert of Molesmes responded to the changes at Cluny by founding an austere new order at Cîteaux, north of Cluny near Dijon, in 1098. The Cistercians (from the Latin for Cîteaux) wore simple undyed wool habits, ate no meat, and worshipped in sparsely decorated churches. Within a century there were 500 Cistercian abbeys. Though the Cistercians had refused lavish endowments, rising land values in the more marginal areas where they established themselves eventually made their order wealthy too. One group of Cistercians in particular became known for their rule of silence. The Cistercians of the Strict Observance, or Trappists, were founded in the 1600s by Armand de Rancé, abbot of the monastery of La Trappe in Normandy. The best known Trappist of the twentieth century was the mystic Thomas Merton (1915–68), who became interested in Asian spirituality, especially Zen Buddhism, and was active in social protest in the 1960s. Other Cistercians helped to found spiritual orders of knights such as the Knights Templar, the Knights of St John, and the Teutonic order. Their members made pilgrimages to the Holy Land and took as their biblical model the Maccabees, the Jewish patriots of the second century BCE.

Carthusians

Also influenced by Robert was a German named Bruno, who turned to the religious life in his mid-forties and followed Robert's spiritual direction before founding his own order in 1084. The

Founded in 1929 by Capuchin friars, the Capuchin Soup Kitchen in Detroit now serves 2,000 people a day in some of the city's poorest neighbourhoods. In 1997 the friars founded a farm that in 2011 harvested nearly 3,000 kilograms (6,000 pounds) of produce for the soup kitchen.

© Jim West/Alamy

Carthusian order (named after its base at La Grande Chartreuse, near Grenoble in France) demanded a vow of silence and considerable austerity from its members. Like the Benedictine abbey of Fécamp, near the English Channel, the Chartreuse abbey supported itself in part by making and selling a famous liqueur, in this instance the brilliant green one that gave its name to the colour chartreuse.

Mendicant Orders

The monastic response to the secular world had been to withdraw from it—even if that withdrawal turned out to be more a matter of theory than of practice. With the growth of towns and cities in Europe, however, came a significant new problem: urban poverty. To respond to the needs of the urban poor, a new type of religious order emerged whose members—called **friars**, from the Latin *frater* ("brother")—dedicated themselves to pastoral work, serving the poor. There were mendicant orders for women and laypeople as well as men. Their members either worked or begged for their living, and were not bound to one convent.

Franciscans

Francis of Assisi (1182–1226) grew up as the privileged son of a wealthy cloth merchant in central Italy, but a serious illness in his twenties led him to rethink his life. On a pilgrimage to Rome, he was so moved by the beggars outside St Peter's Basilica that he exchanged clothes with one of them and spent the day begging for alms. When he returned to Assisi, he dedicated his life to serving the poor. Gradually attracting a small group of like-minded companions, he established a rule of life emphasizing poverty, which received papal approval in 1209. Within a few years, Clara of Assisi had formed a Franciscan women's order known as the Poor Clares. An offshoot of the Franciscans called the Capuchins drew up their own rule in 1529 and are still known today for their soup kitchens, which offer free meals in impoverished neighbourhoods.

In 1224 Francis experienced a vision of an angel from whom he received the "stigmata": wounds in his own body replicating those suffered by Christ on the cross. Proclaimed a saint in 1228—just two years after his death—he quickly became a beloved figure and the subject of many legends, among them several that emphasized his love of the natural world. In one of the most famous tales, he preaches to a flock of birds, telling them how fortunate they are to be provided for by God.

Dominicans

In 1216–17 a priest from northern Spain named Dominic Guzmán received a papal mandate to establish a preaching order dedicated to combatting the "Albigensian heresy." (Named for the city of Albi in southwestern France, Albigensianism was a dualistic doctrine, not unlike **Manichaeism**, centred on a view of existence as a struggle between light and darkness, and was highly critical of Roman Catholicism.) Dominicans such as Aquinas rapidly established their influence as itinerant preachers of doctrine in university towns such as Paris.

Carmelites

The Carmelites, or hermits of Mount Carmel, were organized in Palestine in 1154, during the Crusades, and given a rule by the patriarch of Jerusalem. As the numbers of crusaders in the Holy Land declined, the Carmelites established themselves in Europe and England, where they were termed "White Friars."

Celibacy

The insistence that priests be celibate became stronger in the Middle Ages, and much stronger in Latin Catholicism than in Greek Orthodoxy. Rationales for priestly celibacy included the spiritual benefit of surmounting worldly desires and the practical benefit of freedom from the responsibilities of marriage and parenthood. In addition, since it made a hereditary priesthood impossible, celibacy worked against the tendency for institutional influence to become concentrated in particular families.

Women in Medieval Catholicism

The tradition of women in a consecrated religious life within Christianity had roots in the early Church. However, its most significant period of development was in the Middle Ages. Various forms of religious life for women flourished throughout the period.

Vita Canonica

We have already seen that informal groups of women living a religious life were organized in the time of the early Church. Eventually this way of life came to be known as the Vita Canonica. In response to women's requests for direction on how to order a common religious life, local bishops would write rules ("canons") for them. Communities of "canonesses" were characterized by their diversity, lack of structure, and relative autonomy.

Nuns

The rules governing female monastic communities paralleled those for male communities. Normally, each woman entering the convent as a "bride of Christ" was required to furnish a dowry and relinquish all private property. Nuns lived together under one roof and traditionally took vows of poverty, continence, and obedience that were irrevocable, reflecting a permanent commitment to the religious life. The formal consecration ended with the vow to live always as the bride of Christ.

Over time, it became common for women's communities to separate themselves entirely from contact with the world; by the thirteenth century, the male hierarchy of the Church had imposed this practice, known as cloistering, on all women's communities. The **abbesses** who presided over these institutions were quite powerful. In addition to making and enforcing the community's laws, the abbess was responsible for its landholdings, which in many cases were quite extensive, and so played a significant role in the feudal system. She administered the financial affairs of the estate and also oversaw the lives of tenants who lived on and farmed it. Some abbesses had monks as well as nuns under their care in what were known as double monasteries..

Nevertheless, the power of the abbess and the female monastic community declined by the later Middle Ages. Church property had become important to the wealth of society, and secular princes anxious to limit the autonomy of the Church introduced the principle of double investiture, according to which secular and ecclesiastical powers alike had an interest in local lands and events. In the twelfth century, *Gratium's Decretum* enforced the legal principle that no layperson could exercise control over a cleric. Since no woman could be ordained, even an abbess was by definition a layperson and therefore forbidden to exercise authority over a male cleric, however junior. This put an end to the phenomenon of double monasteries. Increased strictures around cloistering also meant that abbesses, unlike abbots, were not able to leave their monasteries to conduct the business of their communities. Meanwhile, increasing external control by the male hierarchy meant that some female communities disappeared altogether.

Beguines and Beghards

Beguines were groups of unconsecrated women who chose to live a freer type of religious life. They did not follow any of the traditional rules of consecrated religious life, and the fact that their communities did not live under the authority of local bishops automatically made them suspect. This new style of religious life also attracted some men, though in smaller numbers. Like their female counterparts, these **Beghards** came together in small groups, mainly in urban environments, in order to live their lives in poverty, celibacy, prayer, and service, after the model of the gospel.

A number of Beguines are known for their writing in the tradition of love mysticism. Among them are Mechthild of Magdeburg in Saxony (1207–97), whose work was collected under the title *The Flowing Light of the Godhead*, and Hadjewich, a Beguine from Flanders who wrote many letters as well as poems and accounts of visions. A common theme in their work was the supremacy of love. Beguine love poetry celebrates the ecstatic union of the soul with God.

A third notable female mystic who is widely thought to have been a Beguine was Marguerite Porete, who was burned at the stake for heresy in 1310—the first person to be put to death in the Paris Inquisition. Condemned by Church authorities, her book *The Mirror of Simple Souls* is reputed to have influenced Christian mystics for centuries.

🏵 Saints

The expansion of Christianity into Africa, Asia, and Eastern Europe was facilitated by its emphasis on the miraculous power of saints.

Sainthood

Over the centuries the Church developed criteria for sainthood (including the performance of attested miracles), a canonical list of saints, and a rigorous procedure for screening new nominees for the title. The first person to become a saint by papal decree was a German bishop, in 993.

The saints collectively came to be regarded as a kind of heavenly senate or honour society. They were thought to possess merit or virtue, a personal credit in the economy of blessedness that could be drawn on by believers who wanted them to intercede with God on their behalf. By praying to certain saints or making pilgrimages to their shrines, one might win release from punishment in the next existence and from guilt in this one. In short, the saints could be powerful allies in the quest for spiritual benefit.

Particular saints came to be associated with specific conditions or occupations. St Christopher, for example, who was said to have carried the child Jesus across a dangerous river, is one of several patron saints of travellers, and St Cecilia is the patron of musicians because she sang a song to God on her deathbed.

Particular saints also came to be associated with particular symbols. Visitors to Venice, for instance, learn that the lion symbolizes the gospel author St Mark. Similarly, a bishop portrayed carrying a beehive is likely St Ambrose, the fifth-century bishop of Milan, whose name connotes nectar; reportedly, Ambrose's mother dreamed that as a boy he swallowed a bee, which made him sweet of speech. But the beehive is also associated with Bernard of

Document

Mechthild of Magdeburg, "Of the Nine Choirs and How They Sing"

The nine orders or "choirs" of angels were a standard part of the religious imagery of Mechthild's day. The idea that there was a hierarchy of angels was well established from the fifth century, when Pseudo-Dionysius the Aereopagite named the nine orders in his book On the Celestial Hierarchy.

Now listen, my love. Hear with spiritual ears what the nine choirs sing.
We praise You, O Lord.

For you have sought us in your humility,
Saved us by your compassion,
Honoured us by your humanity,
Led us by your gentleness,
Ordered us by your wisdom,
Protected us by your power,
Sanctified us by your holiness,
Illumined us by your intimacy,
Raised us by your love (Madigan, 1998: 138).

Clairvaux, who was called the "honey-mouthed teacher." Keys represent the Apostle Peter, to whom (in a famous passage in Matthew 16) Jesus promises the keys to earth and heaven; but there are at least nine other saints who have also been represented with keys. And the orb appears not only with God but also with Dominic, the twelfth-century founder of the Dominican order, whose mission it was to bring light to the world.

In some places the traditions of particular saints include elements of pre-Christian customs and symbolism. In the eighth century, the English Church historian known as the Venerable Bede reported correspondence from Gregory the Great 100 years before him:

> On the day of the dedication or the festivals of the holy martyrs, whose relics are deposited there, let them make themselves huts from the branches of trees around the churches which have been converted out of shrines, and let them celebrate the solemnity with religious feasts. Do not let them sacrifice animals to the devil, but let them slaughter animals for their own food to the praise of God (*Ecclesiastical History*, ch. 30; Colgrave and Mynors, 1969: 109).

St Ursula was depicted as sailing the Rhine in the fashion of the earlier Teutonic moon goddess Urschel. And St Christopher, "Christ-bearer," was said to have felt he was bearing the weight of the universe when he carried the child Jesus on his shoulder, recalling Hercules and Atlas, who bore the weight of the world in classical mythology.

The Virgin Mary

Pre-eminent among the Christian saints was **Mary**, the virgin who was chosen by God to become the mother of Jesus. By the later Middle Ages it was thought that someone so near to Christ must share especially closely in his redeeming work, that she embodied the virtue of compassion, and that as the Mother of God she would be ready to plead with her son on behalf of sinners. The resulting increase in devotion to Mary reflected a broader theological shift towards a greater concern with the person or humanity of Jesus.

In Latin Europe, artistic depictions of Mary reflected a particular set of conventions. Although some of them can be traced to the cult of the pre-Christian goddess Isis, Mary's role is not limited to that of the devoted young mother. She is also the mature woman who grieves at the martyrdom of her adult son; she is the model of purity and incorruptibility, of devotion and fidelity, of sorrow and compassion. Many statues and paintings of the sorrowful Mary present her as a model of selflessness to which all—male as well as female—might aspire.

Worship in the Medieval Church

Liturgical reforms in the early medieval period fundamentally changed the nature of worship in the Western Church, limiting the opportunities for ordinary people to participate and reserving them for the clergy. Portions of the liturgy that until then had been spoken in the vernacular were increasingly performed in Latin. At the same time, the rules governing the Eucharist were tightened to require a complex process of confession and penitence before receiving the sacrament. This meant that priests could receive communion frequently, but laypeople perhaps only once a year. In addition, only the clergy were allowed to receive the wine (the blood of Christ); laypeople were given only the bread (the body).

Church music also became less accessible to the average person. Gregorian chant or plainsong had been simple and easy for congregations to learn by rote, but as musical forms became more complex, using several voices, participation was increasingly restricted to formal choirs made up of monks and clergy.

Church architecture contributed to the distancing of laypeople from the life of the Church. Between the nave (the main body of the church, where the worshippers gathered) and the altar, another section of seats (the chancel) was added for the choir, and by the later medieval period worshippers' view of the altar had been further obstructed by rood screens erected between the nave and the chancel. Finally, the altar was pushed up against the wall, so that instead of standing behind it, facing the people, while celebrating the Eucharist, the priest now turned his back on them. This change had a theological basis: now the priest was offering the sacrifice on behalf of the people rather than presiding at the Eucharistic banquet of the whole people of God, as when he had faced the people. At the same time, ongoing architectural changes—from the basilica form to the romanesque to the gothic—also contributed to the increasing separation between the altar and the people.

🐚 The Early Modern Era

Humanism

In the course of the fourteenth century, Europe crossed the watershed that divided the medieval from the early modern world. After centuries that one of the first Renaissance humanists, the poet Petrarch, described as the "dark ages," Western culture began to rediscover the philosophy, science, art, and poetry of Greek and Roman antiquity. Among the consequences was a renewed emphasis on life in this world, the celebration of beauty, and the capacity of human beings to govern themselves. This put the humanists in conflict with a Church that had traditionally understood itself to be the primary interpreter and mediator of human experience.

Erasmus (1466–1536)

Erasmus of Rotterdam in the Netherlands laid much of the groundwork for later reform-minded theologians. Ordained a priest in the Augustinian order in 1488, he had studied at the University of Paris, which was zealous in its enthusiasm for reform of traditional Catholic teachings in several areas. He was critical of the Church's abuses and called for demanding new standards of scholarship

in theology, based on new translations of the original sources.

In itself, humanism posed no real threat to the Church. However, the external force of humanism was met with a push toward internal reform from within the Church itself. Together, these external and internal forces for change led to the schism within Western Christianity that came to be known as the Protestant Reformation.

The Protestant Reformation

The English Reformation, although not unrelated to the various strains of reforming activity on the continent, was uniquely linked to the British political context; therefore it will be discussed separately (see p. 197).

The Continental Reformation

In the early sixteenth century the influence of the Church in Europe was all-pervasive. Collectively the Church was Europe's largest landholder. Clergy played more than one vital role in European society, not only dispensing the sacraments and, with them, forgiveness and the hope of salvation, but providing social services such as medical care and education. The religious enthusiasm of the laity was reflected in pilgrimages, ostentatious public devotions, and huge investments in the Church, through paid funeral **masses** and the purchase of **indulgences**: releases from the time that the soul was required to spend in purgatory (a kind of holding area for the departed in the course of their passage from death to the next existence).

At the same time, this period was one of unprecedented advances in lay literacy and engagement in matters of worship and theology. However, there were also concerns with the Church, particularly in Germany. Many German clergy were penniless and ill-educated, while German bishops were often princes of the Church from very wealthy families who used their ecclesiastical positions to reinforce their social status, political power, and wealth.

The combination of a changing intellectual world, engaged religious practice, dissatisfaction with the Church, and the invention of the printing press set the stage for the events of the Reformation.

Martin Luther (1483–1546)

Martin Luther is understood to be the father of the Protestant Reformation. The son of a miner in Saxony, Germany, Luther offered himself at a young age for the religious life as an Augustinian friar. In 1512 he was made a doctor of theology and professor of Scripture at the University of Wittenberg.

Luther struggled with the theological issues of salvation. In the complex system of clerical mediation between God and sinner that characterized the early Church, he feared that he would not be found worthy of salvation. In the course of his struggle, however, he had a sudden revelation, known as his "tower experience," which convinced him of the "essence of the gospel": that humans are justified (set right with God) only by faith, which itself is a gift of God's grace; there are no "works" we can do to earn that justification. His anxieties relieved, from this point forward he argued that if we have faith, then we are assured of salvation.

In October 1517 Luther posted a list of "95 Theses" against indulgences on the door of the church in Wittenberg. This act of public protest sparked a conflict with the Church, which eventually led to Luther's excommunication by the pope and his emergence as the primary agent of the Protestant Reformation: a schism that split the Church into many differing groups, among them one named for Luther himself.

Luther's core doctrine was justification by faith alone, through grace alone: the idea that salvation is a gift of grace that can be received only through faith, and there is nothing the sinner can do to earn it. However, the Lutheran theological tradition also emphasizes the idea, developed by the Apostle Paul, of the priesthood of all believers, whereby all persons have direct access to God through the power of the Holy Spirit, without mediation by a priest. This notion led to the development of a Church that

Sites

Wittenberg, Germany

It was on the doors of what is now All Saints' Lutheran Church in Wittenberg, Germany, that Martin Luther nailed his 95 Theses. Today the church houses Luther's tomb.

This bronze statue by Johann Gottfried Schadow, erected in Wittenberg's town square in 1821, was the first public monument to Luther.

© typo-graphics/iStockphoto

is much less clerical than its Catholic counterpart, less dependent on the traditional threefold order of ministers, particularly bishops.

Luther's theology of Church–state relations is defined by his doctrine of the "two kingdoms." As an Augustinian, Luther had been influenced by Augustine's theology of the city of God as distinct from the city of the profane. Thus he argued that human society was divided into two realms that should not be confused. The whole world belongs to God, but he designates oversight of the secular kingdom to secular princes who administer the rule of law. The second kingdom of God is the place where grace rules in the spirit. This theoretical separation led Luther to support secular princes in their efforts to maintain order. This is most pointedly reflected in a tract he wrote in 1525, in response to the peasant revolts going on in parts of Germany and elsewhere. Luther's fear of anarchy was so great that he advocated ruthless suppression of the peasants.

Jean Calvin (1509–1564)

Jean Calvin represents the second stage of the Reformation. A French Protestant theologian who was trained as a lawyer, he was unwelcome in Catholic France, and so became a refugee who attempted to proclaim his version of Christianity in Geneva between 1536 and 1538. Although that first attempt failed, in 1541 he returned and became the undisputed master of the Genevan Reformation.

Calvin's theology was not expressly innovative. His views remained constant from the beginning to the end of his theological career. Like Luther, he affirmed the importance of scripture in the Christian life of faith. Indeed, he attributed primary authority to scripture—the Word of God—rather than clergy. Also like Luther, he affirmed the justification of the sinner by faith alone. Where Calvin differed from Luther was in his theology of sin and salvation. Calvin believed that, since the fall of Adam, no human could ever freely choose faith and thereby realize his own salvation: only God could bring that about, and even before the creation, he

had predestined some of his creatures to damnation and some to salvation. By contrast, Luther believed that the death and resurrection of Christ made the gift of faith by grace available to all. Calvin's notion of absolute predestination, which echoes Augustine's, emphasizes the absolute omnipotence of God. After Calvin's death, his teachings were developed in a number of emerging Protestant traditions.

Perhaps one of the most interesting aspects of Calvin was his effort to establish a **theocracy** in Geneva. A theocracy is a state ruled by God through religious authorities. Effectively, Geneva reflected Calvin's vision of a reform community, with regular preaching, religious instruction for adults and children, and close Church regulation of the business and moral life of the community.

Under Calvin, the Genevans hoped to convert France to Protestantism. However, the first in a decades-long series of "Wars of Religion" broke out in 1562 between French Roman Catholics and Protestants (Huguenots), who were heavily influenced by Calvin. Under persecution in the seventeenth and eighteenth centuries, the Huguenots sought refuge in Protestant lands throughout Europe and as far afield as present-day South Africa and the Thirteen Colonies that would become the United States, spreading Calvinist theology around the world. As we will see, a variety of denominational traditions, usually identified as "Reformed" or "Presbyterian," resulted from this diaspora.

Ulrich Zwingli (1484–1531)

The father of the Swiss Reformation, Ulrich Zwingli, had been ordained a Roman Catholic priest in 1506. His rupture with Rome came gradually, with early critiques of the Church that were influenced by Erasmus. Inspired by Luther's theology, Zwingli argued that the gospel is the sole basis of truth, and in so doing he rejected the authority of the pope. Until 1522 he accepted the traditional Roman Catholic view of the Eucharist as a ritual of transubstantiation in which the bread and wine of the Eucharist ceased being bread and wine and became the literal body and blood of Jesus.

However, by 1524 he was arguing that the meaning of the Eucharist was strictly symbolic. All notion of the real presence of Christ was rejected. This stand on the meaning of the Eucharist meant that union with other Protestant churches was not possible, as most accepted the idea of the real presence of Christ in some form.

Sixteenth-Century Denominations

The Reformation was marked by division and diversity. Early reformers often advocated their breakaway doctrines with an ideological stridency that was no less authoritarian than the Church they had rejected. At a practical level, redundancy and confusion developed when independent bodies competed for adherents. A denominationally fragmented Church has been the legacy of the Protestant Reformation down to the present day. In continental Europe, two main theological directions leading to new denominations emerged in the sixteenth century: Lutheran and Calvinist. There were also a number of more extreme Protestant movements such as the Anabaptists: the forerunners of denominations such as the Mennonites and, eventually, Baptists, they made up what is known as the "radical Reformation."

Lutherans

The followers of Luther flourished in Germany and Scandinavia. Like him, they stressed the authority of scripture and the guidance of the Holy Spirit. Lutheranism allowed ample scope for rational and intellectual argument in the exposition of scripture, but it also encouraged a deep sense of personal piety. Images of God as friend and companion are just as frequent in the texts of Lutheran hymns as images of God as warrior or judge.

In worship and in ecclesiastical organization, Lutherans departed in only some respects from the Roman Church. They retained a Eucharist-like sacrament, but they celebrated it in the vernacular rather than Latin, and they held that Christ's body was present along with the bread and wine but was not produced out of them. The Lutheran priesthood continued to be governed by bishops, but members of the clergy were permitted to marry. (Only in recent years have Lutheran women been ordained as priests.)

In most parts of Germany and Scandinavia, Lutheran Christianity became the state religion. The **Evangelical** Church, as it is called in Germany, is dominant in the north of the country, while Catholicism is stronger in the south. To this day, Germany provides basic funding for churches out of tax revenues. All taxpayers, including non-believers, pay a flat rate, and the money is directed to Evangelical or Catholic treasuries, depending on the taxpayer's affiliation. Outside Germany and Scandinavia, Lutheranism has spread through migration and missionary activity. It was carried to North America in the nineteenth century by Germans who settled in places such as Pennsylvania, Ohio, Missouri, and Ontario, and by Scandinavians, most of whom settled in Minnesota and Wisconsin. The ethnic character of the North American Lutheran churches has become diluted over time, except in places where it has been refreshed by continuing immigration.

Reformed Churches

From the 1520s to 1560s, the Reformation movement in and around Switzerland departed from Luther's position on several points. While Zwingli in Zürich disputed Luther's Eucharistic theology, Martin Bucer in Strasbourg promoted a more active role for laypeople as ministers, elders, deacons, and teachers.

From Calvin's Geneva the ideas of the Swiss Reformation spread to other lands, notably France, the Netherlands, Hungary, England, and Scotland. In the Netherlands, Calvin's teaching of **predestination** was challenged by Jacobus Arminius, who believed that God's sovereignty was compatible with human free will. Arminian views were condemned by an assembly in Dordrecht (Dort) in 1518, which sentenced their supporter, the scholar and jurist Hugo Grotius, to life imprisonment. (Grotius escaped in a box of books being shipped to his wife and settled for a time in Paris.) In the

Netherlands and Hungary, the Calvinist churches are known as **Reformed Churches**.

In England the Reformed tradition was called Presbyterian because of its form of government by lay elders or "presbyters"; for the same reason, the established state Church of Scotland is termed Presbyterian. Reformed Churches do not have bishops; instead, the regional representative assembly, the presbytery, corporately performs the traditional tasks of a bishop, including the supervision, examination, and ordination of candidates for ministry. Through migration Presbyterianism has taken root on other continents. Presbyterians from England and Scotland settled in eastern Canada and the middle Atlantic American states, as well as in New Zealand and Australia. Dutch Reformed settlers carried their tradition to South Africa, New Amsterdam (New York), and Michigan.

In the nineteenth and twentieth centuries, Presbyterian missions from Britain and North America reached many parts of Asia and Africa, but in most cases the churches they founded remained small, and in Islamic regions they found most of their recruits among Eastern Orthodox Christians. The Presbyterians did become a sizable minority in Korea, however.

Anabaptists

The radical Reformation rejected the broader Protestant movements' affiliations with secular power. Groups such as the Anabaptists shunned politics, military service, and even the taking of oaths. Believing that baptism should be actively sought on the basis of mature personal commitment, the Anabaptists practised adult rather than infant baptism. They also sought to restore the close-knit sense of community of the apostolic era.

Anabaptist groups rely on lay preachers rather than trained clergy and in times of war they have tended to pacifism. Essentially anti-establishment in orientation, the Anabaptist movement emerged in response to dissatisfaction with the pace of change in the first decade of the Reformation. One of the first breaks with the "establishment" Reformation came in 1525, when some of the more radical followers of Zwingli began administering adult baptism in defiance of Zwingli himself.

A decade later, in the northwestern German town of Münster, Anabaptist efforts to establish the kingdom of God by force prompted a crackdown by Catholic and Protestant authorities alike. Thereafter a former Dutch priest named Menno Simons led the movement into a largely otherworldly and non-violent path. Since there was virtually no chance of removing the authorities, he urged his followers to remove themselves from society. Some of his followers—the Mennonites—settled in the Netherlands, where they enjoyed toleration and by the middle of the nineteenth century had largely assimilated to the secular climate of the Enlightenment. As the movement spread eastward through Germany and Austria to the Ukraine, however, hardship and persecution led some to remove themselves from Europe altogether.

Mennonites who migrated to the Americas settled mainly in Pennsylvania, where they came to be known as Pennsylvania Dutch (from *Deutsch*, meaning "German"), and, later, Ontario and the Canadian prairies. Today most Mennonites are fully part of the modern world. Nevertheless, some branches, such as the Old Order Amish farmers in Pennsylvania and Ontario, prefer traditional modes of dress and conduct. They continue to farm with the draft animals and simple tools of a century ago, resisting more modern machinery and gadgetry as part of the moral temptation and corruption of the secular world.

Unitarians

Unitarianism rejects the doctrine of the Trinity. As early as 1527 in Strasbourg, Martin Cellarius preferred to speak of God as a single person. Others expressed similar views. Subsequently, Unitarian communities emerged in several lands, including Poland and Hungary. In England, John Biddle began to publish Unitarian tracts in 1652, but a Unitarian congregation was not organized until 1773–4, when Theophilus Lindsey resigned from the Church of England and opened a Unitarian chapel in London.

In the United States, Unitarianism represented a left-wing theological break with Congregationalists (see p. 199). William Ellery Channing preached a sermon in Baltimore in 1819 that American Unitarians have taken as a kind of denominational manifesto. However, Channing did not think of the Unitarians as a separate group and claimed to belong "not to a sect, but to the community of free minds."

In North America, Unitarianism has appealed mainly to people of a humanist and rationalist bent, often in university circles. In 1961, the Unitarians merged with a kindred group, the Universalists. Because of its minimal creedal demands, Unitarianism has often been the denomination of choice for Jewish–Christian couples.

Women and the Continental Reformation

Although the reformers did not take an egalitarian view of women, their emphasis on the individual believer's direct relationship with God would have huge significance for women over time. For example, although Luther argued that women were inferior to men, he conceded that women might preach if no men were available. Eventually, many Protestant traditions would move to allow the full participation of women in the leadership of their churches. But that is a story for the modern era.

In the sixteenth century, one of the more consequential reform arguments was that celibacy is not the natural state for human beings. Over the course of the reformation, many convents and monasteries were closed, and although most nuns did not renounce their vocations, some did leave and marry, often with former monks. The new role of the "clergy wife" was born. Martin Luther himself married a former nun by the name of Katherine Von Bora. Together they made their home a centre for the new movement, a place both of hospitality and of theological debate and teaching.

Luther advocated public education for both boys and girls, to ensure the basic literacy required for unmediated access to scripture. The invention of the printing press only a few decades before the start of the Reformation made that scripture accessible to the people in a way that could not have been imagined in the era when all written material had to be hand-copied by scribes. Luther's commitment to the idea that ordinary people should have access to scripture also led him to translate the Latin Bible known as the Vulgate into the German vernacular of the people. As well, worship services in the new Protestant churches were conducted in the local language rather than the Latin that had limited the possibility of understanding the liturgy to the educated few.

The Counter-Reformation

The Protestant Reformation had the effect of stimulating reform from within the Roman Catholic Church, which led to its revitalization as an institution. This phenomenon is known as the Counter-Reformation. From the mid-1500s to the Thirty Years War (1618–48), the reforming Church was reinvigorated by the development of new religious orders, the Council of Trent, and a revitalized spirituality.

The defining religious order of the Counter-Reformation was the Society of Jesus (Jesuits), founded by Ignatius Loyola (1491–1563), a knight from a noble Spanish family who had a conversion experience after being wounded in battle. After several years as a hermit, in 1534 he joined with six companions to form the Society of Jesus. Characterized by a rigorous discipline that reflected Loyola's military background, the Jesuits became the spearhead of the missionary forces that carried Christianity to both the Americas and Asia. Ignatius Loyola is also known for having written the Ignatian Spiritual Exercises, a tract that guided the spiritual practice of generations of Christians.

The Council of Trent (1545–63), the Church's nineteenth ecumenical council, was the first to be convened since the Council of Constance in 1417. Meeting in three separate sessions over 18 years, it laid a solid foundation for renewal of both the discipline and the spiritual life of the Church. It would be 300 years before the next ecumenical council was convened. Thus Trent was a watershed that marked the beginning of early modern Roman Catholic practice.

Counter-Reformation Mysticism

During the Counter-Reformation many religious orders experienced a revitalization of spiritual life. The most notable figures in this revitalization were the Spanish mystics Teresa of Avila and John of the Cross.

Teresa of Avila (1515–1582)

Teresa of Avila lived in what has come to be known as the golden age of Spanish mysticism. Educated by Augustinian nuns, she entered a Carmelite convent in 1535. Her personal experience of God fired her with reforming zeal to establish several houses within her order. Teresa wrote extensively about her religious experience. All her spiritual teachings were grounded in intense personal experience of revelation or divine illumination: she experienced the immediacy of God's presence in a physical as well as a spiritual sense. The fact that her writings were received with enthusiasm even in her own day is significant, as her time was one of extreme repression for women.

Teresa's primary themes were self-knowledge, the importance of identifying the attachments that keep us from joining with God, the need for awareness of one's own weakness and vulnerability, the reality of God present always to all life, and the certainty of God's promise of forgiveness and transformation through Christ. For Teresa mysticism was not an escape from reality. What was human was not left behind: rather, humanity was transformed by the unitive experience, set free to be for God and others. From suffering came compassion, and through prayer the person who practised looking inward would be transfigured, released to live a life of active love.

In her most famous work, *The Way of Perfection*, she describes the spiritual path to union with God. She writes of being inundated with spiritual delight and sweetness as the soul joins with God in the bliss of the unitive life, and describes the marriage of the soul to its divine love as two candlesticks joining in one flame. Ten years after writing the *Way* Teresa wrote *The Interior Castle*, which more fully elaborated the path toward the unitive state in

Document

Teresa of Avila and John of the Cross

From Teresa of Avila, *The Interior Castle*

Now let us come to imaginative visions, for they say the devil meddles more in these than in the ones mentioned, and it must be so. But when these imaginative visions are from our Lord, they in some way seem to me more beneficial because they are in greater conformity with our nature. I'm excluding from that comparison the visions the Lord shows in the last dwelling place. No other visions are comparable to these (Madigan 1998: 250).

From John of the Cross, *The Dark Night of the Soul*

[H]owever greatly the soul itself labours, it cannot actively purify itself so as to be in the least degree prepared for the Divine union of perfection of love, if God takes not its hand and purges it not in that dark fire. . . . (Book I, Ch. 3; trans. E. Allison Peers; accessed 22 Oct. 2013 at http://www.ccel.org/ccel/john_cross/dark_night.txt).

a journey through seven "dwelling places," the last of which is the interior castle where God resides in the self. Such an encounter with God fundamentally changes our perception of reality: values and priorities shift, our attachment to material things weakens, we know the virtue of calm and peace in the soul even though turmoil may exist around us, and our understanding of God and our self in relation to God expands.

John of the Cross (1542–1591)

John of the Cross was also a Carmelite, and with Teresa he founded a reform order called the Discalced ("Barefoot") Carmelites. He is best known for the beauty of his writings, which are considered the summit of mystical Spanish literature. His most famous concept is that of the "dark night of the soul." Like Teresa, John experienced the movement toward God as a journey of many stages. The "dark night" comes when the soul, longing for God, becomes disoriented and loses its way. This part of the spiritual journey is painful and can last for years, but it is a necessary stage on the way to union with God.

The English Reformation

The relationship of the English Reformation to the Continental Reformation is complex. England had been acquainted with Christianity since the fourth century, and by the seventh century it was fully embedded in the ecclesiastical system of the Western tradition. However, it was predisposed to the principles behind the Continental Reformation.

A century and a half before Luther posted his 95 Theses, John Wycliffe (1320–84) had written against indulgences as well as the wealth and power of the papacy. Well-trained in the scholastic tradition, Wycliffe used his intellectual skills to raise fundamental questions about key aspects of the ecclesiastical traditions of his day. Perhaps most significantly, he was an early advocate for the use of the vernacular in both scripture and worship, and promoted an early translation of the Bible into the language of ordinary people. Today it is

generally believed that the English translation from the Latin Vulgate known as "Wycliffe's Bible" was not actually made by Wycliffe himself, although he was the main force behind its production. Even though possession of Wycliffe's Bible could lead to a death sentence, many copies were made between the 1380s and 1530s, when it was superseded by a new translation, from the original Hebrew and Greek, that had the benefit of the printing press (as did Luther's German Bible). The main author of that work was William Tyndale (1492–1536). Having left the still-Catholic England of Henry VIII in the 1520s to pursue his translation on the continent, he was arrested in the Netherlands and put to death as a heretic before he could complete it. Just three years later, however, Henry himself authorized a different English translation. What had changed?

The English Reformation was as much political as it was theological (some would say more so). When the continental Reformation began, Henry VIII defended the papacy against the reformers and their teachings, put his name on an anti-Lutheran tract, sentenced priests with reform sympathies to death, and, through his Lord Chancellor of the time, Sir Thomas More, took an active role in suppressing Protestant heresies when they appeared in England. However, things changed when Henry needed a divorce from his wife Catherine of Aragon so that he could marry Anne Boleyn, who herself was significantly influenced by Protestant thinking. The pope's refusal to grant the divorce eventually led to a schism between England and Rome. The Church of England was established as an autonomous entity in 1534, no longer subject to the authority of the bishop of Rome.

The concept of Church–state relations that developed in England was different from the configuration of that relationship in Roman Catholic lands. In England, Henry declared himself the head of the church as well as the head of state. This model was based on the idea that temporal and spiritual authority were united in the person of the monarch. Religion in this system was "established" as the official religion of the state, supported by the state in all ways, including economically, and any changes to it would have to be passed into law by the parliament of the country.

To demonstrate his authority in ecclesiastical matters, and at the same time appropriate their wealth for the Crown, Henry suppressed the monasteries in two waves. First an Act of Parliament in 1536 dissolved the smaller monasteries and confiscated their property. Then from November 1539, with the passing of an act investing the Crown with all monastic possessions, the larger, wealthier monastic houses began to surrender and dissolve themselves by agreement; the last house surrendered in 1540.

England remained Protestant under Henry's young son, Edward VI, but with the succession of Edward's half-sister Mary I (r. 1553–8) England once again became officially Catholic. The contest for power was violent. It was not until the fifth and last monarch of the Tudor dynasty, Elizabeth I (r. 1558–1603), negotiated what came to be known as the Elizabethan Settlement that the situation began to stabilize. The Act of Supremacy passed in 1559 re-established the English Church's independence from Rome and conferred on Elizabeth the title "Supreme Governor of the Church of England." It also re-established the liturgy contained in the *Book of Common Prayer* (BCP) as the standard for the new Church.

First published in 1549 and revised several times in its first decade, the BCP was produced under the direction of Thomas Cranmer (1489–1556), who had been appointed Archbishop of Canterbury (the senior Episcopal seat in England) by Henry VIII, and also served under Edward VI and (briefly) the staunchly Catholic Mary I. Mary had Cranmer burned at the stake for treason and heresy. Nevertheless, the BCP reflects his commitment to negotiated compromise between varying theological positions. Thus many strains of theology, Catholic as well as Protestant, became foundation texts in the BCP. Indeed, Anglicanism itself represents a compromise or middle way between Roman Catholic and Protestant theologies and worship forms.

Puritans

The Puritans embraced a more extreme form of Protestantism and sought further purification of the Church along Calvinist lines. The Puritans were never a majority, but they held considerable economic and political power and were influential in the ecclesiastical landscape of sixteenth-century England. They condemned all forms of church ornamentation, the elaborate robes worn by clergy, and the use of organ music, as well as gestures such as the sign of the cross, while calling for an emphasis on preaching rather than sacraments, and strict observance of Sunday as the Sabbath. As well, Puritans upheld the authority of scripture over clergy and insisted on the Calvinist principle that every individual was predestined by God for either salvation or damnation. The most problematic commitment of the Puritans, however, was their insistence, following Calvin, that the state should be subject to the Church—the inverse of the English insistence that the Church was subject to the state through the headship of the monarch. This would eventually lead to charges of treason against the Puritans.

Seventeenth-Century Denominations

Quakers

Also significantly at odds with the established Church of England was the Religious Society of Friends, better known as the Quakers, a group founded almost spontaneously as people came to adopt the principles and practices of a man named George Fox (1624–91). Fox came of age during the upheaval of the English civil war, which created a context for the re-emergence of religious radicalism such as had been seen in the Reformation. In that context, Fox developed a pacifist approach to life as a Christian. Opposing the established religion of the day, he travelled the countryside as a dissenting (non–Church of England) preacher advocating a Christianity stripped of non-essential trappings, including clergy, ceremonial rites, church buildings, and special holy days.

The name "Quaker" referred to the Friends' tendency to tremble when overflowing with the spirit within. Following the principles outlined by Fox, Friends worshipped together without paid clergy, and sat in silence unless the spirit moved a member to speak. They refused to pay tithes to support the established Church, to take legal oaths (because one should always tell the truth), and to serve in the military (on the biblical principle that we should love our enemies). Embracing simplicity and love of neighbour as a way of life, the Quakers cultivated a practical understanding of mysticism in which union with God was meaningful only in so far as it furthered the goal of service to others.

Congregationalists

The Congregational churches trace their roots to "separatist" clergy in the time of Elizabeth I, but they did not become a significant force in England until the time of Cromwell, in the mid-1600s. As far as doctrine is concerned, there is little to distinguish Congregationalism from Presbyterian Calvinism. Where they differ is in their form of governance. Carrying the notion of the priesthood of all believers to its logical conclusion, Congregationalists reject the idea of elders and accord each individual congregation the ultimate authority to manage its theological and institutional affairs: for them, the only higher power is God.

In England, Congregational churches formed a Congregational Union in 1832 and were active in political and missionary causes throughout the nineteenth century. But the tradition's stronghold was Massachusetts, where Congregationalists founded Harvard University in 1637 in order not "to leave an illiterate ministry to the churches, when our present ministers shall lie in the dust." Yale University (1701) and other educational institutions in the American northeast were also founded by Congregationalists.

Baptists

Like the Anabaptists in continental Europe, the English Baptists practised the baptism of mature believers rather than infants. But they were much more intimately connected with the Puritan movement in England than with the Anabaptists. They believed that people should choose their religion rather than be born into it, and that the individual's choice ought to be private and beyond any interference by the state. By the 1640s, the English Baptist movement had two branches. Calvinist, or "Particular," Baptists reserved redemption for a particular sector of humanity, whereas "General" Baptists proclaimed a general redemption for humanity.

The first Baptist churches in the United States were established as early as 1639, but the Baptist presence remained small until the revival movement of 1740–3 known as the Great Awakening. Though the Baptists were not among its principal protagonists, they made massive numerical gains in its wake. They positioned themselves to become the largest American Protestant denomination partly through their successful appeal to the Black population; by the middle of the twentieth century, two out of every three African-American Christians were Baptists.

Pietism

The term "**Pietism**" designates not a denomination but a movement that rippled through various Protestant denominations, including the Lutherans in Germany and the Reformed (Calvinist) churches in the Netherlands, beginning in the late 1600s. Dissatisfied with the doctrinal and institutional rigidity they perceived in the Protestant churches emerging from the Reformation, Pietists sought a spontaneous renewal of faith accompanied by a feeling of certainty of divine forgiveness and acceptance.

For many, that feeling of certainty was all the evidence they needed to validate their faith. Their position set Pietists against the emerging rationalism of the eighteenth-century Enlightenment, but would find intellectual expansion in the emphasis laid on feeling by the German philosopher Friedrich Schleiermacher (1768–1834). Pietism spread in Lutheran circles both in Europe and in the Americas. In the form articulated by the Moravian Brethren—who traced their origins to the early Czech reformer John Hus—it also influenced the Wesleyan movement in England and contributed to Methodism.

Worship and the Protestant Reformation

Given that the crisis of the Reformation laid bare critiques of the hierarchical authority that had come to characterize Western Christianity, it was to be expected that the worship life of the newly emerging movement would change. As we saw in the medieval era, worship had been increasingly removed from ordinary people. Protestant reformers such as Luther, Zwingli, and Calvin all advocated changes to worship forms that would reduce mediation by clergy and give the people more direct access to God.

Although each of the denominational traditions that grew from the Reformation developed its own liturgical forms, all emphasized the use of the vernacular so that people could worship in their own languages rather than the Latin of the clergy.

New forms of music were designed for full congregational participation, the frequency of communion increased, and in the Lutheran and Anglican traditions, the clergy and congregation shared in both the bread and the wine. As well, worship spaces were reconfigured, especially in the traditions influenced by Calvin, putting clergy and people together in a less hierarchical arrangement that allowed full participation for all. In some traditions, altars were moved away from the wall; in others, they were de-centred entirely and the idea of a movable communion table was introduced. These changes were designed to communicate the theological point that all the baptized have direct access to God, and that the relationship of the disciple to God did not need mediation by clergy.

🐌 The Modern Era
The Enlightenment

By the end of the eighteenth century Christianity was no longer at the centre of Western civilization, and the ties between Church and state had been significantly loosened. The intellectual movement responsible for those changes is generally known as the Enlightenment. At the heart of the Enlightenment was a growing confidence in human reason.

The precise beginning of the Enlightenment is hard to identify, but a crucial early moment came in 1543, when the Polish astronomer Nicolaus Copernicus proposed that the universe revolved around the sun rather than the earth. Half a century later, the Italian mathematician Galileo Galilei confirmed that theory through observation. The Church responded by adding Copernicus's book to its list of prohibited writings and, in 1633, bringing Galileo to trial before the Inquisition. Found guilty of heresy, he was forced to "abjure, curse, and detest" his supposed errors, and to live the remaining eight years of his life under house arrest.

Deism

The growing importance of science was reflected in the rise of Deism. Recognizing that the universe manifests regular patterns or "laws of nature," the Deists did not believe that those laws could be suspended by divine intervention, but they could envision the universe as the product of a divine intelligence. They saw their creator God as a divine clockmaker, who assembles the universe and then leaves it to run on its own. The idea that if one can observe a design, then one can infer the existence of a designer goes back to ancient Greece and is known as the **teleological** argument, or argument from design.

The English philosopher William Paley offered the following example of the Deist position in his *Natural Theology*, published in 1802. If we found a watch on a desert island, we would not need to have seen any other watch in order to posit the existence of a maker; the watch would not even have to work perfectly, nor would we have to understand the function of every part. The same is true of the universe as evidence for God: even if the creation is imperfect, or not fully comprehensible, humans can still reasonably posit the existence of a perfect creator deity.

Philosophy

At the same time, the eighteenth century was a period of philosophical skepticism about claims for the transcendent. Particularly decisive were the critiques of the Scotsman David Hume and the German Immanuel Kant. Thomas Aquinas's argument for God as the First Cause cannot be proved; as Kant argued, causality is not part of the data of the physical world but part of the framework of thought in which human minds interpret it. But what Kant showed to be in principle unprovable is by the same token not disprovable. Whereas earlier thinkers sought to prove the existence of the divine or transcendent itself, many philosophers of religion since Kant have focused instead on experience and feeling—that is, the human response to the transcendent. In the early nineteenth century, Schleiermacher characterized religion as an "intuitive sense of absolute dependence": if we cannot prove the existence of what we intuitively feel that we depend on, at least we can describe that intuition.

Schleiermacher also contributed to a "subjective" understanding of Christ's atonement. In the traditional Christian understanding, it is through Christ's sacrifice that humanity is saved and restored to its proper relationship with God. For Schleiermacher, however, Jesus functions as a moral example, an embodiment of human awareness of God; salvation comes first as a change in spiritual awareness and then atonement follows as a divine–human reconciliation. From Schleiermacher the school of theology known as "liberal" theology was born.

Evolution

At the beginning of the nineteenth century, the scientific worldview was "creationist." Scientists held that every species on earth had been created by God with specific characteristics. This view was challenged by Charles Darwin, whose theory of evolution proposed that new types of organisms were not created by a deity but developed over time

Anti-evolution literature for sale at an outdoor stand in Dayton, Tennessee, in 1925. The creation vs evolution debate continues to rage, particularly where school curricula are concerned.

through a process he called natural selection. Darwin's epoch-making study *On the Origin of Species* was published in 1859, more than 20 years after he had worked out the basics of his theory.

Refining his argument clearly took time, but Darwin may have been especially cautious because he had studied theology and was well aware of the resistance he would encounter. He needed not merely to make a credible case for evolution, but to refute the basic tenets of biological creationism. He also knew that natural selection was antithetical to the teleological argument from design. If the natural world was completely self-regulating, there was no need for a supervising deity.

Because of Darwin, modern Christian theologians assessing the place of human beings in the universe have tended to locate human distinctiveness not in a special physical creation but in a unique intellectual and spiritual capacity for transcendence. For religious thinkers persuaded by Darwin's discoveries, what matters is not so much where we came from as where we are going.

Socio-political Context

Following the intellectual shifts of the Enlightenment, major changes took place in the economic and political landscape of the Western world. Social, political, and economic revolutions precipitated a fundamental shift in the relationship between Church and society, which in turn meant significant internal changes for Christianity. It has been argued that the French Revolution (1789) dealt a fatal blow to the traditional alliance between Church and state in Western Christendom. As the great dividing line in European political history, the French Revolution represents a watershed between the past and modern political systems. The medieval *ancien regime*, in which the monarch and the Church held power as partners in the project of social cohesion, disappeared under the onslaught of new ways of imagining human beings and their relationship to power.

The idea that all men (women were not included at this juncture) should have a voice in the political process carried the day. The violent overthrow of the French monarchy destabilized the Church, which had now lost its partner in power. Meanwhile, the Thirteen Colonies had already thrown off the historic control of the British government and demanded their right to exist as a sovereign nation, overthrowing the Church of England as the established Church. From that point forward, religion would be a choice based on the principle of volunteerism. Running parallel to these political revolutions was the economic revolution whereby an agrarian or property-based system changed to a money-based economy fuelled by consumerism and made possible through the mechanization of industrial production. This shift precipitated several other changes that also affected the role of the Church in the community.

Demographic migration from rural to urban areas, the breakdown of extended family units, and a (paradoxical) slight improvement in the economic situation of many workers intensified exploitation, which created greater job and social insecurity and generally contributed to the increase of human suffering, all affected the Church, which was de-centred from its role as the focal point of community and social norms. At the same time, the exploitation of workers led to the development of a working-class consciousness, which in turn led to the creation of labour unions. Unions became the primary champions of quality of life for the industrial working class, reducing the role of the churches. As well, most denominations did little to respond in a proactive way to the suffering of the industrial poor, which meant that organized religion became predominantly the preserve of the emerging middle class. All these contextual changes contributed to the declining significance of Christianity in Western culture.

Evangelical Great Awakenings

In the face of its declining significance in the Western world, Christianity paradoxically experienced several waves of religious revival in the early years of the modern era. Known as the Great Awakenings, these revivals unfolded in three stages: the first Great Awakening was a movement for religious revitalization that swept Protestant Europe and British America in the 1730s and 1740s. Focusing mainly on people who were already church-going believers, it summoned them to participate actively in the imperatives of the Protestant Reformation, including the divine outpouring of the Holy Spirit, the proclamation of the Word, and the expression of God's love in the world. There was a theological split between preachers of a Calvinist bent and those who took an Arminian perspective. However, all were united in their desire to set the hearts of God's people on fire with love of his gospel.

The second Great Awakening, beginning around 1800, was slightly different in its goals, focused on bringing non-believers to Christ. Many significant missionary organizations trace their origins to this time.

The third Great Awakening spans the period from 1858 to the beginning of the First World War in 1914. In 1858, after two centuries of self-imposed isolation, Japan allowed the first Christian missionary of modern times to enter the country, and David Livingstone published his *Missionary Travels and Researches in South Africa*, which fuelled enthusiasm for global mission. The principle of the priesthood of all believers summoned all disciples of Christ to become active agents of God's saving work. This time the emphasis was on social engagement, whether in the form of lay involvement at the grassroots level, religious education, distribution of the Bible, or social reform (including prohibition of alcohol as protection for the family). Both the movement for women's suffrage and the modern ecumenical movement had their roots in this wave of revival.

John Wesley (1703–91)

The primary catalyst of the first Great Awakening was John Wesley. The fifteenth child of the Rev'd Samuel and Susannah Wesley, at the age of 25 he followed in his father's footsteps and was ordained an Anglican priest. While studying theology at Oxford, he formed a small study group with his brother Charles Wesley and fellow student George Whitfield that was nicknamed the "Methodists"

for their methodical study of thinkers such as the seventeenth-century cleric Jeremy Taylor.

Wesley spent some time in the mission field in Georgia in 1735, but after a love interest went wrong he found himself on a boat sailing back to Europe. It was during that voyage that his life changed by an encounter with a group of Moravians from Germany. Heavily influenced by seventeenth-century Pietism, the Moravians reflected a lively and heartfelt faith that John had not experienced in the Anglican world.

Once back in England, Wesley had a transformative religious experience that he referred to as the moment when his heart "was strangely warmed." From then on, it became his mission to summon practitioners of a lukewarm religion to an engaged experience with the living Christ. Wesley's theology reflected his Anglican heritage in that (like Luther) he rejected the Calvinist theory of predestination in favour of the Arminian view that all who believed would be saved by grace. Unlike Luther, however, Wesley also believed that all who had been saved by faith should continue to become more visibly holy as evidence of their salvation. This notion of "sanctification" was extended into the arena of works. If one was saved, one's work would reflect the transfiguration of one's heart by the saving grace of God. It had not been Wesley's intention to break with the Church of England, but he found that his new way of preaching and teaching was not welcome there. In his commitment to theology as experience, Wesley developed a new expression of Christianity that became known as Methodism, a denomination which has since spread around the globe. Giving priority to the preaching of the Word and the involvement of laypersons at all levels of ministry, the Methodists emphasized engagement with the world as the place where the Kingdom of God was to be made real. The notion of progressive sanctification became central to the denomination.

Jonathan Edwards (1703–58)

Edwards was an American-born revivalist preacher from Puritan Calvinist roots who sparked enthusiasm for the gospel throughout the Thirteen

Colonies. An itinerant preacher, like most in the revivalist mode, he travelled from community to community inspiring new enthusiasm for faith with a dramatic and emotional style.

Where Edwards and Wesley differed was in their primary theological commitment. Wesley was an Arminian, emphasizing (as Luther had) that all could be saved through faith. Edwards, by contrast, was a Calvinist whose theology of salvation was grounded in the assumptions that only some were predestined to be saved, and that God alone knew who they were. Although Edwards died early (from a smallpox inoculation), he made a major contribution to American revivalism not only through his preaching but through his many writings, which remained popular well into the nineteenth century and inspired thousands to pursue a missionary vocation.

Holiness Churches

In time the main Methodist bodies in America became more organized and conventional, more sedate and mainline. But new independent churches and movements continued to spring from Methodism's revivalist roots. Because of their emphasis on the conversion experience, in which they believed that the gift of holiness or sanctification was received, these congregations have often been called **Holiness Churches**.

Like the early Methodists, members of the Holiness movement believed that if one's heart had been changed by God, one's outward behaviour would become progressively more holy as a sign of one's eventual salvation. As holiness preachers promoted this theology at revival meetings, people attracted to it broke away from their more mainstream denominations to form their own Holiness Churches.

Women and Revivalism

Like the Reformation, the Great Awakenings emphasized the ministry of all the baptized, and in so doing created openings for Protestant women to participate more actively in their churches.

Although the majority of revivalist preachers were male, most of the people who filled the tent meetings were women, and once the visiting preachers had moved on, it was the women who found new ways to live their faith, inspired by their experience in the tents. This openness to the religious experience of revival was reinforced by the gender assumptions of the day, whereby men were expected to toil in the often corrupt public world of business, while women made the private world of the home and family a haven of virtue and tenderness.

Led mainly by middle-class women who could afford to take the time away from their household responsibilities, new voluntary associations were developed with a wide range of foci, including the Sunday School movement; the development of missionary societies (which sent both male and female missionaries into the field); the resurrection of the Order of Deaconesses, based on the early Church model; support for the paid employment of single laywomen in a variety of Church ministry contexts; and maintaining connections with other women's groups, both nationally and globally.

All these activities helped to lay the groundwork for later advances, including recognition of their right to vote in Church councils and, eventually, to ordination. The women of the revival era empowered themselves as they learned the skills required for organization-building, fund-raising and disbursement, and strategic planning for the implementation of missionary visions. At the same time, their churches gradually became accustomed to the idea of women in various leadership roles.

Missions

Missionary activity was hardly a new phenomenon. From its beginnings Christianity has been essentially a missionary religion: evangelization in the time of the Apostle Paul; the Christianization of the Roman Empire; early European expansion as more of the continent was converted to Christianity; the age of discovery, when European empires began to explore the world, taking Christianity with them.

What was new in the era of the awakenings was that now the missionaries included zealous Protestants as well as Catholics. The first English-speaking Protestant to enter the global mission field was William Carey (1761–1834) of the Baptist Missionary Society, who left for India with his family in 1793. Other denominations followed suit and soon several missionary organizations were competing for converts abroad.

Although mission societies reflecting their denominational traditions were particular in their scope and focus, several characteristics were typical of the work. These included strong adherence to the exclusive claims of Christianity; commitment to the view that the religions of missionized people were the work of the "devil"; emphasis on preaching a gospel of conversion and distributing Bibles, with little social outreach; translation of the Christian scripture, particularly into the languages of Asia and Southeast Asia; and, in the early years, training of indigenous clergy (this activity declined as the European notion of the "noble savage" was replaced by colonial stereotypes of indigenous people as childlike and in need of both education and civilization).

By the third awakening, both Protestant and Catholic missionaries were not only proselytizing but actively promoting the Christianization of their own society. This led various historic colonial churches to work with the governments of the day on projects of cultural assimilation. In the case of new immigrants, conversion to Christianity and adaptation to the cultural norms of the host society were often presented as one and the same thing. As well, in places such as Canada, the United States, and Australia, the historic colonial churches collaborated with government to promote the assimilation of indigenous people. The most disturbing example of this collaboration is found in the partnership agreements between governments and churches to operate residential or boarding school systems. In this partnership the government set the policies and paid the churches per capita fees to strip indigenous children of their culture and

Focus

Black Elk (1863–1950)

In North America, some today argue that the harm Christianity caused through its role in the process of colonization means that it has no value for the present and future of indigenous people and communities. However, there have been Aboriginal leaders who believed that indigenous wisdom and Christian belief were complementary. An Oglala Lakota man by the name of Black Elk was perhaps the most significant of those who held this view. At the age of nine he fell ill and during his illness was given a vision for his people that was later affirmed by Lakota elders as one of great spiritual power. He became a medicine man (healer) among his people. As an adult he was converted to Christianity by Roman Catholic missionaries, but throughout his life he continued to receive visions that confirmed the experience of his youth, and over time he came to articulate the parallels between Lakota wisdom and Christian teaching. Thus he insisted that the "Great Spirit" or Creator of the Lakota tradition was analogous to the Creator God of the Christian Trinity, and believed that the traditional pipe given to the Lakota people was a way of knowing God prior to the introduction of Christ among Native Americans. He understood that the path of all creation, the "Red Road" in Lakota teaching, was indeed the Christ he had met when he was converted to Christianity. Today his visions and his theology continue to play a significant part in the conversation between indigenous elders and Christian theologians.

assimilate them to Euro-descent norms. Together, the loss of culture and the abuse suffered by these children have harmed several generations of indigenous people. One of the key challenges that now face the churches historically involved in this work is to find ways to repair the damage that was done and mend the broken relationships that have been the result.

Today, awareness of that damage has faced the historic colonial churches with the task of reformulating the mission concept so as to prevent any repetition of the harm done in the past.

Theological Controversies and Denominational Splitting

As we have seen, the intellectual advances of the modern era created a crisis for Christianity in the West. Theologians struggled to find ways of adapting theology to emerging methods of inquiry. The development of historical biblical criticism and "modernist" theology led to the splitting of denominations and the creation of new traditions.

The three schools of thought that shaped the drama of denominational splitting can be identified as liberalism, evangelicalism, and fundamentalism. All three were broad global movements that affected Christianity everywhere in the West. The term "modernist" was first used to refer to a group of Roman Catholic theologians who, towards the end of the nineteenth century, had adopted a critical and skeptical attitude toward traditional Christian doctrines, especially with reference to Christology (who is Jesus?) and soteriology (salvation). This movement fostered a positive attitude toward radical biblical criticism and stressed the ethical rather than the doctrinal dimensions of faith. The term migrated into North American Protestantism fairly rapidly. By the turn of the twentieth

Focus

Christianity in Nazi Germany

When the National Socialists rose to power under Hitler in 1932, the religious landscape in Germany shifted dramatically. Early in the Nazi regime there was increasing pressure on the Christian churches to welcome Hitler as their Führer. Most Christian churches acceded to this directive, some even forming the "German Church," which was directly accountable to Hitler. However, a significant number of Protestant pastors (ordained ministers) resisted. They banded together to form what they called the Confessing Church, and in 1934 they produced the Barmen Declaration, proclaiming that Jesus Christ and no other was the Lord of the Church—an act of resistance to Hitler's insistence that he commanded primary loyalty in the German state and that the church should be subject to him. The influential theologian Karl Barth was a leader in the Confessing Church movement, and one of the great heroes of twentieth-century Christianity, Dietrich Bonhoeffer, a Lutheran pastor and theologian, was among the signatories of the declaration. Unlike Barth, however, he took his insistence on adherence to Christian principles to a point of resistance that led to his arrest in 1942. Bonhoeffer spent the rest of his life imprisoned by the Nazis, and was executed in April 1944 at the age of 39. Continuing to write while imprisoned, he argued that to say "Jesus is Lord" with words was insufficient: all Christians are called to live the meaning of "Jesus is Lord," even to the point of self-sacrifice for love of the other, on the example of Jesus.

century, mainstream Protestant denominations were increasingly influenced by "modernist attitudes," as reflected in a rethinking of the doctrine of creation, an emphasis on God's presence in creation rather than his transcendence, and a shift in atonement theology towards Schleiermacher's view, in which the emphasis is less on Christ's sacrifice as the means to human salvation and more on the example he set for humanity and a consequent emphasis on moral meaning and teaching ("what would Jesus do?").

Historical Biblical Criticism

The eighteenth and nineteenth centuries witnessed the emergence of history as a ruling intellectual discipline. During this period the Bible came to be studied not as a depository of doctrinal truths, but as a historical document like any other. Historical criticism, the product of this development, is a method of biblical interpretation in which the true meaning of a given text is seen as depending on the context of its composition. Thus to understand the meaning of a biblical passage requires knowledge not of Christian doctrine but rather of the historical and social conditions in which it was written. Many Christians saw the rise of historical criticism as the enemy of Christianity, as it undermined the "absolute truth" claims of Christian doctrine and appeared to make faith conditional on historical circumstance.

The Historical Jesus

Some scholars saw in history a means of freeing Christianity from developments that, in their view, Jesus and his earliest followers never intended. Nineteenth-century European theologians used historical methods to write biographies of Jesus that were free of Christian dogma. These scholars were confident that the Gospels, though written at least 30 years after his death, contained enough accurate information to constitute true biographical accounts of the historical Jesus. The German theologian and humanist Albert Schweitzer (1875–1965) noticed that the many lives of Jesus written

in the nineteenth century coincidentally affirmed the values of his biographers. He named these "Liberal Lives of Jesus" to signal that the Jesus of these historians conformed to nineteenth-century hopes for a more liberal society. Schweitzer himself found in the Gospels evidence of an apocalyptic Jesus who is virtually unrecognizable to a modern world so far removed from the one in which Jesus lived. Schweitzer condemned what he called "The Quest for the Historical Jesus" as a largely failed project. After the Second World War, however, the quest was revived with the help of new discoveries about the Judaism of Jesus' day, and in 1985 the Jesus Seminar was formed by 150 scholars who gathered regularly to study each of the sayings and deeds attributed to Jesus and to discuss and debate whether it originated with Jesus or was attributed to him by later followers. Like the earlier questers, the more recent ones have been criticized for "discovering" a Jesus who conforms to the ideals of liberal democracy.

Reactions to Modernism

Evangelicalism

Reactions against modernist theology took two primary forms: evangelicalism and fundamentalism. Evangelical Protestants' resistance to modernism is reflected in their emphasis on the necessity of personal conversion; the desire for personal sanctification overflowing into the desire to work for a better society; lay leadership; and the importance of scripture and preaching. Unlike fundamentalists, however, they have generally not insisted on the literal inerrancy of scripture. In the twentieth century, evangelicalism influenced many Protestant denominations, but was most significant among the Reformed Churches.

Fundamentalism

Fundamentalism represents another theological response to modernism. The term refers to a movement within various Protestant bodies in North

America, which began at the turn of the twentieth century. In reaction against historical biblical criticism and the theory of evolution, fundamentalists sponsored a series of Bible conferences in various parts of the United States. The most famous, the "Niagara Conference," issued a statement of belief containing what later came to be known as the "Five Points of Fundamentals." These five points, which became the defining commitments of fundamentalism, were the inerrancy of scripture; the divinity of Jesus Christ; the virgin birth; the substitutionary theory of the atonement (the idea that Christ died in our place, and in so doing paid the debt we owe God for our sins); and the physical resurrection and second coming of Christ.

The term "fundamentalism" derives from a series of 12 tracts entitled "The Fundamentals," which first appeared in 1909. Written by eminent evangelical leaders, they were widely distributed in the English-speaking world with the aid of American money. Fundamentalism affected a variety of denominations and contributed to denominational splitting by inspiring theological conflicts that became too intense to be contained within a single denominational group.

Pentecostalism

Pentecostalism should not be confused with fundamentalism: they are separate movements with different emphases. Pentecostalism has more in common with the Holiness movement of the nineteenth century. It takes its name from an episode in the Book of Acts in which the Holy Spirit visits a gathering of the Apostles and some others on the Feast of the Pentecost (the fiftieth day after Easter) and bestows on them the gift of **glossolalia**, or "speaking in tongues."

The movement that gave rise to Pentecostalism was led by Charles Parham, an American evangelist who taught that speaking in tongues was evidence of the "baptism of the spirit." One of his students, an African-American pastor named William J. Seymour (1870–1922), adapted his message to be inclusive across racial and gender lines, and began preaching the imminent return of Jesus to mixed-race crowds in Los Angeles in 1906. Seymour's "Azusa Street Revival" was so popular that it sparked similar meetings across the US and eventually around the world. Gifts of the Spirit such as speaking in tongues and interpretation of tongues,

Focus

Secularism

The dramatic decline of Christianity in Europe and North America has been fuelled by a rising secularism. Increasingly people are looking beyond organized religion to answer the questions of purpose and ultimate meaning in their lives. This is true for all major religious groups in the northern hemisphere. As the numbers of people embracing a religious worldview have declined, the numbers embracing other perspectives have grown. Most notable among those other perspectives are Marxism, a political philosophy that attributes all

causation in human society to economic factors, and psychology, which considers human actions and behaviours as reflections of the psyche. One of the great theological challenges of the modern era has been to define the place of Christianity and organized religion generally in a world where questions of ultimate meaning can be so readily answered by alternative modes of thought. Some argue that consumerism itself is replacing organized religion as the vehicle by which people attempt to find meaning in their lives.

Focus

Aimee Semple McPherson (1890–1944)

Spirit-based movements such as Pentecostalism have been more likely than more mainstream denominations to offer women opportunities as preachers and leaders. The reason for this unusual openness has to do with the idea that if God gave someone a gift for a particular kind of ministry, then the Church should affirm that gift.

Aimee Semple McPherson was an important example of this phenomenon. Born in Ontario and converted to Pentecostalism in her teens, she followed her passion to preach all the way to Los Angeles, where in time she became the most famous evangelist of her generation. Unlike other early Pentecostals, she very quickly realized the potential of modern media (especially radio) as vehicles for evangelization. Aimee became renowned for both her preaching and the divine healings that were reported to take place at her revival meetings when, as she saw it, God broke into people's lives and demonstrated his love and mercy by healing them both physically and spiritually. Eventually she built a large church known as the Angeles Temple, which was filled by the thousands for every worship service. She founded an early Pentecostal denomination known as the Four Square Gospel Church, which still exists today. The media-based ministry that she pioneered served as a prototype for later forms of North American Pentecostalism.

Aimee Semple McPherson prays enthusiastically with her congregation at Tom Noonan's Chinatown mission in New York in 1933 (© Hulton-Deutsch Collection/Corbis).

divine healings and prophecy were interpreted as signs to community members that God was with them. Many new denominations were born from this renewal movement, including the Assemblies of God, the Pentecostal Fellowship, and the Church of God. Today Pentecostalism is the fastest-growing sector of Christianity in the world, and is especially prevalent in the Global South.

The Social Gospel

Both evangelical and liberal Protestants developed a keen sense of active faith. Early in the twentieth century, an American Baptist minister named Walter Rauschenbusch (1861–1918) argued that Christianity is by nature revolutionary, that realizing the Kingdom of God that Jesus talked about was not a matter of individuals' getting to heaven but of transforming life on earth into the harmony of heaven. He focused on social sin rather than individual sin, with particular attention to religious bigotry, graft, and the corruption of justice as a perversion of God's intention. This way of approaching the relationship of the gospel to the world captured the imagination of Christians across theological and denominational lines and inspired a new emphasis

Focus

Global Pentecostalism

Of the more than two billion Christians in the world today, more than one-quarter are Pentecostal or "charismatic." Latin Americans, Native Americans, Africans, and Asians say that Pentecostal interpretations of Christianity are more in keeping with their cultural worldviews than other forms of Christianity. However, current studies indicate that the experience of divine healing is the single most important reason for the growth of Pentecostalism. In parts of the world where access to health care is out of reach for most people, Pentecostalism thrives. In addition, Pentecostal churches (unlike the historic colonial churches) offer their congregations help with everyday problems.

on social engagement in a wide range of Christian communities.

The social gospel was enthusiastically embraced in Canada as well as the United States. However, the two nations developed the theology differently. Under Rauschenbusch's leadership, the American social gospel movement had a political dimension that led it to side with labour against big business. By contrast, the Canadian churches tried to encourage business people to treat their workers fairly and humanely. Although this strategy was largely unsuccessful in effecting social change, several significant leaders from the Canadian churches carried a message that was essentially the social gospel into the political arena. The best known of those leaders was Tommy Douglas (1904–86), a Baptist minister who eventually left the ministry to enter politics. As premier of Saskatchewan he led the way to socialized medicine, and the Saskatchewan plan for universal health care was eventually mirrored across Canada.

Theological Diversity in the Modern/Postmodern Era

The rise of liberal theology gave impetus to the development of both fundamentalism and Pentecostalism. Yet there was also a rapid proliferation of theological diversity within the liberal camp.

Particularly in North America, theologians took the basic commitments of liberal theology and developed new forms of theological expression. These included the application of existential philosophy to theology, as in the work of Paul Tillich (1886–1995); the development, by Alfred North Whitehead (1861–1947), Charles Hartshorne (1897–2000) and others, of process theology, which drew on physics to argue for a God who is in some respects changeable, in ongoing relationship with the unfolding universe; and the rise of liberation theologies of various kinds, which focused on the particular concerns of oppressed groups including women, indigenous people, African Americans, and, in Latin America, the poor and politically violated.

In the face of this explosion of diversity among liberal theologies, an opposing theological direction emerged in the period between the two world wars. The primary architect of this "neo-orthodoxy" was the Swiss theologian Karl Barth (1886–1968), who emphasized the transcendence of God and the inability of human beings to work out their own salvation. Barth's radical doctrine of sin and grace found resonance among the Reformed Churches in particular.

The Changing Place of Women

The modern era has seen significant changes in the roles and participation of women in Christian

Focus

The Catholic Worker Movement and Dorothy Day (1897–1980)

The twentieth century saw the birth of many Christian-inspired social movements. Roman Catholics have been particularly devoted to improving life for the poor and oppressed. The Catholic Worker Movement in the United States is an example of this phenomenon. Dorothy Day was a journalist and social activist, heavily influenced by Marxist thought, who as a young woman had a conversion experience in a Roman Catholic worship setting. Through this experience she made the journey from atheist to devout Catholic while remaining a Marxist. With her friend Peter Maurin, she established a movement that spread across the US and continues today. This movement inspired houses of hospitality wherein persons committed to the poor lived with them as companions and friends, sharing their food and shelter, and offering respite from the harsh edge of urban poverty. Persons committed to this movement also worked unceasingly for social change on behalf of the poor and consistently spoke against war. To serve as a platform for this advocacy, Day and Maurin started their own small newspaper; the *Catholic Worker* is still available today at the original price of 1 penny per copy. The pacifist anarchism that characterized Day's theology meant that she was often in conflict with the American government, and the movement often had to defend itself against accusations of un-American activity. Dorothy Day is currently being considered for canonization (elevation to sainthood in the Roman Catholic Church).

© AP Photo/H.B. Littell/CP

Dorothy Day (centre, seated), founder of the *Catholic Worker*, moderates a discussion about the problems of segregation during a radio broadcast at the Louisville Public Library, 10 Sept. 1954.

communities. As surely as the nineteenth century saw the rise of women's leadership in the voluntary and missionary arenas, the twentieth saw questions arise concerning women's roles in the churches. This shift was in large measure precipitated by shifts in cultural understandings of women's roles and place in society. In other words, women were included as full persons under the law, with the right to vote, before their churches began to address the matter of female ordination.

Even today, only a minority of Christians belong to a church that allows women to participate fully in leadership roles. More than half of the world's Christian population is Roman Catholic, another significant sector is Eastern Orthodox, and yet another is conservative Protestant. With minor variations that reflect the particularities of their denominational theologies, women in these churches do not have full ecclesiastical voting rights and are not eligible for ordination. Most historic colonial or mainline Protestant denominations and some evangelical churches do permit women to vote and be ordained on an equal footing with their male colleagues. Yet there are still limitations on the roles that women can play in some mainline denominations. For example, the Anglican Church of Canada has permitted ordination of women as bishops, priests, and deacons since 1976, but in the Church of England women are still restricted to serving as deacons and priests; a motion to permit ordination as bishops was defeated by just six votes in 2012.

Progress towards gender parity tended to follow a standard pattern: first women were given voting rights in all the governing bodies of their churches, and then the question of ordination was tackled. In most denominations those changes took place between the 1960s and the 1990s.

Liberal Protestant denominations in North America were ordaining women as clergy by the middle of the twentieth century, and the Anglican communion began doing so not long after that. Several American and Canadian denominations have had women as presiding officers. The first woman to be ordained a bishop in the Anglican communion was Barbara Harris, who served as an Episcopalian bishop in Massachusetts from 1989 to 2003. Lois Wilson, a minister and former moderator of the United Church of Canada, was a president of the World Council of Churches from 1983 to 1991, as was Madeleine Barot, from France, from 1954 to 1960.

The fact that the Roman Catholic and Eastern Orthodox churches, some conservative evangelical denominations, and some indigenous denominations in Africa, Asia, and Latin America refuse to ordain women at all hearkens back to the early Church's position with regard to the proper place and function of women in Christian leadership, though in some cases it also reflects current views

© Reuters/Corbis

Bishop Barbara Harris of the Episcopal Diocese of Massachusetts at her ordination as the first female bishop in the Anglican Communion, in 1989.

on gender. Although the arguments against the ordination of women vary with theological perspective, both Roman Catholic and Orthodox theologians have argued that women cannot represent Christ because Christ was male. Other justifications for women's exclusion draw on select passages from scripture, and the fact that the early Church did not ordain women to the threefold order of ministry.

Twentieth-Century Movements for Social Change

In the twentieth century, Christians played an active part in several grassroots movements for social change, including the anti-apartheid movement in South Africa, the *Communidades de Base* movement in Latin America, and the civil rights movement in the United States. However, it is interesting to note that in each of these situations there were Christians on both sides of the debate. The churches in question were used both to reinforce the status quo and to demand change in cases involving injustice and oppression, particularly of the poor.

In South Africa, the Afrikaners who justified the seizure of land from indigenous Africans on grounds of manifest destiny were largely members of the Dutch Reformed Church. They argued they had been chosen by God to administer South Africa and prevent miscegenation (the mixing of races through intermarriage). South African Anglicans for the most part, opposed apartheid. However, individual church members disagreed as to tactics for resistance, and some Anglicans of European descent vigorously opposed their church's involvement in politics, while black Anglican clergy such as Desmond Tutu became very public political figures. Methodism, also imported from England, quickly became an overwhelmingly black denomination with an openly anti-apartheid stance, although the aggressive activism of its leaders cost it support from those who feared the power of the apartheid state. The Roman Catholic Church in

South Africa opposed apartheid as well, but a group calling itself the South African Catholic Defence League condemned the Church's political involvement and denounced school integration.

In Latin America the Roman Catholic Church was an agent both of change and of resistance to change. As the official Church of Spain, the colonial power that dominated Latin America from the fifteenth century to the nineteenth, it allied itself with the state in regimes of control and repression, as was the case in processes of colonization everywhere. However, with decolonization the Church–state relationship shifted. When economic crises from the 1960s to the 1990s permitted the rise of military dictatorships, the poor faced crushing poverty and extreme violations of human rights. Although some local Church leaders stood with the military regimes, most positioned themselves in solidarity with the poor and suffering. In 1968, at the second conference of Latin American bishops in Bogota and Medellin, three important documents were generated. Entitled "Justice," "Peace," and "Poverty of the Church," they shattered the centuries-old alliance between the Church, the military, and the wealthy. The key words that emerged as blueprints for the future were "liberation" and "participation." The Church pledged itself to participate in the dynamic action of an awakened community in resistance to the forces that oppressed and denied life.

This consciousness-raising was reflected in the *Communidades de Base*: grassroots Christian "base communities," located in the poorest slums of Latin America, that were often supported by local priests. Offering Bible study, prayer, and fellowship, they became the focal points of both communal resistance and communal renovation, expressions of the Church's theological commitment to the dignity of all human beings. Many Church leaders paid with their lives for their commitment to the poor. The most notable example was Bishop Oscar Romero of El Salvador. Although before his appointment he had been a mild-mannered academic, not involved in the country's political turmoil, as bishop he developed a passion for solidarity with the poor, and he became a recognized leader of the non-violent resistance to the military dictatorship of the day. His assassination, while presiding at worship on 24 March 1980, inspired many others to take up the cause of defending the human rights of political resisters and the poor.

In the United States, the civil rights movement, which demanded equal rights under the law for persons of colour after centuries of slavery and segregation, was largely driven by the Black churches. Historically, through the era of slavery and beyond, Black churches had served as focal points for communal life and empowerment. Thus when the time came for resistance to white repression, the Black churches and their pastors were pivotal in gathering the community and providing leadership in the form of both inspiration and strategy. Most notable of all was the Reverend Dr Martin Luther King, Jr (1929–68), a Baptist pastor whose skills as an orator and insistence on non-violent resistance made him the principal spokesman for the civil-rights movement until he was murdered at the age of 39. The Christian principle that all people are made in the image of God animated social resistance in a world where a significant proportion of the population was not accorded the most basic human rights.

Vatican II

The election of the Italian cardinal Angelo Giuseppe Roncalli as pope in 1958 sparked significant change in the Roman Catholic Church. Though already in his late seventies, John XXIII (the name he chose upon his election) proved to have a vision for his Church and a fearless openness to change. Calling for *aggiornamento*, Italian for "updating," John XXIII convoked the Second Vatican Council, which met from 1962 to 1965.

The changes set in motion at the council ushered in a new era for Catholicism. Latin was replaced by the vernacular as the language of the mass, and the officiating priest now turned to face the congregation (although the doctrine of transubstantiation was retained). The dress of priests and nuns was modernized and in many cases religious dress

was set aside for particular occasions. Whereas the First Vatican Council (1869–70) had emphasized the monarchical aspect of the pope's role, Vatican II emphasized the more collegial nature of his role in council with the bishops. Efforts were also made to improve relations with other branches of Christianity and other religious traditions, especially Judaism.

The Church of Rome Today

More than fifty years later, the council's agenda still has not been completed, and pressing problems remain. The priesthood today is under serious threat, as the numbers of candidates continue to decline. A major breach developed in the Church shortly after the council, in 1968, when John's successor, Pope Paul VI, in his encyclical *Humanae Vitae* ("On human life") prohibited the use of artificial birth control by Catholics. The gap between the Church's official stand on sexuality and the actual practice of the faithful has only widened in the intervening decades. Many Catholics have ceased to follow teachings they consider out of date. But the matter had other implications as well. *Humanae Vitae* intensified the theological tensions between the reform-minded and traditionalist wings in the Church's hierarchy. Progressive Catholics saw the encyclical as an attempt to turn the clock back and reaffirm the papal authority established at Vatican I.

Sexual Abuse

The sexual abuse of children by religious professionals is not uniquely a phenomenon of the modern era or of the Roman Catholic Church alone. However, in recent years the latter has been shaken by a series of scandals involving its clergy and children. Beginning in 2001, such cases were required to be reported to Rome, rather than handled by local Church officials as had previously been allowed. Cases that were tried in secular criminal courts received significant media attention in Canada, the United States, and Ireland in particular, with a preponderance of charges being laid in the United States. As well, thousands of civil lawsuits have been filed against the Church seeking compensation for damages. According to the Associated Press, restitution payments made between 1950 and 2012 are estimated at more than 3 billion dollars. As a consequence, eight dioceses in the US declared bankruptcy between 2004 and 2011, and by 2013 another five had filed for bankruptcy protection. Even more significant than the financial implications are the challenges that these cases have posed to the credibility and authority of the Church.

Changes in the Papal Office

In February 2013 Pope Benedict XVI announced that he would resign from the papal office. The last time a pope had resigned from his office was in 1415, when Pope Gregory XII resigned to end the great Western schism. At the age of 86, Benedict said that he no longer had the physical strength to perform his duties adequately. The following month Jorge Bergoglio, Archbishop of Argentina, was elected as the first pope from the Global South and took the name Francis I. Pope Francis is known for his solidarity with the poor, and for his commitment to social justice. His election has sparked hope in the hearts of Catholics around the world that positive change for the Church is not only possible but imminent.

Recent Developments
Changing Demographics

For several decades the mainline denominations in Europe and North America have been declining, even as Christianity grows rapidly in the Global South. In response to their decline, the traditional churches have been re-evaluating the forms and structures of their worship and organizational life and their relationship to Western culture. Meanwhile, new groups such as the Emergent Church Movement are experimenting with new ways of expressing Christian belief, new forms of urban monastic community, house churches, and participation in environmental and social projects as forms of faith expression. Although continuing immigration from Asia and the Global South is likely to slow the decline to some degree, it will also lead to changes in Church life in the next generation.

Focus

Indigenization of Christian Liturgy

Christian liturgy is understood to reflect the particular culture in which it develops. Thus as cultures evolve over time, so do their liturgies. And as new communities adopt Christianity, they adapt the liturgies they have been given to reflect their own culture, taking key aspects of the faith and integrating them into local life in a reciprocal conversation between history and the present. This basic process of adaptation, or indigenization, can be seen at work today in several places. In Africa, for instance, historic colonial denominations are adapting their liturgies to include traditional local songs and drumming. In Canada, indigenous Anglicans in various parts of the country have developed services in the own languages, incorporating traditional musical forms and language. And in New Zealand, the Anglican Church has developed a prayer book that contains worship services in English, Polynesian, and Maori, with content that reflects the symbol systems of all three cultures.

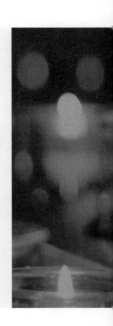

Ecumenism

The historical divisions within Euro-American Christianity made little sense when they were exported to Africa and Asia. For more than a century the mainline Protestant denominations have been working to overcome four centuries of separation.

Part of this movement was rooted in missionary collaboration, beginning with the World Missionary Conference held in Edinburgh in 1910. Denominational mission boards agreed to divide overseas territories among the various denominations to reduce redundant competition. Also significant was collaboration in youth work, through organizations such as the interdenominational Student Christian Movement. In the United States, the Federal Council of Churches was particularly devoted to collaboration on economic and social issues.

By mid-century, a generation of leaders who had grown up with interdenominationalism had moved into positions of responsibility in their own churches. The time was ripe for worldwide collaboration, and in 1948 the World Council of Churches was formed, with representation from most major Protestant and Orthodox bodies. **Ecumenism** (from the Greek meaning "inhabited world") offered a climate of mutual acceptance and common purpose, an emphasis on unity in diversity. However, Protestants agreed to continue disagreeing on many issues that historically had separated them, such as Eucharistic theology and Church discipline (how members of the community are expected to conduct themselves in matters involving ethics). It was much easier to affirm one another's agendas regarding social justice (or, later, ecological concern) than to take communion together.

Nonetheless, a number of denominational mergers did take place in the twentieth century. In 1925 Canadian Methodists, Congregationalists, and a majority of the country's Presbyterians formed the United Church of Canada. A similar group of churches joined to form the Uniting Church in Australia in 1977. In England in 1972, the Presbyterians and Congregationalists merged to form the United Reformed Church. In the United States, a multiple merger in 1961 produced the United Church of Christ.

But more ambitious twentieth-century attempts at Church union remain unconsummated. Consultations in the United States and New Zealand involving Anglicans, Presbyterians, and others were unable to resolve differences over ordination and the Eucharist. Anglicans hesitated to rush into union with Reformed Churches, partly because they also wanted to conduct conversations with Lutherans and the Roman Catholic Church. However, the Church of South India was formed in 1947 by a variety of Protestant denominations, including Anglicans, and it was followed by a number of regionally defined unions in North India, Pakistan, and Bangladesh. And Episcopalians and Lutherans in the United States moved part of the way towards union in 1999.

Among the most significant advances have been the theological agreements reached between various churches. In 1982 the Faith and Order Commission of the World Council of Churches produced a document entitled "Baptism, Eucharist and Ministry," now widely referred to as "BEM," which reflects a significant degree of consensus among member churches of the World Council on these key areas of Church life, while also identifying areas of ongoing difference in belief and practice. In 1992 the Anglican churches of England and Ireland, the Church in Wales and the Episcopal Church of Scotland, the Churches of Denmark, Norway and Sweden and the Evangelical Lutheran churches of Estonia, Finland, Iceland, Latvia, and Lithuania, overcame their theological differences to ratify the Porvoo Common Statement, allowing for co-operation and sharing between Anglicans and Lutherans in areas such as communion and clergy.

Rome's twentieth-century move into ecumenism is associated primarily with the papacy of John XXIII. A permanent Secretariat for the Promotion of Christian Unity was established in 1960. An important item on the agenda of the Second Vatican Council was the drafting of documents and declarations that might bring about a rapprochement with other Christians. The spirit of reunion was in the air. By the end of the 1960s, Protestant and Catholic institutions for the study of theology and the training of clergy were entering into collaborative arrangements of all sorts, while their students were attending the same lectures and reading the same books.

Fission and Fusion

The modern era can be characterized as a period of fission and fusion for Christianity. Reflecting the explosion of theological diversity and the rapid global expansion of Christianity through modern mission activity, historic colonial denominations seeded new churches that developed in their own ways. Currently, according to David Barrett in the *World Christian Encyclopedia*, there are more than 20,000 distinct denominational families in the world, most of which have come into being in the last hundred years. Perhaps ironically, the ecumenical movement, which called for fusion, in fact contributed to division as complicated union negotiations have often left some parties behind, thus creating both a new fused denomination and the persistent remnants of the former denominations, as was the case with the United Church of Canada.

Currently, as we have noted, the single largest Christian denomination in the world is Roman Catholicism and the fastest growing dimension of Christianity is Pentecostalism (not as a denomination but as a way of being Christian in a variety of denominations). These two factors have led demographer Philip Jenkins to conclude that within several decades, despite the rapid explosion of denominational diversity, only two basic forms of Christianity will remain: Roman Catholicism and Pentecostalism.

Together, the rapid expansion of Christianity in the Global South and its rapid decline in the North and West have re-shaped the face of Christian missions. In prior centuries, European and North American denominations sent missionaries to the Far East and the Global South. Today, however, the largest numbers of ministers known as missionaries are being sent from Africa, Latin America, and Korea to take the Christian message to the largely de-Christianized continents of Europe and North America. These missions are heavily reminiscent of mission activity in the eighteenth and nineteenth centuries, in that their purpose is conversion. So we see that while in the North and West that model has been eschewed in favour of partnership and respect for religious pluralism, missionaries from the Global South are reintroducing a conversionist model of Christianity to the northern hemisphere.

Christianity and Pluralism

By the beginning of the third millennium, diversity had become part of the national fabric not only of societies built on immigration, like Canada, the United States, and Australia, but also, increasingly, of European societies where until recently the great majority of citizens shared a common cultural background, including the Christian faith.

One of the great opportunities and challenges of this generation is the religious diversity that characterizes the global landscape. Christians live side by side with people of many faiths in ways previously not known. This has opened up a plethora of opportunities for engagement theologically and spiritually between peoples of different backgrounds. As well, opportunities abound for Christians to work with their neighbours of differing religious commitments for the well-being of local and global communities. Of course, religious difference has also served throughout history to fuel division and violence. However, traditional Christian commitments to love of neighbour, compassion, and mutual respect impel Christian communities, in their best moments, toward new ways of authentically Christian living beside and in partnership with non-Christian neighbours. Arguably, to learn this discipline well will be one of the most significant projects for Christians in the next centuries.

Table 4.1 Professing Christians Worldwide, 2011	
Total Christians as % of world population: 33%	
Affiliated Christians (church members)	2,187,138,999
Church attenders	1,523,229,000
Evangelicals	965,400,000*
Pentecostals/Charismatics/Neocharismatics	612,472,000
Membership By Six Ecclesiastical Megablocs	
Roman Catholic	1,160,880,000
Protestant	426,450,000
Independent	378,281,000
Orthodox	271,316,000
Anglican	87,520,000
Marginal Christian	35,539,000

*Includes Great Commission Christians

Source: Adapted from Johnson, Barrett, and Crossing 2011: 28–9.

✿ Summary

This short consideration of key themes in the history of Christianity has suggested both its complexity and its consistency. From its origins as a Jewish reform movement Christianity grew to embrace the globe, incorporating diversities of cultural and ethnic experience and a wide variety of philosophical perspectives that produced diverse schools of theology and a wide range of ecclesiastical forms and practices. As Christianity begins its third millennium it continues to expand, although differently than in earlier generations. Today, rather than looking back towards Europe, Christianity is looking towards the Global South as the location of its most pressing concern. As it navigates the uncharted terrain of the future, it will carry with it the central message that is the gospel of resurrected life in Jesus Christ. It will fashion its next becoming with the tools of its past learning, honed in the workshop of negotiated difference.

Sacred Texts

Religion	Text	Composition/ Compilation	Compilation/ Revision	Use
Christianity	Old Testament (Genesis, Exodus, Leviticus, Numbers, Deuteronomy, Joshua, Judges, Ruth, 1 Samuel, 2 Samuel, 1 Kings, 2 Kings, 1 Chronicles, 2 Chronicles, Ezra, Nehemiah, Esther, Job, Psalms, Proverbs, Ecclesiastes, Song of Solomon, Isaiah, Jeremiah, Lamentations, Ezekiel, Daniel, Hosea, Joel, Amos, Obadiah, Jonah, Micah, Nahum, Habakkuk, Zephaniah, Haggai, Zechariah, Malachi)	Composed by various individuals and schools, from approximately 625 BCE to the 1st century BCE.	Individual books and sections revised from the 6th to 1st century BCE. At the Council of Yavne (70–90 CE) these writings were brought together and the canon reached final form. However, later writings suggest that debates were ongoing as to which texts belonged in the canon.	Doctrinal, ritual, inspirational, educational
	New Testament: Undisputed Pauline Epistles (1 Thessalonians, Galatians, Philippians, 1 Corinthians, 2 Corinthians, Romans, Philemon)	Composed between approximately 51 and 63 CE, over the course of Paul's career in Ephesus, Corinth, Philippi, Macedonia, and Rome.		Doctrinal, ritual, inspirational, educational
	New Testament: Disputed Pauline Epistles (2 Thessalonians, Colossians, Ephesians)	Composed in Macedonia and Asia Minor between approximately 60 and 85 CE. Scholars doubt that they were actually written by Paul.		Doctrinal, ritual, inspirational, educational
	New Testament: Pastoral Epistles (1 Timothy, 2 Timothy, Titus)	Composed in Asia Minor and perhaps Crete between approximately 90 and 140 CE. These letters are named after the people to whom they were addressed and traditionally attributed to Paul, but their actual authors are unknown.		Doctrinal, ritual, inspirational, educational

Continued

Sacred Texts (Continued)

Religion	Text	Composition/ Compilation	Compilation/ Revision	Use
Christianity	New Testament: Additional Epistolary Writings (1 Peter, 2 Peter, James, Jude, 1 John, 2 John, 3 John)	Composed in Asia Minor and Rome between 64 and 150, and attributed to the disciples after whom the texts are named. Their real authors are unknown, however.		Doctrinal, ritual, inspirational, educational
	New Testament: Hebrews	Composed in either Rome or Alexandria in 63 CE, by an anonymous author.		Doctrinal, ritual, inspirational, educational
	New Testament: Synoptic Gospels (Matthew, Mark, Luke)	Composed in Antioch, Southern Syria or possibly Galilee, and Ephesus between 65 and 85 CE; attributed to the disciples for whom they are named, but their actual authors are unknown.		Doctrinal, ritual, inspirational, educational
	New Testament: Gospel of John	Composed in Ephesus or possibly Alexandria in 90 CE and traditionally attributed to Jesus' disciple John, son of Zebedee; actual author unknown.		Doctrinal, ritual, inspirational, educational
	New Testament: Acts of the Apostles	Composed in western Asia Minor, perhaps Ephesus, between 85 and 140 CE; attributed to Luke the Evangelist, the same disciple named as the author of the Gospel of Luke; the actual author is unknown.		Doctrinal, ritual, inspirational, educational
	New Testament: Revelation	Dated to between 64 and 96 CE and traditionally attributed to John the Evangelist, writing on the Greek island of Patmos, but the actual author is unknown.		Doctrinal, ritual, inspirational, educational

Discussion Questions

1. How has local culture shaped Christian thought and practice at all times and in all places?

2. How did the shift from private to public worship affect what Christianity became?

3. What are some examples of changes in Christian thinking that reflect the changing world in which Christianity has lived?

4. In what contexts has Christianity been a reform movement? How has it served as a stabilizing influence within society?

5. Even though Christianity suffered persecution in its own early days, it has acted as persecutor in other contexts. Discuss.

6. What factors have influenced the place of women in Christianity?

7. How do you imagine the future of Christianity will unfold, based on its past?

Glossary

abbesses Powerful nuns who oversaw the lands owned by their communities, which in many cases were quite extensive; they played a significant role in the feudal manorial landholding system of the day.

anchoritic monasticism The form of monasticism practised by the "desert fathers and mothers," who withdrew from society to pursue a life of silence, prayer and sometimes mortification of the flesh; anchorites may also be known as hermits.

Anselm Eleventh-century Archbishop of Canterbury who moved away from the principle of scriptural authority, asserting that faith itself has a kind of rationality. His most notable contribution to the theological discourse of his age was the **ontological argument** for the existence of God.

Apostles The early followers of Jesus who witnessed his return as the risen Lord and were sent out into the world to proclaim him.

Aquinas, Thomas Dominican theologian considered the greatest of the scholastics, author of the *Summa Theologiae* ("Summation of Theology").

Arius The early theologian who argued (against Athanasius) that Jesus was of like substance with God rather than the same substance.

Athanasius The Bishop of Alexandria who argued (against Arius) that Jesus was of the same substance as God.

atonement Christ's restoration of humanity to a right relationship with God, variously interpreted as divine victory over demonic power, satisfaction of divine justice, or demonstration of a moral example.

Augustine Bishop of Hippo Regius in North Africa, whose theological writings shaped much of what would become the theological tradition of Western Christianity.

baptism The ritual of initiation into the Christian faith; one of the two key sacraments of Christianity. The details vary from one tradition to another, but the ritual typically involves either immersion in water or pouring of water over the head, and the words "I baptize you in the name of the Father and the Son and the Holy Spirit," although some denominations baptize in the name of Jesus alone.

Beghards Men who, like the **Beguines**, came together in small groups, mainly in urban environments, to live their lives in poverty, celibacy, prayer, and service on the model of the gospel.

Beguines Women who adopted a free style of religious life in many areas of Europe from the end of the twelfth century.

Benedict's Rule The prototype for Western monastic life, written in the first half of the sixth century by St Benedict.

Bernard of Clairvaux A monastic leader of the twelfth century who founded a Cistercian monastery at Clairvaux. He was distinguished by the perceived holiness of his life.

bishop The supervising priest of an ecclesiastical district called a diocese.

Body of Christ Term for the worldwide Christian community.

Calvin, Jean The French Protestant theologian, seen as the father of the Reformed Churches, who emphasized a radical doctrine of sin and grace.

canon A standard; a scriptural canon is the list of books acknowledged as scripture; the list of acknowledged saints is likewise a canon. Canon law is the accumulated body of Church regulations and discipline.

Cappadoccian Fathers Three theologians—Gregory Nanzianzus, Gregory of Nyssa, and St Basil—from a region in what is now Turkey that was known for its tradition of desert monasticism.

Carmelites An ascetic monastic order of hermits established on Mount Carmel in Palestine. After the failure of the Crusades, many members migrated to Europe and reorganized themselves as a mendicant order.

Carthusians A monastic order that demanded a vow of silence and considerable austerity from its members.

cenobitic monasticism The form of monasticism practised by religious who live in community with one another.

charisms Spiritual gifts such as preaching, healing, speaking in tongues (glossolalia), and prophesying, which surfaced in local worshipping communities in the period of the early Church. Movements that emphasize such gifts are described as "charismatic."

Christ From *Christos*, the Greek translation of the Hebrew *mashiach* (messiah), "anointed one."

Christology A theory of who Jesus was, by nature and in substance.

Cistercians An austere monastic order, founded in France in 1098; a particularly strict branch of Cistercians, known as Trappists, observe a rule of silence.

City of God Work by Augustine of Hippo, which articulated a vision for the relationship between sacred and secular in the age of the encroaching decline of the Roman Empire.

Cluniac Fathers An order, founded in 910, at the centre of a movement to reform monasticism by bringing its institutions under the control of religious rather than secular authorities.

Constantine The first Christian emperor, who convened the Council of Nicaea in 325 CE.

Council of Chalcedon The fifth-century Church council where the controversies over the nature of Jesus' humanity and divinity were finally resolved.

Council of Nicaea The fourth-century Church council, convened by **Constantine**, that formally established many beliefs about Christ.

creeds Brief formal statements of doctrinal belief, often recited in unison by congregations.

Crusades A series of military actions (1095–late 1200s) undertaken by European Christians to drive Islam out of the Holy Land.

deacon From Greek *diakonia* "service"; the third order of (male) ministry in the early Church.

deaconess The similar, but initially not equivalent, office for women in the early Church, devoted to serving women and children in the community.

Dominicans A **mendicant** preaching order formed in the early 1200s to combat the "Albigensian heresy."

dyophysitism The belief that the two natures of Jesus, human and divine, are united in the second person of the Trinity; affirmed at both Nicaea and Ephesus and proclaimed as orthodoxy for both the Western and Eastern Christian churches.

Easter The festival, held in March or April, celebrating the resurrection of Jesus.

ecumenism The movement for reunion or collaboration between previously separate branches of Christianity.

episcopacy Literally, "oversight"; the foundational office of authority in early Christianity. The first *episcopoi* were the men to whom the original Apostles delegated local authority in early Christian communities.

Erasmus The humanist thinker who laid the groundwork for Reformation theologians such as Luther.

Eucharist The sacramental meal of bread and wine that recalls Jesus' last supper before his crucifixion; a standard part of Christian worship.

Evangelical In Germany, a name for the Lutheran Church. In the English-speaking world, "evangelical" refers to conservative Protestants with a confident sense of the assurance of divine grace and the obligation to preach it.

excommunication Formal censure or expulsion from a church, particularly the Roman Catholic Church, for doctrinal error or moral misconduct.

Franciscans Mendicant order whose monks live by a rule based on the life and example of St Francis of Assisi.

friar A member of a **mendicant** order such as the Carmelites, Dominicans, or Franciscans.

fundamentalism A twentieth-century reaction to modernity, originally among Protestants who maintained the infallibility of scripture and doctrine.

glossolalia Speaking in "tongues"; a distinguishing feature of charismatic groups such as **Pentecostals**, in which people who feel filled with the Spirit begin speaking in what they believe is a special heavenly language. The ability to interpret such speech is also considered a spiritual gift.

Gnosticism A worldview based on a radical dualism, which prioritized reason and spirit over the physical.

Gospel "Good news" (*evangelion* in Greek); the news of redemption that the Hebrew prophets had promised. The Gospels are the accounts of Jesus' life attributed to his disciples Mark, Matthew, Luke, and John.

heresy A belief or practice that is contrary to the accepted orthodoxy.

Holiness Churches Protestant churches that believe their members have already received "holiness" (spiritual perfection) as a gift from God.

humanism The intellectual movement that is seen as a necessary precursor of the Protestant Reformation.

icon From the Greek for "image"; a distinctive Byzantine form of portraiture used to depict Jesus, Mary, and the saints.

incarnation The embodiment of the divine in human form; the Christian teaching that God became human in the person of Jesus.

indulgences Releases from time in **purgatory**; the selling of indulgences by the Church was one of the abuses that led to the Protestant Reformation.

liturgy A prescribed form for public worship.

logos "Word" in the sense of eternal divine intelligence and purpose.

Luther, Martin The father of the Protestant Reformation.

Manichaeism An intensely dualistic religion, founded in the third century, that grew out of Syrian Christianity under the influence of Gnosticism.

martyrs Christians who have died for their faith.

Mary The mother of Jesus; a major saint, deeply venerated by Roman Catholics in particular.

mass The Roman Catholic name for the Eucharist.

mendicant orders Orders that, instead of turning their backs on the world and withdrawing to monasteries, dedicate themselves to pastoral work, serving the people; examples include Carmelites, Dominicans, and Franciscans.

monophysitism The belief that Christ had only one nature, either divine or a synthesis of divine and human; generally abandoned in favour of **dyophysitism**.

mysticism The pursuit of intensely felt spiritual union with the divine.

Nestorianism The position that there was one (divine) nature in Christ and it was separate from the human Jesus.

New Testament The collection of 27 books—accounts of Gospels, Acts of the Apostles, Epistles, and Revelation—written by various authors in the first and early second centuries and determined to be authoritative for the early Christian Church.

Nicene Creed The statement of faith agreed on at the Council of Nicaea.

nuns Women living a common life in a monastic community.

ontological argument Anselm's argument for the existence of God based not on observation but on the logic that such a being must necessarily exist.

original sin The idea that human beings are inherently sinful because our earliest ancestors, Adam and Eve, chose to disobey God.

orthodoxy Literally, the "straight way," meaning correct belief; in any church, the accepted doctrine.

parables Simple stories told to illustrate a lesson.

patriarchs In the early Church, the five bishops who held primacy of authority by geographical region: Rome, Constantinople, Alexandria, Antioch, and Jerusalem. Today the term refers to those bishops in the Eastern Orthodox churches who preside over specific geographical regions and/or historical forms of the churches.

Paul, St The Jewish convert to Christianity (originally known as Saul of Tarsus) who founded a number of Christian communities and wrote them letters of instruction and guidance.

Pauline Epistles Letters attributed to Paul in the New Testament, some of which were probably written by others.

Pelagianism A salvation heresy according to which human nature was not so tainted by **original sin** as to be incapable of choosing good or evil without divine assistance.

Pentecost The fiftieth day after Easter, commemorated as the dramatic occasion when Jesus' followers experienced the presence of the Holy Spirit.

Pentecostals Modern Protestant groups that emphasize **glossolalia** as a sign of the presence of the Holy Spirit and hence of the individual's holiness or spiritual perfection.

Peter, St The "prince of Apostles" who was said to have become the first bishop of Rome.

Pietism A movement that originated in late seventeenth-century Lutheran Germany, expressing spontaneous devotion and a confident certainty of forgiveness.

pope The head of the Roman Catholic Church.

predestination The notion that God anticipates or controls human actions and foreordains every individual to either salvation or damnation.

presbyter Literally, "elder"; a key office that developed in the post-Apostolic period.

Reformed Churches Churches that are Calvinist in doctrine and often Presbyterian in governance; historically strongest in the Netherlands and Scotland but also found in France, Switzerland, and Hungary.

Rules of Faith Compendiums of the main teachings of bishops.

sacrament A ritual action seen as signifying divine grace. The most widely accepted sacraments are baptism and the Eucharist, although the Catholic and Anglican churches also recognize five others.

saints People recognized by the Church for their faith and virtue. Most saints are believed to have worked at least one miracle.

scriptures The holy writings of Christianity, consisting of the Hebrew Bible in Greek translation (the Septuagint), which Christians called the "Old Testament," and the "New Testament" accounts of Jesus' life and the early years of the Christian community.

see One of the five major episcopal areas: Rome, Constantinople, Alexandria, Antioch, and Jerusalem, known as the pentarchy.

soteriological Involving salvation.

Synoptic Gospels The Gospels of Matthew, Mark, and Luke, called "synoptic" ("seen together") because of their many overlapping stories and themes.

teleological argument From Greek *telos*, "end" or "purpose"; an argument inferring the existence of God from the perception of purpose or design in the universe.

theocracy A state in which all of society is controlled by the Church or religious leaders.

Theotokos Epithet for Mary as "God bearer."

transubstantiation The view, held mainly by Roman Catholics, that during the mass the bread and wine of the Eucharist become the literal body and blood of Jesus.

Trinity The doctrine that God exists in three "persons" or manifestations: as Father, as Son, and as Holy Spirit.

widows The earliest known order for women in Christianity, originally a response to the social problem of providing support for poor widows in the community.

Zwingli, Ulrich The father of the Swiss Reformation.

Note

My appreciation to Harry O. Maier for his assistance with the preparation of the New Testament materials. I am also grateful to have been able to incorporate portions of the late Willard Oxtoby's original chapter here.

Further Reading

Beilby, James, ed. 2009. *The Historic Jesus: Five Views*. Downers Grove, IL: IVP Academic. Five scholars present their views of the historic Jesus.

Bettenson, Henry S., and Maunder, Chris, eds. 1999. *Documents of the Christian Church*. 3rd edn. London: Oxford University Press. Strong on the early Church and Anglicanism.

Cross, F.L., and Livingstone, E.A., eds. 2005. *The Oxford Dictionary of the Christian Church*. 3rd edn. New York: Oxford University Press. The best general one-volume reference handbook.

Ehrman, Bart. 2011. *The New Testament: An Historical Introduction to Early Christian Writings*. New York/Toronto: Oxford University Press. An overview of the Christian scriptures in their historical, social, and literary contexts within the Greco-Roman world.

Farmer, David Hugh. 2004. *The Oxford Dictionary of Saints*. New York: Oxford University Press. A comprehensive guide.

Hastings, Adrian. 2000, 2007. *A World History of Christianity*. Grand Rapids: Eerdmans Publishing. A detailed history including Orthodox, Asian, African, Latin American, and North American Christianity.

Holder, Arthur (editor). 2005. *Blackwell Companion to Christian Spirituality*. Oxford, UK; Malden, MA: Blackwell. Essays by various scholars, each of whom represents a different perspective on Christian spirituality and its forms.

Jenkins, Philip. 2007. *The Next Christianity: The Coming of Global Christianity*. New York: Oxford University Press. Explores the implications of the shift in Christianity's centre of gravity from Europe and North America to South America, Africa, and Asia.

Kraemer, Ross. 1988. *Maenads, Martyrs, Matrons, Monastics: A Sourcebook on Women's Religions in the Greco-Roman World*. Philadelphia: Fortress Press. A collection of primary texts relating to women's religion in antiquity.

MacCulloch, Diarmaid. 2010. *Christianity: The First Three Thousand Years*. New York: Viking Adult. A large recent work by a noted Reformation historian.

McGinn, Bernard. 2006. *The Essential Writings of Christian Mysticism*. New York: Modern Library. A wide-ranging anthology.

McManners, John. 2002. *The Oxford Illustrated History of Christianity*. Oxford/Toronto: Oxford University Press. A comprehensive volume detailing the development of Christianity.

Murray, Peter, and Linda Murray. 1998. *The Oxford Companion to Christian Art and Architecture*. New York: Oxford University Press. An illustrated guide.

Sakenfeld, Katharine Doob. 2009. *New Interpreter's Dictionary of the Bible*. 5 vols. Nashville: Abingdon Press. A good reference work on biblical topics.

Schussler-Fiorenza, Elisabeth. 1994. *In Memory of Her: A Feminist Theological Reconstruction of Christian Origins*. New York: Crossroad. Explores the role of women in the development of Christianity; a classic.

Skinner Keller, Rosemary, and Rosemary Radford Ruether. 2006. *Encyclopedia of Women and Religion in North America*. 3 vols. Bloomington: Indiana University Press. A three-volume collection of essays on women's religious experience in North America, past and present.

White, James. 2001. *Introduction to Christian Worship.* 3rd edn. Nashville: Abingdon. The liturgical history of the Christian Church.

Wilson-Dickson, Andrew. 1997. *The Story of Christian Music: From Gregorian Chant to Black Gospel: An Authoritative Illustrated Guide to All the Major Traditions of Music for Worship.* Oxford: Lion Publishing. Traces the development of Christian worship music.

Recommended Websites

www.ccel.org/

Links to many classic Christian texts.

www.newadvent.org/

A Catholic site with links to many primary texts from the time of the early Church.

http://biblos.com/

A tool for Bible study, containing many different translations of the Bible.

www.christianity.com

A comprehensive source of articles, videos, and audio resources on Christian history, theology, and living, as well as Bible study tools.

www.ncccusa.org

Site of the National Council of Churches USA.

www.oikoumene.org/

Site of the World Council of Churches.

www.religionfacts.com/christianity/index.htm

A wide-ranging source of information on Christianity as well as other religions.

www.vatican.va/phome_en.htm

The English-language version of the official Vatican site.

http://virtualreligion.net/forum/index.html

Site of the Jesus Seminar.

www.wicc.org

Site of the Women's Inter-Church Council of Canada.

www.worldevangelicals.org

A global association of evangelical Christians.

References

Barrett, David B., George T. Currian, and Todd M. Johnson. 2001. *World Christian Encyclopedia : A Comparative Survey of Churches and Religions in the Modern World.* Oxford: Oxford University Press.

Bettenson, Henry, ed. 1967. *Documents of the Christian Church.* 2nd edn. Oxford: Oxford University Press.

Bonhoeffer, Dietrich. 2012. *Collected Works V. 1–8.* Minneapolis: Fortress.

Brown, Candy Gunther, ed. 2011. *Global Pentecostal and Charismatic Healing.* New York: Oxford University Press.

Colgrave, Bertram, and R.A.B. Mynors. 1969. *Bede's Ecclesiastical History of the English People.* Oxford: Clarendon Press.

Colledge, Edmund, and James Walsh, eds and trans. 1978. *Julian of Norwich: Showings.* Classics of Western Spirituality. New York: Paulist Press.

Day, Dorothy. 2012. *All the Way to Heaven: The Selected Letters of Dorothy Day.* Random House.

Epstein, Daniel Mark. 1993. *Sister Aimee: The Life of Aimee Semple McPherson.* New York: Harcourt Brace.

Fletcher-Marsh, Wendy. 1995. *Beyond the Walled Garden.* Dundas, ON: Artemis.

Frend, W.H.C. 1965. *The Early Church.* Oxford: Blackwell.

Jenkins, Phillip. 2007. *The Next Christendom.* New York: Oxford University Press.

Johnson, Todd M., David B. Barrett, and Peter F. Crossing. 2011. "Christianity 2011: Martyrs and the Resurgence of Religion." *International Bulletin of Missionary Research* 35, 1 (January): 28–9.

Kavanaugh, Kieran. 1987. *John of the Cross: Selected Writings.* New York: Paulist Press.

King, Martin Luther, Jr. 1964. *Why We Can't Wait.* New York: New American Library.

Lamm, Julia. 2013. *The Wiley–Blackwell Companion to Christian Mysticism.* Hoboken, NJ: Wiley.

Livingstone, David. 1858. *Cambridge Lectures.* Cambridge: Deighton.

McManners, John, ed. 1990. *The Oxford Illustrated History of Christianity.* Oxford: Oxford University Press.

Madigan, Shawn, ed. 1998. *Mystics, Visionaries and Prophets: A Historical Anthology of Women's Spiritual Writings.* Minneapolis: Fortress Press.

Martos, Joseph, and Pierre Hegy. 1998. *Equal at the Creation: Sexism, Society and Christian Thought.* Toronto: University of Toronto Press.

Meyer, Robert T., trans. 1950. *Athanasius, Life of St. Anthony.* Westminster, MD: Newman Press.

Neill, Stephen. 1965. *A History of Christian Missions*. Grand Rapids, MI: Eerdmans.

O'Brien, Elmer. 1964. *Varieties of Mystic Experience*. New York: Holt, Rinehart and Winston.

Petroff, Elizabeth Alvilda, ed. 1986. *Medieval Women's Visionary Literature*. New York: Oxford University Press.

Smith, Wilfred Cantwell. 1963. *The Faith of Other Men*. New York: New American Library.

Steletenkamp, Michael F. 2009. *Nicholas Black Elk: Medicine Man, Missionary, Mystic*. University of Oklahoma Press.

Stevenson, J., ed. 1957. *A New Eusebius*. London: SPCK.

Stokes, Francis G., trans. 1909. *Epistolae obscurorum virorum*. London: Chatto & Windus.

Sykes, Stephen, Jonathan Knight, and John Booty, eds. 1998. *The Study of Anglicanism*. Philadelphia: Fortress Press.

Teresa of Avila. 1979. *The Interior Castle*. Translated by Kieran Kavanaugh and Otilio Rodriguez. New York: Paulist Press.

Von Gebler, Karl. 1879. "Letter to Castelli (excerpt)." Accessed 26 Feb. 2010 at www.law.umkc.edu/faculty/projects/ftrials/galileo/lettercastelli.html.

Ward, Benedicta. 1975. *The Sayings of the Desert Fathers*. Translated and foreword by Benedicta Ward. Trappist, KY: Cistercian Publications.

Whitehead, Alfred North. 1929. *Process and Reality*. Cambridge: Cambridge University Press; New York: Macmillan.

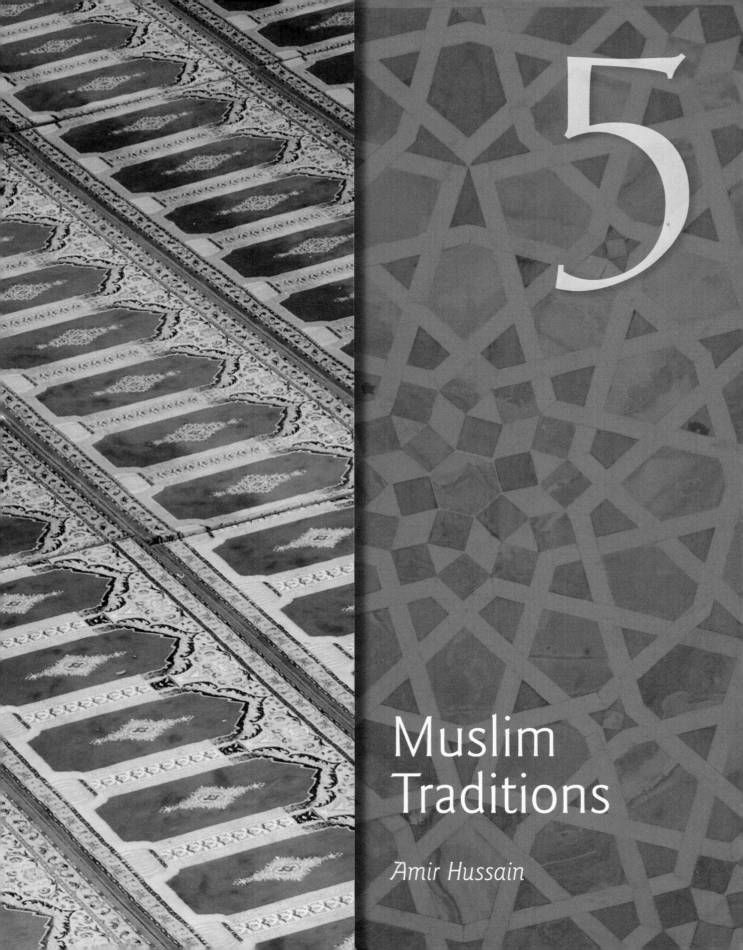

5

Muslim Traditions

Amir Hussain

Traditions at a Glance

Numbers

There are approximately 1.6 billion Muslims around the world, including more than 900,000 in Canada, nearly 3 million in Great Britain, and between 6 and 7 million in the United States.

Distribution

Although Islam originated in Arabia, the largest Muslim populations today are in Indonesia, Pakistan, India, and Bangladesh. Muslims are the second largest religious community (behind Christians) in many Western countries, including Canada, Great Britain, France, and Germany.

Principal Historical Periods

570–632 Lifetime of the Prophet Muhammad
632–661 The time of the four caliphs
661–750 Umayyad caliphate
750–1258 'Abbasid caliphate
1517–1924 Ottoman caliphate

Founder and Principal Leaders

There are two major branches of Islam: Sunni and Shi'a. All Muslims place authority in Muhammad as the last prophet, but the Shi'a give special authority after Muhammad to his son-in-law 'Ali and 'Ali's descendants (the Imams).

Deity

Allah is Arabic for "the God" and is cognate with the Hebrew *'Eloh* (plural *'Elohim*), "deity." Muslims believe Allah to be the same God worshipped by Christians, Jews, and other monotheists.

Authoritative Texts

The essential text is the Qur'an (literally, "The Recitation"), believed to have been revealed by God to Muhammad between the years 610 and 632 CE. Second in importance are the sayings of Muhammad, known collectively as the *hadith* (literally, "narrative").

Noteworthy Doctrines

Islam, like Judaism and Christianity, is a faith based on ethical monotheism. Its prophetic tradition begins with the first created human being (Adam) and ends with the Prophet Muhammad. Muslims believe that the first place of worship dedicated to the one true God is the Ka'ba in Mecca, built by Abraham and his son Ishmael.

In this chapter you will learn about:

- The Arabian environment in which Islam emerged
- The biography of Muhammad and its importance to Muslims
- The story of the Qur'an and its role in Islam
- The basic religious practices of Islam
- The distinctions within Islam, including the Sunni–Shi'a split and the mystic tradition (Sufism)
- The development of Islamic law (*shari'ah*), philosophy, and theology

- Contemporary issues facing Muslim communities in North America.

In the years before the terrorist attacks of 11 September 2001, many instructors would begin their courses on Islam with standard historical introductions to the life of Muhammad and the beginnings of Islam. Their students often knew very little about either Islam itself or the religious lives of Muslims before signing up for the course. Even Muslim students in many cases had never had a formal introduction to their faith, and so the university course provided their first opportunity to study it.

← An imam at the Imamzadeh Helal-ebne Ali Shrine in Kashan, Iran (© ZUMA Press, Inc./Alamy).

After 9/11, however, some instructors found that students were coming in with what they thought was a great deal of knowledge about Islam and the religious lives of Muslims. Unfortunately, most of their "knowledge" came from the popular media and was at odds with what the majority of Muslims understand of their faith. As a result, some instructors decided that they had to begin with a crash course on media literacy, especially in the context of television news, underlining that when ratings take priority, the controversial and provocative is privileged over the thoughtful and accurate. This anecdote shows the power of the media in constructing understandings of the world around us, including of course Muslims and Islam. How many of us come to the study of Islam with our minds already made up, convinced either that it is a religion of peace that can help to heal the ills of modern Western society, or that it is a religion of violence and intolerance, incapable of co-existing with that society?

Islam is the last of the three historic monotheistic faiths that arose in the Middle East, coming after Judaism and Christianity. Its name means "submission" in Arabic and signifies the commitment of its adherents to live in total submission to God. A person who professes Islam is called a Muslim, meaning "one who submits to God." An older term, rarely used today, is "Mohammedan," which misleadingly—and to Muslims offensively—suggests that Muslims worship the Prophet Muhammad himself.

The Qur'an, the Islamic scripture, presents Islam as the universal and primordial faith of all the prophets from Adam to Muhammad, and of all those who have faith in God, the one sovereign Lord, creator, and sustainer of all things. According to the Qur'an, Islam is God's eternal way for the universe.

Who is a Muslim? Inanimate things, plants and animals, even the angels, are all *muslims* to God by nature or instinct. Only human *islam* is an *islam* of choice. Human beings may voluntarily accept or wilfully reject God, but on the Day of Judgment they will face the consequences of their choice. They can expect to be rewarded for their faith or punished for their rejection of it.

Most Muslims are born into Muslim families. But one can also become a Muslim simply by repeating before two Muslim witnesses the **shahadah**, or profession of faith: "I bear witness that there is no god except God, and I bear witness that Muhammad is the messenger of God." Anyone who does this becomes legally a Muslim, with all the rights and responsibilities that this new identity entails.

Document

A *Hadith* (Saying) of the Prophet Muhammad

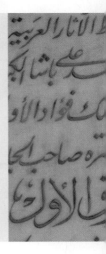

A man sinned greatly, and when death came to him he charged his sons, saying: "When I have died, burn me, then crush me and scatter my ashes into the sea. For, by God, if the Lord takes possession of me, God will punish me in a manner in which God has punished no one else." So they did that to their father. Then God said to the earth "Produce what you have taken!"—and there was the man. God said to the man, "What induced you to do what you did?" The man replied, "Being afraid of you, O my Lord." Because of that, God forgave the man (from the earliest *Hadith* collections of al-Bukhari and Muslim ibn al-Hajjaj).

Timeline

622 CE	Muhammad's *hijrah* from Mecca to Medina
632	Muhammad dies; leadership passes to the caliph
642	Birth of al-Hasan al-Basri, early Sufi ascetic (d. 728)
661	Damascus established as capital of Umayyad caliphate
680	Death of Husayn at Karbala, commemorated as martyrdom by Shi'as
711	Arab armies reach Spain
762	Baghdad established as 'Abbasid capital
801	Death of Rabi'a al-'Adawiyah of Basra, a famous female Sufi
1058	Birth of al-Ghazali, theological synthesizer of faith and reason (d. 1111)
1071	Seljuq Turks defeat Byzantines in eastern Anatolia
1165	Birth of Ibn 'Arabi, philosopher of the mystical unity of being (d. 1240)
1207	Birth of Jalal al-Din Rumi, Persian mystical poet (d. 1273)
1258	Baghdad falls to Mongol invaders
1492	Christian forces take Granada, the last Muslim stronghold in Spain
1529	Ottoman Turks reach Vienna (again in 1683)
1602	Muslims officially expelled from Spain
1703	Birth of Ibn 'Abd al-Wahhab, leader of traditionalist revival in Arabia (d. 1792)
1924	Atatürk, Turkish modernizer and secularizer, abolishes the caliphate
1930	Muhammad Iqbal proposes a Muslim state in India
1947	Pakistan established as an Islamic state
1979	Ayatollah Khomeini establishes a revolutionary Islamic regime in Iran
2001	Osama bin Laden (d. 2011) launches terrorist attacks on America
2006	Orhan Pamuk becomes the second Muslim (after Naguib Mahfouz in 1988) to win the Nobel Prize for Literature
2010	Islamic scholars at the Mardin Conference in Turkey issue a ruling against terrorism
2011	The "Arab Spring"; the governments of Tunisia, Egypt, Yemen, and Libya are overthrown. Tawakkul Karman, a leader of the movement in Yemen, becomes the second Muslim woman (after Shirin Ebadi in 2003) to win the Nobel Peace Prize

🦋 Beginnings

Pre-Islamic Arabia

The long period of pre-Islamic Arab history is called by the Qur'an the age of *jahiliyah* ("foolishness" or "ignorance"). The term designates not so much a state of cognitive ignorance or lack of *'ilm* (knowledge) as it does a lack of moral consciousness. The Arabs before Islam (like the ancient Hebrews) did not believe in an afterlife. To them, the only form of life after death was the ghost of a slain man, which would linger in this world until revenge was exacted, whether from the killer himself or from any man of similar status in his tribe; as a consequence, long and deadly feuds decimated many tribes. Since time would spare no one, they believed that humans ought to make the most of this life while they could. Arab society was thus focused on earthly accomplishments and pleasures, valuing manly prowess and tribal solidarity, and praising the man who made a good name for his tribe to boast of while drowning his existential sorrows in wine, women, and sentimental verse.

Allah is Arabic for "the God." The Arabs before Islam recognized Allah as the supreme creator god,

Sites

Mecca, Saudi Arabia

The place where the Prophet Muhammad was born and received his first revelations, Mecca is also home to the Ka'ba, the first place of monotheistic worship. Muslims believe that the Ka'ba was built by Abraham and his son Ishmael, and when they pray, they face in its direction. The structure is now surrounded by the Great Mosque of Mecca (the Masjid al-Haram) and is the focal point of the annual *hajj* (pilgrimage), when more than two million Muslims visit the site over a period of about ten days. The entire city is permanently closed to non-Muslims.

Recent years have seen controversy over the Saudi government's decision to destroy many historic Muslim buildings in order to erect a luxury hotel and a massive clock tower (modelled on London's Big Ben). Sami Angawi, a Saudi scholar, has documented this destruction at his Hajj Research Centre in the nearby city of Jeddah.

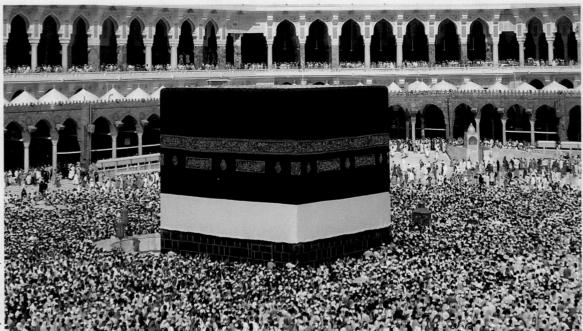

© Jamal Nasrallah/epa/Corbis

During the *hajj*, as many as 500,000 pilgrims gather in the inner courtyard of the great mosque and circumambulate the Ka'ba. Outside the courtyard but still within the Great Mosque there may be almost 2 million more pilgrims.

but he was not the only recipient of worship. Among the many other deities worshipped by the Arabs in and around the city of Mecca (Makkah) were a god named Hubal ("vapour"), who may originally have been a rain god, and three goddesses who were said to be the daughters of Allah: Al-Lat, al-'Uzzah, and Manat (Manat may have been a version of the goddess of love, known to the Greco-Roman world as Aphrodite or Venus). Although the three goddesses were worshipped as intermediaries who might bring devotees closer to their father (see Q. 39: 3), the Qur'an repudiates them as mere "names which you [the Arabs] and your fathers named; God sent down no authority concerning them" (53: 20–3).

Arabs shared the general Semitic idea of a sacred place (*haram*) where no living thing—plant, animal, or human—could be harmed. For Mecca and most of Arabia, the chief *haram* was the shrine called the Ka'ba: an ancient square building that contained many idols or images of gods and goddesses (among them some crudely painted figures that may represent Jesus and his virgin mother Mary) and still contains at one corner an unusual black stone that most think to be a meteorite. The Ka'ba was believed to have been built by the biblical patriarch Abraham and his son Ishmael (Isaac's brother), who had settled with his mother, Hagar, in the valley of Makkah (see Q 14:37). Before Islam, then, the Ka'ba was already a pilgrimage site to which people came from far and wide. The pilgrimage season was also the time of a trade fair, which gave Mecca a special prestige and economic status in Arabia.

When Islam emerged in the seventh century CE, Arabia was bordered to the west by the Christian Byzantine empire and to the east by the Zoroastrian Sasanian Persian empire. The city of Mecca, some 70 kilometres (40 miles) inland from the Red Sea, was dominated mainly by one tribe, the Quraysh, but it was open to a broad range of cultural and religious influences, including the moral and devotional ideas of the Jewish and Christian communities that had been present in the territory for centuries. There were desert hermits who practised holiness and healing, and a group of Meccan Arabs known as **hanifs** ("pious ones") who shared the

ethical monotheism of Judaism and Christianity. The majority of pre-Islamic Arabian society, however, was polytheistic. Pre-Islamic Arabia was also a tribal society, with radical class distinctions and social inequality, including the practice of slavery.

The Life of Muhammad (570–632 CE)

Muhammad was born into the Quraysh tribe around the year 570. His father died before his birth and his mother a few years later. In the paternalistic and tribal society of pre-Islamic Arabia, to be without a family was to be on the margins of society, but the orphaned Muhammad was taken in and cared for by his paternal grandfather, 'Abd al-Muttalib, and then, after his grandfather's death, by his uncle Abu Talib.

Little is known about Muhammad's youth. His family was in the caravan trade, and Muhammad joined his uncle in the family business. By his mid-twenties, however, he was working as a merchant for a rich widow, Khadijah, who proposed marriage to him. Although she was older than he was, and had been married and widowed before, he accepted. Early biographical sources describe him as a contemplative, honest, and mild-mannered young man. He was called al-Amin ("the faithful" or "trustworthy") because of the confidence he inspired in people.

Once a year, during the month of **Ramadan**, Muhammad spent days in seclusion in a cave on Mount Hira, a short distance from Mecca. Tradition reports that it was during one of those retreats that he received the call to prophethood and the first revelation of the Qur'an.

As Muhammad was sitting one night in the solitude of his retreat, an angel—later identified as Gabriel (Jibril in Arabic)—appeared. Taking hold of him and pressing him hard, the angel commanded, "Recite [or read]!" Muhammad answered, "I cannot read." After repeating the command a second and third time, the angel continued, "Recite in the name of your Lord who created, created the human being from a blood clot. Recite, for your

Lord is most magnanimous—who taught by the pen, taught the human being that which s/he did not know" (Q. 96: 1–5). Shivering with fear and apprehension, Muhammad ran home and asked the people of his household to cover him with a cloak, to protect him. Khadijah was the first one to believe in the truth of Muhammad's encounter with Gabriel, but his young cousin 'Ali (the son of Abu Talib) also supported him.

The angel returned to him often, saying, "O Muhammad, I am Gabriel, and you are the Messenger of God." Khadijah consoled and encouraged him, and eventually took him to her cousin, a learned Christian named Waraqah ibn Nawfal. Waraqah confirmed Muhammad in his mission, declaring him to be a Prophet for the Arabs, chosen by God to deliver a sacred law to his people just as Moses had to the Jews.

The idea of a prophet—*nabi* in both Arabic and Hebrew—was not unfamiliar to the people of the region. But for 12 years Muhammad the Prophet of God preached the new faith in the One God with little success. The Meccans did not wish to abandon the polytheistic ways of their ancestors, and they feared the implications of the new faith both for their social customs and for the religious status of the Ka'ba, which as a pilgrimage centre brought significant economic resources to their city. (In many ways, pilgrimage was as lucrative to pre-modern economies as tourism is to modern ones.)

Muhammad's message was not only religious but also moral and social. He instructed the Meccans to give alms, to care for the orphaned, to feed the hungry, to assist the oppressed and destitute, and to offer hospitality to the wayfarer. He also warned of impending doom on the day of the last judgment. The first to accept the new faith, after his wife Khadijah, were his cousin (and future son-in-law) 'Ali ibn Abu Talib, his slave Zayd ibn Harithah (whom he later freed and adopted), and his faithful companion Abu Bakr.

Like Jesus and his disciples, Muhammad and his followers were often vilified. Around 615, one group of Muslims without tribal protection faced such severe persecution from the polytheistic Meccans that the Prophet advised them to migrate across the Red Sea to the Christian country of Abyssinia (Ethiopia), where they were well received. And in 619 the Prophet himself was left without support or protection when both his wife and his uncle died within the space of barely two months. Although he later entered into a number of polygamous marriages (as was the custom in his society), the loss of Khadijah must have been particularly hard: they had been married for almost half his life, she was the mother of their four daughters, and she had been the first person to believe in him. But the death of Abu Talib must have been almost equally hard, for he was the only father figure Muhammad had known, and with his death Muhammad lost the protection that his beloved uncle had provided.

It was soon after these losses that Muhammad experienced what came to be known as the "night journey," travelling from Mecca to Jerusalem in the course of a single night, and the **mi'raj**: a miraculous ascent to heaven, where he met some of the prophets who had gone before him and was granted an audience with God. For Muslims, these miraculous events confirmed that even in times of trouble, the Prophet still had the support of God. Even so, it would be another three years before he was able to find a place for the Muslims to establish their own community, free of the persecution they suffered in Mecca.

The First Muslim Community

Finally, in 622, an invitation was offered by the city of Yathrib, about 400 kilometres (250 miles) north of Mecca. The migration (**hijrah**) to Yathrib, which thereafter came to be known as "the city of the Prophet" or Medina ("the city"), marked the beginning of community life under Islam, and thus of Islamic history. In Medina Muhammad established the first Islamic commonwealth: a truly theocratic state, headed by a prophet whose rule was believed to follow the dictates of a divine scripture.

Medina was an oasis city with an agricultural economy. Its social structure was far more heterogeneous than Mecca's, for its population included a substantial Jewish community as well as two feuding Arab tribes, the Aws and the Khazraj, whose old

Focus

Islamic Dates

The migration to Mecca provided the starting-point for the dating system used throughout the Muslim world. Years are counted backwards or forwards from the *hijrah* and accompanied by the abbreviation AH, from the Latin for "year of the *hijrah*."

Because Muslims use the lunar year—which is 11 days shorter than the solar year—*hijri* dates gain one year approximately every 33 solar years. Thus the year 1400 AH was reached in 1979 CE, and the new year of 1441 will be celebrated in 2019.

rivalries had kept the city in a continuous state of civil strife. Muhammad was remarkably successful in welding these disparate elements into a cohesive social unit. In a brief constitutional document known as the covenant of Medina, he stipulated that all the people of the city should form a single Muslim commonwealth. The covenant granted the Jews full religious freedom and equality with the Muslims, on condition that they support the state and refrain from entering into any alliance against it, whether with the Quraysh or with any other tribe.

The Qur'an's narratives and worldview are closely akin to the prophetic view of history laid out in the Hebrew Bible. The Prophet expected the Jews of Medina, recognizing this kinship, to be natural allies, and he adopted a number of Jewish practices, including the fast of the Day of Atonement (Yom Kippur). But the Medinan Jews rejected both Muhammad's claim to be a prophet and the Qur'an's claim to be a sacred book. The resulting tension between the two communities is reflected in the Qur'an's treatment of the Jews. Some references are clearly positive; for example, "Among the People of the Book are an upright community who recite God's revelations in the night, prostrate themselves in adoration, believing in God and the Last Day . . . these are of the righteous, whatever good they do, they shall not be denied it" (3: 113–15). Others are just as clearly negative: "Take not the Jews and Christians for friends" (5: 51). Increasingly, Islam began to distinguish itself from Judaism, so that within two years of the Prophet's arrival in Medina, the fast of Ramadan took precedence over the fast of Yom Kippur and the **qiblah** (direction of prayer) was changed from Jerusalem to the Ka'ba in Mecca.

Sites

Medina, Saudi Arabia

Medina is the home of the first Muslim community and the place where Muhammad was buried. Unlike Mecca, the city of Medina is open to non-Muslims. The Prophet's Mosque (Masjid al-Nabawi), located in the centre of the city, next to Muhammad's home, was originally quite simple.

But over the centuries it was expanded to its present form, and it is now one of the largest mosques in the world. The graves of the Prophet's first two successors as leader of the Muslims, Abu Bakr and 'Umar ibn al-Khattab, are also located in the Prophet's Mosque.

In the Qur'an the people of Medina who became Muslims are called Ansar ("helpers") because they were the first supporters and protectors of Islam and the Prophet. As the flow of Muslim immigrants from Mecca increased, however, a new social group was added to an already diverse society. The new arrivals, along with those who came with or shortly after the Prophet, were called Muhajirun ("immigrants").

The Conversion of Mecca

The Muslims who had fled Mecca for Medina had left all their goods and property behind. Without the means to support themselves in their new home, they began raiding Meccan caravans returning from Syria. In 624, when the Meccans sent an army of roughly 1,000 men to Medina, they were met at the well of Badr by a 300-man detachment of Muslims.

Though poorly equipped and far outnumbered, the Muslims were highly motivated, and they inflicted a crushing defeat on the Meccans. Thus the Battle of Badr remains one of the most memorable events in Muslim history. It is celebrated in the Qur'an as a miraculous proof of the truth of Islam: "You [Muhammad] did not shoot the first arrow when you did shoot it; rather God shot it" (Q. 8: 17); "God supported you [Muslims] at Badr when you were in an abased state" (Q. 3: 123).

To avenge their defeat, the Meccans met the Muslims the following year by Mount Uhud, not far from Medina, and this time they prevailed. Following the Battle of Uhud, the Jews of Medina were expelled from the city on the grounds that they had formed alliances with the Meccans against the Muslims. But the real reason may have been to free the Muslim state of external influences at a critical stage in its development. —

The Muslims were growing in strength. Meanwhile, they continued to raid the caravans of the Quraysh, and before long they received word that the Meccans were planning to attack Medina itself. On the advice of Salman the Persian, a former slave, the Prophet had a trench dug around the exposed parts of the city, to prevent the Meccan cavalry from entering. Thus when the Quraysh, along with a large coalition of other tribes, tried to invade Medina in 627, the city was able to withstand the attack. The "Battle of the Trench" marked a tipping point in relations between the Muslims and the Meccans, and in 628 the latter were impelled to seek a truce. Two years later, when the Quraysh breached the truce, the Prophet set out for Mecca at the head of a large army. But there was no need to fight. When the Muslims arrived, the Meccans surrendered to them and accepted Islam en masse.

Whenever an individual or tribe accepted Islam, all hostilities were to cease and enemies were to become brothers and sisters in faith. Therefore the Prophet granted amnesty to all in the city. Asked by the Meccans what he intended to do with them, the Prophet answered, "I will do with you what Joseph did with his brothers. Go; you are free." Then he quoted Joseph's words to his brothers: "There is no blame in you today; God forgive you" (Q. 12: 92).

Muhammad took no credit for the conquest of Mecca, attributing the victory solely to God, as prescribed in the Qur'an: "When support from God comes, and victory, and you see people enter into the religion of God in throngs, proclaim the praise of your Lord and seek God's forgiveness, for God is truly relenting" (Q. 110). He returned to Medina and died there two years later, in 632, after making a farewell pilgrimage to Mecca and its sacred shrine, the Ka'ba.

Muhammad was always known as *rasul Allah* ("the Messenger of God") rather than as a ruler or military leader. But he was all of these. He waged war and made peace. He laid the foundations of a community (**ummah**) that was based on Islamic principles. He firmly established Islam in Arabia and sent expeditions to Syria. Within 80 years the Muslims would administer the largest empire the world had ever known, stretching from the southern borders of France through North Africa and the Middle East into India and Central Asia.

At the time of his death, however, no one could have foreseen that future. The majority of Muslims—the **Sunni**, meaning those who follow the *sunnah* (traditions) of the Prophet—believed that he had not even designated a successor or specified how one should be chosen. But a minority community, known as the **Shi'a** (from the Arabic meaning "party"), believed that Muhammad had in fact appointed his cousin and son-in-law 'Ali to succeed him. Muhammad's death therefore precipitated a crisis, which would grow into a permanent ideological rift.

A *khalifah* is one who represents or acts on behalf of another. Thus after Muhammad's death, his close companion Abu Bakr became the *khalifat rasul Allah*—the "successor" or "representative" of the Messenger of God—and Abu Bakr's successor, 'Umar ibn al-Khattab, was at first referred to as the "successor of the successor of the Messenger of God."

From the beginning, the institution of the caliphate had a worldly as well as a religious dimension. As a successor of the Prophet, the **caliph** was a religious leader. At the same time, as the chief or administrative head of the community, he was the *amir* or commander of the Muslims in times of peace as well as war. Perhaps conscious of this temporal dimension of his office, 'Umar is said to have adopted the title "commander of the faithful" in place of his cumbersome original title. Nevertheless, the caliph continued to function as the chief religious leader ("imam") of the community. In all, there were four caliphs who ruled after Muhammad, from 632 to 661. From 661 to 750, the Muslim world was ruled by a hereditary dynasty known as the Umayyads. Then the Umayyads in turn were defeated by the 'Abbasid dynasty, which ruled from 750 to 1258.

❧ Foundations

Prophets and Messengers

According to the Qur'an, God operates through prophets and messengers who convey God's will in revealed scriptures and seek to establish God's sacred law in the lives of their communities. From the Islamic point of view, therefore, human history is prophetic history.

Islamic tradition maintains that, from the time of Adam to the time of Muhammad, God sent 124,000 prophets into the world to remind people of every community of their obligation to the one and only sovereign Lord and warn them against heedlessness and disobedience: "There is not a nation but that a warner was sent to it" (Q. 26: 207). The Qur'an mentions by name 26 prophets and messengers. Most are well-known biblical figures, among them Abraham, Moses, David, Solomon, Elijah, Jonah, John the Baptist, and Jesus. It also mentions three Arabian prophets: Shu'ayb, Hud, and Salih.

Islamic tradition distinguishes between prophets and messengers. A prophet (*nabi*) is one who conveys a message from God to a specific people at a specific time. A messenger (*rasul*) is also a prophet sent by God to a specific community; but the message he delivers is a universally binding sacred law (**shari'ah**). The Torah given to Moses on Mount Sinai was an example of the latter: though delivered to the ancient Hebrews, it remained binding on all those who knew it, Hebrews and others, until the arrival of the next revelation—the gospel of Jesus. In other words, every messenger is a prophet; but not every prophet is a messenger. Among the messenger-prophets, five—Noah, Abraham, Moses, Jesus, and Muhammad—are called *ulu al-'azm* ("prophets of power or firm resolve," Q. 46: 35). Their special significance lies in their having received universally binding revelations from God.

Abraham

In the Qur'an, it is the innate reasoning capacity of the Hebrew patriarch Abraham—Ibrahim in Arabic—that leads him away from his people's tradition of idol worship and towards the knowledge of God. Even as a youth he recognizes that idols made of wood or stone cannot hear the supplications of their worshippers, and therefore can do them neither good nor harm.

One night, gazing at the full moon in its glory, Abraham thinks that it must be God. But when he sees it set, he changes his mind. He then gazes at the bright sun and thinks that, since it is so much

Document

From the Qur'an: Abraham Destroys the Idols

When [Abraham] said to his father and his people, "What are these idols that you so fervently worship?" they said, "We found our fathers worshipping them."

He said, "Both you and your fathers are in manifest error." They said, "Have you come to us with the truth, or are you one of those who jest?"

He said, "Your Lord is indeed the Lord of the heavens and the earth, for your Lord originated them; and to this I am one of those who bear witness. By God, I shall confound your idols as soon as you turn your backs."

He thus destroyed them utterly except for the chief one, so that the people might turn to it [for petition].

They said, "Who did this to our gods? He is surely a wrongdoer."

Some said, "We heard a youth called Abraham speaking of them."

Others said, "Bring him here in the sight of the people, so that they may all witness."

They said, "Did you do this to our gods, O Abraham?"

He said, "No, it was their chief who did it. Question them—if they could speak."

The people then turned on one another, saying, "Indeed you are the wrongdoers!" Then they bowed their heads in humiliation, saying, "You know well, [O Abraham], that these do not speak."

He [Abraham] said, "Would you then worship instead of God a thing that can do you neither good nor harm? Shame on you and on what you worship instead of God; do you not reason?"

They said, "Burn him and stand up for your gods, if you would do anything."

We [God] said, "O fire, be coolness and peace for Abraham."

They wished evil for him, but We turned them into utter losers. And We delivered him and Lot to a land that We blessed for all beings. We also granted him Isaac and Jacob as added favour, and We made them both righteous. We made them all leaders guiding others by our command. We inspired them to do good deeds, perform regular worship, and give the obligatory alms; and they were true worshippers of Us alone (Q. 21: 51–73).

larger, it must be the real God. But that night the sun too sets, leading Abraham to declare: "I turn my face to the One who originated the heavens and the earth, a man of pure faith, and I am not one of the Associators [those who associate other things or beings with God]" (Q. 6: 77–9).

Moses

Because Muslim tradition presents Muhammad in many ways as "a prophet like Moses," Moses occupies more space in the Qur'an than any other prophet, including Muhammad; he is mentioned over 200 times. Like Muhammad, Moses grows up as an orphan, away from his parents' home. His mission, like Muhammad's, begins in solitude with God in the wilderness. The scripture revealed to him, the Torah, is for Muslims second in importance to the Qur'an and most like it in content and purpose.

Moses is sent as a messenger of God not only to his own people, but also to the Egyptians. The Qur'an summarizes Moses' mission thus: "His Lord called out to him, . . . 'Go to Pharaoh, for he has waxed arrogant!' . . . He [Pharaoh] cried out and proclaimed, 'I am your lord most high!' But God seized him with the torment of both the next world and this" (Q. 79: 15–25). Pharaoh persists in the sin of claiming parity with God for himself (a sin known in Islam as *shirk*). But the magicians he brings to counter God's miracles are themselves converted and die as martyrs for their faith. In Muslim tradition, Pharaoh's wife, too, accepts faith in God and dies a martyr. As for Pharaoh, his declaration of faith in "the God of the children of Israel," coming at the point of his death by drowning, is too late to save him (see Q. 10: 90).

Muslims believe that every major prophet is supported in his claim to be sent by God by evidentiary miracles. These miracles must suit the prophet's mission as well as the condition of his people. Thus the miracles of Moses affirm God's power and wisdom against the magic and might of the Egyptians.

Jesus

Jesus is presented in the Qur'an as a miracle in himself. His virgin birth, his ability to heal the sick, feed the hungry, even raise the dead: these miracles affirm God's creative and life-giving power against those—Jews and non-Jews—who deny the reality of the resurrection and life to come. Furthermore, the miracles of Jesus were performed at a time when Greek medicine, science, and philosophy were challenging the sovereignty, power, and wisdom of God as the sole creator and Lord of the universe. The miracles of Jesus therefore serve to assert the power of God over human science and wisdom.

The Qur'an presents Jesus as a messenger of God sent to the children of Israel with the message: "God is surely my Lord and your Lord. Worship him, therefore; this is the straight way" (Q. 3:51). For Muslims, particularly the mystics, Jesus is an example of a world-renouncing ascetic, a wandering prophet of stern piety but deep compassion for the poor, suffering, and oppressed, whoever they might be.

Thus Jesus is a great prophet for Muslims. Although the Qur'an categorically denies his divinity and divine sonship (see Q. 5: 116, 19: 34–5, and 5: 17 and 72), it sees his role as extending far

beyond his earthly existence into sacred history. Jesus, the Qur'an insists, did not die, but was lifted up by God to heaven (Q. 4: 157–8). He will return at the end of time as "a sign of the knowledge of the Hour [that is, the Day of Resurrection]" (Q. 43: 61), kill the anti-Christ (al-Dajjal, the deceiver), and establish true Islam on earth.

It is God's covenant with all prophets that each of them must prepare for and support the prophet to come after him. Thus Jesus in the Qur'an announces the coming of Muhammad, saying, "O children of Israel, I am the messenger of God to you, confirming the Torah that was before me, and announcing a messenger who shall come after me whose name is Ahmad [a variant of Muhammad]" (Q. 61: 6). For Muslims, Muhammad is the last in the long line of prophets.

Muhammad

Muslim tradition regards Muhammad as "the Prophet of the end of time." Just as the sacred book that he receives directly from God, the Qur'an, is God's final revelation for humanity, confirming and supplanting all previous revelations (see Q. 5:48), so Muhammad himself is "the seal of the prophets," and his way or life-example (*sunnah*) is the prophetic model that will guide history until it comes to an end on the Day of Judgment.

For the early Muslims, obedience to the *sunnah* of the Prophet was the same as obedience to God. This was because they understood whatever the Prophet said or did to be on God's behalf and by his command. Muslims believe that God protects all prophets from sin and error. With regard to Muhammad in particular, the Qur'an asserts, "Your companion did not go astray, nor did he err. He speaks not out of capricious desire; rather it is a revelation revealed to him" (Q. 53:2–4).

When the Qur'an asserts that God has sent his Messenger with "the Book and wisdom" (Q. 62: 2), Muslims understand "the Book" to be the Qur'an and the "wisdom" to be the *sunnah* of the Prophet. Muhammad himself is reported to have declared that he "was given the Qur'an and its equivalent [i.e., the *sunnah*] along with it." Hence Muslims believe that his actions and sayings are no less divinely inspired than the Qur'an itself.

The spiritual pre-eminence that Muslims accord Muhammad is reflected in the story of the night journey and *mi'raj*, which is elaborated in a **hadith** (tradition) based on the following short passage from the Qur'an: "Glory be to him who carried his servant by night from the Holy Mosque to the Further Mosque, the precincts of which we have blessed, that we might show him some of our signs" (Q. 17:1). In the course of the same night the Prophet experiences the *mi'raj* ("ladder"), which parallels the heavenly ascents of prophetic figures described in visionary terms in Hellenistic and rabbinic Jewish religious literature.

To show their respect for Muhammad, Muslims speak (or write) the phrase "peace [and blessings of God] be upon him" every time his name or title is mentioned. In writing, the formula is often abbreviated as PBUH. When the prophets as a group, culminating in Muhammad, are mentioned, the formula changes to "peace be on them all."

The Qur'an

The *ayahs* (verses) and **surahs** (chapters) that came to constitute the Qur'an were revealed (literally, "sent down") to Muhammad by the angel Gabriel over a period of 23 years. The Prophet's role as transmitter of those revelations is reflected in the Qur'an's characteristic phrasing: God ("We") instructs the Prophet ("you") to "say" something to the people (that is, to deliver a particular message to them). Yet the first instruction, as we have seen, was the command that Muhammad himself "recite" or "read" (*iqra'*). The term "Qur'an" is derived from the same root: *q–r–'*, meaning "to read" or "recite."

In size the Qur'an is nearly as long as the New Testament. The individual portions revealed to Muhammad vary in length and content from short verses on a single theme or idea to fairly lengthy chapters. The early Meccan *surahs* are generally brief admonitions couched in terse and powerful verses, while the later ones are didactic narratives or illustrative tales of earlier prophets and their communities. Through stories, parables, and exhortations urging good conduct and dissuading evil and indecent behaviour, the Qur'an aims to create an *ummah*: a "community" (that is, a society united by faith).

The *surahs* revealed in Medina are fewer in number but longer, presenting didactic arguments, discourses, and legal pronouncements, often in response to questions or situations arising in the life of the community.

The Status of the Qur'an

Muslims believe that the Qur'an is an immutable heavenly book containing the eternal Word of God. In fact, there is an interesting theological parallel with Christian understandings of Jesus, who in the prologue to John's gospel is proclaimed to be the eternal Word of God made incarnate at a certain moment in history. For Christians Christ is the Word of God made flesh, while for Muslims the Qur'an is the Word of God made into a book.

Muslims understand the Qur'an to have been revealed specifically in the Arabic language—not surprising, given that Arabic was the language of its first audience. Hence any translation is considered to constitute an interpretation, not the Qur'an itself. Even in places where few if any Muslims speak the language, the Qur'an is always recited in Arabic. Of course, each passage is usually followed by a translation in the appropriate language.

The words of the Qur'an are recited in a newborn child's ear as a blessing. They are also recited to bless and seal a marriage contract or a business deal, to celebrate a successful venture, or to express sorrow and give solace in times of misfortune. Throughout the Muslim world, the Qur'an is recited on most special public occasions and daily on radio and television. Qur'anic recitation is an art of great virtuosity and hypnotic power. For private devotional recitation over the course of a month, the Qur'an has been divided into 30 parts of equal length. The words of the Qur'an, in the

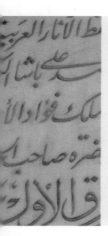

Document

From the Qur'an: On the Day of Judgment

This short surah (chapter) is known by the title "The Earthquake."

In the name of God, the All-merciful, the Compassionate. When the earth shall be shaken with a great quake, and the earth yields up her burdens, and the human being exclaims, "What has happened to her!" On that day the earth shall recount her tidings—as her Lord had inspired her. Whoever does an atom's weight of good shall then see it, and whoever does an atom's weight of evil shall then see it (Q. 99).

form of calligraphy, have also been a central motif in Islamic art, and are used to decorate Muslim homes, mosques, and public buildings.

Compiling the Qur'an

When the Prophet died in 632, there were many people who had committed the Qur'an to memory. But the only physical records were fragments written on stones, bones, palm leaves, and animal parchment, which were held in a variety of private collections. In some cases the same material existed in several versions, and since the vowel marks were not added until later, different readings of certain words or phrases were possible. These variants came to be identified with specific readers through the generations of Muslim scholars.

The process of producing an official text of the Qur'an was completed under the third caliph, 'Uthman ibn 'Affan, within 20 years of the Prophet's death. One of the first copies of the complete text was given to Hafsah, one of his widows.

As an earthly book, the Qur'an has been shaped by Muslim history. Tradition maintains that the verses of each individual *surah* were arranged by the Prophet at Gabriel's instruction, but that the order of the *surahs* in relation to one another—roughly in decreasing order of length—was fixed by a committee that 'Uthman appointed to compile an official version. Of the 114 *surahs*, 113 are preceded by the invocation *bism-illahi ar-rahman*

ar-rahim ("in the name of God, the All-merciful, the Compassionate"); the exception is the ninth *surah*, which commentators generally believe to be a continuation of the eighth.

Qur'anic Commentary (Tafsir)

The term for commentary on the Qur'an, **tafsir**, means "unveiling" or elucidating the meaning of a text. Any such interpretation is based on one of three authoritative sources: the Qur'an itself, Prophetic *hadith*, and the opinions of the Prophet's companions and their successors. Like the Qur'an and the *hadith*, the earliest commentaries were transmitted orally, but by the tenth century Qur'anic interpretation had developed into a science with several ancillary fields of study. In fact, every legal or theological school, religious trend, or political movement in Muslim history has looked to the Qur'an for its primary support and justification. The result has been a wide range of interpretations reflecting the diversity of the sects, legal schools, and mystical and philosophical movements that emerged as the Islamic tradition developed.

The Qur'an's Concept of God

The Qur'an presents its view of the divinity in direct and unambiguous declarations of faith in the one and only God, creator, sustainer, judge, and sovereign Lord over all creation. For Muslims, it is a sin ("*shirk*") to associate any other being with God or to ascribe divinity to any but God alone.

"Allah" is not the name of a particular deity: as we noted earlier, it means "the God," "the Lord of all beings" (Q. 1: 2) who demands faith and worship of all rational creatures. It was used in the same sense by the pagan Arabs before Islam, and is still used in that sense by Arab Jews and Christians today.

Islamic theology holds that God's essence is unknowable, inconceivable, and above all categories of time, space, form, and number. Materiality and temporality cannot be attributed to God. Nor, properly speaking, can masculinity or femininity, although references to God in the Qur'an and throughout Islamic literature use masculine pronouns, verbs, and adjectives.

God is known through attributes referred to in the Qur'an as the "most beautiful names" (sometimes translated as "wonderful names"). These divine attributes are manifested in creation in power and mercy, life and knowledge, might and wisdom. The Qur'an (59: 22–3) declares:

God is God other than whom there is no god, knower of the unknown and the visible. God is the All-merciful, the Compassionate. God is God other than whom there is no god, the King, the Holy One, Peace, the Faithful, the Guardian, the Majestic, the Compeller, the Lofty One.

Faith and Action

Righteousness as it is expressed in the Qur'an has several components. In addition to faith in God, God's angels, books, and prophets, and the judgment of the last day, it includes good works: Muslims should give of their wealth, however much they may cherish it, to orphans and the needy or for the ransoming of slaves and war captives. Righteousness also includes patience and steadfastness in times of misfortune or hardship and war, and integrity in one's dealings with others.

Because all men and women are ultimately part of one humanity, they are all equal before God,

regardless of race, colour, or social status. They may surpass one another only in righteousness: "Humankind, We have created you all of one male and one female and made you different peoples and tribes in order that you may know one another. Surely, the noblest of you in God's sight is the one who is most aware of God" (Q. 49: 13).

The Arabic word *iman* means faith, trust, and a personal sense of safety and well-being in God's providential care, mercy, and justice. On this level of inner personal commitment, *iman* is a deeper level of *islam*: total surrender of the human will and destiny to the will of God. The opposite of *iman* is **kufr**, rejection of faith. To have faith is to know the truth and assent to it in the heart, profess it with the tongue, and manifest it in concrete acts of charity and almsgiving. *Kufr*, on the other hand, means knowing the truth but wilfully denying or obscuring it by acts of rebellion against the law of God. The word *kufr* literally means "to cover up, deny, or obscure."

The Qur'an also makes an important distinction between Islam and faith. Outwardly, Islam is a religious, social, and legal institution, whose members constitute the worldwide Muslim *ummah*, or community. *Iman*—faith—is an inner conviction whose sincerity God alone can judge, a commitment to a way of life in the worship of God and in moral relations with other persons. This is described beautifully in the Qur'an (49: 14), where the Bedouin come to Muhammad and say, "we have faith." Muhammad is commanded to respond: "Do not say that you have faith, rather, say that you have submitted [you have *islam*], for faith has not yet entered your hearts." Faith, as a comprehensive framework of worship and moral conduct, is explicitly depicted in the answer that the Prophet is said to have given to the question "What is faith?": "Faith is seventy-odd branches, the highest of which is to say 'There is no god except God' and the lowest is to remove a harmful object from the road."

Above Islam and *iman* stands *ihsan* (doing good or creating beauty). On the level of human interrelations, *ihsan* is a concrete manifestation of both Islam and *iman*. On the level of the personal relationship of the man or woman of faith with God, *ihsan* constitutes the highest form of worship, expressed in this *hadith*: "*Ihsan* is to worship God as though you see God, for even if you do not see God, God sees you."

❧ Practice

The Five Pillars of Islam

Individual faith and institutional Islam converge in the worship of God and service to others. According to well-attested tradition, the Prophet himself said that Islam was built on five "pillars." With the exception of the first (the *shahadah*, the profession of faith through which one becomes a Muslim), the pillars are all rites of worship, both personal and communal. The Five Pillars are:

- to declare, or bear witness, that there is no god except God, and that Muhammad is the Messenger of God;
- to establish regular worship;
- to pay the **zakat** alms;
- to observe the fast of Ramadan; and
- to perform the **hajj** (pilgrimage to Mecca) once in one's life.

The Five Pillars are the foundations on which Islam rests as a religious system of faith and social responsibility, worship, and piety. Acts of worship are obligatory for all Muslims. Each of the Five Pillars has both an outer or public obligatory dimension and an inner or private voluntary dimension.

Bearing Witness

The first pillar is the *shahadah*: "I bear witness that there is no god except God, and I bear witness that Muhammad is the messenger of God." It consists of two declarations. The first, affirming the oneness of God, expresses the universal and primordial state of faith in which every child is born. The Prophet is said to have declared, "Every child is born in this original state of faith; then his parents turn him

into a Jew, Christian, or Zoroastrian, and if they are Muslims, into a Muslim."

The second declaration, affirming Muhammad's role as messenger, signifies acceptance of the truth of Muhammad's claim to prophethood, and hence the truth of his message.

Prayer

The second pillar consists of the obligatory prayers (**salat**). These are distinguished from voluntary devotional acts, such as meditations and personal supplicatory prayers (which may be offered at any time), in that they must be performed five times in a day and night: at dawn, noon, mid-afternoon, sunset, and after dark. The *salat* prayers were the first Islamic rituals to be instituted.

The *salat* prayers must always be preceded by ritual washing. *Wudu'* ("making pure or radiant") or partial washing includes washing the face, rinsing the mouth and nostrils, washing the hands and forearms to the elbows, passing one's wet hands over the head, and washing the feet to the two heels.

Five times a day—on radio and television, through loudspeakers, and from high minarets—the melodious voice of a **mu'adhdhin** chants the call to prayer, inviting the faithful to pray. Whether praying alone at home or at the mosque, behind the imam, as a member of the congregation, every Muslim is always conscious of countless other men and women engaged in the same act of worship at the same time.

Each phrase of the call to prayer is repeated at least twice for emphasis:

God is greater. I bear witness that there is no god except God, and I bear witness that Muhammad is the Messenger of God. Hasten to the prayers! Hasten to success (or prosperity)! (Shi'as add: Hasten to the best action!) God is greater. There is no god except God.

The prayers consist of cycles or units called *rak'ahs*, with bowing, kneeling, and prostration. The dawn prayers consist of two cycles, the noon

© Charles O. Cecil/Alamy

Women in Fez, Morocco, performing ablutions at the Zawiya (shrine) of Moulay Idris II, who ruled Morocco from 807 to 828.

and mid-afternoon prayers of four each, the sunset prayer of three, and the night prayers of four cycles.

Apart from some moments of contemplation and personal supplication at the end of the *salat*, these prayers are fixed formulas consisting largely of passages from the Qur'an, especially the opening *surah* (*al-Fatihah*):

In the name of God, the All-merciful, the Compassionate:

Praise be to God, the All-merciful, the Compassionate, King of the Day of Judgment. You alone do we worship, and to you alone do we turn for help. Guide us to the straight way, the way of those upon whom you have bestowed your grace, not those who have incurred your wrath, nor those who have gone astray (Q. 1: 1–7).

The **Fatihah** for Muslims is in some ways similar to the Lord's Prayer for Christians. It is repeated in every *rak'ah*—at least 17 times in every 24-hour period.

Unlike Judaism and Christianity, Islam has no Sabbath specified for rest. Friday is the day designated for *jum'ah* ("assembly"), for congregational prayers. In the Friday service the first two *rak'ahs* of the noon prayers are replaced by two short sermons, usually on religious, moral, and political issues, followed by two *rak'ahs*. The place of worship is called the *masjid* ("place of prostration in prayer") or *jami'* (literally, "gatherer"). The English word "mosque" is derived from *masjid*.

Other congregational prayers are performed on the first days of the two major festivals, **'Id al-Fitr** and 'Id al-Adha, at the end of Ramadan and the *hajj* pilgrimage, respectively.

Faithful Muslims see all things, good or evil, as contingent on God's will. Hence many take care to preface any statement about hopes for the future with the phrase *in-sha' Allah*, "if God wills."

Almsgiving

The third pillar of Islam reflects the close relationship between worship of God and service to the poor and needy. Traditionally, all adult Muslims who had wealth were expected to "give alms" through payment of an obligatory tax called the *zakat* (from a root meaning "to purify or increase"). Offering alms in this way served to purify the donor, purging greed and attachment to material possessions.

The *zakat* obligation was 2.5 per cent of the value of all accumulated wealth (savings, financial gains of any kind, livestock, agricultural produce, real estate, etc.). During the early centuries of Islam, when the community was controlled by a central authority, the *zakat* revenues were kept in a central treasury and disbursed for public educational and civic projects, care of orphans and the needy, and the ransoming of Muslim war captives. Now, however, the Muslim world is divided into many independent nation-states, most of which now collect some form of income tax, and as a consequence the *zakat* obligation has become largely voluntary. Many ignore it; others pay through donations to private religious and philanthropic organizations.

In addition to the obligatory *zakat* alms, Muslims are expected to practise voluntary almsgiving (**sadaqah**). The Qur'an calls *sadaqah* a loan given to God, which will be repaid in manifold measure on the Day of Resurrection (Q. 57: 11). *Sadaqah* giving is not bound by any consideration of creed: the recipient may be anyone in need.

The Ramadan Fast

The fourth pillar of Islam is the month-long fast of Ramadan. Fasting is recognized in the Qur'an as a

Focus

A Muslim Ritual: The Call to Prayer

It is Friday afternoon, a few minutes before the start of the weekly congregational prayer. In this mosque in Southern California, perhaps 1,000 men and 100 women are gathered; the difference in numbers reflects the fact that this prayer is obligatory for men but optional for women. A young man walks to the front of the large men's section (the women are seated in a second-floor gallery), raises his hands to his ears, and begins the call to prayer: *"Allahu akbar*, God is greater. . . ."* When he has finished, the people behind him line up in rows and wait for the imam— the person who will lead the prayer—to begin.

Were this service in a different location, the call to prayer might already have been sounded in the traditional way, broadcast from minarets (towers) beside the mosque. But there are no minarets here, as the mostly non-Muslim residents of this neighbourhood wanted a building that would "fit in" with its surroundings. Nor does this mosque have the characteristic dome: it is a two-storey building designed to look more like a school than a mosque. In this non-traditional context, the function of the call to prayer has changed. Instead of being broadcast outside, to let the community know that it is time to pray, the call is broadcast inside to those already assembled for the prayer. This is one of the ways in which the Muslims who come to this mosque have adapted to their surroundings.

Focus

Beginning the Fast

Ms Becker teaches fourth grade in a public elementary school. Eleven of the school's pupils are Muslim, and one of them is in Ms Becker's class. This year, seven of the Muslim students have decided that they will fast during the month of Ramadan. Some of them have fasted before, but for the nine-year-old in Ms Becker's class this will be the first time.

There is no set age at which Muslim children are expected to begin observing the fast. It may be as early as eight or nine, or as late as adolescence. In certain Muslim cultures, girls begin at an earlier age than boys, who are usually exempted on the grounds that they "aren't strong enough." While their non-Muslim classmates have lunch, those who are fasting gather in Ms Becker's classroom to work quietly on school projects. They are also excused from their physical education classes, and instead do a writing assignment about physical fitness. In this way, a public school accommodates the needs of its Muslim students.

universal form of worship, enjoined by scriptures of all faiths. In addition to the Ramadan fast, the Prophet observed a variety of voluntary fasts, which are still honoured by many pious Muslims.

The Ramadan fast is mandated in just one passage of the Qur'an:

> O you who have faith, fasting is ordained for you as it was ordained for those before you, that you may become aware of God. [. . .] Ramadan is the month in which the Qur'an was sent down as a guidance to humankind, manifestations of guidance and the Criterion. Therefore whosoever among you witnesses the moon, let them fast [the month], but whosoever is sick or on a journey, an equal number of other days (Q. 2: 183, 185).

According to this passage, Ramadan was the month in which the Qur'an was revealed to the Prophet.

Ramadan is a month-long fast extending from daybreak till sundown each day. It requires complete abstention from food, drink, smoking, and sexual relations. The fast is broken at sunset, and another light meal is eaten at the end of the night, just before the next day's fast begins at dawn.

With respect to the rules governing the fast, the Qur'an notes that "God desires ease for you, not hardship" (2: 185). Therefore the sick, travellers, children, and women who are pregnant, nursing, or menstruating are exempted from the fast, either altogether or until they are able to make up the missed days.

Before Islam, the Arabs followed a lunar calendar in which the year consisted of only 354 days. To keep festivals and sacred months in their proper seasons, they (like the Jews) added an extra month every three years. The Qur'an abolished this custom, however, allowing Islamic festivals to rotate throughout the year. When Ramadan comes in the summer, particularly in the equatorial countries of Asia and Africa, fasting from sunrise to sunset can be a real hardship. But when it comes in winter, as it did in the 1990s in the northern hemisphere, it can be relatively tolerable.

Ramadan ends with a festival called 'Id al-Fitr, a three-day celebration during which people exchange gifts and well-wishing visits. Children receive gifts and wear brightly coloured new clothes, people visit the graves of loved ones, and special sweet dishes are distributed to the poor. Before the first breakfast after the long fast, the head of every family must give special alms for breaking the fast, called *zakat al-fitr*, on behalf of every member of the household. Those who are exempted from fasting for reasons of chronic illness or old age must feed a poor person for every day they miss.

The fast of Ramadan becomes a true act of worship when a person shares God's bounty with those who have no food with which to break their fast. True fasting means more than giving up the pleasures of food and drink: it also means abstaining from gossip, lying, or anger, and turning one's heart and mind to God in devotional prayers and meditations.

The Pilgrimage to Mecca

The fifth pillar of Islam is the *hajj* pilgrimage, instituted by Abraham at God's command after he and his son Ishmael were ordered to build the Ka'ba. Thus most of its ritual elements are understood by the women and men who perform them as re-enactments of the experiences of Abraham, whom the Qur'an declares to be the father of prophets and the first true Muslim.

Before the pilgrims reach the sacred precincts of Mecca, they exchange their regular clothes for two pieces of white linen, symbolic of the shrouds in which Muslims are wrapped for burial. With this act they enter the state of consecration. They approach Mecca with the solemn proclamation: "Here we come in answer to your call, O God, here we come! Here we come, for you have no partner, here we come! Indeed, all praise, dominion, and grace belong to you alone, here we come!"

Once in Mecca, the pilgrims begin with the lesser *hajj* (*'umrah*). This ritual is performed in the precincts of the Great Mosque and includes the *tawaf* (walking counter-clockwise around the Ka'ba seven times; a form of prayer in which men and women participate together, side by side) and running between the two hills of al-Safa and al-Marwa. In the traditional narrative, Hagar, Abraham's handmaid and the mother of his son Ishmael, ran between these two hills in search of water for her dying child. After the seventh run, water gushed out by the child's feet, and Hagar contained it with

sand. The place, according to Islamic tradition, is the ancient well of Zamzam ("the contained water"). The water of Zamzam is considered holy, and pilgrims often take home containers of it as blessed gifts for family and friends.

The *hajj* pilgrimage proper begins on the eighth of Dhu al-Hijjah, the twelfth month of the Islamic calendar, when throngs of pilgrims set out for 'Arafat, a large plain, about 20 kilometres (13 miles) east of Mecca, on which stands the goal of every pilgrim: the Mount of Mercy (Jabal al-Rahmah). In accordance with the Prophet's *sunnah* (practice), many pilgrims spend the night at Mina, but others press on to 'Arafat. As the sun passes the noon meridian, all the pilgrims gather for the central rite of the *hajj* pilgrimage: the standing (*wuquf*) on the Mount of Mercy in 'Arafat.

In this rite, the pilgrims stand in solemn prayer and supplication till sunset, as though standing before God for judgment on the last day. The *wuquf* recalls three sacred occasions: when Adam and Eve stood on that plain after their expulsion from paradise, when Abraham and his son Ishmael performed the rite during the first *hajj* pilgrimage, and when Muhammad gave his farewell oration, affirming the family of all Muslims.

The sombre scene changes abruptly at sundown, when the pilgrims leave 'Arafat for Muzdalifah, a sacred spot a short distance along the road back to Mecca. There they observe the combined sunset and evening prayers and gather pebbles for the ritual lapidation (throwing of stones) at Mina the next day. The tenth of Dhu al-Hijjah is the final day of the *hajj* season, and the first of the four-day festival of sacrifice ('Id al-Adha). The day is spent at Mina, where the remaining pilgrimage rites are completed.

Tradition says that on his way from 'Arafat to Mina, Abraham was commanded by God to sacrifice that which was dearest to him—his son Ishmael. Satan whispered to him three times, tempting him to disobey God's command. Abraham's response was to hurl stones at Satan, to drive him away. Thus at the spot called al-'Aqabah, meaning the hard or steep road, a brick pillar has been erected to represent Satan. Pilgrims gather early in the morning

Pilgrims throw stones at one of the pillars representing Satan. This ritual is a key part of the pilgrimage.

to throw seven stones at the pillar, in emulation of Abraham. Three other pillars in Mina, representing the three temptations, are also stoned.

Following the stoning ritual, the head of each pilgrim family or group offers a blood sacrifice—a lamb, goat, cow, or camel—to symbolize the animal sent from heaven with which God ransoms Abraham's son (Q. 27: 107). Part of the meat is eaten by the pilgrims and the rest is distributed to the poor, so that they may eat as well. After this, to mark the end of their state of consecration, pilgrims ritually clip a minimum of three hairs from their heads (some shave their heads completely). The *hajj* ends with a final circumambulation of the Ka'ba and the completion of the rites of the lesser *hajj* ('*umrah*) for those who have not done so.

Tradition asserts that a person returns from a sincerely performed *hajj* free of all sin, as on the day when he or she was born. Thus the *hajj* represents a form of resurrection or rebirth, and its completion marks a new stage in the life of a Muslim. Every pilgrim is henceforth distinguished by the title *hajjah* or *hajji* before her or his name.

Religious Sciences

In Arabic a learned person is termed an *'alim*. The plural, *'ulama'*, refers to the religio-legal scholars, or religious intellectuals, of the Islamic world as a group. What Muslims call the "religious sciences" were part of a comprehensive cultural package—including theology, philosophy, literature, and science—that developed as Islam expanded geographically far beyond the religio-political framework of its Arabian homeland. Cosmopolitan, pluralistic Islamic cultural centres like Baghdad,

Sites

Al-Azhar University, Egypt

Located in Cairo, Al-Azhar is the oldest university in the Western world and an important centre of Sunni learning. It was transformed into a modern university, with a newly created faculty for women, in 1961, under the direction of Egypt's President Nasser.

Cordoba, and Cairo offered ideal settings for intellectual growth. Beginning in the eighth century, the development of philosophy, theology, literature, and science continued in different parts of the Muslim world well into the seventeenth.

Islam is a religion more of action than of abstract speculation about right belief. Hence the first and most important of the religious sciences, Islamic law, stresses that the essence of faith is right living. The Prophet characterizes a Muslim thus: "Anyone who performs our prayers [i.e., observes the rituals of worship] and eats our ritually slaughtered animals [i.e., observes the proper dietary laws] is one of us." For Muslims, inner submission to the will of God is God's way for all of humankind. At both the personal and the societal level, Islam is a way of life that is to be realized by living within the framework of divine law, the *shari'ah*: that is, a way of life based on moral imperatives.

Islamic Law (Shari'ah) and its Sources

The Qur'an

The Qur'an and hence the *shari'ah* are centrally concerned with relationships among individuals in society and between individuals and God. The most particular and intimate human relationship is the one between husband and wife; the second is the relationship between parent and child. The circle then broadens to include the extended family, the tribe, and finally the *ummah* and the world.

Islam has no priesthood. Every person is responsible both for his or her own morality and for the morality of the entire Muslim *ummah*: "Let there be of you a community that calls to the good, enjoins honourable conduct, and dissuades from evil conduct. These are indeed prosperous people" (Q. 3: 104).

The Qur'an places kindness and respect to parents next in importance to the worship of God. These are followed by caring for the poor and the needy through almsgiving. Usury is prohibited as a means of increasing one's wealth. But renunciation of material possessions is no more desirable than total attachment to them. Rather, the Qur'an enjoins the faithful to "Seek amidst that which God has given you, the last abode, but do not forget your portion of the present world" (Q. 28: 77).

In short, the Qur'an is primarily concerned with moral issues in actual situations. It is not a legal manual. Of its 6,236 verses no more than 200 are explicitly legislative.

The Sunnah

The life-example of the Prophet includes not only his acts and sayings but also his tacit consent. His acts are reported in anecdotes about situations or events in which he participated or to which he reacted. In situations where he expressed neither approval nor objection, his silence is taken to signify consent. Thus the *sunnah* of consent became a normative source in the development of Islamic law.

Accounts that report the Prophet's *hadiths* (sayings) must go back to an eyewitness of the event. The *hadith* literature is often called "tradition" in English, in a quite specific sense. Islamic "tradition" (or "Prophetic tradition") is the body of sayings traced to the Prophet Muhammad through chains of oral transmission. *Hadith* is the most important component of *sunnah* because it is the most direct expression of the Prophet's opinions or judgments regarding the community's conduct.

To qualify as a *hadith*, a text must be accompanied by its chain of transmission, beginning with the compiler or last transmitter and going back to the Prophet. The aim of the study of *hadith* is to ascertain the authenticity of a particular text by establishing the completeness of the chain of its transmission and the veracity of its transmitters.

There are six canonical *hadith* collections. The earliest and most important collectors were Muhammad ibn Isma'il al-Bukhari (810–70) and Muslim ibn al-Hajjaj al-Nisaburi (c. 817–75). As their names suggest, the former came from the city of Bukhara in Central Asia and the latter from Nishapur in northeastern Iran. Although the two men did not know each other, they were contemporaries and both spent many years travelling across the Muslim world in search of *hadiths*. The fact that their independent quests produced very similar results suggests that a unified *hadith* tradition was already well established.

Both men are said to have collected hundreds of thousands of *hadiths*, out of which each selected about 3,000, discounting repetitions. Their approach became the model for all subsequent *hadith* compilers. Their two collections, entitled simply *Sahih* (literally, "sound") *al-Bukhari* and *Sahih Muslim*, soon achieved canonical status, second in authority only to the Qur'an. Within less than half a century, four other collections—by Abu Dawud al-Sijistani, Ibn Majah, al-Tirmidhi, and al-Nasa'i—were produced. It is worth noting that, like al-Bukhari and Muslim, these four also came from Central Asia and Iran. Each of these collections is entitled simply *Sunan* (the plural of *sunnah*).

As legal manuals, all six collections are organized topically, beginning with the laws governing the rituals of worship and then continuing with the laws regulating the social, political, and economic life of the community.

The Scope of Islamic Law

For Muslims God is the ultimate lawgiver. The *shari'ah* is sacred law, "the law of God." It consists of the maxims, admonitions, and legal sanctions and prohibitions enshrined in the Qur'an and explained, elaborated, and realized in the Prophetic tradition.

The term *shari'ah* originally signified the way to a source of water. Metaphorically it came to mean the way to the good in this world and the next. It is "the straight way" that leads the faithful to paradise in the hereafter. Muslims believe the *shari'ah* to be God's plan for the ordering of human society.

Within the framework of the divine law, human actions range between those that are absolutely obligatory and will bring rewards on the Day of Judgment, and those that are absolutely forbidden and will bring harsh punishment. Actions are classified in five categories:

- lawful (**halal**), and therefore obligatory;
- commendable, and therefore recommended (*mustahabb*);
- neutral, and therefore permitted (*mubah*);
- reprehensible, and therefore disliked (*makruh*); and
- unlawful (**haram**), and therefore forbidden.

These categories govern all human actions. The correctness of an action and the intention that lies behind it together determine its nature and its consequences for the person who performs it.

Jurisprudence (Fiqh)

Jurisprudence, or **fiqh**, is the theoretical and systematic aspect of Islamic law, consisting of the interpretation and codification of the *shari'ah*, or sacred law. A scholar who specializes in this exacting science is called a *faqih* ("jurist").

Islamic jurisprudence, as it was developed in the various legal schools (Hanafi, Maliki, Shafi'i, and Hanbali), is based on four sources. Two of these, the Qur'an and *sunnah*, are its primary sources. The other two are secondary sources: the personal reasoning (*ijtihad*) of the scholars, and the general consensus (*ijma'*) of the community. The schools of Islamic law differed in the degree of emphasis or acceptance that they gave to each source.

Personal reasoning is the process through which legal scholars deduced from the Qur'an and *sunnah* the laws that are the foundations of their various schools of thought. The term *ijtihad* signifies a scholar's best effort in this endeavour, which is based on reasoning from analogous situations in the past: modern software piracy, for instance, would be considered analogous to theft.

Finally, the principle of consensus (*ijma'*) is meant to ensure the continued authenticity and truth of the three other sources. In the broadest sense, *ijma'* refers to the community's acceptance and support of applied *shari'ah*. More narrowly, it has encouraged an active exchange of ideas among the scholars of the various schools, at least during the formative period of Islamic law. Consensus has remained the final arbiter of truth and error, expressed in the Prophet's declaration that "my community will not agree on an error."

Yet even this important principle has been the subject of debate and dissension for the scholars of the various schools. Among the many questions at issue are whether the consensus of earlier generations is binding on the present one, and whether the necessary consensus can be reached by the scholars alone, without the participation of the community at large.

Early Jurisprudence

The Qur'an calls on Muslims to choose a number of individuals to dedicate themselves to the acquisition of religious knowledge and instruct their people when they turn to them (Q. 9:122). The need for such a group was felt from the beginning when some pilgrims visiting Mecca from Medina accepted Islam and on their return took with them Muslims who had acquired religious knowledge to teach the people of Medina the rituals and principles of the new faith. As Islam spread and communities across Arabia became Muslim domains, governors

with special religious knowledge were sent by the Prophet to administer these new domains and instruct their people in Islam.

Among those governors was Mu'adh ibn Jabal, a man of the Ansar (the Prophet's "helpers") who was well known for his knowledge of Islam. Before sending him to Yemen, the Prophet is said to have asked Mu'adh how he would deal with the People of the Book (Jews and Christians), who made up the majority of the population in the region. Mu'adh supposedly answered that he would deal with them in accordance with the Book of God and the *sunnah* of his Prophet. Muhammad then asked what would happen if he did not find the answer to a problem in either of the two sources. Mu'adh is said to have answered, "I would then use my reason, and would spare no effort."

This pious tale no doubt reflects much later developments. It was invoked to bestow on a developing discipline an aura of Prophetic blessing and authority. Nevertheless, the anecdote aptly illustrates the development of Islamic law in its early stages. A number of the companions were known for their ability to deduce judgments from Qur'anic principles, together with the actions and instructions of the Prophet.

As the Muslim domains expanded through rapid conquest, the need for a uniform body of religious law became increasingly evident. For a time, the need was filled by Muslims of the first and second generations (the Companions and their successors), particularly those among them who were distinguished as reciters of the Qur'an and transmitters of the Prophet's *sunnah*. They laid the foundations for subsequent legal traditions. Until the eighth century, these traditions centred in western Arabia, particularly in Medina and Mecca, and Iraq, especially in Kufah and Basrah. It was in these centres that the "living tradition" of jurisprudence was transformed from an oral to a written science, with a rich and ever-growing body of literature.

The Sunni Legal Schools

By the middle of the eighth century, the process of establishing distinctive legal schools with independent legal systems was well under way. Two men in the eighth century and two in the ninth distinguished themselves as the jurists of their time and founders of the earliest Sunni legal schools. After a period of often violent conflict, the four principal Sunni legal schools gained universal acceptance as equally valid interpretations of the *shari'ah* that divided the Muslim world geographically among themselves.

Some less important legal schools died out: for example, the Yahiri school, which was established early by the literalist jurist Dawud ibn Khalaf (d. 884), ceased with the end of Muslim rule in Spain. Others survived, but only in small and isolated communities: among them is the Ibadi school, which was established during the first century of Islam by 'Abd Allah ibn Ibad and is still represented in small communities in North Africa and Oman.

Hanafi Law

The most famous jurist of Iraq was Abu Hanifah (699–767), the son of a Persian slave. Although he left no writings that can be ascribed to him with certainty, his two disciples al-Shaybani and Abu Yusuf, who lived during the early and vigorous period of 'Abbasid rule, developed their master's system into the most impressive and widespread Sunni legal school.

The Hanafi school was for centuries accorded state patronage, first by the 'Abbasid caliphate and then by the Ottoman Empire. It spread to all the domains influenced by these two empires: Egypt, Jordan, Lebanon, Syria, Iraq, Central Asia, the Indian subcontinent, Turkey, and the Balkans.

Maliki Law

Malik b. Anas (c. 715–95), the leading scholar of Medina and founder of the Maliki legal school, developed his system in the framework of the *hadith* and legal traditions he collected in his book *al-Muwatta'* ("The Levelled Path"). The first such collection to be made, it reflects the early development of legal thought in Islam.

Unlike later jurists and collectors of *hadith*, Malik gave equal weight to the *sunnah* of the Prophet himself and the "practice," or living tradition, of the people of Medina. He also relied much more on *ijtihad*—the personal effort to deduce well-considered legal opinions—than did later distinguished religious scholars. He was guided in this effort by the principle of common good (*maslahah*).

Abu Hanifah had also relied greatly on living tradition, along with the principles of deductive analogical reasoning (*qiyas*; for example, deciding that software piracy is analogous to theft) and rational preference (*istihsan*, according to which one may prefer one particular ruling over other possibilities). The work of both Malik and Abu Hanifah indicates that the principle of Prophetic tradition (*sunnah*) as a material source of jurisprudence was still in the process of development. It went hand in hand with the "living traditions" of major cities or centres of learning. Both ultimately traced their judgments back to the Prophet or the first generation of Muslims.

The Maliki school was carried early to Egypt, the Gulf region, and North Africa and from there to Spain, West Africa, and the Sudan.

Shafi'i Law

A decisive stage in the development of Islamic jurisprudence came in the ninth century with the crucial work of the systematizer Muhammad ibn Idris al-Shafi'i (767–820). Although Shafi'i was closer intellectually to the school of Medina, he travelled widely and studied in several different centres without clearly allying himself with any school. He spent his last years in Egypt, where he wrote the first systematic treatise on Islamic jurisprudence. His hitherto unequalled work radically changed the scope and nature of Islamic jurisprudence. Shafi'i advocated absolute dependence on the two primary sources of Islamic law, the Qur'an and *sunnah*. He based his own system on a vast collection of *hadith* and legal tradition, entitled *Kitab al-Umm*, which he compiled for that purpose.

Shafi'i restricted the use of *qiyas* or analogical reasoning, and rejected both the Hanafi principle of rational preference (*istihsan*) and the Maliki principle of common good (*maslahah*). He insisted that all juridical judgments be based on the Qur'an and the *sunnah*, and (unlike most jurists of his time) he preferred *hadiths* transmitted by single authorities to personal opinion. His argument was that jurists should not prefer the opinions of people to the Book of God itself and the *sunnah* of his Prophet.

Although Shafi'i's system was later adopted as the foundation of the school bearing his name, he expressly opposed the idea. He saw himself not as the founder of a new legal school, but as the reformer of Islamic law.

The Shafi'i school took root early in Egypt, where its founder lived and died. From there it spread to southern Arabia and then followed the maritime trade routes to East Africa and to Southeast Asia, where it remains the dominant legal school.

Hanbali Law

Not long after Shafi'i, the well-known *hadith* collector Ahmad ibn Hanbal (780–855), a strict conservative, founded the Hanbali legal school in conformity with Shafi'i's position. The *hadith* collection he produced, the *Musnad*, was arranged not by subject, as other standard collections were, but by the names of primary transmitters, usually the Prophet's Companions and other early authorities. Though the *Musnad* of Ibn Hanbal was not the first work of this genre, it was by far the largest and most important, and it became the foundation of the Hanbali legal system.

The Hanbali school has had a smaller following than its rivals, but also a disproportionately great influence, especially in modern times. It exists almost exclusively in central Arabia (the present Saudi kingdom), with scattered adherents in other Arab countries. Its conservative ideology, however, has been championed by revolutionaries and reformers since the thirteenth century.

The End of Ijtihad

The Prophet is reported to have declared that "The best generation is my generation, then the one that follows it, and then the one that follows that." This judgment expresses the widely held view that after the normative period of the Prophet and the first four "rightly guided" caliphs, Muslim society grew increasingly corrupt and irreligious. Yet there were exceptions to the rule: women and men who modelled their lives and piety on the examples from that normative period. These were the well-known pious scholars, jurists, and *hadith* collectors of the formative period of Muslim history.

With the establishment of the major Sunni legal schools by the tenth century, there was a sort of undeclared consensus that the gate of *ijtihad* had closed. This did not mean that the development of Islamic legal thinking ceased altogether, but it did mean that no new legal systems would henceforth be tolerated.

In fact, the process of exclusion had already begun. It depended not on pious or scholarly considerations, but on the awarding of political patronage to some schools and the denial of it to others. From this time on, only the experts in religious law (*muftis*) of each city or country were empowered to issue legal opinions, called **fatwas**, in accordance with the principles of their respective legal schools. Various collections of famous *fatwas* have been made, which less able or less creative *muftis* use as manuals.

Ja'fari (Shi'i) Law

The Shi'i legal and religious system is named after the man regarded as its founder, Ja'far al-Sadiq (c. 700–65). The sixth in the line of Imams that began with 'Ali—the cousin and son-in-law of the Prophet whom the Shi'a believed to be his only legitimate successor—Ja'far was revered as a descendant of the Prophet's family (*ahl al-bayt*), and, with his father Muhammad al-Baqir (the fifth Imam), was among the leading scholars of Medina. They left no written works, but a rich oral tradition was preserved and eventually codified in the tenth and eleventh centuries as the foundation of the legal system that governs **Imami** or **Twelver** Shi'ism (see Focus box). In the Ja'fari school, Twelver Shi'ism possesses the Shi'i legal school closest to Sunni orthodoxy.

In contrast to Sunni legal schools, which developed first a science of jurisprudence and then a canonical *hadith* tradition to buttress it, the Ja'fari school based its legal system on a vast body of *hadith* centred on the three centuries of traditions associated with the Imams descended from 'Ali. The first of what would become four collections of Imami *hadith* was compiled by Muhammad al-Kulayni (d. 941): entitled *al-Kafi* ("The Sufficient"), it resembles Sunni *hadith* collections in that it consists first of books dealing with the fundamentals of doctrine and worship and then of books on ancillary legal matters.

Where it diverges sharply from the Sunni model is in the section dealing with the imamate, entitled *Kitab al-Hujjah* ("Book of the Proof of God"), which is included among the books dealing with the fundamentals of faith. In fact, the essential point of difference between the Shi'i and Sunni legal traditions is the former's fundamental belief in the necessity of the Imams as guardians of the *shari'ah* and guides to its correct interpretation and implementation by the community. The Imam is believed to be the proof or argument (*hujjah*) of God to his human creatures. Hence the earth cannot be without an Imam, whether he be present and active in the management of the affairs of the community or hidden from human sight and perception (see Focus Box, below).

Following al-Kulayni, important *hadith* collections were compiled by Ibn Babawayh (c. 923–91) of the Iranian holy city of Qom, who was known as al-Shaykh al-Saduq ("the truthful **shaykh**"), and Abu Ja'far al-Tusi (d. 1067), "the jurist doctor of the community."

With Tusi the foundations of the Imami *hadith* and legal traditions were virtually fixed. In the absence of the Imam, his role as guardian of the *shari'ah* had to be filled, however imperfectly, by scholars of the community. This meant that *ijtihad*, or personal reasoning, had to continue, albeit in a limited way, in the form of rational efforts on the part of the scholars not so much to formulate new laws as to comprehend and interpret the Imams' rulings in ways that would apply to new situations, and consensus must be limited to the *ijma'*

Focus

The Twelfth Imam

According to the Shi'i doctrine of *imamah*, the Prophet appointed 'Ali as his vice-regent. 'Ali in turn appointed his son Hasan to succeed him as Imam, and Hasan appointed his brother Husayn. Thereafter, each Imam designated his successor, usually his eldest son.

Mainstream Shi'as believe that the line of Imams descended from Husayn continued until 874, when the twelfth Imam, the four-year-old Muhammad ibn Hasan al-'Askari, disappeared; it is for this reason that they are also known as "Twelvers." They maintain that he went into hiding ("occultation"), but continued to communicate with his followers through four successive deputies, until 941; then the Imam ceased communication and entered a new phase known as the "greater occultation," which will continue until the end of the world. At that time, before the Day of Resurrection, he will return as the **Mahdi**, "the rightly guided one," who with Jesus will establish universal justice and true Islam on earth. In short, Twelver Shi'ism understands the *sunnah* to include not only the life-example of the Prophet Muhammad and his generation, but the life-examples of the 12 Imams—the men they believe to be his rightful successors. Hence the period of the *sunnah* for Twelvers extends over three centuries, until the end of the "lesser occultation" of the twelfth Imam in 941.

of the scholars only (and not to the community as a whole).

For this reason the Imami legal school rejected analogical reasoning as an instrument of *ijtihad*. This does not mean that reason played a secondary role in the growth of Shi'i jurisprudence. On the contrary, the primary sources of law were identified early on as the transmitted tradition (*naql*), including the Qur'an, and human reason ('*aql*). Furthermore, where transmitted tradition and reason come into conflict, reason takes priority over tradition.

Ijtihad has remained in principle a primary source of law for Shi'i jurists to this day. But its use has been circumscribed by the principle of precaution (*ihtiyat*) rooted in the fear of error in judgment in the absence of the Imam. Precaution has tended to minimize the use of personal reasoning to the point that jurists with any measure of originality are few and far between.

Taqlid means following the *ijtihad* of a particular jurist. For the Sunni, it meant following the founder of one of the recognized legal schools, which implied strict adherence to a traditional system with no room for innovation. For the Shi'a, the absence of the Imam made *taqlid* of a living jurist, a *mujtahid*, a legal necessity. This emphasis has had the same effect on the Shi'i community that the closing of the gate of *ijtihad* has had on the Sunni. The development of courageous and sensitive new approaches to the interpretation and application of the *shari'ah* is therefore imperative in both communities today.

Islamic Philosophy and Theology

An important subset of the religious sciences (also known as the transmitted sciences) consisted of the "rational" sciences of philosophy and theology. Theology is discourse about God, God's attributes, and God's creation and nurture of all things. It is also concerned with human free will and predestination, moral and religious obligations, and the return to God on the Day of Resurrection for the final judgment. Insofar as theology addresses human faith and conduct, it is part of the science of *fiqh*, jurisprudence.

In time, however, Islamic theology also came to concern itself with more philosophical questions about the existence of God, creation, and the problems of evil and suffering. In these areas Islamic theology reflects the influence of Hellenistic philosophy, whose principles and rationalistic methodology it adopted.

The rapid spread of Islam out of Arabia into Syria and Mesopotamia brought Muslims into contact with people of other faiths and ethnic backgrounds, including Hellenized Jews and Christians. With the rise of the 'Abbasid dynasty in the mid-eighth century, interest in Greek philosophy, science, and medicine increased, and Arabic translations of Greek works began to appear.

The quest for knowledge reached its peak in the next century under the caliph al-Ma'mun (r. 813–33), whose Bayt al-Hikmah ("House of Wisdom") in Baghdad was the first institution of higher learning not only in the Islamic world but anywhere in the West. Christian scholars had already translated many Greek medical, philosophical, and theological treatises into Syriac and commented on them, but the House of Wisdom, which housed an impressive library of Greek manuscripts, provided additional support for their work. Families of translators worked in teams, rendering into Arabic the ancient treasures of Hellenistic science and philosophy. Smaller centres of philosophical and medical studies in Syria and Iran also made notable contributions.

The Early Period

Early Islamic philosophy had a distinctive character: Aristotelian in its logic, physics, and metaphysics; Platonic in its political and social aspects; and Neoplatonic in its mysticism and theology. Two figures stand out in this early period. The first was the Iraqi theologian-philosopher Abu Yusuf Ya'qub al-Kindi (d. 870), who used philosophical principles and methods of reasoning to defend fundamental Islamic teachings such as the existence and oneness of God, the temporal creation of the universe by God's command out of nothing, the inimitability of the Qur'an, and the necessity of prophets. In his argument for the latter, Al-Kindi underlined the distinction between the philosopher who acquires his knowledge through rational investigation and contemplation and the prophet who receives his knowledge instantaneously, through divine revelation.

In sharp contrast to al-Kindi, Abu Bakr Zakariyah al-Razi ("the one from Rayy, Iran"; c. 865–926) was a thoroughgoing Platonist who rejected the doctrine of creation out of nothing. Rather, drawing on the theory that Plato elaborated in his *Timaeus*, al-Razi argued that the universe evolved from primal matter, floating gas atoms in an absolute void. The universe or cosmos came into being when God imposed order on the primeval chaos, but it will return to chaos at some distant point in the future, because matter will revert to its primeval state.

The Flowering of Islamic Philosophy

Abu Nasr al-Farabi (c. 878–950), who moved to Baghdad from Turkestan, in Central Asia, was not only a great philosopher but an important musical theorist and an accomplished instrumentalist. His Platonic philosophical system was comprehensive and universal. According to al-Farabi, God is pure intellect and the highest good. From God's self-knowledge or contemplation emanates the first intellect, which generates the heavenly spheres and a second intellect, which then repeats the process. Each subsequent intellect generates another sphere and another intellect.

Al-Farabi agreed with al-Kindi that a prophet is gifted with a sharp intellect capable of receiving philosophical verities naturally and without any mental exertion. He then communicates these truths to the masses, who are incapable of comprehending them on the philosophical level.

Although al-Farabi was called "the second teacher," after Aristotle, even he was excelled by "the great master" Ibn Sina (known in Latin as Avicenna, 980–1037). Ibn Sina, who was born in Bukhara, Central Asia, was a self-taught genius who mastered the religious sciences at the age of ten and

by the age of 18 had become a leading physician, philosopher, and astronomer. His encyclopedic manual of medicine, *al-Qanun fi al-Tibb* ("The canon of medicine"), and his philosophical encyclopedia, *al-Shifa'* ("The book of healing"), were studied in European universities throughout the Middle Ages.

Ibn Sina built on al-Farabi's Neoplatonic ideas to produce a comprehensive system of mystical philosophy and theology. He accepted and developed al-Farabi's theory of emanations, placing it in a more precise logical and philosophical framework. Although he affirmed the prophethood of Muhammad, the revelation of the Qur'an, and the immortality of the soul, he rejected the Qur'anic traditions of the resurrection of the body, the reward of paradise, and the punishment of hell.

According to a widely accepted Prophetic tradition, at the beginning of every century God raises a scholar to renew and strengthen the faith of the Muslim community. Such a man is known as a *mujaddid* ("renovator") of the faith. Abu Hamid Muhammad al-Ghazali (1058–1111) of Tus, in Iran, has been regarded as the *mujaddid* of the sixth Islamic century. His work went far beyond theology and philosophy, encompassing mysticism and all the religious sciences.

In 1091 al-Ghazali was appointed a professor of theology and law at the prestigious Nizamiyah college in Baghdad, where he tirelessly defended mainstream Sunni Islam against the innovations of the theologians and the heresies of the philosophers. Just four years later, however, he suffered a deep psychological crisis and gave up teaching. After a long quest, he determined that true knowledge could not be attained through either the senses or the rational sciences, but only through a divine light that God casts into the heart of the person of faith. His reason thus enlightened, al-Ghazali produced one of the most ambitious works in the history of Islamic thought. Appropriately entitled *The Revivification of the Religious Sciences* (*Ihya' 'ulum al-din*), this magnum opus examines all religious learning from a deeply mystical point of view.

In his book *The Incoherence* [or "Collapse"] *of the Philosophers*, al-Ghazali rejected the philosophical principle of causality (which said, for example, that created things could be the efficient causes of events) and in its place proposed a theory of occasionalism, according to which the only cause of anything in the universe is God. Al-Ghazali's critique itself would become the subject of a critique by the Andalusian Aristotelian philosopher Ibn Rushd.

Ibn Rushd (known in Latin as Averroës, 1126–98), who was born in Cordoba, Spain, was the greatest Muslim commentator on Aristotle. He came from a long line of jurists, and was himself a noted scholar of Islamic law. His legal training decisively influenced his philosophy. In his commentary on al-Ghazali's work, entitled *The Incoherence of the Incoherence*, Ibn Rushd methodically criticizes al-Ghazali for misunderstanding philosophy and Ibn Sina for misunderstanding Aristotle. The first to construct a true Aristotelian philosophical system, Ibn Rushd essentially shared his Eastern predecessors' belief in the primacy of philosophy over religion. In his famous double-truth theory, however, he argued that both were valid ways of arriving at truth: the difference was that philosophy was the way of the intellectual elite, while religion was the way of the masses.

The great thirteenth-century philosopher-mystic Ibn 'Arabi will be discussed later, in the context of Sufism. A more empirical philosopher than any of those mentioned so far was the Tunisian-born 'Abd al-Rahman Ibn Khaldun (1332–1406). Through his extensive travels and the positions he held as a jurist and political theorist, Ibn Khaldun gained insight into the workings both of nations and of political and religious institutions. This led him to write a universal history. The most important part of this work is its introduction (*Muqaddimah*), in which Ibn Khaldun presents the first social philosophy of history in the Western world.

Islamic philosophy had a lasting influence on medieval and Renaissance thought in Europe, particularly through its interpretation of Aristotelianism. Europeans came to know many Muslim philosophers by Latinized forms of their names: Rhazes for al-Razi, Alpharabius or Avennasar for al-Farabi, Avicenna for Ibn Sina, Algazel for al-Ghazali, Averroës for Ibn Rushd. Among the Europeans who were influenced by the latter in particular was the great medieval Catholic philosopher and theologian St Thomas Aquinas. In fact, it is impossible to properly understand his thought without appreciating its roots in both the Muslim philosophy of Ibn Rushd and the Jewish philosophy of Maimonides.

Variations

Shi'ism

As we have seen, for Sunnis the term "imam" refers to anyone who serves as the leader of prayer at the mosque—a role that was sometimes performed by the caliph. For Shi'as, however, "Imam" is also the title given to the one individual divinely mandated to lead the Muslim community because he is descended from the Prophet's cousin, son-in-law, and rightful successor 'Ali.

Devotion to the family of the Prophet ("the people of the house") has always been a central characteristic of Shi'ism, which finds support for its position in the Qur'an: "Surely, God wishes to take away all abomination from you, O people of the House, and purify you with a great purification" (Q. 33: 33). Furthermore, Muhammad himself declares that he wishes no reward for his work in conveying God's revelation "except love for [my] next of kin" (Q. 42: 23). The expressions "people of the house" (*ahl al-bayt*) and "next of kin" (*al-qurba*) are usually interpreted as referring to the Prophet's daughter Fatimah, her husband 'Ali, and their two sons, Hasan and Husayn.

The foundation of the Shi'i claim is a *hadith* according to which the Prophet, on his way back from Mecca to Medina, stopped at a place called Ghadir Khumm, took 'Ali by the hand, and made the following declaration:

> O people, hear my words, and let him who is present inform him who is absent: Anyone of whom I am the master, 'Ali, too, is his master.

In the Iranian city of Isfahan, actors perform a *tazieh*, or "passion play," re-enacting the events surrounding the death of Husayn at Karbala in 680. This is part of the commemoration of Ashura among the Shi'a.

O God, be a friend to those who befriend him and an enemy to those who show hostility to him, support those who support him and abandon those who desert him.

On the basis of this and other sayings in which they believe the Prophet directly or indirectly designated 'Ali as his successor, Shi'i specialists on the Prophetic oral tradition constructed an elaborate legal and theological system supporting the doctrine of *imamah*, according to which the source of all legitimate authority is the Imam.

Ashura

In the year 680 the Prophet's grandson Husayn (the son of 'Ali) was leading an uprising against the Umayyad Caliph Yazid when he was killed in battle at Karbala in Iraq. The anniversary of his death, on the tenth day of the month of Muharram, has become a focal point for the Shi'i community's hopes and frustrations, messianic expectations, and highly eschatological view of history.

"Ashura" ("ten"), as the anniversary came to be known, is still commemorated by Shi'as around the world. Blending sorrow, blessing, and mystery, it has inspired a rich devotional literature, as well as numerous popular passion plays re-enacting the events leading up to the death of Husayn. Above all, it is observed by the Shi'a as a day of suffering and martyrdom. Its symbolism is expressed in a variety of devotional acts, including solemn processions, public readings, and a pilgrimage to the sacred ground of Karbala. The Sunni community commemorates "Ashura" with a day of fasting.

Sites

Karbala, Iraq

Home of the Shrine of Imam Husayn (the third Imam and grandson of Muhammad), who was killed at Karbala in 680. It is of special importance to the Shi'a, who during their daily prayers touch their heads to a small disk of clay from the soil of Karbala. Since 2004, numerous suicide bombings near the shrine have killed hundreds of innocent worshippers.

Divisions within Shi'ism

The Shi'a share a general allegiance to the right of 'Ali and his descendants to spiritual and temporal authority in the Muslim community after Muhammad. But "Shi'ism" is a broad term that covers a variety of religio-political movements, sects, and ideologies.

The majority of Shi'as accepted the line of Husaynid Imams down to Ja'far al-Sadiq, the legal scholar who was sixth in the succession. But a major schism occurred when Ja'far's oldest son and successor, Isma'il, predeceased him. Ja'far then appointed a younger son, Musa al-Kazim, as his own successor. The Shi'a who accepted this appointment and went on to revere Musa as the seventh Imam eventually came to be known as Imamis or Twelvers (see Focus Box, p. 255).

Others, though, considered the appointment irregular and insisted that the seventh Imam should be Isma'il's son Ahmad. For this reason they came to be known as **Isma'ilis** or "**Seveners**," The largest faction, called Nizaris, carried on the line of Imams through Ahmad and his descendants down to the present.

Basic to Isma'ili faith and worldview is the doctrine of the divine mandate of the Imam and his absolute temporal and religious authority. Over the centuries Isma'ili philosophers and theologians developed this fundamental teaching into an impressive esoteric system of prophetology. The Isma'ilis have played very conspicuous intellectual and political roles in Muslim history.

For centuries they lived as an obscure sect in Iran, Syria, East Africa, and the Indo-Pakistani subcontinent. Since 1818 their leader, or Imam, has been known as the Agha Khan, an Indo-Iranian title signifying nobility. The third Agha Khan (1877–1957) initiated a movement for reconciliation with the larger Muslim community, and efforts to resolve differences have continued under his Harvard-educated successor, Karim Agha Khan (b. 1936). In modern times Isma'ilis have migrated in large numbers to the West. Prosperous and well-organized, the Isma'ilis now number roughly 15 million and are the best-integrated Muslim community in the West.

Sufism: The Mystical Tradition

The early Muslim mystics were said to wear a garment of coarse wool over their bare skin in emulation of Jesus, who is represented in Islamic hagiography as a model of ascetic piety. For this reason they became known as Sufis (from the Arabic word meaning "wool"). Asceticism was only one element in the development of Sufism, however.

At least as important was the Islamic tradition of devotional piety. Since the ultimate purpose of all creation is to worship God and sing his praises (see Q. 17: 44 and 51: 56), the pious are urged to "remember God much" (33: 41), "in the morning and evening" (76: 25), for "in the remembrance of God hearts find peace and contentment" (13: 28). The Prophet's night vigils and other devotions, alluded to in the Qur'an (73: 1–8) and greatly

The Aga Khan, spiritual leader of the world's 15 million Isma'ili Muslims, received an honorary doctor of laws degree at the University of Toronto in 2004.

embellished by hagiographical tradition, have served as a living example for pious Muslims across the centuries. *Hadith* traditions, particularly the "divine sayings" (*hadith qudsi*) in which the speaker is God, have also provided a rich source of mystical piety. Above all, the *mi'raj*—the Prophet's miraculous journey to heaven—has been a guide for numerous mystics on their own spiritual ascent to God. This journey has been richly illustrated in numerous manuscripts.

The early Muslim ascetics were known as *zuhhad*, meaning "those who shun [the world and its pleasures]." One of the earliest champions of this movement was a well-known theologian and *hadith* collector named al-Hasan al-Basri, who was born in Medina in 642 and lived through both the crises and the rise to glory of the Muslim *ummah*. In a letter addressed to the pious caliph 'Umar ibn 'Abd al-'Aziz, Hasan likened the world to a snake: soft to the touch, but full of venom.

The early ascetics were also called weepers, for the tears they shed in fear of God's punishment and in yearning for God's reward. Significantly, this early ascetic movement emerged in areas of mixed populations, where other forms of asceticism had existed for centuries: places such as Kufa and Basra in Iraq (long the home of Eastern Christian asceticism); northeastern Iran, particularly the region of Balkh (an ancient centre of Buddhist ascetic piety, now part of Afghanistan); and Egypt (the home of Christian monasticism as well as Gnostic asceticism).

Asceticism for its own sake, however, was frowned on by many advocates of mystical piety. Among the critics was the sixth Imam, Ja'far al-Sadiq, who argued that when God bestows a favour on a servant, God wishes to see that favour manifested in the servant's clothing and way of life. Ja'far's grandfather 'Ali Zayn al-'Abidin is said to have argued that God should be worshipped not out of fear of hell or desire for paradise, but in humble gratitude for the gift of the capacity to worship God.

What transformed ascetic piety into mysticism was the all-consuming love of the divine exemplified by an early woman mystic named Rabi'a al-'Adawiyah of Basra (c. 713–801). Born into a poor family, Rabi'a was orphaned and sold into slavery as a child, but her master was so impressed with her piety that he set her free. She lived the rest of her life in mystical contemplation, loving God with no motive other than love itself:

> My Lord, if I worship you in fear of the fire, burn me in hell. If I worship you in desire for paradise, deprive me of it. But if I worship you in love of you, then deprive me not of your eternal beauty (Smith 1928).

Mystics of all religious traditions have used the language of erotic love to express their love for God. Rabi'a was perhaps the first to introduce this

Document

Rabi'a al-'Adawiyah

When Rabi'a's fellow Sufis urged her to marry, she agreed in principle, but only on the condition that the prospective husband—a devout man named Hasan—answer four questions. In the end she remained unmarried, free to devote all her thoughts to God.

"What will the Judge of the world say when I die? That I have come forth from the world a Muslim, or an unbeliever?"

Hasan answered, "This is among the hidden things known only to God. . . ."

Then she said, "When I am put in the grave and Munkar and Nakir [the angels who question the dead] question me, shall I be able to answer them [satisfactorily] or not?" He replied, "This is also hidden."

"When people are assembled at the Resurrection and the books are distributed, shall I be given mine in my right hand or my left?" . . . "This also is among the hidden things."

Finally she asked, "When mankind is summoned (at the Judgment), some to Paradise and some to Hell, in which group shall I be?" He answered, "This too is hidden, and none knows what is hidden save God—His is the glory and the majesty."

Then she said to him, "Since this is so, and I have these four questions with which to concern myself, how should I need a husband, with whom to be occupied?" (Smith 1928: 11).

language into Islamic mysticism. She loved God with two loves, the love of passion and a spiritual love worthy of God alone.

The love that Rabi'a spoke of was the devotional love of the worshipful servant for his or her Lord. A more controversial tradition within Sufism pursued absolute union with God. Among the proponents of this ecstatic or "intoxicated" Sufism was Husayn ibn Mansur al-Hallaj (c. 858–922), whose identification with the divine was so intense as to suggest that he made no distinction between God and himself. For this apparent blasphemy he was brutally executed by the 'Abbasid authorities.

Al-Hallaj had been initiated into Sufism early in life and he travelled widely, studying with the best-known Sufi masters of his time. But in time he broke away from his teachers and embarked on a long and ultimately dangerous quest of self-realization. It began when he went one day to see his teacher Abu Qasim al-Junayd. When the latter asked who was at the door, Al-Hallaj answered, "I, the absolute divine truth" (*ana al-Haqq*)—calling himself by one

of the 99 "wonderful names" of God mentioned in the Qur'an. Al-Junayd reprimanded his wayward disciple and predicted an evil end for him.

At its core, al-Hallaj's message was moral and intensely spiritual, but it was interpreted as suggesting that God takes the form of a human person (as Christians believe of Jesus)—an idea that most Muslims of his time found deeply shocking. Whereas a less extreme predecessor, Bayazid Bistami, had preached annihilation of the mystic in God, al-Hallaj preached total identification of the lover with the beloved:

I am He whom I love, and He whom I love
    is I.
We are two spirits dwelling in one body.
If thou seest me, you see Him; and if thou
    seest Him, you see us both
(Nicholson 1931: 210–38).

After eight years in prison, al-Hallaj danced to the gallows, where he begged his executioners to

Document

Farid al-Din 'Attar

Farid al-Din 'Attar lived in Iran at the turn of the thir-teenth century. In this extract, the words "Ask not" echo a phrase used by theologians to express paradox—bila kayf, "without asking how"—but here they evoke the mystic's sense of ineffability.

His beauty if it thrill my heart
If thou a man of passion art
Of time and of eternity,
Of being and non-entity,
Ask not.

When thou hast passed the bases four,
Behold the sanctuary door;
And having satisfied thine eyes,
What in the sanctuary lies
    Ask not. . . .
When unto the sublime degree
Thou hast attained, desist to be;
But lost to self in nothingness
And, being not, of more and less
    Ask not.
(Arberry 1948: 32–3)

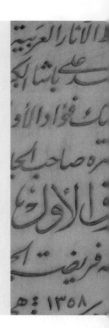

"Kill me, O my trusted friends, for in my death is my life, and in my life is my death." For many Muslims, al-Hallaj lives on as the martyr of love who was killed for the sin of intoxication with God by the sword of God's own *shari'ah*.

The Development of Sufism

The mystical life is a spiritual journey to God. The novice who wishes to embark on such an arduous journey must be guided by a master who becomes in effect his or her spiritual parent. But as Sufism grew, many well-recognized masters attracted too many disciples to allow for a one-to-one relationship. By the eleventh century, therefore, the ideas of the masters were being recorded and transmitted in writing. Perhaps the greatest work of the period was al-Ghazali's *Revivification of the Religious Sciences*.

Roughly half a century after al-Ghazali, Shihab al-Din Suhrawardi (c. 1155–91) became known as the great master of illumination (*shaykh al-ishraq*). He grew up in Iran and eventually settled in northern Syria. Drawing on a verse in the Qur'an (24: 35) that speaks of God as the light of the heavens and the earth, Suhrawardi described a cosmos of light and darkness populated by countless luminous angelic spirits.

The most important Sufi master of the thirteenth century was Muhyi al-Din Ibn 'Arabi (1165–1240), who was born and educated in Muslim Spain and travelled widely in the Middle East before finally settling in Damascus. The central theme of Ibn 'Arabi's numerous books and treatises is the "unity of being" (*wahdat al-wujud*), although he himself never used this term.

According to this doctrine, God in God's essence remains in "blind obscurity," but is manifested in the creation through an eternal process of self-disclosure. Thus even as human beings need God for their very existence, God also needs them in order to be known.

Ibn 'Arabi's doctrine of the unity of being had many implications, among them the idea that, if God alone really is, then all ways ultimately lead to God. This means that all the world's religions are in reality one. Ibn 'Arabi says:

My heart has become capable of every form:
    it is a pasture for gazelles and a convent
      for Christian monks,
And a temple for idols, and the pilgrim's

Ka'ba, and the tables of the Torah and the
book of the Koran.
I follow the religion of Love, whichever way
his camels take. My religion and my faith
is the true religion
(Nicholson 2002 [1914]: 75).

Ibn 'Arabi remains one of the greatest mystic
geniuses of all time.

Rumi

The most creative poet of the Persian language was
Jalal al-Din Rumi (1207–73). Like Ibn 'Arabi, he
was the product of a multicultural, multi-religious
environment. Rumi was born in Balkh, Afghanistan, but as a child fled with his parents from the
advancing Mongols. At last they settled in the city
of Konya in central Anatolia (Turkey), a region that
had been part of the Roman Empire.

In 1244 Rumi met a wandering Sufi named
Shams of Tabriz. The two men developed a relationship so intimate that Rumi neglected his teaching duties because he could not bear to be separated
from his friend. Yet in the end Shams disappeared,
leaving Rumi to pour out his soul in heart-rending
verses expressing his love for the "Sun" (the name
"Shams" means "sun" in Arabic) of Tabriz.

Rumi's greatest masterpiece is his *Mathnawi*
("Couplets"), a collection of nearly 30,000 verses.

The spirit of this vast panorama of poetry is clearly
expressed in its opening verses, which evoke the
haunting melodies of the reed flute telling its sad
tale of separation from its reed bed. In stories,
couplets of lyrical beauty, and at times even coarse
tales of sexual impropriety, the *Mathnawi* depicts
the longing of the human soul for God.

Sufi Orders and Saints

The religious fraternity is an ancient and widespread phenomenon. The earliest Sufi fraternities
were established in the late eighth century, and by
the thirteenth century a number of these groups
were becoming institutionalized. Usually founded
either by a famous *shaykh* (master) or by a disciple
in the *shaykh*'s name, Sufi orders began as teaching
and devotional institutions located in urban centres, where they would often attach themselves to
craft or trade guilds in the main bazaar.

It became a common custom for lay Muslims
to join a Sufi order. Lay associates provided a good
source of income for the order, participated in devotional observances, and in return for their contributions received the blessing (*barakah*) of the *shaykh*.

The truth and authenticity of a *shaykh*'s claim to
spiritual leadership depended on his or her spiritual
genealogy. By the thirteenth century, Sufi chains
of initiation (similar to chains of **isnad** in *hadith*

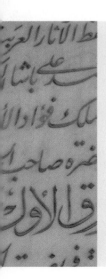

Document

Jalal al-Din Rumi

In this excerpt from the Mathnawi *(Book 3, 3901–3906)
Rumi expresses the mystic's experience of union with
God in terms of the dissolution of individual identity.*

I died as mineral and became a plant
I died as plant and rose to animal,
I died as animal and I was Man.
Why should I fear? When was I less by dying?

Yet once more I shall die as Man, to soar
With angels blest; but even from angelhood
I must pass on: all except God doth perish [Q. 28: 88].
When I have sacrificed my angel-soul,
I shall become what no mind e'er conceived.
Oh, let me not exist! for Non-existence
Proclaims in organ tones, "To him we shall return"
[Q. 2: 151] (Nicholson 1950: 103).

Document

Jalal al-Din Rumi, *Diwan*

Ghazal no. 1827

If anyone asks you about *houris* [heavenly beings], show your face and say, "Like this."
If anyone speaks to you about the moon, rise up beyond the roof and say, "Like this."
When someone looks for a fairy princess, show your face to him.
When someone talks of musk, let loose your tresses and say, "Like this."
If someone says to you, "How do clouds part from the moon?"
Undo your robe, button by button, and say, "Like this."
If he asks you about the Messiah, "How could he bring the dead to life?"
Kiss my lips before him and say, "Like this."
When someone says, "Tell me, what does it mean to be killed by love?"
Show my soul to him and say, "Like this."
If someone in concern asks you about my state,
Show him your eyebrow, bent over double, and say, "Like this."
The spirit breaks away from the body, then again it enters within.
Come, show the deniers, enter the house and say, "Like this."
In whatever direction you hear the complaint of a lover,
That is my story, all of it, by God, like this.
I am the house of every angel, my breast has turned blue like the sky—
Lift up your eyes and look with joy at heaven, like this.
I told the secret of union with the Beloved to the east wind alone.
Then, through the purity of its own mystery, the east wind whispered, "Like this."
Those are blind who say, "How can the servant reach God?"
Place the candle of purity in the hand of each and say, "Like this."
I said, "How can the fragrance of Joseph go from one city to the next?"
The fragrance of God blew from the world of his Essence and said, "Like this."
I said, "How can the fragrance of Joseph give sight back to the blind?"
Your breeze came and gave light to my eye: "Like this."
Perhaps Shams al-Din in Tabriz will show his generosity, and in his kindness display
his good faith, like this (Chittick 2000: 89–90).

transmission) were established. Such chains began with the *shaykh*'s immediate master and went back in an unbroken chain to 'Ali or one of his descendants, or in some cases to other Companions of the Prophet or their successors.

Through this spiritual lineage, a *shaykh* inherited the *barakah* of his masters, who inherited it from the Prophet. In turn, the *shaykh* bestowed his *barakah*, or healing power, on his devotees, both during his life and, with even greater efficacy, after his death.

The *shaykh*s of Sufi orders are similar to the saints of the Catholic Church in that the faithful ascribe miracles or divine favours (*karamat*) to them. Unlike Christian saints, however, they are recognized through popular acclaim rather than official canonization.

Devotional Practices

Although Sufis also perform the five daily prayers, their most characteristic practice is a ritual called the **dhikr** ("remembrance") of God, which may be public or private. The congregational *dhikr* ritual is usually held before the dawn or evening prayers. It consists of the repetition of the name of God, Allah, or the *shahadah*, "There is no god except God" (*la ilaha illa Allah*). The *dhikr* is often accompanied by special bodily movements and, in some Sufi orders, by elaborate breathing techniques.

Often the performance of the *dhikr* is what distinguishes the various Sufi orders from one another. In some popular orders it is a highly emotional ritual (similar to charismatic practices in some Pentecostal churches) intended to stir devotees into a state of frenzy. By contrast, in the sober Naqshbandi order (founded by Baha' al-Din al-Naqshbandi in the fourteenth century), the *dhikr* is silent, an inward prayer of the heart.

Another distinctly Sufi practice is the *sama'* ("hearing" or "audition"), in which devotees simply listen to the often hypnotic chanting of mystical poetry, accompanied by various musical instruments. As instrumental music is not allowed in the mosque, *sama'* sessions are usually held in a hall adjacent to the mosque, or at the shrine of a famous *shaykh*.

Music and dance are vital elements of devotional life for members of the Mevlevi (Mawlawi) order, named after Mawlana ("our master") Rumi and founded by his son shortly after his death. As practised by the Mevlevis—also known as the

© Images & Stories/Alamy

Dervishes at the Galata Mevlevihanesi (Mevlevi Whirling Dervish hall) in Istanbul.

"Whirling Dervishes"—dance is a highly sophisticated art symbolizing the perfect motion of the stars; the haunting melodies of the reed flute and the large orchestra that accompanies the chanting echo the primordial melodies of the heavenly spheres.

Sufism has always shown an amazing capacity for self-reform and regeneration. It was the Sufis who preserved Islamic learning and spirituality after 1258, when Baghdad fell to Mongol invaders, and Sufis who carried Islam to Africa and Asia. Today in the West it is primarily Sufi piety that is attracting non-Muslims to Islam.

Women and Sufism

Women have played an important role in the Sufi tradition, often serving as positive role models and teachers for both men and women. This may help to explain part of the historical tension between orthodox Islam and Sufism. One of the most beloved stories about Rabi'a, the early female Sufi *shaykhah* (the feminine of *shaykh*), has her roaming the streets of Basra carrying a bucket of water and a flaming torch, ready to put out the fires of Hell and set fire to the gardens of Paradise so that people will worship God for the sake of Love alone.

The Sufi tradition provided one of the few outlets for Muslim women to be recognized as leaders. Since the Sufis believed the Divine to be without gender, gender was irrelevant in worship. After Rabi'a, Sufi women could be *shaykahs* for mixed congregations, even though they were prohibited from being imams for mixed gender congregations (women were trained to be imams for groups of other women, however). It's also worth noting that the shrines of Sufi saints, whether male or female, are often cared for by women. As places where women have some measure of control, they tend to attract more women than men, inverting the usual gender breakdown at mosques. It isn't hard to imagine how some men, chauvinistically accustomed to thinking of public space as male space, could feel threatened by a public space in which women are the dominant presence. Thus they might categorize

Sufi women in Srinagar, Kashmir, pray outside the shrine of their order's founder, Shaikh Abdul Qadir Jilani, on the anniversary of his death.

© FAYAZ KABLI/Reuters/Corbis

Sufism as "un-Islamic" not because of doctrines, but because of the power and privilege it accords to women.

The Spread of Islam

Islam, like Christianity, is a missionary religion. Muslims believe that the message of their faith is intended for all humankind, to be practised in a community that transcends geographic, cultural, and linguistic borders.

Ideologically as well as historically, Islam is a post-Jewish, post-Christian religion. Ideologically, it sees itself as a third religion of the Book, one that confirms the scriptures that preceded it, notably the Torah and the Gospels. Historically, Muslims from the beginning responded to and interacted with the communities of other faiths, particularly Christians and Jews. As a religio-political power, therefore, Islam had to regulate its relations with non-Muslim citizens.

As People of the Book, Jews and Christians living in Muslim lands were promised full freedom to practise their faith in return for paying a poll tax that also guaranteed them physical and economic protection and exemption from military service. Legally such communities came to be known as *dhimmis* ("protected people"). In the course of time,

this designation was extended to other communities with sacred scriptures, including Zoroastrians in Iran and Hindus in India.

In its first century Islam spread through conquest and military occupation. Much of the Byzantine and Roman world and all of the Sasanian Persian domains yielded to the Arab armies and came under Umayyad rule. In subsequent centuries, politico-military regimes continued to contribute to Islam's dominance, especially in regions under Arab, Iranian, or Turkish rule.

Over time, however, the influence of mystics, teachers, and traders has reached farther and endured longer than the power of caliphs and

Map 5.1 Language and Culture in the Spread of Islam

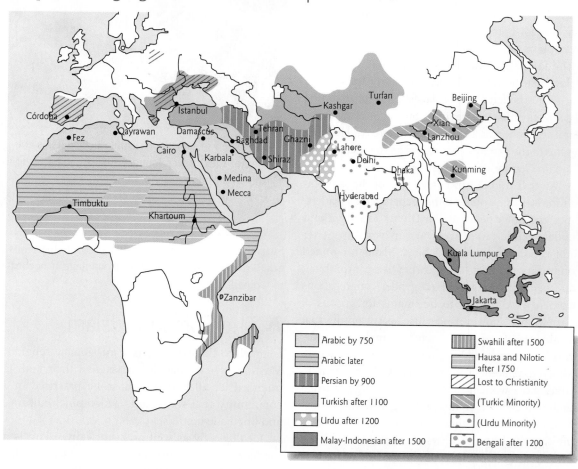

Arabic by 750	Swahili after 1500
Arabic later	Hausa and Nilotic after 1750
Persian by 900	Lost to Christianity
Turkish after 1100	(Turkic Minority)
Urdu after 1200	(Urdu Minority)
Malay-Indonesian after 1500	Bengali after 1200

conquerors. It was principally through the preaching and the living examples of individual Muslims that Islam spread to China, Southeast Asia, and East and West Africa. In modern times, migration and missionary activity have carried Islam to the Western hemisphere as well.

North Africa

After conquering what came to be the historical heartland of Islam—Syria, Egypt, and Iran—the Muslims moved into North Africa in the second half of the seventh century. Before that time North Africa had been first an important Roman province and then an equally important home of Latin Christianity. With its indigenous Berber, Phoenician, Roman, and Byzantine populations, North Africa was rich in cultural and religious diversity, and it has always maintained a distinct religious and cultural identity that reflects its ancient heritage.

The Umayyads had established their capital in Damascus in 661. With the shift of the capital from Damascus to Baghdad under the 'Abbasids in 762, the main orientation of the eastern Islamic domains became more Persian than Arab, more Asian than Mediterranean. Meanwhile, the centre of Arab Islamic culture shifted from Syria to the western Mediterranean: to Qayrawan, the capital of North Africa, in what is today Tunisia; and to Cordoba, Islam's western capital, in Spain, which rivalled Baghdad and Cairo in its cultural splendour. North African mystics, scholars, and philosophers were all instrumental in this remarkable achievement. In the nineteenth and twentieth centuries, North African religious scholars and particularly Sufi masters played a crucial role in the region's struggle for independence from European colonial powers. They helped to preserve the religious and cultural identity of their people and mobilized them to resist Italian and French colonization in Libya and Algeria. In spite of the deep influence of the French language and secular culture, North African popular piety still reflects the classical Islamic heritage.

Spain

When Arab forces arrived on the Iberian Peninsula in 711, Jews who had lived in Spain for centuries were facing harsh restrictions imposed by rulers recently converted to Catholic Christianity. They welcomed the Arabs as liberators.

With astonishing rapidity, Umayyad forces conquered the land of Andalusia, or al-Andalus, as the Arabs called southern Spain, and laid the foundations for an extraordinary culture. Arab men married local women, and a mixed but harmonious society developed that was Arab in language and expression and Arabo-Hispanic in spirit. Muslims, Christians, and Jews lived together in mutual tolerance for centuries before fanatical forces on all sides stifled one of the most creative experiments in interfaith living in human history.

One of the greatest scholars of the *convivencia* ("shared life") between Muslims, Jews, and Christians in medieval Spain was María Rosa Menocal, who died in 2012. In *The Arabic Role in Medieval Literary History* (1987) she traced the linguistic connections between Arabic and Romance languages. Her most famous book, however, *The Ornament of the World* (2002), expanded her work on *convivencia*.

Arab Spain produced some of the world's greatest minds, including not only Ibn 'Arabi, Ibn Tufayl, and Ibn Rushd but the jurist and writer Ibn Hazm (994–1064) and the mystic-philosopher Ibn Masarrah (d. 931). Islamic Spain was the cultural centre of Europe. Students came from as far away as Scotland to study Islamic theology, philosophy, and science in centres of higher learning such as Cordoba and Toledo. It was in these centres that the European Renaissance was conceived, and the great universities in which it was nurtured were inspired by their Arabo-Hispanic counterparts.

In Muslim Spain the Jews enjoyed a golden age of philosophy and science, mysticism, and general prosperity. Jewish scholars, court physicians, and administrators occupied high state offices and served as political and cultural liaisons between Islamic Spain and the rest of Europe. Arab learning

Document

María Rosa Menocal on *Convivencia*

An excerpt from Menocal's essay "The Myth of Western-ness in Medieval Literary Historiography":

In the destruction of the whole of the magnificent National Library and other major collections in Sarajevo in 1992, it now appears one very significant book was rescued, the famous manuscript called the Sarajevo Haggada. A Haggada is of course a prayer book that is, appropriately, the collection of prayers to be said on Passover, on the eve of exodus, but despite its name this gorgeous and elaborately illuminated manuscript, considered the best of its kind anywhere in the world, and much treasured by Jews everywhere, is not "Sarajevan" at all, nor "merely" Jewish, but rather "Spanish." And what can "Spanish" possibly mean, what do I mean it to be that is so different from what it seems to be in most other uses of this and other "identity" tags? Made in Spain in the late thirteenth century, it is, to put it most reductively, one of the many reflections of a Jewish culture that flourished and had its Golden Age, the Golden Age, precisely because it adopted the virtues of exile and found its distinctly impure voice within an Arabic culture that was expansive and promiscuous and often exilic itself. It was thus altogether fitting that the precious object, the book that inscribes the story of the exile from Egypt, was carried out of Spain by members of the exiled Sephardic community in 1492: and remained, for the better part of the subsequent five hundred years, well-protected and cherished inside the Ottoman Empire, itself a remarkable example of the great good of empires, which learn how to absorb and tolerate and intermarry "identities," and which became,

after 1492, the place of refuge of most Sephardic Jews and of many Andalusian Muslims. But the manuscript had to be rescued once again, during World War II, and it was when a Muslim curator in Sarajevo, attached as most Muslims are to the memory of Spain, saved that Spanish Haggada from Nazi butchers.

Surely, the morals of the story are perfectly clear: to understand the richness of our heritage we must be the guardians of the Haggada—the Muslim librarian who was not an Arab, of course, but who in saving the manuscript was fulfilling the best of the promises of Islamic Spain and Europe—and we must be the translators who reveal the exquisite ambivalence and sometimes painful conflict of identity of Judah Halevi, whose poetry is sung in so heavy an Arabic accent, and we must be the guardians and defenders of the interfaith marriage between the Christian girls who sang in corrupt Romance and the refined poets of the Arab courts, which is left inscribed, as a passionate and great love, in the *muwashshahat*. We must, in other words, reject the falsehoods of nations in our work, and reveal, with the exquisite Ibn 'Arabi, the virtues of what he more simply calls love. "My heart can take on any form," he tells us, and then he simply names those temples at which he prays, the temples that inhabit him: the gazelle's meadow, the monks' cloister, the Torah, the Ka'ba. These are the temples whose priests we need to be, if we are to understand what any of this history is about, and it is only in them that there can be any future understanding of the complex "identity" of Europe in the Middle Ages. And almost undoubtedly in its present and future as well (Menocal, 2003: 269–70).

penetrated deep into Western Europe and contributed directly to the West's rise to world prominence.

In addition to symbiotic creativity, however, the 900-year history of Arab Spain (711–1609)

included the tensions and conflicts typical of any multi-religious, multicultural society ruled by a minority regime. In the end, Islamic faith and civilization were driven out of Spain and

Sites

Cordoba, Spain

The city at the heart of the *convivencia* ("shared life") in medieval Spain, Cordoba was described by a tenth-century Benedictine nun as "the ornament of the world."

The Mosque–Cathedral of Cordoba, also known as the Mezquita and the Great Mosque of Cordoba, began as a Visigoth church, was transformed into a medieval Muslim mosque, and is now a Catholic cathedral. Spanish Muslims have been lobbying the Spanish government and the Vatican to be allowed to perform prayers inside its walls.

failed to establish themselves anywhere else in Europe.

Sub-Saharan Africa

Islam may have arrived in sub-Saharan Africa as early as the eighth century. As in other places where it became the dominant religion, it was spread first by traders, and then on a much larger scale by preachers. Finally jurists came to consolidate and establish the new faith as a religious and legal system. Sufi orders played an important part both in the spread of Islam and in its use as a motivation and framework for social and political reform.

Islam always had to compete with traditional African religion. Muslim prayers had to show themselves to be no less potent than the rain-making prayers or rituals of the indigenous traditions. In the fourteenth century, the Moroccan Muslim traveller Ibn Battutah wrote a vivid account of the efforts of Muslim converts in the Mali Empire of West Africa to adapt their new faith to local traditions.

In East Africa Islam spread along the coast, carried mainly by mariners from Arabia and the Gulf trading in commodities and also in slaves. From the sixteenth century onward, after Portuguese navigators rounded the southern cape of Africa, the cultural and political development of East African Islam was directly affected by European colonialism as well.

Unlike the populations of Syria, Iraq, Egypt, and North Africa, the peoples of East Africa did not adopt the Arabic language. But so much Arabic vocabulary penetrated the local languages that at least one-third of the Swahili vocabulary today is Arabic, and until recently most of the major African languages were written in the Arabic script.

An important element of East African society has been the Khoja community. Including both Sevener (Isma'ili) and Twelver (Imami) Shi'as, the Khojas immigrated from India to Africa in the mid-1800s. They have on the whole been successful business people with Western education and close relationships with Europe and North America. These relationships have been strengthened by the migration of many Khojas to Britain, the United States, and Canada.

Central Asia and Iran

Central Asia had a cosmopolitan culture before Islam. Buddhism, Gnosticism, Zoroastrianism, Judaism, and Christianity existed side by side in mutual tolerance. The Arab conquest of the region took more than a century: beginning in 649, less than two decades after the Prophet's death, it was not completed until 752.

Under the Samanid dynasty, which ruled large areas of Iran and Central Asia in the ninth and tenth centuries, Persian culture flourished, as did classical *hadith* collectors, historians, philosophers, and religious scholars working in the Arabic language. Particularly important centres of learning developed in the cities of Bukhara and Samarkand, located in what is now Uzbekistan, which owed much of their prosperity to trade with India, China, and the rest of the Muslim domains. With the first notable Persian poet, Rudaki (c. 859–940), Bukhara became the birthplace of Persian literature.

While their contemporaries the Buyids promoted Shi'i learning and public devotions in the region that is now Iraq, the Samanids firmly established Sunni orthodoxy in Central Asia. Many Sunni theologians and religious scholars lived and worked in Bukhara and Samarkand under Samanid patronage. Among the great minds of the tenth and eleventh centuries were the theologian al-Maturidi, the philosopher Ibn Sina, the great scholar and historian of religion Abu Rayhan al-Biruni, and the famous Persian poet Ferdowsi. In this intellectual environment, Islam was spread by persuasion and enticement rather than propaganda and war.

Early in the eleventh century, the Samanids were succeeded by the Seljuq Turks in the Middle East and the Karakhanid Mongols in Persia and Central Asia. The Mongols profoundly altered the situation in that region as they did in the Middle East a century later. The devastating consequences of the Mongol conquest of Persia and Central Asia were compounded by the loss of trade revenues when the traditional caravan routes were abandoned in favour of sea travel to India and China. Central Asia never recovered from the resulting decline in culture and prosperity.

The Turks

As Turkic tribal populations from Central Asia moved into parts of the Middle Eastern Muslim heartland, they were converted to Islam mainly by Sufi missionaries. The tribes became influential from the tenth century onward in Central Asia, Armenia, Anatolia, and Syria. Mahmud of Ghazna in Afghanistan (r. 998–1030), of Turkish descent,

Sites

Istanbul, Turkey

The city that had been Constantinople under the Byzantines was renamed Istanbul after its capture by the Turkish ruler Muhammad II in 1453. The capital of the Ottoman Turkish Empire and the centre of the sultan's power, it is the site of many imperial buildings, including the famous Topkapi Palace (the principal residence of the sultans from 1465 to 1856) and its successor, the Western-influenced Dolmabahce Palace.

broke away from the Persian Samanid dynasty; his successors, the Ghaznavids, extended Muslim power in northern India. Mahmud was the first person to be called "sultan," a term that until his time had referred to the authority of the state.

The Seljuqs, another Turkic family, prevailed in Iran and farther west a generation after Mahmud. The second Seljuq sultan, Alp Arslan, inflicted a crushing defeat on the Byzantines at Manzikert, in eastern Anatolia, in 1071. Bit by bit, eastern Anatolia (today's Turkey) fell to the Seljuqs, who ruled until they were conquered by the Mongols in 1243.

In 1299 Osman I took over the caliphate from the 'Abbasids, establishing a dynasty—the "Ottomans"—that was to endure until 1924. In the fourteenth century they absorbed former Seljuq territory in eastern Anatolia and took western Anatolia from the Byzantines, and they reached the height of their power in the sixteenth century, occupying the Balkans as far north as Vienna, the Levant (i.e., the Syro-Palestinian region), and all of northern Africa except Morocco. So widespread was their empire that Christian Europe until the nineteenth century thought of Islamic culture as primarily Turkish.

As their imperial emblem the Ottomans adopted the crescent, an ancient symbol that the Byzantines had also used. Conspicuous on the Turkish flag, the crescent thus came to be seen by Europeans, and eventually by Muslims themselves, as the symbol of Islam. Turkic languages still prevail across much of the Central Asian territory that was ruled by the Soviet Union for most of the twentieth century: from Azerbaijan to Uzbekistan and Turkmenistan, a dominant element in the population is Turkic. The same is true of Chinese Central Asia.

China

Islam may have made contact with China as early as the eighth century, although the first written sources referring to Islam in China do not appear till the seventeenth century. For earlier information we have to rely on Chinese sources, which unfortunately focus on commercial activities and have little to say about the social and intellectual life of Chinese Muslims.

The extent of the Muslim presence in a given area may often be gauged by the number of mosques it contains. There seem to have been no mosques in the main inland cities of China before the thirteenth century. Along the coast, however, the minaret of the mosque in Guangzhou (Canton) and various inscriptions in the province of Fujian suggest that maritime trade with the Islamic world was under way considerably earlier, in 'Abbasid times.

From the beginning, Persian and Arab merchants were allowed to trade freely so long as they complied with Chinese rules. But it was not until the thirteenth century that Muslim traders began settling in China in numbers large enough to support the establishment of mosques. The presence of Islam in China before that time was probably limited.

Muslim communities in China prospered under the Mongol (1206–1368) and Ming (1368–1644) emperors. After the Mongol period Chinese Muslims were assimilated culturally but kept their distinct religious identity. Since it was through trade that they kept in touch with the rest of the Muslim *ummah*, however, the decline of the overland trade with Central Asia in the 1600s had the effect of isolating the Chinese Muslim community. It became virtually cut off from the rest of the world, so that our information about Muslims in China after the seventeenth century is largely a matter of conjecture.

Unlike Buddhism, centuries earlier, Islam never came to be seen as culturally Chinese. The Uighurs—the Muslim population of Xinjiang (Chinese Turkestan), in the far northwest of the country—are an identifiable minority in Chinese society, distinguished by their Turkic language as well as their religion. Yet even the Chinese-speaking Muslims in the principal eastern cities of "Han" China are set apart by their avoidance of pork—a staple of the Chinese diet. The presence of *halal* (ritually acceptable) restaurants and butcher shops is a sure sign of a Muslim neighbourhood.

Chinese Muslims experienced their share of repression under the Communist regime, particularly during the Cultural Revolution of 1966–76. Although the overall situation for Muslims has improved since then, Uighur demands for independence have been met with a severe crackdown, and Chinese authorities often describe Uighur nationalists as "terrorists." Today there are approximately 50 million Muslims in China. Like other religious communities in contemporary China, they face an uncertain future, but their ethnic base in China's Central Asian interior is not likely to disappear soon.

South Asia

Islam arrived early in India, carried by traders and Arab settlers. Umayyad armies began moving into the region in the early eighth century, and since that time Islam has become an integral part of Indian life and culture.

The Muslim conquest of India was a long process. In the second half of the tenth century the city of Ghazni, in what is today Afghanistan, became the base from which the armies of the sultan Mahmud of Ghazna and his successors advanced over the famous Khyber Pass onto the North Indian Plain. By the fourteenth century most of India had come under Muslim rule, with the exceptions of Tamil Nadu and Kerala in the far south.

For the Muslim rulers of India, who came from Iran and Central Asia, maintaining and expanding their power over a large Hindu population meant continuous warfare. For Hindus, the Muslim regime was undoubtedly repressive; yet Indian Islam developed a unique and rich religious and intellectual culture.

India was something new in the history of Islam's territorial expansion. For the first time, the majority of the conquered population did not convert to the new faith. In ancient Arabia Islam had been able to suppress and supplant polytheism; but in India it had to learn to coexist with a culture that remained largely polytheistic.

At the same time Islam was something new to India. In a land where people often had multiple religious allegiances and community boundaries were fluid, Islam's exclusive devotion to the one God and clear delineation of community membership represented a dramatically different way of life.

Together, the three countries of the Indian subcontinent—India, Bangladesh, and Pakistan—have the largest Muslim population in the world. The Muslims of India alone make up the world's third-largest Muslim population (after Indonesia and Pakistan), numbering between 100 and 120 million. Even so, they are a minority whose future appears bleak in the face of rising Hindu nationalism.

Southeast Asia

Southeast Asia, when Islam arrived there, consisted of small kingdoms and settlements that were home to a wide variety of languages and cultures, and its religious life had been strongly influenced by the Hindu and Buddhist traditions. These influences can still be seen in the ancient Hindu culture on the island of Bali and the great Buddhist stupa complex of Borobudur in Indonesia.

There is no evidence for the presence of Islam in Southeast Asia before the tenth century. But Yemeni traders are reported to have sailed into the islands of the Malay archipelago before the time of the Prophet, and this suggests that the Malay people may have been exposed to Islam at an early date. Scattered evidence from Chinese and Portuguese travellers, as well as passing references by Ibn Battutah, indicate that Islam had spread widely in Southeast Asia by the 1400s. Two centuries later, when British and Dutch trading companies arrived in the region, Islam was the dominant religion and culture of the Malay archipelago.

Muslim communities in small states ruled by sultans are widely reported by the thirteenth century. The earliest of these was Pasai, a small kingdom on the east coast of northern Sumatra. Some of the states that emerged in the fifteenth century gained considerable prominence both culturally and economically. In every case, prosperity attracted Muslim religious scholars from India to these states. In an effort to expand and strengthen his realm, the sultan Iskandar Muda of Acheh (r. 1607–36) became the first Muslim ruler in Southeast Asia to establish alliances with European powers. Acheh also produced noteworthy Islamic legal scholarship, which is still used in the Malay world today.

In Southeast Asia even more than elsewhere, Sufi orders played a crucial part in the process of Islamization. They were also prominent in later political and social struggles for reform and liberation. In the late nineteenth and early twentieth centuries, reform movements in the Middle East inspired similar movements in Indonesia and other countries of the region. At present Islam is the majority religion in Malaysia, Brunei, and Indonesia (the largest Muslim country in the world today, with at least 180 million Muslims), and there are Muslim minorities in all the other countries of Southeast Asia. Today Southeast Asia can claim at least one-third of the world's Muslims.

❧ Cultural Expressions

Islamic Architecture

The functions of the mosque include not only prayer, implied in the Arabic *masjid* ("kneeling place"), but other community activities, implied in the Arabic term *jami'* ("gatherer"). Early mosques functioned as treasuries, where financial records were kept; as law courts, where judges heard cases; and as educational centres, where classes and study circles were held. In time these other activities moved into their own buildings, but the functions of public assembly and prayer continued to dictate the architectural form of mosques. Two other types of buildings with religious functions—the *madrasah* or religious school, and the tomb or mausoleum—drew on much the same repertory of styles that mosques did.

Every mosque includes four essential features: a fountain for washing hands, face, and feet upon entering; a large area for kneeling and prostration in prayer; a pulpit (*minbar*) from which the leader of Friday noon worship delivers the sermon; and an imageless niche in the middle of the wall closest to Mecca, indicating the *qiblah* (direction of prayer). Not part of the earliest mosques in Arabia but characteristic of Islam in many places is the minaret, the tower from which the *mu'adhdhin* delivers the call to prayer. The Turks in the sixteenth century made much use of the dome, an important feature of church architecture among the Byzantines who had preceded them. A high central dome, resting on four semi-dome apses, enclosed the prayer space. Some major Turkish mosques had four or more minarets marking the corners of the mosque. Central dome architecture, though often simpler and without minarets, is also characteristic of mosques in Malaysia and Indonesia, where the rainy climate dictates that the prayer space must be roofed over.

Ultimately, Islamic architecture tends to reflect the distinctive idioms of different geographic regions. The keyhole arch, for instance, though it appears in the great mosque of Damascus, is

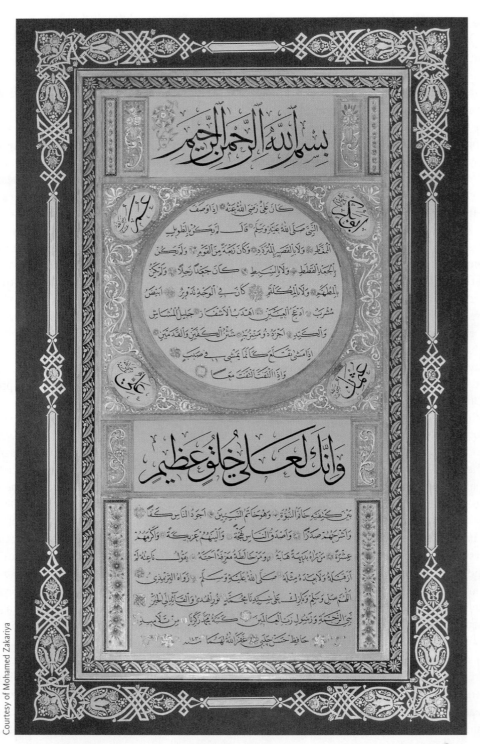

A modern hilye (calligraphic description) of the Prophet by Mohamed Zakariya. The top line reads "In the name of God, Universally Merciful, Specifically Merciful" and the circular section is surrounded by the names of the first four caliphs.

characteristic mainly of North Africa and Islamic Spain. A shallow pointed arch emerged in Iraq, became the predominant form in Iran, and spread to Central Asia and India. The bud or onion domes of Indo-Muslim architecture have been picked up in Southeast Asia. In China many mosques are built like Chinese temples, with tiled roofs resting on wooden columns and bracket structures. A number of Chinese minarets are built in the form of East Asian Buddhist pagodas.

Islamic Art

Islamic art is rich, elaborate, even exuberant. Three elements are particularly distinctive: calligraphy (the decorative use of script and units of text); geometrical decoration (particularly the interlaced motifs called arabesques in the West); and floral designs (especially common in Iran). All three are more abstract than pictorial and therefore point beyond themselves in a way that pictorial images may not. Design using these elements captures the viewer's attention and directs it to the larger structure on which the decoration appears, whether a page of the Qur'an, a prayer rug, or the tiled entrance of a mosque. Religious content is most obvious in the decorative use of calligraphy in mosques, where the texts used are often passages from the Qur'an, but even the craft items sold in bazaars are often adorned with some of the 99 "wonderful names" or attributes of God.

Three-dimensional sculpture is prohibited in Islam, but the two-dimensional representation of living creatures is highly developed. Some Persian carpets include animals in their garden scenes. Persian and Indian manuscripts are illustrated with miniature paintings of legendary heroes and current rulers. Among Iranian Shi'a, portraits of 'Ali

Focus

Mohamed Zakariya

Mohamed Zakariya (b. 1942) is the most celebrated Islamic calligrapher in the United States. Born in Ventura, California, he moved to Los Angeles with his family and saw Islamic calligraphy for the first time in the window of an Armenian carpet store. Travelling to Morocco in his late teens, he became fascinated with Islam and Islamic calligraphy. On his return to the United States he converted to Islam.

He made other journeys to North Africa and the Middle East, and spent some time studying manuscripts in the British Museum in London. After studying with the Egyptian calligrapher Abdussalam Ali-Nour, Zakariya in 1984 became a student of the Turkish master calligrapher Hasan Celebi. In 1988 he received his diploma from Celebi at the Research Center for Islamic History, Art and Culture in Istanbul, the first American to achieve this honour. He received his second diploma, in the *ta'lik* script, from the master calligrapher Ali Alparslan in 1997.

Zakariya lives with his family in Arlington, Virginia. His work has been displayed in various museums and galleries, and is in a number of private collections. He was the artist commissioned by the United States Postal Service to design its Eid stamp, which made its debut on 1 September 2001.

In addition to teaching calligraphy according to the Ottoman method, producing new work, and exhibiting it around the world, Zakariya writes contemporary instructional material and translates classic texts. In 2009, he was commissioned by US President Barack Obama to create a piece of calligraphy that was presented to King Abdulaziz of Saudi Arabia.

Mohamed Zakariya's work shows that American Islam has become an integral part of the Muslim world. Now students from that world travel to the United States to study with an American master of an ancient Islamic art.

are a focus of popular piety. While representations of the Prophet himself are avoided, Buraq—the steed that carried him on his heavenly journey—is portrayed in popular art as a winged horse with a human head; this is a common motif on trucks and buses in Afghanistan and Pakistan. In addition, highly ingenious use has been made of Arabic calligraphy not only in the decoration of mosques and minarets, but in the representation of animals ("zoomorphic calligraphy").

❧ Towards the Modern World

Islam and Modernity

Throughout the history of Islam, many individuals and groups have taken it on themselves to reform the rest of the Muslim community. An external impetus for reform has been Muslim interaction with Western Christendom. The first major Western challenges to Muslim power were the crusades. Determined to liberate Jerusalem from Muslim domination, the armies of the first crusade captured the Holy City in 1099 after massacring its Jewish and Muslim inhabitants. For nearly two centuries, Frankish Christian kingdoms existed side by side with Muslim states along the eastern Mediterranean shores, sometimes peacefully, but most of the time at war.

In the end most of the crusaders returned home, and those who remained were assimilated. But the spirit of the crusades lived on, as did the distorted images of Islam and its followers that the crusaders took home with them. The equally distorted images of Christianity and Western Christendom that the crusaders left in Muslim lands have also lived on, and have been reinforced and embellished in response to Western imperialism.

Premodern Reform Movements

Common to all reform movements has been the call to return to pristine *islam*, the *islam* of the Prophet's society and the normative period of his "rightly guided" successors. Among those who championed this cause was the religious scholar Ibn Taymiyyah (1263–1328), a jurist of the conservative Hanbali school who waged a relentless campaign against Shi'i beliefs and practices, Sufi excesses (e.g., claims that the law was no longer binding on them since they had reached God), and the blind imitation of established legal traditions, while fighting to revive the practice of *ijtihad*. Perhaps his most famous *fatwa* (religious legal opinion) was one that allowed Muslims in the city of Mardin (in what is now Turkey) to wage war against the occupying Mongols, even though the latter Mongols had converted to Islam after their conquest of Baghdad. In so doing, Ibn Taymiyyah contradicted the standard teaching that Muslims should not wage war against Muslim

Sites

Haram al-Sharif, Israel

The area of the ancient city of Jerusalem called Haram al-Sharif (the "Noble Sanctuary"; also known to Jews and Christians as the Temple Mount) contains two sacred buildings: the Masjid al-Aqsa—the "farthest mosque," from a passage in the Qur'an

(17: 1) referring to Muhammad's miraculous journey—and the Dome of the Rock, a sanctuary built on the spot from which tradition says Muhammad made his ascent to heaven.

rulers. The "Mardin fatwa" was to exert a powerful and long-lasting influence on subsequent reform movements.

Some four centuries later, Ibn Taymiyah's ideas became the basis of the reform program advocated by the Wahhabi movement, named for its founder Muhammad Ibn 'Abd al-Wahhab (1703–92). Significantly, this uncompromising and influential revivalist movement began in the highlands of Arabia, the birthplace of Islam. Ibn 'Abd al-Wahhab's long life allowed him to establish his movement on a firm foundation. He allied himself with Muhammad 'Al Sa'ud, a local tribal prince, on the understanding that the prince would exercise political power and protect the nascent movement, which would hold religious authority. This agreement remains operative today: the kingdom of Saudi Arabia is a Wahhabi state, ruled by the descendants of 'Al Sa'ud.

The Wahhabis preached a strictly egalitarian Islam based solely on a direct relationship between the worshipper and God. They repudiated the widely cherished hope that the Prophet and other divinely favoured individuals would intercede with God on behalf of the pious to grant them blessing and succour in this life and salvation in the next. The Wahhabis regarded the veneration of saints, including the Prophet, as a form of idolatry. They even advocated the destruction of the sacred black stone of the Ka'ba, on the grounds that it stood as an idol between faithful Muslims and their Lord.

The Wahhabis held all those who did not share their convictions to be in error. They waged a violent campaign aimed at purging Muslim society of what they considered to be un-Islamic beliefs and practices. They destroyed the Prophet's tomb in Medina and levelled the graves of his Companions. They attacked the Shi'a's sacred cities of Najaf and Karbala, massacred their inhabitants, and demolished the shrines of 'Ali and his son Husayn. They also went on a rampage in Arab cities, desecrating the tombs of Sufi saints and destroying their shrines.

The basic ideals of Wahhabism have appealed to many revivalists and played an especially significant role in provoking reform efforts within eighteenth- and nineteenth-century Sufism (see below). In the present day, however, a number of extremist groups influenced by Wahhabi ideology, including Al-Qaeda and the Taliban, have transformed the internal struggle to "purify" Islam into an external war against all perceived enemies, Muslim and non-Muslim alike.

Nineteenth-Century Revivalism

Jihad—Arabic for "struggle"—has two components. Inner *jihad* is the struggle to make oneself more Islamic; outer *jihad* is the struggle to make one's society more Islamic.

A number of Sufi *jihad* movements arose in the nineteenth century, partly in response to Wahhabi criticisms and partly in reaction against European colonial encroachment on Muslim domains. Several of these movements were able to establish short-lived states, among them those led by Usman ('Uthman) dan Fodio (the Sokoto caliphate, 1809–1903) in Nigeria, Muhammad al-Sanusi (the Sanusi movement, 1837–1969) in Libya, and Muhammad Ahmad al-Mahdi (the Mahdi rebellion, 1881–9) in Sudan. Common to all these movements was an activist ideology of militant struggle against external colonialism and internal decadence. They also strove for reform and the revival of *ijtihad*.

Because of their broad appeal, these Sufi reform movements exerted a lasting influence on most subsequent reform programs and ideologies. In North Africa in particular, Sufi *shaykhs* and religious scholars not only helped to preserve their countries' religious, linguistic, and cultural identity but in some cases spearheaded the long and bloody struggles for independence from French and Italian colonial rule. In the nineteenth century, for example, the Sufi *shaykh* Abdelkader ('Abd al-Qadir) played an important political role in the long campaign for Algeria's independence. King Muhammad V of Morocco, who negotiated his country's independence from France in 1956, was himself a Sufi *shaykh* and a "venerable descendant" (*sayyid*) of the Prophet. And the grandson of al-Sanusi, Idris

I, ruled Libya as king from independence in 1951 until he was overthrown in a revolution in 1969.

The movement begun by al-Sanusi in Libya promoted reform and Muslim unity across North and West Africa. By contrast, the goal of al-Mahdi's movement in Sudan was more eschatological: its founder saw himself as God's representative on earth and set out to establish a social and political order modelled on that of the Prophet. He believed the Ottoman–Egyptian occupation of Sudan to be un-Islamic and waged a war of *jihad* against it. In 1885 he triumphed over Egyptian forces and established an Islamic state based on strict application of the *shari'ah* law. Although al-Mahdi himself died within a few months, the regime lasted until 1889, when it was overthrown by British and Egyptian forces.

Ahmadiyah

The career of Mirza Ghulam Ahmad (1835–1908) reflects both the social and the religious diversity of the Punjab in the 1880s—a time of various movements for renewal of Hindu and Muslim identity, as well as a growing emphasis on self-definition among the Sikhs. To this mix Ghulam Ahmad contributed several volumes of commentary on the Qur'an, as well as claims of his own leadership status.

In 1889 he accepted from his followers the homage reserved for a prophet like Muhammad. Ahmadis, as they are known, have also revered him as the *mujaddid* (renewer) ushering in the fourteenth century of Islam, as the Mahdi of Shi'i expectation, as the tenth incarnation of the Hindu deity Vishnu, and as the returning Messiah of Christianity (Ahmadis also maintain that Jesus did not die in Palestine but went to Afghanistan, in search of the ten lost tribes of Israel, and was buried in Srinagar, Kashmir).

Active proselytizers, Ghulam Ahmad and his followers preached in the streets, engaged in debates, and published translations of the Qur'an. The movement has spread widely. Including 4 million in Pakistan, Ahmadis now total at least 10 million, or 1 per cent of the world's Muslims. Leadership since

the founder's death in 1908 has been termed *khilafat al-Masih* (succession of the Messiah). Although the successor is chosen by election, since 1914 the title has stayed in Ghulam Ahmad's family, held first by a son and then by two grandsons. Because they identified themselves as Muslims, on the partition of India in 1947 the Ahmadis were displaced from Qadian and relocated their centre across the border in Rabwah, Pakistan, west of Lahore.

Many Muslims, however, have not accepted the Ahmadis as fellow Muslims. As early as 1891, Ghulam Ahmad's claim to prophethood was rejected by orthodox Muslim authorities. In Pakistan Ahmadis have been the target of riots and demonstrations; in 1984 they were declared to be a non-Muslim minority (hence ineligible for opportunities available to Muslims); and they have been prohibited from calling themselves Muslims or using Islamic vocabulary in their worship and preaching.

Ahmadiyah's future, therefore, may lie in its diaspora. Missions have been notably successful in lands not historically Islamic, such as West Africa, the Caribbean, and the overseas English-speaking world. The largest mosque in North America, opened in 1992, is the Ahmadi Baitul Islam mosque in the Toronto-area suburb of Maple.

Modern Reformers

As the nineteenth century opened, European influence in the Muslim world was growing. Napoleon, who landed on Egyptian shores in 1798, brought with him not only soldiers but also scholars and the printing press; in this way the Middle East discovered Europe. The great Ottoman Empire, which in the early decades of the sixteenth century had threatened Vienna, had by the nineteenth become "the sick man of Europe." Meanwhile the British Empire was extending its rule in India and its control over much of the Muslim world.

Muslim thinkers everywhere were awed by the West and resentful of the political inertia into which the Muslim *ummah* had apparently fallen. Even so, many areas of the Islamic east did experience an intellectual and cultural revival in the nineteenth century. Egypt, for instance, was the home of an Arab intellectual renaissance. Owing to unsettled social and political conditions in the Levant, a number of Western-educated Syro-Lebanese Christians immigrated to Egypt, where they established newspapers and cultural journals and participated actively in the recovery of the Arabo-Islamic heritage.

The Arab renaissance of the nineteenth century was to a large degree stimulated by the cultural and intellectual flowering that was taking place in the West. Undermined first by the Protestant Reformation and then by the Enlightenment, religious faith and institutions were giving way to secularism and romantic nationalism. The same ideas were attractive to many Muslims. In the eastern Mediterranean they contributed to the rise of Arab nationalism, and they had a similar effect in other Muslim regions, so that nationalistic identities came to compete with, and in some cases even supersede, Islamic identities.

These and other Western influences were reinforced by the proliferation of Western Christian missionary schools and institutions of higher learning throughout the Muslim world. In short, Islamic reform movements of the nineteenth and twentieth centuries in Asia, Africa, and the Middle East arose in a context of widespread cultural and intellectual ferment.

The Indian Subcontinent

The Mughal dynasty in India was founded by Babur in 1526 and reached its peak during the reign (1556–1605) of his grandson Akbar. With the decline of the Mughals in the seventeenth century, demands for reform along traditional lines intensified. One of the strongest voices was that of Ahmad Sirhindi (1564–1624), who called for a return to the shari'ah, regarded Sufis as deviants, and condemned Ibn 'Arabi in particular as an infidel.

The most important movement of Islamic reform on the Indian subcontinent in modern times was begun by Shah Wali Allah of Delhi (1702–62). Although he was a disciple of Ibn 'Abd al-Wahhab,

he was a Sufi himself, and instead of rejecting Sufism he sought to reform it. A man of encyclopedic learning, Shah Wali Allah was a moderate reformer who also sought to reconcile Shi'a–Sunni differences, which had been (and sometimes are still) a source of great friction on the Indian subcontinent in particular.

Shah Wali Allah's grandson Ahmad Barelwi transformed his grandfather's program into a *jihad* movement against British rule and the Sikhs. In 1826 he established an Islamic state based on the *shari'ah* and adopted the old caliphal title "commander of the faithful." Although he was killed in battle in 1831, his *jihad* movement lived on. For Barelwi, India ceased to be an Islamic domain after the end of Mughal rule, and therefore Muslims should wage a *jihad* to liberate it. If independence from infidel sovereignty was not possible, Muslims should undertake a religious migration (*hijrah*) to an area where Muslims did rule.

The shock that Indian Muslims suffered with the consolidation of British rule was intensified by the fact that the British tampered with Islamic law itself. The result was a mixture of Islamic law and Western humanistic rulings known as Anglo-Muhammadan law.

At the opposite end of the spectrum of reaction to British rule from *jihad* movements like Barelwi's was the approach of Sayyid Ahmad Khan (1817–98). Like all reformers, Khan called for modern *ijtihad* or rethinking of the Islamic heritage, but unlike most of them he rejected *hadith* tradition as a legitimate basis for modern Islamic living. He founded the Aligarh Muhammadan College (later Aligarh Muslim University), where he attempted to apply his ideas in a modern Western-style program of education.

Muhammad Iqbal

The ideas of Sayyid Ahmad Khan and his fellows culminated in the philosophy of Muhammad Iqbal (1876–1938), the greatest Muslim thinker of modern India. Central to Iqbal's work is the idea of an inner spirit that moves human civilization.

Iqbal argued that Western science and philosophy were rightfully part of the Islamic heritage and should be integrated into a fresh *Reconstruction of Religious Thought in Islam* (the title of his only major work in English, published in the 1930s). A poet as well as a philosopher, Iqbal frequently repeated this call for a dynamic rethinking of Islamic faith and civilization in his verse.

❧ Recent Developments

Twentieth-Century Secularism

Many of the early Muslim reformers were at once liberal modernists and traditional thinkers. For this reason they are known as *salafis*: reformers who sought to emulate the example of "the pious forebears" (*al-salaf al-salih*). This important ideal of equilibrium between tradition and modernity disappeared by the 1920s. Thereafter, Islamic reform meant one of three things: revivalism, apologetics, or secularism.

Following the Ottoman defeat in the First World War, a young army officer named Mustafa Kemal Atatürk (1881–1938) launched a movement for national liberation. As the first president of the new Republic of Turkey (1923) he abolished the caliphate, transforming the Turkish state from a traditional Islamic domain into a modern secular state. Although for centuries the caliphate had been a shadowy office without any power, it had nevertheless embodied the only hope for a viable pan-Islamic state. Its disappearance therefore had far-reaching consequences for Islamic political thought.

Atatürk banned Sufi orders, dissolved Islamic religious institutions, replaced the Arabic alphabet (in which Turkish had traditionally been written) with the Latin, and mounted a nationwide campaign for literacy in the new script. His express aim was to westernize the Turkish republic and cut it off from its Islamic past. He encouraged the adoption of Western-style clothing and even went so far as to ban the fez—the brimless conical red hat that, like all traditional Muslim headgear, allowed the faithful to touch their foreheads to the ground during prayer.

Though Atatürk's ideology has remained the official state policy in Turkey, his program largely failed, for the people's Islamic roots were not easily destroyed. Islamic faith and practice remain strong among the people of Turkey, and the country has its own powerful revivalist movements.

Twentieth-Century Islamic Revivalism

Islamic reform movements generally seem to have experienced a loss of nerve after the international upheavals of the First World War and the break-up of the Ottoman Empire. Despite their differences, the various reform movements of the nineteenth century shared a dynamic and courageous spirit of progress. The premature stifling of that spirit may have reflected the lack of a coherent program of reform that post-colonialist Muslim thinkers could implement or build upon. In any event, the liberal reform movements of the nineteenth century were transformed into traditional revivalist movements in the twentieth.

On the eve of Atatürk's abolition of the caliphate in 1924, Muhammad Rashid Rida (1865–1935) published an important treatise on the Imamate, or Supreme Caliphate, in which he argued for the establishment of an Islamic state that would be ruled by a council of jurists or religious scholars. Such a state would recognize nationalistic sentiments and aspirations, but would subordinate them to the religio-political interests of the larger community. Rida's Islamic revivalism and Arab nationalism came to represent two major trends in twentieth-century Muslim thinking, and his political plan for a council of jurists would be implemented in Iran following the revolution of 1978–9.

Contemporary Revivalist Movements

It remains the ideal of Islamic reform to establish a transnational Islamic caliphate. The reality, however, has been a proliferation of local movements reflecting local needs and ideas.

Common to most revivalist movements in the second half of the twentieth century was the ideal of an all-inclusive and self-sufficient Islamic order. This ideal had its roots in the Society of Muslim Brothers (Jam'iyat al-Ikhwan al-Muslimin), founded in 1928 by an Egyptian schoolteacher named Hasan al-Banna. The aim of this society was to establish a network of Islamic social, economic, and political institutions through which the total Islamization of society might in time be achieved. Working through social and educational facilities such as schools, banks, cooperatives, and clinics, the Muslim Brothers penetrated all levels of Egyptian society.

The political and militaristic aspects of revivalism also had their beginnings in the Muslim Brothers, particularly after the assassination of the populist and generally peaceful al-Banna in 1949. He was succeeded by hard-line leaders who advocated active *jihad* against the Egyptian state system, which they regarded as un-Islamic. Among the products of the Muslim Brothers' ideology were the young officers, led by Gamal Abdel Nasser, behind the 1952 socialist revolution that abolished monarchical rule in Egypt.

A charismatic proponent of Arab nationalism in the 1950s and 1960s, Nasser nevertheless clashed with the Muslim Brothers, and in the mid-1960s he imprisoned, exiled, or executed most of their leaders. One of those leaders was Sayyid Qutb, who is important as a link to modern Islamist groups. As a theoretician he influenced Islamist ideology; and as an activist whose defiance of the state led to his execution he provided younger militants with a model of martyrdom to emulate. Following the Arab defeat in the six-day Arab–Israeli war of June 1967 and the death of Nasser three years later, the Muslim Brothers were driven underground and superseded by more powerful revivalist movements under Anwar Sadat and his successor Hosni Mubarak, some of which advocated the use of violence to achieve their goals. Although suppressed in Egypt, the Brotherhood has spread in other Arab countries; but in exile, without its social infrastructure, it was more influential on the level of ideology than of social action until the events of the "Arab Spring." A similar organization, the Jama'at-i Islami (Islamic Society), was established in 1941 by Mawlana Sayyid Abu al-A'la Mawdudi. Like Hasan al-Banna, Mawdudi was committed to pan-Islamic unity. But also like al-Banna, he concentrated his efforts on his own community—in this case the Muslims of India and (after 1947) Pakistan. The influence of both organizations spread far beyond their original homes.

While most contemporary revivalist movements, including the two organizations noted above, have been open to modern science and technology, they have rejected many Western values and practices—including capitalist democracy, women's liberation, and the free mixing of the sexes—as decadent. Therefore, unlike the nineteenth-century reformers who looked to the West for ideas and models, contemporary revivalist reformers have insisted on finding Islamic alternatives. Mawdudi, for example, wishing to distinguish his Islamic state model from Western democracies, described it as a "theo-democracy" based on the broad Qur'anic principle of consultation (*shura*) and the *shari'ah* law.

State Islam and the Islamic Revolution

Following a coup in 1969, Gaafar Mohamed el-Nimeiri made *shari'ah* the law in Sudan. The result was a bloody conflict between the Muslim north and the generally Christian south that has reduced a formerly rich agricultural country to famine; although South Sudan became an independent republic in 2011, violent clashes continue along the border that separates the two states. Similarly in Pakistan, which for three decades had been a constitutionally Islamic but modern state, the 1977 introduction of *shari'ah* by General Mohammad Zia-ul-Haq led to violent social and political conflict.

In almost every Muslim country there is at least one revivalist movement advocating some form of

Islamic state. In countries like Malaysia and Indonesia, the governments themselves espouse Islamic national policies in order to silence extremist demands for radical reform. Nevertheless, in most Muslim countries feelings continue to run high between Islamic movements made up of educated middle-class men and women and despotic regimes determined to hold on to power at any cost.

On 19 December 2010, a Tunisian named Mohamed Bouazizi set himself on fire to protest police and government corruption that made it impossible for him to sell fruits and vegetables from a cart without paying bribes to officials. His self-immolation sparked widespread protests that led to the overthrow of the Tunisian president. These dramatic events in turn sparked protests in Algeria and Egypt. The largest coordinated protests began in Cairo in late January 2011, and on 11 February Egyptian President Hosni Mubarak stepped down from power. In 2012 Mohammed Morsi of the Muslim Brotherhood was announced as the new Egyptian president. He served for almost exactly a year before being removed by the Egyptian military on 3 July 2013. Among the other Arab countries swept up in the "Arab Spring" were Syria, Yemen, Bahrain, and Libya. On 18 March 2011 the UN Security Council authorized a resolution to protect civilians under attack in Libya, and the following day the first Western air strike was launched against the military regime of Muammar Gaddafi. He was killed in October 2011, and a new assembly was elected in July 2012. As of late 2013 the violence in Syria continues.

In such highly charged social and political conditions, religion serves as a powerful moral, social, and spiritual expression of discontent—not only for Islamic activists, but for a broad spectrum of the community as well. It was on precisely such mass discontent that Imam Ruhollah Khomeini (1901–89) and his fellow Shi'i *mullahs* (religio-legal functionaries) built the Islamic Republic of Iran, in which social, political, economic, and religious life are all under the control of a religious hierarchy headed by a supreme Ayatollah (*ayat Allah*, "sign of God").

Throughout the long period of secular Shi'i rule in Iran (1501–1979), the authority of the religious *'ulama'* operated in more or less continuous tension with the secular authorities. This tension was greatly increased during the reign of the US-supported Shah Mohammad Reza Pahlavi, who sought to westernize the country and obscure its Islamic identity by emphasizing Iran's pre-Islamic cultural past. In 1963, during the Muharram observances of Husayn's martyrdom, matters came to a head when the Shah's dreaded secret police ruthlessly put down mass demonstrations led by the *'ulama'*. Khomeini, already a prominent religious leader, was sent into exile, where he elaborated his religio-political theory, according to which the jurist should have all-embracing authority in the community. In 1979 Khomeini returned to Iran at the head of the Islamic revolution. The Islamic republic he founded has had a turbulent history, including an eight-year war with Iraq (1980–8), out of which it emerged greatly weakened but still intact. Pro-democracy protests and challenges to the authority of the *'ulama'* came to international attention with the controversy that surrounded the 2009 election and the protests that erupted in March 2011.

Islam in Western Europe

The Islamic presence in western Europe began with the establishment of Umayyad rule in southern Spain in 711. Commercial, political, and cultural relations were initiated with both Latin and Byzantine states, but medieval Europe would not tolerate a permanent Muslim community on its soil. The campaign to drive the Muslims out of Spain succeeded in 1492 with the conquest of Granada. As a result, the Muslim communities in western Europe today are a relatively recent phenomenon.

In the twentieth century some Muslims migrated to Europe from various colonies as students, visitors, and merchants. Many also went as menial labourers and factory workers, especially after the Second World War. The majority of these post-war immigrants were men ranging in age from their teens to their forties.

The ethnic makeup of the Muslim communities in Europe was largely determined by colonial ties. Muslims from the French colonies in North Africa, for example, went to France. Indian and, later, Pakistani and Bangladeshi Muslims tended to go to Britain. Those from Turkey and the former Soviet Turkic republics went to Germany and the Netherlands, while Bosnians went to Austria. These patterns were established in the early decades of the twentieth century and have continued in spite of many restrictions.

Muslim communities in Europe tend to reflect ethnic and linguistic rather than sectarian affiliations. In recent years hundreds of mosques and cultural centres have been established in European cities, and Muslim communities have become a dynamic religious and intellectual force in European society. France and Britain no longer confine Muslims to the status of "guest workers," as most other European countries do. Yet even there, the long histories of European racism, ethnocentrism, and colonialism have ensured that many Muslims continue to be treated as second-class citizens. This has created serious problems.

After the Islamic revolution of 1978–9, many Iranians immigrated to Europe, adding yet another layer of ethnic and religious diversity to European Muslim society. The 15-year Lebanese civil war of 1975–90, as well as the disturbances in other Arab countries, including the Gulf War of 1991, also sent many political and economic refugees to the West. Meanwhile, intermarriage and conversion have infused new blood into the Muslim community in the Western world.

Many Muslims born in Europe to foreign-born parents are assimilating into European society and culture. On the other hand, most European countries have taken legal measures to limit immigration, and since the mid-1980s a number of them have repatriated some of their Muslim immigrants. Such actions may have been prompted in part by economic considerations, but also perhaps by nationalistic fears that Muslim immigrants might alter the social and ethnic character of these countries. In 2009, for example, Swiss citizens voted into their constitution a ban on minarets for new mosques—even though, of the approximately 150 mosques and Islamic centres in Switzerland, only four have minarets. At the same time, European discrimination against ethnic minorities and the Islamic awakening precipitated by the Iranian revolution have made Muslims more aware of their own religious and cultural identity.

Islam in North America

When the first Muslims arrived on American shores is a matter of conjecture. Suggestions that Muslims from Spain and West Africa may have sailed to America long before Columbus should not be discounted, although they have not been proven. Scattered records point to the presence of Muslims in Spanish America before 1550, and it is very likely that the fall of Granada in 1492 and the harsh treatment imposed on Muslims and Jews by the Inquisition led many to flee to America soon after Columbus's historic voyage.

In the sixteenth and seventeenth centuries, hundreds of thousands of Africans were taken as slaves to the Spanish, Portuguese, and British colonies in the Americas. Although the majority were from West Africa, Muslims made up at least 20 per cent of the total. And among the slaves taken from Senegal, Nigeria, and the western Sudan, the majority were Muslims, many of whom were well educated in Arabic and the religious sciences. Some were able to preserve their faith and heritage, and some tried to maintain contact with Muslims in their home areas, but many others were quickly absorbed into American society, adopting their masters' religious affiliations and even their family names.

Islamic customs and ideas can still be traced in the African-American community, and today efforts are underway to reconstruct the story behind them from slave narratives, oral history, and other archival materials, including observations of Islamic activities by white travellers in the mid-1800s.

Beginning in the late nineteenth century, African-Americans made conscious efforts to recover their Islamic heritage. In the early 1930s,

Elijah Muhammad (born Elijah Poole, 1897–1975) founded the Nation of Islam in America (see Chapter 7). He saw Islam as a religion of Black people only, misrepresenting the universalistic and non-racial nature of Islam. But his sons and successors, after travelling in the Muslim world and observing the international and multiracial character of the *hajj* pilgrimage, have drawn closer to classical Islam. African-American Muslims often refer to themselves as Bilalians, after Bilal, an African Companion of the Prophet's time and community. Islam continues to be the fastest-growing religion in America, particularly among African-Americans.

Before the revival of Islam in the African-American community early in the twentieth century, small numbers of Muslims travelled to Canada and the United States, mainly from Syria and Lebanon. These early immigrants were uneducated men who intended only to work in North America for a few years and then return home. Instead, many married Canadian or American women and were soon completely assimilated.

The first Muslim missionary in America was Muhammad Alexander Webb, a jeweller, newspaper editor, and diplomat who converted to Islam in 1888, while travelling in India. On his return, Webb created an Islamic propaganda movement, wrote three books on Islam, and founded a periodical entitled *The Muslim World* (not to be confused with the academic journal of the same name). He travelled widely to spread the new faith and established Islamic study circles or Muslim brotherhoods in many northeastern and midwestern American cities. With his death in 1916, however, his movement died as well.

The numbers of Muslim immigrants coming to Canada and the United States increased markedly during the twentieth century. Most were of South Asian origin. Many were students who later chose to stay, or well-educated professionals hoping to find better opportunities. But others came to escape persecution in their homelands on account of their religious or political activities. Interestingly, many recent newcomers have arrived as staunch anti-Western revivalists but have soon forgotten their hostility and taken up life as peaceful, responsible, and law-abiding citizens.

Although these and other religiously committed Muslim immigrants may have moderated their political convictions, they retained a high degree of religious zeal, which they put to good use in the service both of their own community and of the society at large. They have played a crucial role in preserving the Islamic identity of fellow immigrants and promoting a better understanding of Islam through media activities and academic meetings.

The first mosque in the United States was built in 1915 in Maine by Albanian Muslims; another followed in Connecticut in 1919. Other mosques were established in the 1920s and 1930s in South Dakota and Iowa. In 1928, Polish Tatars built a mosque in Brooklyn, New York, which is still in use. The first Canadian mosque was built in Edmonton, Alberta, in 1938, and a number of smaller towns in Alberta also have Muslim communities. In Toronto, the first Muslim organization was the Albanian Muslim Society of Toronto, founded in 1956; in 1968 this organization purchased an unused Presbyterian church and converted it into a mosque. Toronto currently has Canada's largest concentration of Muslims.

The exact numbers of Muslims in Canada and the United States are a matter of debate. The 2001 Canadian census counted almost 600,000 Muslims, making Islam the second-largest religion in the country. As of 2012, the Muslim population was estimated to be 940,000. The United States has not had a religious census since 1936, but the current Muslim population there is estimated to be between 6 and 7 million. Whatever the numbers may be, Islam in North America is no longer an exotic rarity: it is the faith of many people's co-workers and neighbours.

Issues of gender equality and sexual diversity are rarely discussed in the largest of the Muslim political and religious organizations in North America (such as the Islamic Society of North America), partly because those groups tend to emphasize traditional interpretations of Islam, and partly because they have been preoccupied with matters such as community-building, immigration policy, discrimination, and (to some extent) foreign policy. But as the size of their constituencies has grown, and the range of perspectives within those constituencies has increased, there has been growing pressure to address matters involving gender and sexuality.

Diasporic communities in large urban centres tend to become more open to questions about traditional religious and cultural ideas as they become more deeply rooted (or "assimilated") in their new societies. As contact with the "host" community intensifies, those who question traditional ideas are likely to have much easier access to information and networks of like-minded people than their counterparts in their countries of origin. Some will "exit" their communities of origin and seek full assimilation to the dominant society; but in large communities particularly, some will remain connected and mobilize their challenges to traditionalism from within.

In general, Muslims born and raised in North America are more open to diversity than those born abroad, especially if their communities are not sufficiently homogeneous to support their own separate social institutions (such as schools). The likelihood of dissent is further amplified in the Muslim communities of North America by relatively high levels of education. In general, higher education increases openness to diversity, as well as to equity claims by women and sexual minorities. The fact that Muslim minorities in North America are less economically marginalized than those in Europe also reduces the likelihood of strict adherence to religious belief.

On the other hand, the great majority of Muslims in Canada and the United States are still relatively recent immigrants from places where social norms regarding gender and sexuality are starkly conservative, and the mosques and Islamic centres to which new immigrants become attached are almost invariably conservative on moral questions. Groups seeking to challenge conservative ideas are developing, as we shall see below, but homosexual Muslims in particular continue to face condemnation from mainstream Muslim society.

Marriage and the Family

Marriage under Islam is essentially a contractual relationship negotiated between the prospective husband and the woman's father or guardian. But the Qur'an emphasizes that the true contract is between the husband and the wife, based on mutual consent: the woman's father or guardian, "he in whose hand is the tie of marriage" (Q. 2: 237), is expected to act on her behalf and, ideally, in her interest. Divorce is allowed, but only as a last resort after every effort has been made to save the marriage.

The Qur'an allows polygyny, or simultaneous marriage to more than one wife. But it places two significant restrictions on such marriages. First, it limits to four the number of wives that a man can have at one time (before Islam the number was unlimited). Second, it demands strict justice and equality in a man's material and emotional support for all his wives. If this is not possible, the Qur'an stipulates, "then only one." The Qur'an also warns that "You cannot act equitably among your wives however much you try" (Q. 4: 3 and 129). As a result, the vast majority of Muslim marriages are monogamous.

Even more significantly, the Qur'an changes the nature of polygyny from an entitlement to a social responsibility. The verses dealing with this subject open with a proviso: "If you [men] are afraid that you would not act justly towards the orphans [in your care], then marry what seems good to you of women: two, three, or four" (Q. 4: 3). This statement may be interpreted in two ways. It may mean that a man could marry the widowed mother of orphans in order to provide a family for them. It may also mean that a man could marry two, three, or four orphan girls after they have attained marriageable age, again to provide a home and family for them. In either case, marriage to more than one wife was explicitly allowed as a way of providing for female orphans and widows in a traditional society beset with continuous warfare, where a woman could find the love and security she needed only in her own home.

Adultery, Fornication, and "Family Honour"

The Qur'an (17:32) is explicit in condemning adultery: "And do not come close to adultery—it is truly a shameful deed and an evil way." The punishment provided in the Qur'an (24: 2) for adulterers (married men or women who have sex with someone other than their spouse) or fornicators (unmarried women or men who have sex with anyone) is 100 lashes: "The woman and the man guilty of adultery or fornication, flog each of them with a hundred lashes: Let not compassion move you in their case, in a matter prescribed by God, if you believe in God and the Last Day: and let a party of the Believers witness their punishment." Since the act had to be witnessed by four reliable eye-witnesses, such cases were rarely prosecuted.

Yet there have been cases, especially in recent times, where adultery and fornication have been punished by law, and in some places the penalty has not been a flogging, but capital punishment carried out by stoning. Among those places is Iran, which according to the human rights organization Amnesty International has carried out six such executions since 2006. The scriptural source used to justify stoning is not the Qur'an but the *hadith* literature. Many activists, both Muslim and non-Muslim, have sought to end this barbaric practice.

Another barbaric practice that has attracted increasing attention in recent years is the murder of family members by their relatives, ostensibly to preserve the family's "honour"; the victims in such cases are almost always young women or girls who are perceived to have brought shame on the family by disobeying male authority. In Canada, the 2009 Shafia case was a horrific example, where a father, his second wife in a polygamous marriage, and their son murdered the family's three teenaged daughters (Zainab, Sahar, and Geeti Shafia), as well as the husband's first wife (Rona Mohammed). The three perpetrators were convicted in 2012 and sentenced to life imprisonment. There is nothing in the Qur'an that calls for the taking of an innocent life.

The thinking behind such killings is rooted not in religion but in honour/shame culture.

Women

Of all the social and political issues that are currently being debated within the Muslim community, perhaps the most important is the question of women's rights. The Qur'an (9: 71–2) makes it clear that men and women have the same religious duties and obligations:

> The Believers, men and women, are protectors one of another: they enjoin what is just, and forbid what is evil: they observe regular prayers, practise regular charity, and obey God and God's Messenger. On them God will pour mercy: for God is Exalted in power, Wise. God has promised to Believers, men and women, gardens under which rivers flow, to dwell therein, and beautiful mansions in gardens of everlasting bliss. But the greatest bliss is the good pleasure of God: that is the supreme felicity.

Another example can be found in *surah* 33, verse 35:

> For Muslim men and women, for believing men and women, for devout men and women, for true men and women, for men and women who are patient and constant, for men and women who humble themselves, for men and women who give in Charity, for men and women who fast (and deny themselves), for men and women who guard their chastity, and for men and women who engage much in God's praise, for them God has prepared forgiveness and great reward.

The Qur'an allows women to acquire property through bequest, inheritance, or bride dowry and dispose of it as they please. In the modern world these rights may well be inadequate, but they point to a Qur'anic recognition of women's human dignity that until recently was denied in many societies. Islamic law and social custom have been not been so generous and forward-looking, however: in general, they have tended either to restrict the rights laid out in the Qur'an or to render them virtually inoperative. Although women as well as men are supposed to receive education, some Islamic societies (such as Afghanistan under the Taliban) deny education and employment opportunities for women.

As for the **hijab** or veil, the Qur'an does not refer to it at all. It merely demands that women avoid wearing jewellery and dress modestly; and in the very next verse it also demands modesty of males. The *hadith* tradition indicates that most Muslim communities adopted the practice of veiling during the time of the caliphate, probably under the influence of Eastern Christian and ancient Greek customs. An extreme extension of the practice, which may also be attributable to non-Arab influences, is the seclusion of women. Under the South Asian system of *purdah*, for instance, women are not only veiled but isolated from men. And seclusion became a hallmark of Turkish life under the *harim* system of the Ottoman aristocracy. In Afghanistan, the *burqa* covers the entire body; even the woman's eyes (and her vision) are obscured by a screen.

In the twenty-first century, the *hijab* has become a powerful—and powerfully ambiguous—symbol, widely condemned (especially by non-Muslims) as a limitation on women's rights, but often defended by Muslim women themselves as a freely chosen affirmation of their Islamic identity. The question at issue is to what extent women can be excluded from public life. Around the world, social and economic conditions increasingly demand equal participation and equal rights for women and men alike.

In March 2005 Professor Amina Wadud led a mixed-gender Muslim prayer service in New York

National Hijab Day at the University of Toronto: Sajda Khalil ties a hijab for Mikaela Valenzuela.

Lucas Oleniuk/GetStock.com

City. The event caused a great deal of controversy because it broke at least three Islamic conventions. Traditionally, women have led prayer only among other women or within their own families; some of the women attending the service had their hair uncovered; and men and women were not separated (the only time such interspersing of genders is accepted by all Muslims is during the pilgrimage to Mecca, when as described earlier, men and women circumambulate the Ka'ba and pray beside one another). The New York prayer service started a new trend; similar events have been held in a number of North American cities, including Toronto. Mixed-gender and female-led prayers are likely to become an increasingly important issue for North American Muslims.

Muslim women activists have also acquired a more prominent voice in at least some mainstream Muslim organizations, challenging male leaders to adopt more inclusive language and develop policies to encourage women's participation. They are also becoming more vocal in their engagement with Western feminism over issues such as head covering. Although their positions on questions of gender equality sometimes diverge from those of Western feminists, controversies over issues such as veiling have created significant openings for Muslim women to engage in political debate within their own religious communities.

War, Terrorism, and Violence

Many hoped that the end of the cold war in 1989 and the moves made in the 1990s towards ending the long and bitter conflict between Israelis and Palestinians might allow for better relations between the Western and Muslim worlds in general. But the Israeli–Palestinian conflict has only deepened, and new conflicts have emerged in recent years.

One major political development was the Iranian revolution of 1979. Three decades later, the prospect of an Iran with nuclear weapons has only increased the tensions between the Islamic regime and the West. A second development can also be traced to 1979, when the Soviet Union invaded

Afghanistan. Muslims from around the world volunteered to fight with the Afghans for their liberation, and the United States contributed heavily to their training. They were called *mujahidin* (the word is derived from *jihad*), and at the time—before the end of the cold war—they were seen as "freedom fighters" by much of the world, including the American president, Ronald Reagan.

Among the other contributors to Afghanistan's "holy war" was Osama bin Laden, the son of a wealthy Saudi Arabian family, who created Al-Qaeda ("the base") to help fund and train *mujahidin*. The Soviet troops were withdrawn in 1988. But Al-Qaeda was not disbanded. In 1996 bin Laden issued a *fatwa* calling for the overthrow of the Saudi government and the removal of US forces in Arabia, and in 1998 he declared war against Americans generally. A series of terrorist actions followed, culminating in the attacks on the United States of 11 September 2001. In response, the US and its allies went to war, first in Afghanistan and then in Iraq.

Muslims around the world have repeatedly condemned terrorist activity. Muslim leaders have pointed out that the use of suicide bombers violates mainstream Islamic teachings that prohibit both suicide and the killing of civilians during war, and in March 2005, on the first anniversary of the 2004 Al-Qaeda train bombing in Madrid, Spanish clerics issued a *fatwa* against bin Laden himself. Even so, it would be another seven years before he was tracked down and killed by US forces.

An important reference point in discussions of martyrdom is the Mardin Conference, held in March 2010 in the city that was at issue in Ibn Taymiyyah's famous fourteenth-century *fatwa* legitimizing the use of violence against unjust Muslim rulers. Because many modern terrorists have used this *fatwa* to justify their actions (among them bin Laden), the Mardin conference brought together fifteen senior Islamic scholars from across the Muslim world to discuss the context in which it was issued some 700 years earlier.

In condoning violence against authoritarian rulers in order to re-establish true Islamic rule, Ibn

Anti-US graffiti on the wall of the former US Embassy in the Iranian capital, Tehran.

© Roberto Fumagalli/Alamy

Taymiyyah broke with the teachings of his own conservative Hanbali school. As the scholars who met at Mardin pointed out, however, the *fatwa* was issued in a very particular historical context, in the aftermath of the Mongol conquest and the devastation of Baghdad (the seat of Islamic authority at the time). They concluded that "anyone who seeks support from this *fatwa* for killing Muslims or non-Muslims has erred in his interpretation." They also asserted that "It is not for a Muslim individual or a group to announce and declare war or engage in combative *jihad* . . . on their own."

Unfortunately, extremists seem impervious to mainstream Muslim opinion. Muslims can accomplish much in the West if they work with their non-Muslim neighbours to promote justice and moral consciousness. But many non-Muslims see "Islam" and "the West" as mutually exclusive realities, and do not recognize their shared heritage. If future generations of Muslims are to remain active as Muslims in pluralistic Western societies, it is more important than ever to re-examine old images and ideas.

Summary

A major development in the history of Islam is now underway in the West. Muslims who, through migration, have moved from majority to minority status are being spurred to define the priorities of their faith. Their decisions about what to pass on to their Western-born children will shape the contours of Islam in the twenty-first century and beyond. At the same time, the Western emphasis on open discussion calls on Muslims from different cultural and regional backgrounds to think clearly about what they do and do not share. Muslims living in the West will use Western technology and democratic institutions to help their brothers and sisters revitalize the Muslim communities in their countries of origin, as well as the rest of the Muslim *ummah*. The potential of modern communications to contribute to this process became clear during the "Arab Spring" of 2011.

Sacred Texts

Variation	Text	Composition/ Compilation	Compilation/ Revision	Use
Sunni and Shi'a	Qur'an	Revelations received by Muhammad between 610 and 632 CE	Authoritative Codex produced between 644 and 656 CE	Doctrinal, ritual, inspirational, educational
Sunni and Shi'a	*Hadith*	Sayings of Muhammad and his early companions collected during their lifetimes	Earliest authoritative collection produced by al-Bukhari (d. 870 CE)	Doctrinal, ritual, inspirational, educational
Shi'a only	Nahj al-Balagha ("the peak of eloquence"; the sayings of 'Ali)	Sayings and sermons of 'Ali, the first Shi'i Imam	Collected by Al-Radi (d. 1015)	Doctrinal, ritual, inspirational, educational
Ismaili Shi'a only	Ginans (hymns of praise and worship of God)	Collection begun by Pir Nur in the 12th century	Composition and collection continued until the beginning of the 20th century	Doctrinal, ritual, inspirational, educational

Discussion Questions

1. What is the significance of the *hijrah* in Muslim history? Why is this event so important to Muslims?

2. Muslims consider the life of Muhammad to be of fundamental importance to their faith. Write a brief biography of the Prophet highlighting two events in his life that are particularly significant to Muslims. In your answer, explain why the events you have chosen are so central.

3. What is the Qur'an? What do Muslims understand it to be?

4. Discuss the differences between Sunni and Shi'a Islam. What are the two primary groups within the Shi'a?

5. Outline the development of Sufism, the mystical dimension of Islam.

6. What are the Five Pillars of Islam?

7. What are some of the issues raised by feminist interpretations of the Qur'an and the Muslim tradition?

Glossary

caliph From the Arabic *khalifah* ("one who represents or acts on behalf of another"). The caliph was the Prophet's successor as the head of the Muslim community; the position became institutionalized in the form of the caliphate, which lasted from 632 to 1924.

dhikr "Remembering" God's name; chanted in Sufi devotional exercises, sometimes while devotees dance in a circle.

dhimmis "Protected people": non-Muslim religious minorities (specifically Jews and Christians, as "People of the Book") accorded tolerated status in Islamic society.

Fatihah The short opening *surah* of the Qur'an, recited at least 17 times every day.

fatwa A ruling issued by a traditional religio-legal authority.

fiqh Jurisprudence, or the theoretical principles underpinning the specific regulations contained in the *shari'ah*.

hadith The body of texts reporting Muhammad's words and example, taken by Muslims as a foundation for conduct and doctrine; a *hadith* is an individual unit of the literature.

hajj The annual pilgrimage to Mecca.

halal Ritually acceptable; most often used in the context of the slaughter of animals for meat; also refers generally to Muslim dietary regulations.

hanifs "Pious ones"; a group of pre-Islamic Arabs who shared the ethical monotheism of Jews and Christians.

haram "Forbidden," used especially in reference to actions; similar in its connotations to "taboo."

hijab A woman's veil or head covering.

hijrah The Prophet's migration from Mecca to establish a community in Medina in 622 CE. In dates, the abbreviation AH stands for "year of the *hijrah*" (the starting-point of the Islamic dating system)

'Id al-Fitr The holiday celebrating the end of the Ramadan fast; the festival traditionally begins following the sighting of the new moon.

ijma' The consensus of religio-legal scholars; one of the two secondary principles used in jurisprudence; some legal schools give it more weight than others.

ijtihad Personal reasoning applied to the development of legal opinions.

Imamis ("Twelvers") Shi'is who recognize 12 imams as legitimate heirs to the Prophet's authority; the last, in occultation since 874, is expected to return some day as the **Mahdi**.

Isma'ilis ("Seveners") Shi'is who recognize only seven imams; named after the last of them, Isma'il, whose lineage continues to the present in the Agha Khan.

isnad The pedigree or chain of transmission of a *hadith*, with which the individual unit begins.

jihad Struggle in defence of the faith; some *jihads* are military, waged in response to threats to the community's security or welfare; others are spiritual, waged to improve moral conduct in society.

kufr Rejecting belief; implies lack of gratitude for God's grace.

Mahdi The Shi'i twelfth Imam, understood in his role as the "rightly guided one" who will emerge from hiding at some unspecified future date to restore righteousness and order to the world.

mi'raj The Prophet's miraculous journey to heaven.

mu'adhdhin The person who calls people to prayer.

qiblah The direction of prayer, marked in mosques by a niche inside the wall nearest Mecca.

Ramadan The month throughout which Muslims fast during daylight hours.

sadaqah Alms given voluntarily, in addition to the required *zakat*.

salat The prescribed daily prayers, said five times during the day.

shahadah The Muslim profession of faith in God as the only god, and in Muhammad as God's prophet.

shari'ah The specific regulations of Islamic law (jurisprudence, or theoretical discussion of the law, is *fiqh*).

shaykh The Arabic term for a senior master, especially in the context of Sufism.

Shi'a From the Arabic meaning "party"; Muslims who trace succession to the Prophet's authority through the line of Imams descended from 'Ali; the smaller of the two main divisions of Islam, accounting for about one-sixth of all Muslims today. "Shi'i" is the adjective form.

sunnah The "life-example" of Muhammad's words and deeds, based mainly on the *hadith* literature; the primary source of guidance for Muslims.

Sunni Muslims who trace succession to the Prophet's authority through the caliphate, which lasted until the twentieth century; the larger of the two main divisions of Islam, accounting for about five-sixths of all Muslims today.

surah A chapter of the Qur'an; there are 114 in all, arranged mainly in decreasing order of length except for the first (the *Fatihah*).

tafsir Commentary on the Qur'an.

taqlid Following the *ijtihad* or legal opinion of a particular jurist.

ummah The Muslim community.

zakat The prescribed welfare tax; 2.5 per cent of each Muslim's accumulated wealth, collected by central treasuries in earlier times but now donated to charities independently of state governments; see also *sadaqah*.

Further Reading

Ahmed, Leila. 1992. *Women and Gender in Islam: Historical Roots of a Modern Debate*. New Haven: Yale University Press. A frequently cited contribution on this topic.

Alvi, Sajida Sultana, et al., eds. 2003. *The Muslim Veil in North America: Issues and Debates*. Toronto: Women's Press. A good collection of essays about the issues surrounding *hijab*.

Coulson, N.G. 1964. *A History of Islamic Law*. Edinburgh: Edinburgh University Press. Traces the development of Islamic jurisprudence from its inception in the ninth century through to the influence on it of modern Western legal systems.

Dodds, Jerrilyn D., et al., eds. 2008. *The Arts of Intimacy: Christians, Jews, and Muslims in the Making of Castilian Culture*. New Haven: Yale University Press. A beautifully illustrated book that looks at the *convivencia* ("shared life") between Muslims, Christians, and Jews in medieval Spain.

The Encyclopedia of Islam, rev. ed. 1963–. Leiden: E.J. Brill. (First published in 4 vols, 1913–38.) Vast and technical, but authoritative. Entries appear under Arabic head-words, sometimes in unfamiliar transliterations, and so pose a challenge for the beginner.

Esposito, John, ed. 2009. *The Oxford Encyclopedia of the Islamic World*. New York: Oxford University Press. An indispensable reference.

Grabar, Oleg. 1973. *The Formation of Islamic Art*. New Haven: Yale University Press. Concentrates on Islamic art in the Middle East in the early Islamic centuries.

Haddad, Yvonne Y., and Jane I. Smith, eds. 1994. *Muslim Communities in North America*. Albany: State University of New York Press. An examination of Islamic tradition and identity in the modern Western diaspora.

Mottahedeh, Roy. 2002. *The Mantle of the Prophet: Religion and Politics in Iran*. Oxford: Oneworld Publications. One of the best single-volume studies of the events leading up to the Iranian revolution.

Peters, Francis E. 1994. *A Reader on Islam*. Princeton: Princeton University Press. An anthology of historical source readings.

Qureshi, Emran, and Michael A. Sells, eds. 2003. *The New Crusades: Constructing the Muslim Enemy*. New York: Columbia. An excellent collection of essays on Western representations of Islam and Muslim lives.

Safi, Omid, ed. 2003. *Progressive Muslims: On Justice, Gender and Pluralism*. Oxford: Oneworld. A collection of essays by Muslim scholars of Islam on contemporary topics.

Schimmel, Annemarie. 1975. *Mystical Dimensions of Islam*. Chapel Hill: University of North Carolina Press. A survey of Sufism by one of its most respected Western interpreters.

Taylor, Jennifer Maytorena. 2009. *New Muslim Cool*. Documentary film. Educational DVD available from Seventh Art Releasing at <www.7thart.com>. The story of Hamza Perez, a Puerto Rican American hip hop artist who converted to Islam.

Watt, W. Montgomery. 1962. *Islamic Philosophy and Theology*. Edinburgh: Edinburgh University Press. A masterly survey of Muslim religious intellectuals, especially in the first six centuries of Islam.

Recommended Websites

www.uga.edu/islam/
The best academic site for the study of Islam, presented by Professor Alan Godlas of the University of Georgia.

www.cie.org/index.aspx
The Council on Islamic Education offers useful resources for teachers.

http://acommonword.com/
An interfaith initiative supported by a wide range of Muslim scholars and leaders.

www.msawest.net/islam/
An excellent selection of resources on Islam, including searchable translations of both the Qur'an and the *hadith* literature, presented by the Muslim Students Association.

References

Arberry, Arthur J. trans. 1948. *Immortal Rose: An Anthology of Persian Lyrics*. London: Luzac & Co.

———, trans. 1955. *The Koran Interpreted*. London: Allen and Unwin.

Chittick, William C. 2000. *Sufism: A Beginner's Guide*. Oxford: Oneworld.

Menocal, María Rosa. 2003. "The Myth of Westernness in Medieval Literary Historiography." Pp. 249–87 in Emran Qureshi and Michael Anthony Sells, ed. *The New Crusades: Constructing the Muslim Enemy*. New York: Columbia University Press.

Nicholson, Reynold A. 1931. "Mysticism." In *The Legacy of Islam*, ed. T. Arnold and Alfred Guillaume, 210–38. London: Oxford University Press.

———, trans. 1950. *Rumi: Poet and Mystic*. London: G. Allen and Unwin.

———. 2002 [1914]. *The Mystics of Islam*. Bloomington: World Wisdom.

Smith, Margaret. 1928. *Rabi'a the Mystic*. Cambridge: Cambridge University Press.

6

Indigenous
Traditions

Ken Derry

Traditions at a Glance

Numbers

Reliable statistical information on Indigenous religions is virtually impossible to come by. According to the United Nations, there are approximately 370 million Indigenous people in the world. On average perhaps 15 to 20 per cent practise their ancestral traditions, but the figures are much higher in some communities and much lower in others.

Distribution

Indigenous religious traditions can be found almost everywhere: there are more than 5,000 distinct Indigenous cultures in some 90 countries around the world. By far the largest Indigenous populations are in Asia and Africa; fewer than 10 per cent live in Central and South America, approximately 2 per cent in North America and Oceania, and just a small fraction in Europe.

Recent Historical Periods

Extant written records of most Indigenous traditions begin only after contact with non-Indigenous people occurred, so the only developments we can trace with any certainty are those that have taken place since then. It's important to keep in mind, however, that Indigenous religions had been changing and adapting for millennia before that time.

600–700	First contact between Muslims and Indigenous Africans
1450–1850	First contact between Europeans and Indigenous people of Africa, North America, and Oceania; development of Atlantic slave trade and other colonial practices that devastated Indigenous populations
1930–1960	Several governments begin to reduce restrictions on Indigenous people and religion
1960–present	Revival of many Indigenous traditions around the world; development of global pan-Indigenous movements

Founders and Leaders

Few pre-contact Indigenous traditions identify a human founder, although most attribute key features of their religious life to superhuman ancestors. Virtually all traditions also contain religious authority figures such as elders, as well as ritual specialists such as diviners and healers who invoke spiritual powers to aid their communities. In response to colonialism, several new movements were founded by specific people, such as Wovoka (Paiute) or Nongqawuse (Xhosa).

Deities

Indigenous traditions vary widely in their conceptions of gods. Some recognize a single supreme deity as the source of all life and power. Others do not recognize such a being, but attribute creation to a series of gods, spirits, or ancestors. Almost all Indigenous traditions, however, believe that personal deities (or spirits or ancestors) have an active, ongoing impact on the world.

Authoritative Texts

Most pre-contact Indigenous religions passed along their sacred stories orally. These stories often include accounts of the creation of the present world and/or the origins of the community. Many also recount the ongoing activity of personal spiritual forces in the world. New tales continue to be told (and written), particularly about trickster figures, and some post-contact movements (such as the Handsome Lake religion of the Iroquois) have their own sacred texts.

Noteworthy Teachings

Indigenous traditions are typically bound to specific places where important spiritual forces have

Chief Arvol Looking Horse (see p. 343) at the Cheyenne River Sioux Reservation in South Dakota (© National Geographic Image Collection/Alamy).

manifested themselves (e.g., where acts of creation occurred). They also tend to be more concerned with what happens during life than after death; therefore they place greater emphasis on behaviour than on belief, and assess actions in terms of whether they benefit the community or cause it harm. Indigenous traditions frequently understand time as rhythmic rather than linear, linking the past to the present in a way that responds to changing circumstances; in this conception, the sacred interacts with the world on an ongoing basis, in ways that are both old and new.

In this chapter you will learn about:

- the difficulties involved in defining the term "Indigenous"
- some of the false assumptions that non-Indigenous people have held (and continue to hold) about Indigenous cultures
- the necessity of considering the specific historic and cultural context of any aspect of an Indigenous tradition
- the importance of relationships in Indigenous communities, stories, rituals, and art
- why religious location and practice are much more important than belief for many Indigenous people
- the impact of colonialism on Indigenous religions
- how contemporary Indigenous people around the world are reclaiming, rebuilding, and revising many of their traditions.

So.
In the beginning, there was nothing. Just the water.
Coyote was there, but Coyote was asleep. That Coyote was asleep and that Coyote was dreaming. When that Coyote dreams, anything can happen.
I can tell you that.
—Thomas King (1993: 1), **Cherokee**/Greek

Anything can happen. The possibilities, the complexities, of religions seem to be endless. This is particularly true of Indigenous traditions, which constitute the majority of the world's religions.

They are interwoven with the entire history of humanity, they encompass the whole earth. And they are almost unimaginably diverse. So where to begin?

Perhaps it is best to start with ourselves. Let us approach the task of generalizing about Indigenous traditions with humility, and with the understanding that there are exceptions to every rule. We should also keep in mind that many past interpretations of these traditions have proven to be deeply mistaken. Looking through the lenses of their own assumptions and cultural biases, scholars can easily be tricked into seeing things that are not there, or missing what is right in front of them.

Coyote would not be surprised.

"Indigenous Religion"

Definitions

There is a shared sense of Aboriginality nationally (and internationally with other Indigenous peoples), regardless of the geographical location or socio-economic experience of the individual.
—Anita Heiss (2001: 207), **Wiradjuri**

There is no definitive, agreed-on understanding of "Indigenous religion." In fact, the meanings of the words "Indigenous" and "religion" themselves are open to debate, and it's even possible to question whether they mean anything at all. You might think that trying to define a term made up of two elements that may be meaningless is doomed to failure. But we are going to try anyway.

"Religion"

Many of the difficulties surrounding the word "religion" stem from the effort to find common patterns in such a variety of human practices. Are religions always about gods? (No.) Do all religions have a sacred text, believe in life after death, or promote the same basic values? (No again.) So what exactly are we talking about when we refer to "religion"? Although scholars generally concede that we are unlikely to develop a single definition on which all can agree, they also point out that all definitions are themselves constructs. In other words, often what is most important is simply to be clear about which construct we are using.

The view of religion underlying this chapter is one that focuses on the beliefs, experiences, and practices of specific communities with respect to *non-falsifiable* realities (Cox 2007: 88). A proposition that is falsifiable is one that can be scientifically proven untrue. Religious propositions are of a different kind. It may not be possible to prove them true, but it is equally impossible to prove them false. Rather, religious propositions traffic in the unseeable, the untouchable, the un-measurable. Whenever we step outside of material reality to address questions of spirit, meaning, or divinity, I would say, we are dealing with religion.

This definition is not perfect, of course. Among other potential weaknesses, it implies a distinction between religion and science—as if religion had no scientific components, or science could not function as a religion for some people. This is not a reasonable distinction, in my opinion: religion and science may often overlap. Nor do I mean to imply that scientific knowledge supersedes other forms of knowledge or ways of knowing. Scientists have been proven wrong about aspects of our world that some Indigenous cultures have long been right about.

Still, I believe that the focus on "non-falsifiable realities" as a basis for defining religion can work quite well. In particular—and most relevantly—it is a good fit for the examples of Indigenous religion that this chapter will examine.

"Indigenous"

The term "Indigenous" is also problematic, for it obliges us to ask which cultures and people are "Indigenous" and which are not. This question is not just academic: it is loaded with legal and political implications, and so how it is answered has a direct and lasting impact on the lives of millions of people around the world. If we cannot identify a particular group as Indigenous, for example, how can its members assert their treaty rights, or see their land claims settled fairly?

Unfortunately, it is usually non-Indigenous governments that impose the definitions, and those definitions themselves tend to change over time. In Canada, for instance, it was for many years the case that a "status Indian" woman who married a "non-status" man was no longer legally Indigenous; she automatically forfeited all the rights that the (legally defined) Indigenous people of Canada are entitled to. When this law was reversed after years of protest, not only these women but also their children suddenly "became" Indigenous, virtually overnight.

Other definitions are also problematic. Almost invariably, "Indigenous" is understood to mean "original to the land." Yet many places in the world, including India and Africa, have very ancient histories of migration and interaction between various groups. How could anyone possibly determine the "original" inhabitants of such lands?

Furthermore, we again run into the difficulty of finding patterns among religious beliefs and practices. Some cultures that may be considered Indigenous recognize a single supreme being; some recognize a variety of deities; and some do not bother themselves at all with such things. Among those Indigenous people who do believe in a god or gods, there are some who pray to those higher powers and some who do not. Given the immense diversity of these traditions, how reasonable is it to group them all together?

That said, there is at least one definition that avoids some of these problems by focusing on two elements of central importance to cultures that have typically been considered Indigenous both

Timeline

Although most of the dates below relate to developments in Indigenous traditions since contact with non-Indigenous people, the histories of those traditions began many millennia earlier. Archaeological evidence can identify the early presence of *Homo sapiens* communities in various sites, but dates remain approximate at best. Also note that the events listed here relate only to the cultures discussed in this chapter—a tiny fraction of the thousands that have existed.

c. 190,000 BCE	Earliest evidence of Indigenous people in Africa
c. 70,000 BCE	Earliest evidence of Indigenous people in Australia, Europe, and Asia
c. 12,500 BCE	Earliest evidence of Indigenous people in the Americas
616 CE	First Muslims arrive in Africa (Ethiopia)
c. 1250	First contact between the Ainu and the Japanese
c. 1300	First Indigenous settlers arrive in New Zealand (from Polynesia)
1444	Portuguese exploration of sub-Saharan Africa begins
c. 1480	Atlantic slave trade begins
1492	Christopher Columbus (Italian) arrives in the West Indies, initiating Spanish colonization of the Americas
1642	Dutch explorer Abel Janszoon Tasman arrives in New Zealand
1788	British First Fleet arrives in Sydney, Australia
1799	Handsome Lake experiences his first vision
1819	British and Xhosa (led by Nxele) fight Battle of Grahamstown
c. 1840	Canada establishes residential school system
1856–7	Nongqawuse's vision leads to Xhosa cattle massacre
1869	Australia begins taking Aboriginal children from their families, producing the first of many "Stolen Generations"
1883	Pauline Johnson (Mohawk) publishes first poems; US bans Sun Dance
1884	Canada bans potlatch
1885	European powers partition Africa at Congress of Berlin; intensive Christian missionary efforts begin in non-Muslim areas of Africa; earliest recorded "cargo cult" begins in Fiji
1889	Wovoka revives the Ghost Dance
1890	US Cavalry massacres more than 300 Lakota Sioux at Wounded Knee, North Dakota
1899	Japan appropriates Ainu lands, denies Ainu status as Indigenous people
1934	US lifts ban on Sun Dance and potlatch
1951	Canada lifts ban on potlatch
1956–65	Beginning of African post-independence era

continued

1958	Chinua Achebe (Igbo) publishes *Things Fall Apart*
1969	Kiowa novelist N. Scott Momaday's *House Made of Dawn* wins Pulitzer Prize for Fiction
1970	US returns 194 km² of land to Taos Pueblo
1985	Maori novelist Keri Hulme's *The Bone People* wins the Booker Prize for Fiction
1990	Oka Crisis in Quebec, Canada
1992	Australian High Court overturns *terra nullius* ruling
1994	Nelson Mandela (Xhosa) elected president of South Africa
2007	United Nations adopts Declaration on the Rights of Indigenous Peoples
2008	Australia apologizes for "Stolen Generations"; Canada apologies for residential school system; Japan formally recognizes Ainu as an Indigenous group
2012	Idle No More protests begin; "Mayan Apocalypse" does not

by themselves and by others: kinship and location. To be "Indigenous" (or its synonym, "Aboriginal") in this sense is to belong to a community that is defined both by its members' *genealogical* relations to one another, and by its connection to a particular *place*. The people who make up this community may or may not be the first or "original" inhabitants of this place. They may not even inhabit it now. Yet they see themselves as belonging to it in critical ways, and they distinguish themselves from people who do not share this connection.

Putting our two terms together, then, "Indigenous religion" refers to the beliefs, experiences, and practices concerning non-falsifiable realities of peoples who (a) identify themselves as Indigenous and (b) rely (at least in part) on kinship and location to define their place in the world.

Change and Syncretism

One other issue we need to consider from the outset is the fact that Indigenous religions no longer exist as they did before contact with the "outside" world. This situation is partly the result of **syncretism**, the merging of elements from different cultures. Many Native North American religions have been deeply affected by Christianity; some African rituals have incorporated elements of Islam; the sacred oral stories of Japanese Shinto became written texts under the influence of Chinese Buddhism. Does this mean that "real" Indigenous religions have disappeared?

Definitely not. Change and syncretism have taken place among *all* religions throughout history. It is true that Indigenous religions today are not the same as they were 100, or 500, or 10,000 years ago. But the traditions as they exist now are no less authentic than they were in the past. The forms of Christianity practised in the contemporary United States have likewise been variously influenced by the beliefs and practices of many cultures, including African and Native American. These American forms in turn are quite different from the European Christianity that Martin Luther knew in the 1500s, or the Hellenized Christianity that Paul taught in the first century—a tradition that of course began life as the Palestinian Judaism practised by Jesus. Like everything else in the world, religions change, and none of them are ever exactly what they used to be.

These days, Indigenous religious practices can be found anywhere: **Anishinaubae** drumming ceremonies in Toronto, Canada; **Yoruba** funeral rites in London, England; and **Maori** purification rituals at the opera house in Sydney, Australia. Indigenous people and their religions may be connected to history, but they are not bound (or buried) by it.

Map 6.1 North American Indigenous Language Families

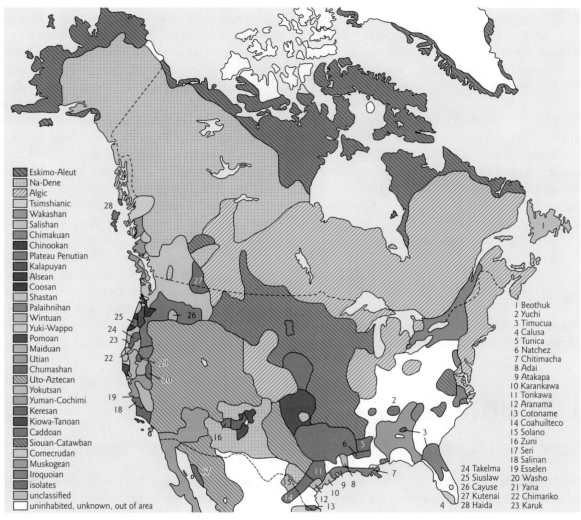

Legend:
- Eskimo-Aleut
- Na-Dene
- Algic
- Tsimshianic
- Wakashan
- Salishan
- Chimakuan
- Chinookan
- Plateau Penutian
- Kalapuyan
- Alsean
- Coosan
- Shastan
- Palaihnihan
- Wintuan
- Yuki-Wappo
- Pomoan
- Maiduan
- Utian
- Chumashan
- Uto-Aztecan
- Yokutsan
- Yuman-Cochimi
- Keresan
- Kiowa-Tanoan
- Caddoan
- Siouan-Catawban
- Comecrudan
- Muskogean
- Iroquoian
- isolates
- unclassified
- uninhabited, unknown, out of area

1 Beothuk
2 Yuchi
3 Timucua
4 Calusa
5 Tunica
6 Natchez
7 Chitimacha
8 Adai
9 Atakapa
10 Karankawa
11 Tonkawa
12 Aranama
13 Cotoname
14 Coahuilteco
15 Solano
16 Zuni
17 Seri
18 Salinan
19 Esselen
20 Washo
21 Yana
22 Chimariko
23 Karuk
24 Takelma
25 Siuslaw
26 Cayuse
27 Kutenai
28 Haida

This map shows the distribution of North American language families north of Mexico at the time of European contact (to the extent that scholars can determine). Language borders are given for the sake of clarity but were in reality much fuzzier than this image suggests. The map points to the tremendous diversity of Native North American cultures, since each *language family* may contain dozens of distinct *languages*. The family of Romance languages, for instance, contains Italian, French, Spanish, Portuguese, Romanian, and Catalan, as well as many regional languages.

The "Patterns" section below will offer a basic overview of some additional features that seem to be common to many, if not all, Indigenous religions, both past and present. Before we can say much more about what Indigenous religions are, however, we first need to briefly consider what they are not. That means breaking down some of the key misconceptions about these religions that many non-Indigenous people have held, and often continue to hold.

"Us" and "Them"

> The people who have control of your stories, control of your voice, also have control of your destiny, your culture.
> —Lenore Keeshig-Tobias, Anishinaubae (in Lutz 1991: 81)

Most of what most people know, or think they know, about Indigenous cultures has come from non-Indigenous people. This reality points to one further element common to Indigenous traditions: **colonialism**. The effects of colonialism will be discussed in some detail later in this chapter, but at the moment it is important to say a few words about one facet of colonialism: namely, academic work on Indigenous people and cultures.

Scholars with Weapons

Over the past few decades, there has been some opposition to the efforts of non-Indigenous scholars to "explain" Indigenous people. The main concern is that, even when such theories bear little relation to reality, they tend to have significant social and political influence. The recent confusion about the "**Mayan** Apocalypse" stems from an academic misunderstanding about Indigenous people. Early discoveries indicated that the Mayans had identified an age of the gods, lasting for over 5,000 years and ending in 3114 BCE. Scholars simply assumed the next age would be of the same duration, calculating that it (the age, not the world) would end on 21 December 2012. In fact, the Mayans understood the period following the age of the gods to be composed of entirely different time periods, rendering the identification of 2012 as the end of *any* Mayan-related phenomenon completely meaningless.

Another, more harmful example of academic impact was outlined by the **Oglala Sioux** lawyer, historian, and activist Vine Deloria, Jr, in his book *Custer Died for Your Sins: An Indian Manifesto*. Anthropologists seeking to explain the social ills plaguing

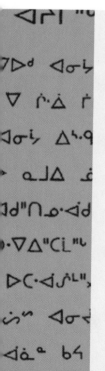

Document

From *Custer Died for Your Sins*, by Vine Deloria, Jr (Oglala Sioux)

Looking at a variety of Native American issues including colonialism, religion, and even humour, and appearing in the early days of the American Indian Movement, Custer Died for Your Sins *remains one of the most influential works of Indigenous non-fiction ever written.*

From lack of roads to unshined shoes, Sioux problems were generated, so the anthros discovered, by the refusal of the white man to recognize the great desire of the Oglala to go to war. Why expect an Oglala to become a small businessman, when he was only waiting for that wagon train to come around the bend?

The very real and human problems of the reservation were considered to be merely by-products of the failure of a warrior people to become domesticated. . . . What use would roads, houses, schools, businesses, and income be to a people who, everyone expected, would soon depart on the hunt or warpath? . . .

The question of the Oglala Sioux is one that plagues every Indian tribe in the nation, if it will closely examine itself. Tribes have been defined as one thing, the definition has been completely explored, test scores have been advanced promoting and deriding the thesis, and finally the conclusion has been reached—Indians must be redefined in terms that white men will accept, even if that means re-Indianizing them according to the white man's idea of what they were like in the past and should logically become in the future (Deloria, Jr, 1988 [1969]: 92).

the Oglala community ignored the "real issue, white control of the reservation," and theorized that the people were simply "warriors without weapons" (Deloria, Jr, 1988 [1969]: 90). In other words, the Oglala were incapable of adapting to a market-economy lifestyle because, deep in their souls, they remained violently primitive. Accordingly, attention was diverted away from the pressing needs of the people in this community—credit, employment, housing, medical services—and focused instead on figuring out how to make "modern Indians" out of them (Deloria, Jr, 1988 [1969]: 92).

Today it is not unusual for concern to be expressed when non-Indigenous scholars speak about Indigenous people. The main objection might seem to be that "outsiders" lack the "insider" knowledge and insight required to speak with authority about a particular community, culture, or tradition. As Deloria suggests, however, the real problem is not so much a matter of accuracy as it is one of *power* and *control*. The fact is that such scholars historically have been in a privileged position of authority to define Indigenous people not only to other non-Natives, but even to Native people themselves.

Unacceptable Terms

Another important problem with academic work about Indigenous people is that it tends to reinforce the idea that "they" are different from "us." Thus the study of Indigenous religions has produced many terms and concepts that typically are applied only to those traditions, and not to "world" religions more broadly. Such terms include:

- animism
- fetish
- mana
- myth
- shaman
- taboo
- totem

This chapter will rarely use any of the above terms, in part because they are not necessary for an introductory understanding of Indigenous religions—but also because they are not used in reference to the other religions discussed in this book, even when they might be relevant. For example, the origin stories of Indigenous people are usually labelled "myth," while similar stories recounted in texts like the Hebrew Bible or the *Mahabharata* are referred to as "sacred literature." Similarly, the rule that prohibits an African mask carver from coming into contact with a woman during his work would normally be called a "taboo"; yet that term is not applied to the rule that forbids a priest from pouring unused communion wine down the drain. In short, it is important not to perpetuate the notion that Indigenous religions are of a different order from non-Indigenous religions.

"Primitives" and the Problem of History

> If I press any anthros in a prolonged discussion on exactly why they study Indians and other tribal peoples and why they study anthropology at all, I am almost always informed that tribal people represent an earlier stage of human accomplishment and that we can learn about our past by studying the way existing tribal peoples live.
> —Vine Deloria, Jr (1997: 214), Oglala Sioux

The More Things Change

For many years non-Indigenous people assumed that Indigenous people and cultures had changed very little over time—at least until the two groups met and colonization began. Until relatively recently, in fact, only anthropologists studied Aboriginal people: historians (including historians of religion) did not, because they assumed there was no Aboriginal history to look at.

The development of anthropology as an academic field can be traced to the European Enlightenment of the seventeenth and eighteenth centuries. Among other factors that led to this development, the Enlightenment was an age of exploration, during which reports were regularly sent back to Europe describing encounters with previously unknown cultures—cultures that were primarily oral in nature, for example, and that used simpler technology.

Assuming that such cultures had remained essentially unchanged from their beginnings, the Europeans referred to them as "primitive" (from the Latin *primus*, meaning "first"). For those people, history was assumed to have begun only when they first encountered "modern/civilized" cultures.

This assumption was supported by the fact that the majority of Europeans at the time of contact were Christians who believed both in the (God-given) superiority of their own culture, and in the divine imperative to spread their religion to those who had not yet heard the gospel. Indigenous cultures were seen as ideal recipients of the Word of God, blank slates with no real history—or religion—of their own. This missionary worldview often went hand in hand with academic inquiry, and tended to colour the scholars' interpretation (in some cases, fabrication) of the details of Indigenous lives.

We know now that those long-standing assumptions about Indigenous cultures as static and ahistorical were completely untrue. All the available evidence shows that Indigenous peoples had dynamic, eventful histories full of change long before they were "discovered." They have also been quite conscious of their histories, using stories, songs, or physical markings to record all manner of past events and conditions, changes in the culture or the land, family genealogies, remarkable natural phenomena, and so on.

A Persistent Problem

One example of the persistent notion that Indigenous cultures are "primitive" is the tendency to think of them as non-literate. This belief is deeply problematic in several ways, which will be discussed in the next section ("Transmission"). For now I simply wish to state three points. First, writing is not inherently more "advanced" than orality. Second, many Indigenous cultures did use a form of writing before contact with non-Indigenous people (see, for example, the Mayan glyphs below). Third, of course, the simple fact is that the vast majority of contemporary Indigenous cultures are fully literate; to ignore this fact is to continue to think of these cultures only in the past tense.

Another example of the tendency to regard Indigenous people as "primitive" is the belief that

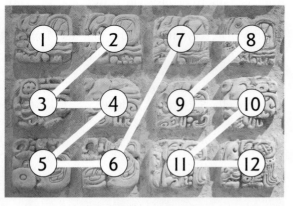

Mayan writing consisted of elaborate images, or glyphs, which were "logosyllabic" (each image represents either a word or a syllable). These images were painted on ceramics, carved in wood, or—as in the image here—moulded in stucco. Most often they were arranged in blocks of two columns, each one to be read from left to right, top to bottom.

© Ariadne Van Zandbergen/Alamy

they do not distinguish between the "religious" and the "non-religious" aspects of their lives—that they consider everything to be sacred. Sometimes this idea is supported by pointing to practices such as the **Navajo** enactment of the "Blessingway" ceremony before a new dwelling is occupied. Commentators claim that for the Navajo, this ceremony transforms the home into a sacred site in a manner that renders every single act of daily life that occurs within it—eating, sleeping, arguing, laughing—equally sacred. This notion is both inaccurate and patronizing. Essentially, Indigenous people are understood to resemble young children, who often believe that everything—trees, stuffed animals, bits of clothing—is alive and sentient.

The fact is that Indigenous cultures are no less able than non-Indigenous ones to form distinctions in relation to the category of religion. Observant Muslims may take their prayer mats wherever they go, but they use the mats only at specific, established times; other times are not for prayer. Similarly, an Australian **Aborigine** knows the difference between a mountain that is sacred and one that is not, and that certain acts are performed only in particular ritual contexts, and not at any other time.

Many non-Indigenous scholars have come to realize that Indigenous cultures were (and are) just as complex and innovative as their own, and that the idea of the "primitive" says much more about the person who holds it than about the people it is applied to. For example, it typically suggests a belief in one's own superiority. As such, it provides justification for the "improvement" of Indigenous cultures through the introduction of writing, technology, or a market economy. In a similar fashion, those who romanticize "primitive" cultures often do so as a way of expressing the belief that their own "civilized" culture has alienated people from themselves, or from the natural world. Again, the concept tells us more about such people—and their culture—than it tells us about the people they imagine to be "primitive."

Still, the idea of the "primitive" is a stubborn one, and it continues to have deeply negative consequences. It is one reason why many world religions courses still ignore Indigenous traditions altogether. It also helps to explain why literary scholars often ignore modern Indigenous writers, while anthropologists continue to pore over transcriptions of ancient tales. As the Anishinaubae author Daniel David Moses has commented: "This image of traditional Native storytelling places Native people in the museum with all the other extinct species" (Moses and Goldie 1992: xiii).

Patterns

> The knowledge imposes a pattern, and falsifies . . .
> The only wisdom we can hope to acquire
> Is the wisdom of humility: humility is endless.
> —T.S. Eliot (1959: 23–4), Euro-American

Eating and Seeing

Dr Clare Brant, a **Mohawk** from southern Ontario, has recounted an experience from the 1970s when his band invited a group of James Bay **Cree** to a sporting tournament they were hosting (Ross 1992: 2–3). The Mohawk—who developed agriculture long before meeting Europeans—had a tradition of always setting out more food than their guests could eat, in order to demonstrate their wealth and generosity. Unfortunately, the Cree had a very different tradition. Coming from a culture of hunting and gathering, they were accustomed to living with scarcity; as a result they would eat all the food offered, thus showing their respect for the skill and generosity of those who provided it.

Of course these two traditions did not mix well. The Cree thought the Mohawk were deliberately forcing them to overeat to the point of severe discomfort, while the Mohawk thought the Cree were grossly self-indulgent and bizarrely determined to insult their hosts. Thus even though both groups were trying their best to be polite, each was seen by the other as intentionally disrespectful.

This story highlights two important points. First, it tells us that not all Indigenous cultures are alike. Even people who live very close to one another can sometimes think or act in very different ways. Consider that New Guinea and its surrounding islands contain more ethnographic diversity than anywhere else on earth, approximately one-fourth of the world's cultures (and languages and religions). It would be the height of arrogance for us to imagine that these cultures are essentially identical simply because the same label ("Indigenous") has been applied to them. The second point is that anyone attempting to understand another culture is in a position similar to that of the Mohawk and the Cree. The eyes we see through are the ones we have inherited from our own cultures, and so we must never forget to use them with caution and humility.

Common Elements

With the above points in mind, in the rest of this chapter we will try to identify some elements common to many (if not necessarily all) Indigenous religions. Among them are the following:

- importance of orality
- connection to specific places
- emphasis on community and relationship
- sense of time as rhythmic
- greater emphasis on what happens during life than after death
- behaviour more important than belief
- authority of **elders**
- **complementary dualism**
- a view of the sacred as ongoing process rather than static revelation
- gendered roles

This last point requires some comment at the outset. Traditionally, everyone in an Indigenous community had clearly defined roles, and often those roles were gendered. In general, hunting and warfare were male occupations, while food preparation and healing were the responsibility of women. Maori carvers were men, and Maori weavers were women. The **Bunu** Yoruba men were responsible for growing cotton, and the women for turning it into cloth. In this way, men and women were dependent

on one another, and yet also independent in certain important ways.

A similar balancing can often be seen in regard to political and social power. The heads of most Indigenous societies have typically been male. Yet in many instances women have been inherently involved with any decisions that affect the entire community. And in some instances such decisions are normally made by women, then carried out by men.

It is also important to note that gender classification could be somewhat fluid in many Indigenous societies. Sometimes women might participate in men's work, and vice versa. Sexual roles and orientations could also be fluid. Accounts of men identifying as women, wearing female clothes, and taking on women's roles in the community, are not unusual. There are also accounts of Indigenous women identifying as men and becoming hunters or warriors.

There is no definitive gender pattern with respect to kinship. Some Indigenous societies are matrilineal, tracing ancestry primarily through the mother's family, while others are patrilineal, focusing on the father. Similarly, important spirits and gods—including the supreme being—may be either male or female.

It was also not uncommon for Indigenous societies to separate the religious activities of women and men in some respects. However, most studies of these societies have looked only at male practices—whether because male scholars were unaware that women had their own religious practices, because they were not permitted to study the women, or because they assumed that the men were the most important members of their communities and hence that the men's practices were the only ones worth investigating. It is only relatively recently that scholars have begun to recognize this error and correct it by also examining what Indigenous women do and think in the context of religion.

Final Concerns

Most of the examples examined below come from three vast regions of the world—Africa, Oceania, and North America—though a few come from Asia and South America. It is important to emphasize that the very idea of the world as composed of these regions was a European invention: their diverse Indigenous inhabitants thought in much more local terms.

Still, this (mis-)perception of the world as made up of a few large regions, rather than thousands of small communities, can serve a useful political purpose for Indigenous people: for example, it can give them a stronger and more unified voice on issues such as land claims or self-government. These and many other matters of general concern were set out in the 2007 United Nations Declaration on the Rights of Indigenous Peoples, a resolution that would not have been possible without a global understanding of what it means to be Indigenous.

Finally, regarding another kind of boundary, please note that the aspects of Indigenous religious life discussed in the next three sections—"Transmission," "Practice," and "Cultural Expressions"—are in reality not as cleanly demarcated as those headings might suggest. As is the case with all religions, there is a good deal of overlap. Oral stories are also ritual performances, for example, while rituals may require, or produce, works of art, which in turn may evoke stories that are critical to a community's religious tradition.

The last point to keep in mind is that the examples in this chapter represent only a tiny sample of the world's Indigenous religious traditions. As such, they say as much about me as they do about Indigenous religions themselves. They represent what I know and what I think is important, arranged into the patterns that I see. An author with different views, experience, or knowledge would have made different choices, and would perhaps have constructed quite a different picture overall. All this is true of any work on any subject, of course, which is why a good dose of skepticism is always helpful. Nothing should be taken at face value. But this point is especially important in relation to Indigenous people, who have consistently been misrepresented, often with harmful results. I have done

my best to avoid grievous errors, and I apologize upfront for any mistakes I may have made.

🐚 Transmission

The Power of Speech

> When you dig in the earth, you find stone and earthen implements, but not words— not the words of our ancestors. Words aren't buried in the ground. They aren't hanging from the branches of trees. They're only transmitted from one mouth to the next.
> —**Ainu** elder (in Shigeru 1994: 154–5)

Orality may not be a defining characteristic of Indigenous religions, but it remains a vital one for the vast majority of them. Even though some Indigenous cultures in the past did have writing, and virtually all of them have it now, most often the things of critical importance to them—including the values and beliefs that would be classified as religious—were (and are still) passed on orally. Typically this transmission happens through stories.

Writing versus Speaking

Unfortunately, many people in contemporary non-Indigenous societies continue to think of orality as "primitive" and writing as a defining characteristic of "civilization." To these people, the development of writing represents a key evolutionary advance that allows for abstract philosophical thought, while oral cultures remain attached to the present and the material world, incapable of sophisticated analysis or extended self-reflection. Writing frees humans to develop science, according to this view, whereas reliance on speaking alone limits us to magic.

Such beliefs are both incorrect and self-interested, and (as mentioned above) they contribute to the construction of Indigenous cultures as primitive. Furthermore, all cultures—including all other world religions—have many crucial oral dimensions. Both the Qur'an and the stories of Buddha were passed along in oral form for many years before they were recorded as texts.

In addition, although in non-Indigenous cultures writing is often assumed to be more important than speaking, there are contexts in which things that are *said* still have a power that the written word does not. There is a world of difference between words on paper and those same words delivered by a skillful comedian, actor, preacher, or politician. Shakespeare's plays literally come alive when the words are voiced, while the sermons of Martin Luther King, Jr, affected the course of history in a way that would not have been possible had they appeared only in print.

There is also the obvious fact that books and newspapers are no longer the standard communications media in many non-Indigenous cultures today. People in these cultures tend to prefer video, film, or television—media that have more in common with Indigenous storytelling than they do with written texts. In keeping with the high value that non-Indigenous societies place on the written word, this preference is usually lamented as proof of civilization's decline.

There may be another explanation, though. Perhaps we are simply more easily and strongly engaged by narratives that are performed than by those that just sit on a page. Perhaps technology has finally caught up with modern living arrangements, and non-Indigenous people can once again readily experience stories in their full power, as Indigenous people have been experiencing them all along.

Stories

> I can recall lying on the earth and wondering what it was all about. The stars were a beautiful mystery and so was the place where the eagle went when he soared out of sight. Many of these questions were answered in story form by the older people. How we got our pipestone, where corn came from and why lightning flashed in the sky, were all answered in stories.
> —Luther Standing Bear, **Lakota** (in Beck et al. 1992 [1977]: 59)

In many cultures stories often serve as vehicles for the transmission of beliefs and values. Yet it is not always easy to determine what is being passed along. This is as true for Indigenous tales as it is for the New Testament parables of Jesus. There are many factors that may undermine our ability to interpret the meaning of a particular story.

The Afterlife

Stories about the afterlife often appear to reveal a culture's beliefs about what literally happens following death, but the truth may be more complex. In a **Kewa** tale from Papua New Guinea, for instance, a young man goes into the bush and finds a tunnel that leads to the underworld. He recognizes many of his dead kinsmen there, residing together in a large house. The men give him many tools and other valuable items to distribute among the living people of his village, but warn him not to say where the items came from. The young man gives everything away but breaks his promise not to speak, and when he returns to the tunnel he finds it sealed.

The Anishinaubae tell the story of a man whose beloved dies just before they are to be married. Distraught, he journeys for months in search of the Path of Souls, so that he may see his love one last time. The people in his community try to dissuade him; they say the quest is hopeless, and that even if he were to succeed, seeing her would only bring more pain. When he finds the path at last, the old man who guards the land of the dead agrees to let him enter only if he promises to return to his regular life once his wish is fulfilled. The man agrees, journeys through a misty forest and across a turbulent river, and finds the woman he loved. Then he turns his canoe around and returns home as instructed, heartbroken but prepared now to continue with his life.

What do these stories tell us about the Kewa and the Anishinaubae? Do the people believe that their dead reside underground, or on the other side of a forest? Perhaps. But in each case the story seems to have more to do with relationships than with metaphysics. In the Kewa tale, ancestors help their descendants, and the young man helps his community but breaks his promise to his dead kinsmen; as a result, life becomes a little harder for everyone. Similarly, the Anishinaubae story depicts the difficulty and necessity of pushing through loss and returning to life after tragedy.

In short, these stories may tell us more about how we should live than about what happens when we die. Even the places where the dead are found have a this-worldly quality to them: our ancestors have not disappeared into some far-off, inaccessible alternative dimension, but are (relatively) nearby, and can affect our lives in direct, material ways.

Truth in Storytelling

As the above afterlife tales suggest, we should not assume that all stories are thought to be literally true by the people who tell them, or that the literal meaning of the story is the most important aspect. Some may well be understood to be fiction, or true only in a figurative or symbolic sense. The Kewa, for example, clearly distinguish between true stories called *ramani* (oral *history*) and fictional tales called *lidi* (oral *literature*). Among their many classifications of oral form, the **Nyanga** of Zaire similarly contrast *nganuriro* (true stories) with *karisi* (epic poems). Not all Indigenous people make this kind of distinction, of course, but many of them do.

We must also recognize that what others see as factual history may include elements that seem fictional to us. One Kewa story classified as *ramani*, for instance, concerns a leper who removes his diseased skin before attending a ceremonial dance, in order to appear healthy and beautiful.

To further complicate the issue, we must be careful about assuming that a particular story is an authorized or transparent reflection of a culture. It may be only a single storyteller's version, and the narrative details may reflect the teller's own preferences as much as they do the values or worldview of his or her culture. In other words, the story may be "true" only to the person who is sharing it.

Context

Perhaps the most important point to remember about interpreting Indigenous stories is that we almost never encounter them in their natural form: spoken to a group in their original language. Instead, most of us read them silently, to ourselves, in a colonial language such as English, in a time and a place that are usually far removed from the circumstances in which they would normally have been performed. It's hard to overestimate the effect of these differences. It would be something like the contrast between reading "Close your eyes and I'll kiss you . . ." and being part of the shrieking studio audience in February 1964 when the Beatles opened their first American television appearance, on *The Ed Sullivan Show*, with "All My Loving."

The shift from community performance to solitary reading has the potential to transform the meaning of a story. The act of telling is itself a ritual—many stories are told only in a particular place and time, and only by certain people. Similarly, not all stories are for everyone—some may be just for women, some for men, and some for children. When we lose all this context and tradition, what else is lost?

Writing the Spoken

Writing also diminishes the capacity of an oral story to change with the teller and the time. The same story told by a cheerful woman on a sunny day will likely seem much different if it is told by an angry man on a rainy night. And the stories themselves can alter or evolve in response to changing circumstances or needs, producing significant variations. But what happens when a story is committed to ink on paper? Is it fixed in place forever?

Perhaps, in certain ways. But writing may be less "fixed in place" than we tend to think. This fact becomes evident when we look at different written accounts of the same oral story. In various collections of Anishinaubae tales, for example, Basil Johnston has several times recounted the fight between the **trickster** Nanabush and his father Epingishmook (the spirit being who represents the

West, old age, and death). In one version, the two appear equally matched, and the battle ends only when Nanabush manages to cut his father with a piece of flint; in another, Epingishmook is the clear winner and stops the fight when Nanabush falls to the ground, exhausted and expecting to be killed by his father at any second.

Together, the two versions of the story emphasize that Nanabush is both a brave, strong warrior and a weak, cowardly one, making a point that might not be so clear in a single story that showed him behaving differently in different circumstances. In addition, the stories together raise the question of what is true about them, whether literally or symbolically.

Multiple versions of the same story also pose an important challenge: how are we to make sense of them all? Generally speaking, every Indigenous culture has thousands of stories, and every story may have many variations. There is no possible way to do justice to such variety here. Instead, we will consider just a few examples of two types of stories: those that in some way explain origins, and those featuring "trickster" figures. Doing so will highlight some of the points already mentioned, and also (with luck) show both the challenges and the rewards of trying to understand what these stories may be saying to—and about—the people who tell them.

Origin Stories

> No matter if they are fish, birds, men, women, animals, wind or rain. . . . All things in our country here have Law, they have ceremony and song, and they have people who are related to them.
> —Mussolini Harvey, **Yanyuwa** elder (in Swain and Trompf 1995: 24)

North America

Among the best-known origin stories are the Native North American "Earth Diver" tales. Several of their key elements are common to cultures across the eastern woodlands areas of Canada and the United States. Typically, the story begins with the world destroyed by flooding; then an animal or deity brings a bit of earth up from beneath the waters to begin rebuilding the land.

In one version Sky Woman, a spirit being, descends to earth during the flood. Seeing that she is pregnant, the giant turtle offers to let her rest on his back. She then asks the other animals to dive for some soil. Many try but fail, and they drown. In the end, it is one of the lowliest animals, the muskrat—who has been ridiculed by the others for offering to help—that succeeds.

Sky Woman breathes into the soil, which spreads across the turtle's back to become what is now called North America. Her breath infuses the earth with the spirit of life, nourishment, shelter, and inspiration for the heart and mind. She gives birth to twins—the ancestors of the people who tell this story—and she awards joint stewardship of the land to all beings who live there, whether human, spirit, or animal.

Africa

The African **Dogon** people also refer to a form of pregnancy in their origin stories, which tell how the supreme being, Amma, created the world (and humanity) essentially by accident. Out of loneliness, Amma transformed himself into a womb holding four new beings called Nummo; two of these were mostly male but partly female, and the other two were mostly female but partly male. Before their 60-year gestation period was complete, one of the males became so impatient to be with his sister that he tore away part of the womb searching for her. This torn part of the womb became the earth.

Life began when Amma sacrificed the sister, scattering the pieces of her body on the ground in order to purify the earth. After the departure of their transgressing brother, the two remaining Nummo clothed the earth with vegetation and infused it with a creative, universal life force called *nyama*. Amma and the Nummo also created eight beings who were placed in separate celestial chambers and prohibited from eating a certain type of

Sites

Bandiagara Escarpment, Western Africa

In the Dogon creation story, the supreme being Amma sacrificed one of the Nummo (his four children) and scattered the body's remains on the earth. The Bandiagara escarpment in Mali is one of the sites where the Dogon people erected shrines to house the pieces. Other such sites can be found throughout Western Africa.

grain. They became lonely and their food ran out, however, and so they gathered together and cooked the forbidden grain. When they were expelled from the heavens and crashed to earth, the world as we know it was created, including human life, culture, and speech.

Australia

The origin stories of the Australian Aborigines centre around events that occurred in a time and place unique to Australian conceptions, a time that nineteenth-century anthropologists famously (mis-)translated as "**The Dreaming**"; a more accurate translation might be "The Uncreated." Although anthropologists understand The Dreaming as archaic time, Aborigines themselves have traditionally given the impression that the events of The Dreaming occurred just a few generations before their own time. In other words, those events are out of reach of living memory, but they are not fixed in time. They are also recent enough to remain vital and meaningful to the communities that speak of them.

Unlike most Africans and Native North Americans, Australian Aborigines generally do not recognize a single divine authority from whom all life, values, rules, and so on, derive. Instead, stories of origin usually concern the first ancestors, whose actions shaped both the physical world and the cultural practices of their descendants.

There are countless stories of The Dreaming, but many tales reflect some basic patterns. For example, "Love Magic" (in the Document box, p. 315) explains how several elements important to the people—including the love magic ritual and a specific sacred site—originated in the actions of two ancestors, while reinforcing the community's prohibitions on incest and rape. The metamorphosis of the ancestors into physical formations on the land is typical of Dreaming tales.

Meanings

What do origin stories mean? It's certainly possible that they were (and perhaps still are) understood to be straightforward historical accounts. I have met many Native people in Canada who refer to North America as "Turtle Island" and who regard it as sacred. But to my knowledge none of them think that the continent was actually formed from a clump of mud on the back of a giant reptile.

In any case, we should also consider what other aspects of these stories might be important. First, as in the Kewa and Anishinaubae "afterlife" stories, relationships are central. Creation in each case results from a desire for community or companionship. Similarly, the central beings in each story are the ancestors of the people who tell it.

Second—and along the same lines—the stories typically underline the inherent relatedness of all aspects of existence. Just as the Australian Aborigines are related to ancestors from The Dreaming who remain connected to the landscape, all of existence is connected along a network of various pathways and intersections. The world in its

Sites

Uluru, Australia

An enormous sandstone formation in central Australia that is sacred to the local Aboriginal people, the Pitjantjatjara and Yankunytjatjara. These communities conduct ceremonies along the rock's base and in its caves, where ancestral markings from Dreamtime events are evident. Uluru itself was the result of such an event, when the earth rose up in grief after a bloody battle. In 1873 the colonial government named the formation "Ayers Rock" after the Chief Secretary of South Australia at the time, Sir Henry Ayers. The landmark became the first site in the Northern Territory to be officially designated in both English and an Aboriginal language in 1993, when it was renamed "Ayers Rock / Uluru"; and in 2002 another name change made it "Uluru / Ayers Rock." There has been much dispute over ownership of the site. In 1985 the Australian government finally agreed to transfer title to the Aboriginal community in exchange for a 99-year lease arrangement and tourist access, but the latter continues to be a point of contention. Aboriginals do not want tourists climbing Uluru, and although it is still permitted, various episodes—some of them involving golf, some nudity—have attracted renewed support for banning the climb.

Document

"Love Magic" (Australian Aborigine)

"Ngarlu" has three meanings in this story from central Australia. It is the flower of the ngarlkirdi (witchetty grub tree) as well as the name of a sacred site and of the ceremonies performed there. A "subsection" is a kinship group, while "hairstring" is string made from human hair, used to make many different items, from belts to wrappings for spears.

There was a Dreaming man named Linjiplinjipi of the Jungari subsection at this site. He had adorned his body with *Ngarlu* and was spinning hairstring. The whirling sound of his spinning tool [made of crossed sticks] attracted a woman of the Ngapangardi subsection [and therefore his mother-in-law]. He climbed the hill and as he was watching her she stopped to urinate. Sexually aroused, he continued to attract her with the noise. Finally, he caught her, forced her legs apart and raped her. Upon ejaculation, however, she closed her legs and her tight vagina dismembered his penis.

Today, at Ngarlu her vagina remains transformed into rock and the severed stone-penis is still embedded in it. *Linjiplinjipi* himself, in agony, went to the other side of the hill where he turned into a large boulder which has paintings upon it depicting his hairstring cross and his erect penis. *Yilpinji* ["love magic"] is performed modelled on *Linjiplinjipi's* methods of attracting his mother-in-law, using sticks from *Ngarlu* and adorning the torso with the flowers of the witchetty grub tree (Swain and Trompf 1995: 22–3).

entirety is infused with the spirit of the ancestors. Specific communities, however, would be more strongly joined to certain stories, and therefore to the specific elements of those stories (locations, rituals, beliefs, etc.).

Third, origin stories typically do not imagine the beginning of time. Instead, they presuppose the existence of the universe, and focus on the origin of certain elements within it—language, culture, landscape—that remain present, connecting us to the actions of our ancestors. Past and present are forever linked, and stories of origin remain deeply meaningful to our contemporary lives.

Finally, it's worth noting that these stories rarely present a simple, idealized picture of nature. They tell us that the world we live in is (at least in part) the product of violence: the result of a torn womb, a rape, a devastating flood. The Dogon tradition associates the creation of humans with loneliness and disobedience, while in North America many animals sacrificed themselves in their efforts to help Sky Woman and her baby. In other words, order, creation, and life in Indigenous origin stories are almost always connected to chaos, destruction, and death.

And, speaking of chaos . . .

Tricksters

"You know what I noticed? Nobody panics when things go according to plan, even if the plan is horrifying. If tomorrow I tell the press that, like, a gangbanger will get shot, or a truckload of soldiers will be blown up, nobody panics. Because it's all part of the plan. But when I say that one little old mayor will die, well then *everyone loses their minds*."
—Joker, in *The Dark Knight* (2008)

The concept of the trickster was developed by scholars to categorize a certain type of character that appears in the stories of many cultures, including those of

Contemporary Yolngu artist David Malangi in 1997, painting the Milmildjark Dreaming on bark. When the Australian government eventually compensated Malangi for using his work "Gurrmirringu's Mortuary Feast" on the one-dollar note, the payment marked the first recognition of Aboriginal copyright.

© Penny Tweedie/Alamy

the non-Indigenous "West"; Loki was the trickster in Norse mythology, while the ancient Greeks had Hermes. Although the people who told these stories did not conceive of such characters as "tricksters," and many trickster figures do not actually seem to have very much in common, the label has stuck.

Tricksters are sometimes referred to as "culture heroes," typically because they are the central figures in many (if not most) of a community's stories, and also because they often serve to teach the most important lessons in history, ethics, and

relationships. Once again, however, the ways in which these lessons are transmitted are not always simple or obvious.

Shape-changers

As their name implies, tricksters are hard to pin down. For one thing, they can usually shape-shift, and many tricksters are explicitly "zoomorphic" (that is, they take the form of animals). Examples include

- badger (Japan)
- coyote (North America)
- crow (North America)
- fox (South America)
- rabbit (Africa and North America)
- raven (North America)
- spider (Africa)
- tortoise (Africa)
- wolf (South America)

In addition, many tricksters are able to change their gender. Invariably the change is from male to female, and in some cases it is biological, though in others the trickster simply puts on women's clothing and uses prosthetics to mimic female sexual characteristics. In one Cree story, Wichikapache physically transforms himself into the perfect woman in order to teach a lesson to a conceited young man, who refuses to marry because he cannot find a woman good enough for him. The trickster even becomes pregnant, but when the children are born as wolf cubs the trick is revealed and the young man is humiliated.

The various changes in the trickster's outer form are reflected in other inconstancies. Tricksters are typically related to both the spirit and material/human worlds; though in general they are more than human, they are almost always less than gods. They can be selfless or greedy, kind or cruel, funny or deadly serious. They may be fools, but they may also reveal fools. And while very often their behaviour is scandalous, explicitly violating the social order, this is not always a bad thing. Sometimes the social order *needs* to be violated, and sometimes the most effective way to make this point is through laughter.

Self and Others

So how do we know when to imitate the trickster's example and when to do the opposite? Often the main clue is the trickster's motivation: whether a particular action is intended to help others or is driven by self-interest alone. In other words, our judgment depends on understanding what is good for the community. One of the most common scenarios centres on the male trickster's efforts to satisfy his enormous sexual appetite. These efforts often

Document

"Red Willows" (Anishinaubae)

Nanabush was wandering in the far north. He was hungry. Nanabush was always hungry.

He was with his mother at the time. That old lady is known by many names. Some call her "Dodomum" or "Dodum"; others call her "Gushiwun" or "Gushih."

They wandered until Nanabush chanced to meet a bear. "Ha!" he announced. "I'm going to eat you!" "Oh no you don't," replied the bear. "I will fight back if you try to kill me. Get out of here, Nanabush."

Nanabush would not leave. "Listen," he pleaded, "I'm hungry. Can't you see that? I'm hungry. I've eaten next to nothing for about three days. Maybe four days! I'm going to kill you."

They started fighting somewhere over there, somewhere near Kenora. They battled tooth and nail. They fought in a number of different places along the way, even where Sault Ste Marie now stands. At the rapids. That really happened. That was all land then. At that time there was no channel of water flowing there.

First, Nanabush would hit the bear; then the bear would hit Nanabush. One time, Nanabush threw the bear so hard against the ground he broke the earth, and water began to flow through. That in fact is the reason the water now flows past Sault Ste Marie.

Finally, Nanabush said to his mother, "You go on ahead and stay there. When I get there too, I will kill this bear." As soon as the word was given, she was gone.

She could hear them battling in the distance. At one point, the bear sent Nanabush flying with such force that he landed on his mother, causing her to fall backwards onto her rump. That is why the lake there is called "The Old Lady Sat Down."

They fought all along the way. The evidence of it is still there. At the place that is now called Sudbury they hurled rocks at one another.

Where they pulled boulders up from the earth, ore was later found. Where they dragged each other along the ground, depressions were made in the land.

Eventually, Nanabush killed the bear, in the general vicinity of Parry Sound.

Meanwhile, his mother came along behind, carrying supplies. She made a fire and put a pot of water over it. Nanabush butchered the bear. When it was cooked, he ate and ate. But he ate too much and very soon suffered the runs.

"Oh!" He ran over there. "Ah!" Such discomfort. He could not stop going to the toilet. When he sat down to defecate, blood also flowed. He couldn't find anything to use to wipe himself, so he grabbed a sapling and used that. Then he stuck the sapling—with the blood and feces on it—into the earth, somewhere near Parry Sound.

A red willow grew at that spot. Its colour came from the blood of Nanabush.

That is how the red willows came to be (Johnston 1995: 33–7).

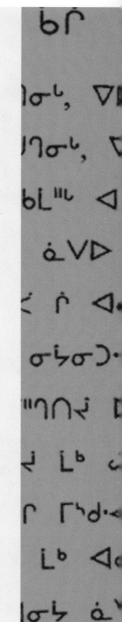

"Red Willows," by contemporary Anishinaubae artist David Johnson.

result in some kind of disaster, either for the trickster himself or for his victim(s). Such stories testify to the understanding that unrestrained (male) sexuality poses a serious threat to society.

In contrast, the Anishinaubae story "Red Willows" shows Nanabush displaying obvious consideration for his mother. He tells her to get out of harm's way while he fights a bear, and he keeps his promise to rejoin her when the battle is done. Presumably these are admirable qualities, as he defeats the bear and assuages his (and his mother's) hunger. However, he is also extremely self-indulgent and shows no restraint when eating the bear—a transgression for which he immediately pays a painful price.

Like many trickster stories, "Red Willows" explains the origins of certain elements of the physical world that was home to the community connected to the tale, from the river at Sault Ste Marie to the rugged terrain around Sudbury. And since those (colonial) towns are named, we know that this is either a modern retelling of an old tale or one of the new stories of Nanabush that continue to appear. Finally, we learn that the red willows got their colour from Nanabush's bloody feces. Here we have another wonderful illustration of a view of nature that is not naively idealized, and that recognizes holistic connections between the beautiful and the ugly or painful.

Chaos and Order

Like the origin stories, trickster tales such as "Red Willows" also attribute the creation of aspects of our world to violent, destructive activity. In other stories the trickster invents the bow and arrow; breaks the teeth in women's vaginas to make intercourse possible; initiates pregnancy and menstruation; and introduces death. Despite his association with chaos, then, the trickster also brings a kind of order to the world.

The Yoruba trickster, Eshu, is an explicit example of such activity. Eshu delights in chaos, and is constantly playing pranks on the Yoruba in the hope that disorder will result. But his tricks work only when the people, forgetting the importance of community stability, become greedy or lazy, or behave stupidly. In one story Eshu wears a special hat, black on one side and red on the other, while walking between two friends; each seeing only one side of the hat, the friends fight over what colour it is and wind up bitter enemies for no reason at all.

Thus trickster stories, like tricksters themselves, can play many roles: they can show us how we *should* behave, or should *not*; they can help to explain the origins of the world, and connect a community more deeply to specific locations; and whether they are funny or scary, thoughtful or silly, simple or complex, they are almost always entertaining and highly provocative. They embody the extremes of humanity, and all of our contradictions: our weaknesses and strengths; our selfishness and compassion; our humiliations and our triumphs.

It's also worth noting again that, while there is greater gender diversity in newer stories, almost all the traditional trickster figures we know of are male. Here too, one reason may be that trickster stories were, until relatively recently, recorded only by male European academics. It is possible that those men had no interest in female trickster stories. It is also possible that if such stories did exist, they were the preserve of women and the male scholars never inquired about them, presuming that any important cultural knowledge was carried by the community's men.

On the other hand, it may be that for some communities most of the trickster's typical activities—hunting, travelling, unrestrained sex—were in fact associated mainly or even exclusively with men. If so, we might be justified in supposing that even though tricksters are specialists in social transgression, gender roles may represent one boundary that (until recently) even these cagey figures have had difficulty transcending.

✿ Practice

Ritual

> If you ask what is the greatest thing
> I will tell you
> It is people, people, people.
> —Maori proverb (in Webber-Dreadon 2002: 258)

Rituals perform the same functions in Indigenous cultures that they do in every culture. They identify and remind us of what is important in life—or, more precisely, what the culture we live in understands to be important. In religious terms, their explicit purpose is to communicate in some way with gods, ancestors, or spirits. At the same time, rituals remain rooted in very *human* needs and relationships.

Varieties

Around the world, followers of virtually every religious tradition affirm their faith through the performance of daily domestic rituals. Many of these rituals involve food—one of the most common and vital elements of life. Thus Jews and Muslims observe kosher and halal regulations; many Buddhists set a portion of each meal aside in a shrine for their ancestors; and the Anishinaubae traditionally put a small amount of food in a dish for the spirits. Australian Aborigines practise rites aimed at maintaining the balance and abundance of the animal species they rely on for food; these ceremonies are often very simple, and may involve nothing more than singing the song of the ancestor while rubbing a pile of stones.

Other rituals are more complex and much less frequent, marking critical moments in the life of individuals (birth, marriage, death), the community (departure of a powerful leader, liberation from

Sites

Bighorn Medicine Wheel, United States

In general, a medicine wheel or sacred hoop is a circular arrangement of stones with radial lines from the centre to the rim, designed to facilitate communication with spirits. Located in Wyoming at an elevation of roughly 3,000 metres (almost 10,000 feet), the Bighorn Medicine Wheel is arguably the most important sacred hoop in North America. Blackfoot, Crow, Cheyenne, Sioux, and Arapahoe communities continue to use the site for vision quests, healing rituals, and prayers for guidance and wisdom.

slavery, completion of a great project), or the natural world (annual cycles, great disasters, rich harvests). Sometimes these rituals mark transformations, and sometimes they help to bring transformation about. It is this less frequent, more dramatic type of ritual that will be discussed in detail in this section.

Meaning and Structure

When someone who has been ill recovers after a ritual healer asks an ancestor spirit to remove the illness, does the healer (or the patient, or the community) believe that the illness has actually been removed by the spirit? Those of us who are not Indigenous may ask the same questions about our own rituals. To what extent does a young Jewish girl change objectively, at the moment of her bat mitzvah, into an adult woman? How many Catholics believe they drink the literal blood of Christ when they take communion?

It seems evident that many people, past and present, have believed in the literal truth of their religious stories and rituals. Once again, though, we often separate Indigenous traditions from other world religions by treating their ritual practices as "magic" rather than "religion," implying that "they" believe in things that obviously are not true, whereas "we" do not. In fact, many Indigenous and non-Indigenous people alike believe in the literal truth of at least some of their religious traditions, and many others in both groups take a more figurative approach.

In either case, when we look closely at the rituals of any Indigenous culture, what we find is a system of formal yet creative activities through which the members of the community relate to the world and to one another. Such activities tap into the people's deepest beliefs about the origins of the world, the existence of order, and the beginnings of life. Repeating them therefore serves in some way to recreate key aspects of the world, of order, of life. In this sense, we can see ritual as an indicator both of the human need for meaning and structure in a world that is often random and frightening, and of the human capacity to create such meaning and structure.

Rites of Passage

All people who go to the sacred bush benefit from it. They may be observers; they may be priests; they may be the initiate. Only we concentrate on the initiate most. Yet everybody is involved, particularly the priests, for there is a belief . . . that we are reborning ourselves. Even we priests, we are getting another rebirth.

—Ositola, **Yoruba** (in Drewal 2002: 133)

The Journey

Many cultures around the world regard life as a journey or quest; this perspective forms the central metaphor of a huge number of pop/rock songs ("Like a Rolling Stone," "Proud Mary," "Born to Run," "Road to Nowhere"), and is also indicated by the sacred Yoruba text in the box on the next page. Rituals highlight points along the way, but they also constitute journeys on their own. This understanding is most clearly evident in rites of passage, rituals that explicitly mark a change of state and that may involve *literal* journeys.

Typically, such rituals take participants away from their community—the site of social order and familiarity—to a new place with unfamiliar rules, where some sort of transformation occurs. For males this place is often outside, in the forest or the bush or the desert, whereas for many female rites of passage it is a domestic space of some sort. Once the ritual is complete the participant returns home, often with a physical change, such as a tattoo, scar, or missing body part to symbolize their new mode of being. While away, he or she exists in a kind of in-between or "liminal" state, after the death of the old self but before the birth of the new, neither the person they once were nor the person they will become.

In South Africa, for example, young **Pondos** are moved into a special, separate hut during their long initiation to become *sangomas*, or sacred healers. If they go into town before the ritual is completed, their faces and bodies must be covered in

Document

Yoruba Verse

This verse from the sacred literature of the Yoruba (known as the Odu Ifa) describes life as a quest.

A small child works his way off the edge of his sleeping mat.
A bird soars high above it all.
They divined for our elderly people,
When they were preparing to leave heaven to go to the world. They said, what are we going to do?
They asked themselves, where are we going?

We are going in search of knowledge, truth, and justice.
In accordance with our destiny,
At the peak of the hill
We were delayed.
We are going to meet success.
We will arrive on earth knowledgeable.
We will arrive on earth in beauty.
We are searching for knowledge continuously.
Knowledge has no end (Drewal 2002: 129).

white—the colour of transformation throughout most of Africa—to indicate that they are in the midst of a journey between the realms of the living and the ancestors. This initiation is most often

Daniel Lainé

Young Pondo women from Transkei in South Africa during their initiation to become sacred healers.

undertaken by women, and is complete only when the initiates receive a dream of a particular animal, the incarnation of the ancestor who will authorize them to become a *sangoma*.

Many Anishinaubae undertake a similar initiation, known as a **vision quest**. After years of guidance and preparation for this ritual, a young man on the verge of adulthood travels far from home to a designated site in the wilderness where the spirits dwell. Typically, this is the first time he has ever been completely alone in his life.

The boy has no food, only water. He endures cold and hunger, as well as fear of the wilderness and of harmful unseen forces. With luck, the spirits will give him dreams or visions that reveal his true self and the role he is to play in his community. After several days, an adult male will arrive with food and take the initiate home. If the religious leader determines that the boy did experience true spirit visions during the quest, the ritual is complete and the boy is accepted into the group as an adult man.

Behind the Curtain

The rite of passage for Wiradjuri males in eastern Australia also involves a literal journey, along with fear and pain. At the appointed time, the women and children of the village are covered with branches and blankets. They hear a roaring sound, identified as the voice of the spirit being Daramulun; they feel burning brands being thrown about. Daramulun then takes the boys away to the bush, where he will devour them and regurgitate them back as men. The boys are led away looking only at the ground, with the roaring all about them. While they are covered with blankets, each one has an incisor tooth knocked out. Then fires appear again and the boys are told that Daramulun is coming to burn them.

At the height of their terror, however, the boys receive a shock. Their blankets are removed and the men of the village reveal that they have been acting as Daramulun all along. It was the men who took the boys' teeth, who set the fires, and who made the voice of the spirit being using bull-roarers. It's much like Toto pulling aside the curtain to show Dorothy that the Great and Powerful Oz is simply an old man, except that in this case the deceivers reveal themselves.

When the boys return to the village, therefore, they are truly transformed. They have been initiated into a secret (male) knowledge about the spirit world. They have also formed a bond with one another through their shared experiences of fear and revelation. When they return to the village they do so as men, are given new adult names, and take up residence outside their parents' homes.

In revealing that the initiates have been tricked, doesn't this ritual expose the community's religious beliefs as false? Not necessarily. Sam Gill argues that its point is to demonstrate that what is genuinely meaningful lies beyond the surface of reality, beyond what we can see, hear, feel, taste, and touch. By exposing their trickery, the men produce "a disenchantment with a naive view of reality, that is, with the view that things are what they appear to be" (Gill 1982: 81). In this way, the boys experience a true death of their old selves—their youthful view of the world.

Sacrifice

We are imitating what the gods or holy people have done. It is a return to the beginning.
—Blackhorse Mitchell, Navajo (in Beck et al. 1992 [1977]: 76)

In Mel Gibson's film *Apocalypto* (2006), Mayan priests cut out the beating hearts of captured villagers, cook them, and make offerings of them to appease the gods and end the famine that is afflicting the people. Although it is true that some Indigenous cultures did perform human sacrifices, there are still several problems with the scenario presented by Gibson. Aside from the historical inaccuracies that some scholars have pointed out, *Apocalypto* perpetuates common misunderstandings about the nature of sacrifice itself. These issues become clearer when we consider some real examples of the practice.

Bears, Men, and Cows

Sacrificial rituals are extremely common among Indigenous cultures. At one time the central religious ceremony of the Ainu of northern Japan, for example, was bear sacrifice. They would capture a young cub, raise it for two or three years, shoot it with ceremonial arrows, and then finally kill it. The carcass was specially prepared—often the head was emptied out and filled with flowers—and then the animal was cooked and eaten by the entire village.

Among the Aboriginal peoples of the North American plains, the **Sun Dance** is an annual ritual lasting several days. Inside a specially created lodge, people who have vowed to take part in the ritual dance to the point of exhaustion while the community provides support and encouragement. In some cultures, such as the Sioux, the Sun Dance includes a kind of self-sacrifice: male dancers fast, pierce their chests and backs, and attach themselves to a central pole with ropes tied to sticks that are inserted through the piercings. They may be partially or entirely suspended off the ground, and they dance until they pass out or their fastenings tear loose.

In Africa, the **Nuer** regularly sacrifice an ox for purposes that range from celebration to healing to atonement for moral transgressions. The **Xhosa** people perform a similar but more complex ritual when a young woman falls ill and a **diviner** determines that she is being punished by an ancestor spirit. To restore good relations between the woman's home and the ancestor, a cow is consecrated and then speared. The cry of the animal opens up the path of communication with the spirit world, along which the words of the ritual elder requesting help can travel. Inside the woman's home, a special piece of the animal is cooked. One part is given to the woman, who sucks it and throws it to the back of the house as a sign that she is throwing away her illness. The woman is given a second piece of meat, which she holds while being chastised for behaving in a manner displeasing to the ancestor(s). She consumes the meat and is congratulated for having "eaten the ancestor." Then the rest of the cow is cooked and eaten by the entire community in group celebration.

Community and Ritual Action

When we compare these rituals to the sacrifice in *Apocalypto*, two major differences become clear. First, there is no real social significance to the film's ritual, no communal participation beyond a sense of general bloodlust. For the Ainu, the Sioux, and the Xhosa, however, communal participation is crucial. Even though the sacrifice itself is performed by designated people, everyone becomes involved in some way, whether by providing guidance and support to the dancers during their ordeal or simply by sharing in the group meal. The ritual ultimately brings people together. By contrast, the priests in the film are portrayed as corrupt and the ritual ultimately helps to tear the community apart.

The second difference is that *Apocalypto* presents the sacrifice as a simple offering made to the gods or spirits in return for some reward. The Mayans in the film want food, and apparently the gods want human hearts—it's a simple exchange. Yet in many cultures, the object of sacrifice itself is clearly not of such central importance. When necessary, the Nuer can replace the ox with a cucumber. Similarly, if no suitable cow is available to the Xhosa, beer is used instead.

The fact that such substitutions are possible suggests that, in some cases at least, the item used is far less meaningful than the ritual actions themselves. When the Xhosa do sacrifice a cow, for example, why don't they just kill and eat it? Why go through all the complex stages? What appears to be primarily at stake here is the woman's behaviour in relation to notions of social order set down by the ancestors and reinforced by (male) ritual elders. The community thus shares both in naming the transgression that led to her illness, and in the meal generated by the ritual that heals her.

Why is a special lodge built for the Sun Dance? The creation of the lodge replicates the creation of the world, and is accompanied by songs that tell of this creation. The pole used in the dance is a newly-cut cottonwood tree; in its state between life and death and its physical positioning at the centre of the lodge, it links our material world to the world of the spirits. Physically attached to this tree, the dancers are thus also tied to the spirits and to the earliest times.

Why did the Ainu fill the bear's head with flowers? Because, in their eyes, the animal was not a regular bear but the mountain god in disguise, and the ritual killing of his bear form was necessary to release the god's spirit back to his own realm. The Ainu were not offering a bear to the god; rather, from primordial times onward the god became a bear, over and over again, as a gift to the Ainu. The flowers were an expression of the community's gratitude.

In each case, the ritual actions relate to the spiritual and sometimes physical establishment of the community, or of the world itself. Like rites of passage, sacrificial practices thus play a key role in (re-)creating order and meaning. In re-enacting ancient events, these rituals clearly join people to the past, and yet they also respond to current situations and needs. Thus they reflect and re-establish the common Indigenous sense of time as rhythmic, neither purely linear nor entirely cyclical. Individuals and communities are always changing over time; nothing ever repeats exactly. But in the course of their journeys, people do need to be replenished, and through ritual they return to a source that sustains them.

♨ Cultural Expressions

The array of art forms traditionally produced by Indigenous cultures is extraordinarily rich and diverse, including (among others) architecture, songs, baskets, clothing, statues, paintings, drums, pipes, mats, headdresses, amulets, masks, and tapestries. In each community, some art forms will exist almost entirely for religious purposes; some will be entwined with religion at specific times only; and others may have very little to do with religion.

What You See

> If you don't live the things that go with it, then it's only a design. It's not a *moko* [traditional Maori tattoo].
> —George Tamihana Nuku, Maori (in Mitchell 2003)

With a good deal of Indigenous creative work, what you see is not at all what you get. In some cases, you don't see (or get) anything at all by the time the work is done, because the piece has been consumed by the same process that brought it into being.

A key element of the *malagan* death rituals of Papua New Guinea, for example, is the creation and burning of delicate sculptures made from fibre, wood, bark, and feathers. Likewise, the beautiful and complex Navajo sand paintings must be erased the day they are made if they are to perform their healing function; through ceremony, the cosmic pictures become identified with the patient's

sickness, and it is only through the sand painting's destruction that health can be restored.

Other works, like those discussed below—cloth, **totem poles**, *mbari* shrines—are created from natural materials that decay over time. The works are very often understood as living things, which can (and should) dissolve back into the world when their time is done. Even when the work remains, it may still be relatively bereft of meaning (and life) when we look at it, especially if it is completely removed from its native context. Without knowing what an African mask or Native American basket is used for, and why, we can hardly have any idea what it represents.

In this respect, "art" in Indigenous cultures is fundamentally about relationships. There is a network that connects an object to the person or people who created it; to the ritual in which it is used; to the community it is meant to serve; to the stories that underlie their worldview. These relationships are in many ways vital to the culture in question, and, depending on the context, some or even all aspects of the network—object, creation, ritual, stories—may be considered religious. To illustrate the varied, complex ways in which Indigenous art forms are related to Indigenous religion, we will consider three examples: weaving, carving, and building.

Weaving

> It all starts from the beginning with roots. How the basket makes itself. Like two people meeting. . . . What I'm talking about when I'm talking about my baskets is my life, the stories, the rules, how this things is living, what they do to you.
> —Mabel McKay, **Pomo** (in Sarris 1992: 23–4)

The relationships that are central to Indigenous creative work are well symbolized by weaving. To weave is to intertwine, to connect. Even in modern English, we speak of the "social fabric," the "warp and weft" of history, friendships, or community life. In most cultures, traditional weaving is a social activity; weavers work together, helping (and watching) one another, sharing stories, passing on their skills to younger generations. In addition, the products of weaving often have both a religious meaning and a practical purpose. These functions reflect and reinforce the bonds among the people of a community, as well as the bonds between the people and their environment, their ancestors, and their gods.

Sacred Thread

In Maori tradition, all weavers are female. A prospective weaver is selected as a baby and a special prayer is spoken over her. As she grows up, she learns from her mother, her aunts, her grandmothers, until the art becomes a natural part of her. But her destiny is not fixed. The more she learns, the more the women *discourage* her from weaving. This is a test. The girl must persevere, to demonstrate her true commitment. When her elders are satisfied, she is at last initiated into the *whare pora* ("house of weaving"), which is not a physical building but the collective of weavers in the community. Only then does she come to understand why the weft used to create the pattern and design in Maori weaving is *te aho tapu*—"the sacred thread."

The *whare pora* women are the caretakers of the weaving traditions. These include not only the physical techniques and skills, but the rituals that are essential to every aspect of the craft. For example: materials used in weaving must be specially prepared; sex is prohibited the night before dyeing fibres; no food may be consumed while weaving; fine garments must be woven during daylight; and no strangers can view any work until it is completed.

To weave is to be part of an ancient trust, a gift brought to humanity by Niwareka, daughter of the lightning god Uetonga. The patterns and techniques that she gave the Maori people became the foundation of all future works. The goddess of weaving is Hine-te-iwaiwa, who also presides over healing and childbirth and is often associated both with the moon and with menstruation.

The traditional colours used in Maori weaving—black, red, and white—symbolize the basic forces of creation. Black represents the realm of potential being, the darkness from which the earth emerged; white represents the process of coming into being, the energies that make life possible; and red represents the realm of being and light, the physical world itself. The sacred thread thus runs not only through all garments, which join the members of the community together, but also through time, linking past and present, and through the various realms of existence, entwining people in the divine nature of the cosmos itself.

Undying Cloth

Of course it is not just the process of weaving that has religious significance, but the final product itself. Around the world, a key function of clothing is to declare who we are, how we fit into the "social fabric." Are we Muslim or Hindu, artist or lawyer, man or woman, heterosexual or homosexual, poor or rich? And yet clothing literally has two sides: it can hide as much as it reveals, helping us to construct a public face while obscuring certain aspects of both our bodies and our identities.

Lady Gaga is a great (if perhaps extreme) example of the double-sided nature of clothing. Her costumes and masks hide her private self from view, but reveal those aspects of her identity that she wishes to make public. Part of the woman is Lady Gaga the performance artist, but another part is Stefani Germanotta, graduate of a Catholic private school in Manhattan. In addition, Gaga's apparel announces her individuality while also showing her connection and indebtedness to a community of modern pop figures that includes Madonna and Michael Jackson, and even—through the crown she wears in her "Bad Romance" video—the artist Jean-Michel Basquiat.

In virtually all societies, special cloths are also associated with important rituals—baptisms, graduations, weddings, funerals. These cloths help to set such occasions apart from everyday life. Ideally, the outer form of the cloth reveals (rather than hides) one's true self at these moments, as it announces to the community that a genuine inner change has taken place. Given that rites of passage represent

Sites

Ife, Nigeria

The ancient site in Nigeria where the Yoruba deities Oduduwa and Obatala began the creation of the world. Many Yoruba communities still celebrate this act at the annual Itapa festival in Ife—now a city of roughly 500,000.

a symbolic death and rebirth, it is fitting that the Bunu Yoruba, of central Nigeria, consider the special cloth worn for such rites to be a kind of womb, enveloping the body as if it were a fetus waiting to be born.

The Bunu have a key saying in this regard: "Cloth only wears, it does not die" (Renne 1995: 9). The saying reflects a belief that, just as old cloth is continually replaced by new, so the spirits of the ancestors are reborn into the bodies of children. A special ritual cloth, *orun pada*, is used to divine the identity of such ancestors. Once a child is understood to be a reborn spirit, he or she may at any time wear the *orun pada* used in the divination ritual.

Many people picture very colourful fabrics when they think of African textiles—such as the famous Kente cloth from Ghana—but in fact the most common traditional cloth is white. There are various reasons for this, but among the Bunu Yoruba one important reason has to do with religious meaning. The Bunu understand white to represent any colour from transparent to light grey; thus "white" describes a range of items, from human secretions (milk, semen) to aspects of nature (air, water), and religious phenomena (spirits, heaven).

White cloth—traditionally woven by Bunu women only—is thus used in many instances to bridge the gap between the physical world and the spirit world, between living people and their ancestors. For example:

- wearing white cloth remedies certain types of disorder caused by destructive spirits (miscarriage, anger, illness);
- wrapping white cloth around the trunks of sacred trees may appease the spirits living inside them;
- a white cloth is wound around a pot of objects used to help bring rain;
- at burial, people are swathed in white cloth to facilitate rebirth as an ancestor; and
- the supreme being *Olorun* is sometimes described as "The One clothed in white."

For the Bunu Yoruba, then, white cloth plays a key role in helping members of the community cope with—and find meaning in—the disruptions and pain of disease, drought, conflict, and even death. From the outside, one would likely never suspect that this simple-looking material could have such meaning and power.

Spirit Baskets

Basket weaving is one of the oldest and most widespread of all the arts. Because the tradition goes back so far, and because the baskets themselves decay into nothingness, much of the history of basket weaving cannot be traced. Baskets come in a staggering variety of patterns, colours, materials, sizes, and shapes. They may also be used to hold an enormous array of items, from food and babies to spirits and prayers, and have been used in ceremonies for all stages of life from birth to death.

Baskets also figure in the sacred stories of many cultures. The Hebrew Bible tells how the infant Moses' mother put him in a basket and set it in the river, to be found by Pharaoh's daughter (Exodus

2: 3–5). Tane, the Maori god of light and wisdom, climbed to heaven to bring three baskets of knowledge back to earth (knowledge of all ritual matters; of acts of harm and aggression among people; and of peace and well-being). A Navajo story describes the origin of small birds such as wrens, warblers, and titmice: a woman plucked the feathers of several winged monsters and put them in her basket, but when she passed through a forbidden territory filled with sunflowers, the feathers were transformed into tiny birds and flew out of the basket.

Mabel McKay (1907–91) was a traditional healer of the Pomo people, and one of the most famous basket makers in the world. Her work is collected in various museums, including the Smithsonian. In addition to holding jobs as a washerwoman, factory employee, and seasonal fruit picker, for much of her adult life Mabel gave lectures on baskets and Native American culture at universities in California.

Mabel's basket making was interwoven with her healing practices, as she would give each patient a tiny basket for health and protection, or instruction in making one. Some of her miniature baskets were the size of a pea, and it was impossible to see their intricate patterns without a magnifying glass.

In Pomo communities, men traditionally wove the heavy baskets used for work like hunting and fishing; women were responsible for the baskets that had more explicitly religious purposes, and therefore had to follow specific rules in creating them. As in most Indigenous communities, rituals were prescribed for obtaining and preparing the materials to be used, and the weaving process was surrounded by restrictions. Thus weavers were forbidden to make baskets at all when menstruating or consuming alcohol. They were also forbidden to include representations of humans in their designs, or to reproduce the designs of medicine weavers such as Mabel.

This last rule reflected the fact that those designs were the product of personal spiritual visions. Such visions were for the weaver alone, and were relevant to particular situations. Although Mabel followed the traditions of her culture, and wove with respect for the people, history, and stories of her community, her baskets were always individual, unique.

Even more than usual, then, her baskets were living things, which both reflected and communicated her sacred visions. Thus, when asked if she had been taught to weave baskets by her grandmother or mother, she replied: "No, spirit teach me, since I was small child" (Sarris 1992: 25).

Carvings

What annoys me is that a lot of totem poles that go up have no plaque or information. People who come by wonder, "Who did this? What's it all about?" Every time I carve a totem pole, there's always a kind of signature to identify my family or my nation, the Nisga'a.
—Norman Tait (1993: 11), **Nisga'a**

Masks

The difference that context makes in understanding the meaning of cultural objects is well illustrated by African masks. Non-Africans usually encounter these masks only in museums, where they exist as shadows of their former selves. Used as intended, the masks come alive as part of the community's most important ritual activities: initiations, weddings, hunting celebrations, funerals, harvests, war preparations. There is no comparison between the lifeless husk stuck on a post behind glass, and the fully animate ritual object that links its wearer with the world of spirits, ancestors, and gods.

Across Africa there are thousands of mask designs, created from a great variety of materials including wood, brass, ivory, bronze, copper, glazed pottery, and textiles. Some aspects of their meaning may be apparent even to the outsider, but we always need to be cautious in our interpretations. Although masks are typically meant to bring a spirit into the community, it is important to remember that in African traditions the supreme being is never represented by any physical object: therefore masks can relate only to lesser deities.

Also, the fact that certain masks clearly represent certain animals does not mean (as was once assumed) that the people who use them worship those animals. In Mali, both the Dogon and Bamana cultures use antelope masks in agricultural ceremonies that have little to do with actual antelopes. And even in this instance, the symbolic meanings are not identical: for the Dogon the antelope represents hard work, whereas for the Bamana the animal's horns symbolize tall sprouts of grain.

When we focus only on the form of a mask, without reference to the context in which it is used, we can easily miss the meaning of certain critical elements. The Epa masks of the Yoruba, for example, are not only complex and intricately carved, but also extremely heavy. The weight reflects their function in rituals celebrating the male passage into adulthood. The strength required to dance with such a mask is a literal representation of the wearer's ability to take on his responsibilities as an adult member of the community.

Another unseen—but equally important—aspect of the mask is the process of its creation. Carvers have traditionally been male, trained as apprentices to master carvers who hold positions of high esteem in their societies. Ritual formalities are no less central in the creation of a mask than they are in the final ceremony for which it is made. Typically, for example, carvers must work in isolation while fasting, abstaining from any sexual activity, and avoiding contact both with women and with anything connected to death.

Totem Poles

Produced by the Aboriginal peoples of the Pacific Northwest Coast, totem poles pose similar challenges of context and symbolism. As with the masks, the various markings and carving styles are highly specific to particular communities and locations; those familiar with these traditions would immediately know, on encountering a totem pole, whose territory they had entered.

Yet for many years now, totem poles have been removed from their homes. Poles with little or no connection to one another, from different cultures and with different functions, are often gathered together in a kind of outdoor museum such as

Stanley Park in Vancouver. Some groups have fought this trend—in 2006 the **Haisla** of northern British Columbia successfully retrieved from Sweden's Museum of Ethnography a sacred totem pole that had been stolen from them almost 80 years earlier.

Ironically, the word "totem" is derived from the Anishinaubae word *dodaem*, which has been variously translated as "heart," "nourishment," and "kinship group." But the Anishinaubae (who live thousands of kilometres to the east) never made totem poles, and the cultures of the Pacific Northwest themselves never used the word "totem." The **Tsimshian** people—to pick just one example—call such a pole a *ptsan*.

Normally carved from a single cedar tree, a pole can survive for a century or so. It is traditionally regarded as a living thing and is allowed to rot naturally; some believe that to physically preserve a totem pole is to interfere with the natural order of the world. Certain communities even forbid the "preservation" of poles in drawings or photographs.

The meaning of a particular totem pole depends on its intended use. Some were designed primarily to serve as supporting structures or grave markers; others, as symbols of status or power. Most, however, tell stories. Some stories are mainly historical, recounting achievements, murders, arguments, victories, defeats, marriages, ancestral lineages, and so on. But other stories are more explicitly religious, relating to particular beliefs, or to the tales of great figures such as Raven or Thunderbird (among the most powerful of all North American spirits, Thunderbird is responsible for great storms).

The photos on page 329 show two totem poles. The pole on the left may appear more ornate than the other but is actually much simpler, depicting only two main figures. Grizzly Bear is at the base, holding a human, which usually represents self-preservation or survival. Thunderbird, a symbol of strength, is at the top. The pole's relative simplicity reflects the fact that it was one of a pair created to serve as house posts, holding the roof beam of a building.

The pole on the right, carved by Norman Tait (with Robert and Isaac Tait), tells a more

Totem poles in Vancouver's Stanley Park reflect different creative ends: to support a roof (left), and to tell the story of the Tait family crest (right).

complicated story. The family is first of all represented by the man at the top, who is holding Eagle to signify their clan. There are five disembodied faces on the pole representing five ancestral brothers who one day saw two beavers emerge from their home, remove their skin, and become men (the two figures beside the hole at the base of the pole). The figures told the five brothers that they were being slaughtered by the humans, so the brothers sang a sad song that froze the river, protecting the beavers (who can be seen climbing the pole). This is how the Tait family came to adopt the Beaver for its crest.

Moko

Maori carvings are less likely than totem poles or masks to be displayed outside their original physical context. This is because many of them are an integral part of the ancestral meeting house, or *whare whakairo* (literally, "carved house"), for which they were created. The figures that decorate these houses are ancestors such as Tihori, of the Ngati Awa in Bay of Plenty, New Zealand. The carving of Tihori in the Bay of Plenty meeting house holds a *taiaha*, a weapon used in hand-to-hand combat, which symbolizes his role and accomplishments as a warrior. Tihori is also covered with traditional Maori tattoos, or **moko** (literally, "to strike" or "to tap"). These same markings can be seen on some contemporary Maori men and women, including the famous **Tuhoe** activist Tame Iti.

Originally chiselled (not just inked) into the skin, these markings identify both the individual and his or her relationship to the community. Some *moko* elements may signify education level, personal and family rank, tribal history, or ancestral

Tame Iti, an outspoken and sometimes controversial Maori activist who is well known for his full facial *moko*.

connections; other designs may simply be marks of beauty or ferocity in battle. Traditionally, women were allowed tattoos only on or around their lips and chin, while men could receive markings on their entire face.

A key design that is repeated on Iti's face is the *koru*, or frond/spiral, the most common (and important) of all *moko* elements. A Maori proverb helps explain its meaning: "As one fern frond dies, another is born to take its place." This suggests that the *koru*'s primary meaning has to do with birth, regeneration, and sustainability, but that it can also represent the ancestors themselves, who gave birth to the Maori and who continue to sustain them.

Beyond this symbolism, the art of *moko* itself is directly linked to the Maori ancestors. Uetonga, the god of lightning, developed *moko* in imitation of the marks that his grandfather Ru, god of

earthquakes, had left on the face of the primal parent, the earth. One day Uetonga's daughter Niwareka (who brought weaving to humanity) journeyed to the world of the living and fell in love with the Maori ancestral chief Mataora. The two married and lived together until Mataora, in a jealous rage, hit Niwareka and she fled home. In sorrow, Mataora followed her and came upon Uetonga tattooing a man by cutting deep patterns into his flesh. When Mataora asked to have his own story marked on his face in the same way, Uetonga agreed.

To ease the pain of the carving, Mataora sang of his loss and regret, and the sound reached Niwareka, who forgave her husband. The couple reunited and received permission to return to the surface world. But Mataora neglected to leave an appropriate offering for the guardian of the portal between the two realms, and so from then on living humans were forbidden to enter the underworld. *Moko*—in fact, all traditional carvings—thus remind Maori people of their ancestors, of the importance of meeting one's obligations, of the need to treat one another with respect, of the power of the natural world, and of the boundaries between life and death.

Buildings

> The way into the shrine was a round hole at the side of a hill, just a little bigger than the round opening into a henhouse. Worshippers and those who came to seek knowledge from the god crawled on their belly through the hole and found themselves in a dark, endless space in the presence of Agbala.
> —Chinua Achebe (1996 [1958]: 12), **Igbo**

Ancestral Houses

The Maori meeting house (*whare whakairo*) is part of a larger complex called a **marae**, a cleared area containing several other structures such as a dining room, shelters, and a site where the recently deceased are placed to lie in state. The *marae* is the religious and social home of a Maori person, the site of ritual ceremonies such as weddings, funerals, family celebrations, and formal welcomes for visitors. Authority on the *marae* is held by the community's elders, who use the space to pass on traditions, stories, and arts such as weaving and carving.

As in the case of African masks, the builders and carvers of the *whare whakairo* were traditionally male; the rest of the community was banned from the site until the work was officially declared complete at a public ceremony. The workers themselves operated under a number of ritual restrictions and obligations from the moment the first trees for the building were cut down. Traditionally, *marae* artists were held responsible to such a degree that they could be put to death if the community did not judge the completed work to be acceptable.

The location of the *marae* is critical: it must be a place where previous generations carried out the religious and social activities that continue to define and restore the world itself. This connection to the land is not merely metaphorical, as it is Maori custom to bury the placenta in the ground at birth, as well as the bones after death. The *marae* is also identified with a single common ancestor to whom all members of the community are ostensibly connected.

This identification is given physical form in the *whare whakairo*, which represents the body of the ancestor. On the front of the house, where the roof slopes meet, is the mask-head of the ancestor; the boards along the front of each side of the roof are his arms; the central ridge of the roof is his spine, with ribs/rafters spreading out from it; the front door is his mouth; and the window is his eye. Non-Maori may be able to appreciate the beauty and intricacy of the *whare whakairo*'s construction, but they cannot grasp what such a building truly means to a community without a deeper understanding of its cultural roots.

Three Points, and a Shrine

That said, the attention to detail in the construction of the *whare whakairo* is so great that even a casual observer might still be able to recognize that such a building is imbued with great significance. Many other Indigenous religious structures—including the majority of those in Africa and North America—are so plain that it may be difficult for outsiders to understand how they could have any deeper meaning.

There are three main points at issue here. First, the majority of Indigenous people throughout history have performed all or most of their rituals out of doors, in the natural world. Specific locations can be critically important; when the object of the ritual is to make contact with particular gods or spirits, for example, the ritual must generally be performed where they dwell or intersect with our world. Although some communities may erect a simple structure to mark such sites, to do anything more elaborate would in many instances simply hold no meaning to them, it would not be in keeping with their religious worldview.

Second, it may be helpful to think about the functions of the elaborate religious structures erected by various non-Indigenous groups. One reason the Catholic Church blanketed Europe with grand cathedrals, for example, was the simple fact that for a very long time it was the ultimate authority in that part of the world. Such buildings symbolized the Church's wealth and political power. Small Indigenous communities that did not rule entire continents had no occasion (or resources) for such displays.

Finally, we come back to the point made at the beginning of this section: what you see is often not what you get. An African shrine may contain nothing more than a couple of small, plain, human-shaped carvings, but if the community understands that from time to time particular ancestors or spirits inhabit them, then at those times the figures become visible manifestations of the gods.

Other shrine statues may have quite a different meaning, however. Consider the *mbari* shrine in the photo at the right. How would you interpret these figures? Are they gods? Which one is the most important? Who is the man sitting in front of the statues, and why is he there?

The statues represent the founder of the community in the lower middle, with his wife above and servants on either side. He was renowned as a great healer some two centuries ago, but was attacked by another community and forced to flee across the marshes, carrying his wife on his shoulders. Relics of the healer are kept with the statues and protect members of the society from disease. Because most of the *mbari* shrines in this region have been destroyed, an elder stands guard here at all times.

The guard signifies the presence not only of religious conflict in this region but also of religious change. The idea of defending or preserving this particular type of religious building is actually a modern development. Traditionally, *mbari* shrines were formed out of earth and clay, and—like totem poles—were never repaired once their ceremonial unveiling was done; after several rains, they would simply dissolve back into the earth.

Daniel Lainé

A *mbari* shrine in southeastern Nigeria.

Hogans

The Navajo **hogan** is our final example of a structure that is much more than it appears. It is also the only one that is not "explicitly" religious: although many ceremonies are performed there, a hogan is also simply a traditional dwelling, the kind of building in which any Navajo family might live. As such it is the site of all the daily activities that go on in a home, some of which are religious and some of which are not.

Before a newly constructed hogan is occupied, the community will perform the Blessingway ceremony. This ritual includes a song that begins by referring to "a holy home" (Gill 1982: 10), although this term merely hints at what the hogan represents. The point becomes slightly clearer when we learn

Document

From the Nightway Prayer (Navajo)

*Like the Blessingway song performed as part of the cre-
ation of a new hogan, the first part of this prayer connects the ordinary with the extraordinary through the
central symbol of the home. And like the Yoruba verse in
the box on page 321, its concluding section envisions life
as a journey.*

In Tse 'gíhi
In the house made of the dawn
In the house made of the evening twilight
In the house made of the dark cloud
In the house made of the he-rain
In the house made of the dark mist
In the house made of the she-rain
In the house made of pollen

In the house made of grasshoppers
Where the dark mist curtains the doorway
The path to which is on the rainbow. . .
In beauty (happily) I walk
With beauty before me, I walk
With beauty behind me, I walk
With beauty below me, I walk
With beauty above me, I walk
With beauty all around me, I walk
It is finished (again) in beauty
It is finished in beauty
It is finished in beauty
It is finished in beauty
(Matthews 1995 [1902]: 143–5)

that the Blessingway ceremony is in many ways the
foundation of Navajo religious thought and practice. Before any other ritual can be conducted, for
example, some version of the Blessingway must
be performed.

The Blessingway song names four divine beings:
Earth, Mountain Woman, Water Woman, and
Corn Woman. But the song also speaks of everyday
things: vegetation, fabrics, long life, happiness. In
this way it represents a joining of perspectives, the
cosmic with the mundane.

The cosmic–mundane connection is furthered
by the song's identification of the four deities with
the four main supporting poles of the hogan. And
in Navajo cosmology, the same deities provide support for the world itself. In fact, the Navajo understand the creation of the world to have begun with
the building of a structure; which is to say that the
world *is* a structure—a hogan. It should come as
no surprise that creation was accompanied by the
first performance of the Blessingway ritual. Thus
to build a hogan is to reproduce the origin of all

things, and to fulfill one's ongoing (sacred) responsibility to continually make and re-make the world.

Despite its apparent simplicity, then, the Navajo
hogan—like Pomo baskets and Nisga'a totem
poles, like Yoruba white cloth and Dogon shrines,
like Maori tattoos and *whare whakairo*—is a vital
link between present and past, between community and place, between our world and the world of
the spirits.

Colonialism

"Colonialism" refers both to the process in which
people from one place establish and maintain a settlement in another, and to the effects of this process
on any people already living there. Typically, those
effects include their subjugation, if not removal, and
the imposition of new laws, economies, and social
practices that are controlled by, and often modelled
on, those of the colonists' home territory.

An enormous amount of colonial activity
occurred between the fifteenth and twentieth

centuries, when western Europeans were exploring parts of the world such as Africa, North and South America, Australia, and the islands of the Pacific Ocean. Until this activity began, western Europe was a relatively insignificant region in terms of global influence; afterwards, it was the centre of the world.

The quests for power and profit have often been the key factors driving colonialism. Religion has also played a critical role, however, both as a motivating factor and as a justification for the conquest of other peoples. The consequences for the religious traditions of the conquered peoples have been profound. It is not possible to understand Indigenous traditions today, therefore, without understanding colonialism.

Invasion

> They do not bear arms, and do not know them, for I showed them a sword, they took it by the edge and cut themselves out of ignorance. . . . They would make fine servants. . . . With fifty men we could subjugate them and make them do whatever we want.
> —Christopher Columbus, Italian (in Zinn 1995: 1)

Columbus

The journals of Christopher Columbus offer an insider's account of the start of the most devastating colonial project in history. His first contact with the **Arawaks** foretells much of what happened later: "As soon as I arrived in the Indies, on the first Island which I found, I took some of the natives by force in order that they might learn and might give me information of whatever there is in these parts" (Zinn 1995: 1).

What was it that Columbus most wanted to learn from his captives? He wanted to know where the gold was. Unfortunately for the Arawaks, there was very little gold for the Europeans to find, but Columbus was not deterred. Those who managed to bring him a specified amount of gold were given a copper token to hang around their necks; those who were then found without a token had their hands cut off and were left to bleed to death.

Eventually Columbus came to see that the islands' most valuable "resources" were the people themselves, and he shipped them back to Europe by the boatload. Thus he exclaimed: "Let us in the name of the Holy Trinity go on sending all the slaves that can be sold" (Zinn 1995: 4). Within two years of his arrival, roughly half of the estimated original population of 250,000 had been either exported or killed. A century later, all of the Arawaks on the islands were gone.

Genocides

Colonial efforts elsewhere—in Africa, Australia, New Zealand, the Americas—were similarly catastrophic. Millions upon millions of people, representing thousands of distinct cultures, were wiped out entirely.

In Africa, as in the West Indies, the chief source of wealth for the Europeans was the population itself. By the late nineteenth century, upwards of 20 million Africans had been taken from their homes and sent to the Americas as slaves, though only about 11 million made it there alive. Scholars estimate that by the time the trans-Atlantic slave trade ended, the population of Africa had been reduced by half.

In Australia, less than half of the original population of about 500,000 remained after just a few years of contact with Europeans. The southeast—where the First Fleet arrived in 1788—was hit the hardest. During the first year of colonization, approximately two-thirds of the estimated 250,000 Aboriginals in this region were killed by a smallpox epidemic. By 1850, 96 per cent were dead.

In the Americas, records suggest that by 1600 as many as 90 million Indigenous people—more than 90 per cent of the original population—had died as a direct result of the arrival of the Europeans. More people had been killed than existed in all of Europe at the time (approximately 60 to 80 million). The destruction of the original inhabitants of the Americas was a genocide on a scale that has not been seen in human history before or since.

The biggest single cause of the depopulation of both Australia and the Americas was disease, but other factors included military action, mistreatment (including torture and forced labour) starvation or malnutrition, loss of will to live (e.g., suicide, abortion), and slavery. And the destruction has not ended yet. Most South American countries continue to remove or kill their Indigenous citizens whenever the governments want more land.

Of course, humans have been killing and conquering other humans for as long as humans have existed. This, sadly, is what we do. Indigenous people are no exception to the rule; violence and warfare certainly existed in North America, Africa, and Oceania before the Europeans showed up. But it did not exist on nearly the same scale.

"Masters of the Continent"

Almost everywhere the Europeans went, they occupied the land they found. In many parts of North America, this occupation was initially accomplished through relatively peaceful negotiations with the original inhabitants. After all, the first settlers were greatly outnumbered, and the Indigenous people possessed valuable knowledge and skills. As the settler population grew, however, and the Indigenous population declined, the negotiation process became less friendly. Eventually it ceased entirely in most instances, and Native people living on land that Europeans wanted were either forcibly removed or simply killed.

Colonists justified this behaviour in many ways, some of which were explicitly religious. Many equated their situation with that of the Jews who were ordered by God to destroy the native inhabitants of Canaan. Only then could they inherit the Promised Land.

The notion of **terra nullius** ("no one's land") was also frequently invoked by European settlers in several places, including New Zealand, western Canada, and (most notably) Australia. Colonists argued variously that Indigenous people were not "really" using the land; or that they could not own the land because they did not have any concept of ownership; or that because of their "primitive" nature, they simply did not count as people and therefore the land on which they lived was technically unoccupied. All these arguments are, of course, specious, self-serving, and inherently racist.

By the late nineteenth century, it was widely assumed that the Indigenous people of North America were on the way to extinction. A newspaper editor in South Dakota named L. Frank Baum—the future author of *The Wizard of Oz*—wrote an editorial in December 1890 that carried the theory of the "vanishing Indian" to a brutally logical conclusion:

> The Whites, by law of conquest, by justice of civilization, are masters of the American continent, and the best safety of the frontier settlements will be secured by the total annihilation of the few remaining Indians. Why not annihilation? Their glory has fled, their spirit broken, their manhood effaced; better that they die than live the miserable wretches that they are (Baum 1890).

In effect, Baum was calling for his fellow Euro-Americans to complete the genocide begun by Columbus.

Just nine days after Baum's editorial, the US Calvary moved to relocate an encampment of Lakota Sioux near Wounded Knee Creek, South Dakota, in order to free up the land for colonial settlers. The result was a massacre. More than 300 Sioux were killed, among them unarmed women and children; some were shot as they tried to run away.

Around the world, Wounded Knee remains a powerful symbol of colonialism and its consequences for Indigenous people. A similar conjunction of land acquisition and extreme violence can be found at some point in the history of virtually every encounter between colonial interests and Indigenous people.

Conversion

I thought I was being taken just for a few days. I can recall seeing my mother standing on the side of the road with her head in her hands, crying, and me in the black FJ Holden wondering why she was so upset. . . . . I see myself as that little girl, crying myself to sleep at night, crying and wishing I could go home to my family. Everything's gone, the loss of your culture, the loss of your family, all these things have a big impact.

—Lyn Austin, Australian Aborigine (in Cooke 2008)

As a result of colonialism, the majority of Indigenous peoples in the world were converted to the religion of one colonial power or another. That religion was usually some form of Christianity, but other missionary religions took hold in some areas of the world, notably Islam in parts of Africa and Buddhism throughout Asia.

Accurate information on adherence to Indigenous religions is virtually impossible to come by. Such data are normally obtained from national censuses. On the topic of religion, however, many countries have run into serious problems either with their census questions or with the answer choices they offer. In Indonesia, for example, adherence to an Indigenous religion is simply not recognized by law; thus Indigenous people are counted as members of the dominant tradition (Islam) by default. As well, Indigenous people in many parts of the world have expressed justifiable concern about what they reveal to government officials, and so may give the answers they think are desired, in order to avoid any possible reprisals or repercussions.

That said, the general pattern is that approximately 70 per cent of Indigenous people in the world today identify with a colonial religion, while only 15 to 20 per cent continue to practise an Indigenous religion. The rest declare adherence either to an alternative tradition or to none at all.

Loss of Religion

In the early years of contact, some European missionaries tried to persuade Indigenous communities that Christianity simply made more sense than their own traditions, but that approach was rarely successful. A more effective strategy was to demonstrate the "superiority" of Christian beliefs in practical terms. In many cases, that task was accomplished through the association of military strength with religious authority. The message was simple: Our people are stronger than your people because our god is stronger than yours.

Another major factor in the decline of Indigenous religions was the people's belief that, in order to integrate themselves into the new system, they needed the education that in most cases was available only through missionaries. Then, as colonial abuses accumulated, many oppressed Native people looked to the missionaries for *protection* from the new system. In both situations, Christianity flourished at the expense of traditional beliefs and practices.

Sometimes colonial governments simply made the practice of Indigenous religions illegal. This was invariably the case whenever such religions were suspected of involvement with any sort of anti-colonial resistance. And sometimes such laws were put into effect in a more pre-emptive manner.

In 1883, for example, the United States imposed a federal ban on many Native ceremonies, including the Sun Dance. The next year, Canada amended its **Indian Act** and criminalized the **potlatch**. In both cases the governments claimed that their motive was not to regulate religion but to protect Aboriginal citizens—from physical harm in the case of the Sun Dance, and from economic hardship in the case of the potlatch, which was depicted as driving people into poverty.

Finally, it is important to note that the conversion of Indigenous people had an enormous impact on gender relations, which in turn has had repercussions in all areas of life. Most colonial powers brought a form of patriarchy with them that resulted in the gendered stratification of the

Document

From *Things Fall Apart*, by Chinua Achebe (Igbo)

Achebe's 1958 novel—which focuses on an Igbo man named Okonkwo from a fictional village in Nigeria in the late 1800s—is the most influential work of African literature ever written. In this passage Okonkwo has just returned home after a seven-year exile, and his best friend Obierika is explaining the dramatic changes that have taken place during his absence as a result of colonialism.

"Perhaps I have been away too long," Okonkwo said, almost to himself. "But I cannot understand these things you tell me. What is it that has happened to our people? Why have they lost the power to fight?"

"Have you not heard how the white man wiped out Abame?" asked Obierika.

"I have heard," said Okonkwo. "But I have also heard that Abame people were weak and foolish. Why did they not fight back? Had they no guns and machetes? We would be cowards to compare ourselves with the men of Abame. Their fathers had never dared to stand before our ancestors. We must fight these men and drive them from the land."

"It is already too late," said Obierika sadly. "Our own men and our sons have joined the ranks of the stranger. They have joined his religion and they help to uphold his government. If we should try to drive out the white men in Umuofia we should find it easy. There are only two of them. But what of our own people who are following their way and have been given power? They would go to Umuru and bring the soldiers, and we would be like Abame." He paused for a long time and then said: "I told you on my last visit to Mbanta how they hanged Aneto."

"What has happened to that piece of land in dispute?" asked Okonkwo.

"The white man's court has decided that it should belong to Nnama's family, who had given much money to the white man's messengers and interpreter."

"Does the white man understand our custom about land?"

"How can he when he does not even speak our tongue? But he says that our customs are bad, and our own brothers who have taken up his religion also say that our customs are bad. How do you think we can fight when our own brothers have turned against us? The white man is very clever. He came quietly and peaceably with his religion. We were amused at his foolishness and allowed him to stay. Now he has won our brothers, and our clan can no longer act like one. He has put a knife on the things that held us together and we have fallen apart" (Achebe 1996 [1958]: 124–5).

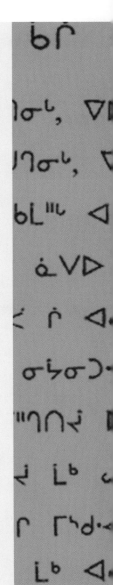

local societies, and the devaluation of women and their roles. As the Métis author Maria Campbell has pointed out, this devaluation was often supported at the deepest levels by colonial religious teachings:

The missionaries had impressed upon us the feeling that women were a source of evil. This belief, combined with the ancient Indian recognition of the power of women, is still holding back the progress of our people today (Campbell 1973: 168).

Loss of Language

As a result of colonialism, an untold number of Indigenous languages have disappeared forever. It has been estimated that Australia had almost 300 distinct Aboriginal languages at the time of first contact; today all but 20 are either extinct

Sites

Nibutani, Japan

The site where the Ainu god Okikurmikamuy arrived on earth, at the midpoint of the Saru River in Hokkaido, Japan. This is also the site where the Ainu author Kayano Shigeru built the Nibutani Museum of Ainu Cultural Resources, dedicated to preserving and revitalizing his people's culture.

Focus

The Potlatch

A ritual dating back thousands of years, the potlatch is practised by many peoples of the Pacific Northwest, including the Haida, Kwakwaka'wakw, Salish, Tlingit, and Tsimshian. To a significant extent the ceremony is about demonstrating hospitality and redistributing wealth; it typically consists of a feast at which the hosting family presents the guests with gifts. Before contact with Europeans, these gifts included items such as tools, blankets, carvings, and dried food (e.g., pemmican); gifts today usually consist of manufactured goods, especially practical household items, as well as artwork and cash.

Each community has its own way of potlatching, but the practice typically marks important moments such as marriage, childbirth, or death, and may include music, theatre, and ceremonial dancing. The potlatch also frequently serves to indicate social status: families demonstrate their wealth and importance by giving away (or even destroying) more resources than other families.

Christian missionaries saw the potlatch as useless and "uncivilized," but also recognized it as a central element of many Native cultures. Getting rid of the practice, they thought, would facilitate assimilation. Their governments agreed: the potlatch was made illegal in Canada in 1884, and banned in the United States a few years later.

In October 1886, the anthropologist Franz Boas recorded a famous comment about the potlatch ban by Chief O'waxalagalis of the Kwakwaka'wakw people on Vancouver Island:

We will dance when our laws command us to dance, and we will feast when our hearts desire to feast. Do we ask the white man, "Do as the Indian does"? No, we do not. Why then do you ask us, "Do as the white man does"? It is a strict law that bids us dance. It is a strict law that bids us distribute our property among our friends and neighbours. It is a good law. Let the white man observe his law, we shall observe ours. And now, if you come to forbid us dance, be gone. If not, you will be welcome to us (Bunn-Marcuse 2005: 322).

As it turned out, the law was hard to enforce. Indigenous communities were large and widespread, and so could often hold potlatches in secret. Even when non-Natives discovered a potlatch, it was not easy for them to distinguish this event from a regular (legal) feast. In addition, many non-Natives—including the government agents tasked with enforcing the ban—regarded the law as harsh and unnecessary. The potlatch ban was finally lifted in the US in 1934 and in Canada in 1951.

or endangered. According to the United Nations, as many as 90 per cent of all existing languages are in danger of becoming extinct within 100 years; the vast majority of these languages are Indigenous.

For cultures that rely heavily on oral traditions to transmit their beliefs and values, this loss of language constitutes a devastating blow to their religion. In his memoir *Our Land Was a Forest*, Kayano Shigeru tells a story about the last three fluent Ainu speakers in his town, one of whom was his father. The three agreed that the first among them to die would be the luckiest, because the other two would be able to perform the death ritual for him in the Ainu language and thereby ensure that he would "return to the realm of the gods" (Shigeru 1994: 107).

What has caused this situation? In many cases, as communities died their languages died with them. In other cases, the process of language loss was accelerated by government programs designed specifically to promote assimilation. Thus in Canada Aboriginal children were taken from their families, often by force, and placed in church-run **residential schools** where they were forbidden to speak their own languages. In Australia children were sent either to foster homes or (much more often) to government- or church-run institutions, where they remained as wards of the state until they reached the age of 18. Record-keeping was often either inadequate or non-existent, with the result that some children never found their families, never returned to their homes.

In both countries, agents of the institutions involved—including teachers and administrators, priests and nuns—inflicted physical, psychological, and/or sexual abuse on many Indigenous children. Taken from their families and told they were worthless, heathen, primitive, these children grew up with no knowledge of their language and culture; at the same time they were deprived of the social knowledge required to establish healthy relationships and raise their own families. It is no wonder that Aboriginal children in Australia who endured such practices for more than a century have been termed the "**Stolen Generations**."

Loss of Land

We have already noted how closely Indigenous religions are tied to specific locations: the sacred places where gods, spirits, and ancestors become present in the lives of each community. Limiting or preventing access to such locations, therefore, undermines the very foundations of Indigenous religion.

Around the world, thousands of Indigenous religious sites have been taken over or destroyed as a result of colonialism; no doubt there are many more such sites that we know nothing of, because the people who held them sacred have themselves been destroyed. Yet even where both the people and the land survive, gaining recognition of land rights is an ongoing problem.

Canada and Australia have particularly poor track records in this respect. When these countries became independent from Great Britain, they

Sites

Tiwanaku, Bolivia

The most sacred place for the Aymara people of Bolivia. Located roughly 70 kilometres (45 miles) west of La Paz, it is the centre of the world, the site of humanity's creation, and the place where the local

Indigenous people go to communicate with their ancestors. Because Tiwanaku is considered a major archaeological site, access to it has been severely restricted; even the Aymara must pay an entrance fee.

Sites

Kanesatake, Canada

The home of the Mohawk community that objected when the neighbouring town of Oka, Quebec, planned to expand a golf course onto land that the Mohawk considered sacred, resulting in armed confrontation. After a 78-day standoff in the summer of 1990, the government of Canada bought the site and stopped the development.

essentially refused to recognize any titles granted to Indigenous people by the British. In 1971, an Australian judge upholding the concept of *terra nullius* went so far as to rule that Aborigines had no land rights at all—a decision that was not overturned until 1992. The situation for Natives in Canada remains in many ways very poor. As recently as 2011, the federal government created the Navigation Protection Act (NPA), which in fact offers "protection" only for corporate projects such as oil pipelines. In other words, the NPA specifically deregulated many waterways that pass through First Nations territory.

In the United States, more than 90 per cent of the land had been taken from its Indigenous inhabitants by 1890. A key (negative) moment in the Native Americans' struggle to reclaim some of this territory came almost a century later, when the Forest Service proposed putting a paved road through the Chimney Rock area of the Six Rivers National Forest in Northern California, in order to open the space for commercial logging. The project would effectively destroy the centre of religious existence for two Native communities, the **Yurok** and the **Karuk**.

The case was brought to the Supreme Court. The Native people were not asking that the land in question be returned to them—only that they retain access to it. Yet the court found that their attachment to the disputed territory was no different from the attachment that any individual might feel for any space. Thus to agree to their request would set a precedent allowing anyone to request

protection of any site on religious grounds. The petition was denied.

This case highlights two central problems in the understanding that many non-Indigenous people have of Indigenous religions. The first problem is that religion in general is frequently seen primarily as an individual commitment to a set of beliefs. Indigenous religions, by contrast, are communal and are as much about practice as they are about belief.

The second problem is the difficulty that non-Indigenous people have in understanding why Indigenous practices are often critically bound to (and dependent upon) access to particular sites—unlike, say, Muslim prayer or Buddhist meditation, which can be performed anywhere at all. If the Vatican were destroyed, Catholics would be upset, but they would not be separated from God or the sacraments. There is an important difference between religions that see the world as a unity—all people are loved equally by Allah; all have equal access to the Four Noble Truths—and religions that see the world in more particular, or locative, terms. For most Indigenous people, specific places are related, and sacred, to specific people, not to everyone in the world. For such people, one might say that the place itself *is* the religion; without it, the religion is fundamentally different.

Appropriation

We lost most of our land, most of our "Aboriginal" rights, many of our languages, most of our traditional cultural ways, our

religion, our relationship to the land and the spirits of the land, and, it seems, that we've even lost control of much of our identity through the process of "trade-marking" images of us, and elements of our culture.
—Philip Bellfy (2005: 30), Chippewa

Identity

For some people, a match between the Cleveland Indians and the Atlanta Braves is not just a baseball game: it's a stark reminder of the ongoing legacy of colonialism, of all that has been taken from Indigenous people and all that continues to be taken from them. Adding insult to injury, the Braves' fans are known for doing the "tomahawk chop," while the Indians' mascot is a degrading caricature named "Chief Wahoo."

Of course this phenomenon is not limited to baseball. Many North American sports teams—such as the Chicago Blackhawks and Washington Redskins—have taken Indigenous-oriented names. And many other types of companies have used "Indigenous" names or logos to market their products, from Eskimo Pie ice cream to the Ford Thunderbird. In effect, the dominant colonial culture has appropriated Indigenous identities and reconstructed them to evoke whatever "primitive" stereotype is best suited to the product in question: the primal "warrior" for a sports team, the noble "chief" for tobacco, or the pure, natural "Indian maiden" for a line of dairy products or even beer.

© Chris Szagola/NewSport/Corbis

The Washington Redskins are the only major professional sports team named after a racial slur. The name, logo, and mascot "Chief Zee" have been the subject of ongoing controversy and legal action. Some Native Americans have proposed that, if the team will not change its name, it could at least change its mascot—to a red-skinned potato.

Such appropriation is thus not simply arrogant, impolite, or politically incorrect. It serves to perpetuate an image of Indigenous people that is far removed from current reality and, in so doing, helps to blind non-Indigenous people to ongoing injustices. To the extent that these people continue to see Indigenous cultures as primitive, savage, and uncivilized, as vanished or vanishing, they will have difficulty recognizing the reality of modern communities and their concerns. Whether they are celebrating or protesting, laughing or grieving, practising Indigenous traditions or Christianity, Indigenous people should at least have the right to ownership and control of their own identity.

Religion in the Movies

From the "Indian burial ground" of Stephen King's *Pet Sematary* to the baboon "shaman" Rafiki in *The Lion King*, to Betty White's "tribal" chanting in *The Proposal*, American films are filled with false ideas about Indigenous religious life. The best-known portrayals of Native culture likely remain those from the classic Hollywood Westerns—most of which used Italian or Spanish actors to play the "Indians." Again and again, Indigenous people are portrayed either as fierce/savage warriors or as the noble/dying people of a lost age.

Similar patterns are evident in movies from both Oceania and Africa. In the highest-grossing Australian film of all time, *Crocodile Dundee*, the extinction of Indigenous culture is signalled by Dundee's Aboriginal friend Neville, who is repeatedly shown to have left his roots behind ("God, I hate the bush," he mutters). More disturbingly, Dundee himself proclaims that "Aborigines don't own the land. They belong to it." It is precisely this view of traditional Aboriginal conceptions of place that the Australian government used to help deprive people of their land rights.

The Gods Must Be Crazy remains the most commercially successful movie about Indigenous people ever made. Released in 1980, the film grossed over $100 million worldwide and focused directly on the (imagined) religious beliefs of the (real) **Ju/'hoansi**

people, in the Kalahari Desert in southern Africa. The movie presents them as "noble savages" living in a simple, idyllic society whose peace is shattered when a Coke bottle falls out of a plane and upsets the balance of Indigenous life, prompting the film's hero, Xi, to set off for the end of the world in order to return the offending object to the gods who sent it. In other words, the movie presents the Ju/'hoansi as naive, superstitious, and innocent, and then uses them to criticize modern non-Indigenous culture.

Catching Dreams and Burning Men

Around the world, sacred Indigenous items continue to be turned into souvenirs for cultural tourists. There is a lot of money to be made by selling cheap versions of African masks to non-Africans. Imitation Maori *moko* have attained a similar level of popularity among non-Indigenous tattoo enthusiasts, and were even used on fashion models for a 2007 Jean-Paul Gaultier collection. Even more striking is the proliferation of dream catchers. Originally used in Anishinaubae culture to help protect children from nightmares, they are now sold by the thousands to non-Native people for use as decorative knick-knacks. Often they can be seen hanging from a rearview mirror like a pair of fuzzy dice.

Indigenous opinion concerning the commercial use of religious objects and symbols is divided. Some people see it as disrespectful and damaging; others argue that it has some value, not only in economic terms but in helping to educate the public about Indigenous culture. Still, there are forms of appropriation that almost all can agree are inappropriate. Some of these are part of what is often referred to as the **New Age** movement.

Many New Age teachings that seem to reflect Indigenous religions in reality turn them upside down. Thus elements of a locative and communal tradition are co-opted to promote notions of universal truth and individual fulfillment. Non-Indigenous people are often willing to pay New Age "shamans" lots of money for the opportunity to get in touch with a "primal" part of themselves and overcome their own psychological and emotional problems. To this end they engage in all manner of pseudo-Indigenous rituals: they tell stories, chant, pass around the talking stick, bang drums, dance, and yell in a forest.

These imitative practices are not simply misguided: they can actually be quite dangerous. In October 2009, three people died and 18 more were hospitalized when self-help guru James Arthur Ray conducted a New Age **sweat lodge** ceremony in Arizona. In the traditional practice, participants sit in an enclosed space and water is poured over rocks heated in a fire to create steam. The ritual is used for various medicinal and religious purposes, including purification and reconnection to the spirits. Many Native communities, including the Anishinaubae, Lakota, **Crow**, and **Chumash**, conduct sweat lodge ceremonies safely in enclosures covered with hides, dirt, or blankets, but it seems that Ray's lodge was covered with plastic sheeting. On 3 February 2010, Ray was arrested and charged with manslaughter for the three deaths.

The largest and most famous Indigenous-themed New Age event is the week-long Burning Man festival held every summer in northern Nevada. The festival takes its name from its central ceremony, when a large wooden effigy is set aflame. Since 2007 well over 40,000 people have attended each year to take part in activities that range from making art and

Document

Statement by Chief Arvol Looking Horse (Lakota) on the Sweat Deaths in Arizona

Chief Looking Horse's statement was issued on 16 October 2009, one day prior to the third death resulting from this incident.

As Keeper of our Sacred White Buffalo Calf Pipe Bundle, I am concerned for the two deaths and illnesses of the many people that participated in a sweat lodge in Sedona, Arizona that brought our sacred rite under fire in the news. I would like to clarify that this lodge and many others are not our ceremonial way of life, because of the way they are being conducted. My prayers go out for their families and loved ones for their loss.

Our ceremonies are about life and healing. From the time this ancient ceremonial rite was given to our people, never has death been a part of our *inikaga* (life within) when conducted properly. . . .

Our First Nations People have to earn the right to pour the *mini wiconi* (water of life) upon the *inyan oyate* (the stone people) in creating *Inikaga* by going on the vision quest for four years and four years Sundance. Then you are put through a ceremony to be painted, to recognize that you have now earned that right to take care of someone's life through purification. They should also be able to understand our sacred language, to be able to understand the messages from the Grandfathers, because they are ancient, they are our spirit ancestors. They walk and teach the values of our culture; in being humble, wise, caring, and compassionate.

What has happened in the news with the makeshift sauna called the sweat lodge is not our ceremonial way of life. . . .

At this time, I would like to ask all Nations upon Grandmother Earth to please respect our sacred ceremonial way of life and stop the exploitation of our *Tunka Oyate* (Spiritual Grandfathers).

In a Sacred Hoop of Life, where there is no ending and no beginning, *namahu yo* (hear my words).

Chief Arvol Looking Horse,
19th Generation Keeper of the Sacred White Buffalo Calf Pipe Bundle (Looking Horse 2009)

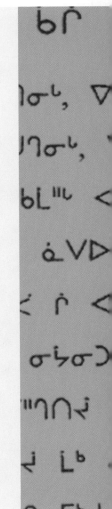

music to self-expression, communal living, gift-giving, and public nudity.

On occasion, some have complained about the degree to which Burning Man (and/or its participants) seem to be appropriating Indigenous cultures. For example, in April 2009 organizers of an offshoot Burner party in Oakland, California, circulated an online flyer encouraging participants to "GO NATIVE" and offering a discount to anyone who showed up "in Native costume." In addition, the party was to feature four "elemental rooms": "Water: Island Natives (Maori); Air: Cliff Natives (Anasazi); Earth: Jungle Natives (Shipibo); Fire: Desert Natives (Pueblo)."

Given the immense popularity of Burning Man and its offshoots, it is impossible to over-estimate the degree to which such appropriation influences the views of non-Natives about Native people—and thereby affects the actual lives of those people.

🌿 Recent Developments

There are references to Gen. Custer and the US Cavalry, to John Wayne and to US policies toward Indians over the years, but *Smoke Signals* is free of the oppressive weight of victim culture; these characters don't live in the past and define themselves by the crimes committed against their people.
—Roger Ebert (1998), Euro-American

Given that Indigenous traditions are the world's oldest religions, changes that have taken place since the emergence of colonialism a few hundred years ago certainly qualify as "recent developments." Also, as a result of colonialism, the religious traditions of Indigenous people have arguably changed more dramatically over the last centuries than the traditions of any other cultures in the world. That said, in what follows it is important to bear two key points in mind.

First, there is a critical difference between recognizing that awful things have been done (and continue to be done) to Indigenous people in the name of colonialism and defining Indigenous

people as "victims," a label that robs them of full humanity. Second, and relatedly, Indigenous people were never simply the passive objects of colonialism: they engaged with it at every step, and they have remained active agents in the developments that have shaped their histories, including recent developments in their religions.

Interaction and Adaptation

I picture oppressors . . . coming into our garden of Eden like a snake. Satan used the snake as his instrument to tempt God's people and to try to destroy God's plan for his people. The bad influence came in breaking our relationship with God, with man, and the Land. We never dreamed that one day the bulldozers would come in.
—Djiniyini Gondarra, **Yolngu** (in Swain and Trompf 1995: 107)

Dualisms

In most Indigenous religions, the process of change began soon after contact with Europeans. Typically, Indigenous people would gradually incorporate some elements of the colonial religion into their own traditions. One of the most important examples of this process was the shift that sometimes took place from the more typically Indigenous worldview of **complementary dualism** (seeing the universe as necessarily including both creative and destructive forces, which can work together), to the "Western" worldview of **conflict dualism** (seeing the universe as divided between good and evil forces that are in constant battle with one another).

Such a shift occurred in the late sixteenth and early seventeenth centuries among many of the Indigenous people of Peru, people who previously had no real concept of "evil." In certain regions, the invading Spanish characterized the local populations as the demonic enemies of Christ, giving them licence to use extreme violence in order to subjugate and convert the people. The plan worked: many of the Indigenous Peruvians who suffered great cruelty at the hands of the invaders did adopt basic Christian beliefs, including the good–evil dualism promoted by the Spanish. However, while they came to regard Jesus as a positive and humane figure, they saw the Spanish as the true embodiments of evil.

A similar change took place among the **Iroquois** in the late eighteenth century. A man in his sixties named Ganioda'yo, or Handsome Lake, experienced a series of visions in which he met Jesus as well as four angels sent by the creator, Tarachiawagon. As a result of these visions, Handsome Lake taught the Iroquois that they should publicly confess their sins; that they should avoid evil (including witchcraft and alcohol); and that they should worship only Tarachiawagon, not his

Sites

Saut d'Eau, Haiti

A group of waterfalls about 95 kilometres (60 miles) from Port-au-Prince, Haiti, where Yoruba spirits are understood to dwell along with several Catholic saints. Voudou adherents make an annual pilgrimage to Saut d'Eau in June, a journey that is required of those seeking to join the priesthood.

A young man worships at Saut d'Eau in July 2008 as part of the annual Voudou pilgrimage to the site.

malevolent brother, Tawiskaron. This division of the world between the good and evil brothers represented a potent fusion of Indigenous religion with Christian conflict dualism. Ganioda'yo's teachings were so influential that today approximately a third of all Iroquois practise what came to be called the Handsome Lake or Longhouse religion.

The Diaspora and the Diviner

The Atlantic slave trade carried African traditions to the Americas, where they mixed with elements of both Christianity and Native American religions. Many relocated Africans continued to worship Yoruba gods under the guise of praying to Christian saints, but in time elements of the two traditions often merged in fact, giving rise to new religions such as Macumba (in Brazil), Voudou (in Haiti), and Santeria (in Cuba).

Many Africans who blended elements of traditional and colonial religion also moved towards a mode of conflict dualism. In the early nineteenth century, in the region that became South Africa, a Xhosa diviner named Nxele experienced what he understood to be an intervention by Christ. Although he continued to practise divination, he also began preaching a message that echoed the teachings of the nearby Christian missionaries.

Like the Indigenous Peruvians, however, Nxele came to see the Europeans as Christ's betrayers. Preaching that the god Mdalidiphu, who lived underground with the ancestors, was on the Xhosa's side, Nxele led 10,000 warriors against the British at Grahamstown. The attack failed and Nxele was imprisoned. He later drowned off the Cape coast while attempting to escape.

Cargo Cults

One of the most famous examples of an Indigenous religion changing in response to contact with outsiders is also one of the most recent: the **cargo cult**. Most cargo cults developed in the region of the southwest Pacific Ocean, although a few similar groups have also appeared in Africa and the Americas. The cargoes that gave rise to these groups were the regular shipments of supplies and manufactured goods that arrived for non-Indigenous foreigners.

Colonists and missionaries first appeared on many of the Pacific islands in the late nineteenth and early twentieth centuries, but activity intensified during the Second World War as the Japanese and later the Allied forces set up (and then abandoned) military bases. The local people believed that the goods arriving for these groups were provided by deities or ancestors, and that in order to receive shipments themselves they should imitate the newcomers. Thus they painted military insignia on their bodies, marched like soldiers, and constructed mock buildings and equipment, making guns from wood and radios from coconuts. Some

Sites

Tanna, Vanuatu

An island belonging to the archipelago nation of Vanuatu in the South Pacific Ocean, and home to one of the last remaining Melanesian cargo cults. The Jon Frum movement began in the 1930s urging a return to traditional practices, and evolved into a cargo cult during the Second World War when approximately 300,000 American troops were stationed in Vanuatu. Its followers still hold a military-style parade every year on 15 February.

Indigenous groups built replicas of airplanes, control towers, and headphones, waved landing signals, and lit torches along runways at night, all in the hope that the gods would send more cargo.

This hope was fuelled by two related goals. First, attaining the desired goods would allow for reciprocal exchanges with the Europeans—a practice that for many Indigenous cultures was central to establishing relationships. Second, cargo cults often came to believe that attaining these goods would help bring about a new age of social harmony, healing the wounds caused by the arrival of the colonists.

Unfortunately, this focus on obtaining cargo eclipsed other elements of the local religions. Even though the Indigenous participants followed the content of their traditions (which explained the cargo as originating with gods or ancestors), they radically changed its form (their ritual behaviour). In the end, many of those traditions disappeared.

Paths of Resistance

Not all Indigenous religions changed so dramatically or so quickly. For many years after first contact with Europeans, several Australian communities did not attempt to merge their tradition with the colonial one; but neither did they reject one or the other. Instead, they were able to declare the simultaneous, contradictory truth of both Christian and Indigenous views of existence. The Aborigines referred to this way of thinking as having "Two Laws." Some have suggested that the Aborigines were better able than most to entertain two radically different cosmologies because their own cultural heritage had accustomed them to paradoxes and non-linear thinking.

In a number of instances where the two were combined, it was Christianity that was subsumed by the Indigenous tradition. The Warlpiri of Central Australia, for example, used ritual song and dance to tell Bible stories, just as they did with Dreaming tales. They also tended to conflate events, as if Adam, Abraham, and Jesus had lived at the same time as the Warlpiri's own ancestors. In effect, by

telling the biblical stories in their own way, they reconfigured the stories to focus on place rather than the chronological order of events.

This emphasis on place is a clear indication that the Aboriginal worldview took precedence over the Christian. To most Christians, for example, it is theologically critical to understand the sequence in which the stories of Adam, Abraham, and Jesus occur. For the Aborigines, however, this sequence was irrelevant; the biblical figures were thus easily incorporated into their universe. In other words, unlike the cargo cult practitioners, they kept the form of key elements of their traditional religion (how stories were told), even though aspects of its content had been altered (those stories now included biblical references). It is possible that, because of this approach, these Aborigines were able to resist conversion longer than many other communities.

"The End Is Near"

They [the Ghost Dancers] danced in rings, the men outside circling to the right, the women and children inside circling to the left. Some of the songs came from Siletz [a community in Oregon], others were dreamed by the people when they were in a trance. All the songs were wordless. The dancers wore the old-time dress. Most of them went crazy and then they would see the dead.
—Robert Spott, Yurok (in Beck et al. 1992 [1977]: 176)

In the wake of the destruction wrought by Europeans, many Indigenous cultures experienced a religious crisis. One response was to understand colonialism as punishment for inadequate observance of Native traditions. Among the people who took this view were some who reasoned that if they repented they might help to usher in a new golden age. In some cases this view may have reflected the influence of Christian eschatology—the idea that the end of the world was near and the kingdom of God would soon arrive. Of course, it may also have derived from the fact that the world as Indigenous people had known it really was coming to an end.

The Cattle Massacre

In the mid-1800s—a time when the Xhosa were suffering greatly under the British—a young woman named Nongqawuse had a vision in which her ancestors told her that, because some of her people had practised witchcraft, the British had been sent to punish them all. If the Xhosa renounced witchcraft and destroyed their food supplies, then the Europeans would be destroyed, the ancestors would return, their food would be replaced, and their land would be restored to them.

Many Xhosa responded by burning their granaries and slaughtering their cattle; in fact, almost half a million cows were ultimately killed. As a result, thousands of Xhosa died of starvation—their population declined within a year from 105,000 to 27,000—and any hope of resisting the British died with them. Many blamed the tragedy on those who had failed to heed Nongqawuse's prophecy, although there was a later backlash against Nongqawuse herself. In the end, most of the survivors turned to Christianity.

The Ghost Dance

Nongqawuse's vision shares some basic similarities with a vision promoted in 1889 by a **Paiute** religious leader named Wovoka in the region that is now Nevada. Reviving a movement from two decades earlier, he prophesied that in a few years the ancestors would return, the buffalo herds would be restored, and the settlers would disappear. To hasten the coming of this new world, Wovoka was told that his people must live peacefully, and that they must perform a ritual focused on the spirits of their ancestors. The Lakota Sioux termed this ritual the "spirit dance," which the Euro-Americans translated as "**Ghost Dance**."

Delegates from various Native communities were sent to hear Wovoka. The Navajo, who were enjoying a period of relative stability, were not convinced.

But the Lakota were on the verge of starvation after the US government had broken a treaty and given away their fertile reservation lands to white settlers. With the bison gone, crops scarce, and government supplies running low, the Lakota were strongly attracted to Wovoka's message, in particular the idea that the whites could be made to disappear. They danced with greater urgency as their situation deteriorated, and many took to wearing "Ghost Shirts," which they believed would repel bullets.

Alarmed, the Bureau of Indian Affairs dispatched thousands of US Army troops to the Lakota territory to put an end to the dancing and protests and force any remaining Sioux to leave areas that had been set aside for white settlers. Among the consequences of this response were the death of Sitting Bull and the massacre at Wounded Knee.

From Earth to Sky

The British arrived in Australia in 1788 at the site that would become Sydney. They then proceeded to devastate the original inhabitants of the region and appropriate their territories so efficiently that, within a decade, the people were desperate to drive them out. Therefore the Aborigines developed a number of special rituals, including ceremonial rebellions against mock colonizers, and appeals to the serpent Mindi to destroy the British with (fittingly) an outbreak of smallpox.

But these efforts failed to produce the desired results, and as the British continued to destroy the bonds between local people and their ancestral lands, a religious crisis developed. Some Aborigines came to believe not only that the world would soon end, but that the source of sacred power and authority had moved from the earth to the sky, a heavenly utopia beyond the clouds. Evidence suggests that these beliefs were a direct result of exposure to Christianity.

Traditionally, the Aborigines had understood that after death their spirits would return to their homelands. Now, in a sad irony, they found comfort in the colonizers' notion that their spirits would instead journey to a paradise in the sky. The only difference was that, for the Aborigines, that paradise would be free of Europeans.

Autonomy and Equality

"If God be for us, who can be against us?"
—Archbishop Desmond Tutu, Xhosa (quoting Romans 8: 31; in Allen 2008: 334)

After various unsuccessful efforts to resist colonialism, many Indigenous people eventually found more effective ways of pursuing autonomy, equality, and fair treatment. In one way or another, religion has often been at the heart of these efforts.

Non-Indigenous Religions

Often the religion involved in the quest for equity has been Indigenous, but not always. Many Indigenous Christians, for example, have fought passionately against colonial (and Christian) abuses using ideas from the imported religion itself. Like Archbishop Desmond Tutu of South Africa, they have drawn on biblical notions of justice, sympathy for the oppressed, and deliverance from evil to support their campaigns for equality and redress.

By the same token, some Indigenous Christians have also incorporated Indigenous views into their critiques of colonial attitudes and practices. To this end Desmond Tutu has frequently cited the African concept of **Ubuntu**, according to which all human beings are interconnected and therefore to harm others is to harm oneself. Stan McKay (Cree), an ordained minister and former moderator of the United Church—the first Native person in Canada to head up a mainline denomination—similarly draws on Aboriginal notions of the inter-relatedness of all life in his censure of Christianity's contributions to current environmental problems. In contrast to such Aboriginal notions, McKay writes, Christian theology for hundreds of years "denied the integrity of creation" (McKay 1996: 55).

Land Claims

McKay's position combines a general concern for the environment with more specific concerns related to the appropriation and destruction of sacred Indigenous lands and efforts to reclaim such lands wherever possible. Some of these efforts have failed completely, some have done well, and others have had more complex results.

Sites

Blue Lake, New Mexico

For the Taos Pueblo, Blue Lake is the site of their most sacred rituals and their most important stories. It is part of the Blue Lake watershed, 194 square kilometres of land in northern New Mexico confiscated in 1906 to create the Carson National Forest. For more than 60 years the Taos Pueblo worked patiently to regain this land. In the 1960s they launched an intense multi-pronged effort that included public support, a national letter-writing campaign, publicity events, and the endorsement of the National Council of Churches. On 2 December 1970, the US Senate voted 70 to 12 to award title of the Blue Lake watershed to the Taos Pueblo. The victory is widely considered one of the most important moments in the post-contact history of Native Americans.

Juan de Jésus Romero, the Pueblo's religious leader in the late 1960s and 1970s, once said: "The story of my people and the story of this place are one single story. No man can think of us without also thinking of this place. We are always joined together."

One early success came in 1970, when 194 square kilometres (48,000 acres) of land in New Mexico were returned to the Taos **Pueblo** by President Richard Nixon. Originally confiscated by President Theodore Roosevelt and designated the Carson National Forest, the region includes Blue Lake, which Taos tradition holds to be the site of creation.

In Canada, a major land dispute erupted in the summer of 1990 between the Mohawk community of Kanesatake and the town of Oka, Quebec. At issue was the town's plan to expand a golf course onto land containing sites sacred to the Mohawk, including a cemetery. After a court ruling allowed construction to proceed despite the community's objections, some Kanesatake people erected a barricade denying access to the disputed territory.

The 78-day standoff eventually pitted Native people from across North America against the Canadian army. The federal government ultimately purchased the land and stopped the golf course development. But the Mohawk regarded this victory as only partial, since ownership of the land still did not rest with them.

Australian Aborigines have perhaps had more success at reclaiming land than any other Indigenous group. Since a High Court case in 1992 overturned the idea of Australia as *terra nullius*, Aborigines have successfully negotiated approximately 3,000 land claims. In the Northern Territory, for example, most of the coastline and more than 40 per cent of the land area is now (once again) owned by Indigenous people.

Other Victories

Most countries have also repealed their laws inhibiting the practice of Indigenous religions. The bans on the Sun Dance and potlatch were lifted decades ago. Much more recently, when a local government in Florida outlawed animal sacrifice in an effort to stop the practice of Santeria and Voudou, the US Supreme Court ruled the legislation unconstitutional.

On a much larger scale, South Africa's apartheid laws were eliminated and its colonial regime overturned in 1994, and in 2008 Australia's Prime Minister Kevin Rudd officially apologized to the Aboriginal people for the policies and practices that had created the Stolen Generations. Later that same year, Canada's prime minister, Stephen Harper, issued an official apology for the residential school system, acknowledging that "it was wrong . . . to separate children from rich and vibrant traditions."

Such victories are reflected in more local but equally important changes in attitude. School teams in countries around the world have replaced their Indigenous-themed names or mascots. An especially imaginative solution was devised in 2006 for the Syracuse Chiefs, a triple-A baseball team in New York State, which kept its name but changed its logo from an "Indian chief" to a silver locomotive (with a "chief engineer"). The change actually made the team's name more relevant to the town's history as a railway hub.

In April 2009, when several Native people got wind of the "GO NATIVE" party in Oakland, California, promoting the Burning Man festival, they decided to attend and use the occasion to explain why they believed the event was harmful to all. They reportedly spent more than four hours lecturing the participants about colonialism and the history of invasion, genocide, and appropriation associated with it. Apparently they made their point: most of those present apologized for their actions, and several broke down sobbing with regret and embarrassment.

The work of Indigenous people and their allies to right previous, ongoing, and new wrongs is a continuous and evolving process. In November 2012, four Saskatchewan women (Jessica Gordon, Sylvia McAdam, Sheelah Mclean, and Nina Wilson), outraged by the implications of an omnibus budget implementation bill (C-45) for Aboriginal treaty rights and the environment, decided to be "idle no more" and organized a protest for 10 December, sparking a wave of similar demonstrations across Canada. The movement attracted international attention and support, and was still active in the summer of 2013. Two days after the first Idle No More rally, partly in protest against

Andre Forget/QMI Agency

More than 2,000 people marched on Parliament Hill for the Idle No More protest in Ottawa on 21 December 2012.

Bill C-45's changes to the Navigation Protection Act, **Attawapiskat** Chief Theresa Spence began what was to become a six-week hunger strike. As a result of these actions, Prime Minister Stephen Harper agreed to meet with First Nations leaders on 11 January 2013.

Contemporary Indigenous Traditions

The people nowadays have an idea about the ceremonies. They think the ceremonies must be performed exactly as they have always been done. . . . But long ago when the people were given these ceremonies, the changing began, if only in the aging of the yellow gourd rattle or the shrinking of the skin around the eagle's claw, if only in the different voices from generation to generation, singing the chants. You see, in many ways, the ceremonies have always been changing.
—Betonie, a character in the novel *Ceremony* by Leslie Marmon Silko (1977: 132), Laguna Pueblo

Resurgence

Not surprisingly, with increasing legal and social recognition of Indigenous traditions has come an increase in the actual practice of those traditions. Most of the varieties of religious expression discussed in this chapter have experienced a resurgence in recent decades, from carving masks in Africa to telling Dreamtime stories in Australia to performing the Sun Dance in North America.

The revival of the Maori *moko* tradition may be especially significant, symbolically. As we saw, *moko* is said to have originated in the underworld and then been brought to the surface. When the practice was abolished by colonial rulers, the tradition returned underground in a political and figurative way; and thus its modern "resurfacing" can be seen as a re-enactment of the ancestral story.

The resurgence of Indigenous religions is understood, at least in part, as a way of coping with the cultural damage done by colonialism. At the same time some people—Indigenous and non-Indigenous—have pointed out that the more material consequences of colonialism must be addressed as well. For many Indigenous people around the world, these consequences include extreme poverty and deprivation; therefore it is important not to focus on "spiritual" issues at the expense of economics and politics. Ideally, the aim is to channel the positive effects of revitalized religious practices in ways that will also contribute to the improvement of Indigenous living conditions.

It is also important to remember that Indigenous people themselves are not of one mind on the revival of traditional religions. There are many who do not wish to return to their ancestral traditions, whether because they do not find value in them or because they now practise another religion. Nevertheless, growing numbers of Indigenous people do seem eager to make traditional beliefs and practices an important part of their lives.

Always Been Changing

The ways in which Indigenous traditions are practised today are generally not identical with the ways in which they were practised in the past, for several reasons. First, of course, all religions—and cultures—change over time. Second, the disruptions caused by colonialism have been so severe that in many instances it is not possible to recover pre-colonial traditions even in part. Third, Indigenous traditions are typically interested in the manifestation of the sacred in the here and now; the intersection of spirits and ancestors with the world did not end sometime in the ancient past but is an ongoing reality that necessitates adaptation.

A couple of simple changes in Yoruba practice may illustrate the above points. For one thing, the roles of many traditional spirits have altered somewhat. Thus the Yoruba god of iron and war, Ogun, has come to be associated with the protection of welders, car mechanics, and chauffeurs. Also, as a result of the lifestyle upheavals caused by colonialism, very little cloth is now woven by hand. Mass-produced fabric is thus used for many rituals, and at times younger people in particular will wear American clothing to ceremonial events. Some communities such as the Bunu, however, still ascribe great religious and social value to hand-woven cloth, and so continue to produce it for the most important occasions.

Trickster stories frequently embody the ways in which Indigenous religions have continued to respond to historical developments. New tales are always appearing. When colonization began, some tricksters used their powers to get the better of the newcomers; others imitated colonizing practices—for example, negotiating worthless agreements—to fool the Indigenous people into giving them things they wanted. Tricksters in modern stories may appear in any number of non-traditional guises, from politician to bartender to university teacher. In addition, there are now many female tricksters.

Gender shifts are evident in other areas of Indigenous life as well. In the past, men and women often had quite different, though interdependent, functions; but because of the severe disruptions to traditional lifestyles over the past few centuries, the same role differentiation is often not possible. For example, if at one time women in a community were responsible for preparing the food that the men killed or grew, the whole arrangement fell apart once their land was taken. This dissolution combined with the advent of colonial patriarchies to put severe stress on Indigenous gender relations.

Some communities are now addressing this situation by moving towards more balanced gender representation in similar roles, many of them related to religious practices. Thus increasing numbers of Native American men are weaving ritual baskets. Similarly, there are now several female *moko* artists, and it is no longer uncommon for women to receive full *moko* themselves (not just on their lips or lower face). Such changes are among the ways in which Indigenous people are working to overcome the gender hierarchies that developed under colonialism.

Cultural Expressions

One especially notable recent development is the presence of Indigenous religions in art forms that originated in non-Indigenous cultures, including film, written literature, oil painting, and electronic music. Works *by* Indigenous people *about* Indigenous people are appearing with increasing frequency and receiving much attention and acclaim. Religion has been employed in some of these works both to engage issues arising from colonialism (past or present) and to highlight or explore aspects of Indigenous life on their own terms.

An example of the latter approach is the painting "Red Willows" by David Johnson (Anishinaubae), which appears on page 318. The work is clearly modern, produced in the mid-1990s to accompany Basil Johnston's retelling of the traditional story. The pairing of art and text adds meaning to both, often in a way that highlights the religious aspects of the tale. Thus the significance of the colour red in the painting is revealed only by the text, while the branch that appears both inside and outside the man suggests the interrelatedness of all things, a theme that readers of the story—distracted by its vivid, humorous physicality—could easily miss.

Prominent recent films that focus primarily on Indigenous religion include *Atanarjuat: The Fast Runner* (Canada, 2001), *Whale Rider* (New Zealand, 2002), and *Ten Canoes* (Australia, 2006). Two notable documentaries that consider the appropriation of Indigenous religion are *White Shamans and Plastic Medicine Men* (US, 1996), which looks at the theft and commercialization of Native American traditions by non-Natives, and *Reel Injun* (Canada, 2009), which explores the depictions of Native people in movies.

Several other films refer to Indigenous religion while focusing primarily on the consequences of colonialism, among them *Dance Me Outside* (Canada, 1994), *Rabbit-Proof Fence* (Australia, 2002), *Moolaadé* (Senegal/France/Burkina Faso/Cameroon/Morocco/Tunisia, 2004), and, perhaps most famously, *Once Were Warriors* (New Zealand, 1994). Directed by Lee Tamahori (Maori) and starring mostly Maori actors, *Once Were Warriors* presents a complex picture of the return to Indigenous traditions. For some key female characters, this return is beneficial, helping them to regain a sense of dignity, community, and self-worth in the wake of the personal and cultural havoc wreaked by colonialism. For a number of male characters, however, the return is clouded by anger and misunderstanding, and sadly helps to perpetuate the domestic and communal violence resulting from colonialism.

Literature

One of the first Indigenous writers to be recognized internationally was the poet Pauline Johnson (Mohawk), who began publishing in 1883. In fact, she was described by critics of her time as "perhaps the most unique figure in the literary world on this continent," and even "the greatest living poetess" (Francis 1992: 113). In 1961 Johnson also became the first Canadian writer, the first Canadian woman, and the first Canadian Aboriginal person to be honoured by a commemorative stamp. Her poetry covered a range of topics but very often returned to the sacred theme of place, as in her most famous work, "The Song My Paddle Sings."

The modern era of Indigenous literature began in earnest in 1958 with the appearance of Chinua Achebe's *Things Fall Apart*. Focusing on the life and family of Okonkwo, an Igbo man from a fictional village in Nigeria around the turn of the nineteenth century, the novel depicts the effects of British colonialism, and particularly Christian missionaries, on the life and religion of the Indigenous people of Africa. *Things Fall Apart* was a landmark, undeniably the most influential work of modern African literature to date, and regularly appears high on the lists of the top 100 books of all time (including *Newsweek*'s 2009 "meta-list," on which it ranked number 14).

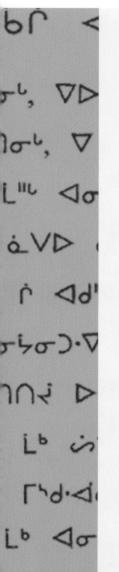

Document

From *The Bone People*, by Keri Hulme (Maori)

Published in 1983, this Booker Prize–winning novel follows three interconnected characters—Simon, Joe, and Kerewin—whose experiences are symbolically linked to Maori religious beliefs and practices. These characters are briefly introduced in the book's prologue.

He walks down the street. The asphalt reels by him. It is all silence.
The silence is music.
He is the singer.
The people passing smile and shake their heads.
He holds a hand out to them.
They open their hands like flowers, shyly.
He smiles with them.
The light is blinding: he loves the light.
They are the light.
. . .
He walks down the street. The asphalt is hot and soft with sun.
The people passing smile, and call out greetings.
He smiles and calls back.
His mind is full of change and curve and hope, and he knows it is being lightly tapped. He laughs. Maybe there is the dance, as she says. Creation and change, destruction and change.
New marae from the old marae, a beginning from the end.
His mind weaves it into a spiral fretted with stars.

He holds out his hand, and it is gently taken.
. . .
She walks down the street. The asphalt sinks beneath her muscled feet.
She whistles softly as she walks. Sometimes she smiles.
The people passing smile too, but duck their heads in a deferential way as though her smile is too sharp. She grins more at the lowered heads. She can dig out each thought, each reaction, out from the grey brains, out through the bones. She knows a lot.
She is eager to know more.
But for now there is the sun at her back, and home here, and free wind all round.
And them, shuffling ahead in the strange-paced dance. She quickens her steps until she has reached them.
And she sings as she takes their hands.
. . .
They were nothing more than people, by themselves. Even paired, any pairing, they would have been nothing more than people by themselves. But all together, they have become the heart and muscles and mind of something perilous and new, something strange and growing and great. Together, all together, they are the instruments of change (Hulme 1983: 3–4).

Achebe's novel was part of the first wave of a flood of modern Indigenous writing around the world. Hundreds of authors have since produced a huge variety of compelling works of fiction, poetry, autobiography, and drama. Among those authors are

- José María Arguedas (Quechua)
- Maria Campbell (Métis)
- Jack Davis (Noongar)
- Louise Erdrich (Anishinaubae)
- Tomson Highway (Cree)
- Keri Hulme (Maori)
- Thomas King (**Cherokee**)
- N. Scott Momaday (Kiowa)
- Sally Morgan (Palku)
- Leslie Marmon Silko (Laguna Pueblo)
- Wole Soyinka (Yoruba)

Religion is a central issue in the works of most Indigenous authors. The very title of Momaday's breakthrough novel *House Made of Dawn*—winner of the 1969 Pulitzer Prize for Fiction—is taken from the Navajo Nightway Prayer.

Keri Hulme's novel *The Bone People* similarly displays elements characteristic of the resurgence of Indigenous traditions in general and Maori traditions in particular. Many of these elements are evident even in the book's brief prologue:

- a rhythmic sense of time, the past connected to the present;
- complementary dualism (the "dance" of "creation and change, destruction and change");
- allusion to the central *koru* (frond/spiral) element of Maori *moko*; and
- the importance of community, of rebuilding the *marae*.

Like other works of contemporary Indigenous art, *The Bone People* taps into the existential possibility of Indigenous religions, applying traditional views and practices to current situations. With both pathos and humour, it shows us characters struggling with their place in the world as individuals and as part of a community. Some of them manage better than others; some of them make terrible mistakes. But nothing is forever, and, as in many Indigenous stories—both past and present—when we get to the end, we are also very clearly at a beginning. For there are always new stories to tell.

✿ Summary

A key problem in understanding Indigenous people and their religions is that they have long been defined, regulated, altered, and in many instances destroyed by non-Indigenous people, often through processes associated with colonialism. The destruction was immense and it continues today in different places around the world. In addition, many incorrect and damaging views of Indigenous people and their traditions have been passed along. Among those incorrect views is the belief that, before colonialism, Indigenous cultures were unchanging and illiterate—which is to say, "primitive."

There is enormous diversity among Indigenous cultures, but many of them share certain broad beliefs and social structures, including a vital connection to specific places; an emphasis on community and relationship; and a view of the sacred as an ongoing process in the world (recall the list on p. 308). In addition, although some Indigenous cultures were literate long before colonialism, orality remains important to virtually all of them. Stories continue to serve as vehicles for the transmission of beliefs and values, although questions of interpretation remain tricky. As with all religious texts, for example, it is difficult to know which stories people understand to be literally or objectively true, and which ones they think about in a more figurative way. Indigenous creation stories, unlike those of the major "Western" religious traditions, often presuppose the existence of the universe and focus on certain elements within it. Repeated themes in these stories include the importance of relationships, as well as the interaction of chaos and order, life and death.

Notwithstanding the patterns that exist among many Indigenous religions, it is crucial to consider the contexts of specific beliefs, practices, and creative expressions. Different communities may perform similar rituals but attribute entirely different meanings to them. There is also, as we have noted, great diversity among Indigenous religions. Some may involve very ornate buildings, for example, while others create much more simple holy structures that easily dissolve back into the landscape.

Despite the dramatic and often harmful changes that have taken place in Indigenous communities over the past several hundred years, many of these communities are reviving and recreating their religious traditions in a variety of ways. Not only are Indigenous religions being presented in new forms or contexts—novels, paintings, films—but, perhaps most important, religious activity is increasingly linked with political activism. Indigenous people are working passionately to reclaim the lands and rights taken from them, and religion continues to be a critical component of those efforts.

Discussion Questions

1. Are all Indigenous religions essentially the same? Why or why not?

2. Why was the colonial appropriation of land so harmful to Indigenous religions?

3. What are some ways in which Indigenous religions have incorporated aspects of contemporary non-Indigenous cultures?

4. How do some trickster tales use chaos to promote social order in a community?

5. What is the literal and symbolic significance of a "journey" in Indigenous rites of passage?

6. What meaning is lost when Indigenous art is examined in a museum?

7. With reference to religious beliefs and practices, how did Indigenous gender relations become more unequal because of colonialism? What are some instances in which gender relations have recently become more equitable?

Glossary

Aborigine An Indigenous person; often the term specifies an Indigenous person of Australia.

Ainu The Indigenous people of northern Japan; not officially recognized as such by the government of Japan until 2008. Current population estimates range widely, from about 25,000 to as high as 200,000.

Anishinaubae The term (roughly translating as "the people") traditionally used by the Odawa, Ojibwe, and Algonkin peoples to refer to themselves. The Anishinaubae are located mainly around the Great Lakes area in Canada and the US.

Arawak The Indigenous people encountered by the Spanish (led by Columbus) in the West Indies in 1492. Most Arawaks were killed by the Spanish or died as a result of other aspects of colonialism, but a few small populations remain in northeastern South America.

Attawapiskat An isolated community of about 2,800 **Cree**, located on James Bay in northern Ontario, Canada. In December 2012 the community's chief, Theresa Spence, began a hunger strike to protest the treatment of Aboriginal people by the government of Canada.

Bunu One of four **Yoruba** groups in central Nigeria, living near the city of Lokoja, where the Niger and Benue Rivers converge.

cargo cults Religious movements, mainly in Melanesia, inspired by the shipments of goods that local Indigenous people saw arriving for foreigners; founded on the belief that one day the spirits would send similar shipments to them, initiating a new age of peace and social harmony.

Cherokee The largest federally recognized Native American group, with more than 300,000 members. Most currently live in the southeastern US, with band headquarters in Oklahoma and North Carolina.

Chumash A Native American people traditionally based along the southern California coast, from Morro Bay to Malibu. Although only about 200 Chumash remained in 1900, recent estimates put their numbers at around 5,000.

colonialism The process in which people from one place establish and maintain a settlement in another, and the consequences of this process for the people who were already there. Historically, those effects have often included the destruction of Indigenous people and cultures.

complementary dualism A worldview in which the universe necessarily comprises both creative and destructive forces, and the two can work together; a feature of many Indigenous religions.

conflict dualism A worldview in which the universe is divided between good and evil forces that are in constant battle with one another; a feature of many Western religions.

Cree The largest Aboriginal group in Canada, numbering more than 200,000. Formerly based in central Canada, Cree populations are now well established in every province from Alberta to Quebec, as well as parts of the northern US such as Montana.

Crow A Siouan-speaking Native American people historically based in the Yellowstone River valley, and now concentrated in Montana.

diviner A religious specialist who uses various ritual tools and practices to gain insight into the hidden or spiritual aspects of particular circumstances, events, problems, etc.

Dogon A West African people living mainly in the central region of Mali, with a population of about half a million. Their first contact with Europeans was in 1857, but the Dogon have been more successful at preserving their traditional religious practices than many other Indigenous Africans.

The Dreaming The term that anthropologists gave to the time and place of Australian Aboriginal origin stories. Although often assumed to represent the archaic past, The Dreaming is actually understood by many traditional Aborigines to lie just out of reach of living memory.

elders Men or women whose wisdom and authority in cultural matters are recognized by their community. Elders are not necessarily old in years, but are understood to possess greater knowledge of tradition than others, and often to be more closely in touch with spiritual forces.

Ghost Dance A religious movement that emerged in the western US in response to the colonial destruction of Indigenous people and cultures. Launched in 1869 by Wodziwob and revived in 1889 by Wovoka, the Ghost Dance was performed in an effort to hasten both the removal of the settlers and the restoration of what Native people had lost. Smaller revivals occurred periodically throughout the twentieth century.

Haisla First Nation on the North Coast of British Columbia, Canada, whose name translates roughly as "living at the river mouth, living downriver." The population of the Haisla reserve in Kitimaat Village is less than 2,000.

hogan A traditional **Navajo** home. The first hogan was the earth itself, and so building a new home reproduces the creation of the world. This structure is at the centre of the community's domestic, social, and religious life. If anyone dies inside a hogan it is never used again, and in fact is often burned.

Igbo One of the largest Indigenous groups in Nigeria, based in the southeastern region of the country. Worldwide population estimates range between 20 million and 40 million.

Indian Act Canadian federal legislation created in 1876 that defines and regulates Native people and their lands and outlines the federal government's responsibilities towards them. The act is administered by the Department of Indian and Northern Affairs and has undergone several amendments and revisions.

Iroquois Also known as the Six Nations; a North American Native confederacy based in the northeastern US and southeastern Canada, originally composed of five Iroquoian-speaking groups (Mohawk, Oneida, Onondaga, Cayuga, and Seneca) and joined in 1722 by the Tuscarora.

Ju'hoansi Indigenous African group with a population of about 30,000 in northeast Namibia and 5,000 in northwest Botswana. Until 50 years ago, the Ju'hoansi were nomadic hunters and gatherers, but since then most of them have adjusted to settled lives and occupations.

Karuk A community from the region of the Klamath River in northwestern California, with a population of about 3,500. "Karuk" translates as "upstream people," in contrast to their downstream neighbours, the **Yurok**.

Kewa Indigenous people from the Southern Highlands province of Papua New Guinea, with a current estimated population of about 65,000.

Lakota The largest of the three Native American groups that make up the **Sioux Nation** (the others are the Eastern and Western Dakota). The Lakota were originally based near the Great Lakes, but moved to the Great Plains in response to the influx of European settlers.

Maori The Indigenous people of New Zealand, who appear to have arrived there in the late thirteenth century from elsewhere in Polynesia. Current estimates put the Maori population at around 700,000.

marae The religious and social home of a Maori community: a cleared area bordered with stones or wooden posts and containing several structures including the *whare whakairo* ("carved house"), dining room, shelters, and a site where the dead are placed in state.

Maya A Mesoamerican civilization (c. 2000 BCE–late 1600s), noted for their highly developed written language, art, architecture, mathematics, and astronomy. Despite the Spanish conquest, Maya people today make up a large portion of the population throughout the region, and millions continue to speak Mayan languages.

mbari A mode or style of cultural practice, especially architecture; principally identified with the Owerri **Igbo** of Nigeria.

Mohawk The most easterly of the Iroquoian Six Nations, based near Lake Ontario and the St Lawrence River.

moko Traditional Maori tattoos originally chiselled into the skin that identify both the individual and his or her relationship to the community. Said to have been brought to earth from the underworld by the ancestors, *Moko* was prohibited by colonial rulers but has resurfaced with the revival of other Maori practices.

Navajo The second-largest Native American group in the US (after the **Cherokee**), with an estimated population of almost 300,000. The Navajo occupy extensive territories in Arizona, New Mexico, and Utah.

New Age A common term for Western spiritual movements concerned with universal truths and individual potential. New Age teachings are drawn from a wide range of religions and philosophies, including astrology, Buddhism, metaphysics, environmentalism, and Indigenous traditions. The term was used in the early 1800s by William Blake and gained wide popularity in the mid-1970s.

Nisga'a Indigenous people of the Nass River valley of northwestern British Columbia. In 1998 the Nisga'a reached a historic settlement with the provincial and federal governments acknowledging their sovereignty over 2,000 square kilometres of land; the Nisga'a agreement was the first formal Native treaty signed in BC since 1854.

Nuer A confederation of peoples in southern Sudan and western Ethiopia; the largest Indigenous group in East Africa, with a population of about 33 million. The Nuer successfully fought off colonial forces in the early twentieth century and have largely resisted conversion to Christianity.

Nyanga Indigenous people from the highlands of east-central Zaire, near the borders of Rwanda and Uganda. Part of the larger Bantu group in Africa, their current population is about 35,000.

Oglala One of seven groups that make up the Lakota Sioux; based at the Pine Ridge Indian Reservation in South Dakota, the second-largest reservation in the US.

Paiute Two related Native American groups, the Northern Paiute (based in California, Nevada, and Oregon) and the Southern Paiute (based in Arizona, California, Nevada, and Utah). Wovoka, the leader of the 1889 Ghost Dance movement, was a member of the Northern group.

Pomo Native people of the northern California coast who, though connected by geography and marriage, traditionally lived in small separate bands rather than as a large unified group. The Pomo linguistic family once comprised seven distinct languages, but few Pomo speakers now remain.

Pondo South African Indigenous group who speak the Xhosa language and live along the southeastern coast of Cape Province.

potlatch A ritual practised by many Indigenous groups of the Pacific Northwest Coast (e.g., Haida, Salish, Tlingit, Tsimshian), in which a family hosts a feast and offers guests a variety of gifts. The ritual typically marks important moments such as marriage, childbirth, or death, and may include music, theatre, and ceremonial dancing.

Pueblo Native people from the southwestern US, particularly New Mexico and Arizona, who traditionally lived in small villages ("pueblos" in Spanish). Approximately 25 separate Pueblo communities remain, including the Hopi, Taos, and Zuni.

residential schools Church-run schools, funded by the Canadian federal government, designed to facilitate the assimilation and Christian conversion of Indigenous people. Families were forced to send their children to the schools, where they remained for months or even years at a time, forbidden to speak their own languages and often subjected to neglect or abuse. The system was established in the 1840s and the last school did not close until 1996.

Sioux Native people with reserves in the Dakotas, Minnesota, Montana, Nebraska, Manitoba, and southern Saskatchewan, and comprised of three main groups: Lakota, Eastern Dakota, and Western Dakota. The Sioux have been central to many key moments of American colonial history, including the Battle of the Little Bighorn, and Sioux writers and political leaders remain among the most influential members of the larger Native North American community.

Stolen Generations The generations of Australian Aborigines who as children were taken from their families by the government and sent either to foster homes or to government- or church-run institutions. Because records were frequently lost or not kept at all, many children were never able to reconnect with their families. The practice continued from approximately 1869 to the early 1970s.

Sun Dance Annual summer ritual practised by peoples of the North American plains (e.g., Blackfoot, Cheyenne, Crow, Kiowa, Sioux). The details of the ritual vary from one community to the next, as does the meaning of the solar symbolism. In the late nineteenth century the Sun Dance was severely discouraged by the Canadian government and outlawed in the US; it has experienced a revival since the 1960s.

sweat lodge A structure traditionally covered with skins, blankets, or dirt, used to induce sweating by pouring water over heated stones to create steam. Sweat lodge ceremonies are performed by several Native North American communities for various medicinal and religious purposes, including purification and reconnection to the spirits.

syncretism The combination of elements from two or more different religious traditions. Too often the term is used negatively to suggest that the "purity" of a particular religion has been compromised or contaminated.

terra nullius Latin for "no one's land," referring to territory over which no person or state has ownership or sovereignty; a concept invoked in several instances by European colonists to claim land occupied by Indigenous people. In Australia, the High Court invalidated this justification in a 1992 ruling.

totem pole A tall pole traditionally carved from a single cedar tree by an Indigenous community of the Pacific Northwest Coast (e.g., Haisla, Nisga'a, Tsimshian) to record historical events, indicate social status, represent ancestral lineage, support a physical structure, etc. Markings are often highly symbolic and specific to particular communities and locations.

trickster Term coined by scholars to classify a variety of usually superhuman figures who appear in the stories of cultures around the world; tricksters disrupt the norms of society and/or nature and often serve to teach important lessons about what kinds of behaviour a particular community considers appropriate.

Tsimshian Indigenous people of the Pacific Northwest Coast, from British Columbia to southeast Alaska. The current Tsimshian population is approximately 10,000.

Tuhoe A Maori community of about 40,000, named for the ancestral figure Tuhoe-potiki. Tuhoe translates as "steep" or "high noon," and the people are known for their dedication to Maori identity and heritage: about 20 per cent continue to live on their traditional lands on the steep eastern North Island of New Zealand, and 40 per cent still speak their native language.

Ubuntu The African concept that all human beings are interconnected, employed most famously by Nelson Mandela and Archbishop Desmond Tutu as one of the founding principles of the new South Africa. *Ubuntu* has since gained prominence in the US as well.

vision quest Fasting ritual undertaken in many Native North American communities to induce visions through contact with spirits. A vision quest typically lasts several days and involves a solitary journey into the wilderness; it may be undertaken as a rite of passage to adulthood or during other key life events, such as preparation for war.

Wiradjuri The largest Indigenous group in New South Wales, Australia, who have lived in the central region of the state for more than 40,000 years. No known native speakers of the Wiradjuri language remain.

Xhosa Indigenous people living mainly in southeast South Africa. There are currently about 8 million Xhosa, and their language is the second most common in South Africa after Zulu. Nelson Mandela and Archbishop Desmond Tutu are both Xhosa.

Yanyuwa A small group of Aborigines located mainly in the Northern Territory of Australia. Fewer than ten speakers of the Yanyuwa language currently remain.

Yolngu Aboriginal community from northeastern Arnhem Land in Australia's Northern Territory. For more than 50 years, Yolngu leaders have been centrally involved with land claims.

Yoruba One of the largest Indigenous groups in west Africa, with a population of approximately 30 million based mainly in Nigeria. Yoruba traditions have had an enormous influence on the religions of African communities around the world; because so many African slaves were Yoruba, their impact has been especially significant in the Americas.

Yurok Native American community, with a population of about 6,000, who have lived near the northern California coast for more than 10,000 years. Yurok translates as "downstream people," in contrast to their upstream neighbours, the **Karuk**.

Further Reading

Ballinger, Franchot. 2004. *Living Sideways: Tricksters in American Indian Oral Traditions*. Norman: University of Oklahoma Press. An excellent, engaging introduction to the roles, meanings, and diversity of Native American trickster figures; focuses on traditional (oral) stories but also includes references to contemporary literature.

Baum, Robert M. 1999. *Shrines of the Slave Trade: Diola Religion and Society in Precolonial Senegambia*. New York: Oxford University Press. This detailed study is one of the few to examine the pre-contact history of any African Indigenous religion.

Bell, Diane. 1983. *Daughters of the Dreaming*. Melbourne: McPhee-Gribble. An accessible (and bestselling) work of groundbreaking scholarship on the religious lives of Aboriginal women in central Australia.

Bockle, Simon. 1993. *Death and the Invisible Powers: The World of Kongo Belief*. Bloomington: Indiana University Press. An insider's introduction to the religious life of the Kongo people of Lower Zaire and to African religions generally, focusing on views and behaviours concerning death.

Deloria, Vine, Jr. 1994 (1972). *God Is Red: A Native View of Religion*. 2nd ed. Golden: Fulcrum. Indispensable overview of Native American religious perspectives, particularly regarding the importance of sacred places and the effects of colonialism.

Francis, Daniel. 1992. *The Imaginary Indian: The Image of the Indian in Canadian Culture*. Vancouver: Arsenal Pulp. A detailed, accessible discussion of the ways in which non-Natives in Canada have appropriated Native identity.

Gill, Sam D. 1982. *Beyond the "Primitive": The Religions of Nonliterate Peoples*. Englewood Cliffs, NJ: Prentice-Hall. Still one of the best general introductions to Indigenous traditions; especially useful on what religious practices mean to their communities.

Jacobs, Sue-Ellen, Wesley Thomas, and Sabine Lang, eds. 1997. *Two-Spirit People: Native American Gender Identity, Sexuality, and Spirituality*. Urbana and Chicago: University of Illinois Press. A vital collection of essays examining the connections between Native North American religions and constructions of gender and sexuality, from the traditional acceptance of diversity in many communities to current efforts to reclaim that acceptance.

LeRoy, John, ed. 1985. *Kewa Tales*. Vancouver: University of British Columbia Press. A valuable collection of traditional oral narratives from Papua New Guinea, catalogued to highlight various story patterns.

Mead, Hirini Moko. 2003. *Tikanga Maori: Living by Maori Values*. Wellington, NZ: Huia. A useful overview of Maori *tikanga* ("way of doing things"), especially the connections between religion and the creative arts; promotes *tikanga* as a guide for non-Maori people.

Olajubu, Oyeronke. 2003. *Women in the Yoruba Religious Sphere*. New York: State University of New York Press. Examines women's roles—along with issues of gender and power relations—in both traditional and contemporary Yoruba thought and practice.

Olupona, Jacob K., ed. 2004. *Beyond Primitivism: Indigenous Religious Traditions and Modernity.* New York: Routledge. One of the very few works to look at the contemporary situation of Indigenous religions; contributors from a broad range of backgrounds consider traditions from across America, Africa, Asia, and the Pacific.

Renne, Elisha P. 1995. *Cloth That Does Not Die: The Meaning of Cloth in Bùnú Social Life.* Seattle: University of Washington Press. A clear, insightful look at the role of a key material object in the culture (and especially religion) of the Bunu Yoruba people.

Rosaldo, Renato. 1980. *Ilongot Headhunting 1883–1974: A Study in Society and History.* Stanford: Stanford University Press. An influential analysis of the meaning and function of headhunting for the Ilongot people in the Philippines; discredits the notion that Indigenous societies were/are static, as opposed to European societies that changed over time.

Ryan, Allan. 1999. *The Trickster Shift: Humour and Irony in Contemporary Native Art.* Vancouver: University of British Columbia Press. The first book-length study of the influence of trickster conceptions in modern Native art, with photos of recent work alongside commentaries from the artists.

Shigeru, Kayano. 1994. *Our Land Was a Forest: An Ainu Memoir.* Trans. Kyoko Selden and Lili Selden. Boulder: Westview. A moving personal account by an Ainu man who has spent much of his life documenting his people's culture and history, as well as creating a school to ensure the continuation of the Ainu language.

Smith, Jonathan Z., et al., eds. 1995. *The HarperCollins Dictionary of Religion.* San Francisco: Harper-Collins. The following entries provide an excellent brief introduction to particular topics relevant to the study of Indigenous religions: "Africa, traditional religions in"; "Australian and Pacific traditional religions"; "circumpolar religions"; "Mesoamerican religion"; "Native Americans (Central and South America), new religions among"; "Native Americans (North America), new religions among"; "non-literacy"; "North America, traditional religions in"; "Religions of Traditional Peoples"; "South American religions, traditional"; "traditional religions, Western influence on."

Swain, Tony, and Garry Trompf. 1995. *The Religions of Oceania.* London: Routledge. The first (and possibly best) book in English on the religions of the southwest Pacific as a whole; provides clear interpretive tools and general information on the history and content of these traditions, from before colonialism through to modernity.

Wright, Ronald. 1992. *Stolen Continents: The "New World" through Indian Eyes.* Boston: Houghton Mifflin. Powerful, accessible account of the colonization and survival of five American civilizations—Aztec, Maya, Inca, Cherokee, and Iroquois—that includes much Indigenous testimony.

Recommended Websites

http://cwis.org
Center for World Indigenous Studies Virtual Library: a list of websites offering further information on Indigenous cultures and current issues, organized by region.

www.everyculture.com
Countries and Their Cultures: contains brief but substantive information on most Indigenous cultures, including an overview of religious beliefs and practices, and a bibliography for further research on each group.

http://indigenouspeoplesissues.com
Indigenous Peoples Issues and Resources: articles, updates, and information on current issues affecting Indigenous communities around the world, provided by a global network of scholars, activists, and organizations.

www.hanksville.org/sand/index.html
A Line in the Sand: information and resources about (and critiques of) the appropriation of Indigenous cultural property, particularly religious images and practices.

www.nativeweb.org
NativeWeb: news and information from and about Indigenous people and organizations around the world. Initiated the NativeWiki project, a library of Indigenous data to which users can also contribute.

www.peoplesoftheworld.org.
Peoples of the World: education for and about Indigenous people; includes lists of resources such as documentaries and volunteer programs, as well as detailed information about Indigenous people organized by language, country, and name.

References

Achebe, Chinua. 1996 (1958). *Things Fall Apart.* Oxford: Heinemann.
Allen, John. 2008. *Desmond Tutu: Rabble-Rouser for Peace: The Authorized Biography.* Chicago: Lawrence Hill.

Baum, L. Frank. 1890. *Aberdeen* (South Dakota) *Saturday Pioneer,* 20 December.

Beck, Peggy V., Anne Lee Walters, and Nia Francisco. 1992 (1977). *The Sacred: Ways of Knowledge, Sources of Life*. Redesigned ed. Tsaile: Navajo Community College Press.

Bellfy, Philip. 2005. "Permission and Possession: The Identity Tightrope." In Ute Lischke and David T. McNab, eds. *Walking a Tightrope: Aboriginal People and Their Representations*, 29–44. Waterloo: Wilfrid Laurier University Press.

Bunn-Marcuse, Kathryn. 2005. "Kwakwaka'wakw on Film." In Ute Lischke and David T. McNab, eds. *Walking a Tightrope: Aboriginal People and Their Representations*, 305–34. Waterloo: Wilfrid Laurier University Press.

Campbell, Maria. 1973. *Halfbreed*. Halifax: Goodread.

Cooke, Dewi. 2008. "'Sorry' Statement Should Acknowledge Cultural Loss, Says State Leader." *The Age* (1 February). Accessed 11 Oct. 2009 at www.theage.com.au/articles/2008/01/31/1201714153311.html.

Cox, James L. 2007. *From Primitive to Indigenous: The Academic Study of Indigenous Religions*. Aldershot: Ashgate.

Deloria, Vine, Jr. 1988 (1969). *Custer Died for Your Sins: An Indian Manifesto*. Norman and Lincoln: University of Oklahoma Press.

———. 1997. "Conclusion: Anthros, Indians, and Planetary Reality." In Thomas Biolsi and Larry J. Zimmerman, eds. *Indians and Anthropologists: Vine Deloria, Jr., and the Critique of Anthropology*, 209–21. Tucson: University of Arizona Press.

Drewal, Margaret Thompson. 2002. "The Ontological Journey." In Graham Harvey, ed. *Readings in Indigenous Religions*, 123–48. London: Continuum.

Ebert, Roger. 1998. Review of *Smoke Signals*. rogerebert.com (3 July). Accessed 17 Jan. 2010 at http://rogerebert.suntimes.com/apps/pbcs.dll/article? AID=/19980703/REVIEWS/807030303/1023.

Eliot, T.S. 1959. *Four Quartets*. London: Faber and Faber.

Francis, Daniel. 1992. *The Imaginary Indian: The Image of the Indian in Canadian Culture*. Vancouver: Arsenal Pulp.

Gill, Sam D. 1982. *Beyond the "Primitive": The Religions of Nonliterate Peoples*. Englewood Cliffs: Prentice-Hall.

Heiss, Anita. 2001. "Aboriginal Identity and Its Effects on Writing." In Armand Garnet Ruffo, ed. *(Ad)dressing Our Words: Aboriginal Perspectives on Aboriginal Literatures*, 205–32. Penticton, BC: Theytus.

Hulme, Keri. 1983. *The Bone People*. Wellington: Spiral.

Johnston, Basil. 1995. *The Bear-Walker and Other Stories*. Illustrated by David Johnson. Toronto: Royal Ontario Museum.

King, Thomas. 1993. *Green Grass, Running Water*. Toronto: HarperCollins.

Looking Horse, Arvol. 2009. "Concerning the deaths in Sedona." *Indian Country Today* (16 Oct.). Accessed 20 Feb. 2010 at www.indiancountrytoday.com/opinion/columnists/64486777.html.

Lutz, Hartmut. 1991. *Contemporary Challenges: Conversations with Canadian Native Authors*. Saskatoon: Fifth House.

McKay, Stan. 1996. "An Aboriginal Christian Perspective on the Integrity of Creation." In James Treat, ed. *Native and Christian: Indigenous Voices on Religious Identity in the United States and Canada*, 51–5. New York: Routledge.

Matthews, Washington. 1995 (1902). *The Night Chant: A Navaho Ceremony*. Salt Lake City: University of Utah Press.

Mitchell, Ryan. 2003. "Maori Chief on Facial Tattoos and Tribal Pride." *National Geographic News* (14 Oct.). Accessed 21 Mar. 2009 at http://news.nationalgeographic.com/news/pf/84577710.html. 2009.

Moses, Daniel David, and Terry Goldie. 1992. "Preface: Two Voices." In Daniel David Moses and Terry Goldie, eds. *An Anthology of Canadian Native Literature in English*, xii-xxii. Toronto: Oxford University Press.

Renne, Elisha P. 1995. *Cloth That Does Not Die: The Meaning of Cloth in Bunu Social Life*. Seattle: University of Washington Press.

Ross, Rupert. 1992. *Dancing with a Ghost: Exploring Indian Reality*. Markham: Octopus.

Sarris, Greg. 1992. ""What I'm Talking about When I'm Talking about My Baskets": Conversations with Mabel McKay." In Sidonie Smith and Julia Watson, eds. *De/Colonizing the Subject: The Politics of Gender in Women's Autobiography*, 20–33. Minneapolis: University of Minnesota Press.

Shigeru, Kayano. 1994. *Our Land Was a Forest: An Ainu Memoir*. Trans. Kyoko Selden and Lili Selden. Boulder: Westview.

Silko, Leslie Marmon. 1977. *Ceremony*. New York: Penguin.

Swain, Tony, and Garry Trompf. 1995. *The Religions of Oceania*. London: Routledge.

Tait, Norman. 1993. Foreword to Hilary Stewart, *Looking at Totem Poles*, 9–11. Vancouver: Douglas & McIntyre.

Webber-Dreadon, Emma. 2002. "He Taonga Tuku Iho, Hei Ara: A Gift Handed Down as a Pathway." In Graham Harvey, ed. *Readings in Indigenous Religions*, 250–9. London: Continuum.

Zinn, Howard. 1995. *A People's History of the United States: 1492–Present*. New York: HarperPerennial.

Note

I would like to express my very great thanks to all those who read, commented upon, or inspired any part of this chapter: Meagan Carlsson, Ted Chamberlin, Michel Desjardins, Graham Harvey, Amir Hussain, Agnes Jay, Kelly Jay, Daniel Heath Justice, Sarah King, Sally Livingston, Jennifer Mueller, Michael Ostling, Keren Rice, and Mark Ruml. I also wish to dedicate this chapter to Willard Oxtoby, who defined much of my time at the University of Toronto and who was always generous with both his scholarship and his humour.

7

New Religions and Movements

Roy C. Amore

In this chapter you will learn about:

- The differences between a religion, a sect, and a cult
- The origins, beliefs, and practices of Eastern movements that are now established in the West, such as Soka Gakkai, Falun Dafa, and the International Society for Krishna Consciousness
- The origins, beliefs, and practices of Western movements such as the Church of Jesus Christ of Latter-Day Saints, the Baha'i Faith, the Nation of Islam, and the Kabbalah Centre
- The origins, beliefs, and practices of new Western movements such as Wicca (modern witchcraft), Scientology, the Raëlian Movement, and New Age traditions.

The youngest of the Abrahamic religions covered in this volume is well over 1,000 years old, but innovations in religion did not end with Islam. The early nineteenth century saw the emergence of many new faiths, and more have developed since then. This chapter explores a selection of those newer religions. First, though, we need to consider what distinguishes a "religion" from a "sect" or a "cult."

❧ Defining New Religions, Sects, and Cults

What is a "new religion"? The question might be easier to answer if scholars could agree on what constitutes a religion. But there are hundreds, if not thousands, of ideas on that subject. Even a definition as seemingly basic as "belief in a god or goddess" would not take into account non-theistic traditions such as Buddhism and Jainism. Fortunately, it is not our task here to define religion, but to understand what is meant by the terms "sect" and "cult," and how those terms are applied to new religious movements.

Sociologists of religion such as Max Weber, writing in the early 1900s, used the word "**sect**" to refer to Christian splinter groups, new institutionalized movements that had broken away from mainstream denominations, usually in order to practise what they considered to be a purer form of the faith. Often the breakaway group would denounce the parent institution and adopt stricter rules, new modes of worship, or distinctive clothing to set itself apart. With the passage of time, however, most sectarian movements either faded away or moved back towards the mainstream. In

Timeline

1830 CE	Church of Jesus Christ of Latter-day Saints (United States)
1844	Baha'i Faith (Iran)
1929	Nation of Islam (United States)
1930	Soka Gakkai (Japan)
1940s	Wicca (England)
1954	The Church of Scientology (United States)
1965	International Society for Krishna Consciousness (ISKCON) (United States)
1965	The Kabbalah Centre (United States)
1974	Raëlian Movement (France)
1990	Falun Dafa (China)

← Baha'i "Lotus" temple, New Delhi (© Prisma Bildagentur AG/Alamy).

other words, new movements would begin as sects (or sectarian movements) and evolve into churches (new denominations). A similar process can be seen in the history of many other religions.

As for "**cult**," it was originally a neutral term, used as a synonym for "worship" or even "religion." Today, though, its connotations—at least in the popular media—are almost always negative: a cult is generally assumed to be a small group under the control of a charismatic leader who is suspected of brainwashing followers (especially the young) and promoting self-destructive, illegal, or immoral behaviour.

A movement that is accepted by outsiders as a "new religion" will enjoy all the constitutional protections and tax exemptions afforded to established religions. But a movement that gets labelled as a "cult" is likely to attract scrutiny if not harassment from legal authorities and taxation officials. In divorce cases where custody of the children is in dispute, it is not unusual for one parent to use association with a "cult" to argue that the other parent is unfit. And in the 1994 race for the California Senate, one candidate received damaging media attention because his wife was thought to be associated with a cult (Lewis 2003: 208).

Yet the definitional lines between a cult and a sect (or new religion) are quite vague. By the usual definitions, for example, the **Hare Krishna** movement was a sect of Hinduism in India, but in the West its members' unusual practice and dress soon led to their branding as a cult. This suggests that the "cult" label has less to do with the nature of the movement itself than with how sharply it differs from the mainstream religious culture—in other words, that one person's religion is another person's cult.

At the same time, it is possible to identify several traits that many cults seem to share. Cults typically claim to have some special knowledge or insight, perhaps based on a new interpretation of an old scripture or revealed through contact with spirits (or even aliens). Their practice often includes rituals designed to promote ecstatic experiences, and they tend to focus more on individual spiritual

experience than institutional organization (see Dawson 2006: 28–9).

Perhaps the most widely shared characteristic, however, is a charismatic individual leader who demands extreme loyalty. Adherents may be required to work long hours for little or no pay, cut ties with family and friends from the past, denounce former religious beliefs and practices, or even submit sexually to the leader. In extreme cases, leaders may go so far as to demand that followers be willing to die for the cause. The mass suicide (forced or voluntary) of more than 900 members of the Peoples Temple at Jonestown, Guyana, in 1978 is one famous example. Others include the succession of murders and suicides in the mid-1990s associated with the Solar Temple cult, in which more than 70 people in Switzerland, France, and Canada died; the suicides of 37 Heaven's Gate adherents in California in 1997, and the murder-suicide of 780 members of a breakaway Catholic cult called the Movement for the Restoration of the Ten Commandments in Uganda in 2000 (Dawson 2006: 13). The 1993 murder-suicide of 80 people at the Branch Davidian compound near Waco, Texas, was somewhat different in that it was precipitated by an assault on the compound by law enforcement officers. In most of these mass suicides, whether coerced or voluntary, the underlying belief was that the current world order was about to end and be replaced by a new order in which the cult's members would be rewarded for their loyalty. That is, the movements had a **millenarian** belief in an imminent "End of Time" leading to the dawning of a "New Age."

What gives rise to new religious movements? It has often been noted that new religions tend to appear at times of serious cultural disruption or change. The Indigenous prophetic movements discussed in Chapter 6 are classic examples, emerging in societies whose traditional cultures were breaking down under the pressure of European colonization. Similarly, the massive cultural changes of the 1960s gave rise to several new religions in North America.

Hundreds of new religions and movements have established themselves in the West over the past two centuries. This chapter focuses on a small selection of the ones that have been most successful or have attracted the most attention. We will discuss them in three groups, organized according to their spiritual roots: traditional Asian religions, Abrahamic traditions, and other forms of spirituality.

🙏 New Religions from the East

Soka Gakkai

Soka Gakkai was founded in Japan in the years leading up to the Second World War and emerged as an important force only after the war—a period that saw a flowering of new Japanese religions. However, its roots lie deep in Buddhist history, in the tradition of the controversial thirteenth-century monk Nichiren.

The dominant tradition of Nichiren's day was the Pure Land school of Mahayana Buddhism, which taught its followers to trust in the saving power of Amida Buddha. Nichiren, however, believed that a Mahayana scripture called the *Lotus Sutra* represented the culmination of all Buddhist truths, and warned that Japan would be doomed if the people ignored its teachings. At the same time he became increasingly critical of the Pure Land sects of the time, so angering their leaders that they persuaded the emperor to exile him to a remote island. While in exile, he continued to write tracts criticizing other Buddhist sects and promoting his own.

Nichiren's prophecies of impending doom seemed to come true when the Mongols attempted to invade Japan in 1274. Thus he was allowed to return from exile and, with his followers, establish a sect based on his teachings, together with the *Lotus Sutra*. It is to this sect, eventually known as Nichiren Shoshu ("True Nichiren"), that Soka Gakkai traces its roots.

Soka Gakkai ("Association for Creating Values") was established in 1930 as a lay organization within Nichiren Shoshu. Its founder was a reform-minded schoolteacher named Makiguchi Tsunesaburo, who wanted to promote moral values among young people. Many of its leading figures were imprisoned during the Second World War because they refused to recognize the divinity of the Emperor as required by the officially Shinto Japanese state, and Makiguchi himself died in prison before the war ended.

The organization's new leader, Toda Josei, adopted an aggressive recruitment strategy based on an ancient Buddhist missionary principle. To break down resistance to their message, Soka Gakkai members might gather outside the home of a potential convert and chant all day and all night, or point out to shop-owners that their business would improve if they converted because Soka Gakkai members would shop at their stores. Although critics complained that these tactics amounted to harassment and coercion, the approach was effective, and Soka Gakkai grew exponentially under Toda's leadership. Meanwhile, small groups of practitioners began to establish themselves throughout much of Asia, Europe, and the Americas. Often the leaders of these local groups were ethnic Japanese, but the majority of the members were not. As usual with new religious movements, young people made up the majority of the converts.

Today Soka Gakkai International (SGI)—founded in 1975 as a worldwide organization under the umbrella of Soka Gakkai in Japan—claims 12 million members. Most "new religions" in Japan promise this-worldly happiness, and Soka Gakkai is no exception. In particular, it stresses the here-and-now benefits of chanting the sacred mantra *namu myoho renge kyo* ("Hail the marvellous teaching of the *Lotus Sutra*," or, as the Sokka Gakkai website translates it, "I devote myself to the Lotus Sutra of the Wonderful Law"): passing a test, getting a promotion, improving one's outlook on life. Soka Gakkai is also active in youth activities and the enjoyment of nature, sponsoring summer camps designed to give urban youth a taste of Japan's natural beauty and a chance to experience life in a more traditional setting.

At the core of Soka Gakkai is the belief that the practice of Nichiren Buddhism can bring about a personal transformation or "human revolution" that will empower the individual to take effective action towards the goals of peace, justice, social harmony, and economic prosperity. An example of the organization's economic perspective can be seen in a 2008 speech by SGI President Daisaku Ikeda, in which he called for "humanitarian competition" in a new economic order that would avoid both the excessive greed of capitalism and the lack of competition historically associated with socialism (Ikeda 2008).

An emphasis on social engagement had been a central feature of Soka Gakkai from the beginning, and in 1964 it led some prominent members to form a political party. Known as **Komeito**, the new party was not officially affiliated with Soka Gakkai, but its unofficial association with the organization was well recognized. It had socialist leanings, took a strong stand against corruption in Japanese politics, and worked with several other parties in opposition to the long-ruling Liberal Democratic Party (LDP). Finally, in 1993, the LDP government was replaced by a short-lived centre–left coalition of which Komeito was part. When the coalition fell apart, however, the LDP returned to power and Komeito itself soon fragmented as well. The New Komeito party (1998–) is more conservative than its predecessor, with a platform of reducing the size of central government, increasing transparency, and promoting world peace through nuclear disarmament. It is part of the ruling LDP coalition.

Meanwhile, in 1991, Nichiren Shoshu had officially severed its links with Soka Gakkai. It was the most dramatic event in recent Japanese religious history, and the climax of a long dispute between the conservative clergy and the reform-minded lay organization. Following the split, the priests of Nichiren Shoshu even tore down the Grand Hall that Soka Gakkai had built on the grounds of the main Nichiren temple.

The profile of Soka Gakkai in Japan has been somewhat diminished because of the split. But the international organization has continued to grow, even establishing a university in California in 1995, and the split has not affected Soka Gakkai's

practice. Members continue to follow the religious teachings of Nichiren Shoshu, studying the *Lotus Sutra* and chanting the sacred mantra. The emotional power of the chanting grows with repetition as the pace and volume increase, rising to a crescendo.

Falun Dafa (Falun Gong)

Falun Dafa ("Energy of the Wheel of Law"), popularly known as Falun Gong, developed out of a Buddhist qigong tradition in China in the early 1990s. The term *qi* (pronounced "chi" and often spelled *chi* in the older transliteration system) refers to unseen energy flowing through the body, while *qigong* refers to various techniques of breathing and movement designed to permit energy to flow properly through the body, promoting healing, health, and long life. Although Western science has been reluctant to incorporate the flow of energy into its worldview, the belief in *qi* and the various ways to strengthen it have been part of Chinese and other East Asian cultures for centuries. In addition to exercise techniques designed to enhance the flow of *qi*, the Chinese have developed eating patterns that are thought to maintain the proper balance between the *yin* (feminine, cold, wet, dark) and *yang* (masculine, warm, dry, light) forces in the body. Even skeptics have trouble explaining why acupuncturists are able to anesthetize patients by inserting needles at various energy points in the body.

A man named Li Hongzhi brought Falun Dafa to prominence in China in 1992. He explains it as a system of Buddhist cultivation passed down through the centuries, and considers himself only the most recent in a long line of teachers. The system's Buddhist roots are reflected in its name, for the *falun* or Dharma Wheel and its symbols, among them the swastika, are auspicious symbols in Buddhism. Li's teachings of compassion and self-development are based on Buddhist principles and he uses Buddhist symbols and terms, but Falun Dafa is not officially recognized as a traditional school of Chinese Buddhism. As a consequence, the Chinese government has been able to outlaw Falun Dafa without contravening its policy on the five religions it does recognize.

Although Falun Dafa has traditional roots, Li Hongzhi was the first to turn it into a popular practice adapted to everyday life, and the practice spread quickly among the people of China, for whom it was simply a new variation on a familiar theme. Unfortunately, its rapid growth in popularity attracted the attention of the Communist Party, which in 1999 counted a total party membership of just over 63 million. With as many as 70 million members in that year, Falun Dafa was seen as a threat to the party, and the fact that it was increasingly popular among younger party members and their children was particularly disturbing. When some senior party officials began expressing alarm over Falun Dafa in 1998 and early 1999, the leaders

The Falun Dafa symbol. Note the Daoist yin–yang (*taiji*) symbols and Buddhist rotating swastikas. The outer symbols rotate individually, and together they rotate around the central swastika, first in one direction and then in the other. The colours are said to vary depending on the level of visions experienced by the practitioner. (Photo: Falun Dafa Association, http://en.falun dafa.org/introduction.html.)

of Falun Dafa made a fateful decision. They organized a demonstration in April 1999 in the section of Beijing where the top government officials live and work. Sitting silently in orderly rows, without banners or placards, they intended to show that Falun Dafa was not a political threat to the government or the social order. But their silent demonstration had the opposite effect. The government was alarmed by the sudden presence of so large a gathering in the heart of Beijing.

Government officials persuaded the Falun Dafa leadership to send the demonstrators home. Then, three months later, the organization was banned on the grounds that it was an unregistered religion and had the effect of discouraging people from seeking proper medical attention. Falun Dafa members throughout China were arrested, fired, imprisoned, sent to prison camps, tortured, or killed.

Under pressure from the government, Li Hongzhi had left China two years before the ban was imposed. He now lives in New York City, which has become the base of a worldwide organization claiming more than 100 million followers in over 100 countries. Its literature has been translated into more than 40 languages.

Practice

Whereas some people practise *qigong* purely for its physiological benefits, Falun Dafa practitioners seek both physical and spiritual purification through meditation and *qigong* exercises. The organization describes Falun Dafa as "a high-level cultivation practice guided by the characteristics of the universe—Truthfulness, Benevolence, and Forbearance" ("Introduction"). And Li Hongzhi himself refers to it specifically as a "buddhist practice" (Li 2000).

Practitioners are said to develop a *falun* or "law wheel" in the abdomen. This is not the same as the *qi*, which is naturally present in everyone. Once acquired, the *falun* spins in synchrony with the rotation of the planets, the milky way, and other objects in the universe. When rotating clockwise, the *falun* absorbs and transforms energy from the universe, and when rotating counter-clockwise, it dispenses salvation to oneself, to others, and to the universe. According to Li, healing comes not from the *qi* but from the *falun* when it is rotating counter-clockwise. The *falun* changes its rotational direction according to its own dynamics, and it continues to rotate even when one is not actually practising the Dafa exercises. Li writes that this is a unique feature of Dafa practice, setting it apart from other cultivation systems. The energy cluster emitted by the *falun* is called *gong*—hence the alternative name Falun Gong. The *gong* is said to glow like light.

Li divides Falun Gong practices into five sets, with names such as "Buddha showing a thousand hands," which is the foundational set of exercises. It is repeated three times and is meant to open the body's energy channels. When it is done properly, the body will feel warm; this is said to indicate that the energies have been unblocked and that energy is being absorbed from the universe.

Reflecting the practice's Buddhist background, one of its goals is to cultivate "mind-nature" (*xinxing*); that is, to build a character that is kinder, more honest, and more patient.

Although Falun Dafa teaches and practises non-violence, along Buddhist lines, practitioners have faced serious persecution in China, and therefore it remains an underground movement, regularly denounced as an evil cult working against the good of the people. Curiously, it has not been banned in Hong Kong, which has been a part of China since 1997. However, when the organization wanted to hold a major international rally there in 2007, Beijing blocked the event by refusing to grant visas to Falun Dafa members from abroad.

Outside China, Falun Dafa is openly practised and has mounted a campaign of severe criticism of the Chinese government. According to Falun Dafa many practitioners are imprisoned in long-term work camps, where they are used as what amounts to slave labour to produce various goods that are sold in the West. The organization also claims that organs are involuntarily removed from prisoners to be used for transplants. Organizations such as

Amnesty International have lent some credence to these accusations (Amnesty International).

International Society for Krishna Consciousness (ISKCON)

In September 1965 a 70-year-old Hindu holy man arrived by freighter in New York City with virtually nothing but a short list of contacts. A few weeks later, he sat under a now famous tree in Tompkins Square Park and began to chant:

Hare Krishna Hare Krishna,
Krishna Krishna Hare Hare,
Hare Rama Hare Rama,
Rama Rama Hare Hare.

He had learned this *Maha Mantra*, "great mantra," from his guru in India, who had learned it from his guru, and so on—it was said—all the way back to a sixteenth-century Hindu mystic named Chaitanya, who was reputed to enter a state of mystical ecstasy while chanting the three names of his god: Krishna, Hare, Rama. Within a year of his arrival, A.C. Bhaktivedanta Swami Prabhupada had established the International Society for Krishna Consciousness (**ISKCON**) and the "Hare Krishna" movement had begun to take root in America.

The Hare Krishna movement was new to the West, but it was not a new religion. Rather, it was a Western mission of **Vaishnava** Hinduism, the school that emphasizes devotion to Vishnu. Traditional Vaishnavas worship Vishnu both as the Supreme Godhead and in the forms of his ten major avatars—the animal or human forms he has assumed at different times to "come down" (*avatara*) to earth to save humanity. In this system, Krishna, "the dark-complexioned one," is the eighth avatar. However, Prabhupada belonged to a regional (Bengali) variant known as Gaudiya Vaishnava, in which the Cowherd (Gopala) Krishna is the Supreme Godhead—the source of everything, including other divine forces. As the Supreme Personality, Krishna is understood to encourage a very personal relationship between the devotee and himself. Like other forms of Hinduism, ISKCON teaches that the soul is eternal and subject to reincarnation according to the individual's karma; however, those who practise loving devotion to Krishna will go to his heaven when they die and thus escape the cycle of rebirth. The fundamental texts for ISKCON are the *Bhagavad Gita* and a collection of stories about Krishna's life called the *Srimad Bhagavatam*.

Between the founding of ISKCON in 1966 and his death only 11 years later, Srila Prabhupada travelled throughout North America and around the world spreading his version of Hinduism. His recorded addresses and voluminous writings laid down the fundamental beliefs and practices of the movement. Soon the Hare Krishna movement was establishing centres in cities across North America and abroad. Schools were started to educate the children of devotees in Vedic culture, and some devotees studied "Vedic architecture." Each centre included a temple with an altar area featuring images of Krishna and his consort Radha, as the male and female aspects

of the divine, as well as pictures of the guru, Prabhupada. In addition to the temples, located mostly in large cities, farms were established that undertook to work the land in traditional ways consistent with Vedic (ancient Hindu) ways.

It is not uncommon for new religions to undergo a difficult period of institutional adjustment after the death of the charismatic founder/leader. Following Prabhupada's death, ISKCON vested authority not in a new guru, but in a Governing Body Commission (GBC). Eleven devotees who had risen to high positions under Prabhupada's leadership were recognized by the GBC as gurus, each of whom was authorized to ordain recruits and oversee operations in one of 11 regional zones. Some of the 11 got into trouble with the law over matters including illegal guns, drugs, child abuse, and murder, and by the 1980s six of the original 11 had quit or been removed from office by the GBC. Those who were following in the tradition of Prabhupada had to deal with the bad publicity attracted by those who were not.

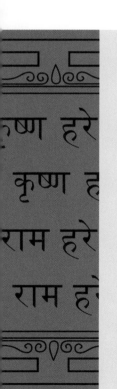

Document

From Swami Prabhupada

On the potential for God-consciousness in all:
This love of God is now in a dormant state in everyone's heart. And, there, love of God is manifested in different ways, but it is contaminated by the material association. Now the material association has to be purified, and that dormant, natural love for Krishna has to be revived. That is the whole process (Prabhupada 1972:606).

On the ethical ideals of Krishna Consciousness:
A person in Krishna Consciousness, fully devoted in the transcendental loving service of the Lord, develops many good qualities. . . . Lord Chaitanya described only some of them to Sanatan Goswami: A devotee of the Lord is always kind to everyone.

He does not pick a quarrel with anyone. He takes the essence of life, spiritual life. He is equal to everyone. Nobody can find fault in a devotee. His magnanimous mind is always fresh and clean and without any material obsessions. He is a benefactor to all living entities. He is peaceful and always surrendered to Krishna. He has no material desire. He is very humble and is fixed in his directions. He is victorious over the six material qualities such as lust and anger. He does not eat more than what he needs. He is always sane. He is respectful to others; but for himself he does not require any respect. He is grave. He is merciful. He is friendly. He is a poet. He is an expert. And he is silent. (Prabhupada 196:104).

Sites

New Vrindaban, West Virginia

Located in a rural area near Moundsville, West Virginia, New Vrindaban is modelled after Vrindaban, India—an area sacred to ISKCON because of its associations with Krishna. New Vrindaban's temple, constructed using traditional Indian tools and techniques, is a popular stop for tourists, and (like most Hare Krishna temples) includes a vegetarian restaurant that is open to the public. The community also grows its own organic food.

Practice

In the *Gita*, Krishna is the charioteer for a heroic royal leader named Arjuna. On the eve of a great battle between two factions of the royal family, Arjuna is troubled at the thought of fighting his own kin. His charioteer counsels him, and in the course of their conversation he reveals his identity. He tells Arjuna that he, Krishna, is the highest of all gods, and informs him that although the yoga (spiritual practice) of good karma actions and the yoga of spiritual wisdom are both valid paths, the best and highest path is **bhakti** yoga: loving devotion to Krishna.

These ideas—that Krishna is the supreme deity and that devotional faith is the best spiritual path—combined with Chaitanya's mystical practice of chanting the praises of Krishna while dancing in ecstasy, are at the heart of the tradition that Prabhupada introduced to the West. Devotional services, *pujas*, to Krishna are held several times a day. One male or female devotee acting as *pujari*, the *puja* leader, stands near the altar and makes offerings of fire and vegetarian food to the images on the altar, which include, in addition to Krishna himself, his consort Radha and his brother Balarama. While the *pujari* performs these rituals, the other devotees chant and dance to the accompaniment of hand-held cymbals and drums or a small organ called a harmonium. As the pace builds, the chanting becomes louder and the dancing more feverish, and when it reaches a climax, many devotees jump high into the air.

Devotees are given a Sanskrit name by their guru. They wear saffron-coloured robes and show their devotion to Krishna by adorning their bodies with painted marks called *tilaka*, made of cream-coloured clay from the banks of a holy lake in India that is associated with the life of Krishna. Two vertical marks represent the feet of Krishna, or the walls of a temple, and below them is a leaf representing the sacred *tulasi* (basil) plant. The diet is strictly vegetarian, and recreational drugs of all kinds, including alcohol and caffeine, are avoided.

Great effort is put into keeping the temple clean, and every activity is to be done "for Krishna," as an act of devotional service. In this way the mental state known as Krishna consciousness is developed. Some devotees are congregational members, living away from the temple and attending only for major temple activities, but others live in or near the temple. Single male and female devotees have separate living quarters, while married couples and families often live in nearby houses or apartments. Sexual activity is allowed only within marriage and for the purpose of procreation. Some devotees have outside employment and turn their wages over to the temple. Others work full-time for the movement.

Most temple-based male devotees shave their heads except for a pigtail at the back of the head. Women are required to dress very modestly. Devotees carry a small bag containing a string of 108 chanting beads (*japa mala*), similar to a Christian rosary, made from the *tulasi* plant. The number 108

Hare Krishna devotees try to recruit new members by chanting their mantra in public places; here, in front of a mural by R. Cronk at southern California's popular Venice Beach.

is sacred in India partly because it represents the multiple of the 12 zodiac houses and 9 planetary bodies as understood in Indian astrology. Using the beads if their hands are free, devotees chant the Hare Krishna mantra hundreds of times each day as they go about their duties at the temple.

ISKCON has a full cycle of festivals, including Gita Jayanti, celebrating the conversation between Krishna and Arjuna. They have staged some lavish festival parades in India and abroad, following the style of traditional Indian religious processions.

The Hare Krishna movement provoked strong reactions, both positive and negative. On the positive side was the enthusiasm shown by celebrities like George Harrison of the Beatles. Harrison's 1970 song "My Sweet Lord" contributed greatly to the acceptance of the movement. But there were many negative reactions as well. One reason was

simply that the movement was so foreign to Western culture and that its members were so keen to adopt Indian styles of dress, music, and worship. The practice of chanting in public places such as airports while trying to raise money generated bad publicity. Another reason was the fact that in the early years ISKCON discouraged any contact between devotees and their former friends and family. As a consequence, the media quickly branded the movement a "cult," and a new profession known as "deprogrammer" came into existence. Hired by concerned parents to kidnap their offspring from the movement, deprogrammers would hold their subjects in a motel room for days and try to break the "cult program" that had been "brainwashed" into them. Sometimes these efforts succeeded, but many young people returned to the Hare Krishnas as soon as they were free to do so.

The schools operated by ISKCON for children of devotees have also generated controversy, initially from concerned outsiders and eventually from former students. Efforts were made to correct the problems and address the concerns of former students. But in 2000 a class action suit (Children of ISKCON vs ISKCON) was filed in Dallas by 44 former students who claimed to have been victims of physical, emotional, and sexual abuse in ISKCON-operated schools in the United States and India. Although the case was initially dismissed on technical grounds, it was refiled in another court. By the time the final settlement was reached, hundreds of others had joined the list of plaintiffs and ISKCON had been forced to seek bankruptcy protection. The claims, totalling $20 million, were settled by 2008, and ISKCON emerged from bankruptcy protection.

ISKCON now runs approximately 350 temples and centres worldwide. It has been especially successful in the former states of the Soviet Union, including Russia. South America has also proven receptive to ISKCON. The spread of ISKCON back to India has been a remarkable development. After starting his mission in America, Prabhupada frequently returned to India, where he established temples in Mumbai as well as various places associated with either Krishna or Chaitanya. Having established a strong presence in the West, ISKCON has been welcomed in India as a movement reviving Gaudiya Vaishnava devotion. Indian devotees now may outnumber Western ones. New temples have been built and major festivals have been organized.

❧ Religions Arising from the Abrahamic Lineage

We now turn our attention to some new religions arising from the three Abrahamic religions. The Church of Latter-day Saints can be classed either as a branch of Protestant Christianity or as a new religion developing out of Christianity. Our second example, the Baha'i Faith, originated in Iran in the context of Shi'i Islam. The Kabbalah Centre draws on a Jewish mystical tradition that is centuries old, while the Nation of Islam was established in the United States by leaders raised in the Christian tradition.

Church of Jesus Christ of Latter-day Saints (Mormons)

The founder of the Church of Jesus Christ of Latter-day Saints, Joseph Smith, Jr (1805–44), claimed that in 1820, as a boy in upstate New York, he had experienced a vision of God and Jesus in which he was told not to join any of the existing denominations. In subsequent visions, he said, an angel of God named Moroni had persuaded him that he had been divinely chosen to restore the true Church of Christ. The new Church was founded in 1830.

As a textual basis for the enterprise, Smith published the *Book of Mormon*, which he said he had translated from gold plates inscribed in "reformed Egyptian" that had been entrusted to him by Moroni during a hilltop meeting near Palmyra, New York. Though subsequent editions referred to Smith as the "translator," the title page of the 1830 first edition declared him "author and proprietor." He said that he was aided in translating the *Book* by two special stones he called "Urim and Thummin"—the names given in the Old Testament to two unidentified objects used by the Hebrew high priests to determine the will of God.

The *Book of Mormon* uses the language and format of the 1611 King James translation of the Bible to tell the previously unknown, and otherwise undocumented, story of two groups, both descended from one of the lost tribes of Israel, that supposedly migrated from the Near East to the New World around 600 BCE and became the ancestors of the Indigenous peoples of the Americas. Including accounts of visitations by Christ sometime after his crucifixion, the book is understood by **Mormons** to be a scriptural account of God's activity in the western hemisphere, parallel with the Bible and its account of divine events in the eastern hemisphere.

Also scriptural for Mormons are Smith's *The Pearl of Great Price*, a book of revelations and

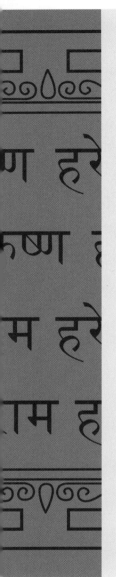

Document

From *The Book of Mormon*, Chapter 1

Here the prophet-historian named Mormon explains how he was instructed to recover the texts hidden by Ammaron, a record-keeper among the Nephites—one of four groups said to have migrated from Jerusalem to the Western hemisphere more than five centuries before the time of Jesus.

1. And now I, Mormon, make a record of the things which I have both seen and heard, and call it the Book of Mormon.

2. And about the time that Ammaron hid up the records unto the Lord, he came unto me, (I being about ten years of age, and I began to be learned somewhat after the manner of the learning of my people) and Ammaron said unto me: I perceive that thou art a sober child, and art quick to observe;

3. Therefore, when ye are about twenty and four years old I would that ye should remember the things that ye have observed concerning this people; and when ye are of that age go to the land Antum, unto a hill which shall be called Shim; and there have I deposited unto the Lord all the sacred engravings concerning this people.

4. And behold, ye shall take the plates of Nephi unto yourself, and the remainder shall ye leave in the place where they are; and ye shall engrave on the plates of Nephi all the things that ye have observed concerning this people.

5. And I, Mormon, being a descendent of Nephi, (and my father's name was Mormon) I remembered the things which Ammaron commanded me.

15. And I, being fifteen years of age and being somewhat of a sober mind, therefore I was visited of the Lord, and tasted and knew of the goodness of Jesus.

. . .

Chapter 4

22. And it came to pass that the Nephites did again flee from before them, taking all the inhabitants with them, both in towns and villages.

23. And now I, Mormon, seeing that the Lamanites were about to overthrow the land, therefore I did go to the hill Shim, and did take up all the records which Ammaron had hid up unto the Lord.

The Book of Mormon. 1961. Salt Lake City. The Church of Jesus Christ of Latter-day Saints. 460–7.

translations, and *Doctrine and Covenants*, a collection of his revelatory declarations. Passages in the latter work address specific moments in the Church's early years. General reflection is interspersed with guidance for particular circumstances in a manner reminiscent of the letters of Paul or certain *surah*s of the Qur'an.

Smith and his small band of followers faced ridicule and persecution from mainstream Christians in New York, and so Smith led them westward in search of a safer place. They established settlements in Ohio and Missouri, and, when driven out of Missouri in 1839, moved on to Nauvoo, Illinois, on the Mississippi River. By now the Mormons were calling themselves the Church of Jesus Christ of Latter-day Saints. It was in Nauvoo that Smith secretly introduced "plural marriage" (polygamy), rumours of which added to the suspicions of outsiders. He also declared himself a candidate for the American presidency in the 1844 elections, advocating a blend of democracy and religious authority that he called "theodemocracy." Some of these innovations caused strife between factions of the Latter-day Saints, and in 1844 Smith and his brother were killed by an anti-Mormon mob.

A number of the traditionalist, anti-polygamy Mormons stayed in the Midwest as the Reorganized Church of Latter-day Saints, with headquarters in Independence, Missouri. For years, this branch of the Mormons was led by descendants of Smith, who prided themselves on remaining true to his legacy. In 2001 they renamed themselves the Community of Christ. Although relatively small in numbers, the Community of Christ is very active in spreading its message around the world. Its members continue to regard the *Book of Mormon* and the *Doctrine and Covenants* as scripture, but emphasize the Bible and its teachings about Jesus. It sees itself not as a "new religion," but as a branch of Christianity in the line running from the Hebrew prophets through Jesus to Joseph Smith.

The larger branch of the Mormons, the Church of Jesus Christ of Latter-day Saints, has a separate history. In 1847 most of them moved to Utah under the leadership of Brigham Young, who had been president of an inner council of 12 that Smith had organized on the pattern of the apostolic Church and who continued to lead the Mormons for the next 30 years. Although they were unsuccessful in their bid to make Utah a Mormon state, they dominated the region and Young was chosen by the US government to serve as governor of the Utah Territory.

Practice

The Mormons set their community apart with a code of behaviour that included not only a rigid sexual morality but strict abstinence from stimulants, including tea and coffee as well as alcohol and tobacco. Young adults are expected to serve as volunteer missionaries for two years after completing high school—a practice that has helped spread awareness of the faith and attract new members around the world. Distinctive Mormon doctrines

include the notion that God is increasing in perfection as human beings improve. Distinctive practices include the augmentation of the spiritual community through baptism (by proxy) of the deceased; because of this practice, Utah has become a world centre for genealogical research. Mormons have also taken a keen interest in western-hemisphere archaeology, in the hope that physical evidence of the events described by the *Book of Mormon* will be found.

The most controversial Mormon practice, however, was plural marriage, which was officially adopted in 1852 and officially dropped in 1890 after the federal government threatened to abolish it. The practice soon faded among mainstream LDS members. But a few congregations refused to accept the change and broke away from the Church of Jesus Christ of Latter-day Saints to form independent sects known collectively as "Fundamentalist Mormons." The largest of these sects, the Fundamentalist Church of Jesus Christ of Latter-day Saints (FLDS), in particular is known for allowing its male leaders to have multiple wives. Because the women involved are often quite young, FLDS congregations have come under intense scrutiny by government officials and concerned women's organizations. In 2007, FLDS leader Warren Jeffs was sentenced to 10 years in prison for being an accomplice to rape.

Whether the Mormons constitute a new religion or merely a new denomination of Christianity is open to question. Joseph Smith saw himself as reforming the Christian Church, and the fact that Mormons keep the Bible as scripture argues for inclusion under the umbrella of Christianity. On the other hand, the Mormons' belief in new, post-scriptural revelations, new scriptures, and new modes of worship (e.g., using water rather than wine for the communion sacrament) suggests a new religion. The issue came into focus during the lead-up to the 2000 electoral primaries, when Massachusetts governor Mitt Romney was seeking nomination as the Republican party's candidate for president. Some conservative Christians who admired his strong family values were nevertheless reluctant to support his candidacy because of his

Mormon faith. However, in the 2012 presidential campaign, the Billy Graham Evangelistic Association removed Mormonism from its list of cults following a visit between Romney and Billy Graham.

The Baha'i Faith

Baha'i developed out of Islam in the mid-nineteenth century, when Islam was already more than 1,200 years old. Although it has many elements in common with Islam, it gives those elements a new and more nearly universal configuration. The main point of divergence is that Baha'is believe that their leader, Baha'u'llah, was a new prophet, whereas Muslims believe there can never be another prophet after Muhammad.

The roots of Baha'i lie in the particular eschatology of Iranian Shi'ism. Ever since the last imam disappeared in 874, Twelver Shi'a had been waiting for a figure known as the **Bab** ("gateway") to appear and reopen communication with the hidden imam. After 10 centuries, most people no longer expected this to happen anytime soon. But seeds of messianic expectation germinated in the soil of political unrest.

Thus in 1844 Sayyid 'Ali Muhammad declared himself to be the Bab, the gateway to a new prophetic revelation. Although he himself was imprisoned in 1845, his followers, the Babis, were not discouraged. They repudiated the Islamic *shari'ah* law and in 1848 the Bab proclaimed himself the hidden Imam. He was executed by a firing squad in 1850, but he left behind a number of writings that have been considered scriptural.

The leadership momentum passed to Mirza Husayn 'Ali Nuri (1817–92), whose religious name was Baha'u'llah, "Glory of God." He had not met the Bab personally, but had experienced a profound feeling of divine support while imprisoned in Tehran in 1852. On his release the following year, he was banished from Iran to Baghdad in Turkish-controlled Iraq, where he became a spiritual leader of Babis in exile. Then, since he was still near enough to Iran to be seen as a threat, in 1863 he was moved to Istanbul. Before going, he declared himself to be

© E Simanor/Robert Harding World Imagery/Corbis

Baha'is have a major temple in every major region of the world. Architects are instructed to take their inspiration from the traditional culture and building styles of the region, while incorporating the number 9 (sacred to Baha'is) and formal gardens in the Iranian style. The temple above, in Haifa, Israel, is Middle Eastern in design. By contrast, the "Lotus temple" in New Delhi (p. 362) evokes the sacred flower that is a symbol of Indian culture.

"the one whom God shall manifest" as foretold by the Bab. He also claimed to have had a "transforming" 12-day mystical experience in 1862.

This transfer to the Mediterranean world expanded the sphere of Baha'u'llah's spiritual activity well beyond the horizons of Iranian Shi'ism. Now he was in a position to address the entire Ottoman Empire. Although he was banished to Acre in Palestine a few years later, his following continued to grow. Nearby Haifa, today in Israel, remains the world headquarters of the Baha'i faith today.

Baha'u'llah wrote prolifically throughout his years in Acre, producing more than 100 texts. Baha'is believe his writings to be God's inspired revelation for this age. Among the most important are *Kitab-i Aqdas* ("The Most Holy Book," 1873), containing Baha'i laws; *Kitab-i Iqan* ("The Book of Certitude," 1861), the principal doctrinal work; and *Hidden Words* (1858), a discourse on ethics. *The Seven Valleys* (1856), a mystical treatise, enumerates seven spiritual stages: search, love, knowledge, unity, contentment, wonderment, and seventh, true poverty and absolute nothingness.

For 65 years after Baha'u'llah's death in 1892, authority in interpreting the tradition was passed on to family heirs. His son 'Abbas Effendi was considered an infallible interpreter of his father's writings, and on his death the mantle of infallibility was bequeathed to his grandson, Shoghi Effendi Rabbani. Shoghi Effendi appointed an International Baha'i Council, and from 1963 leadership was vested in an elected body of representatives called the Universal House of Justice.

Baha'i teachings are based on Baha'u'llah's writings. The soul is believed to be eternal, a mystery that is independent both of the body and of space and time; it can never decay. Yet it becomes individuated at the moment of the human being's conception.

The Baha'i notion of prophethood is in line with the Abrahamic religions. Prophets are sent by God to diagnose spiritual and moral disorder and to prescribe the appropriate remedy. Islam affirms that God sent prophets to various peoples before Muhammad with a message to each. Similarly, Baha'is believe that the world has known a sequence of prophets. They do not believe the prophets' messages to have been community-specific, however: instead, they understand the prophets to speak to the entire world. They also believe that the series remains open; according to their doctrine of "progressive revelation," more prophets will come in future ages.

It may well be their ideal of world community that has done the most to energize Baha'is and make their tradition attractive to serious searchers. Baha'u'llah himself wrote that he came to "unify the world," and Baha'is have asserted the unity of religions. Over a doorway to one Baha'i house of worship is the inscription, "All the Prophets of God proclaim the same Faith." Various religions are seen as corroborating the Baha'i faith itself.

But there is more to unity than doctrinal teaching; Baha'is actively advocate economic, sexual, and racial equality. Extremes of poverty and wealth are to be eliminated, and slavery rooted out—along with priesthood and monasticism. Women are to enjoy rights and opportunities equal to men's, marriage is to be strictly monogamous, and divorce is frowned on. Baha'is have consultative status with the United Nations as an official NGO (non-governmental organization). World peace is to be achieved through disarmament, democracy, and the rule of law, along with the promotion of international education and human rights. Although these goals are clearly compatible with modern secular values, they have a spiritual quality for Baha'is, who cite Baha'u'llah as saying that human well-being is unattainable until unity is firmly established, and Shoghi Effendi as saying that "Nothing short of the transmuting spirit of God, working through His chosen Mouthpiece [Baha'u'llah], can bring it about."

Unity of the races in the human family is actively proclaimed, and interracial marriage welcomed. In recent decades this emphasis has been a major factor in the appeal of the Baha'i Faith to African-Americans. Once the United States eliminates racism at home, some Baha'is claim, it will be the spiritual leader of the world.

Practice

Baha'is strive to live a peaceful and ethical life. Personal spiritual cultivation is encouraged, and recreational drugs and alcohol are forbidden. Since the Baha'i Faith sees itself as the fulfillment of other religions, Baha'is are unusually open to dialogue with other faiths.

Baha'is follow a distinctive calendar, in which the number 19 (which figured in the tradition's early mystical thinking) plays an important role. Beginning with the spring equinox, Iran's traditional time for the new year, there are 19 months of 19 days each, with four additional days (five in leap years) to keep pace with the solar year. Local Baha'i societies assemble for a community feast on the first day of each month, and the final month, in early March, is devoted to dawn-to-dusk fasting, as in the Muslim observance of Ramadan.

Although the 19-day calendar does not recognize the seven-day week, Sunday gatherings for study and reflection have become common among Baha'is in the West. Important days in the annual cycle are essentially historical, marking events in the founding of the religion: several days in April and May are associated with Baha'u'llah's mission, for instance. In addition, the Bab's birth, mission, and martyrdom are commemorated, as are the birth and passing (or ascension) of Baha'u'llah.

Baha'i devotions at the monthly feasts feature a cappella singing but no instrumental music. Prayers are in Farsi (Persian), Arabic, or other languages. Readings are mainly from Baha'i scriptural writings by Baha'u'llah or the Bab, but they may be supplemented with devotional readings from other traditions. Among life-cycle rituals there is a simple naming ceremony, and many who grow up as Baha'is may make a personal profession of faith at the age of 15. Converts simply sign a declaration card. Baha'i weddings vary depending on the tastes of the couple, but always include the declaration "We will all, truly, abide by the will of God." At funerals there is a standard prayer for the departed, which is virtually the only prayer said in unison by Baha'is.

Personal devotions are similar to Islamic practice: the faithful wash their hands and face before praying, and set prayers are said at five times of the day. Also reminiscent of Islam is the practice of repeating the phrase *Allahu-'l Abha* ("God is the most glorious"). These similarities notwithstanding, the Baha'i faith has gone its own way. Its revelation does not conclude with the Qur'an, and its ideals for society depart from those reflected in the *shari'ah*. There have also been political tensions with Islam. Muslims have tended to see the Baha'is as Israeli sympathizers, and in Iran the Baha'i community suffered serious losses in lives and property after the Islamic revolution of 1979.

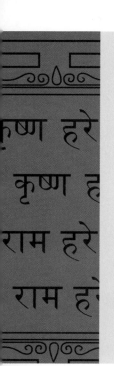

Document

Baha'i Prayer

A prayer, composed by 'Abdu'l-Bahá, reflecting the Baha'i belief that the oneness of humankind overrides any religious, racial or national divisions.

Oh kind Lord! Thou Who art generous and merciful! We are the servants of Thy threshold and we are under the protection of Thy mercy. The Sun of Thy providence is shining upon all and the clouds of Thy mercy shower upon all. Thy gifts encompass all, Thy providence sustains all, Thy protection overshadows all and the glances of Thy favour illumine all. O Lord! Grant unto us Thine infinite bestowals and let Thy light of guidance shine.

Illumine the eyes, make joyous the souls and confer a new spirit upon the hearts. Give them eternal life. Open the doors of Thy knowledge; let the light of faith shine. Unite and bring mankind into one shelter beneath the banner of Thy protection, so that they may become as waves of one sea, as leaves and branches of one tree, and may assemble beneath the shadow of the same tent. May they drink from the same fountain. May they be refreshed by the same breezes. May they obtain illumination from the same source of light and life. Thou art the Giver, the Merciful! (*Baha'i Prayers*, 1969: 43–4).

Since the end of the nineteenth century, the Baha'i Faith has spread around the world. It now claims some 7 million adherents in 235 countries. These include 750,000 in North America and several times that number in India. More than one-quarter of local councils are in Africa and a similar number in Asia. There are nearly as many councils in the southwestern Pacific as in Europe.

The Nation of Islam

It is estimated that at least 20 per cent of the Africans taken as slaves to the Americas were Muslims. One early promoter of Islam—or a version of it—among African-Americans was Noble Drew Ali, who in 1913 founded the Moorish Science Temple of America in Newark, New Jersey. By the time of his death in 1929, major congregations had been established in cities including Chicago, Detroit, and Philadelphia.

Whether Wallace D. Fard (1893–1934?) was ever associated with the Temple is unclear; his followers say he wasn't. But the idea that Islam was the appropriate religion for African Americans was in the air when he established the Nation of Islam (NOI) in Detroit in 1930. Fard's version of Islam bore little resemblance to either the Sunni or the Shi'i tradition. For Muslims, who understand Allah to be a purely spiritual entity, the most fundamental difference lay in the NOI's claim that Allah took human form in the person of Fard himself. In fact, Fard was identified as the second coming of Jesus as well. These claims may have originated in Fard's first encounter with Elijah Poole (1897–1975), a young man who had felt called to a religious mission of some kind, but did not think of it as a Christian one and had stopped attending church before his fateful 1923 meeting with Fard. He later described the meeting:

> when I got to him I . . . told him that I recognized who he is and he held his head down close to my face and he said to me, "Yes, Brother." I said to him: "You are that one we read in the Bible that he would come in the last day under the name Jesus." . . . finally he said; "Yes, I am the one that you have been

looking for in the last two thousand years" (quoted in Sahib 1951: 91–2).

Fard was so impressed with the young man—whose name he later changed to Elijah Muhammad—that he authorized him to teach Islam with his blessing. Elijah quickly became Fard's favourite disciple.

The men who developed the theology of the Nation of Islam were more familiar with the Bible than the Qur'an, but the story they told was no more familiar to mainstream Christians than it was to Muslims. They maintained that all humans were originally black and had lived in harmony as one tribe called Shabazz for millions of years, until an evil man named Yakub rebelled and left Egypt for an island where he created a white race by killing all dark babies. Eventually, the evil white race returned to Egypt and subjugated the blacks, bringing oppression and disunity to humankind. God sent Moses to try to redeem them, but that effort failed. Now the blacks needed to undergo a "resurrection" and recognize themselves as proud members of the Shabazz people who once had a great and peaceful society.

Martha Lee has argued that the Nation of Islam is a millenarian movement (1996: 3). In the NOI version of history, white rule has lasted more than 6,000 years and is approaching the "end time," when the Mother of Planes—a huge aircraft base in the sky—will destroy the "white devils." The "Fall of America" is to be expected soon. In fact, Elijah Muhammad originally prophesied that the fall would occur in the mid-1960s. When that prediction failed to come true, NOI thinking about the "end time" became less literal.

An economic as well as a religious movement, the NOI advocates black economic self-sufficiency and teaches a strict ethical way of life. It followed the Islamic prohibitions on pork and alcohol, but did not until much later practise Friday prayers (services were generally held on Sunday) or follow the *shari'ah* law. Although Elijah Muhammad called for a separate state, such a demand was too impractical to pursue seriously.

The Nation of Islam came to the attention of the authorities in Detroit when it was rumoured that

Fard had promised life in heaven for anyone who killed four whites. This was most likely not true, although he was known to have preached that anyone who killed four devils would go to heaven. In any event, Fard disappeared after he was arrested and expelled from Detroit in 1933. Elijah Muhammad took over the leadership, but the movement fragmented, and some factions were quite hostile to him. Leaving Detroit in 1935, he settled in Washington, DC, where he preached under the name Elijah Rasool (Lee 1996: 26).

In 1942, however, he was convicted of sedition for counselling his followers not to register for the draft. His wife, Clara, directed the organization during the four years he spent in prison, and after his release in 1946 the NOI's numbers soon began to grow. Much of the credit for the movement's expansion in the 1950s has been given to a convert named Malcolm X.

Malcolm X

Malcolm Little (1925–65) was born in Nebraska but spent much of his childhood in Lansing, Michigan. When he was six, his father was run over by a streetcar; the coroner ruled it a suicide, but the Little family believed he had been killed by a white supremacist group. After his father's death, the family was impoverished and his mother suffered a nervous breakdown, so the children were put in foster care. Later, Malcolm moved to Boston and became involved with criminals. It was while he was serving time for theft that he was encouraged by his brother to join the NOI. He read widely and after his release in 1952, he became a key disciple of Elijah Muhammad. Like other converts at that time, he took the surname X to protest the absence of an African name and to recall the X branded on some slaves. Before long Malcolm X had become the leader of the Harlem temple. His eloquence brought him national attention as an advocate for Black Power, and he came to symbolize the black defiance of white racism in America.

Despite his success, however, Malcolm X became increasingly alienated from the movement.

Finally in 1964 he broke away from the NOI and founded Muslim Mosque, Inc. Increasingly aware of the differences between NOI theology and that of traditional Islam, he converted to Sunni Islam and made the pilgrimage to Mecca, where he learned that Islam was not an exclusively black religion, as the NOI had taught. It was a life-changing experience. Changing his name to El Hajj Malik El-Shabazz, he began to teach an understanding of Islam as a religion for all races. Less than a year later, in February 1965, he was assassinated while giving a speech in New York. Three members of the NOI were convicted of the murder, although some people suspected that the FBI's Counter Intelligence Program might have played a role in instigating the assassination (Lee 1996: 44).

Warith Deen Muhammad

The early 1970s also saw a softening of the NOI's attitude towards whites and an increasing willingness to work with other black organizations. When Elijah Muhammad, known as the Messenger, died in 1975, the leadership passed to his son Wallace, who moved the NOI further towards the mainstream. He declared an end to the idea that all whites were devils, withdrew the demand for a separate black state, and helped put the NOI on a more solid financial basis. He also renamed the temples, adopting the Arabic word for mosque, "masjid." This, together with a new emphasis on studying the Qur'an, brought the NOI into Sunni Islam. In 1975 Wallace renamed the organization the World Community of al-Islam in the West (WCIW), and in 1981 it became the American Muslim Mission. In 1985 the name was changed again to the American Society of Muslims. He also renamed himself as Warith Deen Muhammad (the inheritor of the religion of Muhammad), and became a mainstream American Sunni leader until his death in 2008.

Louis Farrakhan

Not all members of the former NOI agreed with these reforms, however. Among the dissenters was

Minister Louis Farrakhan. In 1978 he broke with WCIW and formed a new organization modelled on the NOI. He restored the original name, reinstituted the Saviour's Day festival—formerly the most important holiday—and attracted a large number of members.

In 2001 a former member of the revived NOI published an account of his experience that was particularly critical of Farrakhan's financial dealings. According to Vibert L. White, Jr, members were pressured to donate large sums, and many struggling black-owned businesses were left with unpaid bills for their services to the organization, even as substantial amounts of money were finding their way to various members of the Farrakhan family (White 2001).

At the same time, Farrakhan appears to have courted African Muslim leaders, including Libya's Muammar Gaddafi, for support. Perhaps this helps to explain why he has moved the NOI towards the Islamic mainstream by encouraging Islamic-style daily prayers and the study of the Qur'an. The most difficult change he made was to drop the doctrine that identified Fard as Allah and Elijah Muhammad as his Messenger. In a 1997 conference, Farrakhan publicly affirmed that Muhammad was the last and greatest prophet of Allah (Walker 2005: 495).

In 1995 Farrakhan organized a "Million Man March" on Washington, DC, to draw attention to the role of the black male and to unite for social and economic improvement. The March was a joint effort sponsored by many black organizations, and most of the participants had a Christian background. As the main organizer, however, Farrakhan set the agenda. Dennis Walker writes:

> The March was an Islamizing event. A range of Muslim sects were allowed to appear before the multitude and recite the Qur'an in Arabic on a basis of equality with the Christian and black Jewish clerics whom Farrakhan had inducted. It was a recognition in public space of Islam as part of the being of blacks that had had no precedent (Walker 2005: 508).

Although the March was criticized for excluding black women and promoting a Muslim agenda, as well as its lack of transparency in accounting, it did bring several African-American organizations into fuller cooperation and helped draw public attention to the challenges faced by African Americans.

The Kabbalah Centre

The Kabbalah Centre in Los Angeles teaches a new form of spirituality based on traditional Jewish mysticism. As an organization, it traces its roots to a centre for **Kabbalah** studies founded in Jerusalem in 1922 by Rabbi (or Rav) Yehuda Ashlag. But the tradition stretches back through the sixteenth-century master Isaac Luria to the (probably) thirteenth-century text called the *Zohar* and beyond. The Centre itself claims that its teachings go back some 4,000 years.

The National Institute for the Research of Kabbalah (later renamed the Kabbalah Centre) was founded in 1965 by Rabbi Philip S. Berg. Raised in New York City, he had trained as a rabbi but was not practising when, during a trip to Israel in 1962, he met Rabbi Yehuda Brandwein, the Kabbalist dean of a *yeshiva* in Jerusalem's Old City, and a descendant of many famous Hasidic scholars. With Brandwein as his mentor, Berg became an active Kabbalist.

Berg's followers claim that he succeeded Rabbi Brandwein as leader of the entire Kabbalah movement, including leadership of the Jerusalem yeshiva. At the yeshiva itself, however, Brandwein's son Rabbi Avraham Brandwein is considered the leader, and the Kabbalah taught there is in no way new.

In itself, Berg's Kabbalah is not new either, but his approach to it is radically different. Traditionally, the study of Kabbalah was restricted to mature male Jews, aged 40 or older, who had already completed years of Talmudic studies. Yet Berg taught Kabbalah to his secretary, who would later become his wife and a leading figure in the movement herself. Within a few years, the Bergs set out to make Kabbalah available to the world at large: young and old, male and female, Jews and Goyim alike. This was the new dimension of Berg's Kaballah, and it sparked a great deal of controversy in traditional Jewish circles.

On its website the Centre defines Kabbalah as "ancient wisdom and practical tools for creating joy and lasting fulfillment now." The emphasis on "practical tools" is significant, for the purpose of Kabbalah study, as the Centre presents it, is to unlock the human potential for greatness. In fact, it is a fundamental tenet of Kabbalah (as it is of Eastern traditions such as Hinduism and Buddhism) that humans will be reincarnated over and over again, returning to this world as many times as necessary "until the task of transformation is done" (Kabbalah Centre).

Another fundamental principle is that the reality perceived by our five senses is only a tiny portion of the totality, and that events occurring in the knowable 1 per cent of reality are the product of events in the unknown 99 per cent. Berg's followers maintain that his teachings enable people to perceive the 99 per cent of reality that normally remains unknown.

Practice

Kabbalists experience God in the world as the energy that underlies and permeates all things.

As the sixteenth-century Kabbalist Moses Cordovero put it, even a stone is "pervaded by divinity." (A similar idea can be found in the non-canonical Christian Gospel of Thomas, which quotes Jesus as saying, "Li[f]t the stone and there you will find me. Split the wood and I am there"; Saying 30 + 77b [pOxy. 1.23–30]).

To illustrate the way God and the material world interrelate, Kabbalah uses a diagram usually referred to as the Tree of Life. The space above the tree represents God as *Ein Sof*, "The Endless"—a common Kabbalah term calling attention to the infinite nature of God. The tree itself pictures the 10 **spherot**, shining circles of fire, representing the 10 attributes of God in the world. The topmost circle represents the Crown (*Keter* or *Kether*). Below it the other nine circles are arranged in three sets, each with a circle in the left, centre, and right columns. Read from the top down, these three sets represent the spiritual, intellectual, and material (earth-level) qualities of creation. The *spherot* in the right-hand column represent masculine attributes of God and those on the left feminine attributes. The *spherah* in the centre of the nine *spherot* is "Glory," which brings harmony and interconnectedness among the lower nine *spherot*. Lines connecting the *spherot* show how they interact.

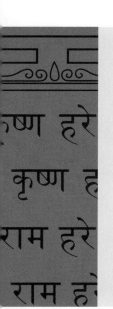

Document

Kabbalah: Thoughts on God

God's only desire is to reveal unity through diversity. That is, to reveal that all reality is unique in all its levels and all its details, and nevertheless united in a fundamental oneness (Kabbalist Aharon Ha-Levi Horowitz, 1766–1828; in Levi 2009: 929).

The essence of divinity is found in every single thing—nothing but It exists. Since It causes everything to be, no thing can live by anything else. It enlivens them. *Ein Sof* exists in each existent. Do

not say, 'This is a stone and not God.' God forbid! Rather all existence is God, and the stone is a thing pervaded by divinity (Moses Cordovero, 1522–70; in Levi 2009: 937).

Shards of Light are drawn out of the destructive entities that reside within my being. Their life force is cut off and I am then replenished with Divine energy. Life grows brighter each and every day as billions of sacred sparks return to my soul! ("Focus in Front").

The 10 *spherot* are numbered from top to bottom, and the 22 connecting lines are numbered 11 to 32, also from top to bottom. The total number of connecting lines corresponds to the number of letters in the Hebrew alphabet.

In an interesting twist on most theological systems, Kabbalah practitioners believe that their practices using the tree facilitate the flow of divine energy into the world. Whereas mainstream Judaism, Christianity, and Islam stress the absolute power of God, in Kabbalah God needs human effort to work in the world.

Kabbalists do not attempt to interpret the Bible literally; instead, they use a complex kind of numerology. The ancient Hebrews used regular letters as numbers, assigning their numerical value according to their position in the 22-letter Hebrew alphabet. Totalling the numbers in certain words could reveal hidden connections between them and lead to new interpretations. For example, it turns out that the numerical values of YHWH, the name for God revealed to Moses, and *aleph*, the first letter of the alphabet, are both 26. For Kabbalists, this is significant because one of the words for Lord or Master in Hebrew, *aluph*, is based on the word *aleph*. Inspired by the numerological practices of ancient Kabbalah, modern Kabbalists maintain that determining the numerical value of one's name can lead to new insights.

One of those practices involves meditating on the 72 names for God, based on combinations of Hebrew letters that Kabbalah finds hidden in *Exodus* 14: 19–21, the biblical account in which Moses calls to God for help before leading the people into the sea as the Egyptian army pursues them. Kabbalists took these three verses, each having 72 letters in Hebrew, and developed 72 names of God by combining them into triads of three letters each. To get the first name, they took the first letter of verse 19, the last of verse 20, and the first of verse 21. The next name is composed of the second letter of verse 19, the second from last of verse 20, and the second of verse 21, and so on for a total of 72. These 72 names are then arranged in a grid with 8 columns and 9 rows. According to the Kabbalah

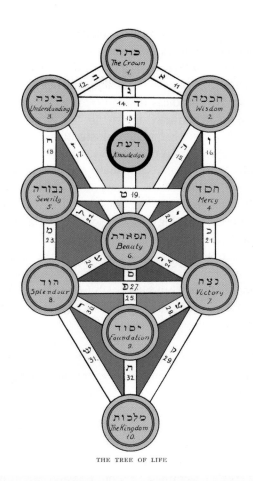

THE TREE OF LIFE

The Tree of Life (Photo: Mary Evans Picture Library).

Centre, the 72 Names of God "work as tuning forks to repair you on the soul level"; each three-letter sequence "act[s] like an index to specific, spiritual frequencies. By simply looking at the letters, as well as closing your eyes and visualizing them, you can connect with these frequencies" ("72 Names").

Traditional Kabbalah employs a dualistic symbolism of light and darkness, and many of the Centre's teachings focus on moving from darkness to light. For example, it stresses that instead of running away from adversaries, one should confront and learn from them, just as the biblical Jacob wrestled with the angel and gained light from the experience. Kabbalists see Jacob's angel as a personification of the personal darkness with which every individual must struggle in order to reach the light. The ego is seen as covered with a garment of darkness. Kabbalah practice helps to remove the darkness that covers the ego so as to reveal the light, the spark.

Like many other religious institutions, the Kabbalah Centre claims that its spiritual understanding fulfills other religions. In sharp contrast to most, however, it does not require its members to give up their former religious identities.

Like **Scientology** (see below), the Kabbalah Centre has benefitted from the media attention attracted by some of its adherents. At the head of the celebrity list is Madonna, who has sometimes included references to Kabbalah in her lyrics (Huss 2005). However, with this notoriety, and the large sums of money donated by celebrities, have come questions about the Kabbalah Centre's finances and accounting.

There are now Kabbalah Centres in over 40 cities worldwide. Some Jews have accused the Centre of exploiting Kabbalah for worldly gain, which the Kabbalist tradition explicitly forbids. Other criticisms have focused on the Centre's claims linking worldly happiness with Kabbalah practice. One leader of the Centre in London, England, was criticized for suggesting that Jews died in the Holocaust because they did not follow Kabbalah.

✤ Religions Inspired by Other Forms of Spirituality

Not all new religions are offshoots of established mainstream religious traditions. We turn now to a selection of new religions deriving from unconventional sources. **Wicca** is a modern phenomenon inspired by pre-Christian European traditions, with a significant feminist component. Scientology and the Raëlian Movement draw on more secular sources, including science fiction and new forms of depth psychology. Finally, we will look at some spiritual manifestations of the New Age movement.

Wicca: The Witchcraft Revival

In the late Middle Ages, after centuries of condemning the remnants of "pagan" tradition in northern Europe as "witchcraft," the Roman Catholic Church mounted a systematic campaign to eradicate those remnants once and for all. Although accusations of witchcraft were frequent well into the 1700s, by the early twentieth century witchcraft was widely considered a thing of the past in industrialized societies—a matter of historical curiosity, but not in any way a living tradition.

Around the time of the Second World War, however, a movement emerged in England that claimed witchcraft to be the original religion of Britain and sought to revive the tradition. The leading figures in this movement were two men, Gerald B. Gardner and Aleister Crowley, but women's interest increased after 1948, when Robert Graves published *The White Goddess*, a work on myth that posited a mother goddess in European prehistory. In 1953 Doreen Valiente was initiated into the movement and wrote *The Book of Shadows*, a kind of a liturgical handbook for witchcraft.

The first modern use of the Old English word "Wicca" is attributed to Gardner in 1959. Within a few years, an Englishman named Alex Sanders, who claimed descent from witches in Wales, was attracting media attention to the movement; a 1969 film entitled *Legends of the Witches* was based on his writing. Sanders also initiated many witches who in turn founded covens (assemblies of witches) in Great Britain and continental Europe, but it is a Gardner initiate named Ray Buckland who is credited with introducing Wicca to the United States. Soon people with no connection to the Gardner lineage were establishing covens, and the name Wicca was becoming known outside the movement or "Craft" itself.

It is difficult to estimate the current size of the Wicca movement, but publications sales and various claims regarding coven attendance suggest that there are at least 85,000 adherents in North America, and perhaps four times as many around the world. The Covenant of the Goddess, which was organized in California in 1975, is a kind of umbrella organization, but it enlists no more than one coven out of every 20 in the United States.

The feminist movement had a major impact on Wicca in North America. Zsuzsanna Budapest established a female-only coven in 1971; her book *The Holy Book of Women's Mysteries* (1980) focuses on goddesses and rituals for women. Journalist Margot Adler became interested in the movement after listening to a tape sent by a witchcraft circle in Wales. Investigating other women's involvement in the Craft, she found that the visionary or aesthetic element played an important part, along with the mysteries of birth and growth, a concern for the natural environment, and particularly a sense of feminist empowerment. Feminism is also central to Starhawk (Miriam Simos), for whom the religion of the Goddess is the pulsating rhythm of life, and human sexuality a reflection of the fundamentally sexual nature of the earth itself. At a lake high in the Sierra Nevada Mountains of California, she writes,

> it seems clear that earth is truly Her flesh and was formed by a sexual process: Her shakes and shudders and moans of pleasure, the orgasmic release of molten rock spewing forth in fiery eruptions, the slow caress of glaciers, like white hands gently smoothing all that has been left jagged (Starhawk 1982: 136).

In general, this kind of neopagan witchcraft seeks a return to primal nature and repudiates the classical Western religions that it holds responsible for repressing human sexuality. At the same time, its feminist emphasis challenges the patriarchal traditions of Judaism and Christianity. Although men can take an active part in it, Wicca is particularly empowering for women, and this has surely been part of its appeal.

Wiccans celebrate the winter solstice at Stonehenge.

AP Photo/Matt Dunham/CP

Practice

Wiccans celebrate as many as eight *sabbats* (festivals) during the annual cycle or "wheel of the year." Four have fixed dates: Candlemas (1 February), May Day (1 May), Lammas (1 August), and Hallowe'en (31 October). The other four mark the important days of the solar cycle: the Spring and Autumn equinoxes and the Fall and Winter solstices.

Ideally, every Wiccan service would be held in the open air, but this is not always possible. Although practices vary in their details, standard activities include healing rituals and celebration of important life-cycle events: birth, coming of age, marriage, death. Among the most important symbols are the circle, the four directions, and the four elements (earth, water, fire, air). Some of the rituals are symbolically sacrificial, paralleling (or parodying) the Christian Eucharist. Some covens announce upcoming services only by word of mouth and require that strangers be introduced by a trusted friend.

In 1993 members of the Covenant of the Goddess took part in the centennial World's Parliament of Religions in Chicago. In an age of interfaith acceptance, Wiccan priestesses and priests sought public and governmental recognition of their work as institutional chaplains, in hospitals, prisons, universities, and military units, but they could not provide any formal documentation of clerical training. To obtain the necessary credentials, some Wiccan leaders enrolled in Unitarian theological seminaries. Since then, the term "witch" has begun to be used to distinguish credentialled clergy (group leaders) from lay adherents.

Scientology

The Church of Scientology was founded in 1954 by L. Ron Hubbard (1911–86). Official biographies emphasize the breadth of his experience and learning. As a boy in Montana, for instance, he was exposed to the traditional teachings of the Blackfoot nation. In his youth he was introduced to Freudian psychology by a mentor who had trained with Freud and, travelling to Asia with his family, learned about a variety of ancient spiritual traditions. As an adult he not only became a prolific author in various genres, including science fiction, but served as a naval officer in the Second World War and, after being severely wounded, assisted his return to health by discovering how to remove deep-seated blocks in his mind. Following his recovery he began to advocate a new theory of what the soul does to the body. He called this theory **dianetics**, from the Greek *dia* (through) and *nous* (mind or soul).

Hubbard's 1950 book *Dianetics: The Modern Science of Mental Health* sold millions of copies. Soon followers were forming groups across the US, and in 1954 they became the first members of the Church of Scientology. The Church's official website defines Scientology—a word derived from the Latin *scio* (knowing) and the Greek *logos* (study)— as "knowing about knowing" and describes it as an "applied religious philosophy".

The Creed of Scientology begins with several generic statements about human rights, including freedom of expression, association, and religion. Reflecting Hubbard's belief that the underlying principle of all life forms is the drive to survive, it asserts that all humans have the right to survive and defend themselves, and the duty to protect others. At the same time it affirms that "the laws of God forbid" humans to destroy or enslave the souls of others; that the spirit can be saved; and that the spirit alone can heal the body.

Scientologists understand the universe to consist of eight intersecting planes or "dynamics," beginning with the self, the family, and so on at the bottom and moving up to the spiritual universe (the seventh dynamic) and the Supreme Being or Infinity (the eighth). The nature of the Infinity or God dynamic is not clearly defined. However, it seems to have less in common with the "personal God" of Christianity, who knows, wills, and acts like a (super) human person, than with "impersonal" principles or divinities such as the Dao of Daoism, the Brahman of the Hindu *Upanishads*, and the transcendent cosmic Buddha of some forms of Mahayana Buddhism.

Scientology uses the term "**thetan**" (pronounced "thay-tan") for the soul. Each thetan is thought to be billions of years old. Like the Atman of Hindu belief, the thetan is reincarnated, passing from one body to another at death.

Scientologists prefer to think of the movement as originating with its practitioners rather than with Hubbard himself. But he was its inspiration, he gave it direction from the first, and his writings and lectures constitute its religious literature. In a sense, the spread of Scientology began with the publication of *Dianetics* and its translation into numerous languages, even before the official founding of the Church in 1954. Various publications helped to spread Scientology to Britain and Europe. Today Scientologists have an organized presence in most countries.

As a strategy for spreading Scientology's influence, Hubbard decided to focus on high-profile celebrities. "Celebrity Centers" offering posh facilities for practice and training, established in major cities of North America and Europe, succeeded in attracting several celebrities, whose names have added credibility to the organization.

Credibility was important because the movement was haunted by controversy. Several Scientologists, including Hubbard's wife, Mary Sue, were convicted of criminal activity involving the infiltration of various government agencies and theft in an effort (referred to by Scientology leaders as Operation Snow White) to remove documents thought to reflect badly on the operation. L. Ron Hubbard was named as an unindicted co-conspirator (*United States vs Mary Sue Hubbard et al.,* 1979).

After Hubbard's death in 1986, the leadership passed to David Miscavige. As a boy growing up in Philadelphia, Miscavige had suffered from allergies and asthma, but was apparently cured following a dianetics training session. He joined Scientology in 1976, right at the time of Operation Snow White, and within three years rose from a cameraman filming Hubbard to an executive role, restructuring the various divisions so as to better conform to various laws and to protect Hubbard from personal liability. In the aftermath of the trial, Mary Sue Hubbard resigned from her leadership role and a new division was created under the leadership of Miscavige, who became chairman of the board of the Religious Technologies Center, charged with protecting the integrity of Hubbard's teachings. From this power base, he has served as the organization's paramount leader since 1986, although his role is that of an administrator rather than a spiritual leader.

As early as 1982, some dissenting followers of Hubbard were beginning to form alternative organizations outside the Church of Scientology. This activity increased after Hubbard's death. These "heretical" organizations are known collectively as the "Free Zone." The name comes from Hubbard himself, who claimed that planet Earth, under the galactic name Teegeeack, had been declared a "free zone" millions of years ago. In that context, "free" meant free of political or economic interference from other planets in the galaxy, but in the organizational context it meant free to follow the teachings of Hubbard without either payment to or interference from the Church of Scientology. RON's Org was one of the first of the Free Zone groups. Other Free Zone groups sprang up in Germany and elsewhere. The Church of Scientology tries to maintain exclusive rights to Hubbard's practices and refers to any unauthorized scientological practices as "squirreling" and to **Free Zoners** as "squirrels," which corresponds to the term "heretics" in Christianity. On the other hand, Free Zoners such as The International Free Zone Association claim that it is the Free Zoners who are faithful to the original teachings and practices of Hubbard.

Practice

In the 1960s Hubbard developed a step-by-step method for clearing the mind, or thetan, of mental blocks (called **engrams**) and restoring it to a state referred to as "clear." Engrams are the result of traumatic experiences, and they remain with the thetan until they are cleared, even carrying over from one life to the next. In some ways they are comparable to bad karma in the religions of India. Hubbard's process for clearing engrams, called

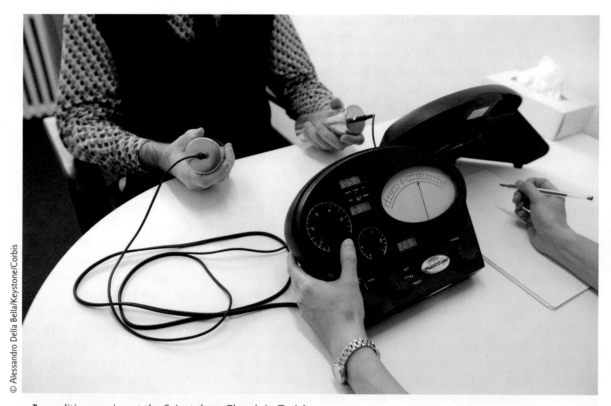

An auditing session at the Scientology Church in Zurich.

"auditing," involves the use of a device called an "**E-meter**," which is supposed to indicate when an engram blockage has been discovered in the mind. The E-meter (electro-psychometer) was originally developed by a polygraph expert named Volney Mathison, who had noticed while doing lie detection sessions that subjects tended to give readable responses to words that triggered unconscious as well as conscious thoughts. Mathison and Hubbard knew each other because they both wrote science fiction, and Hubbard began to use the "Mathison E-meter" in his dianetics practice. Although Mathison later distanced himself from Hubbard, the latter was able to get a patent on a modified version of the device. The Hubbard E-meter is manufactured at the movement's California headquarters and sold to members for their use in auditing.

Another important practice—the equivalent of scriptural study—is the study of Hubbard's thought and writings (an area in which the movement works hard to preserve orthodoxy). This study is known as "training," and students are encouraged to continue it, striving to reach ever-higher levels. Progress is termed "moving along the bridge" to total freedom, and it can take years of expensive auditing. After sufficient progress has been made to be called a Clear, the "advanced training" begins. This instruction introduces some of Hubbard's imaginative science fiction concepts, among them the idea that an extraterrestrial named Xenu, the ruler of a galactic confederation, came to Teegeeack (Earth) 75 million years ago, bringing with him thousands of aliens who had tried to revolt against his leadership. He put these political prisoners around volcanoes in which he detonated H-bombs. Then he captured the souls of the dead, now known as Thetans, and subjected them to brainwashing, implanting in them various ideas that we now associate with other religions. However, traces of their essences remain to this day, and some of their souls accumulated on the few bodies that were left. They are known as "body thetans." Those who complete all seven levels of this training are known as Operating Thetans (OTs).

Scientologists try to minimize the formation of new engrams in themselves and others. For example, Scientologist women are encouraged (though not required) to give birth in silence, in order to minimize the trauma of birth and therefore the creation of engrams in the baby thetan. Gestures are used for communication between the mother and attendants, and the mother is urged to minimize her cries of pain. Since Scientology prohibits drugs, the mother is also encouraged to give birth without the aid of painkillers.

Since Scientology does not anticipate any form of divine judgment after death, funeral services focus on celebrating the life of the deceased and wishing his or her thetan well in the next incarnation. After the funeral, friends and relatives of the deceased are encouraged to undergo auditing to rid themselves of the engrams resulting from grief. Scientologists may opt for cremation or burial. Hubbard was cremated, and before his death he discouraged the building of any elaborate memorials to him.

Scientology has come under intense public scrutiny and criticism for several reasons. Professional psychologists and other scientists are not sympathetic to the underlying claims of dianetics, and the fact that every step along the bridge costs additional money has given rise to accusations that it is just a pyramid scheme designed to bilk money from the rich and gullible. Some observers have claimed that Hubbard once suggested to a meeting of science-fiction writers that, instead of writing for a penny a word, they could make millions by starting a new religion.

Marc Headley, a former Scientology believer and employee, broke with the movement after 15 years, escaping on a motorcycle with security personnel chasing him in a van until he crashed. Later he returned to rescue his Scientologist wife as well. In 2009 Headley published an autobiographical exposé of his years in Scientology. In *Blown for Good: Behind the Iron Curtain of Scientology* he describes his early years as a child of Scientologists who sent him to Scientology schools whenever they could afford it. Eventually he took a job with the organization. Promoted to the headquarters where the tapes, E-meters, and other equipment were manufactured, he happened to be chosen as the subject on whom Tom Cruise would practise auditing. In an interview with *The Village Voice*, Headley explained that, as Cruise's trainee, he was instructed to tell inanimate objects such as bottles or ashtrays to move in a certain way; then, when they did not move, Headley was instructed to move the objects himself and then thank them for moving. The purpose of this exercise, according to Headley, was to rehabilitate the mind's ability to control things and be controlled (Ortega 2009). He also claimed that employees lived and worked in sub-standard conditions for little or no pay, and were not allowed to leave the premises. In Scientology circles, critics such as Headley are known as Suppressive Persons, or SPs.

Despite the controversies that surround it, Scientology has been recognized as a valid new religion in several countries, including South Africa, Spain, Portugal, and Sweden. According to Headley, when the Internal Revenue Service of the United States granted Scientology tax-free status as a religious organization in 1993, Miscavige held a big meeting to announce that "the war" was over.

The movement has had problems elsewhere, however, especially in France. In 1977 five Scientology leaders were found guilty of fraudulently coercing money from members, and the next year Hubbard himself was found guilty of fraud. A well-known owner of a computer company lost a large order from the ministry of education after the French media ran a story about his Scientology affiliation in 1991, and in 2009 six leaders of the Scientology Celebrity Center of Paris were convicted of fraud and fined almost 1 million dollars, although the court stopped short of banning the organization, as the prosecution had requested, on the grounds that the law regarding fraud did not extend that far (Erlanger 2009). In such cases, even the prosecution is careful to focus on Scientology's money-raising tactics rather than its spiritual beliefs.

Although it was founded only in the mid-twentieth century, Scientology now claims more than 12 million followers in over 100 countries. Critics who believe that number to be grossly exaggerated suggest that it is based on the numbers of people who have ever bought a book or taken a Scientology course since the movement's inception. Based on the quantities of E-meters and other supplies shipped during his time with the organization, Headley estimates that there were roughly 10,000 to 15,000 active Scientologists in the 1990s.

The Raëlian Movement

The Raëlian Movement traces its origins to a winter day in 1973 when a French journalist and racing enthusiast named Claude Vorilhon impulsively decided to drive to the site of an old volcano where he had enjoyed family picnics in the past. There he saw a small flying saucer hovering near the ground. An extraterrestrial creature—approximately 1.2 metres (4 feet) tall and resembling a bearded human with a greenish skin tone—then walked over and spoke to Vorilhon in French. In the course of this and subsequent encounters, the alien—named Yahweh (same as the name of God as revealed to Moses according to some scholars)—recounted details of Vorilhon's own life and explained that he had telepathically drawn the Frenchman to this spot. Yahweh invited him inside the spaceship and told him that all life on earth was originally created in a laboratory by aliens called Elohim—the plural form of the word for a god in biblical Hebrew (*eloh*), frequently used in the Torah to refer to the one God. The International Raëlian Movement translates "Elohim" as "those who came from the sky," replacing the traditional idea of creation by a deity with creation by sky people.

Yahweh explained that a few weeks earlier he had used telepathy to urge Vorilhon to refresh his memory of the book of Genesis because he wanted to talk to him about it; now Vorilhon understood why he had recently, for no apparent reason, purchased a Bible and started to read it. The alien interpreted the reference to God's creation of heaven and earth (in Genesis 1: 1) as a reference to the aliens "from the sky," and the verse saying that the spirit of God moved over the face of the earth (Genesis 1: 2) as a reference to the alien spacecraft. Continuing to instruct Vorilhon on the proper interpretation of Genesis, Yahweh said that a "day" in the context of the six days of creation was equal to 2,000 earth years; that since the earth at that time was covered in water, the aliens had caused explosions in order to form the continents; and that they had used advanced scientific techniques to create the first plants and animals on earth in such a way that they would be able to reproduce themselves thereafter.

Despite minor differences in physical appearance (explained as the result of differences in the methods used by the various teams of Elohim scientists to create each group), the humans were formed "in the image of" the Elohim themselves. This alarmed the Elohim back on the home planet, who feared that humans' intelligence might someday allow them to travel to the alien planet and cause trouble. Therefore it was decided to keep humans' scientific knowledge at a very primitive level. The team of scientists working in what is now Israel, however, had created an unusually intelligent group of humans, and wanted to give them greater scientific knowledge. That team, Yahweh explained, was what Genesis refers to as the "serpent" that tempted Eve, and the "Garden" from which Adam and Eve were expelled was in fact the laboratory of the Elohim. Similarly, the idea of the Jews being a "chosen people" was a reflection of the way the Elohim scientists had realized their genius. However, Genesis 6: 4—in which "the sons of Elohim" mate with the daughters of men—is interpreted literally.

The story of Noah and the flood in Genesis 7 is also given a novel twist. In the Raëlian interpretation, the flood is the result of nuclear explosions set off by the Elohim on the home planet who fear that humans have been given too much knowledge, and Noah thwarts their plan by taking cells of each creature aboard an orbiting satellite. Then, after the flood, Noah waits for the nuclear fallout to settle before returning to earth with a cargo that includes a pair of humans from each of the races created by the Elohim scientists.

The biblical story of the Tower of Babel gets a new interpretation as well. Traditionally, the Tower was built by a great king to reach to the heavens—a symbol of arrogance, which God punished by making humans (who until then had all spoken the same language) unable to understand one another. In the alien's account, the "Tower of Babel" is the name of a spaceship built by the Hebrews in partnership with the Elohim scientists who had been banished to earth for making humans too intelligent. This project so alarms the Elohim on the home planet that they thwart the progress of human science by scattering the Hebrews throughout the world. Similarly, the cities of Sodom and Gomorrah are destroyed not by normal fire in punishment for sexual sin, but by nuclear explosion in response to the threat posed to the home planet by scientific progress on earth. And God's order that Abraham sacrifice his son is translated into a test by the Elohim to see if the leader of the Hebrew scientists was still loyal to them. The New Testament gets some novel interpretations as well: for example, the resurrection of Jesus is attributed to cloning.

Yahweh told Vorilhon that he had been chosen to receive the truth because he had a religious background, with a Jewish father and a Catholic mother, and was a free-thinking opponent of traditional religion. As a result of his UFO encounter, Vorilhon was told to change his name to Raël, "messenger of the Elohim." Feeling called to prophecy, he was told to write down the message in book form, and to spread the word in anticipation of the Elohim's return.

Two years after his initial encounter, Raël reports, he was taken aboard a spaceship and transported to the planet of the Elohim, where he received further instruction and met with past religious leaders. He wrote an account of the visit in his book *They Took Me to Their Planet*.

In 1974 Raël called a press conference in Paris, at which he introduced his movement to the media. By 1980 the International Raëlian Movement had

taken on most of the features of an organized religion: scripture, rituals, festival days, a communal building. It is organized hierarchically on the model of the Roman Catholic Church, with Raël himself at the pinnacle, like a pope, and various lesser officials with titles such as Bishop Guide and Priest Guide. Susan Jean Palmer (1995) notes that although the movement advocates gender equality and is libertarian about sexuality and gender roles, women are not well represented in the leadership hierarchy, especially at the upper levels.

The leadership hierarchy may reflect Roman Catholicism, but the Raëlian cosmology is nothing like that of traditional Christianity. Not only does it reject belief in gods of any kind, but it teaches that the whole of the observable universe is just a small atom of a larger structure, which is itself part of a larger one, and so on infinitely. At the same time every atom is itself a universe on the next smaller scale, with structures descending in size infinitely. Time and space are infinite in this cosmos, which runs on scientific principles without any need for divine command or intervention.

The Elohim are expected to return by 2035, but only on condition that humans are ready to welcome them, have tolerance for one another, and show respect for the environment. The Movement hopes one day to create an "embassy" that would function as a place for the Elohim to interact with humans in a helpful way; ideally, this embassy would be located in Israel.

Raëlians reject the theory of evolution. Instead, they believe that the Elohim brought all life to earth from another planet 25,000 years ago, and that just as the Elohim were themselves created by previous entities, we earthlings may someday take life to yet another planet. The term "Intelligent Design," which some conservative Christians have promoted as an alternative to Darwinian evolution, has been adopted by Raëlians. But whereas for conservative Christians Intelligent Design is a way to get God and creationism back into the post-Darwinian picture, for Raëlians the term represents a third option for those who, like themselves, reject both evolution and creation by a god. The latest collection of

Raël's writings about his UFO encounters has been published under the title *Intelligent Design: Message from the Designers*. In a postscript, Raël calls his approach a Third Way, between Darwin and Genesis. Since Raël holds that humans were created in a laboratory, he is confident this Third Way will one day be replicated in a laboratory by humans.

The Raëlian symbol is a swastika—best known today as the symbol of Nazism in Hitler's Germany—inside a six-pointed star that is said to be based on a design of interlocking triangles displayed on the spaceship during Raël's UFO encounter. In fact, though, it seems identical to the Star of David: the symbol of Judaism. To avoid offending Jews, the symbol was changed for a few years to a swirling galaxy image inside the hexagram. But now the movement has returned to the original symbol. Raëlians claim that their swastika has nothing to do with Nazism, and point out that for thousands of years before its adoption by Hitler, it was a symbol of good luck and prosperity used in Buddhist, Jaina, and other religious traditions. They say that the symbol as a whole stands for the Elohim, while the swastika part represents infinite time and the hexagram infinite space. It reflects the Raëlian belief that the universe is cyclical, without beginning or end.

Practice

During Raël's second encounter with the Elohim he was taught a spiritual technique known as "sensual meditation" or "meditation of all senses," in which the meditator turns inward to experience the lesser universes within the atoms of his or her own body, and then turns outward to experience the greater universes beyond our own; eventually, the most adept will be able to visualize the planet of the Elohim. The goal is to awaken humans' highest spiritual potential by first awakening their physical sensibilities.

There are four main Raëlian holidays: the first Sunday in April, celebrated as the day the Elohim created Adam and Eve; 6 August, the day of the Hiroshima bombing, which for Raëlians is the beginning of the Apocalypse; 7 October, the date that Raël met with Jesus, Buddha, and other past prophets aboard a spaceship during the second encounter; and 13 December, the day when Raël first encountered the Elohim.

Raëlians are expected to avoid mind-altering drugs, coffee, and tobacco, and to use alcohol either in moderation or not at all. They celebrate sensuality, advocate free love, and discourage traditional marriage contracts. The movement's liberal policy regarding marriage and sexual partners has made it an attractive religious home for gays and lesbians.

Becoming a Raëlian involves two ceremonies. First, initiates must renounce all ties to theistic religions. After this "Act of Apostasy" comes a baptismal ceremony in which information about the initiate's DNA is supposedly transmitted to the Elohim.

As part of his effort to free humans from the constraints imposed by traditional religions, Raël has called for a massive "de-baptism" campaign across Africa or (as he prefers to call it) the United Kingdom of Kama. He argues that "spiritual decolonization" is a prerequisite for future development. The Movement has also been active in denouncing the practice of clitorectomy, which is common in some parts of Africa, and has started a fundraising effort to pay for restorative surgery.

Although Raëlians reject the concept of the soul, they believe that a kind of everlasting life can be attained through cloning. Clonaid, a Raëlian enterprise founded in France in 1997, claims to be the world's first human cloning company. Since then, it has announced the births of several cloned babies; none of these claims have been substantiated, however.

Because Raëlians do not believe in gods, the International Raëlian Movement is not officially classified as a religion, although some jurisdictions do recognize it as a non-profit organization (the first to do so was the province of Quebec, in 1977). Important religious leaders such as Jesus and Buddha are recognized as prophets, however, inspired by the Elohim to communicate as much of the truth as humans were able to absorb in their time. Raël

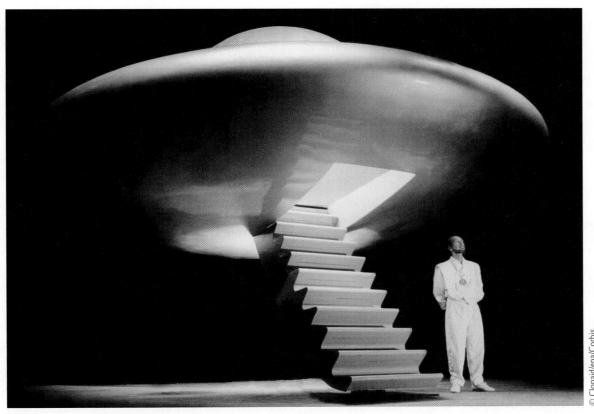

Raël with a full-scale model of the spaceship he encountered in 1973.

© Clonaid/epa/Corbis

himself is identified with Maitreya, the future Buddha who is expected to come when the world needs him, although Buddhists themselves do not accept this claim.

Despite its partial recognition of traditional religious leaders, the Movement is exclusivist in terms of allegiance, as the Act of Apostasy indicates. Just as Christianity sees itself as completing Judaism, and as Islam sees Muhammad as the "seal of the prophets," Raëlians see their Movement as the culmination of earlier religions, which incorrectly understood the role of the Elohim.

According to Raël, the Elohim told him that only 4 per cent of humans were advanced enough to understand the truth about them, so it is not surprising that the Raëlian mission has not made converts by the millions. Nevertheless, the movement claims more than 65,000 members in 84 countries.

The New Age Movement

The expression "New Age" has a wide range of connotations, including the biblical notion of an apocalypse in which God will intervene to restructure society, reward the righteous, and (in some scenarios) smite the wicked with long-overdue punishment. The nineteenth century saw the rise of several millenarian Christian movements, among them the Jehovah's Witnesses, that looked forward to the literal fulfillment of the prophecies in the biblical books of Daniel and Revelation. On the whole, the idea of a "new age" for these movements meant a reconstitution of society. For the Nation of Islam, however, the "new age" would be one in which African Americans would emerge strong and triumphant. And various loosely defined organizations have emerged under the generic name New

Age. As we will see, New Age draws on both Eastern and Western traditions.

The term "New Age" was in use as early as 1907 as the title of a progressive British political and literary journal that introduced its readers to topics such as Freudian psychoanalysis. But the "consciousness revolution" of the 1960s brought expectations of a different sort of "new age." The transpersonal psychology movement, for instance, emphasized spiritual insights and therapeutic techniques that were diametrically opposed to the mechanistic approach of orthodox Freudianism. One centre of transpersonal psychology was the Esalen Institute in Big Sur, California, founded in 1962 as a retreat centre offering seminars, workshops, and encounter groups.

Not all New Age seekers were so disciplined. In 1967 the musical *Hair!* popularized the idea that the dawning of the Age of Aquarius would usher in a universal religion to replace the Christianity of the Piscean age. To some, the Aquarian age meant little more than freely available rock music or drugs. Those expectations came together in 1969, when as many as half a million young people congregated in a farmer's field near Woodstock, New York. By the late 1980s, "New Age" had become a kind of shorthand term for a cluster of trends that included a quest for individual spiritual insight, expectations of both personal transformation and worldly success, the pursuit of physical healing and psychological peace through various self-help disciplines, and in some cases reliance on astrology and psychic powers. Many New Age enthusiasts have published accounts of their personal transformations through some combination of New Age disciplines, diets, and cures.

Scholars looking for the historical roots of New Age spirituality often point to Emanuel Swedenborg, an eighteenth-century Swedish mystic who wrote about the evolution of the human soul; the nineteenth-century American Transcendentalist Ralph Waldo Emerson; or the Russian founder of the Theosophical movement, Helena P. Blavatsky, who claimed to have discovered the wisdom of the ages in Asian teachings such as Hindu Vedanta. Those looking for antecedents of New Age

therapeutic techniques, for their part, often point to the Swiss physician Paracelsus (Philippus Aureolus Theophrastus Bombast von Hohenheim; 1493–1541), who claimed that humans were subject to the magnetism of the universe. Two centuries later, the German physician Franz Anton Mesmer postulated that healing takes place through a kind of magnetism in bodily fluids, analogous to ocean tides, and sought to manipulate these with magnets or the wave of a wand or a finger. The effort to direct their flow, called mesmerism after him, was reflected in the development of hypnosis in the nineteenth century. As for what New Agers call "channelling," the roots can be traced back at least as far as the nineteenth-century practice of the séance, in which the bereaved sought to make contact with their deceased loved ones through a "spirit medium." The use of gems and crystals was promoted in the first half of the twentieth century by the medium Edgar Cayce.

None of these earlier developments in itself constituted the New Age. But together they fertilized the spiritual soil of the English-speaking world, so that after the 1960s the New Age fascination with the exotic, the occult, the experiential, the curative, and the futuristic could take root and spread rapidly. Subjects that had been left on the sidelines of a scientific and technological age—astrology, hypnosis, alternative healing—were resurrected and, at a time of growing interest in subjects such as nutrition, ecology, and altruistic business ethics, entered the mainstream. All these could be seen as alternatives to orthodox religion, medicine, and society generally, and perhaps also to the exclusivist claims made by mainstream orthodoxies.

If any of the metaphysical and therapeutic resources sketched so far had a connection with the major Western religious traditions, it was marginal at best. So how did the New Age movement come to be so closely associated with religion? At least part of the answer can be found in its connections with Eastern religious traditions.

A prominent feature of the search for alternative modes of consciousness in the 1960s was a fascination with depths of awareness that Hindu yoga and

Japanese Zen Buddhism in particular were believed to offer. The *Yijing* (or *I Ching*), an ancient Chinese divination manual, became a bestseller, and many people were introduced to Asian religious symbolism through the writings of the Swiss psychologist Carl G. Jung and the Jungian comparative-religion scholar Joseph Campbell. "Exotic" religions seemed to offer something that the familiar traditions of the West did not.

Across North America and Europe, practitioners turned to Chinese *qigong* and acupuncture, Indian yoga and ayurvedic medicine, and Buddhist meditation techniques. In India, Maharishi Mahesh Yogi's Transcendental Meditation movement attracted high-profile entertainers, including the Beatles, Mia Farrow, and Clint Eastwood, as devotees. Deepak Chopra, an endocrinologist practising in the West, returned to his native India to explore traditional ayurvedic medicine and proceeded to write and lecture about its compatibility with modern Western medicine. The Thailand-born and Western-educated Chinese master Mantak Chia, working in New York, has written extensively on the potential of Daoist techniques for healing and sexual energy. And the list goes on.

A recurring temptation, in the promotion of Asian disciplines and therapies, is to divorce the techniques from a comprehensive understanding of the cultural vocabularies in which they had developed. It is a temptation not only for consumers of these wares, but also for their providers. For example, **Eckankar**, a new religion introduced in the 1960s by the American Paul Twitchell, takes its name from "Ik Onkar" ("the one om-expression"), a name for the transcendent God in the Sikh tradition. But though Twitchell claimed to have studied with a Sikh master in India, it was only one episode in a lifetime of "soul travel" to supposed invisible worlds on levels above our earthly one. Eckankar holds that there has always been a living Eck master on earth, among whom have been ancient Greek and Iranian Muslim figures, and that Twitchell was the 971st in the series.

The New Age movement is thoroughly eclectic, and its diversity is part of its appeal. It is open to many possibilities, including exploration, expression, and leadership by women. As such, it stands in sharp contrast to the male-dominated structures of the established religions and professions. This may constitute one of its lasting contributions.

Is there any single word that sums up the spirit of the New Age? One candidate would be "holistic." Implying a quest for wholeness, sometimes with an overtone of holiness, it was coined in the context of evolutionary biology to refer to the whole as something more than the sum of its parts. Thus holistic diets and therapies seek to treat the whole person, body and mind, and holistic principles are fundamental to the ecological movement; the Gaia hypothesis, for instance, sees the earth as a single organism whose survival depends on the interaction of all its components (a perspective central to James Cameron's film *Avatar*). New ages yet to come are bound to view ecological holism as an increasingly urgent goal.

Summary

The new religions we have discussed cover the spiritual landscape, from East to West to outer space. None of these new religions is seriously challenging the traditional religions for influence. Some of them seem to have already peaked in numbers, at least in North America. Since new religions typically need a strong, charismatic leader, most such organizations have trouble sustaining their growth and unity after their founders have left or died. But others are still making significant gains in numbers, wealth, and influence.

The few that survive and prosper eventually become established as normal parts of the religious landscape. They become just "religions," rather than "new religions." Judaism, Christianity, and Islam made this transition long ago. The Baha'i Faith and the Mormons have made it more recently. Which, if any, of the new religions that emerged in the late twentieth century will survive into the twenty-second is impossible to tell from this vantage point, but is surely an interesting topic for debate.

Sacred Texts

Religion	Texts	Composition/ Compilation	Compilation/ Revision	Use
Soka Gakkai	The *Lotus Sutra*	Probably composed in the early 1st century CE; considered the highest expression of Mahayana thought	Supplemented by writings of Nichiren and modern leaders	Read and chanted; the phrase "Homage to the Lotus Sutra" is chanted as a mantra
Falun Dafa (Falun Gong)	*Falun Gong* by Li Hongzhi	First published in 1993. Li's works have been translated into most major languages	The English translation has been revised several times	Li's books and videos are used as guides to practice
ISKCON ("Hare Krishnas")	*Srimad Bhagavatam*, *Bhagavad Gita*, and other Krishna-centred devotional texts	Ancient Hindu texts of debatable date, now available in English and other major languages	Commentaries by Swami Prabhupada	Studied and chanted during puja
LDS (Mormons)	The Bible, plus Smith's *The Book of Mormon*, *Doctrine and Covenants*, and *The Pearl of Great Price*	*The Book of Mormon* was published in 1830. *Doctrine and Covenants* (selected writings) in 1835; *The Pearl of Great Price* was compiled by F.D. Richards and published in England in 1851	All three texts have been revised at various times	Used in worship and for life guidance
Baha'i	The *Most Holy Book*, *The Book of Certitude*, *Hidden Words*, and *The Seven Valleys*	Written by Baha'u'llah between 1856 and 1873	Edited by 20th-century Baha'i leaders	The *Most Holy Book* is used as a source of legal guidance, The *Book of Certitude* for doctrine, *Hidden Words* for ethical guidance, and *Seven Valleys* for mystical guidance

Religion	Texts	Composition/ Compilation	Compilation/ Revision	Use
Nation of Islam	The Qur'an, plus Elijah Muhammad's *Fall of America* and *Message to the Blackman*	Elijah Muhammad's works date from the 1950s and '60s	Louis Farrakhan's *A Torchlight for America* (1993)	The Qur'an is studied, recited and used in Sunni services, along with *Muslim Daily Prayers*
Kabbalah Centre	Hebrew Bible, The Zohar	The Kabbalah Centre attributes the Zohar to Rav Shimon Bar Yochai rather than Moses de Léon	The Bible is interpreted through numerology and the 72 names of God	Spiritual practices of Zohar and related approaches are used to guide daily life
Wicca	Important early works include Graves' *The White Goddess* (1948) and *The Book of Shadows* (c. 1950)	Other publications added a feminist emphasis, such as *The Holy Book of Women's Mysteries*	Newer writers such as Starhawk have popularized the movement	Used in rituals and sabbats
Scientology	Hubbard's *Dianetics: The Modern Science of Mental Health* and *Scientology: The Fundamentals of Thought*	1950s		Used in "auditing" process
Raëlian Movement	*Intelligent Design: Message from the Designers*	Published in 2005: a compilation of Raël's publications from the 1970s–80s	Other texts include *The Maitreyya* and *Sensual Meditation*	Teachings are studied and used as guidance for sensual meditation practice

Discussion Questions

1. What kinds of social and economic factors may contribute to the rise of new religious movements?

2. Why is the line between a "cult" and a "religion" so difficult to define?

3. Why do Eastern religions appeal so strongly to many people in the West?

4. Do all "religions" have to involve belief in deities?

5. Can a set of beliefs and practices centred on extraterrestrial aliens be considered a "religion"?

6. What do you think are some of the factors that might attract some people to new religious movements?

7. How do new religious movements gain acceptance?

8. How do new religious movements tend to change over time?

Glossary

Bab The individual expected to appear as the "Gateway" to the new prophet in the **Baha'i Faith**.

Baha'i The religious tradition of those who call themselves Baha'i, meaning "adherents of Baha ('u'llah)"

bhakti Devotional faith, the favoured spiritual path in ISKCON.

Church of Jesus Christ of Latter-day Saints The formal name of the largest Mormon organization, abbreviated as "LDS."

cult Term for a new religion, typically demanding loyalty to a charismatic leader.

dianetics L. Ron Hubbard's term for the system he developed to clear mental blocks.

Eckankar A new religion based on the teachings of Paul Twitchell.

E-meter A device used in **Scientology** to detect mental blocks.

engrams The term for mental blocks in **Scientology**.

Falun Dafa A "law wheel" said to be acquired through Dafa practice.

Free Zoners Individuals or groups teaching Hubbard's thought independently of Scientology International.

Hare Krishnas Informal name for the members of ISKCON, based on their chant.

ISKCON International Society for Krishna Consciousness.

Kabbalah Traditional Jewish mysticism.

Komeito A Japanese political party loosely associated with **Soka Gakkai**.

Mormons Another name for members of the **Church of Jesus Christ of Latter-day Saints**.

millenarian Term used to refer to the belief that the current social order will soon come to an end.

Nation of Islam (NOI) An African-American movement that originated in Detroit in 1930. Its practice of Islam has become more aligned with the Sunni tradition in recent years.

New Age A vague term embracing a diversity of religious or spiritual movements providing alternatives to mainstream Western religions.

qi (or **chi**) Spiritual energy.

qigong Exercises to cultivate **qi**.

Raëlian Movement A new religion originating in France in the 1970s, based on the belief that an alien revealed previously unknown information about the creation of life on earth to a man named Raël.

Scientology A new religion devoted to clearing mental blockages; founded by L. Ron Hubbard.

sect A sociological term for a group that breaks away from the main religion.

Soka Gakkai A lay movement that originated in the 1930s among Japanese adherents of Nichiren Shoshu Buddhism; now an independent new religion teaching the power of chanting homage to the *Lotus Sutra*.

spherot The 10 attributes of God in **Kabbalah**.

thetan Term for the soul or mind in **Scientology**.

Vaishnava A Hindu who worships Vishnu and related deities.

Wicca A name for witchcraft or the Craft.

Further Reading

Baha'u'llah. 1952. *Gleanings from the Writings of Baha'u'llah*, rev. edn. Wilmette, IL: Baha'i Publishing Trust. A good selection of Baha'i writings.

Barrett, David V. 2003. *The New Believers: A Survey of Sects, Cults and Alternative Religions*. London: Octopus Publishing Group. A good place to start on the topic of cults versus new religions.

Dan, Joseph. 2005. *Kabbalah: A Very Short Introduction*. Oxford: Oxford University Press. A useful introduction.

Drew, A. J. 2003. *The Wiccan Bible: Exploring the Mysteries of the Craft from Birth to Summerland*. Franklin, NJ: Career Press. An overview of Wicca.

Esslemont, John E. 1979. *Bahá'u'lláh and the New Era: An Introduction to the Bahá'í Faith*. 4th edn. Wilmette, IL: Baha'i Publishing Trust. The standard survey recommended by Baha'is.

Gallagher, Eugene V., William M. Ashcraft, and W. Michael Ashcraft, eds. 2006. *An Introduction to New and Alternative Religions in America*. 5 vols. Westport: Greenwood Press. Scholarly introductions to religious movements from colonial era to the present.

Headley, Marc. 2009. *Blown for Good: Behind the Iron Curtain of Scientology*. Burbank: BFG Books. The autobiography of a former Scientologist turned critic.

Hubbard, L. Ron. 1956. *Scientology: The Fundamentals of Thought*. 2007. Los Angeles: Bridge Publications. The basic introduction, by Scientology's founder.

Lewis, James R., and J. Gordon Melton, eds. 1992. *Perspectives on the New Age*. Albany: State University of New York Press. One of the best assessments of the New Age phenomenon.

Li Hongzhi. 2000. *Falun Gong*. 3rd edn. New York: University Publishing Co. Master Li's introduction to Falun Dafa.

Miller, William McElwee. 1974. *The Baha'i Faith: Its History and Teachings*. Pasadena: William Carey Library. An outsider's view of Bahai.

Muster, Nori J. 2001. *Betrayal of the Spirit: My Life behind the Headlines of the Hare Krishna Movement*. Champaign: University of Illinois Press. A former member's critical view of ISKCON.

Ostling, Richard, and Joan K. Ostling. 2007. *Mormon America—Revised and Updated Edition: The Power and the Promise*. New York: HarperOne. An overview of the issues.

Porter, Noah. 2003. *Falun Gong in the United States: An Ethnographic Study*. N.p.: Dissertation.Com. Argues against the "cult" label based on interviews and publications.

Seager, Richard H. 2006. *Encountering the Dharma: Daisaku Ikeda, Soka Gakkai, and the Globalization of Buddhist Humanism*. Berkeley: University of California Press. A scholarly overview.

Shinn, Larry D. 1987. *The Dark Lord: Cult Images and the Hare Krishnas in America*. Philadelphia: Westminster Press. An objective account, based on extensive interviews.

Starhawk. 1982. *Dreaming the Dark*. Boston: Beacon Press. One of many works by an important Wicca leader.

White, Vibert L., Jr. 2001. *Inside the Nation of Islam: A Historical and Personal Testimony by a Black Muslim*. Gainesville: University Press of Florida. Particularly interesting because the author was involved both in the NOI and in the organization of the 1995 March.

Wright, Lawrence. 2013. *Going Clear: Scientology, Hollywood, and the Prison of Belief*. New York: Alfred A. Knopf. A balanced but critical overview of Scientology, its leaders and celebrity followers.

Recommended Websites

www.bahai.org
Site of the Baha'i religion.

www.falundafa.org
Site of Falun Dafa.

www.finalcall.com
News site of the Nation of Islam.

www.internationfreezone.net
Portal for the Free Zoner alternative to Scientology.

www.iskcon.org
Site of the International Society for Krishna Consciousness.

www.kabbalah.com
Site of the Kabbalah Centre International.

www.lds.org
Site of the Church of Jesus Christ of Latter-day Saints, the Mormons.

www.komei.or.jp
Site of the New Komeito party, loosely affiliated with Soka Gakkai.

www.rael.org
Site of the International Raëlian Movement.

www.scientology.org
Site of the international Scientology organization.

www.sgi.org
Site of Soka Gakkai International.

www.wicca.org
Site of the Church and School of Wicca.

References

Amnesty International. "Human Rights in China." Accessed 10 March 2010 at www.amnesty.ca/blog2.php?blog=keep_the_promise_2& page=7.

Dawson, Lorne L. 2006. *Comprehending Cults: The Sociology of New Religious Movements*. Toronto: Oxford University Press.

Erlanger, Steven. 2009. "French Branch of Scientology Convicted of Fraud." *New York Times*. Accessed 10 March 2010 at www.nytimes.com/2009/ 10/28/world/europe/28france.html? _r=1.

"Focus in Front." Accessed 10 March 2010 at www.kabbalah.com/news letters/weekly-consciousness-tune-ups/focus-front.

Huss, Boaz. 2005. "All You Need is LAV: Madonna and Postmodern Kabbalah." *Jewish Quarterly Review* 95, 4: 611–24.

Ikeda, Daisaku. 2008. "Toward Humanitarian Competition: A New Current in History." Accessed 10 March 2010 at www.sgi.org/ peace2009sum.html.

"Introduction: What Is Falun Dafa?" Accessed 10 March 2010 at www.falundafa.org/eng/intro.html.

Kabbalah Centre. "Reincarnation." Accessed 10 March 2010 at www.kabbalah.com/node/434.

Lee, Martha F. 1996. *The Nation of Islam: An American Millenarian Movement*. Syracuse: Syracuse University Press.

Levi, Jerome M. 2009. "Structuralism and Kabbalah: Sciences of Mysticism or Mystifications of Science?" *Anthropological Quarterly* 82, 4 (Fall).

Lewis, James R. 2003. *Legitimating New Religions*. Rutgers: Rutgers University Press.

Li Hongzhi. 2000. *Falun Gong*. 3rd edn. New York: University Publishing Co.

Ljungdahl, Alex. 1975. "What Can We Learn from Non-Biblical Prophet Movements." In *New Religions*, ed. Haralds Biezais. Stockholm: Almqvist & Wiksell International.

Olyan, Saul M., and Gary A. Anderson. 2009. *Priest-hood and Cult in Ancient Israel*. Sheffield: Sheffield Academic Press.

Ortega, Tony. 2009. "Tom Cruise Told Me to Talk to a Bottle: Life at Scientology's Secret Headquarters." *The Village Voice*. Accessed 10 March 2010 at http://blogs.villagevoice.com/runninscared/archives/2009/11/ tom_cruise_was.php.

Palmer, Susan Jean. 1995. "Women in the Raelian Movement: New Religious Experiments in Gender and Authority." In *The Gods Have Landed: New Religions from Other Worlds*, ed. James R. Lewis. Albany: State University of New York Press.

Sahib, Hatim A. 1951. "The Nation of Islam." Master's thesis. University of Chicago. Cited in Lee 1996: 23.

"72 Names of God, The." Accessed 15 March at www.kabbalah.com/node/432.

Starhawk. 1982. *Dreaming the Dark*. Boston: Beacon Press.

Walker, Dennis. 2005. *Islam and the Search for African-American Nationhood: Elijah Muhammad, Louis Farrakhan and the Nation of Islam*. Atlanta: Clarity Press.

White, Vibert L., Jr. 2001. *Inside the Nation of Islam: A Historical and Personal Testimony by a Black Muslim*. Gainesville: University Press of Florida.

Note

Parts of this chapter, especially in the sections on the Mormons, the Baha'i Faith, Wicca, and New Age movements, incorporate material written by the late Will Oxtoby for earlier editions of the work.

8

Current Issues

Amir Hussain and
Roy C. Amore

In this chapter you will learn about:

- some of the ways in which religion and politics have interacted in recent decades
- fundamentalism
- how religious traditions around the world are responding to issues such as bioethics, environmental responsibility, gender, and sexuality
- religious diversity.

Most of the chapters in this book have concentrated on individual religious traditions. In this concluding chapter we broaden our focus and look at some general issues relevant to religions around the world.

Religion and Politics

Once upon a time, many in the West regarded religion as a kind of cultural fossil. Aesthetically rich or anthropologically intriguing? Yes. But relevant to today's hard-nosed world of economics and politics? Hardly at all. Those of us who studied religion were often asked how we could waste our lives on something that had so little to do with the modern world. In the secular intellectual climate of the 1960s, some philosophers and even theologians announced that God was dead. That announcement proved to be premature.

Religion has been a major factor in many of the events that have shaken the world since 1970. One such event occurred in 1979, when the Shah of Iran was deposed in an "Islamic Revolution." That a nation of 40 million people would be ready to sacrifice lives and livelihoods to defend religious values was a concept utterly alien to development economists and politico-military strategists in the West. Meanwhile, not only in Iran but elsewhere, Muslims were turning their backs on modernity and secularism in general and the modern West in particular. In increasing numbers, Muslim men from Algeria to Zanzibar started to grow beards and wear turbans, and more Muslim women than ever before adopted the *hijab* (head scarf).

A second event of 1979 that was to have profound repercussions was the Soviet Union's invasion of Afghanistan. From across the Muslim world, volunteers were taken to Afghanistan and trained by the United States to fight for the country's liberation. They were called *mujahidin*, and at the time—before the end of the cold war—they were widely seen as what US President Ronald Reagan called "freedom fighters."

Among the supporters of Afghanistan's "holy war" was Osama bin Laden (1957–2011), a wealthy Saudi who helped fund and train *mujahidin*. The Soviet troops were withdrawn in 1988, but bin Laden emerged as the leader of Al-Qaeda ("the base"), an extremist organization. In 1996 bin Laden issued a *fatwa* (religious legal opinion) calling for the overthrow of the Saudi government and the removal of US forces in Arabia; in 1998 he declared war against Americans generally; and in 2001 he was accused of masterminding the 9/11 attacks. In response to those attacks, the United States went to war first in Afghanistan and then in Iraq. To understand the modern world, we now realize, we need to take into account the meanings that traditional religions have for their adherents.

Another eventful year was 1989, when the communist order of eastern Europe and the Soviet Union began to crumble. Hopes for democracy, peace, and progress were high. But when the restraints of the socialist order were loosened, old identities resurfaced, and with them passions that most outsiders had assumed to be long dead. Feuds and ethno-religious divisions in the Balkans, the Caucasus, and Central Asia erupted into bitter conflict. Samuel Huntington, in his book *The Clash of Civilizations and the Remaking of World Order*, argued that the old world order based on the conflict between communism and capitalism has been replaced by a new one based on the differences among civilizations defined primarily along religious lines.

In India, Hindu nationalists have for decades demanded the construction of a Hindu temple in Ayodhya on the hill that is sacred to Hindus generally because of its association with the princely hero Rama. Since 1527, however, that hill had been

The Dalai Lama meeting with US President Barack Obama in February 2010 (Official White House Photo by Pete Souza).

Sites

Ayodhya, India

A city in the Indian state of Uttar Pradesh that is sacred to Hindus as the birthplace of Rama—the hero of the epic *Ramayana* who is said to be an incarnation of the god Vishnu and is worshipped by some devotees as the supreme deity himself. For nearly 500 years, Ayodhya was also the site of the Babri Mosque, named for the first Mughal emperor, Babur, and hence an important site for Indian Muslims. The city also has many other temples associated with characters from the *Ramayana*, as well as other mosques and former Buddhist sites.

occupied by the Babri mosque. Then in 1992 a Hindu rally at the site turned violent: the mosque itself was destroyed, and more than 2,000 people, mostly Muslims, were killed in the nation-wide rioting that followed. Among the forces suspected of provoking the violence was the Hindu nationalist Bharatiya Janata Party (BJP). It has become the main opposition to the Congress Party, and although it has never won a majority of seats at the national level, it did lead a coalition government from 1998 to 2004.

In Sri Lanka the struggle of Hindu Tamil **separatists**, led by the Liberation Tigers of Tamil Eelam, to establish an independent homeland led to a bitter and protracted civil war (1983–2009) that ended in the defeat of the separatists. Although the war was originally a struggle for regional autonomy, it took on a religious dimension because the Tamil Tigers and their supporters were mostly Hindu, whereas the central government was dominated by ethnic Sinhalese, who were mostly Buddhist. This sparked a resurgence of Buddhist fervour among the Sinhalese majority. For the first time in history, monks ran for public office, leading to the formation of a pro-Buddhist party that elected several monks to parliament. Now that the civil strife has ended, the challenge is to rebuild a state in which Sri Lankans of all religions can feel welcome and represented in parliament.

A similar separatist movement has led to separatist strife against the majority Buddhist government by Islamic groups in the southern part of Thailand that borders Malaysia and has a majority ethnic Malay, Muslim population.

In China religious minorities such as the Muslim Uighurs and the Buddhist Tibetans have renewed their struggles against the repressive tendencies of the national government.

Fundamentalism

In most cases the leading figures in the resurgence of religious fervour have come from the ultraconservative or "**fundamentalist**" end of the religious spectrum. A brief review of the rise of fundamentalism may help to explain why.

Now widely used to refer to ultraconservative religious movements, the term "fundamentalism" originated in the United States, where a series of booklets entitled *The Fundamentals* was published from 1910 to 1915. Affirming the "inerrancy" (infallibility) of the Bible and traditional Christian doctrines, the booklets were distributed free to Protestant clergy, missionaries, and students through the anonymous sponsorship of "two Christian laymen" (William Lyman Stewart and his brother Milton, both of whom were major figures in the Union Oil Company of California). By 1920, defenders of biblical inerrancy were being described as "fundamentalists."

Fundamentalism is a modern phenomenon, a reaction against the values associated with secularism and modernity. Above all, perhaps, what

In June 2012, opponents of US President Obama's health-care plan in Charleston, SC, argued that requiring employers to provide insurance coverage for contraception would infringe on their religious freedom.

fundamentalists reject is the modern tendency to locate ultimate authority in human institutions such as courts and legislatures rather than divine scriptures and religious leaders. If they interpret their scripture as condemning homosexuality, for example, they resist all efforts to legalize same-sex marriage as a human right. Fundamentalists do not necessarily denounce science, but on specific issues where science differs from their interpretation of scripture, they side with scripture as the ultimate authority. For Christian fundamentalists, the main conflict with science has centred on the perceived conflict between the biblical stories of creation and the consensus of modern science. They understand the Bible to affirm that the world was created by

God in six days, only a few thousand years ago, and that everything in existence originated at that time. By contrast, science maintains that the universe has existed for many billions of years, that our planet formed some time later, and that all life on earth is the product of evolution through countless generations.

The test case for fundamentalism came in 1925, when a Tennessee high-school teacher named John T. Scopes was brought to trial for violating a newly enacted state law that banned the teaching of evolution on the grounds that it contradicted the Bible. The court found for the prosecution, conducted by the famed orator William Jennings Bryan (1860–1925) against the defence of Clarence Darrow

(1857–1938), and fined Scopes $100. So extensive was the news coverage of the case, however, that fundamentalism itself was effectively put on trial in the court of public opinion, where Darwin, Scopes, and Darrow emerged the clear victors. What earned the Scopes case the nickname the "monkey trial" and made it a *cause célèbre* was the idea that humans were not the special creations of God but a species of primate descended from the same common ancestor as gorillas and chimpanzees. Although Scopes's conviction was overturned in 1927 on the technical grounds that the fine was too high, it would be another 40 years before the Tennessee law banning the teaching of evolution was repealed.

The word "fundamentalism" can have various meanings, but almost all of them are pejorative: even conservative Protestants tend to describe their own views as "evangelical" and use "fundamentalist" only to refer to more extreme views. In addition to denoting an orthodoxy based on the inerrancy of scripture, "fundamentalism" generally suggests orthopraxy—conformity to a straitlaced code of social and personal conduct—and a militant defence of their tradition as they understand it. Fundamentalists have been known to attack as diabolical those they believe to be subverting that tradition by expressing doubt or taking more liberal positions on some issues.

Fundamentalists perceive a struggle between good and evil forces in the world, and they have a greater-than-average readiness to believe that evil is tangibly manifested in social groups and forces with which they take issue, such as advocates of homosexual rights or free choice in abortion. They

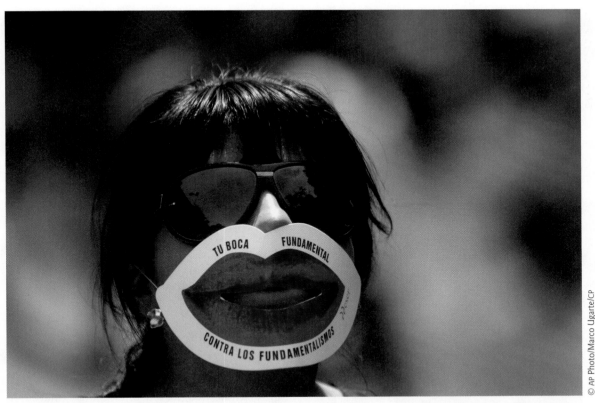

At a demonstration in Mexico City in 2011 in favour of legalizing abortion, an activist wears a mask that reads "Your mouth is fundamental against fundamentalism".

also tend to believe that the apocalypse—a final battle between the forces of good and evil in this world—is imminent.

Since the 1970s the term "fundamentalist" has been widely used to describe ultraconservative movements in religious traditions other than Christianity—especially those movements that have taken their beliefs into the political realm. Some scholars object to the use of a term with specifically Christian roots to refer to different traditions. Nevertheless, from the popular perspective there are enough similarities among the various ultraconservative movements around the world to justify the term's extension to other cultures.

The term "fundamentalist" has also been applied in India to the conservative Hinduism embraced by the Sangh Parivar ("family of associations"), a collective term for Hindu nationalist organizations, including the BJP. The most important "parent" in this was the RSS, "National Volunteer Association," founded in 1925 by K.B. Hedgewar (1889–1940) to promote the idea of India as a Hindu nation. To counter the growing strength of the All-India Muslim League (a political party that was calling for the creation of a separate Muslim state), Hedgewar started a boy's club that met early in the morning for military style drills, physical exercises and instruction in traditional Hindu values. His emphasis on the Hindu nation inspired the formation of many other Hindu nationalist organizations.

Central to Hindu nationalist thought is the concept of **Hindutva**, a term coined in the 1920s by the writer and independence activist V.D. Sarvakar. It literally means "Hindu-ness" and refers to an attitude that can manifest itself in a wide range of ways, from taking pride in Hindu traditions to claiming that Hinduism is the only true Indian religion, demanding that Indians of other faiths accept Hindu dominance, and promoting sectarian violence.

❧ Bioethics

An important challenge facing religious communities in the twenty-first century is the unprecedented power over human life and death made available by developments in biological research and medical technology. This power is especially troubling for the Western religions, which have traditionally considered humans to be sacred, set apart from all other beings. In Islam, for example, the human being is created expressly to serve as God's representative on earth:

> Behold, your Lord said to the angels: "I will create a vicegerent on earth." They said: "Will You place therein one who will make mischief there and shed blood while we celebrate Your praises and glorify Your holy name?" God said: "I know what you do not" (Q. 2: 30).

Central to the notion of the human being as sacred is the notion of the soul. The Christian understanding of the soul was economically expressed by the Anglican writer C.S. Lewis: "You don't have a soul, you are a soul. You have a body." Hinduism likewise teaches that the soul (*atman*) is the eternal and therefore the more important part of the human being; in fact, one of the Hindu terms for soul is *dehin*, meaning "that which possesses a body." In Islam, the soul is believed to enter the body at a certain stage of its development in the womb:

> And truly We created the human being out of wet clay, then we made it a drop in a firm resting place, then We made the seed a clot, then We made the clot a lump of flesh, then We made (in) the lump of flesh bones, then We clothed the bones with flesh, then We caused it to grow into another creation, so blessed be God, the best of the creators" (Q. 23: 12–14).

Modern Muslims take great pride in the history of science and medicine associated with Islam. Following an injunction of the Prophet Muhammad "to seek knowledge even unto China" (that is, to the end of the then-known world),[1] Muslims never really experienced the kind of tension between religion and science that Western Christianity did. To

© AP Photo/Anupam Nath/CP

Demonstrating against the gang rape and death of Jyoti Singh Pandey in December 2012, a protestor in Gauhati, India suggested a link between violence against women and the selective abortion of female fetuses.

discover scientific truths about the world was to learn more about God who created the world. Thus universities were established in the Islamic world as early as the ninth century; one of the earliest accounts of the duties of the doctor was written by a ninth-century physician named Ishaq ibn Ali Rahawi; and in the tenth century another Muslim physician named al-Razi (known in the West as Rhazes) wrote numerous treatises on medicine, pharmacy, and medical ethics.

The situation with Eastern religious traditions is somewhat different. One reason is that modern medical technologies have only recently arrived in Asia, and still are not readily available to many people. Abortion, however, has long been an issue for Buddhists and Hindus. Even though all Eastern traditions condemn it, abortion is relatively common in most Asian countries, especially Japan,

India, China, and South Korea. According to the World Health Organization and The Guttmacher Institute, the abortion rate in Asia in the period from 1995 to 2008 was approximately the same as for the whole world: approximately 28 induced abortions for each 1,000 women of child-bearing age (Sedgh, 2012).

The Buddhist scriptures have little to say about abortion itself, but the Buddhist ethic of non-violence has been understood to apply to abortion no less than to any other form of harm. In the Theravada countries of Southeast Asia abortion is typically illegal, but covert abortions are common. Japanese Buddhists have developed a special memorial service, called *mizuko kuyo*, for aborted fetuses, and some temples set aside special areas where family members may go to honour their memory.

As well as all the usual motivations for abortion, Hindus in India face two additional pressures. One is the persistence of an unusually onerous **dowry** system under which the family of a bride is expected to provide the groom's family with generous compensation. Because the family can rarely afford to pay the entire debt before the wedding, the payments are often spread over several years, like a mortgage. The dowry system is not sanctioned in traditional Hindu law, but neither governmental legislation nor the condemnation of some Hindu leaders has been able to put an end to it. Thus the birth of a daughter means that the family faces the prospect of a terrible burden when she comes of marital age: not only will it have to pay for both the wedding and the dowry, but after marriage the girl will go to live with—and work for—the family of her husband. Conversely, a baby boy brings the prospect not only of receiving a significant financial reward when he marries, but of gaining an additional labourer or income earner in the form of his wife.

Under these circumstances, many families use modern medical technology to find out the sex of a prospective child before birth, and some give in to the economic pressures and abort female fetuses. The other factor contributing to the rise of abortion in India is the government's ongoing effort to control the growth of the country's population. Unlike China, India has not resorted to forced birth control, but it has put in place incentives to limit reproduction. For example, a village that manages to keep its birth rate low is eligible to receive special grants for community development projects, such as roads, wells, or community centres. Thus community leaders sometimes put heavy pressure on women who already have children to undergo sterilization in order to prevent additional pregnancies. This approach may have the unintended effect of encouraging abortion.

The Environment

After creating the first humans, according to the Bible (Genesis 1: 28), God gave them "dominion . . . over all the earth": the fish of the sea, the birds of the air, and every living thing. This verse was traditionally interpreted as a grant of power and a licence for unlimited exploitation of the earth's resources, but today it is generally understood differently, as a command to take responsibility for the environment.

An influential early advocate of this "greener" interpretation was Lynn White, who in 1967 published an article entitled "The Historical Roots of Our Ecologic Crisis." In it he argued that the traditional reading of Genesis had played a significant part in the degradation of the earth. This article prompted a shift in attitude among many Jews and Christians, towards an understanding of "dominion over the earth" that emphasized stewardship of God's creation rather than exploitation of it. This awareness can be seen in churches such as the Canadian Memorial Church in Vancouver, which has embraced an environmental mission: "To cultivate a spiritual understanding of Creation, and to adopt and promote awareness of a spiritually-principled approach to planetary sustainability."

According to the Qur'an, God offered the responsibility for this universe as "a Trust to the heavens and the earth and the mountains; but they refused to undertake it, being afraid thereof" (Q. 33: 72). Thus the "Trust" passed from the physical world to the one part of creation that was willing to take it: the human being. The verse concludes with the following words: "The human being was indeed unjust and foolish." In suggesting that we would behave foolishly and without justice to the earth, this passage underlines the necessity of wisdom and justice in the exercise of the profound responsibility that humans have been given.

Faced with the evidence of humans' failure to serve as responsible stewards, Muslims, Jews, and Christians are reflecting on their fundamental religious teachings and discovering in them the bases for a new environmental ethic.

In sharp contrast to their Western counterparts, most Eastern religious traditions have never made any radical distinction between humans and nature or between humans and other animals. Hinduism understands all animals to have a soul (*atman*), and holds that reincarnation may take place in either a human or an animal body. Jainism goes even

© Roy C. Amore

Monks at Drepung Monastery near Lhasa, Tibetan Autonomous Region, China, use solar heaters to boil water in kettles, which they will pour into the waiting containers for their morning tea break.

further, teaching that plants as well are animated by a kind of soul. Jainism and Buddhism alike emphasize the ethic of non-violence and denounce any human activity that causes unnecessary harm to living things.

Ajai Mansingh (1995) defends Hinduism's "natural theology," based on reasoning and observation of nature rather than revelation, as better equipped to understand the dynamic relationship between the divine and the world than the more static Creator/creation approach of most Western religions. Certainly attitudes towards the environment may be shaped by practical as well as theoretical concerns. As Bina Agarwal (1992) points out, rural women in India have more at stake in the environmental arena than do most people in the West,

male or female, since so many of them still have the daily chore of fetching water for their households. The distances they must travel, especially in the dry months, are often increased by the pressures of human population growth and environmental degradation. The same is true for women who have to make regular trips to gather fodder for their animals. Their understanding of environmental issues is informed by direct experience.

A number of Buddhists, including the Dalai Lama and Sulak Sivaraksa, have applied the Buddhist ethic of moderation to environmental issues. Sulak argues that human greed is responsible for the redirection of vast quantities of natural resources to support cash crops, causing suffering on the part of local people as well as harm to the

Document

The Dalai Lama on the Common Ground between Buddhism and Science

On the philosophical level, Buddhism and modern science share a deep suspicion of any notion of absolutes, whether conceptualized as a transcendent being; as an eternal, unchanging principle such as soul; or as a fundamental substratum of reality. Both Buddhism and science prefer to account for the evolution and emergence of the cosmos and life in terms of the complex interrelations of the natural laws of cause and effect.

From the methodological perspective, both traditions emphasize the role of empiricism. . . . This means that in the Buddhist investigation of reality, at least in principle, empirical evidence should triumph over scriptural authority, no matter how deeply venerated a scripture may be. . . . I have often remarked to my Buddhist colleagues that the empirically verified insights of modern cosmology and astronomy must compel us now to modify, or in some cases reject, many aspects of traditional cosmology as found in ancient Buddhist texts. . . .

So, a genuine exchange between the cumulative knowledge and experience of Buddhism, and modern science on wide-ranging issues pertaining to the human mind, from cognition and emotion to understanding the capacity for transformation inherent in the human brain, can be deeply interesting and potentially beneficial as well. . . . The compelling evidence from neuroscience and medical science of the crucial role of simple physical touch for even the physical enlargement of an infant's brain, during the first few weeks powerfully brings home the intimate connection between compassion and human happiness (His Holiness The Dalai Lama 2008: 190–2).

environment. One of the first to bring these ecological concerns to wide public attention was the economist E.F. Schumacher, in his book *Small Is Beautiful* (1973). Schumacher called for a "Buddhist economics" designed to meet the needs of all the planet, as opposed to a traditional business economics designed to maximize profits. But of course this approach is not confined to Buddhism: M.K. Gandhi's preference for small-scale, locally based technology, together with his call for all to work for the benefit of all, has inspired organizations around the world dedicated to environmental responsibility and human-centred development.

🕉 Gender and Sexuality

In 2000, two advertising campaigns in Los Angeles featured images of veiled women. One campaign was for the opening of the renovated Aladdin Hotel and Casino in Las Vegas, a day's drive across the desert. Billboards featured the head and shoulders of an attractive Middle Eastern woman with an enticing smile, wearing a delicate veil that covered her hair and lower face. The image was a classic example of the "erotic Orient" myth—the harem girl whose sensuality so shocked (and sometimes titillated) the Victorians.

The other campaign was for the *Los Angeles Times*. Entitled "Connecting Us to the Times," it included television commercials as well as print ads and billboards. In each case, an image of bikini-clad women on a beach was juxtaposed with an image of women covered from head to toe in full black robes. In many ways, this campaign was more troubling than the first example. It's no surprise that a Las Vegas casino would use sex to sell itself, but why would a respected newspaper choose that approach? In this case, the veiled women suggested a suppressed sexuality that underlined the overt sexuality of the women in bikinis. The ads were criticized not only by Muslim groups, but also by 200 *Times* employees who objected to the use of women's bodies—covered or uncovered—to sell their product. As a result, the *Times* cancelled the campaign.

These examples are recent and specifically North American, but the distorted images they present point to a tendency to distort the image of Muslim women that is rooted in prejudice and misunderstanding.

When discussing the roles and lives of women today, it is essential to keep in mind that individual circumstances vary just as widely for them as for any other group. To be a woman in North America is a very different experience for a university professor than it is for an unemployed mother of four who never finished high school. Or look at the roles of women in political life. In both Canada and the United States, women are theoretically equal to men, yet neither country has elected a female leader. (Kim Campbell's short stint as prime minister in 1993 was the result of the midterm resignation of Brian Mulroney, not a national election.) By contrast, Indonesia, Pakistan, Bangladesh, and Turkey (all predominantly Muslim), India (predominantly Hindu) and Sri Lanka (predominantly Buddhist) have elected women as leaders. It would be no less simplistic to assume that North America is necessarily progressive in its treatment of women than it would be to assume that the other regions of the world are necessarily oppressive.

Many religious traditions are also beginning to rethink their positions on sexuality. Islam is among the majority of Western religious traditions that recognize only heterosexual relationships as valid, and Muslims often speak out against homosexuality. However, there are Muslims who identify themselves as lesbian–gay–bisexual–transgendered–intersex–questioning (LGBTIQ), and they are forming support groups. One such group, with branches in several Canadian cities including Toronto and Vancouver, is Min al-Alaq, which takes its name from a Qur'anic phrase (96: 2) that translates literally as "from the clot." The implication is that members consider all believers, whatever their sexual orientation, to come "from the same clot of blood."

Homosexuality has played a major role in Christian church politics as well. The international family of churches led by the Archbishop of Canterbury, the head of the Church of England, has been particularly hard hit by controversy over homosexuality. Until recently these churches constituted one big family known as the Anglican Communion, but in recent years a major split has taken place, largely over the question of whether or not the Church should bless same-sex marriages and ordain persons openly living in same-sex relationships. James Packer, a well-known conservative Anglican theologian, officially resigned his membership in a Vancouver-area diocese in 2008 because its head favoured allowing the ritual blessing of same-sex unions. Earlier that year several conservative congregations broke away from the Anglican Church of Canada to form the Anglican Network of Canada. They recognize a South African bishop as their spiritual head and pride themselves on adhering to biblical tradition, which in their view considers homosexuality a sin. (In fact, although some local divisions of the Anglican Church of Canada have endorsed same-sex blessings, so far the Church as a whole has not done so.)

Among Jews, the Union for Reform Judaism has been at the front of the struggle for LGBTIQ rights. In 2011 they participated in the "It Gets Better" campaign for teens.

Most Eastern traditions are just beginning to discuss such issues. In fact, it is only recently that India has officially recognized the existence of homosexuality within its borders. Buddhist ordination rules prohibit the admission to the sangha of a category of persons that has been understood to include homosexuals and transsexuals. But most sanghas insist that monks and nuns remain celibate in any case, so questions about sexual orientation rarely arise. (The one exception is Japan, where married Buddhist priests are common.) In general, Buddhist societies in Asia are socially conservative and frown on homosexual relationships, although the Buddhist culture of Thailand has a

Document

Reform Judaism and LGBTIQ Teens

Statement by Rabbi David Saperstein, Director of the Religious Action Center of Reform Judaism:

Unfortunately, even as we celebrate the growing acceptance of marriage equality and the end of "Don't Ask, Don't Tell," we know that members of the LGBT community still face stigma and discrimination. This is especially true for teens who, all too often, are bullied because of their real or perceived sexual orientation or gender identity.

When we hear the word "bullying" we often think merely of name calling, but LGBT youth sadly endure far much worse than that. According to the Suicide Prevention Resource Center, more than sixty percent of LGBT youth reported that they felt unsafe at school as a result of bullying related to their sexual orientation; more than forty percent were physically harassed (i.e. shoved or pushed) and nearly twenty percent were assaulted (i.e. punched, kicked, attacked with a weapon). The effects of enduring this are severe: the Center estimates that 30% of all lesbian, gay, bisexual, and transgender youth have attempted suicide at some

point—a rate that is three times that of their heterosexual counterparts.

That is why messages of hope, not hate, are so vital.

As Jews we believe in the inherent dignity of all people, for we read in the Torah, "So God created the human beings in [the divine] image, creating [them] in the image of God, creating them male and female" (Gen. 1:27). As human beings, we have a responsibility to ensure that the spark of the Divine presence in each individual is respected. To that end, we hope that our participation in the It Gets Better campaign will remind LGBT youth who are struggling that they are valued and loved.

In addition, we will continue our efforts to make it better for LGBT youth, as we advocate for passage of legislation to enhance anti-bullying efforts in schools, including the Safe Schools Improvement Act and the Student Non-Discrimination Act. [This statement] is a continuation of the Reform Movement's decades of work on behalf of LGBT equality and rights as well as our longstanding commitment to fighting bigotry, wherever it may arise.

long tradition of accepting males who cross-dress as females.

A major factor in India's movement towards greater openness has been the **Bollywood** film industry. Just a few years ago, the leading lady in an Indian film could not even be kissed on camera, but now physical expressions of affection—even suggestions of gay or lesbian sexuality—are increasingly common. Still, many traditionally minded Hindus and Muslims are shocked by the new openness.

Chinese society is also becoming more open and permissive about homosexuality. China no longer lists homosexuality as a mental illness, and gay–lesbian pride parades are now held annually in Shanghai. In the past, in China as elsewhere, many gay males married and raised families, but now gay men's wives—called *tongqi*—are forming support groups and calling attention to their plight ("Gay marriage gone wrong," 2012).

Japanese society has traditionally avoided any public discussion of homosexuality, but that is starting to change. One indicator of the change is that Tokyo Disneyland now allows same-sex marriages to be performed at its theme park (Westlake, 2012).

🐦 Religious Diversity

"Aren't all religions pretty much the same?" Most students of religion will be asked this question, or some version of it, more than once in their careers. As scholars we might want to unpack the proposition. What aspect of religion are we talking about—teachings? practices? implications for society? Still, it would probably be safe to assume that the questioner considers all religions to be of equal value and deserving of equal respect. And in the multicultural society of twenty-first-century North America, most of us would probably agree. This was not the case 100 years ago, when North American society was overwhelmingly Christian and most of the Christian churches were actively engaged in missionary work. Missionary activity presumes a difference among religions—a difference so consequential that believers cannot keep silent about it, but must spread the word.

For its first three centuries, Christianity was an affinity-based movement whose members were not born into it but actively chose to join. In the early fourth century, however, with the imperial favour of the emperor Constantine (r. 306–37), the missionary religion became a state religion as well. Christianity converted several entire populations by first converting their rulers. In its earlier centuries, Islam likewise succeeded in persuading a significant number of nations to convert, perhaps partly because it offered improved juridical status, including especially tax exemption, to those who became Muslims. Christianity's spread after the 1490s was closely associated with European military and cultural expansion. Priests accompanied soldiers in Mexico and Peru, and the sponsoring Spanish and Portuguese regimes took it as their responsibility to save the souls of the Indigenous peoples whose bodies they enslaved. The cultural–religious imperialism of Catholic countries in the sixteenth century was matched in the nineteenth by that of Protestant England, notably in Africa.

Muslim rule in northern India began with the establishment of the Delhi sultanate in the thirteenth century. This was the first region where Islam did not succeed in converting the entire population. Only in the Indus Valley, Bengal, and the mid-southern interior did Muslims become the majority; the rest of the subcontinent remained predominantly Hindu.

In the later centuries of its expansion, Islam grew not through military conquest, but through trade and the missionary activity of the Sufis in particular. The devotional life of the Sufis resonated with the Hindu and Buddhist meditational piety already present in Southeast Asia and provided Islam with an entrée to that region, in which it became dominant. Similarly in Africa south of the Sahara, traders and Sufis were the principal vehicles of Islam.

Dialogue in a Pluralistic Age

Today we often use the term "**pluralism**" to denote a combination of two things: the fact of diversity, and the evaluation of that diversity as desirable. This use of the word, which has become standard since the mid-twentieth century, reflects a convergence of developments and trends.

But let us be clear about what we mean by it. First, pluralism is not the same thing as diversity. People from many different religions and ethnic backgrounds may be present in one place, but unless they are constructively engaged with one another, there is no pluralism.

Second, pluralism means more than simple tolerance of the other. It's quite possible to tolerate a neighbour about whom we know nothing. Pluralism, by contrast, demands an active effort to learn.

Third, pluralism is not the same thing as relativism, which can lead us to ignore profound differences. Pluralism is committed to engaging those differences, to gain a deeper understanding both of others' commitments and of our own. It is also important to recognize that pluralism and

Focus

Missionary Religions

The fact that a mere three traditions—Buddhism, Christianity, and Islam—claim the allegiance of over half the world's population reflects the success of their missionary activities. All three are "universal" rather than "ethnic" religions: that is, they direct their messages to all human beings, regardless of heredity or descent. And all three were strongly motivated from the start to spread their messages far and wide.

By the time Buddhism emerged in what is now northern India, Indian society was already stratified into four broad social classes. Whether those distinctions had ethnic connotations in the time of the Buddha may be debated. What is clear is that Buddhism set caste and class status aside as irrelevant to the achievement of spiritual purity and liberation.

Christianity began as a sect of Judaism, a religion focused almost exclusively on the relationship of one particular nation to God. But the early Christians decided that it was not necessary to be a Jew in order to become a Christian. Early Christian teaching understood the new covenant to apply to all humans who accepted Jesus as their Lord, regardless of ethnicity.

Islam believes the Prophet Muhammad to have been the last in a long line of prophets sent by God to different peoples. And although the Qur'an explicitly addresses the people of Arabia, it was understood from the start to incorporate the messages delivered to other groups by earlier prophets and to represent God's final revelation to humanity at large.

In general, Buddhist, Muslim, and Christian missionaries have been more successful in recruiting converts from the traditional religions of small-scale tribal societies than from the other major religions. The reasons may have something to do with the material culture and technologies—including writing systems—of the major civilizations, which have conferred powerful advantages on those who possess them. Scriptural literatures have given the major traditions a special authority among cultures that were primarily oral, allowing them to use the content of their scriptures to shape social values. The early missionary spread of Theravada Buddhism is credited to King Ashoka. We do not know enough about the Indigenous traditions in many of the regions where Theravada spread to determine why its teachings were accepted. In the case of China, however, it seems that the Daoist interest in magic and healing techniques may have helped Mahayana Buddhism gain an initial foothold.

In the twentieth century, some Christian denominations began to curtail their missionary activity, partly because the returns on the resources invested were too small. Generations of European missionary effort in the eastern Mediterranean had made almost no inroads into Islam. And in the years around 1960, when many African countries were struggling for independence from European rule, Christian missionaries in West Africa particularly suffered from identification with colonial interests as well as the former slave trade. Thus Christian missionaries in Africa were largely replaced by an emerging generation of Indigenous church leaders. Another factor in the Christian churches' retreat from missionary work, however, was an increasing respect for other communities and traditions.

A coalition of diverse American faith leaders came to Washington, DC, for a day of interfaith action to urge the US Congress and President Obama to protect the poor and the vulnerable in the "fiscal cliff" negotiations of December 2012.

dialogue are happening around the world, not just in North America.

The current situation has been shaped by increasingly intimate intercultural contact. Within the lifetimes of people still alive today, transportation and communication have been transformed almost beyond recognition. As late as 1950, travel between North America and East Asia was rare, but now tens of thousands of people fly across the Pacific every day. And new technologies allow us to be in touch with almost any part of the world in an instant. Migration has also increased significantly. Since the end of the Second World War, the demographic profile of European and North American cities has been transformed by the arrival of populations from other parts of the world who

have brought their Muslim, Hindu, Buddhist, and other traditions with them. Though apprehensive at first, Western societies have made some progress towards understanding those traditions.

Change in the evaluation of diversity is reflected in many aspects of contemporary life, large and small. In some cases old institutions have been retained, but with new rationales. For instance, Sunday—the Christian day of religious observance—remains the day of reduced business activity in many jurisdictions. The arguments for legislation preserving Sunday store closing, however, now revolve around issues such as fairness, family time, and opportunities for recreation.

We should distinguish pluralism from secularism. Secularism means the exclusion (in principle) of all religious groups, institutions, and identities from public support and public decision-making. Pluralism, on the other hand, means equal support, acceptance, and participation in decision-making for multiple religious groups. Whereas recreational arguments for Sunday closing are secularist, arguments for school holidays on the Jewish New Year or the Muslim festival ending the Ramadan fast are pluralist. Up to a point, secularism and pluralism go hand in hand in the West because both seek to limit the role that Christianity can play in setting the society's standards. Where they differ is in what they propose as alternatives. Pluralism places a parallel and a positive value on the faith and practice of different communities. It often does so on the assumption that any religion is beneficial to society so long as it does no harm to other religions. It can also presume that the effort to understand a neighbour's religion—whatever it may be—is beneficial to society. Essentially, pluralism downplays the differences between religions and focuses instead on the values they share. In its scale of priorities, harmony in the society as a whole is more important than the commitments of any particular religion.

Interfaith Dialogue

The word "dialogue" comes from a Greek root meaning to argue, reason, or contend. Some Christian writers have pointed to the apostle Paul as an early proponent of interfaith dialogue because he is described as "arguing and pleading about the kingdom of God" with the Jews (*Acts* 19: 8–9). Paul was a missionary, however, and missionaries—by definition—believe they are possessed of a truth that it is their mission to spread. Missionary argumentation therefore bears little resemblance to dialogue in the modern sense, which demands openness to other points of view.

Dialogue is also a literary form, almost always designed to advance the author's point of view. The Greek philosopher Plato was a master of the dialogue form, using questioners and objectors as foils (or comedic "straight men") to demonstrate the

invincible logic of his own ideas and those of his mentor Socrates.

The Hindu *Upanishads* also take the form of dialogues: yet they too were composed to advance specific arguments. Similarly, in the Buddhist story of the sage Nagasena answering the questions of King Milinda, the questioner is like a puppet whose only function is to bring out the views that the author is already committed to.

True openness to alternative points of view is rare in any of the premodern traditions, but we do find instances of it. One highly significant example was Akbar, the Mughal emperor of India from 1556 to 1605. As a Muslim ruler of a mainly Hindu population, Akbar could have taken a tolerant stance towards Hindu spirituality on purely practical grounds, but he was a genuine seeker of religious insight. Therefore he summoned to his court representatives of all the religious communities within his domain and pursued conversations with them late into the night. From those conversations Akbar drew the components of an eclectic new religion that he called Din-i Ilahi ("divine faith"). Although Akbar's synthesis did not endure for long after his death, it reflected a remarkable phenomenon in his society: a widespread perception that despite their communal boundaries, Hindus and Muslims shared a devotional spirituality.

Conservative Muslims disapproved of Akbar's openness to heretical views. This is nothing new. Traditional religions may encourage disputation when the outcome is not in question. But Akbar's explorations were open-ended. A dialogue in which both sides are equal is something that orthodoxy cannot control. To those committed to a fixed position, such dialogue implies a threat.

The World's Parliament of Religions, convened in Chicago in 1893, was an adventure in dialogue that brought together representatives of many—though not all—of the world's faiths to present their religious goals and understandings. The conference reflected the existing religious scene and at the same time affected its future development by creating opportunities for Vedanta to present itself as the definitive form of Hinduism, Zen to claim to represent Buddhism, and the Baha'i faith to appear as an overarching synthesis of religion.

Understanding of interfaith dialogue has grown considerably since 1948, when the World Council of Churches was formed. Experienced dialogue participants emphasize that such exercises require both parties to set aside their claims to exclusivity: each must work to understand the other on his or her own terms. Both participants must also be open to the possibility of revising their views in the light of what they learn in the encounter—though this is easier said than done. Even the best-intentioned participants may be tempted to read their own views into others'. The influential Roman Catholic theologian Karl Rahner (1904–84), for instance, referred to people of other faiths as "anonymous Christians"—Christians who simply did not recognize the fact. By the same token, could not Rahner himself have been an anonymous Buddhist?

The goal of dialogue in the modern sense is "understanding." But "understanding" can be a slippery term in the context of religion. Academic students of religion understand particular traditions by explaining them: by describing as accurately as possible what they require of their adherents and how they have developed to become what they are. For those people, understanding may be informed by sympathy, but it is not the same as participation or identification. Similarly, the participants in dialogue understand each other by identifying one another's commitments, but that is not to say that they identify with those commitments. Particularly in the area of Jewish–Christian–Muslim dialogue, there have been calls for complete solidarity on complex and hotly debated issues, characterized by one critic as "ecumenical blackmail." Does true understanding of Judaism require uncritical endorsement of Israel's policies towards the Palestinians? If one truly "understands" Islam, must one agree with Iran's theocratic government and its suppression of democracy? Does understanding Hinduism mean accepting polytheism or animal sacrifice? No. Real understanding is not a matter of agreement or acquiescence, but a quest for a patient and appreciative relationship that can persist despite disagreement.

The Question of Value

For more than three decades, the 1978 Jonestown tragedy—in which 914 members of a religious community called the Peoples Temple died in a mass suicide—has stood as a challenge to the idea that all religions are equally valuable and deserving of respect. The community's founder, the Reverend Jim Jones (1931–78), who took his own life alongside his followers, had aspirations to overhaul the world order that were compatible with a reformist and utopian strand in Protestant (and Marxist) thought; one of his objectives in founding the movement had been to improve the living standards of the poor. But he also sought from his followers an uncritical dedication to his personal leadership that many found disturbing. Having moved the community from the US to rural Guyana in 1972, Jones ordered the mass suicide when he became convinced that evil forces were closing in and the only honourable escape was death.

History repeats itself. The Jonestown story recalls the Jewish Zealots at the fortress of Masada who are said to have committed mass suicide when they were surrounded by Roman troops in 73 CE. Suicide and the psychology of martyrdom have been linked at various times by Christian groups, and in other traditions as well. A similar interpretation has been applied to the conduct of the followers of David Koresh (Vernon Wayne Howell, 1959–93), 85 of whom perished with him when their heavily armed religious commune outside Waco, Texas, was stormed by US law enforcement forces for firearms violations in 1993. To approve of Masada's defenders while condemning the "Branch Davidians" at Waco would amount to deciding what constitutes a provocation worth resisting to the death.

Jim Jones and David Koresh were both leaders of movements that sought to recruit and retain converts. That is not unusual in missionary religions: Buddhism, Christianity, and Islam have all done the same, as have numerous "new religious movements" since the late 1960s. If modern pluralistic society proclaims the freedom to preach or follow religion without state intervention, fairness demands that the same freedom be extended to all.

Nevertheless, my freedom to practise or promote a religion is limited by the freedom of others to know what I am offering and to refuse it if they so choose. In a pluralistic society, religious groups forfeit their right to acceptance if they engage in coercion (psychological or physical) or illegal activities (such as narcotics abuse, firearms abuse, or tax fraud). Critics of movements such as the Unification Church (the "Moonies"), or ISKCON (the Hare Krishna movement), or the Church of Scientology are particularly alarmed when recruits are instructed to sever all ties with their families—even though there have been parallels to such demands in the early Christian movement and in some religious orders—and the families of such recruits have often resorted to equally coercive methods to retrieve and "deprogram" them.

By the early twenty-first century, some of the new religions had achieved a degree of institutional maturity and public acceptance. Most of these organizations are compatible with mainstream religions in that they help their members cope with their lives and encourage good citizenship. Like mainstream religions, in one way or another they address the human condition.

The last point is important. Religions are not all the same, but many may be humanly acceptable if they in fact benefit human beings; an appropriate test is suggested by Jesus' words in the Sermon on the Mount: "you shall know them by their fruits" (Matthew 7: 16). On some occasions, when they have lived up to their ideals, all the major traditions have passed that test; on other occasions, when they have fallen short of their ideals, the same traditions have failed. Typically, though, the various traditions see their distinguishing features as eminently valuable in themselves. If all religions were of equal worth, if there were no fundamentally important differences, why would anyone choose one of them over another? Pluralism may be socially desirable, but it poses a serious theological challenge. Does it really require us to modify our own doctrinal claims?

We personally are convinced that it does. Affirmations of religious "truth" that used to be understood as statements of fact are now increasingly regarded as perspectival—true "for me"—rather than universal claims. Today, thinkers from various backgrounds are presenting their traditions as symbolic accounts of the world and metaphorical narratives of the past. What is more, they argue that this is the way the various traditions should have been seen all along, and that literal interpretation has always been a mistake.

Pluralism demands that religious traditions adapt to a world that is becoming ever more interconnected. Here we think of the work of Wilfred Cantwell Smith, perhaps the greatest Canadian scholar of religion in the twentieth century. Professor Smith founded the Institute of Islamic Studies at McGill University in Montreal. He then moved to Harvard University, where he directed the Center for the Study of World Religions. One of his most important books was *Towards a World Theology: Faith and the Comparative History of Religion* (1981). In it he argued that our various religious traditions were best understood in comparative context, "as strands in a . . . complex whole":

> What those traditions have in common is that the history of each has been what it has been in significant part because the histories of the others have been what *they* have been. This truth is newly discovered; yet truth it has always been. Things proceeded in this interrelated way for many centuries without humanity's being aware of it; certainly not fully aware of it. A new, and itself interconnected, development is that currently humankind *is* becoming aware of it, in various communities (Smith 1989: 6).

Although current events make us painfully aware of the differences that separate the world's religions, it is more crucial today than ever to appreciate the complex connections they share. That is exactly what we are trying to do in this book: to deepen understanding of our interconnected religious worlds.

Discussion Questions

1. What are some of the points of intersection of religion and politics?

2. What did the word "fundamentalism" originally mean, and how is it used today in connection with the world's religions?

3. How are Western religious traditions dealing with issues of sexuality, especially challenges to traditional heterosexual norms?

4. Have religious traditions helped or hurt the environment?

5. Is religious pluralism the same thing as relativism?

6. How does the Eastern view of animals compare with the traditional Western one?

Glossary

Bollywood India's thriving film industry, from "Bombay" and "Holly-wood."

dowry The price paid by the bride's family to conclude a marriage contract; traditionally paid before the marriage, but now often spread over many years.

fundamentalism A very conservative form of religion that typically affirms the literal truth of its scriptures and doctrines and attributes ultimate authority to them.

Hindutva "Hindu-ness" or "India-ness," an affirmation of pride in traditional Indian culture and Hinduism.

pluralism A cultural attitude that welcomes a variety of political, religious and other stances.

separatists Persons who advocate to separating a region to form a new nation.

References

Agarwal, Bina. 1992. "The Gender and Environment Debate: Lessons from India." *Feminist Studies* 18, 1 (Spring 1992), 119–58.

Brockopp, Jonathan. 2003. *Islamic Ethics of Life: Abortion, War and Euthanasia*. Columbia: University of South Carolina Press.

Dalai Lama, His Holiness The. 2008. *In My Own Words: An Introduction to My Teachings and Philosophy*. Trans. Rajiv Mehrotra. London: Hay House.

"Gay marriage gone wrong." 2012. Retrieved 6 Feb. 2013 from www.economist.com/blogs/analects/2012/07/attitudes-towards-homosexuality.

Mansingh, Ajai. 1995. "Stewards of Creation Covenant: Hinduism and the Environment." *Caribbean Quarterly* 41, 1 (March 1995), 59–75.

Sajoo, Amyn. 2004. *Muslim Ethics: Emerging Vistas*. London: I.B. Tauris in association with The Institute for Ismaili Studies.

Saperstein, David. 2011. "Reform Movement Reminds LGBT Teens that 'It Gets Better.'" Retrieved 6 Feb. 2013 from Religious Action Center

of Reform Judaism, http://rac.org/Articles/index.cfm?id=22448&pge_prg_id=11071&pge_id=2541.

Schumacher, E.F. 1973. *Small Is Beautiful: Economics as if People Mattered*. New York: Harper and Row.

Sedgh, Gilda et al. 2012. "Induced Abortion: Incidence and Trends Worldwide from 1995 to 2008." Retrieved 6 February 2013 from www.thelancet.com/journals/lancet/article/PIIS0140-6736%2811%2961786-8/fulltext.

Smith, Wilfred Cantwell. 1981. *Towards a World Theology: Faith and the Comparative History of Religion*. London: Macmillan, and Philadelphia: Westminster.

Westlake, Adam. 2012. "Gay Marriage Debate: Japan Next, Hope Equal Rights Activists." Retrieved 6 Feb. 2013 from http://japandailypress.com/gay-marriage-debate-japan-next-hope-equal-rights-activists-307751.

Note

1. Some Islamic scholars have questioned the authenticity of this *hadith*.

Credits

The authors gratefully acknowledge the use of the following material:

Document box, page 114: From *A Treasury of Jewish Folklore*, edited by Nathan Ausubel, copyright 1948, renewed 1975 by Crown Publishers, Inc. Used by permission of Crown Publishers, a division of Random House, Inc. Any third party use of this material, outside of this publication is prohibited. Interested parties must apply directly to Random House, Inc. for permission.

Document box, page 164: from http://www.creeds.net/ancient/nicene.htm

Document box, page 270: Menocal, María Rosa. "Ten Years After: The Virtues of Exile", *Scripta Mediterranea*, Vols. XIX–XX 1998–9, 55. Published by the Canadian Institute for Mediterranean Studies. Used with permission.

Document box, page 304: Reprinted with the permission of Scribner Publishing Group from *Custer Died for Your Sins: An Indian Manifesto* by Vine Deloria Jr. Copyright © 1969 by Vine Deloria Jr. Copyright renewed © 1997 by Vine Deloria Jr. All rights reserved.

Extract, page 320 and Document box, page 321: Drewal, Margaret Thompson. 1992. *Yoruba Ritual: Performers, Play, Agency*. Indiana University Press.

Document box, page 343: Looking Horse, Arvol. 2009. "Concerning the Deaths in Sedona." *Indian Country Today*, October 16, 2009 at http://indiancountrytodaymedianetwork.com/2009/10/16/concerning-deaths-sedona-84570.

Document box, page 354: Hulme, Keri. 1983. *The Bone People*. Wellington: Spiral. Used with permission of the author.

Box Design Photos

Chapter openers, Timelines, and running heads: Chapter 2: Kirill Zdorov/Thinkstock.com; Chapter 3: Comstock/Thinkstock.com; Chapter 4: Michael Luhrenberg/Thinkstock.com; Chapter 5: Ingram Publishing/Thinkstock.com; Chapter 6: Cenk Unver/Thinkstock.com; Chapter 7: tnotn/iStockPhoto.com

Focus box: moggara12/Thinkstock

Sites boxes: Chapter 1: Margaret and Alan Smeaton/Thinkstock.com; Chapter 2: Nickolay Vinokurov/Thinkstock.com; Chapter 3: Paul Prescott/Thinkstock.com; Chapter 4: Olegusk/Dreamstime.com/GetStock; Chapter 5: José Antonio Sánchez Poy/Thinkstock.com; Chapter 6: Bernardo69/Dreamstime.com/GetStock; Chapter 7: Fabrizio Troiani/Thinkstock.com; Chapter 8: Nenand Cerovic/Dreamstime.com

Document boxes: Chapter 1 and 8: David Crowther/Thinkstock.com; Chapter 2: Yalçin Yener/Thinkstock.com; Chapter 3: Arkadiusz Komski/Thinkstock.com; Chapter 4: Spaceheater/Dreamstime.com/GetStock; Chapter 5: Bbbar/Dreamstime.com/GetStock

Index